READINGS IN
Russian History

VOLUME I

From Ancient Times to
Nicholas I

Readings in Russian History
IN TWO VOLUMES

Volume I: From Ancient Times to Nicholas I

Volume II: From Alexander II to the Soviet Period

Among other works by Warren B. Walsh are:

The Development of Western Civilization, 1940
Readers' Guide to Russia, 1945
Russia under Tsars and Commissars, 1946
Russia and the Soviet Union: A Modern History, 1958
Perspectives and Patterns: Discourses on History, 1962

READINGS IN
Russian History

From Ancient Times to the Post-Stalin Era

VOLUME I

From Ancient Times to
Nicholas I

Compiled and edited by

WARREN B. WALSH

Professor of Russian History, Chairman of
the Department of History, and former
Chairman of the Board of Russian Studies
at Syracuse University

FOURTH EDITION

Extensively Revised

SYRACUSE UNIVERSITY PRESS . . . 1963

To
Elizabeth Cantril Walsh

Library of Congress
Catalog Card: 63–14771

FOURTH EDITION

*Manufactured in the United States of America
by Kingsport Press, Inc., Kingsport, Tennessee*

Contents

* indicates primary source

Part III: THE RISE OF MUSCOVY

Part IV: THE SEVENTEENTH AND EIGHTEENTH CENTURIES

* indicates primary source

* indicates primary source

* indicates primary source

* indicates primary source

A Note on Translations, Transliterations, and Spellings

The originals of the selections which comprise this anthology range in age from a few years to seven centuries. The language of the originals ranges from Old Slavonic and Latin to modern Russian and French, and some of the translations were made many years ago. All translations which are not the work of the editor are attributed to the translators of record. Styles in translation vary from generation to generation, as well as from country to country, and no attempt to achieve uniformity has been made. Variations in translation, however, are less likely to be troublesome than differences in transliteration and in spelling.

There has never been any uniformly accepted system for the transliteration of Russian personal and place names, and none exists today. At least seven major systems of transliteration were in use in the United States and the United Kingdom in 1962. The French have been wont to transliterate in one fashion, the Germans in a second, the British in a third, and so on; and some of the fashions, moreover, have changed from time to time. National habits, changing styles, accepted conventions (such as the use of Moscow instead of Moskva), and personal idiosyncracies—not to mention errors in writing and in typography—have combined to produce a multiplicity which can be puzzling. The same general comments apply to spellings of English words. To have achieved uniform, consistent transliterations and spellings would have required numerous alterations in almost every selection of this anthology. This seemed neither feasible nor desirable, so—to the dismay of compositors, proofreaders, and copy editors—the transliterations and spellings of the originals have not been changed. Only by pronouncing them to himself will the beginning reader learn that the following pairs, for example, are not different objects or persons, but only variant transliterations: boyar, boiar; vieche, veche; mir, meer; czar, tsar; Lwoff, Lvov; Kluchevsky, Klyuchevskii; and even Rus and Russe.

Preface

This anthology originated in a series of mimeographed "Readings" produced for students in my courses in Russian history. When it became apparent that the need for such supplementary materials was not confined to one campus I prepared the first edition of *Readings in Russian History* (1948). Its chronological scope was from very early times to the February/March Revolution in 1917. Critics soon pointed out that the collection would be more useful if it contained materials on the Soviet period. Selections dealing with the development of the Leninist program and with events after 1917 were added in the second edition (1950).

In the third edition (1959) the coverage of the Soviet period was more than doubled. Other changes included the elimination of those selections which had proved least useful, the addition of new material, and a reorganization of the last part of the book.

The chronological coverage in the fourth edition is now from prehistory to the post-Stalin era. This edition is also different from its predecessors in other ways, but the original emphasis on primary sources continues. There are, in all, 205 selections—many of them having several parts—and over two-thirds of the total are from primary sources. Sixty-one selections are new, twenty-five of these having been translated from Russian specifically for this book. An additional twenty-six items, selected from secondary sources, are of Russian or Soviet origin. All the editorial notes have been reviewed, and many have been revised. The Table of Contents has been expanded to facilitate the finding of specific items, additional suggestions for further reading have been made, and the general organization has been altered to accommodate the new material and to improve the balance among the eight sections into which the book is now divided.

All these changes stem from experience—either firsthand or generously shared with me by students and colleagues throughout the country. I am grateful for their criticisms, their suggestions, and their advice. I am regretful that it was not always feasible to accept or to implement their counsel. The final choice as to what to print and what to omit obviously had to be mine. I was guided by three specific criteria as well as by my general philosophy of history.

History is, to me, primarily the study of people; or, to put it a little more formally, it is the study of the continuous interactions of multiple and shifting variables, the most important of which are people. I have therefore sought out reports concerning the ways in which people lived, the manner and content of their thinking, their habits of action, their customs, their social norms, and their value judgments—in short, their reality worlds. "People" includes the rulers as well as the ruled, and in an autocracy the characteristics of the autocrat and his associates affect the lives of all. I have therefore included materials which reveal some aspects of the rulers' personalities and policies.

Since social, political, economic, and other institutions also form a part of a society's norm and value pattern, some selections deal with the origins and development of such institutions. Not all institutions nor all aspects of Russian and Soviet history have equal coverage. Legal and military history and the arts, for example, receive relatively little attention. Descriptions of Soviet norms and values are comparatively limited, not because these are unimportant but simply because materials dealing with them are generally available.

Probable availability, or, more accurately, probable unavailability was one of the three specific criteria. Except in a few instances, I have not included selections from materials which seem likely to be readily available. This criterion alone ruled out many basic documents of the Soviet period, such as the constitutions and the Communist party programs and statutes, which have been printed and distributed in large quantities and many forms. The second specific criterion was that an item be of intrinsic interest; the third, that it make a particular contribution toward an increased understanding of some aspect of Russian and Soviet history.

The general organization and the mechanics are essentially the same as in the preceding editions. Each selection is introduced by an editorial note which identifies the source, establishes the relation of the selection to the whole, or comments on the subject or the source. Suggestions for further reading are made at the end of each part under the title, "Where to Find More Information." Emphasis is on items likely to be found in institutional and personal libraries. To assist teachers and students, I have included page or chapter references to textbooks and some other standard sources. Additional bibliographical information is available in many of the books listed, including my *Russia and the Soviet Union* which contains extensive "Bibliographical Notes."

All copyrighted material is used by agreement with the copyright owners to whom I here express my appreciation. I am the author or the translator of all material not specifically accredited to others.

WARREN B. WALSH

Syracuse, New York
21 December, 1962

Part I

Ancient History—The Early Peoples

~~~~~~

The Legendary Account: "The Tale of Bygone Years"

The written sources for ancient Russian history are varied but fragmentary. They are also frequently imprecise, obscure, and confusing even to experts. Archeological evidence is likewise incomplete, imperfect, and only partially understood. Trying to synthesize these materials into a history is like trying to put together several similar but separate jigsaw puzzles, the pieces of which have been thoroughly jumbled. Some pieces are missing, some are broken, and some are suspected of being fraudulent. The consequence is that historians who try to recreate the events and occurrences of the ancient period have to rely heavily upon conjecture and inference.

The oldest native written records are found in medieval chronicles which were kept in all the major centers from the late eleventh century until the sixteenth or seventeenth centuries. Most of these contain, in addition to local items, a fairly uniform account of traditional origins and of events which happened prior to the late eleventh century. The oldest extant version of this account is a copy made in 1377 by a monk named Lawrence, and known in his honor as the Laurentian text. Long called "The Chronicle of Nestor," this document is now generally referred to by scholars either as "The Tale of Bygone Years," or as "The Primary Chronicle."

The following selections from the most recent, scholarly, English language version of *The Primary Chronicle* were chosen to give the flavor of the whole as well as to provide illustrative samples from this important primary source.

Reprinted by permission of the publishers from: Samuel Hazard Cross, *The Russian Primary Chronicle. Harvard Studies and Notes in Philology and Literature, XII.* Cambridge, Mass.: Harvard University Press, 1930. Pp. 136–143, *passim.*

These are the narratives of bygone years regarding the origin of the land of Rus, who first began to rule in Kiev, and from what source the land of Rus had its beginning.

1

Let us accordingly begin this narrative. After the flood, the sons of Noah (Shem, Ham and Japheth) divided the earth among them. . . . In the share of Japheth lie Rus, Chud, and all the gentiles; . . . For the following nations are also part of the race of Japheth: the Varangians, the Swedes, the Normans, the Russes, the Angles, the Gauls, the Italians . . . and so on.

After the destruction of the tower [of Babylon] and the division of the nations . . . the sons of Japheth [occupied] the western and northern lands. . . . the Slavic race is derived from the line of Japheth, since they are the Noricians, who are identical with the Slavs.

For many years the Slavs lived beside the Danube, where the Hungarian and Bulgarian lands now lie. From among these Slavs, parties scattered throughout the country and were known by appropriate names, according to the places where they settled. [The account lists a dozen such "parties," including the Polyanians and the Derevlians.] The Slavs also dwelt about Lake Ilmen, and were known there by their appropriate name. They built a city which was called Novgorod.

When the Polyanians lived by themselves among the hills, a trade-route connected the Varangians with the Greeks. Starting from Greece, this route proceeds along the Dnieper, above which a portage leads to the Lovat. By following the Lovat, the great lake Ilmen is reached. The river Volkhov flows out of this lake and enters the great lake Nevo. The mouth of this lake opens into the Varangian [Baltic] Sea. Over this sea goes the route to Rome, and on from Rome overseas to Tsargrad [Constantinople]. The Pontus [Black Sea], into which flows the river Dnieper, may be reached from that point. The Dnieper itself rises in the upland forest, and flows southward. The Dvina has its source in this same forest, but flows northward and empties into the Varangian Sea. The Volga rises in this same forest, but flows to the east, and discharges through seventeen mouths into the Caspian Sea. It is possible by this route to the eastward to reach the Bulgars and the Caspians, and thus attain the region of Shem. Along the Dvina runs the route to the Varangians, whence one may reach Rome, and go on from there to the race of Ham. But the Dnieper flows through various mouths into the Pontus. This sea, beside which taught St. Andrew, Peter's brother, is called the Russian Sea.

When Andrew was teaching in Sinope and came to Kherson . . . he observed that the mouth of the Dnieper was nearby. . . . Thence he ascended the river, and by chance he halted beneath the hills upon the shore. Upon arising in the morning, he observed to the disciples who were with him, "See ye these hills? So shall the favor of God shine upon them that on this spot a great city shall arise, and God shall erect many churches therein." He drew near the hills, and having blessed them, he set up a cross. After offering his prayer to God, he descended from the hill on which Kiev was subsequently built, and continued his journey up the Dnieper.

He then reached the Slavs at the point where Novgorod is now situated. He saw these people existing according to their customs, and on observing how they bathed and drenched themselves, he wondered at them. . . . "Wondrous to relate," said he, "I saw the land of the Slavs, and while I was among them, I noticed their wooden bathhouses. They warm them to extreme heat, then undress, and after annointing themselves with tallow, they take young reeds and lash their bodies. They actually lash themselves so violently that they barely escape alive. Then they drench themselves with cold water, and are thus revived. They think nothing of doing this every day, and actually inflict such voluntary torture upon themselves. They make of the act not a mere washing but a veritable torment." When his hearers learned this fact, they marveled. . . .

The Polyanians lived apart and governed their families, for thus far they were brethren, and each one lived with his gens on his own lands, ruling over his kinsfolk. There were three brothers, Kii, Shchek, and Khoriv, and their sister was named Lybed. Kii lived upon the hill where the Borich trail now is, and Shchek dwelt upon the hill now named Shchekovitza, while on the third resided Khorio, after whom this hill is named Khorevitza. They built a town and named it Kiev after their oldest brother. Around the town lay a wood and a great pine-forest in which they used to catch wild beasts. . . .

Some ignorant persons have claimed that Kii was a ferryman, for near Kiev there was at that time a ferry from the other side of the river, in consequence of which people used to say, "To Kii's ferry." Now if Kii had been a mere ferryman, he would never have gone to Tsargrad. He was then chief of his kin, and it is related what great honor he received from the Emperor when he went to visit him. . . .

Now while the Slavs dwelt along the Danube, as we have said, there came from among the Scythians, that is, from the Khazars, a people called Bulgars, who settled on the Danube and oppressed the Slavs. Afterward came the White Huns, who inherited the Slavic country. . . . The Avars . . . also lived at this period. They made war upon the Slavs, and harassed the Dulebians, who were themselves Slavs. They even did violence to the Dulebian women. When an Avar made a journey, he did not cause either a horse or a steer to be harnessed, but gave command instead that three or four or five women should be yoked to his cart and be made to draw him. Even thus they harassed the Dulebians. The Avars were large of stature and proud of spirit, and God destroyed. They all perished, and not one Avar survived. There is to this day a proverb in Rus which runs, "They perished like the Avars." Neither race nor heir of them remains. The Pechenegs came after them; and the Black Huns passed by Kiev later during the time of Olga. . . .

[The account mentions ten Slavic tribes, and continues.] There was a multitude of them, for they inhabited the banks of the Dniester almost down to the sea, and to this day there are cities in that locality which still belong to them. Hence they are called Great Scythia by the Greeks.

These Slavic tribes preserved their own customs, the law of their forefathers, and their traditions, each observing their individual usages. For the

Polyanians retained the mild and peaceful customs of their ancestors, and showed respect for their daughters-in-law and their sisters, as well as for their mothers and fathers. . . . The Derevlians [another Slavic tribe], on the other hand, existed in bestial fashion, and lived like cattle. They killed one another, ate every impure thing, and there was no marriage among them, but instead they seized upon maidens by capture. The Radimichians, the Vyatichians, and the Severians [also Slavic tribes] had the same customs. They lived in the forest like any wild beast, and ate every unclean thing. They spoke obscenely before their fathers and their daughter-in-laws. There were no marriages among them, but simply festivals among the villages. When the people gathered together for games, for dancing, and for all other devilish amusements, the men on these occasions carried off wives for themselves, and each took any woman with whom he had arrived at an understanding. . . .

After this time, and subsequent to the death of the three brothers in Kiev, the Polyanians were oppressed by the Derevlians. . . . Then the Khazars came upon them as they lived in the hills and forests, and demanded tribute from them. After consulting among themselves, the Polyanians paid tribute of a sword from each hearth. The Khazars bore the tribute to their prince and their elders, and said to them, "Behold, we have found new tribute." When asked whence it was derived, they replied, "From the forest on the hills by the river Dnieper." The elders inquired what tribute had been paid, whereupon the swords were exhibited. The Khazar elders then protested, "Evil is this tribute, prince. We have won it with a one-edged weapon called a sabre, but the weapon of these men is sharp on both edges and is called a sword. These men shall impose tribute upon us, and upon other lands." All this has come to pass, for they spoke thus, not of their own will, but by God's commandment. . . . so it has also come to pass that the Russes rule over the Khazars even to this day.

Modern Accounts: The Slavic Peoples

Reports of Soviet Archeologists

Soviet archeologists have delved diligently and extensively into the pre-historic remains of their ancestors. The following excerpt from a synthesis by P. Tretyakov illustrates the general nature of their findings. The source is: "Archeological Studies on the Origins of the Eastern Slavs," *VOKS Bulletin.* No. 6. Moscow, 1945. Pp. 21–28, *passim.*

In their attempt to penetrate to the depths of the East Slavonic past, former historians always proceeded from the theory of a single Slavonic culture, regarding the East Slavonic tribes as a homogeneous body in regard to the social order, culture and economy. Contemporary archaeology, which now actually deals with traces of the real Slavonic past, holds different views. While Slavs of the second half of the first millennium of our era possessed characteristic traits which on the whole distinguished them sharply from Leto-Lithuanian, North Chud, the Volga tribes and the nomads of the steppes, within the East Slavonic tribes themselves numerous local differences existed both of a cultural-ethnic character and with regard to different rates of historical development, primarily in the north and south. This makes comprehensible to archaeologists the apparent contradictions in the descriptions of Eastern Slavs, given by Arabian and other ancient authors who had dealings with Slavs from the most varied regions.

On the middle Dnieper and the regions on the right bank of the Dnieper, Slavonic tribes had evidently done away with the clan order as far back as the first centuries of our era. The territorial commune (*verv*) was their prevailing form of social relations. Its economic basis consisted of field agriculture, comparatively developed crafts, and barter. The Roman coin represented a very important element in the economic life of the forefathers of the Anti tribes, who had undoubtedly conducted extensive trade with peoples from the Black Sea area. Information gleaned from Byzantine authors with regard to the economic and social life of the Anti supports this.

Things had been quite different in the north. While in the Black Sea area, during the first centuries before and after our era historical development had been rapid, in the north, life continued to preserve its ancient rhythm. In the middle of the first millennium of our era a patriarchal clan order held sway along the tributaries of the Dnieper and the upper Oka. Small fortified settlements, patriarchal nests similar to the upper Volga settlements, on the River Sonokha, were the basic form of settlements. They practised the most primitive forms of agriculture (by clearing plots in the forests); an important place in their economy, beside agriculture and stock raising, was fishing and hunting.

Gradually they took up metal working. Their trade with remote countries was very inconsiderable and had hardly any effect on the social and economic life of the northern tribes.

After the sixth century of our era, the picture began to change considerably. The tribes of the right bank of the Dnieper, having reached the highest stages of the primitive communal order under complicated and difficult conditions imposed by the invasion of the Huns, the Balkan Wars, their struggle against the Avars and the Bulgarian tribes, had, as it were, slackened their development, accumulating strength for the future. As a result of the Balkan events of the fifth-seventh centuries, the centre of political life had evidently shifted to the west of the Dnieper, where a tribal union of the Dulebs arose which is presumed to have had the form of a primitive state. Unfortunately, archaeological science is as yet unable to say anything about the Dulebs, or about their archaic state, for archaeological remains along the Western Bug are still waiting to be explored.

During the same period, other East Slavonic tribes had been experiencing a period of rapid economic and social development as though in pursuit of their southern brothers. On the basis of archaeological material, it is possible to state that in the territory of the upper Dnieper, in the basin of the Desna and the upper Volga, Slavonic tribes had in the course of the sixth-eighth centuries been gradually abandoning the clan order; the terri-

torial commune was becoming the prevailing form of social order. So far
the paths of this process are far from clear, but one thing is certain—that
a tremendous role was played by the transfer from ancient primitive agriculture to field agriculture, and by the development of crafts and barter.
Archaeologists are well aware of the fact that precisely during these centuries the ancient forms of fortified settlements began to disappear and
were replaced by huge new settlements. An example of these can be seen
in the remarkably preserved material of the Voronezh settlement of the
eighth-tenth century, studied by P. P. Efimenko. During this period, too,
the first iron ploughshares and other implements of field agriculture put in
their appearance; from being a meat-providing beast, the horse became a
draught animal and little by little the use of horse meat was discontinued.

It was in a situation such as this that there began the above-mentioned
migration of the northern Slavonic tribes to the Volkhov and the Volga, to
the lands of the ancient Meri, and, what was particularly important, to the
south and the southeast; to the Don, the Donets and the Taman. This was
due to the fact that at this particular time the northern Slavs had reached
the same order of life as that which two centuries earlier had forced the
Anti to migrate southward. They had now become interested in fertile
lands.

In this way, by the eleventh-twelfth centuries, different groups of Eastern Slavs had to a considerable degree reached the same stage of development with regard to their social, economic and cultural life, and had become still more consolidated ethnically. Thus, in the course of centuries,
the ground had been prepared among Eastern Slavs for the appearance of
the Kiev State.

The Eastern Slavs

> Much of the history of the early Slavs remains obscured by the mists
> of time. The following account of them is based upon a comparison of
> the earliest native sources with accounts by early foreign observers
> and with analogous usages as observed among modern Slavic peoples.
> The selection is an abridgment and slight adaptation of a study by
> the late Professor Samuel H. Cross of Harvard. The source is: "Primi-
> tive Civilization of the Eastern Slavs," *The American Slavic and East
> European Review.* Vol. 5, nos. 12/13 (1946). Pp. 51–87, *passim.*

The social organization of the Eastern Slavs at the beginning of their history contained elements of primitive groupings. Some of the small rural
townships preserved phases of ancient patriarchal and other relationships,
and the tribes, which had long since developed beyond the stage where
kinship was the only bond, also retained some traces of their evolutionary
development. The union of several small rural townships produced agricultural communities, each extending over a considerable area with the original community lying in the midst. It was such groups which formed the
Vervi mentioned in the *Russkaya Pravda.* Upon the combination of the
small rural communities into larger groups, the authority formerly wielded
by the individual father or elder was vested in a council sometimes known

as *vieche*. As Slavic settlement expanded into less occupied areas the concept of communal tenure which is found in the rural village groups weakened so that the conception of property as the possession of an individual family was promoted. Such scattered settlements were isolated in vast stretches of primeval forests in which the settlers hunted and collected wild honey. For defense the settlers constructed small palisaded enclosures in which rudimentary public life and commerce were concentrated. Sometimes circular, sometimes quadrangular, fortified by a single rampart if on level ground, or by concentric ramparts if placed on a high or otherwise naturally defensible spot, such fortified places are found all through the middle Dnieper basin. The Chronicle preserves the legend that Kii and his two brothers each settled at a strategic point on one of the hills of Kiev. However doubtful the legend itself may be, it accurately illustrates the practice of the early Eastern Slavic settlers, and the reputed foundation of a common strongpoint named after Kii reflects the function of these settlements as a place of refuge and a center of defense.

The Eastern Slavic communities of the ninth century were not, however, exclusively rural. The area occupied by the Eastern Slavs was traversed from north to south by the Dnieper, which had been since time immemorial an artery of trade. The primeval significance of the Dnieper as a trade route is crystallized in the early chronicle account of a "road from the Varangians to the Greeks," by which the Dnieprian Slavs were drawn into the currents of medieval commerce. As is proved by finds of extensive caches of eighth century coins, the medieval development of river-borne commerce in the Kiev area dates from this period, and coincides with the growth of commerce and the Khazar auspices.

Under the stimulation of commercial activity, some of the little fortified places originally founded by the Eastern Slavs for defense and security became trading posts (*pogosti*) where merchandise accumulated and traders foregathered. Those situated at river junctions rapidly became the chief urban nuclei. Their economic functions made them politically the county towns, as it were, of the areas from which their staple articles of trade were drawn. As these towns grew in importance, the rise of a wealthy and influential commercial class tended to wipe out survival of the primitive patriarchal and tribal organizations both in the cities and in the areas closest to them.

Prior to the evolution to a commercial and later an official ruling class, the primitive Slavic population was divided into three distinguishable levels. The lowest level was the slaves, composed of indigenous natives, subjected by Slavic colonists, captives taken in war, ... slaves purchased in the open. and the descendants of slaves. At least in their early history, the attitude of the Slavs toward their slaves was exceptionally mild.

Above the slaves stood the great group of free men (*smerdi*). This term in Russia originally extended to all free elements of the population below the rudimentary aristocracy, but later became restricted to the free agricultural population, dwelling on communal or private land holdings. Since the communal lands were eventually regarded as the Prince's, the free rural population on such lands became the Prince's peasants, rendering to him certain duties, but still free.

Above the free men stood an ill-defined class which probably developed from among the elders of the more primitive units. After the evolution of the Russian commercial towns, the mercantile leaders played a conspicuous role in this connection, eventually allying themselves with the immigrant Varangian warrior-merchants who formed the entourage of the Viking Princes established in Russian territory.

• • •

By the ninth century, the Eastern Slavs had been so exposed to various foreign influences that much of the technique which they possessed was not uniquely Slavic, but common to all adjacent groups of equivalent culture. By the arrival of the Varangians at this epoch, they had passed far beyond rudimentary communism and nomadic agriculture to a system of private property rights, and were exchanging the products of their domestic industries and trades, either by barter or for cash, with itinerant merchants of oriental origin or even transporting these products themselves to the markets on the Black Sea coast. The mass of Slavs was familiar with iron, gold, silver, and lead at least from the second half of the first millennium B.C., and cauldrons are found in Russian tombs of the pagan period, while iron and steel arms were a favorite importation from Scandinavia before the Russian smiths could produce them themselves. Most of the gold and silver found in the primitive tombs appear to have been objects of import, or at least imitations of foreign articles. The Slavs were imitators rather than pioneers in ceramics also.

Among the chief domestic industries were spinning and weaving. Rich silks were imported by the wealthy, but the masses were clothed in homespun fabrics prepared from wool, flax, and hemp. The early Slavs were not expert bleachers, and the resulting fabrics were mostly grayish in color. All finely-dyed fabrics were imported.

There is abundant evidence that in an early stage of their existence the pagan Slavs possessed a knowledge of agriculture considerably in advance of what is attributed to them in this connection by frequently cited historical sources. The content of the general Slavic vocabulary with respect both to agriculture and to cattle-raising is in itself sufficient to vitiate any conception of the Slavs at the dawn of their history as a race of agricultural nomads. Early medieval sources which represent the Slavs as poorly fed and clad nomads should be taken as referring to their economic status during the uncertain period of migration. The common Slav vocabulary shows that as feed-grains, the Slavs knew barley, wheat, millet, rye, and oats; among fruits they knew apples, pears, cherries, and plums, and of vegetables they consumed peas, beans, lentils, onions, garlic, and beets. Flax and hemp were familiar textile fibers. Among domestic animals were horse, bull, steer, sheep, goat, pig, and dog, and among domestic fowl, ducks, geese, chickens, pigeons.

The primitive plow of the Slavs was at first only a forked branch with one fork lopped short, and cut into a point. This type of plow, drawn by two oxen, was in use as late as the tenth century, for by that time the primitive implement had been somewhat improved. The more complex plow was a Roman invention which did not reach the Slavs before the ninth century. At the close of the pagan period the Slavs were practicing the three-field system of culture familiar from the German and Roman usage, in which wheat or rye was sown in one field in the autumn of the first year, then oats or barley in the spring of the second, and finally the field was left fallow during the third season. The prevalence of bee-keeping among the Eastern Slavs was noticed by early tenth century Arabic travellers. The honey was used for brewing mead, chief intoxicant of the early Russians, and the wax was exported along with furs supplied by native trappers (chiefly beaver, sable, fox, and squirrel).

Early Slavic villages were extremely simple. The houses were either scattered throughout the extent of the rural community in proximity to the fields of their occupants, or strung out on either side of a path or a road which formed the main thoroughfare. One early type of house consisted of a trench dug in the ground, the sides of which were raised by walls of logs stuffed with earth; the wooden roof was also coated with earth as an additional protection. By the beginning of the historical period, the Eastern Slavic house had developed beyond this humble form. Kievan houses show an unheated entrance hall or enclosed porch, which later develops into a reception room, and then received a porch of its own. The main room back of this contained at first an open fire, later a hearth. The houses frequently show a separate shed used as a storehouse or a barn, and sometimes having a second story. The evolution of a second story for the whole house first took place in northern Russia and is attributed to later Varangian influence. The use of small sheds as bathing houses in which steam was produced by pouring water over heated stones is also attested for Russia of the pagan period.

The costume of the men among the pagan Eastern Slavs at the time of the Varangian infiltration consisted of a coarse shirt of hemp or flax, falling to the knees, with sleeves and an opening for the neck, combined with tight trousers supported at the waist by a belt of rope or leather, and tied in at the ankles. For the shirt was sometimes substituted a short tunic which was frequently embroidered. This tunic either might be of light material or of coarse wool, in which case it could be worn over the shirt. There existed a considerable variety of these heavier outer garments. The long coat, or caftan, was a characteristic feature of Eastern Slavic garb. It might be trimmed or even lined with fur, while the common people ordinarily used sheepskins or bear or wolf pelts for protection against the cold. After closer contact with the Orient and Byzantium, more expensive fabrics and styles borrowed from foreign costumes were frequently used by the wealthier classes. Women of the people were clad in a long shirt of rough linen hempen material, often representing merely a cylinder of fabric held up by straps over the shoulders. From the waist down they also wore a double apron attached to a belt, while the upper part of the body might be clad in a coarse woolen jacket along with a cloak of similar material around the neck and shoulders. Footwear consisted of rough leather slippers held by a strap over the ankle, or of slippers made of warm bast fiber. The usual male headgear was a high felt hat, or a type of beret edged with fur. Married women wore a kerchief or bonnet, but maidens habitually were bareheaded. Married women cut their hair short; the maidens wore theirs braided and long. Men also wore their hair long, and mustaches were common.

The primitive Slavs, a peaceful race, were unskilled in the use of weapons, but the constant warfare of the migratory epoch and the necessity for defense produced in the succeeding centuries a marked increase of Slavic military equipment. Much of this was borrowed from the Germans, the Franks, and the Scandinavians. Although the Slavs borrowed the sabre from the Orient, most of their swords were from German origin. They also employed an ax probably copied from that used by the Scandinavians. Armor, including chain mail, helmets, and shields also were introduced from the West.

The chief avenue by which foreign cultures in general reached the Eastern Slavs were supplied by commerce. The most ancient trade route in Russian territory, used at least from the second century A.D., is the Volga. Caches of Roman coins and other Roman objects indicate the existence of a very considerable trade between the Slavs and the Roman West from as early as the first century. This was continued and expanded during the period of Gothic hegemony. From the time of the Gothic withdrawal until the beginning of Arab and Scandinavian commerce in the eighth century, there was an interval when trade relations between the Slavs of the Dnieper and the rest of the early medieval world were in abeyance. This interval coincides with the epoch of Slavic migration and dispersion. Its conclusion is marked in turn by the stabilization of the Slavs.

The era between 700 and 1000 saw the evolution of all the medieval Slavic states and their advance to the level of contemporary material and intellectual culture which culminates in their conversion to Christianity under Roman or Constantinopolitan auspices. It likewise witnessed an expansion of trade both in Central Europe and with the Orient. The articles exported by the Eastern Slavs were largely the products of their rudimentary industries: furs, honey and wax, grain, salted and smoked fish. These staples were largely bartered for weapons, jewelry, beads, glassware, perfumes, silk, and luxury articles in general, though the omnipresence of coin shows that sales for cash were also current by the eighth century. While the slaves had not played a large part in the primitive Slavic social economy, they became an important item of commerce at the close of the pagan period, and were sold chiefly to the Orient. Apart from the internal trade routes of the Volga and Dnieper, communication between Russia and Central Europe went over the Carpathian passes to the Danube valley, while the route from Kiev into Galicia was particularly important for the Russian salt supply.

The religion of the pagan Slavs was primarily animistic in its origin, and the animistic personification of powers of nature is further exemplified by abundant references to water and forest spirits. Numerous traces of manistic conceptions are visible in the widespread belief in a house spirit, but the association of nature spirits with the impure dead in modern folklore points rather to Christian contamination than to any manistic belief. In any case, the belief of the pagan Eastern Slavs in a future life of some sort is indicated by the funeral ceremonies attributed to the tribesmen of the ninth century by the *Primary Chronicle*. With the introduction of Christianity, the cult of the major deities faded out, but traces of paganism long endured among the masses in their superstitious beliefs in minor household and nature spirits, and in the old gods of luck and fortune.

An interesting problem connected with the primitive culture of the Eastern Slavs is a determination of the time at which they learned to write. While there have been some fruitless though entertaining attempts at forgery of specifically Slavic runes and at the identification as genuinely Slavic of certain runic texts more probably of North German origin, it is on the whole unlikely that letters of any sort were known in the pre-Christian period apart from cases where a more or less educated Slav managed to write down a few phrases of his language in Greek or Latin characters.

Modern Accounts: Non-Slavic Peoples (I). A Western Study

The following selection is a slightly abridged excerpt from a scholarly study of the early peoples of the Russian plain by an outstanding American anthropologist, the late Ales Hrdlicka. The source is: *The Peoples of the Soviet Union. War Background Studies # 3*. Washington, D.C.: The Smithsonian Institution, 1942. Pp. 2–10.

The Peopling of Russia

Prehistory—Up to the middle of the Quaternary period or Ice Age, the vast stretches of European as well as Asiatic Soviet Union were still devoid of human occupation. According to present-day evidence, it was only during the Mousterian or Neanderthal phase of man, and later, that sparse human contingents began to spread over the more southern parts of these regions. At the end of the last glaciation or soon thereafter the early comers had reached the Crimea, other southern parts of European Russia, and as far at least as Uzbekistan, where recently (1938) the Leningrad anthropologist Okladnikov found in a cave, with Mousterian implements, the remains of a Neanderthal child. Farther east, along the upper Yenisei, Angara, and Lena Rivers and in the Lake Baikal region, occur the remains of later, upper paleolithic and highly interesting neolithic populations, the latter offering close resemblances to some of the American Indians. Upper paleolithic and especially neolithic men reached also over a large part of the European as well as the more southern Asiatic portions of the country.

Early and later historical data.—From the time of the neolithic men to the dawn of historical times, both the European and Asiatic parts of what is now the Soviet Union were extensively although sparsely peopled, and there began taking place in the more southern parts of the country in Europe and Siberia some large-scale displacements.

About 600 B.C., the European region of what was to become Russia comprised the area now occupied by Finland, Karelia, Estonia, Livonia, the higher Volga, and the main central regions, peopled sparsely by the "Finno-Ugrians," a somewhat Mongoloid stock speaking Finno-Ugrian (Uralo-Altaic) dialects, and connected with the original Hun, Magyar, Turic and other related elements of Asia. At the same time the region that is now southern Russia, aside from some older tribes such as the Cimmerians and Taurids, was occupied by partly nomadic (east), partly sedentary and agricultural (west) tribes known to the old Greeks collectively as "Scythians." The more eastern nomadic parts of this loose complex were doubtless Tatar, the sedentary western portions probably early Slavic. Lithuania, then occupying the territory that after the thirteenth century became Eastern Prussia, had an old and probably already mixed European population of its own, while Poland was always essentially Slav.

It was in these earliest historical times also that the Greeks established a number of trading posts and small colonies along the southern coasts of the territory, particularly in the Crimea, the names and remains of which exist in those parts to this day.

In the Arctic regions lived the Mongoloid forefathers of the Lapps, and farther east the Samoyeds.

In the Asiatic portion of the present Soviet Union, over the southern steppes, roamed the Tatars, Kirghiz, and related groups; while more to the south were the Turkmenian and related central Asiatic aggregations.

In Siberia, the neolithic population had passed apparently into the numerous paleo-Asiatic groups, and well before the beginning of the Christian era these were being pushed northward by the Mongol groups from farther south. This large movement of peoples, of which there are many evidences, resulted in many displacements, leading perhaps even to immigrations into the American continent.

As to earlier movements of peoples over what are now the European Soviet territories, many details are lost or obscure. Facilitated by the vast unobstructed grassy southern flats, many such movements occurred, some of much importance. These movements were from all directions except from the Arctic and the northeast, but particularly from the east westward, from the south northward, and eventually from the west eastward.

The "drives" from the east were those by more or less powerful groups of the Mongoloid nomads from the less hospitable Asiatic regions, where the climate was becoming drier. The invaders were the descendants of the old nomadic "Scythians," now known as the Hun, Bolgar, Magyar, Ugrian, Avar, Polovetz, Tatar, and Mongol, and their incursions plagued eastern and even central Europe from the fourth to the thirteenth centuries and even later. They overran generally parts of what is now

Ukrainia, and some reached as far as Poland, eastern Germany, and Pannonia (a larger part of which became "Hun-land, Hungary"). The Huns under Attila penetrated in fact as far as northern France, where in 451 on the "champs de Chalôns," near the Marne, they suffered a fatal defeat.

The advances from the south were made by the Greeks, Venetians, Genoese, Khazars, and Turks; those from the northwest by the Goths, Varangians (Swedes), and Germans; and from the west by the Slavs, who eventually spread over wide areas, with later immigrations of varying magnitude of Jews, Germans, Poles, Czechs, and Rumanians. The more important of these processes deserve more detailed attention.

Movements of Peoples in European Russia. The Scythians

The peoples of what are now the European parts of the Soviet Union first began to be better known as a result of the famous march into their country of Darius Hystaspes—the first "Napoleon"—about 512 B.C., and more especially through the writings of Herodotus, about 450 B.C. Of those populations that were mainly of Asiatic origin, by far the most prominent were the "Scythians," whose territory embraced practically the whole present southern Russia below about 50° N. latitude. Peoples of related origin covered the country from the Urals to Finland, and from the Volga to the Baltic. They were subdivided into numerous tribes and differed somewhat in blood, but all belonged to the Turkish, Tataric, Finno-Ugrian, and Laplandic subdivisions of the great Ural-Altaic stock of Asia. All these peoples, including the Scythians proper, had in common more or less marked Mongoloid features, many were nomadic or semi-nomadic, none originally being strictly agricultural, and except where they were in prolonged contact with other peoples, such as in the case of the Scythians with the Greeks, the Bolgars with the Khazars, or the Finns with the Scandinavians, their culture was of a primitive order.

The term "Scythians" deserves a few comments. Owing to their warlike qualities and the direct intercourse with them by the earlier Greeks, few "barbaric" nations of the pre-Christian era have been more discussed and few peoples since have given rise to more speculation as to their ethnic identity. On the basis of present historical and archeological knowledge it may safely be said that the early Greeks applied the term "Scythians" not to a race, but to a mass or conglomerate of peoples, partly nomadic and partly agricultural, who occupied the southern part of Russia when the Greeks began to explore and colonize the coasts of the Black Sea. The main strains of the more eastern nomadic Scythians were undoubtedly Tatar and Turkic. To the west of the Borythenes (Dneiper), however, and particularly in present Volhynia, Bukovina, and Galicia, the principal and possibly exclusive element of the population from the earliest times was of European extraction, and this stock it seems could in the main have been no other than Slav. To it belonged tribes such as the "Neuri" (Nestor, the earliest Russian historian, mentions "Norici, who are the same with the

Slavs"), the Alazones or Halizones (which in Russian would be Galitshani, from which Galicia received its name), and probably the Borysthenitae husbandmen.

The Scythians claimed to have roamed over or occupied for many centuries the country in which they were found by the Greeks. As shown by their customs described by the Greeks, and by the remains of their culture uncovered by archeological exploration, they were not wholly barbaric people; and contrary to what may be observed regarding later Tatar tribes, their warlike activities were directed mainly toward Persia and Asia Minor rather than toward Europe. It was to avenge their invasion of Medea and Persia that Darius undertook his memorable incursion into their country. Crossing the Hellespont into Thrace and proceeding then northward to and across the Danube, he reached as far as the "Oarus" River (supposed to have been the Volga, but more probably the Dnieper), only to find his great effort against the nomads quite futile. He finally barely escaped with the famished remnants of his army back across the Danube.

The Goths

The first of the historic invasions into Scythia is that of the Goths, ...

The Goth sovereignty in southwestern Russia was not an occupancy of a waste region by a new race. The territories in question were peopled, even though not densely, and remained so after the Goth domination; and their sedentary population was not Goth but in all probability Vendic or Slav, though there are also mentioned the Callipidae (Gepidae), the Alans, and Heruli, may have been some of Alpine and some of Nordic extraction.

The Goths were warlike northerners, who invaded Scythia in some force and brought with them their families. Owing to their favorable original geographical position and their sea activities, they were more advanced in general culture and especially in military art and equipment than the inland populations, who were being only slightly affected by the rest of the world. As a consequence of all this the northmen found no great difficulty in overrunning large areas occupied by the sedentary as well as the nomadic tribes, which had little political unity and no adequate powers of resistance. Some such tribes could even be employed against others, though of their own blood, and the invader finished by becoming the ruler. There are ample illustrations of similar processes elsewhere, such as many centuries later on the American continent, in Mexico and Peru. But the invaders, though they may create a state under their own banners, are seldom strong enough to give the conquered people their language, and though their name may remain, as happened later in Bulgaria and Rumania, the conquerors themselves disappear, either by being driven out or more commonly through amalgamation with the old population. Thus the Goths who gave way before the Huns were merely the usurping and then the ruling class, through their military organization; and when this power was overcome and they were driven westward, they left little behind them that would permanently affect the type of the indigenous populations. Moreover, they doubtless carried with them, in their families, households, and the army, many elements and perhaps even whole groups of the indigenous people.

The Huns

The great Hun invasion which overcame and drove out the Goths and which was one of the most sustained and serious of the Asiatic incursions of all times, obliterated Scythia and disorganized the whole region of the present Ukrainia and Bessarabia. The nomadic Scythians apparently receded to Asia; at all events they vanished completely as a power and entity. They left thousands of kourgans or burial mounds over southern Russia, though some such mounds may have been made also by other people.

The Hun swarm came from beyond the lower Don and Volga. In blood they were of Tatar or "Ugrian" derivation. Their language, like that of all the native population east of the Slav Russia, belonged to the Ural-Altaic. Contemporary accounts show them to have been typical Mongoloid nomads. From southern Russia they extended their incursions over most of western Europe. Soon after their defeat in France their dread chief Attila died, the power which they had established in Pannonia and central Europe rapidly crumbled, their confederates, among whom were some of the Germans and even Ostrogoths, broke away, and what remained of the horde, no longer able to hold its ground, retraced its steps eastward and was lost to sight. Exactly what effect this Hun invasion and occupation had on the population of southern Russia and central Europe is difficult to gauge, but it was probably mainly that of destruction or dispersion.

The Khazars

What remained of the population in southern Russia-to-be after the Hun invasion now became gradually infiltrated with a new ethnic unit, the Khazars. The Khazars, according to many indications, were of Caucasian or anterior Asian extraction, and were related to the Georgians and Armenians. There were with them, however, also the so-called "black Khazars," who have not yet been identified. Their history in southeastern Russia extends over a considerable period of time—to the eleventh century. Between 600 and 950 the territory they controlled is said to have spread from the Caspian Sea to the Don and later even into the Crimea. They were relatively civilized people, who built small towns and engaged extensively in sea trade, which earned them the name of the "Phoenicians" of the Caspian and Black Seas. In the earlier part of the seventh century their power was such that they compelled the agricultural Slavs of the Dnieper and even those of the more northern regions to pay tribute. About 740 they accepted Judaism. But during the ninth and tenth centuries they were slowly outnumbered by the Russians, and in the eleventh century they practically disappear from the stage. Remnants of them probably still exist under different name or names in the Caucasus.

Turkish and Tatar Tribes

The Khazar occupation of the regions which now form southeastern Russia was, however, far from uniform, dense, or continuously peaceful. The waves of incursion of the Turkish and the Tatar tribes from farther east followed at greater or shorter intervals, and over approximately the same roads—the broad open steppes traversed before by the Huns. Some of these invasions it is not necessary to enumerate in detail. The more important ones were those of the Bolgars in 482, of the Avars in 557, and those of the Polovtsi (Kumans), Ugri (Magyars), Pechenegs, and related tribes, in the ninth and tenth centuries. Whatever the name under which they came, they were all of the Tatar or of Turkish extraction, with some admixtures. All were more or less nomadic and destructive, bent mostly on spoliation, but in the case of the major movements also on penetration toward the richer more central and southern parts of Europe, rather than on the conquest of Russia and the establishment there of a permanent new home; though some, such as the Polovtsi, Pechenegs, and others, became for a longer or shorter period settled in the territory. Taken collectively, these invasions resulted in a great retardation of the settlement of the southern parts of Russia. The hordes did not colonize or mix readily except through captives, and although remnants of them and mixtures were left, they made no very great impression on the sedentary population of the region.

Modern Accounts: Non-Slavic Peoples (II). A Soviet Study

Hrdlicka's brief account may be compared with a Soviet study of the same subjects, written by Yu. V. Got'e. The selection is an excerpt from a chapter, "Vostochynaya Evropa v III–VII vv" ("Eastern Europe, 3d–7th Centuries"), in a multivolumed history of the USSR. The translation is the work of my colleague, Professor Kenneth I. Dailey, and I am indebted to him for making it available to me. The source is: Boris D. Grekov (Ed.), *Istoriya SSSR—Tom I (History of the USSR—Vol. I)*. Moscow, 1947. Pp. 42–47. The publication was sponsored jointly by the Historical Institute of the Academy of Sciences of the USSR and the Historical Faculty of Moscow State University.

The Goths and the Huns

In the third century, the Goths, relatives of the Eastern Germanic Tribes, appeared in the steppes to the north of the Black Sea. The Gothic historian of the 6th century, Jordanes, relates that the Goths, after having surmounted the forests and the marshes, (apparently those of the Pripet) came from the estuary of the Vistula to the regions of southeastern Europe and threw themselves upon the Greek colonies on the shores of the Black Sea, heavily damaging their ancient civilization. From here, the Goths, often allied with the tribes of this region, attacked the territory of the Eastern Roman Empire. The Slavic tribes also were subject to their attacks.

The Goths did not settle down permanently in the southern steppes. Their level of social and cultural development was no higher than that of the native population. The culture of the Black Sea regions from the third to the fifth centuries is often erroneously called the Gothic Culture, although it was in fact the culture of the local population, the Sarmatians. The contention of the German fascist historians regarding the organizing role of the Goths in the political and cultural life north of the Black Sea is absolutely without foundation.

The Goths were not sufficiently strong to meet the pressure of the Huns. Beaten by the Huns, they retreated, part of them to the west, and part of them into the mountains of the Crimea, where some groups of the Sarmatians also found shelter. A handful of the Goths remained in the Crimean hills for a long time.

The invasion of the Huns into eastern Europe can be compared as to its force and consequences only with that of the Mongol-Tatars of the 13th century. Other tribes which had been conquered by the Huns, marched with them. In the year 375, the Huns under (Tsar) Balamer crossed the Don River and met and crushed the Goths and the Sarmatians. Soon they occupied the plains of the middle Danube, which became the center of their dominion under (Tsar) Attila. After the death of Attila, the Hunnic Empire fell to pieces (453 A.D.).

While passing through the steppes of southeastern Europe, the Huns exterminated part of the local population, and reduced part of them to slavery and took them with them. A Sarmatian tribe, the Alans, suffered most, but nevertheless, part of them survived in the northern Caucasus, in the Don Basin, and in the Crimean mountains.

The Bulgars and the Avars

In the 6th and 7th centuries the tribal union of the nomadic Bulgars played a considerable role in the southern steppes. They became very well known at the end of the fifth century when the Byzantine emperor asked for their help against other nomads, the Avars. Byzantine historians mention that the Bulgarians for many years lived a nomadic life north of the Sea of Azov.

The Turko-Avars were leading a nomadic life somewhere near the Caspian Sea at the end of the 5th century. In the 6th century they moved swiftly to the west, to the plains of the middle Danube, and from there they attacked the Byzantine Empire and the Slavs. In the Russian Chronicles there is a statement that the "Avars tortured completely" the Slavic tribe of the Dulebs. In the second quarter of the 7th century, the power of the Avars was completely broken by the united forces of the Franconian Empire and the revolting tribes. In the second half of the 7th century the Bulgar tribal union also disintegrated. The Bulgars retreated from the steppes north of the Sea of Azov and near the Don River. One group of them under the leadership of Khan Asparuch, taking advantage of the difficult situation of the Byzantine Empire, forced the emperor to cede them a part of the empire between the lower Danube and the Balkan mountains in the year 679. Thus Danubian Bulgaria was established. After an amalgamation with the local Slavic population, the Bulgars created the present Bulgarian nation, which occupies a considerable part of the Balkan peninsula where a Slavic language very close to Russian is spoken. Another group of the Bulgars moved in a northeasterly direction and settled at the lower part of the Kama and the central part of the Volga rivers.

The Khazars

The sources of Khazar history are poor and fragmentary. Of the Khazar towns, of which three are known, only Sarkel in the lower Don Valley has been investigated by archeologists. The capital of the Khazar state was on the site of Tatar Astrakhan. It was named Itil. The ruins of this town were later washed away by the flood waters of the Volga. Arabian, Georgian, Byzantine, and Armenian historians tell us much about the Khazars, but a definitive historical study of the Khazar State is not available. An original written document can be found in the letter of the Khazar Tsar Joseph, written about the year 860, shortly before the collapse of the Khazar state. This document is written in the Hebrew language to a Spanish rabbi. It furnishes very valuable information about the country, about the nations under Khazar rule at the height of their power, and about Khazar history. However, not all historians regard this source as a reliable one.

The Territory of the Khazar State

The Khazar nation, which the Byzantine historians mention at the beginning of the 7th century, was then living on the western shores of the Caspian Sea. During the 8th and 9th centuries, the center of the Khazar Empire was on the lower Volga. The territory over which the Khazars ruled consisted of the northern Caucasus, the shores of the Sea of Azov, and also a part of the Crimea. The Khazars also conquered the territories of the ancient Bosphorus kingdom, and sometimes even for short periods Kherson, the stronghold of the Byzantine Empire on the northern coast of the Black Sea. Until the second half of the 9th century also, some Slavic tribes—the Polyans, the Severians, and the Vyatiches,—paid tribute to the Khazars, as did also some tribes of the central Volga region—the Bulgars of the Kama, the Burtsy, the Ztarmis, and the Arisu. The Khazars also ruled the steppes between the Mangyshlak Peninsula and the Aral Sea which gave them control over the ancient caravan route to Khoresm.

The Occupations of the Khazars

Agriculture spread among the Khazars in the 10th century, and therefore their life was semi-nomadic. The Arabs relate that during the winter the population lived in cities; but with the spring they went out into the steppes where they remained until the fall. There were no settlements near the capital, but nevertheless, the country was covered with cultivated parcels of land. In the summer, the inhabitants of Itil gathered the crops and transported them into the city with vehicles or barges. This is confirmed also by the letter of Tsar Joseph which asserts, that in April, he himself and his people left for their fields and gardens. Every clan had its inherited properties where its members settled down. At the end of November they returned to their residences. Thus the Khazar city was a kind of winter place from whence the inhabitants went out in the summer. As they lived on the shores of the Volga and the Caspian Sea, the Khazars were also fishermen.

Cities

The Khazar cities—Semender in the Caucasus, Itil on the Volga, and Sarkel on the Don—were centers of commerce and various cultural activities. According to Arabian writers:

"There were many gardens. It is said that they contained 40,000 vineyards. . . . The Moslems have their mosques, the Christians their churches, and the Jews have their synagogues. The town of Itil is surrounded by a wall. It is divided into two parts and each part has two gates, one to the river and one to the steppes. The town has markets and bathhouses. The houses are dispersed and are huts built of wood and felt. Clay is seldom used. Only the palace of the Tsar (Khagan) on the island, which is connected with the town with a floating raft, is made of bricks. The western shore is only for members of the Court. The other is inhabited by Christians, Moslems and Jews, and Pagans and it is larger."

The excavations at Sarkel also show that it was divided into two parts. On the right bank there was a high fortress of white stones, and on the left a widely spread commercial city, which apparently had a large population.

Commerce

The Khazars did not produce anything for export except fish and fishglue. The Khazar Tsar, say the Arabs:

"Has no ships and no men to man them. All that goes southward from Khazaria, honey and furs imported from the Russes and the Bulgars, swords from the more remote Slavonic countries, Russian merchants bring down the Volga and the Khazar Tsar takes his tenth part of them. To this must be added the human commodity, slaves. From the east and from Byzantium, come the products of craftsmen. The Khazars do not manufacture fabrics. Those who use them get them from the southern shores of the Caspian and from the Roman Empire, and from other countries."

Its situation at the crossroads of the Volga-Caspian, Don-Volga, and Mangyshlak-Khoresm trade routes, made Itil a central market for Southeastern Europe.

The Political Order

The Khazar nation was headed by a khan who was surrounded by privileged groups of begs (princes) and tarkhans. The tsar compelled the wealthy ones to provide him with horses according to their wealth, and these warriors went out with banners and spears, clad in solid armour. Together with the supreme ruler, the chagan or khagan, there was his deputy, malik or chakhan-beg, as the oriental writers called him. It was he who had the power of the state practically in his hands. The supreme ruler was regarded, nearly as a God, and only his deputy and two or three other high officials could see him. The title and the functions of the khagan and of his deputy were inherited, but they came from two different families.

Culture

Thanks to its position at the crossroads of many commercial routes which connected the Khazar state with Persia, Azerbaidzhan, the Black Sea, Byzantium, and with the interior regions of the Volga and the Don, Khazar culture shows various traits of manifold influences from the above-named countries. The excavations at Sarkel produced items of the most varied origins—Central Asian, Persian, Trans-Caucasian, Byzantine, and Russian of the 10th and 12th centuries. In the Khazar cities, especially in the capital, Itil, the Orient with its Moslems and Jews; and the Occident with its Byzantine Christians met, and all religions were tolerated. The Arabian writer Masudi says that in Itil there were seven judges; two for the Moslems, two for the Khazars who judge in accordance with the Torah (Jewish Law), two for the local Christians who judge in accordance with the Indgila (Gospel), and one for the Slavs, Russes, and other pagans who were judged in accordance with the pagan law, i.e. the law of common sense. Both the tsars and the greatest part of the Khazar nobility belonged, in the later days, to Judaism. The Judaic influence came from the Crimea, where already the first centuries A.D. in the Bosphorus state, large Jewish colonies were mentioned.

Relations with the East and with Byzantium

After the dissolution of the Bulgarian tribal union in the 7th century, the southern steppes came under Khazar domination for about two hundred years. For a long time, the Khazars managed to resist the pressure of the Pechenegs from the regions beyond the Don and the Volga and they also subdued the Magyars who had come from the slopes of the Urals to the shores of the Black Sea in the 8th century and remained there until the second half of the 9th century. The Khazars had to do not only with the steppes. Their commerce with the trans-Caucasian countries, with Byzantium, and with the Slavic regions was considerable. Their attempts to penetrate into the trans-Caucasian lands were thwarted by the Arabs and by the Persians.

For a long time, Khazar relations with the Byzantine Empire were influenced by the fact that Byzantium and Khazaria had common enemies:

the Persians and the Arabs. Several wars against one or the other were conducted in common alliance. These friendly relations were tightened by marriages. In the 830's, Byzantine engineers and builders, at the request of the Khazars, were helping to build the fortress of Sarkel in order to check the Pechenegs, who were then moving between the Volga and the Ural rivers. There was a hard struggle between the Khazars and the Pechenegs, and the Khazars prevailed against them only with great difficulty. At the beginning of the 10th century, the Pechenegs were moving between the Don and the Danube, and toward the middle of the 10th century, signs of decay of Khazar power can already be noted. The military potential of Khazaria decreased. According to the Arabian writer, Ibn-Ruste, the cavalry of the Khazars was not stronger than ten thousand men. In order to strengthen it, the Khazar rulers were obliged to keep a guard troop of mercenary soldiery of whom the best were Moslems from Central Asia. Invasions by the Russian princes during the second half of the 10th century definitely destroyed the Khazar state.

Where to Find More Information

ALLEN, W. E. D. *The Ukraine: A History.* Cambridge: Cambridge Univ. Press, 1941. Ch. 1.

CHARQUES, R. D. *A Short History of Russia.* N.Y.: Dutton, 1956. Ch. 1.

CLARKSON, J. D. *A History of Russia.* N.Y.: Random House, 1961. Chs. 1 & 2.

HARCAVE, S. (Ed.) *Readings in Russian History.* 2 vols. N.Y.: Crowell, 1962. Vol. 1, sections 1–8.

HRUSHEVSKY, M. (O. J. Fredericksen, Ed.) *History of Ukraine.* New Haven: Yale Univ. Press, 1941. Chs. 1–3.

KERNER, R. J. *The Urge to the Sea.* Berkeley: Univ. of Calif. Press, 1942. Ch. 1.

LYASHCHENKO, P. I. (L. M. Herman, Tr.) *History of the National Economy of Russia to the 1917 Revolution.* N.Y.: Macmillan, 1949. Pp. 17–81, 89–118.

MARTIN, J. S. *Picture History of Russia.* N.Y.: Crown, 1945. Pp. 2–16.

MAZOUR, A. G. *Russia Tsarist and Communist.* Princeton: Van Nostrand, 1962. Ch. 1.

MILIUKOV, P. N. (M. M. Karpovich, Ed.) *Outlines of Russian Culture.* 3 vols. Philadelphia: Univ. of Penna. Press, 1941. Vol. 1, ch. 1.

NABOKOV, V. (Tr.) *Song of Igor's Campaign.* Signet Classic.

NOWAK, F. *Medieval Slavdom and the Rise of Russia.* N.Y.: Holt, 1930. Pp. 3–8, 35–38.

PARES, B. *A History of Russia.* N.Y.: Knopf, 1953. Intro. & ch. 1.

PEISKER, J. "The Expansion of the Slavs," *Cambridge Medieval History.* N.Y.: Macmillan, 1911–1929. Vol. 2, ch. 14.

RAMBAUD, A. *History of Russia.* 3 vols. (Many editions.) Vol. 1, chs. 1–3.

VERNADSKY, G. *Ancient Russia.* (Vol. I in his *History of Russia.*) New Haven: Yale Univ. Press, 1943.

WALSH, W. B. *Russia and the Soviet Union.* Ann Arbor: Univ. of Mich. Press, 1958. Ch. 1.

WREN, M. C. *The Course of Russian History.* N.Y.: Macmillan, 1958. Chs. 1–3.

NOTE: The author's initials, the full title, and the information about the publisher are given only in the initial listing. Thereafter, the author's last name and an abbreviated title are used.

Part II

Kievan Rus

~~~~~~

The Primary Chronicle: Selected Annals

> The first part of *The Primary Chronicle* (see the first selection in
> Part I) is a wholly legendary account. The annual entries in the
> Laurentian text begin with 852 which the unknown chronicler mis-
> takenly believed to be the year when Michael ascended the throne.
> (The correct date is 842.) Scholars have traced this chronological
> error to the ancient Greek accounts from which the chronicler, or
> compiler, drew his information. The first date given by the chronicler
> is *Anno Mundi* (A.M., Year of the World); the second, *Anno Domini*.
>
> Some of the excerpts give the chroniclers' versions of such major
> events as the coming of the Varangians, the beginnings of Kiev, and
> the conversions of Olga and Vladimir. Other excerpts illustrate the
> chroniclers' interest and belief in the supernatural, and other char-
> acteristics of the time.
>
> The source is: Cross, *The Russian Primary Chronicle*, pp. 144–
> 147, 149–151, 157, 168–169, 173, 201, 204–205, 212, 224–225,
> 231–232, 235, *passim*. Reprinted by permission of the publishers,
> Harvard University Press.

In the year 6360 (852) [*sic*] . . . at the accession of the Emperor
Michael, the land of Rus was first named. . . .

6367 (859). The Varangians from beyond the sea imposed tribute
upon the Chuds, the Slavs, the Merians, the Ves, and the Krivichians. But
the Khazars imposed it upon the Polyanians, the Severians, and the
Vyatichians, and collected a squirrel-skin and a beaver-skin from each
hearth.

6368–6370 (860–862). The tributaries of the Varangians drove them
back beyond the sea and, refusing them further tribute, set out to govern
themselves. There was no law among them, but tribe rose against tribe.
Discord thus ensued among them, and they began to war one against
another. They said to themselves, "Let us seek a prince who may rule
over us, and judge us according to the law." They accordingly went overseas to the Varangian Russes: these particular Varangians were known as
Russes, just as some are called Swedes, and others Normans, Angles, and

Goths, for they were thus named. The Chuds, the Slavs, and the Krivichians then said to the people of Rus, "Our whole land is great and rich, but there is no order in it. Come to rule and reign over us." They thus selected three brothers, with their kinsfolk, who took with them all the Russes and migrated. The oldest, Rurik, located himself in Novgorod; the second, Sineus, in Byeloozero; and the third, Truvor, in Izborsk. On account of these Varangians, the district of Novgorod became known as the land of the Rus. The present inhabitants of Novgorod are descended from the Varangian race, but aforetime they were Slavs.

After two years, Sineus and his brother Truvor died, and Rurik assumed the sole authority. He assigned cities to his followers, Polotzk to one, Rostove to another, and to another Byeloozero. . . . Rurik had dominion over all these districts.

With Rurik there were two men who did not belong to his kin, but were boyars. They obtained permission to go to Tsargrad with their families. They thus sailed down the Dnieper, and in the course of their journey they saw a small city on a hill. Upon inquiry as to whose town it was, they were informed that three brothers, Kii, Shchek, and Khoriv, had once built the city, but that since their deaths, their descendants were living there as tributaries of the Khazars. Oskold and Dir [the two boyars] remained in this city, and after gathering together many Varangians, they established their domination over the country of the Polyanians at the same time that Rurik was ruling at Novgorod.

6378–6387 (870–879). On his deathbed, Rurik bequeathed his realm to Oleg, who belonged to his kin, and intrusted to Oleg's hands his son Igor, for he was very young.

6388–6390 (880–882). [Oleg and his warriors captured the cities of Smolensk and Lyubech.] He then came to the hills of Kiev, and saw how Oskold and Dir reigned there. He hid his warriors in the boats, left some others behind, and went forward himself bearing the child Igor. He thus came to the foot of the Hunnish hill, and after concealing his troops, he sent messengers to Oskold and Dir, representing himself as a stranger on his way to Greece on an errand for Oleg and for Igor, the prince's son, and requesting that they should come forth to greet him as members of their race. Oskold and Dir straightway came forth. Then all the soldiery jumped out of their boats, and Oleg said to Oskold and Dir, "You are not princes nor even of princely stock, but I am of princely birth." Igor was then brought forward, and Oleg announced that he was the son of Rurik. They killed Oskold and Dir. . . . Oleg set himself up as prince in Kiev, and declared that it should be the mother of Russian cities. Varangians and Slavs accompanied him, and his retainers were called Russes. Oleg began to build stockaded towns, and imposed tribute on the Slavs, the Krivichians, and the Merians. He commanded that Novgorod should pay the Varangians tribute to the amount of 300 grivni a year for the preservation of peace. This tribute was paid to the Varangians until the death of Yaroslav. [Oleg also conquered the Derevlians and imposed tribute upon them.]

6392 (884). Oleg attacked the Severians, and conquered them. He imposed a light tribute upon them and forbade their further payment of tribute to the Khazars, on the ground that there was no reason for them to pay it as long as the Khazars were his enemies.

6411 (903). As Igor grew up, he followed after Oleg, and obeyed his instruction. A wife, Olga by name, was brought to him from Pskov. [Following Igor's death at the hands of the Derevlians in 945, Olga took over his place and power.]

6412–6415 (904–907). Leaving Igor in Kiev, Oleg attacked the Greeks [with the tribes called Great Scythia by the Greeks]. With this entire force, Oleg sallied forth by horse and by ship, and the number of his vessels was two thousand. . . . [Arriving before Tsargrad,] The Russes inflicted many other woes upon the Greeks after the usual manner of soldiers. Oleg commanded his warriors to make wheels which they attached to the [beached] ships, and when the wind was favorable, they spread the sails and bore down upon the city from the open country. When the Greeks beheld this, they were afraid, and sending messengers to Oleg, they implored him not to destroy the city and offered to submit to such tribute as he should desire. Thus Oleg halted his troops. . . . [He exacted tribute and when the Greeks "prayed for peace"] The Russes proposed the following terms: "The Russes who come hither shall receive as much grain as they require. Whosoever come as merchants shall receive supplies for six months, including bread, wine, meat, fish, and fruit. Baths shall be prepared for them in any volume they require. When the Russes return homeward, they shall receive from your Emperor food, anchors, cordage, and sails, and whatever else is needful for the journey." The Greeks accepted these stipulations, and the Emperors and all the courtiers declared: "If the Russes come hither without merchandise, they shall receive no provisions. Your prince shall personally lay injunction upon such Russes as journey hither that they shall do no violence in the towns and throughout our territory. Such Russes as arrive here shall dwell in the St. Mamas quarter. Our government will send officers to record their names, and they shall then receive their monthly allowance, first the natives of Kiev, then those from Chernigov, Pereyaslavl, and the other cities. They shall not enter the city save through one gate, unarmed and fifty at a time, escorted by soldiers of the Emperor. They may purchase wares according to their requirements and tax-free." Thus the Emperors Leo and Alexander made peace with Oleg. . . .

6416–6419 (908–911). A great star appeared in the west in the form of a spear.

6421 (913). Igor succeeded Oleg and began his reign. . . . The Derevlians declared war on Igor after Oleg's death.

6422 (914). Igor attacked the Derevlians, and after conquering them, he imposed upon them a tribute larger than Oleg's. . . .

6423 (915). The Pechenegs attacked the land of Rus for the first time, but when they had made peace with Igor, they went their way to the Danube. . . .

6456–6463 (948–955). Olga went to Greece, and arrived at Tsargrad. The reigning Emperor was named Tzimiskes. Olga came before him, and when he saw that she was very fair of countenance and wise as well, the Emperor wondered at her intellect. He conversed with her and remarked that she was worthy to reign with him in his city. When Olga heard his words, she replied that she was still a pagan, and that if he desired to baptize her, he should perform this function himself; otherwise, she was unwilling to accept baptism. The Emperor, with the assistance of the Patriarch, accordingly baptized her. When Olga was enlightened, she rejoiced in soul and body. . . . At her baptism she was christened Helena. . . . After her baptism, the Emperor summoned Olga and made known to her that he wished her to become his wife. But she replied, "How can you marry me, after yourself baptizing me and calling me your daughter? For among Christians that is unlawful, as you yourself must know." The Emperor then said, "Olga, you have outwitted me." He gave her many gifts of gold, silver, silks, and various vases, and dismissed her, still calling her his daughter.

[According to the chronicler, Olga died in 6477 (969) having failed to convert her son, Svyatoslav, to Christianity, but] She was the first from Rus to enter the kingdom of God, and the sons of Rus thus praise her as their leader, for since her death she has intervened with God in their behalf.

6496 (988). [The Tale relates at length how Vladimir, Grand Prince of Kiev, after a life of exceeding licentiousness ("Now Vladimir was overcome by lust for women. . . . He was insatiable in vice."), made a study of many religions, calling to him "Bulgarians of Mohammedan faith," German emissaries of the Pope, "Jewish Khazars," and scholars of the Greek faith. While he was still considering the matter, Vladimir captured the Greek city of Kherson, and demanded that the Greek emperors give him their sister to be his wife. They refused to comply unless Vladimir would be baptized. He agreed, and the Princess Anna was sent to Kherson. The Tale continues.]

By divine agency, Vladimir was suffering at that moment from a disease of the eyes, and could see nothing, being in great distress. The Princess declared to him that if he desired to be relieved of this disease, he should be baptized with all speed, otherwise it could not be cured. When Vladimir heard her message, he said, "If this proves true, then of a surety is the God of the Christians great," and gave order that he should be baptized. The Bishop of Kherson, together with the Princess's priests, after announcing the tidings, baptized Vladimir, and as the Bishop laid his hand upon him, he straightway received his sight. Upon experiencing this miraculous cure, Vladimir glorified God, saying, "I have now perceived the one true God." When his followers beheld this miracle, many of them were also baptized.

[After the baptism, Vladimir and Anna were married, the groom's wedding gift to his bride being the return of Kherson to the Greeks. Back in Kiev, Vladimir immediately ordered the chastisement and destruction of the pagan idols.]

Thereafter Vladimir sent heralds throughout the whole city to proclaim that if any inhabitant, rich or poor, did not betake himself to the river, he would risk the Prince's displeasure. When the people heard these words, they wept for joy, and exclaimed in their enthusiasm, "If this were not good, the Prince and his boyars would not have accepted it." On the morrow, the Prince went forth to the Dnieper with the priests of the Princess and those from Kherson, and a countless multitude assembled. They all went into the water: some stood up to their necks, others to their breasts, the younger near the bank, some of them holding children in their arms, while the adults waded farther out. The priests stood by and offered prayers. There was joy in heaven and upon earth to behold so many souls saved. . . .

When the people were baptized, they returned each to his own abode. . . . [Vladimir] ordained that churches should be built and established where pagan idols had previously stood. He thus founded the Church of St. Basil on the hill where the idol of Perun and the other images had been set, and where the Prince and the people had offered their sacrifices. He began to found churches and to assign priests throughout the cities, and to invite the people to accept baptism in all the cities and towns. He took the children of the best families, and sent them to schools for instruction.

6520–6522 (1012–1014). When Yaroslav [Valdimir's son] was in Novgorod, he paid two thousand grivni a year as tribute to Kiev, and distributed one thousand to his courtiers in Novgorod. All the viceroys of Novgorod had always paid like sums, but Yaroslav ceased to render this amount to his father. Then Vladimir exclaimed, "Repair the road and build a bridge," for he proposed to attack his son Yaroslav, but he fell ill.

[After a decade of internecine warfare among the sons of Vladimir, warfare marked by treachery and violence, a settlement was reached.] 6534 (1026). Yaroslav recruited many soldiers and arrived at Kiev, where he made peace with his brother Mstislav near Gorodetz. They divided Rus according to the course of the Dnieper. Yaroslav took the Kiev side, and Mstislav the other. They thus began to live in peace and fraternal amity. Strife and tumult ceased, and there was a great calm in the land.

6536 (1028). A portent visible to the whole country appeared in the heavens.

6537 (1029). Peace prevailed.

6562 (1054). Yaroslav, Great Prince of Rus, passed away. While he was yet alive, he admonished his sons with these words: "My sons, I am about to quit this world. Love one another, since ye are brothers by one father and mother. If ye dwell in amity with one another, God will dwell among you, and will subject your enemies to you, and ye will live at peace. But if ye dwell in envy and dissension, quarreling with one another, then ye will perish yourselves and bring to ruin the land of your ancestors, which they won at the price of great effort. Wherefore remain rather at peace, brother heeding brother. The throne of Kiev I bequeath to my eldest son, your brother Izyaslav. Heed him as ye have heeded me, that he may take my place among you. To Svyatoslav I give Chernigov, to Vsevolod Pereyaslavl, to Igor the city of Vladimir, and to Vyacheslav Smolensk. Thus he divided the cities among them, commanding them not to violate one another's boundaries, not to despoil one another. He laid upon Izyaslav the injunction to aid the party wronged, in case one brother should attack another. Thus he admonished his sons to dwell in amity.

6576 (1068). A multitude of those nomads known as the Polovcians attacked the land of Rus, and Izyaslav, Svyatoslav, and Vsevolod went forth against them as far as the Alta. They joined battle in the dead of night, but since God had let loose the pagans upon us because of our transgressions, the Russian princes fled and the Polovcians were victorious.

The Novgorod Chronicle: Selected Annals

The mixture of legend, fact, and various sorts of political and ec-clesiastical propaganda which characterizes *The Primary Chronicle* is also found in *The Chronicle of Novgorod*. Only the most expert spe-cialists can disentangle fact from legend, and even the experts disagree on many points. The following selection consists of samples taken from the Michell-Forbes translation, and exemplifying the various types of entries from the eleventh through the fifteenth centuries. English words have been substituted, whenever possible, for the Rus-sian terms which appear profusely in this translation. Such substitu-tions are indicated in this selection by enclosure in brackets.

The source is: Robert Michell and Nevill Forbes (Trs.), *The Chronicle of Novgorod, 1016–1471*. Camden Third Series. Vol. 25. London: The Camden Society, 1914. *Seriatim et passim*.

A.D. 1016. A.M. 6524. [There was] a fight at Lyubets, and [the sons of Vladimir] won; and Svyatopolk fled to Poland. And at that time Yaroslav was keeping many Varangians in Novgorod, fearing war; and the Varangians began to commit violence against the wives of the townsmen. The men of Novgorod said: 'We cannot look upon this violence,' and they gathered by night and fell upon and killed the Varangians in Poromon's Court; and that night [Prince] Yaroslav was at Rakomo. And having heard this, [Prince] Yaroslav was wroth with the townsfolk, and gathered a thousand soldiers in Slavno, and by craft falling on those who had killed the Varangians, he killed them; and others fled out of the town. And the same night Yaroslav's sister, Peredslava, sent word to him from Kiev, say-ing: 'Thy father is dead, and thy brethren slain.' And having heard this, Yaroslav the next day gathered a number of the men of Novgorod, and held an [assembly] in the open air, and said to them: 'My beloved and honourable [bodyguard], whom yesterday in my madness I slew, I can-not now buy back even with gold.' And thus he said to them: 'Brethren! my father Volodimir is dead, and Svyatopolk is [Prince] in Kiev; I want to go against him; come with me and help me.' And the men of Novgorod said to him: 'Yes, [Prince], we will follow thee.' And he gathered

4,000 soldiers: there were a thousand Varangians, and 3,000 of the men of Novgorod; and he went against him.

And Svyatopolk having heard this, gathered a countless number of soldiers, and went out against him to Lyubets and encamped there in the open country with a number of soldiers. And Yaroslav having come, halted on the bank of the Dnieper; and they stood there three months, not daring to come together (i.e. in conflict). Svyatopolk's [General] by name of Wolf's Tail, riding along the river-bank, began to reproach the men of Novgorod: 'Wherefore have you come with that builder of wooden [houses]?

'You are carpenters, and we shall make you build houses for us.' And the Dnieper began to freeze. And one of Yaroslav's men was on friendly terms with Svyatopolk. And Yaroslav sent one of his attendants to him by night, and he spoke to him. And this is what he said to him: 'What dost thou advise to be done now? There is but little mead brewed, and the [bodyguard] is large.' And that man said to him: 'Say thus to Yaroslav, if there is little mead, but a large [bodyguard], then give it in the evening.' And Yaroslav understood that he was advising him to fight at night; and that evening Yaroslav with his troops crossed the other bank of the Dnieper, and they pushed the boats away from the bank, and prepared to make battle that night. And Yaroslav said to his [bodyguard]: 'Put a mark on you, wind your heads in kerchiefs.' And there was a terrible fight, and before dawn they conquered Svyatopolk, and Svyatopolk fled to the Pecheneg people.

And Yaroslav went to Kiev, and took his seat on the throne of his father Volodimir. And he began to distribute pay to his troops: to the [elders] ten [half pounds of silver each], to the [foot soldiers] one [half pound of silver] each, and to all the men of Novgorod ten each, and let them all go to their homes.

A.D. 1068. A.M. 6576. The wrath of God came on us; the Polovets people came and conquered the Russian Land. The same year the men of Kiev rescued Vseslav from prison. The same year Svyatoslav defeated the Polovets people near Snovsk, and Izyaslav fled to Poland.

A.D. 1093. A.M. 6601. Vsevolod died; and Svyatopolk took his seat in Kiev. The same summer the Polovets people defeated Svyatopolk and Mstislav at Trepol.

A.D. 1107. A.M. 6615. The earth trembled on February 5.

A.D. 1111 A.M. 6619. Svyatopolk, Volodimir and David and the whole Russian Land to a man went against the Polovets people and defeated them and took their children, and rebuilt the fortified towns of Surtev and Sharukan.

At the same time the Lower town at Kiev was burnt, as well as Cherigov, Smolensk and Novgorod. The same year Ioan, Bishop of Chernigov, died. The same year Mstislav went against Ochela.

A.D. 1124. A.M. 6632. On the 11th day of August before evening service;
the sun began to decrease and it totally perished; oh, there was great terror
and darkness! There were stars and the moon; then it began to re-appear
and came out quickly in full; then all the city rejoiced.

A.D. 1135. A.M. 6643. [Mayor] Miroslav went from Novgorod to make
peace between the people of Kiev and those of Chernigov, and he came
back without having achieved anything; for the whole Russian Land was
in great disorder; Yaropolk called the men of Novgorod to his side; and
the [Prince] of Chernigov to his; and they fought, and God helped the
son of Oleg with the men of Chernigov and he cut up many of the men of
Kiev and others they captured in the month of August. And this was not
the whole of the evil; the Polovets people and everyone began to muster
fighting men.

The same year, Vsevolod with [Archbishop] Nifont founded a stone
church of the Holy Mother of God in the Market Place.

The same year, Irozhnet founded a church to St. Nicholas in Yakov
Street. The same year in the winter, [Archbishop] Nifont with the best
men went into Russia, and found the men of Kiev and the men of Chernigov ranged against each other, and a quantity of troops; and by the will of
God they were reconciled. And Miroslav died before the return of the
[Archbishop] in January 28; the Bishop came on February 4. And they
gave the [Mayor]-ship in Novgorod to Kostyantin Mikultsits.

A.D. 1141. A.M. 6649. On April 1 there was a very marvellous sign in the
sky; six circles, three close about the sun, and three other large ones outside the sun, and stood nearly all day.

The same year they came from Vsevolod from Kiev for his brother
Svyatoslav to take him to Kiev; 'and receive my son as your [Prince],' he
said. And when they sent the Bishop and many best men for his son, they
said to Svyatoslav: 'Thou wait for thy brother, then thou shalt go:' but he,
fearing the men of Novgorod, 'whether they are going to deceive me,' fled
secretly in the night; Yakun fled with him. And they took Yakun on the
[river] Plisa, and having brought him hither with his brother Procupi, they
nearly did him to death, having stripped him naked, as his mother bore him,
and they threw him down from the bridge; but God saved him, he waded
to the bank, and they beat him no more, but took from him 1,000 [half
pounds of silver] and from his brother 100 [half pounds of silver], likewise they took from others; and they exiled Yakun with his brother to the
Chud people, having chained their hands to their wives from Novgorod,
and kept them by him in favour. And Vsevolod was wroth, and he detained all the emissaries and the Bishop and the Merchants.

And the people of Novgorod went without a [prince] nine months;
and they summoned Sudila, Nezhata and Strashko from Suzhdal, who
had fled from Novgorod on account of Svyatoslav and Yakun; and they
gave the [Mayor]-ship in Novgorod to Sudila; and they sent to Suzhdal
for Gyurgi to be [Prince] and he did not go, but sent his son, Rostislav,
who had been before.

The same year Rostislav went on the throne at Novgorod, on November 26.

A.D. 1177. A.M. 6685. Gleb, [Prince] of Ryazan, died in captivity in Volodimir. At the same time [Prince] Mstislav was blinded, with his brother Yaropolk, by their Uncle Vsevolod, and he let them go into Russia. And the two blind [men], being led with rotting eyes, when they reached Smolensk they came to Smyadino into the Church of the Holy Martyrs Boris and Gleb; and there forthwith the Grace of God and of our Holy Sovereign Lady the Mother of God and of the newly manifested holy Martyrs Boris and Gleb descended on them and there they saw clearly. The same year in the autumn the Nerev end from Ivankova took fire and five churches were burnt down. And in the winter [Prince] Mstislav with his brother Yaropolk came to Novgorod, and the men of Novgorod set Mstislav on the throne, and Yaropolk in Novitorg, and Yaroslav in Volok-Lamsk, and thus they arranged [things] according to their will.

A.D. 1203. A.M. 6711. Rurik with the sons of Oleg and the heathen Polovets people, with Kontsyak and Danila Byakovits captured Kiev, on January 1, St. Vasili's Day; and whomever their hands reached, whether monk or nun, priest or priest's wife, these they led off to the heathen; and all foreign merchants and foreigners of every country shut themselves up in the churches, and they granted them their lives; but their merchandise they divided with them by halves; but everything in the monasteries and in all the churches, all valuables and ornaments and ikons the pagans tore off and carried away into their own land; and they set fire to the town. Then, too, the Russian [princes] Rurik, Roman, Mstislav and many other [princes] went against the Polovets people. And then the winter was very cruel; and they took much plunder and drove away their herds. The same year Roman sent Vyacheslav ordering him to have Rurik shorn [a monk]. The same year the sons of Oleg defeated the Lithuanians, and did to death seven hundred and a thousand of them. The same year Miroshka, [Mayor] of Novgorod died, he was shorn in St. Georgi's, and then they gave the [Mayor]-ship to Mikhalko Stepanits. The same year for our sins all the horses died in Novgorod and in the villages so that it was not possible to go anywhere for the stench.

A.D. 1238. A.M. 6746. The wife of Semen Borisovich made a monastery at the Church of St. Paul. That same year foreigners called Tartars came in countless numbers, like locusts, into the land of Ryazan, and on first coming they halted at the river Nukhla, and took it, and halted in camp there. And thence they sent their emissaries to the [princes] of Ryazan, a sorceress and two men with her, demanding from them one-tenth of everything; of men and [Princes] and horses—of everything one-tenth. And the [princes] of Ryazan, George Ingvor's brother, Oleg, Roman Ingvorevich, and those of Murom and Pronsk, without letting them into their towns, went out to meet them to Voronazh. And the [princes] said to

them: 'Only when none of us remain then all will be yours.' And thence
they let them go to Yuri in Volodimir, and thence they let the Tartars at
Voronazh go back to the Nukhla. And the [princes] of Ryazan sent to
Yuri of Volodimir asking for help, or himself to come. But Yuri neither
went himself nor listened to the request of the [princes] of Ryazan, but
he himself wished to make war separately. But it was too late to oppose
the wrath of God, as was said of old by God, to Joshua the son of Nun,
when leading them to the promised land, then he said: 'I shall before you
send upon them perplexity, and thunder, and fear, and trembling.' Thus
also did God before these men take from us our strength and put into us
perplexity and thunder and dread and trembling for our sins. And then
the pagan foreigners surrounded Ryazan and fenced it in with a stockade.
And [Prince] Yuri of Ryazan, shut himself in the town with his people,
but [Prince] Roman Ingorovich began to fight against them with his own
men. Then [Prince] Yuri of Volodimir sent Yeremei as *Voyevoda* with a
patrol and joined Roman; and the Tartars surrounded them at Kolomno,
and they fought hard and drove them to the ramparts. And there they
killed Roman and Yeremei and many fell here with the [Prince] and with
Yeremei. And the men of Moscow ran away having seen nothing. And the
Tartars took the town on December 21, and they had advanced against it
on the 16th of the same month. They likewise killed the [Prince] and
Knyaginya, and men, women and children, monks, nuns and priests, some
by fire, some by the sword, and violated nuns, priests' wives, good women
and girls in the presence of their mothers and sisters. But God saved the
Bishop, for he had departed the same moment when the troops invested
the town. And who, brethren, would not lament over this, among those of
us left alive when they suffered this bitter and violent death? And we, indeed, having seen it, were terrified and wept with sighing day and night
over our sins, while we sigh every day and night, taking thought for our
possessions and for the hatred of brothers. And the accursed godless ones
then pushed on from Torshok by the road of Seregeri right up to Ignati's
cross, cutting down everybody like grass, to within 100 and [66 miles] of
Novgorod. God, however, and the great and sacred apostolic cathedral of
St. Sophia, and St. Kyuril, and the prayers of the holy and orthodox [Arch-
bishop], of the faithful [princes] and of the very reverend monks of the
hierachical [assembly], protected Novgorod. And who, brothers, fathers,
and children, seeing this, God's infliction on the whole Russian Land, does
not lament? God let the pagans on us for our sins. God brings foreigners on
to the land in his wrath, and thus crushed by them they will be reminded
of God. And the internecine war comes from the prompting of the devil:
for God does not wish evil amongst man, but good; but the devil rejoices
at the wicked murder and bloodshed. And any other land which has sinned
God punished with death of famine, or with infliction of pagans, or with
drought, or with heavy rain, or with other punishment, to see whether we
will repent and live as God bids; for He tells us by the prophet: 'Turn to
me with your whole heart, with fasting and weeping.' And if we do so we
shall be forgiven of all our sins. But we always turn to evil, like swine ever
wallowing in the filth of sin, and thus we remain; and for this we receive

every kind of punishment from God; and the invasion of armed men, too, we accept at God's command; as punishment for our sins.

A.D. 1311. A.M. 6819. The men of Novgorod went in war over sea to the country of the [Germans], against the Yem people, with Prince Dmitri Romanovich, and having crossed the sea they first occupied the Kupets river, they burned villages, and captured people and destroyed the cattle. And there Konstantin the son if Ilya Stanimirovich was killed by a column that went in pursuit. They then took the whole of the Black river, and thus following along the Black river they reached the town of Vanai and they took the town and burned it. And the [Germans] fell back into the [citadel]: for the place was very strong and firm, on a high rock, not having access from any side. And they sent with greeting, asking for peace, but the men of Novgorod did not grant peace, and they stood three days and three nights wasting the district. They burned the large villages, laid waste all the cornfields, and did not leave a single horn of cattle; and going hence, they took the Kavgola river and the Perna river, and they came out on the sea and returned all well to Novgorod.

The same spring, on May 19, a fire broke out at night in Yanev Street, and forty less three houses were burnt and seven people. Then in the night of June 28 Glebov's house in Rozvazha Street caught fire, and the Norev quarter was burnt, on one side so far as the fosse, and on the other beyond Borkov Street; and the Church of SS. Kosma and Demyan was burnt, also that of St. Sava, and forty churches were damaged by fire and several good houses. Oh, woe, brethren, the conflagration was fierce, with wind and hurricane! And wicked and bad men having no fear of God, seeing peoples run, plundered other men's property. Then on July 16 a fire broke out at night in the Ilya Street, and here likewise was a fierce conflagration with a high wind, and crashing noise; the market place was burnt, and houses up to Rogatitsa Street, and the churches burnt were—seven wooden churches: St. Dmitri, St. Georgi, S.S. Boris and Gleb, St. Ioan Ishkov, St. Catherine, St. Prokopi, and of Christ; and six stone churches were damaged by fire, and the seventh was the Varangian Church. And accursed men likewise having no fear of God, nor remembering the judgement of God, and having no pity for their fellows, plundered other people's property. Repay them, Lord, according to their deeds!

The same year they took the [Mayor]-ship from Mikhail and gave to Semen Klimovich. The same year [Archbishop] David erected a stone church at the gate of the Nerev quarter, to St. Volodimir.

A.D. 1327. A.M. 6835. The same winter a very great force of Tartars came, and they took Tver and Kashin and the Novi-torg district, and to put it simply, laid waste all the Russian Land, God and St. Sophia preserved Novgorod alone, and [Prince] Olexander fled to Pleskov, and his brother Kostyantin and Vasili to Dadoga. And the Tartars sent envoys to Novgorod, and the men of Novgorod gave them 2,000 in silver, and they sent their own envoys with them, with numerous presents to the [generals].

A.D. 1349. A.M. 6857. The King of Cracow with a large force seized the country of Volynia by deceit, and did much injury to the Christians, and he converted the sacred churches to the Latin service hated of God.

A.D. 1379. A.M. 6887. The same year the Tartars came into the Russian Land, against the [Great Prince] Dmitri. And the [Prince] went out against them, and it was on the Ovosha river, and there both forces met and God aided the Great Prince, and the Tartars turned shoulder and fled. The same year they founded two stone churches: one to the Holy Mother of God in the Mikhalitsa [Street] and the other to the Holy Frola and Lavra in Lyudogoshcha Street.

The same year the Lithuanian [Prince] Yuri Narimantovich came to Novgorod.

A.D. 1380. A.M. 688. The same year, in the month of August, news came to the [Great Prince] Dmitri and to his brother [Prince] Volodimir from the Horde that the pagan race of Ishmaelites was rising against the Christians; for there was some weak man *Tsar* among them, and [Prince] Mamai was controlling all their affairs and he was savagely enraged against the [Great Prince] and all the Russian Land.

And having heard this, that a great Tartar force was coming against him, the [Great Prince] Dmitri Ivanovich gathered many soldiers and went against the godless Tartars, trusting in the mercy of God and in His Immaculate Mother, the Mother of God, the eternal Virgin Mary, calling to his aid the honourable Cross. For he entered their country beyond the Don, and there was a clean field at the mouth of the river Nepryadva, and there the pagan Ishmaelites had ranged themselves against the Christians. And the Moscovites, of whom many were inexperienced, were frightened and in despair for their lives at sight of the great numbers of Tartars, others turned to flight, forgetful of the Prophet's saying that one shall reap one thousand, and two shall move ten thousand, if God does not abandon them.

And the [Great Prince] Dmitri with his brother Volodimir ranged their troops against the pagan Polovets people, and raising their eyes humbly to heaven, and sighing from the depth of their hearts, said, in the words of the psalm: 'Brothers, God is our refuge and our strength.' And both forces immediately met, and there was a fierce battle for a long time, and God terrified the sons of Hagar with an invisible might, and they turned their shoulders to wounds, and they were routed by the Christians, and some were struck down with weapons, and others drowned in the river, a countless number of them.

And in the encounter [Prince] Fedor Belozerski was killed, also his son [Prince] Ivan; and other [princes] and captains went in pursuit of the aliens. The godless Tartars fell from dread of God and by the arms of the Christians; and God raised the right hand of the [Great Prince] Dmitri Ivanovich and of his brother [Prince] Volodimir Andreyevich for the defeat of the aliens.

And this was because of our sins: the aliens take up arms against us, that we might renounce our wrong-doings and hatred of our brethren, from our love of silver, and from wrong judging and violence; but God is merciful and man-loving; He is not angry with us utterly, and is not at enmity forever.

A.D. 1382. A.M. 6890. The Tartar *Tsar* Tektomysh came against the Russian Land with a large force, and ravaged much of the Russian Land; he took Moscow town and burned it; also Pereyaslavl, Kolomno, Serpukhov, Dmitrov, Volodimir and Yurev.

A.D. 1420. A.M. 6928. The men of Novgorod began to trade with silver coins, and sold the [Swedish copper coins] to the Germans, having traded with them nine years.

A.D. 1432. A.M. 6940. The Russian [princes] Vasili Vasilievich and Yuri Dmitrievich came away from the Horde; *Tsar* Mahmed gave the title of [Great Prince] over the whole Russian Land to Prince Vasili Vasilievich.

The same autumn [Prince] Yuri Simeonovich with his wife arrived in Novgorod from the Lithuanian country.

A.D. 1434. A.M. 6942. [Prince] Yuri Dmitrievich seized the town of Moscow and took his seat as [Great Prince].

And the same year, in the spring, on April 1, in Holy Week, the [Great Prince] Vasili Vasilievich came to Novgorod.

A.D. 1441. A.M. 6949. In the winter the [Great Prince] Vasili Vasilievich of Moscow turned his wrath on Novgorod the Great; he sent a declaration of war and ravaged many Novgorod districts. And the men of Novgorod sent out [Archbishop] Eufemi with *Boyars* and men of property who fell in with him in Dereva near the town of Demyan, and concluded peace with him on the old terms, and gave him 8,000 *roubles*.

And the men of Pskov aided the [Great Prince] Vasili in ravaging the Novgorod lands and they did no little damage.

At the same time Novgorod [generals] with men from the country beyond the *Volok* ravaged many lands of the [Great Prince] for those he had ravaged of the districts of Novgorod.

The same winter the Metropolitan Isidor returned to Russia from the Eighth [Assembly] in Rome, and began calling himself *Legatos* from the rib of the Apostolic seat of Roman power, and Roman Metropolitan: he also began the naming of the Pope of Rome in his services, and other new things which we have never heard since the baptism of the Russian Land; and he ordered Russian priests to perform his service in the Polish churches, and chaplains to serve in Russian churches. But Lithuania and Russia did not support this.

A.D. 1445. A.M. 6953. The same winter the [Great Prince] Vasili went against the Tartar *Tsar* Mohmed; many Christians died from cold, others were slain by the Tartars who laid waste the country. But God aided the [Great Prince] Vasili, and the Tartars fled, other being slain.

Bread was dear in Novgorod, and not only this year but during ten whole years: one [half-rouble] for two [baskets]; sometimes a little more, sometimes less; sometimes there was none to be bought anywhere. And amongst the Christians there was great grief and distress; only crying and sobbing were to be heard in the streets and market place, and many people fell down dead from hunger, children before their parents, fathers and mothers before their children; and many dispersed, some to Lithuania, others passed over to Latinism, and others to the *Besermeny* and to the Jews, giving themselves to the traders for bread.

At the same time there was no law or justice in Novgorod; calumniators arose and turned obligations and accounts and oaths to falsehood; and began to rob in the town and in the villages and districts; we were exposed to the rebukes of our neighbours, who were around us. There was much confiscation, frequent demands for money, throughout the districts, with weeping and anguish and with outcries and curses on all sides against our seniors and our town: because there was no grace in us, nor justice.

A.D. 1471. A.M. 6979. The [Great Prince] Ioan Vasilievich marched with a force against Novgorod the Great because of its wrong doing and lapsing into Latinism.

Medieval Towns and Cities

The necessity for trying to supplement incomplete and imperfect evidence by conjectures and reasoned analogies obviously leads to imprecision and uncertainty. It has also led, in the field of Russian history, to many controversies. Some of these have been honest differences of opinion among reasonable men; others reflect antipathetic nationalisms or equally antipathetic philosophies and schema of history. Some of the excerpts from a study by a Soviet scholar illustrate all these characteristics. He writes, of course, from within the framework of historical materialism and its ramifications, including what seems to non-Marxists to be a highly artificial periodization of history.

The source is: M. (N.) Tikhomirov (D. Skvirksy, Ed., Y. Sdobnikov, Tr.), *The Towns of Ancient Rus.* Moscow: Foreign Languages Publishing House, 1959. *Seriatim et passim.* Very much abridged.

In Scandinavian sources, Rus is called Gardariki, a land of towns. That agrees with reports by an anonymous 9th century Bavarian geographer, a fragment of whose writings has come down to us in a late 11th century manuscript. His information antecedes [antedates] that of the Russian chronicle. . . . The towns were unquestionably very small, for he says that the Attorosi tribe . . . had 148 towns. Even at a much later date, such a number of sizable urban settlements could scarcely have found room along the Dnieper and the Bug, where, according to the manuscript . . . [this tribe] lived.

The Slav settlements were situated close to each other but were poorly fortified. They are the "cities" mentioned by the anonymous Bavarian author, who reckons them in the hundreds for some Slav tribes. The conclusions made on the strength of written sources have recently been borne out by the spade. Various artifacts discovered in the Dniester basin indicate that there were handicraft industries in that area in the early centuries of our era. Researchers point to the continuity in the culture of the Dniester country and Kiev Rus. Some strongholds were well fortified but small. They were embryonic towns where the population of the surrounding area sought shelter from enemy raids. . . .

The mist enveloping the history of 8th century Rus because of the total absence of written sources, lifts in the 9th and 10th centuries when the testimony of the chronicles comes to our aid. Nevertheless, the number of ancient Rus cities cannot be established with any certitude even for that period, because our chief source of information, the chronicle, contains only scattered and vague data on the subject. . . . Judging from the chronicle, there were more than a score of Russian cities in the 9th and 10th centuries . . . but this is obviously incomplete. . . .

The slanderous theories describing the Eastern Slavs as a wild people whose culture originated only after the appearance of the Normans in the north and of the Khazars in the south, naturally induce us to find out who built the first Rus cities. The overwhelming majority of Russian cities bear Slavic names. . . . It follows therefore that the earliest Russian towns were founded by Eastern Slavs . . . [who] were the first and principal founders of towns and urban life in Kiev Rus. Since towns are wellsprings of culture, it is the Slavs who are mainly to be credited with the development of Russian culture. . . .

M. K. Karger . . . believes that there were at least three "independent settlements in the 8th–10th centuries" [on the site of Kiev]; this agrees with the legend about the three brothers. It was only late in the 10th century that they [i.e., the settlements] merged into a single town. . . . [Excavations on the site confirm the chronicler's statements] that the fortified locality, the town proper, occupied a very small territory. The town was extended by Yaroslav, who in 1037 founded "the great city of Kiev" with its Golden Gates. . . . [That the initial town was small] is indicated by the remains of an ancient moat . . . which surrounded 8th–9th century Kiev. Traces of mud huts dating from that same period were also discovered. . . . Kiev occupied a small territory . . . [but] It had already ceased to be a small town and had become the "mother of Russian cities.". . .

The earliest of the Kiev tumuli [burial mounds] date back to the 9th century. Male burials contain iron knives with bone hafts, spear and arrow heads, stirrups, and so forth. Female burials yield miscellaneous silver, copper, and, rarely, gold ornaments, as well as necklaces and crosses. . . . Byzantine coins and Arab dirhems date the sepultures to the 9th–10th centuries. . . .

On the whole, the Kiev of that period appears to be a town with a handicraft industry and trade, but scarcely with a considerable population of handicraftsmen. In essence, it was a city of princes and their escorts. The *lyudi,* or citizens, make up a large section of the population but are closely associated with the prince's court and his retinue, while the handicraftsmen as such are mostly bondsmen. This is also true of other early Rus towns, primarily Novgorod. . . .

Russian chronicles of the 11th–13th century mention a large number of towns. [Tikhomirov enumerates 58 from these sources.] But only an incomplete list can be drawn up on the strength of written sources. [Adding names from other sources, he concludes.] We have 64 new towns for the 11th century which with those earlier mentioned brings the total to 89 (or close to a hundred.) [Tikhomirov estimates that there were certainly 224 "urban centers" in Rus "by the end of the 12th century"; and "close to 300 towns in Rus on the eve of the Mongolian [Tatar] invasion."] . . .

With time the towns in Rus became bigger and more numerous. The earliest of them were confined to their . . . citadel, around which separate settlements sprang up and eventually merged into [*i.e.,* formed] suburbs, or *posads.* The bulk of the population lived near the walls of the citadel which was usually situated on a hill at some distance from the river. The choice of site for a citadel was dictated by military considerations, but the development of the handicrafts and trade inevitably drew the artisans and the merchants from the hills to the lowlands—from the *gora* to the *podol.* The latter [term] became the usual name for urban riverside districts as opposed to the aristocratic *gora.* . . . The appearance of urban posads was a milestone in the history of Russian towns. This development is not traced above [*sic* prior] to the late 10th century. . . . As the handicraftsmen and merchants settled beyond the walls of the citadel, two urban worlds—the royal and the free (merchants and craftsmen)—arose side by side. . . .

Urban *posads* began to spring up approximately in the 9th century, in Kiev earlier than elsewhere. In most Russian towns they appeared in the 11th century. [Where did the people come from?] . . . mostly from the countryside and fugitive *kholops* (indentured people). . . . *Ruskaya Pravda* mentions *kholops* who settled in town to take up the handicrafts or engage in trade. . . . *Ruskaya Pravda* also proves that fugitive *kholops* helped to increase the urban population. They were probably not only *kholops* in the narrow sense of the word but also bondsmen in general, including enslaved *smerds.* . . . The steady influx of people into the towns was kept up by the privileges usually extended by the princes to settlers. . . . There is data showing that a part of the urban population was made up of former prisoners of war.

[What caused the rise of towns?] The best known theory of the origin of Russian towns belongs to Klyuchevsky. . . . "They were the direct results of Rus's thriving foreign trade.". . . this theory is in line with Klyuchevsky's idea that trade was the motive force behind the emergence of the early Russian towns. . . . Klyuchevsky has not substantiated his theory. . . . [his] views spring from his belief that hunting and local industries were extensively developed in Kiev Rus. As a result, the first volume of his famous *Course* ignores the economic structure of Russian lands in the 10th–13th centuries. There is no need to probe the role of agriculture in Kiev Rus after everything that has been written on the subject by B. D. Grekov, but it should be noted that the latter, while criticizing Klyuchevsky, agrees that the major Slav towns sprang up along the great waterways.

A closer look at Klyuchevsky's theory . . . shows that it does not hold water [because many towns were not situated on the waterway from the Varangians to the Greeks, and some towns which were so situated failed to survive]. . . . These examples suffice to disprove Klyuchevsky's contention that the earliest Russian towns were necessarily linked with trade along the waterways. Naturally, waterways did contribute to the supremacy of some towns over others, but they were not the primary cause of the emergence of towns. . . .

[S. V. Yushkov] shows that towns were built by princes and not by merchants and enterprising people. . . . He thinks that the Russian town of the 11th–13th centuries . . . was primarily a feudal administrative center . . . a rallying point for the armed forces of the area and a financial and administrative centre. . . . Yushkov's conclusions are highly valuable. . . . [but] His exposition is much too general . . . [he] underestimated the importance of the urban *posads* . . . showing a traditional disregard for the history of towns.

The end of the 9th and the beginning of the 10th century, when the number of towns multiplied and when *posads* clustered around them, was a momentous period of Russian history. . . . Feudalism was established as a social system. . . . Agriculture and the crafts in the economic sphere, and feudal relationships were the real motive forces which caused the emergence of Russian towns.

The medieval town in Rus . . . was first and foremost a walled enclosure. This was what initially distinguished a town from a village. . . . Excavations in 11th–12th century Rus towns confirm that the townsfolk were permanently connected with agriculture. . . . agriculture was the main occupation of the inhabitants, a fact proved by the discovery of hoes, sickles, scythes and so on. Vegetable gardens and orchards were an integral part of every urban homestead. . . . Animal breeding was a major occupation of the townsfolk. . . . [Agriculture] prevailed in small towns . . . [but] was less developed in such major centres as Kiev and Novgorod. . . . Nevertheless, it was the handicrafts and trade, and not agriculture, that dominated the economy of Russian towns in the 10th–13th centuries. The chief urban centers could not exist without constant intercourse with the nieghboring agricultural areas.

Summing up the testimony of the written sources we get the following [incomplete] list of Russian crafts: whitewashers, nailmakers, potters, fortification builders, woodworkers, locksmiths, architects, goldsmiths, iconographers, stonehewers, stonemasons, hoodmakers, tanners, shipwrights, boilermakers, smiths, silversmiths, coppersmiths, bowmakers, bridge builders, tinsmiths, weavers, painters, scribes, carpenters, catapult makers, sempsters, spinners, saddle makers, silverers, glaziers, quiver makers, bootmakers, shield makers.

Trade was one of the main features of urban economy in Ancient Rus. . . . The market was just as important to Ancient Rus towns as their battlements. . . . Internal trade was so commonplace that it scarcely aroused the interest of contemporary writers. That is why we have such scanty and fragmentary reports. . . . Foreign, "overseas" trade is described in far greater detail. [The word *gost* was used to denote a foreign merchant or a merchant who traded with foreign countries; an ordinary tradesman, or merchant, was called *kupets*.] . . . We learn of Russian merchants visiting. . . Central Asia, Constantinople, Denmark, Gottland, while Venetian, Czech, Greek, Central Asian, German, and other merchants came to Kiev, Smolensk, Novgorod, and other Ancient Rus towns. . . . Foreign trade was centered in the towns, mostly in the bigger ones, but foreign goods also trickled into the countryside. . . . In spite of the limited turnover in Ancient Rus between the 9th and the 13th centuries, trade duties were the main items of royal revenue.

It is practically impossible to determine the size of the population of towns in ancient Rus, and only the most general statement can be made on the subject. . . . the population of Kiev at the height of its prosperity reached into the tens of thousands. This was a giant city according to medieval standards. . . . Novgorod's population in the early 11th century was between 10 and 15 thousand, and between 20 and 30 thousand in the early 13th century. . . . Chernigov, both Vladimirs, Galich, Polotsk, and Smolensk [had] populations practically equal to that of Novgorod. They were closely followed by Rostov, Suzdal, Ryazan, Vitebsk, Pereyaslavl Russky. . . . The population of other towns rarely exceed 1,000. . . .

The Beginnings of Kievan Rus

Soviet historians who must work within the arbitrary Marxist-Leninist periodization of history are bound thereby to insist upon the feudal and agricultural character of Kievan society. (Examples of this will be found in this anthology in the selections from the writings of Grekov and Tikhomirov.) A contrary view was set forth in a pre-Soviet work, *Kurs Russkoi Istorii (Course of Russian History)*, by Vasilii O. Klyuchevskii, the most famous Russian historian and one of the great historians of the world. Klyuchevskii, member of the Faculty of Moscow University from 1879 until his death in 1911, was interested almost exclusively in domestic developments and particularly in the social and economic history of the Russian people. His monumental

Kurs Russkoi Istorii covers these aspects, virtually ignoring all others, from the beginnings to 1825. The selection below links the beginnings of Kievan Rus with trade. The findings of more recent scholarship suggest that Klyuchevskii overemphasized this connection, but most non-Soviet scholars still accept his thesis as generally sound though in need of some modifications.

There have been several editions of Klyuchevskii's *Kurs,* including an English translation by C. J. Hogarth. The selection below has been translated from the most recent Russian edition: V. O. Klyuchevskii, *Sochineniya (Works).* Eight volumes. Moscow, 1956–1959. Vol. 1, pp. 146–148. Slightly adapted.

Kiev served both as the center of the Russian export trade and as the main outpost for the defense of the country against the steppes. Therefore, when Kiev later fell into the hands of the Varangians it did not remain only a local Varangian principality, which was happening at about the same time to Novgorod, Izborsk and Byeloozero and, later, to Polotsk and Turov. Bound by commercial ties to Byzantium, the Arabian East, and the markets of the Black Sea, the Sea of Azov, and the Caspian; the labor of her people turned toward the exploitation of the country's forest resources, Kiev was dependent on the amount of trading done. It was indispensable for the protection of this trade to have secure frontiers and open trade routes along the rivers of the steppes. It was also necessary, now and again, to exert armed force upon the markets themselves in order to assure conditions of free trade. All this could be accomplished only by the combined power of all the East Slavic tribes; that is, by their forced cooperation with Kiev because those tribes who lived at a distance from the major trade routes did not voluntarily choose to support the Kievan princes. This explains why our records, and those of others, stress the aggressive acts of the first Kievan princes. The researches of the Academician Vassilev into the lives of St. George of Amastrid and St. Stephen of Surozh show clearly that Rus raided the Black Sea coasts, even the southern coasts, in the first half of the ninth century (A.D.). Rus did not, however, risk attacking Tsargrad itself [*i.e.,* Constantinople] until the time of the Patriarch Fotius [Photius]. Fotius had previously heard some accounts concerning significant changes in Rus, especially and specifically in Kiev, and in his sermon delivered at Tsargrad on the occasion of the Rus attack, and in a subsequent epistle to the neighboring districts, he explained this Russian boldness. An unknown people—insignificant, in Fotius' words, before this attack—suddenly became notorious and celebrated after this daring deed. Such audacity also suggested why the Russes had subjugated the surrounding tribes and why they became overly proud and bold. The meaning is that as soon as the Varangian principality of Kiev was formed, it concentrated the strength of the country, and that the first general Russian undertaking was the securing of trade relations.

These were the conditions, the furthering of which brought about the rise of the Kievan principality. It began as one of many Varangian holdings. Askold and his brother settled in Kiev simply as Varangian chieftains, guarding the security and trading interests of their prize. Oleg followed in their footsteps and continued their policies, but the military-industrial position of Kiev gave these policies a wider significance. The Kievan land, situated at the southern end of the trade route from the Varangians to the Greeks, blocked the rest of the country from access, and the rest of the country shared Kiev's interest in the trade. The other Varangian princes and cities of the Russian region were therefore forced to unite under the power of the Kievan prince, whether they liked it or not, and so the Kievan principality acquired the prestige of the Rus state. The downfall of Khazar power left these princes and town-provinces no alternative to accepting economic and political subordination to Kiev. It therefore seems to me that the arrival of Rurik at Novgorod should not be considered to be the beginning of the Rus state. Novgorod at that time arose as a local and short-lived Varangian principality. The Rus state was established at Kiev through the efforts of Askold and, later, Oleg. The political federation of the Slavs of Russia originated not from Novgorod, but from Kiev. Varangian Kiev, principality of these two stalwarts, was the seed from which grew the union of the Slavs and their neighbors with the Finnish tribes which may be recognized as the first form of the Russian state.

Kievan Rus at Its Peak

This summary description of Kievan Rus at the height of its power has been translated and slightly adapted from the 1956–59 edition of Klyuchevskii's *Sochineniya* (*Works*), vol. 1, pp. 162–164.

The first princes of Kiev thus continued the activities of the Rus trading centers which they had conquered, namely, maintaining trade with overseas markets and protecting the trade routes and the frontiers of Rus against her neighbors on the steppes. Having described the activity of the first Kievan princes, we shall summarize its results and give a cursory glance at the condition of Rus at about the middle of the eleventh century. Kiev was the political center of a rather wide circle of land which the Kievan princes delimited by their swords. The territory had a rather mixed population. Not only the Eastern Slavic tribes but gradually several of the Finnish tribes . . . came to be a part of it. Rus towns appeared early among these alien tribes. Thus there sprang up among the Baltic Chud' in the time of Yaroslav Yurev (Dorpat), so-called after the Christian name of Yaroslav. Other centers of Rus power (Rostov, Murom, and Belozorsk) had appeared even earlier among the Finnish tribes in the east—the Merya, the Muroma, and the Vyes. On the bank of the Volga, Yaroslav built another city which was called by his princely name, Yaroslav. The territory of Rus stretched from Lake Ladoga to the mouths of the right and left tributaries of the Dnieper. From east to west, it ran from the mouth of the Klyasma, on which in the time of Vladimir Monomakh there sprang up the town of Vladimir (Zaleski), to the upper reaches of the Western Bug where there arose even earlier (in the time of St. Vladimir) another town called Vladimir (Volinski). Galicia, the country of the ancient Croats, was a disputed territory in the tenth and eleventh centuries, passing from hand to hand between Poland and Rus. The lower part of the Oka River, which was the eastern border of Kievan Rus, and the lower reaches of the southern rivers—the Dnieper, the Eastern Bug, and the Dniester—were apparently beyond the power of the Kievan princes. Kievan Rus still retained its one-time colony, Tmutorakan, though this was outside the Kievan boundaries. The connection was maintained by water routes along the left tributaries of the Dnieper and the rivers of the Sea of Azov.

The people of different races who dwelt in all this territory became part of the Great Principality of Kiev, or the Rus State, but this Rus State was not a nation of Russian people because such a people did not yet exist. By the middle of the eleventh century there existed only ethnographic elements from which, by a long and difficult process, the Russian nationality would form. All these disparate elements were only mechanically united. The moral bond, Christianity, spread slowly and did not yet unite even all the Slavic tribes of the lands of Rus—the Vyatchi, for example, were still not Christians at the beginning of the twelfth century. The main mechanical bond of part of the population of the Rus lands was the princely administration with its officials, its tributes, and its taxes. The Great Prince of Kiev stood at the head of this administration. The nature and the genesis of his power are already known to us. He came from among the Varangian Vikings, a military and trading group which had begun to appear among the Rus in the ninth century. Beginning as a military guard, they were paid by the population in food and fodder for protecting Rus, its trade, its trade routes across the steppes, and its foreign markets; conquests and contacts with alien political institutions added new features to the power of this hired military group, complicating it and giving to it the character of a supreme governmental authority. In the tenth century, our princes, under the influence of the Khazars, loved to call themselves "Kagans." It is clear from the writings of Ibn-Dast that the usual title for a Rus prince in the first half of the tenth century was "Khakan-Rus," Rus Kagan. The Metropolitan of Rus, Ilarion, who wrote in the middle of the eleventh century, in eulogizing St. Vladimir gives even this prince the Khazar title of Kagan.

A new stream of political ideas and attitudes came into Rus along with Christianity. The newly arrived clergy transferred to the Kievan prince the concept that a sovereign was appointed by God not only to defend the state against external dangers, but also to establish and maintain the domestic social order. The same Metropolitan Ilarion writes that Prince Vladimir, "having only recently become aware of God, with great humility often consulted with the bishops about how to establish law among his people." An account in the first chronicles (the entry for the year 996 in the Laurentian text of The Primary Chronicle) relates how the bishops in counseling Vladimir explained the necessity for a prince to execute robbers

on the ground that a prince was appointed by God to do away with evil
and show mercy to the good.

Russkaya Pravda

> The earliest legal code of Russia was the so-called *Russkaya Pravda.*
> The most common modern meaning of *pravda* is *truth,* but the word
> once also carried the sense of *justice,* or *equity.* Its inspiration was
> partly the secular legal codes of Byzantium, but these were modified
> by Rus customs and circumstances. The first of the two selections
> below consists of seven brief excerpts from the *Russkaya Pravda*
> chosen because they both illustrate the nature of the code and also
> succinctly describe certain aspects of Kievan society. They are taken
> from Leo Wiener, *Anthology of Russian Literature.* Two volumes.
> New York: G. P. Putnam's Sons, 1903. Vol. 1, pp. 45–48, *passim.*
> The second selection is Klyuchevskii's interpretation of the code,
> translated and slightly adapted from the 1956–59 edition of his
> *Sochineniya (Works),* vol. 1, pp. 247–249.

If a man kill a man, let him be avenged by his brother, or father, or
son, or nephew. If there is no one to avenge him, let the price on his head
be 70 grivnas, if he be a prince's man, or a prince's thane's man. If he be a
Russ, or henchman, or merchant, or boyar's thane, or swordsman, or hap-
less man, or Slovene, let the price on his head be 40 grivnas.

· · ·

If a bloodstained or bruised man comes to the court, he need not bring
any witnesses, but the fine shall be 4 grivnas; but if he have no marks upon
him, let him bring a witness. If both parties complain, let him who has begun pay 6 kunas. If the bloodstained man be he who has begun the quarrel, and there are witnesses to the quarrel, let his bruises be his reward.

· · ·

If one gives money on interest, or money as a loan, or grain, let him
have witnesses, and then receive as has been agreed.

· · ·

If a hired servant runs away from his master, he becomes a slave; but
if he goes to collect his money, and does so openly, or runs to the prince
or the judges on account of injury done him by his master, he is not enslaved, but gets his right.

· · ·

If a free peasant assault another without the prince's permission, the
fine is 3 grivnas to the prince and one grivna of kunas for the wounds.
If he assault a prince's or boyar's man, the fine is 12 grivnas, and a
grivna for the wounds. If one steal a boat, the fine is 6 kunas, and the

boat is to be returned; for a seafaring boat, 3 grivnas, and for a warboat, 2 grivnas; for a smack, 8 kunas, and for a barge, a grivna.

o   o   o

If one steal in the hunting ground a falcon, or hawk, the fine is 3 grivnas, and to the owner, one grivna.

o   o   o

If one puts fire to a barn, he is to be banished, and his house confiscated; first the damage is to be made good, and then the prince shall banish him. The same, if he puts fire into a house. And who maliciously injures a horse or beast, the fine is 12 grivnas, and for the damage, one grivna.

* * * * *

One can see in the main features of the *Pravda* an expression of the interests of the ruling groups, of the basic *motifs* of the life of the old Kievan society. The *Russkaya Pravda* was primarily a code of capital. Capital was the object of especially intense consideration by the lawmaker. Human labor was considered only as an instrument of capital; one may say that capital was the most privileged entity in the *Russkaya Pravda*. The most important judicial attitudes which form the law were dictated by capital. Crimes against property were more severely punished than crimes against a person. The very system of punishment and penalty was based upon capital which provided the means for making retribution in these and other crimes and civil misdemeanors. An individual was considered by the *Pravda* less as a member of society than as an owner or producer of capital. A person who neither owned nor produced capital did not possess the rights of full citizenship, and the life of a woman was valued at only half that of a man.

Borrowed capital was extremely expensive. The law did not limit the amount of monthly interest on short-term loans, but annual interest was defined by an article in the *Pravda* as "a third" for two-thirds, that is, 50 per cent. After Vladimir Monomakh became the Great Prince, he limited the yearly interest to half the principal sum, and held that such interest could be collected for only two years. Thereafter, the creditor might recover only the principal, that is, the debt ceased to bear interest. The right to recover the principal was lost if interest were taken the third year. An annual interest of 40 per cent was, however, permitted by Monomakh for long-term loans. But these limitations were rarely observed. . . . Monomakh himself soon came to regard an annual interest of 60 to 80 per cent—half again or twice as much as the legal rate—as "charitable." Somewhat later, in the thirteenth century, when the trading town had lost its pre-eminence in the peoples' economic life, the clergy found it possible to demand a "light" interest of 12 to 14 per cent.

This deference to capital is indicative of the harsh and bourgeois character of the *Russkaya Pravda*. It is clear that the social environment which served as the basis of the *Russkaya Pravda* was the great trading city. The village remained in the shadow; only a short series of articles in the last section of the *Pravda* dealt with rural property. Foremost in the earlier sections of the code were the interests and attitudes of the well-to-do urban classes, that is, the serf-owning, mercantile-industrial strata. Thus, studying the civil order and the private legal relations of people through the medium of the *Russkaya Pravda* we meet again the same force which so powerfully affected the establishment and the continuation of the political order during the first period. The political system of the trading city and the private lives of the citizens of the city were dominated by commercial-industrial capital.

The Diplomatic Relations of Kievan Rus

Because of Western unfamiliarity with the history of Kievan Rus, it was long assumed and asserted that medieval Russia lived in isolation or, at least, only in relations with the Byzantines. The following excerpts help to correct this misconception. The first selection suggests some of the political and diplomatic aspects of Vladimir's conversion to Christianity, and thus supplements the account given in *The Primary Chronicle*. The second selection describes the expansion of Kievan relations with the West and cites numerous matrimonial alliances. Kievan relations with Byzantium and with the Holy Roman (German) Empire are the subjects, respectively, of the third and fourth excerpts; commercial connections with the German trading towns, of the fifth; and the effects of the Tatar conquest, of the final section.

The source is: V. P. Potemkin (Ed.), *Istoriya Diplomatii* (*History of Diplomacy*). Three volumes. Moscow, 1941–1945. Vol. I, pp. 113–114, 120–123, 128, *passim.*

Returning to Kiev from a second campaign against the Bulgars, Svyatoslav was killed by the Pechenegs at the instigation of Greek [Byzantine] diplomats. This did not prevent the Byzantines, when the ambitious and brilliant captain Vardas Focas revolted against them at the end of 987, from again engaging in correspondence "with the Rus tsar," and seeking aid from Svyatoslav's son, Vladimir. In order to ensure a lasting alliance, Vladimir was promised the hand of one of the princesses of the imperial household. Vladimir, for his part, agreed to become a Christian and to baptize his people. Baptism was considered in Byzantine politics as an indirect recognition of vassalage to the emperor. This cunning Byzantine policy did not, however, succeed against the Rus. The Kievan princes contrived to preserve their independence. . . .

Later, a detachment of Rus, sent by Vladimir, assisted the government at Constantinople in suppressing the revolt of Vardas Focas. But when the emperors Vasily and Constantine refused to implement the clauses of the treaty, especially in relation to the marriage with the princess, Vladimir besieged the Byzantine colony of Kherson in the Crimea, and so forced the emperors to honor their promises. Under these conditions, the conversion of the Rus to Christianity did not make them vassals of Byzantium.

* * * * *

After the conversion, Kiev's international ties expanded and grew in significance. The Kievan state entered into relations not only with Byzantium, but also with the Catholic countries of Central Europe. Vladimir Svyatoslavovich, according to the *Chronicle,* "dwelt at peace with the neighboring princes—with Boleslav the Pole, with Stefan the Hungarian, with Andrew the Bohemian, and there was peace and love among them." These words apply accurately to Kiev's nearest neighbors, including Scandanavia with which ties were not severed in the eleventh century.

Political relations were maintained by matrimonial alliances. Prince Boleslav the Brave of Poland sought in marriage a daughter of Vladimir; his successor, Kasimir, married Maria, another of Vladimir's daughters. Anastasia, youngest daughter of Yaroslav, was wed to King Andrew of Hungary, while an older daughter, Elizabeth, was married to Harold, the famous Norwegian king. Yaroslav himself married Ingrid, a daughter of the Swedish King Olaf. Kiev's political relations were not restricted to these states. Yaroslav sought to involve the German emperor in the struggle against Poland, their common enemy. To achieve this aim, Yaroslav sent an ambassador to Hoslar to offer the hand of a Rus princess to the German emperor. This attempt failed, but shortly thereafter, Yaroslav married his daughter Anna to King Henry I of France.

* * * * *

A strong tie was maintained with Byzantium due to the subordination of the Russian Church to the Patriarch of Constantinople. The bond, however, was not wholly ecclesiastical. The Rus and the Byzantines had a common foe—the Polovtsi, who threatened the welfare of both countries. If in the tenth century the [Byzantine] emperor had set the Pechenegs against the Rus, at this later period he needed an alliance with the prince of Rus in order to reduce the threat of the Polovtsi to the country. Offensive-defensive alliances were concluded between the Byzantine emperors and the princes of Rus. In 1073–1074, at the request of the Emperor Michael VII, the princes of Rus under the leadership of Vladimir Monomakh intervened to suppress an uprising of the Khersonese against the Byzantines. The Emperor Michael Comenus, in 1160, besought the Kievan Prince Rotislav Mstislavich for aid against the Hungarians "by virtue of the peace made between the Rus and the Greeks." The Galician Prince Vladimir Volodarevich and his son Yaroslav Osmonisl were also allied with Michael Comenus. The Metropolitan of Kiev carried out Byzantine policies in Rus. He was appointed by the patriarch of the Greek clergy, and was, in fact, the agent in Kiev of the government at Constantinople.

* * * * *

The German Empire and the papacy—the two most powerful forces in medieval Europe—were not excluded from the circle of Kievan diplomacy. In 1073, Izyaslav, son of Yaroslav the Wise, then engaged in a struggle against his brothers, sought the help of the Emperor Henry IV. Svyatoslav escaped this threat only by his own direct negotiations with the emperor. Svyatoslav's success was due only to his marriage to the sister of one of the greatest vassals of Germany, Burkhard, Bishop of Trier, who served as an intermediary in the negotiations. Yaroslav's third son, Vsevolod, also sought German friendship. His daughter, widow of the Margrave of Brandenburg, took as her second husband the Emperor Henry IV.

Eager to reconquer Kiev which his brother had taken from him, Izyaslav sent his son to Rome, thus acknowledging himself a tributary to the Holy See; he took an oath of fealty to the "Prince of the Apostles" and received "his realm as the gift of St. Peter" from the hands of Pope Gregory VII. Thanks to Gregory's intervention with King Voleslav of Poland, Izyaslav was able to regain mastery of Kiev.

* * * * *

From their establishment, the German commercial cities on the Baltic entered into relations with Rus towns and signed commercial treaties regulating their mutual connections. The treaties of Novgorod (1195, 1257, 1270) and Smolensk (1229) with the Baltic towns still retained some of the stipulations [which had been] characteristic of the tenth century. The foreign merchant who was temporarily in one or the other of these towns had to establish his connections with the native population through diplomatic channels which handled civil, criminal, or political matters. The importance attached to the settlement of suits and various other conflicts was notable. The basis of the regulation was Russian law, which had already by this time been brought into a code called the *Russkaya Pravda*. After the Treaty of Smolensk in 1229, all matters had to be resolved in accordance with the *Smolenskaya Pravda* which was only a variant of the *Russkaya Pravda*. The Novgorod treaties, however, in order to avoid subjecting foreigners completely to Russian law, permitted trial by combat, leaving the judgment to God—a procedure which continued to exist for foreigners in northeast Russia until into the sixteenth and seventeenth centuries.

[Other provisions guaranteed the personal security of foreign merchants and proclaimed the neutrality of trade and the right of free passage across the lands of belligerents.] Purely commercial matters bulked large in the treaties concluded with the Baltic Germans; the itineraries which alien traders had to follow, the method of payment of debts, standardization of weights and measures, the importance of taxes on trade, etc., were all prescribed.

* * * * *

After the invasion and conquest of the Rus lands by the Mongol-Tatars, the international importance of the Rus state declined markedly. The Rus lands in the southwest fell under the domination of the grand princes of Lithuania and Poland and lost their independence for a long time. Northeast Rus, cut off from Western Europe by Lithuania and the Teutonic knights, fell under the Tatar yoke. . . . During the course of the fourteenth and first half of the fifteenth century, the foreign relations of northeast Rus were restricted to the Golden Horde, Byzantium, Lithuania, and the trading connections of Novgorod with the Baltic Germans and Swedes. . . . The relations of Novgorod with the Baltic towns which united in the fourteenth century to form the Hanseatic League remained the same as they had been during the two preceding centuries.

The Tatars: a Thirteenth-Century Description

Although Tatar troops had defeated those of the Russian princes in 1228, this had been only a reconnaissance in force and the Tatars had withdrawn without attempting to follow up the victory. They returned in 1236, however, and within less than four years brought all the Russian principalities, except Novgorod, under their dominion. Tatar control of the Russian lands lasted almost two and one-half centuries and had very important, far-reaching consequences. The following description of the Tatars was written in 1243. The source is: Richard Hakluyt, *The Principal Navigations, Voyages, Traffiques and Discoveries of the English Nation.* Ten volumes. New York: E. P. Dutton & Co., 1927. Vol. 1, pp. 91–93.

But concerning their maners and superstitions, of the disposition and stature of their bodies, of their countrey and maner of fighting &c, he protested the particulars following to be true: namely, that they were above all men, covetous, hasty, deceitfull, and mercilesse: notwithstanding, by reason of the rigour and extremitie of punishments to be inflicted upon them by their superiors, they are restreined from brawlings, and from mutuall strife and contention. The ancient founders and fathers of their tribes, they call by the name of gods, and at certaine set times they doe celebrate solemne feasts unto them, many of them being particular, & but foure onely generall. They thinke that all things are created for themselves alone. They esteeme it none offence to exercise cruelty against rebels. They be hardie and strong in the breast, leane and pale-faced, rough and hug-shouldred, having flatte and short noses, long and sharpe chinnes, their upper jawes are low and declining, their teeth long and thinne, their eye-browes extending from their foreheads downe to their noses, their

eies inconstand and blacke, their countenances writhen and terrible, their
extreame joynts strong with bones and sinews, having thicke and great
thighes, and short legs, and yet being equall unto us in stature: for that
length which is wanting in their legs, is supplied in the upper parts of
their bodies. Their countrey in olde time was a land utterly desert and
waste, situated far beyond Chaldea, from whence they have expelled
Lions, Beares, & such like untamed beasts, with their bowes, and other
engines. Of the hides of beasts being tanned, they use to shape for themselves light but yet impenetrable armour. They ride fast bound unto their
horses, which are not very great in stature, but exceedingly strong, and
mainteined with little provender. They used to fight constantly and val-
iantly with javelins, maces, battle-axes, and swords. But specially they are
excellent archers, and cunning warriers with their bowes. Their backs are
slightly armed, that they may not flee. They withdraw not themselves
from the combate, till they see the chiefe Standard of their Generall give
backe. Vanquished, they aske no favour, and vanquishing, they shew no
compassion. They all persist in their purpose of subduing the whole world
under their owne subjection, as if they were but one man, and yet they are
more then millions in number. They have 60000. Courriers, who being
sent before upon light horses to prepare a place for the armie to incampe
in, will in the space of one night gallop three dayes journey. And suddenly
diffusing themselves over an whole province, and surprising all the people
thereof unarmed, unprovided, dispersed, they make such horrible slaugh-
ters, that the king or prince of the land invaded, cannot finde people sufficient to wage battell against them, and to withstand them. They delude
all people and princes of regions in time of peace, pretending that for a
cause, which indeed is no cause. Sometimes they say, that they will make
a voyage to Colen, to fetch home the three wise kings into their owne
countrey; sometimes to punish the avarice and pride of the Romans, who
oppressed them in times past; sometimes to conquere barbarous and
Northern nations; sometimes to moderate the furie of the Germans with
their owne meeke mildnesse; sometimes to learne warlike feats and strat-
agems of the French; sometimes for the finding out of fertile ground to
suffice their huge multitudes; sometimes againe in derision they say that
they intend to goe on pilgrimage to S. James of Galicia. In regard of
which sleights and collusions certain undiscreet governors concluding a
league with them, have granted them free passage thorow their territories, which leagues notwithstanding being violate, were an occasion of
ruine and destruction unto the foresayd governours &c.

Kievan Decline and Political Fragmentation

The late Boris D. Grekov, who wrote the selection below, was among
the most prominent Soviet historians of the mid-twentieth century.
A specialist in Kievan history, Grekov successfully and skillfully combined a high degree of scholarly erudition with a marked deftness in
satisfying the Soviet political leaders. The selection forms the final
section of one of Grekov's major studies. The book is based mostly

on primary source materials, but it also demonstrates Grekov's thorough familiarity with relevant studies by both pre-Soviet and Soviet historians. It is useful to compare Grekov's analysis with the selections from Klyuchevskii which follow it.

The source is: B. (D.) Grekov (Dennis Ogden, Ed., Y. Sdobnikov, Tr.), *Kievan Rus.* Moscow: Foreign Languages Publishing House, 1959. Pp. 674–685. Footnotes omitted.

Similar to other early feudal states, Ancient Rus did not exist for long. The vast territory, with its motley economic, ethnical and cultural elements held together by Kiev's rule, began to show a tendency to fall apart at a very early date. But Kiev always triumphed over the centrifugal forces so long as the balance of power was in its favour and so long as the local nobility was in favour of a strong ruler at Kiev. Kiev's claims to seniority over the other principalities were very much alive even in the early 12th century, despite the fact that the Lubech Congress of 1097 had officially recognized the new political system. Vladimir Monomakh and, to some extent, his son Mstislav (1125–32) succeeded in upholding Kiev's prestige for some time.

But we should bear in mind that the dismemberment of Ancient Rus was primarily the result of the growth of her component parts, each of which began to follow its own policy and strive to achieve its own goals. Kiev lacked the means to further the growth of these lands, and unquestionably retarded their development by its demands for men and money.

Their inevitable isolation deprived the Kiev prince of tributary payments which he was wont to receive from his dependent tribes and peoples since time immemorial. This occurred at a time when Kiev was particularly in need of material means to finance its struggle against these separatist tendencies. But that was not all. International events were afoot which eventually dealt Kiev's economic position a telling blow.

A movement began in Europe in the 11th century which resulted in shorter trade routes from Byzantium and Asia Minor to Western Europe, bypassing the Dnieper.

In 1082, Byzantine Emperor Alexus Comnenus granted a deed to Venice which had given him military aid in the war in Sicily. This gave Venice greater advantages in its trade with Byzantium than were enjoyed by the Emperor's own subjects. Venetian merchants were freed from all duties and a special district and wharves were assigned them in Constantinople. This helped Venice to become a merchant Power of the first magnitude. Kiev's trade, mainly in transit goods, became of secondary importance.

The Crusades were also highly conducive to the development of trade by Italian, South-French and Rhine cities. The latter gained control of the Mediterranean routes which had until then been in the hands of the Arabs and the Byzantines. Eastern goods were carried to Europe by the Italians along the Mediterranean and reached Central Europe via the Rhine. A trade alliance, which set up its officers throughout the Baltic, was organized by the Rhine cities. Novgorod was at its north-eastern terminus

and was one of the Russian cities which received compensation for its
weakened position on the great water-way "from the Varangians to the
Greeks" due to this displacement of world trade routes.

The cities along the middle reaches of the Dnieper decayed after this
shift in the trade routes. Kiev was the most striking illustration of this
process. Deprived of its old economic importance it began simultaneously
to lose its political importance.

By the middle of the 12th century (particularly in its second half) the
consolidation and separation of the new political centres, on the one hand,
and Kiev's weakening on the other, was so far gone that Kiev not only
ceased to be the capital of a large though unstable state, but became of
secondary importance even among the local centres. Yet in the eyes of
the Rus people it continued to be a symbol of Ancient Rus's former grandeur.

This emergence of the separate feudal principalities which eventually
led to the fragmentation of Ancient Rus was by no means peaceful.

Summing up Rus's historical development in the late 11th or early
12th centuries, the chronicler deemed it necessary to underline the difference between the present and the past. He is manifestly in favour of the
past. In olden times (he means the period of the growth and prosperity of
the state of Ancient Rus) the princes and their men expanded the territory
of the Russian land, but led a frugal life. Turning to his own times, he
stresses the marked change in the attitude of the ruling classes to their de-
pendents. He speaks of their insatiable greed and, addressing the rich,
says: "For our greed, has God sent the heathen on us, and our cattle, and
our manors and estates are in their hands, but we do not desist from our
evil ways."

It is fitting to recall later comments on that period. The author of the
Lay of Igor's Host bewails the disastrous state of the feudally disintegrated Rus and turns to the glorious past recalling the "initial years" and
the "first princes." Why could not "old Vladimir" have for ever remained
in Kiev? This historic topic inspired the author of yet another poetic work,
the *Discourse of the Fall of the Russian Land.*

Indeed, many new developments which could not be ignored appeared in social and political relations late in the 11th century.

We have already seen that changes had occurred in the forms of exploitation of the dependent population. The economic and political role of
the local notables was enhanced. We shall have a clear picture of what
was going on in Kiev Rus in the 11th century (the process noted by the
chronicler in his peculiar yet forceful way), if we take into account the
growth of the cities and the attendant awakening of the *veche* assemblies,
particularly in the leading cities whose *veche* decisions were obligatory
for the surrounding countryside, and if we bear in mind that these cities
were the seats of the landowning nobility which entered into certain relationships with the urban masses. The chronicler had good reason to un-
derscore the sharp distinction between his time and the relatively recent
past.

The struggle of the Russian people for their independence was particularly acute at this time. The changes which were afoot in Ancient Rus, and above all the weakening of her military might as a result of the isolation of the lands, raised hopes among her neighbours, who were eager to expand their territories at her expense.

The Polovtsy, who were driven beyond the Don in Monomakh's time, reappeared in Rus's southern territories. This onset of the nomads gained great force in the 60's of the 12th century.

Rus's historical development did not continue on the territories she initially possessed. There was a displacement to the north and north-east, north-west and west, with the southward trend in territorial expansion gradually losing its momentum and the lands grouping themselves around a number of new centres.

Each new independent land became a political system with its own landowning hierarchy (princes and boyars) and highly involved relationships. These separate cells were increasingly concentrating on their local interests, which were extremely narrow compared with the sweep of Ancient Rus's international political activities. They were shrinking perceptibly. However, these entities led an intensive existence and prepared the groundwork for the formation of new states in Eastern Europe, including the biggest among them—the Russian centralized state.

I have noted the sharpening struggle between the two systems in the 11th century, namely, between the old, which stood for Kiev's supremacy over a vast territory inhabited by Russians and partially by non-Russians, and the new, which rejected Kiev's right to dispose of all the forces of the state and advanced a new principle of sovereign existence for every *volost* become principality.

We have seen how this struggle progressed under the first Yaroslavichy. Monomakh and his son could merely retard the Rus's fragmentation but could not stop it altogether.

It would be natural to expect that Mstislav should hand Kiev on to his son in the way he himself got it from his father Monomakh. But that was not so.

The *Lavrenty Annals* for 1132 say the following: "Vladimir's son Mstislav died on the 14th day of April and was succeeded by his brother Yaropolk, for the people of Kiev had sent for him." The successor to the Kiev throne was chosen by the people of Kiev themselves, *i.e.*, the Kiev urban *veche*. Nothing of the kind would have occurred in Ancient Rus's hey-day.

The children of Mstislav Vladimirovich found themselves in the custody of their uncle Yaropolk. He tried to provide for them and appoint them to more profitable cities, but met with determined resistance from his own brothers. Yury, who was nicknamed Dolgoruky, was particularly active in this respect. He had his seat in the Rostov and Suzdal land, but never ceased to dream of Kiev.

One of Yaropolk's nephews, Izyaslav Mstislavich, who considered himself wronged by his uncles Yaropolk and Yury, signed a compact with

the Chernigov princes, the famous Olegovichy, the descendants of Svyatoslav Yaroslavich, one of the "triumvirs." This was an alliance which
boded evil for Kiev, because they were the most vigorous and confirmed
proponents of the new political order of things, so clearly set out in the
resolution of the Lubech Congress ("each one shall hold his own demesne"). The Olegovichy told Yaropolk that they wished to hold what
their father held before them ("what our father held . . . that also we
wish.") If Yaropolk insisted on his right to rule the entire Rus land, they
could not be made answerable for the consequences: ". . . you shall be
to blame, the blood shall be on your head." Novgorod also protested
against Yaropolk's actions: the Novgorod *veche* condemned Vsevolod
Mstislavich for having obeyed Yaropolk and left Novgorod for Pereyaslavl. It expelled him and invited Svyatoslav Olegovich who was a champion of the sovereignty of the separate principalities. The people of Novgorod wished to put an end to the strife and sent their vice-gerent to Kiev
to "establish peace between the Kievties and the Chernigovites."

Yaropolk was attacked by the Olegovichy of Chernigov who were
allied with Izyaslav and his brother Svyatopolk Mstislavich as well as by
the Polovtsy. The latter were victorious. They consolidated their positions
in the Chernigov land and in 1139, after Yaropolk's death, Vsevolod Olegovich even took Kiev and ousted Vyacheslav, Yaropolk's brother, who
tried to gain a foothold there.

This struggle resulted in greater independence from Kiev not only for
the Chernigov, but also for the Galich and Polotsk, and the Rostov
and Suzdal lands. The Olegovichy became a powerful force, which meant
that the new order had manifestly triumphed.

Vsevolod Olegovich (1139–46) rose to great heights as a politician.
He was a vigorous and skilful man who could find his way in the most
difficult and involved situations and knew how to pit his enemies against
each other. Being the prince of Chernigov, he held sway over the greater
part of the former state of Ancient Rus. But the nature of his rule in Kiev
shows that he regarded it as his prize, and no wonder the Kiev masses
were hostile to him. Deprived of the possibility of rising up against him,
they made short shrift of his henchmen as soon as he died. The general
feeling against the Olegovichy was expressed as follows: ". . . We do not
wish to be the hereditary possession of the Olegovichy." The Kievites,
who had got an inkling of their own strength in the choice of their prince,
were dissatisfied with being treated as a hereditary possession by Vsevolod and his brother Igor, whom the former was intent on foisting on the
city.

The twelve days after Vsevolod's death are highly indicative. Vsevolod
had laid the groundwork for his brother Igor's succession to the Kiev
throne. Depending on his strength and having won the support of Kiev's
upper classes, he underestimated the enhanced importance of the city's
merchants and handicraftsmen, who annulled his will.

The city's lower orders convened a *veche* and resolutely repudiated
the decisions of the previous assemblies of Igor's aristocratic supporters.

This *veche* brought to trial Vsevolod's henchmen, above all Prince Igor himself. The latter feared the *veche* but dared not ignore "the invitation" to attend it. He took his men-at-arms along and prepared an ambush, meanwhile sending a more neutral figure, namely, his brother Svyatoslav, to attend the assembly. The latter had to listen to the people's complaints against the violence rife in the previous reign and to promise, on his brother's behalf, to eliminate the abuses of Vsevolod's henchmen. On these conditions the *veche* agreed to recognize Igor as their prince. But it was obvious that the decision was not unanimous, because the city's lower orders immediately launched an attack upon the princely administrators and apparently concluded an agreement with Izyaslav Mstislavich, Monomakh's grandson, who was prince of Pereyaslavl and was more acceptable to them.

Izyaslav advanced against Kiev at the head of an army, defeated Igor and entered the city "with great glory and honour." Igor was deposed and arrested. Izyaslav did not prevent the expression of popular wrath ("much property was taken from the houses and monasteries.")

The Olegovichy attempted to organize a coalition against him. An agreement was reached between Svyatoslav, the brother of the deposed Igor, and Yury Dolgoruky, prince of the Rostov and Suzdal land.

A stubborn struggle ensued, involving not only Russians, but also Hungarians, Poles, "black hoods" and Polovtsy.

The enhanced role of the cites once again becomes manifest in the course of this struggle. Izyaslav was convinced that the citizens of Kiev and also the *smerds* would side with him against Svyatoslav Olegovich and Yury Dolgoruky, since the *veche* decision of the leading city was obligatory to the outlying areas and villages. He was quickly proved wrong. The citizens of Kiev and Vladimir-on-Klyazma had their own opinion of the struggle and Izyaslav's suggestion that the Kievites join him against Yury and Svyatoslav was firmly rejected by the Kiev *veche*. Yury thrice seized Kiev in the course of this struggle and finally entrenched himself there in 1156. He remained in Kiev until his death on May 15, 1158.

A popular movement flared up as soon as Yury died. "Much evil was done that day," says the chronicler, "his magnificent palace was plundered, and another one plundered beyond the Dnieper, which he himself called a 'paradise,' and the palace of his son Vasilyok was plundered in the city; the Suzdal people were assaulted in town and village, and their goods seized." This movement came as no surprise. Yury had seized Kiev by force and the people of Kiev and long since declared that "they could not live with Yury."

What was it Yury had in the South, in the Kiev land? This is no idle question. Yury possessed only a small strip of land along the Goryn River, the Turov and Pinsk land which, incidentally, became isolated very soon, Kiev with the surrounding territory, and Pereyaslavl, Kiev's threshold. He could not claim more because the other lands had already won their independence and were strong enough to defend it.

When Yury arrived in Kiev, he appointed his sons to the surrounding cities: Andrei to Vyshgorod, Rostislav to Pereyaslavl, Boris to Belgorod, Gleb to Kanev, and only Vasilyok was sent to Suzdal.

The *volosts* beyond Kiev's frontiers were leading an independent existence regardless of the Kiev prince.

Yury's reign may be called a period of history in which Rus's fragmentation had been completed. In this system of feudally divided Rus, the Kiev land occupied a very insignificant place. It did not even have the chance of becoming a polity with its own system under a local dynasty. The princes who had their seats in the *udels* saw to it that the Kiev land did not fall to any of them as an independent principality. Yury was succeeded on the Kiev throne by Izyaslav Davidovich of Chernigov, a descendent of the Chernigov Svyatoslavichy (1158–60), Rostislav Mstislavich of Smolensk (1160–68) and Mstislav Izyaslavich of Volyn (1168–69). All of them, while ruling Kiev, remained lords of their own demesnes.

When Mstislav Izyaslavich of Volyn got Kiev, Volyn remained his strongpoint to fall back on in time of crisis and his permanent possession. Kiev, which had previously striven to control Volyn, and actually did so, now changed places with it.

Mstislav was a vigorous and enterprising man, a lover of books, as well as a fearless and capable military leader. He succeeded in organizing a campaign against the Polovtsy in which 13 princes, enumerated by the chronicle, took part. They were owners of principalities and "many others." The "black hoods" also took part in the campaign, for they had long before linked their destiny with Rus. The Polovtsy suffered a crushing defeat. But Mstislav likewise failed to protect Kiev from the force which had in the meantime appeared in the area between the Volga and the Oka.

It was Novgorod that sparked off the war between Andrei of Vladimir and Mstislav of Kiev. The Vladimir prince, intent on possessing Novgorod, could not stand by and see Mstislav take steps to retain Novgorod under his control, for the latter had appointed his son Roman to Novgorod although Andrei had a vice-gerent in the city. Moreover, Roman was inimical to Andrei's allies and the latter decided to crush both Novgorod and Kiev. Novgorod succeeded in defending itself and celebrated its victory over the Suzdal and Vladimir army on February 25, 1170. However, Kiev fell to the enemy on March 8, 1169.

Prince Andrei (1157–74), a son of Yury Dolgoruky (Kiev prince since 1154), had a seat near his father's city in the ancient princely castle at Vyshgorod. He refused to live in the South and preferred the Rostov and Suzdal land. He secretly left Vyshgorod and went to Vladimir-on-Klyazma (he built himself a new castle at Bogolubov, a few miles from Vladimir, and was known as Bogolubsky after that place). In 1169, he organized a big campaign against Kiev.

During the sack of "the mother of Russian cities" there were great material losses and our scholars were deprived of an abundance of written sources.

In 1203, some 30 years later, Kiev was sacked for the second time. Batu's sacking consummated the work begun by the feudal wars. This largely explains the paucity of written sources pertaining to that highly eventful period of our history.

Here is what Solovyov wrote of Andrei's campaign: "It was not of his own accord that Andrei brought his troops to Kiev, the capital city of his ancestors, and later gave it, devastated, to his younger brother, himself remaining in the North, at his old seat in Vladimir-on-Klyazma. Andrei's action was an event of momentous importance, a turning-point in history which marked the beginning of a new order of things." That order, however, was ushered in by foregoing events.

In this case, too, Solovyov correctly noted the fact but explained it from his "tribal" point of view. He believed that until then Rus had been held by a major princely family among whose "princes there was a community of interests." Then Andrei Bogolubsky, Solovyov thinks, established an independent and powerful seat at Vladimir.

We have seen that it was no princely family which controlled Ancient Rus, and that the princes, in spite of being kinsmen, had long since each begun to aspire to an "independent" seat, and that many of them had succeeded in achieving this before Andrei did. He was no exception, but merely one of the more striking illustrations of an order of things which entailed changes in the superstructure under the impact of changes in the basis. If Andrei had any distinctive trait, it was his strength, with which other princes were forced to reckon.

However, Andrei displayed certain traits which make him kin to future Moscow statesmen who succeeded in achieving what Andrei lacked the means to do. Moscow won its successes on a new basis which did not yet exist in the 12th century.

The high standing of the Vladimir prince was the result of favourable circumstances which encouraged the growth of princely authority in the North-East. Strong princely rule in that period of "general confusion" was undoubtedly conducive to the formation of a national state. But before it had made any progress to speak of, Rus fell victim to the Tatar khans, whose rule for long checked the further development of the Russian people.

Klyuchevskii on the Causes and Consequences of the Decline of Kievan Rus

> Professor Klyuchevskii attributed the decline of Kievan power and what he called the "territorial and political change" primarily to internal socio-economic inequalities, princely feuds, and barbarian incursions. The main points of his analysis are printed below in the form of excerpts from his *Course in Russian History*. The source is the 1956–1959 edition of his *Sochineniya (Works)*, vol. 1, pp. 271–291, *passim*. Adapted.

There were two radical changes in Russian life during the period from the thirteenth to the mid-fifteenth century. In the preceding period, the main mass of the population was concentrated in the region of the Dnieper; in this period it is located in the region of the Upper Volga. In the preceding period, the great trading city was the architect and leader of the political and social order; in this period these functions devolved upon the prince—the landlord of an hereditary estate. A new historical scene thus appears in the period now under consideration, involving new territory and a new supreme political force: Dnieper Rus changes into Upper Volga Rus; the *volost* city [an administrative division consisting of the city and its environs] yields its place to the prince against whom it had formerly competed. This political and territorial change creates in Upper Volga Rus a political and economic way of life which does not resemble that of Kievan Rus. Because of the new political force, Upper Volga Rus is divided not into urban regions, but into princely appanages. Because of the territorial shift and the external environment in which the main mass of the Russian people found itself, the driving force of the economy in the Upper Volga becomes the agricultural exploitation of the land with the help of the voluntary labor of serf-tenants instead of foreign trade. . . .

This movement caused the destruction of the social order which had been established in Kievan Rus. The rather complicated reasons for this destruction inhered as much in the nature of life in Kievan Rus as in her external circumstances. I will indicate, in cursory fashion, the main reasons.

Conditions disruptive of the social order and economic prosperity of Kievan Rus became noticeable after the middle of the twelfth century. If one judges this Rus in terms of the upper classes, one may suggest it enjoyed significant success in material prosperity, civilization, and enlightenment. The strength of the economy and of foreign trade indicated a vigorous life and brought great wealth to Rus. Material prosperity found expression in art and bookish education as shown by the artistic and literary monuments of the twelfth century; by churches, schools, books, literary schools, and the use of the Greek language. Prince Vladimir Monomakh, son of Vsevolod, knew the Greek language. . . .

But all this was a façade which concealed a seamy side: the condition of the lower social classes upon whom the social order was based. The economic prosperity of Kievan Rus in the eleventh and twelfth centuries rested upon slave-holding, which reached immense proportions toward the middle of the latter century. As early as the tenth–eleventh centuries, slaves constituted the main item of Rus export to the Black Sea and Volga-Caspian markets. The Rus merchant of that time invariably appeared everywhere with slaves as his principal wares. Eastern writers of the tenth century paint for us a vivid picture of the Rus trader selling slaves on the Volga. Having disembarked, he set up shop in the Volga bazaars, in the cities of the Bulgars, or in Itil; and on his benches sat a living commodity—a slave. He appeared in Constantinople with the same commodity, and when a Greek "man-in-the-street" of Tsargrad had to buy a slave he went to the market where "non-resident Rus merchants are selling slaves." Thus we read in one mid-eleventh century source.

As far as we can judge the matter by the *Russkaya Pravda,* slaveowning was one of the principal subjects upon which the ancient Rus lawmaker focused his attention. The articles about slaveowning form one of the longest and best thought out sections of the *Pravda.* Slaveowning was evidently the original economic and judicial source of landowning in Rus. The ruling class of Rus society remained urban as to domicile and habits of life until the end of the tenth century. Government and trade conferred sufficient benefits so that this group did not think of landowning. But, having become firmly established in the great city on the Dnieper, the ruling class turned its attention to this economic resource. Military campaigns resulted in the accumulation of a multitude of slaves; the urban holdings being surfeited with them, the surplus was marketed overseas. From the tenth century on, as we have seen, the slaves, along with furs, were the main articles of Rus export. Then people of the upper class began to employ the slave on the land, making slaveowning synonymous with landowning. By the twelfth century we find several types of private landowners: princes and members of their retinues, prince-consorts, churches, monasteries, and bishoprics.

But in all the twelfth century records of private landownership, the necessary condition of the ownership was that the land be populated and exploited by slaves; thus, "villages with slaves." Slaves evidently were a necessary economic condition for private landowning, whether secular or ecclesiastical, large or small. It is possible to conclude from this that the very concept of the right of property in land, of the possibility of owning land as one owned other propery, had its source in slavery, and was a development of thought concerning the rights of slaveowning. This land is *mine* because *my* people are cultivating it: this appears to have been the rationalization from which the judicial concept concerning the right of property in land was formed in our country. The agricultural slave—the *stradnik* as he was termed in the economic jargon of ancient Rus—was both the judicial link between the master and the land, and the instrument by which the master exploited the land. Thus arose the ancient Russian *boyar-votchina* [the hereditary boyar estate]. The privileged merchant-prince and his men-at-arms [retinue] of the tenth century were thus transformed into boyars, as privileged landowners were called in the words of the *Russkaya Pravda.* As a consequence of the settlement of slaves on the land in the eleventh and twelfth centuries, the land rose in value; but until the death of Yaroslav, the law permitted the killing of any foreign slave who had struck a free man. This was prohibited by Yaroslav's children. . . .

This servile legal and economic condition of the working class was one of the conditions which disrupted the prosperity and the social order of Kievan Rus. A social order which works only to the disadvantage of the lower classes cannot count on their support. . . . A second disruptive force was the internecine feuds of the princes. . . . And the foreign relations of Kievan Rus added to these conditions still another which acted most destructively on its social order and prosperity.

It should not be forgotten for a moment, in studying the life of Rus, that it was founded at the outskirts of the world of Christian culture, on the edge of Europe, and that beyond it stretched the shoreless sea of the steppes, threshold to Asia. The steppes, with their nomadic population, were the traditional scourge of ancient Rus. The steppe was cleared for a little while after the defeat of the Pechenegs by Yaroslav in 1036, but after Yaroslav's death in 1061, ceaseless attacks on Rus were begun by her new neighbors on the steppes, the Polovtsi, Rus battled against them incessantly during the eleventh and twelfth centuries, and this struggle formed the main subject of the heroic epics and the chronicles. Polovtsian attacks left terrible scars on Rus. We find in the annals of this time vivid descriptions of the disasters which Rus experienced—abandoned fields overgrown by grass, wild beasts settled where herds had grazed.

This two-century struggle of Rus against the Polovtsi had significance in the history of Europe. Rus, by its battles on the steppes, covered Europe's left flank at a time when the Crusaders of Western Europe were undertaking an offensive war against Asia, and a similar movement against the Moors was in progress on the Iberian Peninsula. This historic contribution of Rus cost her dearly. The struggle displaced her from her settled location on the Dnieper, and changed the course of her future life. From the mid-twelfth century, noticeable signs of the desolation of Kievan Rus, of the Dnieper region, grew under the pressure of these three unfavorable conditions—the legal and economic depreciation of the lower classes, the interecine feuds of the princes, and the attacks of the Polovtsi. . . .

The flow of population from the region of the Dnieper moved in two opposite directions. One stream flowed west, toward the Western Bug, into the regions of the Upper Dniester and Upper Vistula, deep into Galicia and Poland. Thus the south Russian population of Dnieper returned to the long-forgotten site which its ancestors had abandoned in the seventh century. . . . The other stream was directed toward the opposite corner of the Rus Land, toward the northeast beyond the Ugra river, in the region between the Oka and the Upper Volga. . . .

The depopulation of Rus of the Dnieper, which began in the twelfth century, was completed by the Tatar attack of 1229–1240. Thenceforward, the former area of Rus, never very thickly settled, was changed into a desert with only a scant remnant of its one-time population. For the next two or three centuries, Kiev underwent many transformations, rose and fell several times. Having barely recovered from the crushing defeat in 1240, it again suffered in 1299 from Tatar depredations. The remnants of her one-time neighbors—the Pechenegs, the Polovtsi, and other aliens— roamed along the former steppe borderlands of Kievan Rus. The southern regions—Kiev, Pereyaslav, and part of Chernigov—remained in such desolation until the middle of the fifteenth century. . . .

Just as the preceding period had opened with a movement of the Slavs from the slopes of the Carpathians to the region of the Dnieper, so the second period was marked by the movement of the population from the

region of the Middle Dnieper to two opposite corners of the Rus Land.
. . . I confine myself in this study to the stream of colonization which
moved to the northeast. This was the source of all the fundamental
phenomena in the life of Rus of the Upper Volga after the mid-twelfth
century. The results of this colonization determined the political and social
existence of this Rus. The consequences were extremely varied, but I shall
note only . . . that the Russian nationality, after having begun to form
in the first period, was broken into two parts during the second period. The
bulk of the Russian people, having retreated from the Dnieper and the
southwest to the Oka and the Upper Volga, gathered and strengthened
itself in the forests of Central Russia and, having established a firm government, returned once again to the southwest to rescue from foreign domination and influence the remnants of the weakest part of the Russian people.

The Appanage Period

> There was a period in medieval Russia, as there was also in medieval
> France and England, when sovereigns granted lands or other wealth
> to their younger sons. The old French name for such grants, derived
> from the verb meaning to nourish or to support, passed into the English
> language as appanage. Its Russian equivalent is *udel*. The period in
> Russian history when such grants were common, *i.e.*, the period of
> the appanages, has been regarded generally by historians as the transi-
> tion between the fall of Kievan Rus and the rise of Muscovy. One of
> the prime exponents of this interpretation was Professor Klyuchevskii.
> His views are summarized in the following selection from his *Kurs
> Russkoi Istorii* (*Course in Russian History*) in *Sochineniya* (*Works*),
> vol. 1, pp. 338–339, 346, 349–350, 369. Adapted.

Appanage ownership is the initial and basic fact from which, or under the
influence of which, flowed all other phenomena in the history of Suzdalian
Russia, and on which was founded the way of political life that took shape
there toward the middle of the fifteenth century. A pair of signs marks the
establishment of this order. First, the movement of princes from principality to principality ceases. The princes become settled owners, living and
dying in their own appanage towns which they do not leave even when by
right of seniority they accede to the throne of Grand Prince. (The temporary owner of this or that *volost* had no incentive to enlarge its boundaries.
The northern prince of the thirteenth century, having inherited his own
appanage, applied all his efforts to its territorial expansion in order to
bequeath to his children more than he had received from his father.
Henceforward, there developed among the northern princes a striving for
aggrandizement, for the acquisition of land, which sometimes took on the
nature of land-greed.) Second, the order of princely inheritance, the
method of passing a volost on to a successor, changes. A prince of old
Kievan Rus could not bequeath his volost to his own son unless the son
followed him in the line of seniority. Northern princes of the thirteenth
and fourteenth centuries, secure in the possession of their volosts, could

bequeath their volosts at will to their sons, or—in the absence of sons—to wife or daughter, or even to a distant relative.

We find many instances in the records of the thirteenth and fourteenth centuries of legacies in the absence of direct successors. For example, the appanage prince, Yaroslav, great-grandson of Vsevolod III, died in 1249 leaving as his only heir his daughter, Maria. At the same time, the princes of Smolensk, in dividing their patrimony, offended their younger brother, Feodor. Feodor thereupon went to the principality of Yaroslav, married the Princess Maria, receiving the principality along with her hand, and in this manner became the progenitor of a new, independent princely line. Yaroslav, third son of Vsevolod, received as his appanage the volost of Pereyaslav which thereafter descended from father to eldest son. Ivan Dimitrievich, dying childless in 1302, willed his appanage to his neighbor, Prince Daniel of Moscow. Semyon Gordiy, Great Prince of Moscow who died in 1353, willed all of his appanage to his wife who later passed it on to her brother-in-law, Semyon's brother, Ivan. Such are the signs showing the development of a novel order of princely ownership in the newer regions of Suzdal. . . .

Once upon a time, the Russian Land was considered to be the inheritable possession of the whole princely family, and the family shared supreme power over it. Individual princes, although they were participants in this collective authority, were only temporary owners of their particular appanages. There was no thought that this collective ownership conferred on an individual prince rights of the nature commonly accorded to private landownership. The princes ruled principalities in accordance either with seniority or by agreement between themselves and the volost cities, and they exercised supreme authority within their principalities, but neither as a group nor as individuals did the princes hold that their authority derived from right of ownership. Moreover, they neither mortgaged their principalities, nor gave them as dowries for their daughters, nor devised them, nor bequeathed them.

The Land of Rostov, however, although originally held as the common heritage of the family of Vsevolod, did not remain a family collective. It was broken into separate principalities, independent of each other and considered to be the personal and hereditary property of their respective owners. The owners ruled the free population of their principalities like sovereigns, held them as private possessions with all authority derived from the fact of ownership. Such holdings were appanages in the fullest and clearest development; a development observable only in the hereditary holdings of the family of Vsevolod in the region of the Upper Volga during the thirteenth to the fifteenth centuries. Under the appanage system, therefore, the holder of power is the individual, not the family; princely ownership becomes individual, does not forfeit supreme authority, merges or becomes identical with private, personal property. . . .

The appanage system was based on two foundations, one geographical, the other political. It was created by a combination of the nature of the country and the nature of its settlement. The physical peculiarities of the

Upper Volga region—that is, the small, secluded river basins—determined the political divisions of the country, that is, its splintering into appanages. The appanages of the Upper Volga during the thirteenth and fourteenth centuries were these small river basins. Under the conditions of settlement, the first prince of an appanage customarily found that his holding was not a settled and established society, but a wasteland on which he had to erect a society. He was the sower and the founder of his appanage, as well as its owner, and his authority derived from these facts. Thus do I explain the historical origin of the appanage system. . . .

The principal results of the appanage system may be summed up in a brief formula. The operation of the system in northern Rus loosened such weak ties of political unity as existed and produced a steadily increasing political fragmentation; this, in turn, caused a steadily increasing weakness among the princes who consequently isolated themselves more and more on their estates and became more and more estranged from each other; as the estrangements grew, they lost their sense of general responsibility and territorial unity until each, in his own manner, became simply a lord of a private manor. These results of the appanage system were very significant in terms of the later political history of northern Rus because they opened the way for subsequent political unification. On the one hand, when a strong prince finally emerged from among the many, poor, appanage princelings, he found among them no support for unification; but, on the other hand, he was able to subdue each in turn by taking advantage of their mutual isolation and their inability to join in common action. . . . The inherent nature of the appanage system made it less able to defend itself than the rota system had been. It was therefore easier to destroy in order to establish a unified state upon its ruins. The appanage system thus represents the transitional political form which allowed the Land of Rus to develop from a mere national entity to a political unity. The history of that development is the history of one princely appanage— Muscovy.

Where to Find More Information

ALLEN, *Ukraine,* ch. 2.
BLACK, C. E. (Ed.) *Rewriting Russian History.* N.Y.: Praeger, 1956. Chs. 5 & 6.
CHARQUES, *Short History,* chs. 2 & 3.
CLARKSON, *History,* ch. 3.
CURTISS, J. S. *Church and State in Russia.* N.Y.: Columbia Univ. Press, 1940. Pp. 1–15.
ECK, A. *Le moyen âge Russe.* Paris, 1933. Chs. 1 & 2. ("Introduction.")
FLORINSKY, M. T. *Russia: A History and an Interpretation.* 2 vols. N.Y.: Macmillan, 1955. Vol. 1, chs. 1, 2 & 5.
HARCAVE, *Readings,* vol. 1, sections 9–11.
HRUSHEVSKY, *Ukraine,* chs. 4–6.
LYASHCHENKO, *National Economy,* pp. 136–169.
MARTIN, *Picture History,* pp. 17–30.
MAZOUR, *Russia,* ch. 2.
MILIUKOV, *Outlines,* vol. 1, ch. 2; vol. 2, ch. 1.
NOWAK, *Medieval Slavdom,* pp. 38–42.
PARES, *Russia,* chs. 2 & 3.
RAMBAUD, *Russia,* vol. 1, chs. 4–7.
VERNADSKY, G. *Kievan Rus.* (Vol. II in his *History of Russia.*) New Haven: Yale Univ. Press, 1948.
————. *The Mongols and Russia.* (Vol. III in his *History of Russia.*) New Haven: Yale Univ. Press, 1953.
WALSH, *Russia,* chs. 2 & 3.
WREN, *Course,* chs. 4–6.

Part III

The Rise of Muscovy

The Transition from Appanages to a Unified Autocracy

> The first three articles, hitherto available in English only in a very much abridged form, have been newly translated from an outstanding history textbook of the tsarist period. Its author was the distinguished scholar, Sergei Fedorovich Platonov, Professor of History at the University of St. Petersburg and tutor to the brother and sister of Nicholas II. Platonov, son of a workman and grandson of a serf, specialized in the history of the seventeenth century, but he brought to all of Russian history an unusual perceptiveness and a sound scholarship so that his work is of enduring merit.
>
> Sentences and phrases which appear below in quotation marks or printed in italics were so printed in the original. A few words, translatable only as cumbersome phrases, have been left in Russian and therefore need definition. A *volost* was a small political or administrative unit, comprising several villages. A *votchina* was a private, hereditary estate, and a *votchinnik* was an owner of such an estate. A *pomestie* was an estate granted by the prince on conditional tenure and in return for service, and a *pomeshchik* was the holder of such a grant. *Dvoryanin*, which meant originally a person attached to the court, came to mean a member of the gentry or nobility who owned land and serfs. Platonov used the terms, *servant, serving people,* and *serving princes* to designate not domestic servants, but those who served the prince or the state. This usage has been retained in the translation.
>
> The source is: S. F. Platonov, *Uchebnik Russkoi Istorii* (*Textbook in Russian History*). Two parts in one volume. Prague, 1924 and 1925. Part I, pp. 128–137.

Autocracy in the Moscow State and the Theory of Moscow as the Third Rome

The Moscow state, as we have seen, was formed by the annexation to the princely appanage of Moscow of neighboring appanages in northern Russia and, later, of the Land of Novgorod and the *volost* of the Grand Prince of Lithuania. The Muscovite princes regarded their appanage as a personal possession, just as the owner of an estate looks upon it as his hereditary landholding. When the Great Principality of Vladimir was acquired permanently, the Moscow princes designated it as their hereditary holding. Later, when they demanded that Lithuania yield the old Rus towns to them, they instructed their envoy to declare that all the lands of Rus had once been part of their patrimony. In such fashion, the Muscovite princes expanded the claims of proprietorship from their appanage to the whole country, and staked out claims to possess and control the whole vast state. This view was generally accepted; the people of Moscow always declared that they belonged to the great sovereign because they lived on his lands. When property was sold, the deed read: "I have sold the land of the sovereign and of my possession." The authority of the Moscow princes thus took on the character of the authority of a lord of a manor over its land and people, and was, therefore, complete and very autocratic. The prince was not only the ruler of the country; he was also its owner. In the course of time, when the Moscow princes took the leadership in gathering together and unifying all of northern Russia, they received recognition as the main leaders of all the people and acquired power which was public, democratic, and national in character. To gain public sympathy and mass support, the Moscow princes presented themselves as entitled to pride and power only as representative of the people and of national independence. Ivan III refused the Emperor's offer of a royal title because he would not accept "ordination" by an alien power in "his own country." Ambassadors later said of Vasili III that he exercised more power than any other monarch of the period, and added that the Muscovites compared their ruler to God, saying, "We do not know; God and the Prince know." So was created in Moscow a powerful autocracy, patrimonial in origin and national in magnitude.

This took place at a time when other Orthodox governments were moving toward their decline and fall. The awesome Turkish conquerors were encroaching upon the Orthodox East. Having seized the Asiatic provinces of the Byzantine (Greek) Empire, the Turks moved on Europe. At the close of the fourteenth and start of the fifteenth century, they conquered the Balkan Slavs and encircled Constantinople. We have seen how the Greeks, in apprehension of this, had sought far and wide for aid. To no avail, however; no help came, and in 1453 Constantinople fell to the Turks. There then remained in the East only one Orthodox state, only one independent bishopric; all the others were captured by the Godless infidels, as the Turks were called. The Moscow state alone retained its Orthodox prince and an independent metropolitan. They alone stood steadfast and strong, forming a powerful union of the Great Russian tribes, and maintaining the last barrier against the Tatar yoke.

For a long time—since the conversion of the Rus to Christianity—the notion had been held in Russia that all "Orthodoxy," that is to say, all Orthodox Christians, had for untold centuries been united under the one supreme power of the Greek [Byzantine] Sovereign ("caesar," "tsar") and the Greek Church. Constantinople, seat of the Greek Patriarch and of the tsar, was therefore called Tsargrad by the Russians, and was looked upon as the capital of all "Orthodoxy." When Constantinople and all the eastern states and churches were in the hands of the Turks and were subordinated to them, the Orthodox recognized no other capital than free Moscow. The people of Moscow awoke to this soon after the fall of Constantinople. The Muscovite princes Ivan III and Vasili III regarded themselves as the heirs and successors of the Greek tsars. Ivan III married a Greek princess, adopted for himself the Greek coat-of-arms, crowned his grandson Dmitri "to the Tsardom." He himself, like Vasili III, sometimes titled himself "Tsar." This view was shared and spread from the Russians to the Greeks and to the Balkan Slavs who saw in the Prince of Moscow the only defender of the faith. They sought the help and support of the Moscow princes, and openly called them the heirs of the [Byzantine] emperor.

The Russian literature of that time shows that the Russians had a great interest in the subject of the relations between Rus and Byzantium. Proceeding from the theory of the Divine One-ness of the entire Christian world, one of the writers of that period, the Monk Philotheus of Pskov, wrote an epistle to the Grand Prince Vasili III in which he argued that Ancient Rome had been the original center of the world; after this appeared a new Rome (Nova Roma—Constantinople), and in the most recent time, a Third Rome—Moscow. "Two Romes have fallen," said Philotheus, "but the third stands, and a fourth shall not be." Thus arose the important theory of the universal role of Moscow—the Third Rome.

After Philotheus, other writers expanded on the same theme, calling the Grand Prince of Muscovy the tsar of all "Orthodoxy"; Moscow, "the new city of Constantinople (*i.e.,* the new Tsargrad)"; and the Russian people, "new Israel," whom God Himself had chosen to lead all the Orthodox. The theory of the transfer of world supremacy from Tsargrad to Moscow having been accepted, it was argued and expounded in every way. It was pointed out that many sacred objects had been miraculously transferred from Byzantium, where Orthodoxy dimmed, to Russia, where it shone as before. They transmitted the tradition that the Apostle Andrew had been in the land of Rus, had blessed the site of Kiev, and had prophesied that Russia would thrive in the true faith; on this basis they concluded that the Russian Church owed its origin to the apostles and was, therefore, a proper successor to the Greek Church. They related further how the symbols of tsarist authority had long ago been given by a Byzantine tsar, namely, Constantine Monomakh, to the Grand Prince of Rus, Vladimir Monomakh, and from him had descended in natural line to the grand princes of Moscow. There actually existed in Moscow (and still exists) Monomakh's cap and cape which were placed on the grand princes at their coronations before the altar. There was revived, eventually, the ancient myth that the Russian dynasty was descended from the first Roman emperors inasmuch as Riurik was the descendant of Prussus, brother of the Emperor Augustus. The legends of unbroken succession gave strength to Muscovite claims such as the following: the state of Moscow is the foremost in all "Orthodoxy"; the Muscovite prince is the

"Orthodox Tsar"; and the Muscovite Church preeminently among all Orthodox churches preserves its independence and purity so that it stands above the older, Eastern Patriarchate.

Adopting this majestic theory, the Muscovite princes raised themselves to great heights. Conscious of their absolute power over their estates and their lands, feeling themselves to be the national leaders of a strong and numerous people, they now sought to play a larger role as tsars of all the Orthodox world. Such mighty and autocratic power seemed to them to be naturally theirs. But this autocratic power was not pleasing to all, and was not everywhere recognized. Markedly opposed to it was a fifteenth-century movement among the Muscovite boyars.

Boyars and Princes: Their Claims

An attachment of the boyars to the prince had been formed, as has been said, during the first years of the rise of the Moscow principality. Ancient custom gave boyars and the "free servants of the prince" the right to retire from the prince's service if the boyar or servant was displeased with his "sovereign" (master). Moreover, distinguished servants and boyars considered that they had a legal place in the princely council where were thrashed out all matters of government and politics. In the fourteenth century, boyars did not leave the Muscovite prince because in Moscow they were better off in the prince's service. On the contrary, many servants of other princes voluntarily came to Moscow and sought service at the Muscovite court. Identifying their own success with the success of Moscow, the boyars originally exerted all their strength to increase the power of the princes whose loyal followers they were.

The boyars more than once governed the principality for young or incompetent princes and took care that they did not suffer harm. The princes, on the other hand, appreciated and rewarded their boyars. It is said that the dying Dmitri Donskoi advised his children, "Love your boyars, do them honor, never act without their counsel." Especially prominent among the Moscow boyars of this time were the families of Fedor Kosh (ancestors of the Romanovs and Sheremetevs), of Byakon (ancestors of the Pleshcheevs and others), of Murz-Chet (ancestors of the Saburovs, Godunovs, and others), and the families of the Golovnins, Morozovs, Vel'gaminovs, and many others. At the beginning of the fifteenth century, large numbers of appanage princes from northern Russia and even Lithuanian princes enlisted themselves among the boyars of Moscow.

The appanage princes who entered the service of the Muscovite prince but still owned their appanages were allowed by the Grand Prince to keep them as ordinary boyar estates. If the Lithuanian princes who left their principalities to come to Moscow came without lands, the Grand Prince gave them some of his lands. These new servants of the Moscow state were thus provided with land in return for which they were obligated to serve Moscow as warriors, or in other capacities, and to answer the state's summons, together with their "people" (serfs), whenever and wherever called upon. Holding various offices at court and in miltary service, these "serving princes" were equal in duties to ordinary state servants, but, on the ground that they were scions of princely families and were descended from Riurik and Gedymin, they refused to accept ordinary boyars as their equals.

[Platonov describes the jealousy with which each prince insisted on his rank. "They knew from the book of genealogy exactly who was a scion of an older lineage, and who of a younger, and who was related to whom." They demanded that the highest appointments be reserved for those descended from the oldest and most illustrious families. Such demands were unpopular with the native Moscow boyars who were not willing to yield precedence to any "princes," some of whom were poverty-stricken. Ambition and pride of pedigree led to tedious disputes about seniority. Men refused assignments unless certain that they would not be humiliated by being subordinate to someone of less illustrious pedigree and rank. The custom of making assignments according to pedigree was called *mestniche-stvo* which may be freely rendered as appointment-by-pedigree.]

In this way, there gradually developed in fifteenth-century Moscow a new boyar group at the head of which, by virtue of their "grand pedigrees," stood the descendants of those appanage princes who had "made submission to Moscow." Claiming that they were of no lower lineage nor less illustrious birth than the Grand Prince, but were of the same blood as he, these boyars refused to accord him sovereign primacy over them. In the ancient expression, the sovereign granted lands and rewards but not lineage. But the Muscovite sovereign was no longer content with his new boyars because he was less dependent on them. The prince-boyars kept in mind that they were of the same ancestry as the sovereign, the Moscow prince, and were therefore also "sovereign," and not ordinary servants of the state. They claimed equal right to govern the state as co-regents related to the Muscovite prince and not inferior to him. They felt themselves equal in their patrimony to appanage princes like their fathers and grandfathers. In a word, the new Moscow boyars assumed the airs of an hereditary, landed aristocracy, and cherished pretensions to share in governing the state. Such were the relations at this time between the Muscovite autocrat and his boyars.

Ivan III and Vasili III both rejected the claims of these "princelings," as they were titled in Moscow. They confiscated some of the princelings' estates, forbid them to sell their lands without special permission, to leave the land except under such conditions as to retain the appanage lands for Moscow, or to leave the state service. Ivan and Vasili did not consult the princelings in their private council nor admit them to their confidential matters but, instead, entrusted such matters to ordinary "clerks" (secretaries). When the princelings complained, they were disgraced, banished to monasteries, or executed. If any princeling plotted to desert to the Grand Prince of Lithuania (there being nowhere else to flee) he was seized and charged with treason and apostasy. In such manner, the Muscovite sovereigns took away the old rights of advising the sovereign and of free departure from him—rights which the boyars had always had. The princelings did not accept such decisions. As times changed and new institutions developed in the state, they rebeled and spread discord. The Moscow princes found domestic foes among their boyar-princes.

Serving People and Taxpayers: the Pomestie System and the Attachment of the Peasants to the Land

Other privileged groups were formed in the Moscow state simultaneously with the formation of the princely aristocracy. In the appanage period, at the time when the princes were colonizing the Slavic tribes of the northeast, class lines within the principality were very blurred. During the whole flow of colonists from the Dnieper and Lake Ilmen to the Volga region, people did not settle permanently, but shifted and wandered, moving gradually east and northeast. Only the princes, the masters of the appanages, remained settled on their appanage domains. Being forced to maintain their forces and their entire economy under conditions of continuous mobility, a "fluidity" of the entire population, the princes developed unusual economic and governmental modes. They were unable immediately to stop the flow of migrations, to keep people within the volost and attach them to the appanage. People freely entered and left the appanage without informing the prince or obtaining his permission. The princes therefore tried to attach individuals to themselves. They either took them freely into their retinue under an agreement (in the case of boyars and free "servants") or (in the case of "people" and the unfree) bought them and held them as slaves. The princely court—like the bodyguard of the Kievan period—was formed from these persons and others.

The appanage prince governed his appanage, defended it, and carried on its economic life with the help of his court. The boyars and the free servants were his advisers and agents. The "people" supplied the troops and were the workers in his fields and enterprises. The prince often invited poor freemen to settle on his lands on condition that they work for the prince and serve him, it being understood that if such a servant did not fulfill his obligations he would be deprived of the land which had been given him. A special middle class of prince's people, neither slaves nor wholly free, arose from those who served "under the court," that is, as inferiors. To recapitulate, the prince's "servants," whether boyars or slaves, were direct subordinates; but the "people" were the prince's subjects in our meaning of that word, that is, they were bound to him by ties of allegiance. Those who left him to serve another prince either lost their lands, if they were "servants under the court," or kept all their lands, if they were free "servants."

Such were the relations to the appanage prince of those who served him. All other persons living in the prince's appanage were known generally as "Christians" or "Cross-bearers" [peasants], and were not considered among those dependent upon the prince. They were governed, both in towns and in rural districts, by communes, or "mirs." The prince was aware that the peasants resided in some of his volosts (living, for example, in some of the river valleys). He had a count made of the number of peasants, appointed one among them to collect all poll taxes and "assessments on individual land allotments," and charged these peasants to deliver the taxes to him on certain dates. The people came and went, to and from the volost, without harm or authorization by the prince. The mir admitted and released the peasants, set and collected all taxes, and chose an "elder" to collect the taxes and deliver them to the prince. Thereafter, from year to year, account was taken of increase or decrease of peasant households in a given volost, and the amount which the mir had to pay was increased or decreased accordingly. By custom, the peasant dealt not with the prince but with the mir, and the prince was quite indifferent to the peasant even if the latter went over to a neighboring prince. The prince was not directly affected by such action, but the free movement of peasants did affect the private lands of the boyars. Arriving on an estate, the peasants entered into formal leases, setting their obligations and payments to the master; on leaving, they formally renounced the lease. Law and custom set St. George's day (the 26th of November) as the normal date for renunciation. When we understand that the movement of people from one class to another—from peasant to townsman or from slave to freeman—was very easy and was possible for all, then we also understand that the social organization in the appanage period was very vague and informal.

This vagueness could not survive the transition which took place in the appanage state. The Moscow sovereigns were the first to reconstruct their "court." We have seen that they imposed restrictions on the lands given to their "serving princes," and demanded that these lands "should not go out of service" (that is, out of the prince's jurisdiction). The same conditions were, in general, applied to all estates. *Everyone who possessed land was obligated to defend the state.* At the sovereign's demand, every estate was required to furnish military forces, "mounted and armed." Princelings and boyars, owners of large estates, brought an entire "army" of their followers. Lesser landowners rode out to serve with just "their own heads," or with a few slaves. But, because of wars against the Tatars, the Lithuanians, and the Germans, larger military forces were required. The traditional way of raising forces was not adequate; the Moscow sovereign required from his serving people more "hale and hearty" (that is, fit-to-fight) recruits; and he bestowed on them crown lands so that they could support and provide larger military forces.

At first, these lands were given out of the prince's private holdings. When these became insufficient, he gave "black" lands (that is, taxable state lands.) The lands given to the serving people were originally known as "service lands"; later, they were called pomestie, and their owners were called pomeshchiks, or younger boyars, or dvoryanin. *In contrast to the votchina, which was the private, hereditary possession of the votchinnik, a pomestie was a temporary possession.* The pomeshchik possessed the land only so long as he served the prince; when the service was broken off through the remissness of the pomeshchik, or by his death, the pomestie reverted to the prince. By the beginning of the sixteenth century, the pomeshchiks numbered thousands, and the pomestie system reached into all sections of the country. A great many people were in the service of the state. New pomeshchiks were settled on lands near the frontiers—at Novgorod, at Smolensk, at Seversk, along the Oka and, finally, in the central districts of Muscovy itself. There was established at Moscow a "pomeshchik izba" [literally, cottage] for the management of pomestie affairs; and for administering the services of pomeshchiks and votchinniks —"Razryad."

The "serving people" were, from time to time, given monetary rewards in addition to pomestie land, and the best known among them were given "kormlen'ya." This meant that some were sent to cities as viceregents or to volosts as administrators. They governed, served as judges, looked after affairs, and, in return, secured "kormyi" and "poshlinyi" [literally, food and taxes] from the people. Kormyi were gifts at specific times (on major feast days), but poshlinyi were fees for helping people in court or in other business. *Thus the government illegally derived income from the volosts and the cities and described it as "feeding."* Such was the organization of the new serving class. This class now consisted of: 1) the princelings and the boyars, constituting the aristocracy; 2) the gentry and the junior boyars—votchinniks and pomeshchiks; and 3) the garrison "people" (musketeers, arquebusiers and cannoneers) assigned to the land in small groups of individual "villages" for the defense of the cities.

The growth of the pomestie system necessitated a very widespread taking possession of peasant lands for transfer to pomeshchiks. This resulted in making the peasants dependent upon the landowners. *Moreover, just as the landowners were required to serve the state in return for their lands, the peasants were under obligation to work for the landowners, tilling their plough-lands and paying fees (obrok) to them.* Soon, neither a pomeshchik nor the government found it convenient to permit the free departure of a peasant from the land or from work on the land and, later, both tried to hold the peasants in their places. The peasants were registered, together with the lands, in individual "cadastres" [official registers] and those who were "caught in the book" were regarded as being attached to the land on which they were registered. These "inscribed" peasants could not leave their jobs nor move from place to place like "uninscribed" persons, that is, those not registered in the cadastres. Peasants on the lands of private landowners (that is, unregistered peasants) were given letters of contract in an effort to attach them to the land in some manner—particularly by giving loans of cash, seeds, or draft animals, loans which did not have to be repaid as long as the peasant did not work for other landowners.

The right of moving on St. George's Day was not abolished at this time, and was used by those peasants who had not tied themselves to a landowner. It is necessary to note that not only did the requirement of defending the country cause the landowners to oppose peasant migration, but also that the peasant communes did not like to lose their "tax-payers" because the loss of taxable people caused trouble in the collection and payment of the taxes demanded by the state. Those who went away paid no taxes; those who remained were obliged to pay more and this produced hardships. Therefore, the peasant mirs themselves besought the government not to allow registered peasants to leave the community. Thus, little by little, measures were taken which bound the peasants in place, forced them to pay fees on the estates, obligated them to pay taxes to the government, and required them to work and to provide services to the landlords.

Herberstein's "Notes on Russia" (1517 and 1526)

The Baron Sigismund von Herberstein went as ambassador to the court of the Grand Prince Vasili Ivanovich (Vasili III) in 1517 and again in 1526. His *Rerum Moscovitarum Commentarii* is the first authentic description of Muscovy based upon personal residence and experience by a European observer. It is accounted a major source for the period. The following brief excerpts will give the flavor of von Herberstein's work as well as some description of Muscovy and its people. The source is: R. H. Major (Ed. and Tr.), *Notes Upon Russia: Being a Translation of the Earliest Account of that Country, entitled Rerum Moscovitarum Commentarii, by the Baron Sigismund von Herberstein.* Two volumes. London: The Hakluyt Society, 1851– 1852. Vol. 1, pp. 95–96, 105–106; vol. 2, pp. 131–132.

All confess themselves to be Chlopos, that is, serfs of the prince. Almost all the upper classes also have serfs, who either have been taken prisoners, or purchased; and those whom they keep in free service are not at liberty to quit at their own pleasure. If any one goes away without his master's consent, no one receives him. If a master does not treat a good and useful servant well, he by some means gets a bad name amongst others, and after that he can procure no more domestics.

This people enjoy slavery more than freedom; for persons on the point of death very often manumit some of their serfs, but they immediately sell themselves for money to other families. If the father should sell the son, which is the custom, and he by means become free or be manumitted, the father can sell him again and again, by right of his paternal authority. But after the fourth sale, the father has no more right over his son. The prince alone can inflict capital punishment on serfs or others.

Every second or third year the prince holds a census through the provinces, and conscribes the sons of the boyars, that he may know their number, and how many horses and serfs each one has. Then he appoints each his stipend, as has been said above. Those who have the means to do so, fight without pay. Rest is seldom given them, for either they are waging war against the Lithuanians, or the Livonians, or the Swedes, or the Tartars of Cazar; or if no war is going on, the prince generally appoints twenty thousand men every year in places about the Don and the Occa, as guards to repress the eruptions and depredations of the Tartars of Precop. He generally summons some also every year by rotation out of his provinces, to fill the various offices in his service at Moscow. But in war time, they do not serve in annual rotation, or by turns, but each and all are compelled, both as stipendiaries and as aspirants to the prince's favour, to go to battle.

. . .

The testimony of one nobleman is worth more than that of a multitude of low condition. Attorneys are very seldom allowed: every one explains his own case. Although the prince is very severe, nevertheless all justice is venal, and that without much concealment. I heard of a certain counsellor who presided over the judgments being apprehended, because in a certain case he had received bribes from both parties, and had given judgment in the favour of the one who had made him the largest presents: when he was brought to the prince he did not deny the charge, but stated that the man in whose favour he had given judgment was rich, and held an honourable position in life, and therefore more to be believed than the other, who was poor and abject. The prince revoked the sentence, but at length sent him away with a laugh unpunished. It may be that poverty itself is the cause of so much avarice and injustice, and that the prince knowing his people are poor, connives at such misdeeds and dishonesty as by a predetermined concession of impunity to them.

The poor have no access to the prince, but only to the counsellors themselves; and indeed that is very difficult. *Ocolnick* holds the place of a praetor or judge appointed by the prince, otherwise the chief counsellor, who is always near the prince's person, is so called. *Nedelsnick* is the post of those who summon men to justice, seize malefactors and cast them into prison; and these are reckoned amongst the nobility.

Labourers work six days in the week for their master, but the seventh day is allowed for their private work. They have some fields and meadows of their own allowed them by their masters, from which they derive their livelihood: all the rest is their master's. They are, moreover, in a very wretched condition, for their goods are exposed to plunder from the nobility and soldiery, who call them Christians and black rascals by way of insult.

A nobleman, however poor he might be, would think it ignominious and disgraceful to labour with his own hands; but he does not think it disgraceful to pick up from the ground and eat the rind or peeling of fruits that have been thrown away by us and our servants, especially the skins of melons, garlic, and onions; but whenever occasion offers, they drink as immoderately as they eat sparingly. They are nearly all slow to anger, but proud in their poverty, whose irksome companion they consider slavery. They wear oblong dresses and white peaked hats of felt (of which we see coarse mantles made) rough from the shop.

. . .

The prince often honours his guests by sending them dishes and drink. He never meddles with matters of serious moment during dinner; but when the dinner is over, it is his custom to say to the ambassadors, "Now you may depart." When thus dismissed, they are escorted back to their hotels by the same persons who had conducted them to the palace, who state that they have orders to remain with them in the hotel, to make merry with them. Silver goblets, and various other vessels containing liquor, are then produced, and all strive to make each other drunk; and very clever they are in finding excuses for inviting men to drink, and when they are at a loss for a toast to propose, they begin at last to drink to the health of the emperor and the prince his brother, and after that to the welfare of any others whom they believe to hold any position of dignity and honour. They think that no one ought or can refuse the cup, when these names are proposed. The drinking is done in this fashion. He who proposes the toast takes his cup, and goes into the middle of the room, and standing with his head uncovered, pronounces, in a festive speech, the name of him whose health he wishes to drink, and what he has to say in his behalf. Then after emptying the cup, he turns it upside down over his head, so that all may see that he has emptied it, and that he sincerely gave the health of the person in honour of whom the toast was drunk. He then goes to the top of the table and orders many cups to be filled, and then hands each man his cup, pronouncing the name of the party whose health is to be drunk, on which each is obliged to go into the middle of the room, and, after emptying his cup, to return to his place. He who wishes to escape too long a drinking-bout, must pretend that he is drunk or sleepy, or at least declare that, having already emptied many cups, he cannot drink any more; for they do not think that their guests are well received, or hospitably treated, unless they are sent home drunk. It is common practice for nobles and those who are permitted to drink mead and beer, to observe this fashion.

Chancelour's Description of Muscovy in the Sixteenth Century

The Englishmen, Sir Hugh Willoughby and Richard Chancelour, were sent out in 1553 by the Muscovy Company of England to search for a northeast passage to Asia. Willoughby and all his people perished, but Chancelour made his way into the White Sea and to the shores of Muscovy. With the permission of Ivan Grozny, he and his party made their way to Moscow where they were well received by the tsar. The following selection is taken from Chancelour's description of Ivan and his realm. The source is: Hakluyt, *Principal Navigations, etc.,* vol. 1, pp. 254–266, *passim.*

The booke of the great and mighty Emperor of Russia, and Duke of Moscovia, and of the dominions orders and commodities thereunto belonging: drawn by Richard Chancelour.

FORASMUCH as it is meete and necessary for all those that minde to take

in hande the travell into farre or strange countreys, to endevour themselves not onely to understande the orders, commodities, and fruitfulness
thereof, but also to applie them to the setting foorth of the same whereby it
may incourage others to the like travaile: therefore have I nowe thought
good to make a briefe rehearsall of the orders of this my travaile in Russia
and Muscovia, and other countreys thereunto adjoyning; because it was
my chance to fall with the North partes of Russia before I came towards
Moscovia, I will partly declare my knowledge therein. Russia is very
plentifull both of land and people, and also welthy for such commodities
as they have. They be very great fishers for Salmons and small Coddes:
they have much oyle which wee call treine oyle, the most whereof is made
by a river called Duina. They make it in other places, in seething of salte
water. To the Northparte of that countrey are the places where they have
their Furres, as Sables, marterns, greese Bevers, Foxes white, black, and
redde, Minkes, Ermines, Miniver, and Harts. There are also a fishes teeth,
which fish is called a Morsse. The takers thereof dwell in a place called
Postesora, which bring them upon Hartes to Lampas to sell, and from
Lampas carie them to a place called Colmogro, where the hie market is
holden on Saint Nicholas day. To the West of Colmogro there is a place
called Gratanove, in our language Novogorode, where much fine Flaxe
and Hempe groweth, and also much waxe and honie. The Dutch marchants have a Staplehouse there. There is also great store of hides, and at
a place called Plesco: and thereabout is great store of Flaxe, Hempe,
Waxe, Honie; and that towne is from Colmogro 120 miles.

There is a place called Vologda; the commodities whereof are Tallowe,
Waxe, and Flaxe: but not so great plenty as is in Gratanove. From Vologda to Colmogro there runneth a river called Duyna, and from thence it
falleth into the sea. Colmogro serveth Gratanove, Vologda and the Mosco
with all the countrey thereabout with salte and saltfish. From Vologda to
Jeraslave is two hundreth miles: which towne is very great. The commodities thereof are hides, and tallowe, and corne in great plenty, and some
Waxe, but not so plentifull as in other places.

The Mosco is from Jeraslave two hundreth miles. The countrey betwixt
them is very wel replenished with small Villages, which are so well filled
with people, that it is wonder to see them: the ground is well stored with
corne which they carie to the citie of Mosco in such abundance that it is
wonder to see it. You shall meete in a morning seven or eight hundred
sleds comming or going thither, that carrie corne, and some carie fish. You
shall have some that carie corne to the Mosco, and some that fetch corne
from thence, that at the least dwell a thousand miles off; and all their carriage is on sleds. Those which come so farre dwell in the North partes of
the Dukes dominions, where the cold will suffer no corne to grow, it is so
extreme. They bring thither fishes, furres, and beastse skinnes. In those
partes they have but small store of cattell.

The Mosco it selfe is great: I take the whole towne to bee greater then
London with the suburbes: but it is very rude, and standeth without all
order. Their houses are all of timber very dangerous for fire. There is a

faire Castle, the walles whereof are of bricke, and very high: they say they are eighteene foote thicke, but I doe not believe it, it doth not seeme, notwithstanding I doe not certainely know it: for no stranger may come to viewe it. The one side is ditched, and on the other side runneth a river called Moscua which runneth into Tartarie and so into the sea called Mare Caspium: and on the North side there is a base towne, the which hath also a bricke wall about it, and so it joyneth with the Castle wall. The Emperour lieth in the castle, wherein are nine fayre Churches, and therin are religious men. Also there is a Metropolitane with divers Bishops. I will not stande in description of their buildinges nor of the strength thereof because we have better in all points in England. They be well furnished with ordinance of all sortes.

The Emperours or Dukes house neither in building nor in the outward shew, nor yet within the house is so sumptuous as I have seene. It is very lowe built in eight square, much like the olde building of England, with small windowes, and so in other poynts.

Now to declare my comming before his Majestie: After I had remained twelve daies, the Secretary which hath the hearing of strangers did send for me, advertising me that the Dukes pleasure was to have me to come before his Ma. with the kings my masters letters: whereof I was right glad, and so I gave mine attendance. And when the Duke was in his place appointed, the interpretour came for me into the utter chamber, where sate one hundred or moe gentlemen, all in cloth of golde very sumptuous, and from thence I came into the Counsaile chamber, where sate the Duke himselfe with his nobles, which were a faire company: they sate round about the chamber on high, yet so that he himselfe sate much higher then any of his nobles in a chaire gilt, and in a long garment of beaten golde, with an emperial crowne upon his head, and a staffe of Cristall and golde in his right hand, and his other hand halfe leaning on his chaire. The Chancelour stoode up with the Secretary before the Duke. After my dutie done and my letter delivered, he bade me welcome, & enquired of me the health of the King my master, and I answered that he was in good health at my departure from his court, and that my trust was that he was now in the same. Upon the which he made me to dinner. The Chancelour presented my present unto his Grace bareheaded (for before they were all covered) and when his Grace had received my letter, I was required to depart: for I had charge not to speake to the Duke, but when he spake to me. So I departed unto the Secretaries chamber, where I remayned two houres, and then I was sent for againe unto another place which is called the golden palace, but I saw no fayrer then it in all poynts: and so I cam into the hall, which was small and not great as is the Kings Majesties of England, and the table was covered with a tablecloth; and the Marshall sate at the ende of the table with a little white rod in his hand, which boorde was full of vessell of golde: and on the other side of the hall did stand a faire cupborde of plate. From thence I came into the dining chamber, where the Duke himselfe sate at his table without cloth of estate, in a gowne of silver, with a crowne emperiall upon his head, he sate in a chaire

somewhat hie: There sate none neare him by a great way. There were
long tables set round about the chamber, which were full set with such as
the Duke had at dinner: they were all in white. Also the places where the
tables stoode were higher by two steppes then the rest of the house. In the
middle of the chamber stoode a table or cupbord to set plate on; which
stoode full of cuppes of golde: and amongst all the rest there stoode foure
marveilous great pottes or crudences as they call them, of golde and silver:
I thinke they were a good yarde and a halfe hie. By the cupborde stoode
two gentlemen with napkins on their shoulders, and in their handes each
of them had a cuppe of gold set with pearles and prescious stones, which
were the Dukes owne drinking cups: When he was disposed, he drunke
them off at a draught. And for his service at meate it came in without
order, yet it was very rich service: for all were served in gold, not onely he
himselfe, but also all the rest of us, and it was very massie: the cups also
were of golde and very massie. The number that dined there that day was
two hundred persons, and all were served in golden vessell. The gentlemen
that waited were all in cloth of gold, and they served him with their caps
on their heads. Before the service came in, the Duke sent to every man
a great shiver of bread, and the bearer called the party so sent to by his
name aloude, and sayd, John Basilivich Emperour of Russia and great
Duke of Moscovia doth reward thee with bread: then must all men stand
up, and doe at all times when those wordes are spoken. And then last of all
he giveth the Marshall bread, whereof he eateth before the Dukes Grace,
and so doth reverence and departeth. Then commeth the Dukes service of
the Swannes all in pieces, and every one in a severall dish: the which the
Duke sendeth as he did the bread, and the bearer sayth the same wordes
as he sayd before. And as I sayd before, the service of his meate is in no
order, but commeth in dish by dish: and then after that the Duke sendeth
drinke, with the like saying as before is tolde. Also before dinner hee
changed his crowne, and in dinner time two crownes; so that I saw three
severall crownes upon his head in one day. And thus when his service was
all come in hee gave to every one of his gentlemen waiters meate with his
owne hand, & so likewise drinke. His intent thereby is, as I have heard,
that every man shall know perfectly his servants. Thus when dinner is done
hee calleth his nobles before him name by name, that it is wonder to heare
howe he could name them, having so many as he hath. Thus when dinner
was done I departed to my lodging, which was an hower within night. I
will leave this, and speake no more of him nor his houshold: but I will
somewhat declare of his land and people with their nature and power in
the wars. This Duke is Lord and Emperour of many countreis, & his
power is marveilous great. For he is able to bring into the field two or three
hundred thousand men: he never goeth into the field himselfe with under
two hundred thousand men: And when he goeth himselfe he furnisheth his
borders all with men of warre, which are no small number. He leaveth
on the borders of Liefland fortie thousand men, and upon the borders of
Letto 60 thousand men, and towarde the Nagayan Tartars sixtie thousand,
which is wonder to heare of: yet doeth hee never take to his warres neither

husbandman nor marchant. All his men are horsemen: he useth no foot-men, but such as goe with the ordinance and labourers, which are thirtie thousand. The horsemen are all archers, with such bowes as the Turkes have, and they ride short as doe the Turkes. Their armour is a coate of plate, with a skull on their heads. Some of their coates are covered with velvet or cloth of gold: their desire is to be sumptuous in the field, and especially the nobles and gentlemen: as I have heard their trimming is very costly, and partly I have seene it, or else I would scarcely have beeleved it: but the Duke himselfe is richly attired above all measure: his pavilion is covered either with cloth of gold or silver, and so set with stones that it is wonderfull to see it. I have seene the Kings Majesties of England and the French Kings pavilions, which are fayre, yet not like unto his. And when they bee sent into farre or strange countreys, or that strangers come to them, they be very gorgious. Els the Duke himselfe goeth but meanly in apparell: and when he goeth betwixt one place and another hee is but reasonably ap-parelled over other times. In the while that I was in Mosco the Duke sent two ambassadours to the King of Poleland, which had at the lest five hun-dred horses; their sumptuousnes was above measure, not onely in them-selves, but also in their horses, as velvet, cloth of golde, and cloth of silver set with pearles and not scant. What shall I farther say? I never heard of nor saw men so sumptuous: but it is no dayly guise, for when they have not occasion, as I sayd before, all their doing is but meane. And now to the effect of their warres: They are men without al order in the field. For they runne hurling on heapes, and for the most part they never give battell to their enemies: but that which they doe, they doe it all by stelth. But I beleeve they be such men for hard living as are not under the sun: for no cold wil hurt them. Yea and though they lie in the field two moneths, at such time as it shall freese more then a yard thicke, the common souldier hath neither tent nor any thing else over his head: the most defence they have against the wether is a felte, which is set against the winde and weather, and when Snowe commeth hee doth cast it off, and maketh him a fire, and laieth him down thereby. Thus doe the most of all his men, ex-cept they bee gentlemen which have other provision of their owne. Their lying in the fielde is not so strange as is their hardnes: for every man must carie & make provision for himselfe & his horse for a moneth or two, which is very wonderful. For he himselfe shal live upon water & otemeale mingled together cold, and drinke water thereto: his horse shal eat green wood, & such like baggage, & shal stand open in the cold field without covert, & yet wil he labour & serve him right wel. I pray you amongst all our boasting warriors how many should we find to endure the field with them but one moneth. I know no such region about us that beareth that name for man & beast. Now what might be made of these men if they were trained & broken to order and knowledge of civill wars? If this Prince had within his countreys such men as could make them to understand ye things aforesaid, I do beleeve that 2 of the best or greatest princes in Christen-dome were not wel able to match with him, considering the greatnes of his power & the hardnes of his people & straite living both of people and horse, and the small charges which his warres stand him in: for he giveth no wages, except to strangers. They have a yerely stipend & not much. As for his own countrey men every one serveth of his owne proper costes and charges, saving that he giveth to his Harcubusiers certaine allowance for powder & shot: or else no man in all his countrey hath one pennie wages. But if any man hath done very good service he giveth him a ferme or a piece of lande; for the which hee is bound at all times to bee readie with so many men as the Duke shall appoynt: who considereth in his mind what that lande or ferme is well able to finde: and so many shall he bee bound to furnish at all and every such time as warres are holden in any of the Dukes dominions. For there is no man of living, but hee is bound likewise, whether the Duke call for either souldier or labourer, to furnish them with all such necessaries as to them belong.

Also, if any gentleman or man of living do die without issue male, immediately after his death the Duke takes his land, notwithstanding he have never so many daughters, and peradventure giveth it foorthwith to another man, except a small portion that he spareth to marrie the daughters with all. Also if there be a rich man, a fermour, or man of living, which is striken in age or by chance is maimed, and be not able to doe the Duke service, some other gentleman that is not able to live and more able to doe service, will come to the Duke and complayne, saying, your Grace hath such an one, which is unmeete to doe service to your Highnes, who hath great abundance of welth, and likewise your Grace hath many gentlemen which are poore and lacke living, and we that lacke are well able to doe good service, your Grace might doe well to looke upon him, and make him to helpe those that want. Immediately the Duke sendeth forth to inquire of his wealth: and if it be so proved, he shall be called before the Duke, and it shall bee sayd unto him, friend, you have too much living, and are unserviceable to your prince, lesse will serve you, and the rest will serve other men that are more able to serve. Whereupon immediately his living shal be taken away from him, saving a little to find himselfe and his wife on, and he may not once repine thereat: but for answere he will say, that he hath nothing, but it is Gods and the Dukes Graces, and cannot say, as we the common people in England say, if wee have any thing; that it is Gods and our owne. Men may say, that these men are in wonderful great awe, and obedience, that thus one must give and grant his goods which he hath bene scraping and scratching for all his life to be at his Princes pleasure and commandement. Oh that our sturdie rebels were had in the like subjection to knowe their duety towarde their Princes. They may not say as some snudges in England say, I would find the Queene a man to serve in my place, or make his friends tarrie at home if money have the upper hand. No, no, it is not so in this countrey: for hee shall make humble sute to serve the Duke. And whom he sendeth most to the warres he thinketh he is most in his favour: and yet as I before have sayde, he giveth no wages. If they knewe their strength no man were able to make match with them: nor they that dwel neere them should have any rest of them. But I thinke it is not Gods will: For I may compare them to a young horse that knoweth not his strength, whome a little childe ruleth and guideth with a bridle, for all his great strength: for if hee did, neither childe nor man could rule him. Their warres are holden against the Crimme Tartarians and the Nagaians.

I will stand no longer in the rehearsall of their power and warres. For it were too tedious to the reder. But I will in part declare their lawes, and punishments, and the execution of justice. And first I will begin with the commons of the countrey, which the gentlemen have rule on: And that is, that every gentleman hath rule and justice upon his owne tenants. And if it so fall out that two gentlemens servants or tenaunts doe disagree, the two gentlemen examine the matter, and have the parties before them, and soe give the sentence. And yet cannot they make the ende betwixt them of the controversie, but either of the gentlemen must bring his servant or tenant before the high judge or justice of that countrey, and there present them, and declare the matter and case. The plaintiffe sayth, I require the law; which is graunted: then commeth an officer and arresteth the party defendant, and useth him contrarie to the lawes of England. For when they attach any man they beate him about the legges, untill such time as he fineth suerties to answere the matter: And if not, his handes and necke are bound together, and he is led about the towne and beaten about the legges, with other extreme punishments till he come to his answere: And the Justice demaundeth if it be for debt, and sayth: Owest thou this man any such debt? He will perhaps say nay. Then sayth the Judge: art thou able to denie it? Let us heare how? By othe sayth the defendant. Then he commandeth to leave beating him till further triall be had.

Their order in one point is commendable. They have no man of Law to pleadeth his owne cause, and giveth bill and answere in writing: contrarie to the order in England. The complaint is in maner of a supplication, & made to the Dukes Grace, and delivered him into his owne hand, requiring to have justice as in his complaint is alleaged.

The duke giveth sentence himself upon all matters in the Law. Which is very commendable, that such a Prince wil take paines to see ministration of justice. Yet notwithstanding it is wonderfully abused: and thereby the Duke is much deceived. But if it fall out that the officers be espied in cloking the trueth, they have most condigne punishment. And if the plaintife can nothing proove, then the defendant must take his othe upon the crucifixe whether he bee in the right or no. Then is demanded if the plaintife be any thing able further to make proofe: if hee bee not; then sometimes he will say, I am able to proove it by my body and hands, or by my champions body, so requiring the Campe. After the other hath his othe, it is graunted as well to the one as to the other. So when they goe to the field, they sweare upon the Crucifixe, that they bee both in the right, and that the one shall make the other to confesse the trueth before they depart foorth of the field: and so they goe both to the battel armed with such weapons as they use in that countrey: they fight all on foote, & seldome the parties themselves do fight, except they be Gentlemen, for they stand much upon their reputation, for they wil not fight, but with such as are come of as good an house as themselves. So that if either partie require the combate, it is granted unto them, and no champion is to serve in their roome: wherein is no deceit: but otherwise by champions there is. For although they take great othes upon them to doe the battell truely, yet is the contrary often seene: because the common champions have none other living. And as soone as the one party hath gotten the victory, hee demandeth the debt, and the other is carried to prison, and there is shamefully used till he take order. There is also another order in the lawe, that the plaintife may sweare in some causes of debt. And if the partie defendant be poore, he shalbe set under the Crucifixe, and the partie plaintife must sweare over his head, and when hee hath taken his othe, the Duke taketh the partie defendant home to his house, and useth him as a bond-man, and putteth him to labour, or letteth him for hier to any such as neede him, untill such time as his friends make provision for his redemption: or else hee re-maineth in bondage all the dayes of his life. Againe there are many that will sell themselves to Gentlemen or Marchants to bee their bond-men, to have during their life meate, drinke and cloth, and at their comming to have a piece of mony. Yea and some will sell their wives and children to bee bawdes and drudges to the byer. Also they have a Lawe for Fellons and pickers contrary to the Lawes of England. For by their law they can hang no man for his first offence; but may keepe him long in prison, and oftentimes beate him with whips and other punishment: and there he shall remaine untill his friends be able to bayle him. If he be a picker or a cut-purse, as there be very many, the second time he is taken, he hath a piece of his Nose cut off, and is burned in the forehead, and kept in prison till hee finds sureties for his good behaviour. And if he be taken the third time, he is hanged. And at the first time he is extremely punished and not released, except hee have very good friends, or that some Gentleman re-quire to have him to the warres: And in so doing, he shall enter into great bonds for him: by which meanes the countrey is brought into good quiet-nesse. But they be naturally given to great deceit, except extreme beating did bridle them. They be naturally given a hard living as well in fare as in lodging. I heard a Russian say, that it was a great deale merrier living in prison then foorth, but for the great beating. For they have meate and drinke without any labour, and get the charitie of well disposed people: But being at libertie they get nothing. The poore is very innumerable, and live most miserable: for I have seene them eate the pickle of Hearring and other stinking fish: nor the fish cannot be so stinking nor rotten, but they will eate it and praise it to be more wholesome then other fish or fresh meate. In mine opinion there be no such people under the sunne for their hardnesse of living.

A Soviet Interpretation

By way of contrast to the contemporary accounts of sixteenth-century Russia by non-Russians, here is a modern and very different interpretation by R. Iu. Vipper. Latvian by birth, Vipper was first a Russian, then a Soviet subject. He returned to the then independent Latvia in 1924, but again became a Soviet subject when Latvia was annexed to the USSR in 1941. Vipper's monograph, *Ivan Grozny,* was first published in 1922, and was reissued in several editions after 1942. The following excerpt is from a translation by J. Fineberg which was published at Moscow in 1947. Pp. 29–32. Slightly abridged.

In the course of continuous fighting to repel the attacks of external foes . . . Moscow built up institutions which had much in common with the strategy, armaments, fortifications, road systems and administrative practice of the great Asiatic empires.

• • •

To the forms borrowed from the enemy, the Moscow State, in the course of time, added its own original institutions, built up, however, on the same lines of a centralized military monarchy. Hence the similarity, in some respects, between Muscovy and the Ottoman Empire, the last great creation of the Asiatic warriors who gained predominance in the Levant. Both Russian and western observers were struck by the similarity between Muscovy and Turkey.

• • •

Foreigners regarded the similarity . . . as the main ground for their attacks upon the Russian system. An anonymous French liberal writer of the period of Ivan Grozny's Oprichnina (Life Guards) [*sic*] observed that institutions for protecting the law and defending the people against tyranny existed in all countries except Muscovy and Turkey. The English observers Horsey and Fletcher also harped on this theme. Failing to understand the Muscow system of administration, they described it as a despotism guided by caprice, often bordering on perverseness, and meeting with no opposition in the "barbarous" society which fully deserved such a system of administration.

Nevertheless, there were institutions in this "oriental despotism" which roused the envy of the West-Europeans and fired their imaginations. Such were the building of roads and the mail service, which helped to keep the regions which had not yet been fully subdued under observation, and also the system of dispatching diplomatic notes and envoys to foreign courts. . . . The speed of traveling and the splendour of the equipages employed astonished foreigners. . . . The government fully appreciated the value of this instrument of administration. In his testament to his children, Ivan III urged them to preserve the yamas (Yama: post station) and stagecoaches on the roads which had been opened during his reign. At the opening of

the Livonian War Ivan Grozny had at his command a splendidly organized
official postal service, which a Nürnberg newspaper, in 1561, described in
the following terms of admiration expressed by a diplomatic mission which
had just returned from Moscow: "In Livonia, near Reval and Riga, the
Tsar has agents who bring him information to Moscow within five days, so
that the Court of Moscow is kept informed about all that which takes place
in the Baltic, and is able closely to watch affairs in Western Europe."

There is another feature of the military organization that prevailed in
Moscow in the fifteenth and sixteenth centuries which attracts our attention, and which was also noted by foreigners. We refer to the systematic
preparations for big campaigns that were made in conformity with a widely
conceived plan. For these campaigns military forces were called up in good
time from the remote provinces and border regions, arms and stocks of provisions were concentrated at definite centers, and so forth. A number of
operations that were prepared for in order to strike the enemy a crushing
military blow and to deprive him of more territory bear evidence of the
strategical methods, characteristic of Moscow, of building fortresses on the
very frontiers, and even in enemy territory. Thus, in 1492 Ivan III built
Ivangorod, opposite the Livonian town of Narva, in preparation for the
occupation of the Finnish coast, which was undertaken by his grandson
Ivan IV sixty-six years later. Ivan III's successors moved up to Kazan by
the same methods. Vasili III built Vassilsursk, and Ivan IV built Svi-
yazhsk. Having in view the subjugation of the Western Dvina region, the
Moscow voyevodas, in 1535, built another Ivangorod on the Sebezh, and in
1536–1537 they built Zavolochye and Velizh. When the armistice was
concluded with Lithuania the fortresses were ceded to the latter as structures erected on alien territory. Later, after depriving Lithuania of the
Polotsk region, Ivan Grozny restored these fortifications, which had
formerly belonged to Moscow. These systematic building operations
show that the Court of Moscow worked out its plans of conquest long before the respective campaigns were launched. . . .

"Of Muscovie"

> The following account by Clement Adams, one of Chancelour's pilots,
> supplements the report made by Chancelour. It also returns the reader
> from Soviet historiography, with its nationalistic slant, to a sixteenth-
> century source. Hakluyt, *Principal Navigations, etc.*, vol. 1, pp. 285,
> 292.

NOVOGORODE. Next unto Mosco, the Citie of Novogorode is reputed the
chiefest of Russia: for although it be in Majestie inferior to it, yet in great-
nesse it goeth beyond it. It is the chiefest and greatest Marte Towne of all
Moscovie. . . . This towne excels all the rest in the commodities of flaxe
and hempe: it yeeldes also hides, honie, and waxe. The Flemings there
sometimes had a house of Marchandize, but by reason that they used the
like ill dealing there, which they did with us, they lost their privileges, a

restitution whereof they earnestly sued for at the time that our men were there. But those Flemings hearing of the arrivall of our men in those parts, wrote their letters to the Emperour against them, accusing them for pirats and rovers, wishing him to detaine, and imprison them. Which things when they were knowen of our men, they conceived feare, that they should never have returned home. But the Emperour beleeving rather the Kings letters, which our men brought, then the lying and false suggestions of the Flemings, used no ill intreatie towards them.

Of the forme of their private houses, and of the apparell of the people.

The common houses of the countrey are every where built of beames of Firre tree: the lower beames doe so receive the round holownesse of the uppermost, that by the meanes of the building thereupon, they resist, and expell all winds that blow, and where the timber is joined together, there they stop the chinks with mosse. The forme & fashion of their houses in al places is foure square, with streit and narrow windoes, whereby with a transparent casement made or covered with skinne like to parchment, they receive the light. The roofes of their houses are made of boords covered without with ye barke of trees: within their houses they have benches or griezes hard by their wals, which commonly they sleepe upon, for the common people knowe not the use of beds: they have stooves wherein in the morning they make a fire, and the same fire doth either moderately warme, or make very hote the whole house.

The apparell of the people for the most part is made of wooll, their caps are picked like unto a rike or diamond, broad beneath, and sharpe upward. In the maner of making whereof, there is a signe and representation of nobilitie: for the loftier or higher their caps are, the greater is their birth supposed to be, and the greater reverence is given them by the common people.

Ivan Grozny and His Court

As a direct result of the Willoughby-Chancelour expedition and the negotiations between England and Russia which grew out ot it, Queen Mary sent one Osep (Joseph) Napea as ambassador to Ivan's court. A portion of one of Napea's reports is given below. Hakluyt, *Principal Navigations, etc.,* vol. 1, pp. 420–425, *passim.*

The 14 of September, 1557, we were commanded to come unto the Emperour, and immediately after our comming we were brought into his presence, unto whom each of us did his duetie accordingly, and kissed his right hand, his majestie sitting in his chaire of estate, with his crowne on his head, and a staffe of goldsmiths worke in his left hand well garnished with rich and costly stones: and when we had all kissed his hand and done our dueties, his majestie did declare by his interpreter that we were all welcome unto him, and into his countrey, & thereupon willed us to dine with him: that day we gave thanks unto his majestie, and so departed untill the dinner was readie.

When dinner time approached, we were brought againe into the Emperours dining chamber, where we were set on one side of a table that stoode over against the Emperours table, to the end that he might wel behold us al: and when we came into the foresayd chamber, we found there readie set these tables following.

First at the upper end of one table were set the Emperour his majestie, his brother, & the Emperour of Cazan, which is prisoner. About two yardes lower sate the Emperour of Cazan his sonne, being a child of five yeeres of age, and beneath him sate the most part of the Emperors noble men.

And at another table neere unto the Emperours table, there were set a Monke all alone, which was in all points as well served as the Emperour. At another table sate another kind of people called Chirkasses, which the Emperour entertaineth for men of warre to serve against his enemies. Of which people and of their countrey, I will hereafter make mention.

All the tables aforesayde were covered onely with salt and bread, and after that we had sitten a while, the Emperour sent unto every one of us a piece of bread, which were given and delivered unto every man severally by these words: The Emperour and great Duke giveth the bread this day, and in like manner three or foure times before dinner was ended, he sent unto every man drinke. All the tables aforesayd were served in vessels of pure and fine golde, as well basons and ewers, platters, dishes and sawcers, as also of great pots, with an innumerable sorte of small drinking pottes of divers fashions, whereof a great number were set with stone. As for costly meates I have many times seene better: but for change of wines, and divers sorts of meads, it was wonderfull: for there was not left at any time so much void roome on the table, that one cuppe more might have bin set, and as far as I could perceive, all the rest were in the like maner served.

In the dinner time there came in six singers which stood in the midst of the chamber, and their faces towards the Emperor, who sang there before dinner was ended three severall times, whose songs or voices delighted our eares little or nothing.

The Emperour never putteth morsell of meate in his mouth, but he first blesseth it himselfe, & in like maner as often as he drinketh: for after his maner he is very religious, & he esteemeth his religious men above his noble men.

This dinner continued about the space of five houres, which being ended, and the tables taken up, we came into the midst of the chamber, where we did reverence unto the Emperors majestie, and then he delivered unto every one of us with his own hands a cup of mead, which when every man had received and drunke a quantity thereof, we were licenced to depart, & so ended that dinner. And because the Emperour would have us to be mery, he sent to our lodging the same Evening three barrels of meade of sundry sortes, of the quantitie in all of one hogshed. . . .

The Emperors majestie useth every yeare in the moneth of December, to have all his ordinance that is in the citie of Mosco caried into the field which is without the Suburbs of the citie, and there to have it planted and bent upon two houses of Wood filled within with earth: against which two houses there were two faire white markes set up, at which markes they discharge all their ordinance, to the ende the Emperour may see what his Gunners can doe. They have faire ordinance of brasse of all sortes, bases, faulcons, minions, sakers, culverings, cannons double and royal, basiliskes long and large, they have sixe great pieces whose shot is a yard of height, which shot a man may easily discerne as they flee: they have also a great many of morter pieces or potguns, out of which pieces they shoote wild fire.

The 12 of December the Emperors Majestie and all his nobility came into the field on horsebacke, in most goodly order, having very fine Jennets & Turkei horses garnished with gold & silver abundantly. The Emperors majestie having on him a gown of rich tissue, & a cap of skarlet on his head, set not only with pearles, but also with a great number of rich and costly stones: his noble men were all in gownes of cloth of gold, which did ride before him in good order by 3. & 3. and before them there went 5000 harquebusiers, which went by 5 and 5 in a rank in very good order, every of them carying his gun upon his left shoulder, and his match in his right hand, and in this order they marched into the field where as the aforesayd ordinance was planted.

And before the Emperors majestie came into the field, there was a certaine stage made of small poles which was a quarter of a mile long, and about threescore yardess off from the stage of poles were certaine pieces of ice of two foot thicke, and sixe foote high set up, which ranke of ice was as long as the stage of poles, and as soone as the Emperors majestie came into the field, the harquebusiers went upon the stage of poles where they setled themselves in order. And when the Emperors majestie was setled where he would be, and where he might see all the ordinance discharged and shot off, the harquebusiers began to shoot off at the banke of ice, as though it had bin in any skirmish or battel, who ceased not shooting, untill they had beaten all the ice flat on the ground.

After the handguns, they shot off their wild fire up into the aire, which was a goodly sight to behold. And after this, they began to discharge the smal pieces of brasse, beginning with the smallest and so orderly bigger and bigger, untill the last and biggest. When they had shot them all off, they began to charge them againe, and so shot them al off 3 times after the first order, beginning with the smallest, and ending with the greatest. And note that before they had ended their shooting, the 2 houses that they shot unto were beaten in pieces, & yet they were very strongly made of Wood and filled with earth, being at least 30 foote thicke. This triumph being ended, the Emperour departed and rode home in the same order that he came foorth into the field. The ordinance is discharged every yeare in the moneth of December, according to the order before mentioned.

The Centralization of Power

> Vipper, like the older historians Platonov and Solovyev, justified and
> explained many of Ivan Grozny's actions as having been necessary for
> the good of the state. Vipper, who approved of Ivan's expansion into
> neighboring lands as being the counterpart of European overseas ex-
> pansion, believed that only centralization of power made Ivan's ex-
> pansion possible. The source is: Vipper, *Ivan Grozny,* pp. 50–51.

Ivan III first introduced the system of distributing lands among the medium and minor officers of the army after Novgorod was incorporated in
the Moscow State in 1478. By this means a result was achieved of extremely important political consequences. These landowners from around
Moscow were planted on the dismembered patrimonies of the vanquished
Novgorod boyars. In this way the power of the aristocracy was completely
undermined and the separatist tendencies of the regions in which they
ruled were checked.

The new squires became the most reliable props of the central Moscow
authority. At the same time, the elevation of this class was a first step in the
direction of building up a new military system and prepared the ground
for the growth of a new type of economy. . . . In the Moscow State this
form developed into a broad, harmonious, centralized system which lasted
for nearly three hundred years. It left in the government's hands a vast
land fund, permitted it to establish also fiscal unity and to regulate all grants
and rewards for services out of a central Treasury. It enabled the government to send soldier squires to any front no matter how distant, while at
the same time keeping them under strict discipline and under its constant
administrative and economic control. Looking back now it seems to us
that the most important feature of this system was the ownership of land
on condition of rendering constant service. This prevented the land from
being converted into private property. . . .

A Tatar Attack

> The Crimean Tatars in 1571 successfully attacked and burned the
> city of Moscow. The first of the following accounts of this incident is
> from a letter written at the time; the second, from the famous report
> by Giles Fletcher. The source for both is: Hakluyt, *Principal Naviga-
> tions, etc.,* vol. 2, pp. 135–136, 315.

The Mosco is burnt every sticke by the Crimme the 24. day of May last,
and an innumerable number of people: and in the English house was
smothered Thomas Southam, Tofild, Waverley, Greenes wife and children,
two children of Rafe, & more to the number of 25. persons were stifeled in
our Beere seller: and yet in the same seller was Rafe, his wife, John
Browne, and John Clarke preserved, which was wonderful. And there went

into that seller master Glover and master Rowley also: but because the heate was so great, they came foorth againe with much perill, so that a boy at their heeles was taken with the fire, yet they escaped blindfold into another seller, and there, as God's will was, they were preserved. The Emperour fled out of the field, and many of his people were caried away by the Crimme Tartar: to wit, all the yong people, the old they would not meddle with, but let them alone, and so with exceeding much spoile and infinite prisoners, they returned home againe. What with the Crimme on the one side, and his crueltie on the other, he hath but few people left. . . .

The greatest and mightiest of them is the Chrim Tartar, (whom some call the Great Can) that lieth South, & Southeastward from Russia, and doth most annoy the country by often invasions, commonly once every yere, sometimes entring very farre within the inland parts. In the yere 1571 he came as farre as the citie of Mosco, with an armie of 200000 men, without any battel, or resistance at al, for that the Russe Emperor (then Ivan Vasiliwich) leading forth his armie to encounter with him, marched a wrong way. The citie he tooke not, but fired the suburbs, which by reason of the buildings (which are all of wood without any stone, brick, or lime, save certaine out roomes) kindled so quickly, and went on with such rage, as that it consumed the greatest part of the citie almost within the space of foure hours, being of 30 miles or more of compasse. Then might you have seene a lamentable spectacle: besides the huge & mighty flame of the citie all on light fire, the people burning in their houses and streetes, but most of all of such as laboured to passe out of the gates farthest from the enemie, where meeting together in a mighty throng, & so pressing every man to prevent another, wedged themselves so fast within the gate, and streets neere unto it, as that three rankes walked one upon the others head, the uppermost treading downe those that were lower: so that there perished at that time (as was said) by the fire & the presse, the number of 800000 people or more.

Oprichnina: the Classic Interpretation

Kasimerz Waliszewski wrote prolifically and brilliantly, if not always accurately, about Russian history. His ten monographs, based upon extensive research, deal with the major persons and events from the time of Ivan Grozny through that of Alexander I. This selection is from: *Kazimerz Waliszewski* (Lady Mary Loyd, Tr.), *Ivan the Terrible*. Philadelphia: J. B. Lippincott Co., 1904. Pp. 240–246.

On December 3, 1564, a Sunday, Ivan had all his treasures, his money, his plate, his gems, his furniture, and his ikons, packed on to waggons, and, followed by a huge train, many boïars chosen out of various towns, and his whole Court and household, he left his capital with his second wife, Maria Temrioukovna, a half-savage Circassian, as violent and passionate as himself. For some time, nobody in Moscow heard anything of him, and no man knew whither he had betaken to the village of Kolemskoié, where bad weather detained him for a fortnight. He then spent some days at Taï-ninskoié, another village in the neighbourhood of Moscow, and near the Troïtsa, and finally took up his quarters in a suburb of the little town of Alexandrov, north of Vladimir. There he revealed the motives and object of his unwonted exodus. On January 3, a courier reached Moscow with a letter from the Tsar to the Metropolitan. In it the monarch, after dwelling at length on the misdeeds of the *voievodes* and officials of every degree, and the clergy, upper and lower, declared he had 'laid his anger' on them all, from the greatest to the least. This was what was called the *Opala,* a sort of ban, which placed all those affected by it in a state of disgrace and incapacity to perform any active function, whether about the Court or in the service of the State. At the same time Ivan announced his determination to leave the Empire and establish himself 'wherever God should counsel him to go.' There was something contradictory in the terms of the message. The Tsar was abdicating, then? And yet he used his authority to punish his subjects. But his message, again, was accompanied by another, addressed to the merchants and 'the whole Christian population of Moscow,' and its contents were to the effect that, as far as they were concerned, the Tsar had no cause of complaint, nor any feeling of displeasure.

What was the meaning of it all? Probably people knew that as partially then as they do now. But so accustomed were the Russians of that day to riddles, that they did not hesitate as to the course they should pursue. The Tsar, displeased with a certain section of his subjects, was meditating some dark design against them, the nature of which would not be revealed till its effects made themselves felt. What was apparent at the present moment was merely the usual setting of the scene. Obediently all men prepared to bear their part in the coming comedy. The boïars betrayed the correct amount of emotion, the populace rose up, shouted aloud, and was much affected. The merchants offered money, the most eloquent fashion of prov-ing their share in the general feeling, and the Metropolitan was called upon to intercede with the Sovereign. Ivan was entreated not to forsake his peo-ple, but to rule as best pleased him, and mete out such treatment as he deemed fit to those of whom he thought he had reason to complain. A deputation took its way to Alexandrov, and the Tsar allowed himself to be mollified, but he made his own conditions; he intended to keep all traitors and rebels in disgrace, to put some to death, and confiscate their fortunes, and he would not go back to Moscow till he had organized his *Opritchnina.*

This, in the common parlance of that day, was the name applied to the dowry paid to the wives of the great Princes. At banquets, certain special dishes which the amphitryon kept in front of himself, and the contents of which he divided amongst his chief guests, were called *Opritchnyié.* And a particular class of peasants settled on the lands belonging to certain mon-asteries were known as *Opritchniki* (from *opritch,* a part). Let my readers now cast their minds back to the ukase of October 10, 1550, which gave the district of Moscow a territorial and political constitution of its own, and settled a selection of *sloojilyié lioodi,* taken from every rank of the nobility and every province of the Empire, within its borders. Without any essential modification of the existing order of things, solely by virtue of this transplanting process and of a change in the nature of the tenure, Ivan had summoned the men just transplanted to form the nucleus of a court, an administration, and an army, all reorganized on a new basis. The *Opritchnina* of 1565, in its fundamental idea, was neither more nor less than the extension and wider application of this original plan.

Ivan now divided his Empire into two parts. One of these was to preserve its ancient organization and its ancient government—in other words, the *voiévodes,* lieutenants, bailiffs, and *Kormlenchtchiki* of every kind were to carry on the administration as it had been carried on hitherto, a college presided over by two boïars taking the place of the Supreme Council as the centre of the various services. The other part, which comprised various portions of the country, a certain number of towns, and several quarters of the capital city, was converted into a sort of dowry or appanage, which the Tsar kept for himself, and on which, with a thousand boïars or boïars' sons, chosen by himself, he was about to follow up the experiment of 1550.

I must insist here on the scope of this experiment, which may be summed up in two principal features: the transformation of the freehold properties into fiefs, and the removal of owners from one holding to another. To take the proprietor of an hereditary freehold, subject to no charges of any kind, to tear him out of the corner of the soil on which, for centuries past, his fortune and importance had sprouted, grown, and struck their roots; to part him from his natural adherents, break off all his natural connections, and, having thus uprooted him, isolated him, and removed him from his own sphere, to set him down elsewhere, as far as possible from his native place, to give him another property, but on a life interest, and on terms exacting service, and the payment of the usual taxes from him, and thus to make a new man of him, a man without a past, without backing, defenceless—this was the constitution of the system. So, at least, we may suppose, for Ivan never revealed his secret. But, though the fact has hitherto passed unnoticed, the evident connection between the two decrees, that of 1550 and that of 1565, does indicate a *system,* and all we know of the two measures, of their character and their application, is in favour of the correctness of the conjecture I have adopted, after the example of Monsieur Platonov, who seems to me to have approached nearest to the truth ('Essays on the History of the Political Disturbances of the Sixteenth and Seventeenth Centuries,' St. Petersburg, 1899, i. 137, etc.), and Monsieur Milioukov, whom I am inclined to think a little further removed from it ('Essays on the History of Russian Culture,' 1896, i. 147, etc.), by his determination to see nothing, either in Ivan's reforms or in Peter the Great's, except financial expedients.

Ivan's horizon was certainly wider than this. During his lifetime, and even after his death, silence has been kept, by superior order, concerning all this undertaking. Questions on the subject must have been foreseen when an embassy from the Tsar went into Poland in 1565. Muscovite diplomacy was in the habit of providing against possible indiscretions by foreseeing such inquiries, and dictating the replies beforehand. Thus, if the envoys were asked what the *Opritchnina* was, they were to answer, 'We do not know what you mean. There is no *Opritchnina*. The Tsar is living in the place of residence he has been pleased to choose, and such of his servants as have given him cause for satisfaction are there with him, or are settled close by; the others are a little farther off—that is all. If peasants, who know nothing about anything, talk about an *Opritchnina*, people should not listen to them.' The same orders were given to other embassies, in 1567 and 1571 ('Collections of the Imperial Society of Russian History,' vol. lxxi., pp. 461, 777).

But facts began to speak in their turn. The part of the Empire originally given up to the *Opritchnina* was gradually increased till it comprised a good half of the Tsar's dominions, and till the *Opritchniki* number 5,000, instead of 1,000, men. In 1565, the provinces of Vologda, Oustioug, Kargopol, Mojaïsk, and Viazma were added; in 1566, all the Stroganov properties; in 1571, part of the province of Novgorod. Each fresh extension was accompanied by a distribution of freehold lands or fiefs, taken from their original possessors. These received territorial compensation exchange, the *Opritchnina* who had been substituted for themselves on their old holdings —unless, indeed, they had the good luck to be received into the *Opritchnina* without undergoing expropriation or exile. And the districts claimed by the *Opritchnina* in the central provinces were just those in which the remnants of the old appanage system were largest and strongest. It laid its hand, thus, on the hereditary patrimonies of the Dukes of Rostov, Starodoub, Souzdal, and Tchernigov. It swallowed up, too, the territories 'beyond the Oka.' The ancient inheritance of yet another group of appanaged Princes—the Odoiévski, the Vorotynski, and the Troubetskoï. Some of these, Prince Feodor Mikhaïlovitch Troubetskoï, Prince Nikita Ivanovitch Odoiévski, allowed themselves to be enrolled under the banners of the new system, and proved its zealous servants. The rest were forced to migrate. Thus, in exchange for Odoiév, Prince Michael Ivanovitch Vorotynski received Starodoub-Riapolovski, some hundred miles further west. Other landowners in that country were given lands in the districts near Moscow, round Kolomna, Dmitrov, and Zvenigorod.

One instance will suffice to show the practical consequences of this moving to and fro. Out of 272 freehold domains in the district of Tver, the proprietors of 53 gave the State no service of any sort or kind; some of these were the lieges of Prince Vladimir Andreiévitch, the Tsar's cousin, the others owed service to descendants of the old appanaged Princes, one to an Obolenski, another to a Mikoulinski, or a Mstislavski, a Galitzine, a Kourliatev, or even to some plain boïar. The *Opritchnina* altered all this. It brought about a general devolution of everything that was owed on the one and only master who had set himself in the place of all the others. At the same time it suppressed the local military bodies, thanks to which the Tsar's unruly vassals frequently made themselves more dangerous to him than to his foes; it proclaimed the law of individual service, and over all the country its rule affected, it established a system of direct and indirect taxation levied for the benefit of the Treasury.

Swayed, too, by economic and financial considerations which I do not dream of denying, it most particularly sought to obtain possession of the towns along the great trade routes of the Empire, and to this change of system—this is worth observing—the traders affected were by no means opposed. The representatives of the English company craved admission to it as a favour. The Stroganovs followed the same course. The only roads between the capital and the frontier which escaped the *Opritchnina's* attention were those running southward, through Toula and Riazan, and these were probably omitted because no apparent advantage was to be derived from their inclusion.

It is only with the greatest difficulty that any full inventory of the territories annexed by the *Opritchnina* has been drawn up, for documents precise enough to serve as a foundation for the calculation do not exist. It seems to have ended by comprising a great slice of the central and northern provinces, bailiwicks, and towns, and of the coast as well (*pomorié*) all the districts of the *Zamoskovié* (Moscow region), all the regions 'beyond the Oka,' and two districts (*piatiny*) out of the five which constituted the province of Novgorod—those of Obonéjé and Biéjetsk. The *Opritchnina*, the northern boundaries of which thus rested on the 'great ocean-sea,' as it was called in those days, cut cornerwise into the territory handed over to the old system, the *Ziémchtcina* (*ziémia,* land), as it was called, while it ran southward as far as the Oka, eastward towards Viatka, and westward up to the Lithuanian-German frontier. The provinces of Perm, Viatka, and Riazan on the east, and the dependencies of Pskov and Novgorod, with the frontier towns, Vielikié-Louki, Smolensk, and Siéviérsk, on the west, were not included in the new organization. Southwards the two zones of the *Ziemchtchina* were connected by the Ukraine and by wild steppes (*dikoié pole*).

In the centre of the country, as I have just said, the *Oprltchnina* only affected certain localities, and the bailiwicks, towns, and town quarters under its jurisdiction were mingled in unimaginable and indescribable confusion with those of the Ziemchtchina. But of the important towns, the old system only kept Tver, Vladimir, and Kalouga, and it may be said generally speaking, to have been pushed back towards the far ends of the Empire. This was a reversal of the history of Rome, which assumed immediate authority over her most distant provinces, so as to draw the steel-clad circle of her legions round the heart of the Empire.

Towards the year 1572, the *Opritchnina* lost its original name. It was then called the Court (*dvor*). At that moment it already possessed all the characteristics of a regularly constituted State organization, and in its working, indeed, it preserved all the administrative forms of the old system, so much so that it is not easy to discover, from any document of that period, which of the two branches thus wedded together has issued it. In principle the *Opritchnina* did not even suppress the *Miestnitchestov:* it simply forbade the application of that system within its own borders. Its action and that of the *Ziemchtchina* ran on parallel and concerted lines, and both possessed a common centre in the Offices of War and Finance. *Diaks* attached to these two branches of the Government overlooked the distribution of the business connected with each. It seems probable, at least, that affairs followed this course, for the coexistence and concerted labours of the two sets of officials are an established fact, which suffices to destroy the legend of an *Oprritchnina* confined to the duties of a mere political police force. In 1570, authentic documents show us the *Oprritchnina* and the *Ziémchtchina* summoned to deliberate, through their respective representatives—all of them boïars—on questions connected with the Lithuanian frontier. The discussions were held separately, but an agreement was reached. There is no trace of any enmity or conflict. That very same year, and the next, detachments furnished by both organizations went campaigning together against the Tartars, and perfect harmony appears to have reigned between them.

The solution of the problem confronting Ivan furnished by the *Oprritchnina* was certainly not wholly satisfactory. What was needed was something which would have annulled the twofold contradiction which afflicted his whole Empire: a contradiction in politics arising out of the fact that the historical march of events had endued the Sovereign with an absolute power founded on a democratic basis, which he was obliged to exercise through an aristocracy; a social contradiction resulting from the fact that this same Sovereign, in his quest of fresh food for the growing ambitions of his Empire, and to insure it, was forced into making over his productive class, bound hand and foot, to the arbitrary will of his non-producers, his 'men who serve,' his soldiers, and his tax collectors.

As far as the destruction of the aristocratic element is concerned, the *Oprritchnina* proved a failure. But it shook it sorely, and Ivan's plan probably did not go beyond this result. Apart from the great and mighty lords it enrolled, and by enrolling disarmed them, only an elect few of the aristocratic class escaped, such as Prince Ivan Feodorovitch Mstislavski and Prince Ivan Dmitriévitch Biélski, both of them placed at the head of the *Ziémchtchïna*—two inoffensive utility actors. It destroyed all the political importance of the class, and the effect of this was to be manifest, even after Ivan's death, in the preponderating part played by parvenus created by him, such as Zakharine and Godounov. Others of his subjects, of yet humbler extraction, peasants, Cossacks, Tartars, recruited in increasing numbers to fill the gaps caused by his confiscations and wholesale executions, not to mention his *transplantings,* ended by forming a comparatively numerous body, and a powerful weapon for levelling and democratic purposes. 'My father's boïars, and my own have learnt to be traitors,' wrote Ivan to Vassiouchka Griaznoï, 'so we have resolved to call on you, vile varlets, and from you we expect fidelity and truth!' Vasiouchka replied: 'You are like unto God! You make a little man into a great man!'

This revolution—for a revolution it certainly was—could not be accomplished without some kind of struggle. Everywhere, in the lowest classes, where it broke bonds that were centuries old, in the towns and country places, into which it introduced strange elements, on the great landed properties which it divided up, calling a new agricultural and industrial proletariat into existence, it wounded innumerable feelings and interests. I have already shown how, by destroying the ancient administrative autonomy of the peasants, now made subject to their new proprietors in all those matters as to which they had hitherto dealt directly with the State, it contributed, indirectly, to the establishment of serfdom. It had a more immediate effect in quickening the current of emigration amongst the elements thus disaggregated, and hastening, through the increase of the calls made on them, the exhaustion of the resources dependent on those elements. From this point of view, Ivan's undertaking is open to much blame, and his conflict with Poland was soon to demonstrate the weak side of a work in other respects useful, and no doubt even necessary. Its execution was attended by excesses of various sorts, which cannot fail to attract severe judgment. But the historian cannot regard the *Opritchnina* from one point of view only. . . .

Oprichnina: a Marxist Interpretation

Ablest of the Marxist historians was Professor Mikhail Nikolaevich Pokrovskii who became actively associated with the Bolsheviks at the time of the 1905 Revolution. Forced to emigrate, Pokrovskii lived in exile from 1908 to 1917 and during the period wrote his chief historical work, *A History of Russia from the Earliest Times*. After the Bolshevik Revolution he became a very powerful leader in the People's Commissariat of Education and was responsible for the persecution of some of his non-Bolshevik professional colleagues. As editor, archivist, and bureaucrat he was the dominant figure in Soviet historiography until his death in 1932. Not long thereafter the party line changed and Pokrovskii and his school were condemned as "Trotskyite agents of fascism" and "enemies of the people."

The following excerpt presents a Marxist interpretation of the struggle between Ivan Grozny and his boyars. It is presented here by way of contrast to the more familiar accounts. The source is: M. N. Pokrovsky (J. D. Clarkson and M. R. M. Griffiths, Eds. and Trs.), *History of Russia*. New York: International Publishers, 1931. Pp. 142–150.

There is nothing more unjust than to deny that there was a principle at stake in Ivan's struggle with the boyars or to see in this struggle only political stagnation. Whether Ivan IV was himself the initiator or not—most probably he was not—yet this "oprichnina" was an attempt, a hundred and fifty years before Peter's time, to found a personal autocracy like the Petrine monarchy. The attempt was premature, and its collapse was inevitable; but he who ventured it unquestionably ranked above his contemporaries. The "warriors' " road lay over the dead body of old Muscovite feudalism, a fact which made the "warriors" progressive, whatever the motives that immediately guided them. The old votchinas within the realm

were now the only source of land at the expense of which middling
pomestye landholding might expand, the tsar's treasury, the only source of
money capital. But to enjoy either it was necessary to take into their own
hands the power that was in the hands of a hostile group, which held it not
only with all the tenacity of secular tradition but also with all the force of
moral authority. Peresvetov might have the audacity to declare that politics
is higher than religion, "justice" than "faith," but his rank-and-file partisans would not have countenanced such a sentiment, much less have expressed it, and still less have acted upon it. The coup of January 3, 1565,
was an attempt, not to infuse a new content into old forms, but to set up
new forms alongside the old and, without touching old institutions, so to act
that they might serve merely as a screen for new men who did not have
the right to enter these institutions as actual masters. Peter was bolder; he
simply seated his officials in the boyar duma and called it the Senate, and
every one made the best of it. But by Peter's time the boyars were in the
eyes of all already a "riven and falling tree." A hundred and fifty years
earlier the tree had, it is true, begun to lose its foliage, but its roots were
still firmly fixed in the ground and were not to be torn out at the first
wrench.

Denying to the "oprichnina" significance in principle, historians have,
on the other hand, depicted its appearance in most dramatic form. How
Ivan the Terrible, on an unusually solemn expedition, suddenly left for
Alexandrovsk (they generally explain the location of this mysterious place
that so unexpectedly bobs up in Russian history), how from there he began
to exchange letters with the "people" of Moscow, and what effect this
produced—all this of course, you have read many times, and there is no
need to repeat the story. In fact, like everything in the world, the event
was much more workaday. Alexandrovsk had long been Ivan's summer
residence; in the chronicle we constantly find him there in the intervals
between military campaigns and his very frequent trips through the Muscovite provinces, on pilgrimage and for economic purposes. The sudden-
ness of his departure is considerably weakened by the fact that Ivan IV
took with him all his valuable movables—all the "holy things, icons and
crosses, with gold and precious stones adorned," his gold and silver vessels,
his whole wardrobe and his whole treasury, and mobilised his whole guard
—"the nobles and knights selected from all the towns, whom the sovereign
had taken to be with him." All these preparations could not have been
made in one day, or in two—especially since the tsar's courtiers were
ordered to "go with wives and with children." Setting forth, Ivan did not
disappear somewhere for a whole month; the Muscovites knew very well
that the tsar celebrated the day of Nicholas the Miracle-Worker (December 6) at Kolomensk, that on Sunday, the 17th, he was at Taininsk, and
that on the 21st he arrived at Troitsa to spend Christmas. In a word, this
was the customary itinerary of his trips to Alexandrovsk, except for the
passing visit at Kolomensk, explained by the thaw and the overflow of the
rivers, unusual in December. While the fact that matters moved so swiftly
at Moscow—on the 3rd the courier arrived with the tsar's letter, on the 5th

the embassy from Moscow was already at Alexandrovsk—clearly shows
that the month had not been wasted, that while the tsar was travelling, his
partisans had been carefully preparing the dramatic effect that so beguiles
modern historians. If during this month Ivan the Terrible really grew grey
and aged by twenty years, as foreigners relate, it was, of course, not because he had been quaking all this time for the success of his unexpected
"prank," but because to break with the whole past was not an easy thing
for a man reared and educated in a feudal environment. Peter was born in
a different environment, and from childhood was accustomed to think and
act without reference to custom. Ivan in his thirty-fifth year had to smash
everything; that was something to grow grey over. That material strength
lay in his hands, that the external, so to speak, physical success of the
coup was assured for the tsar and his new counsellors,—this was so evident to all that we find not the least attempt at resistance on the part of the
old counsellors. And, of course, not because in their servility they did not
dare think of resistance; flight from the tsar of all the Orthodox to the
service of the Catholic king of Poland-Lithuania was a leap incomparably
greater than would have been an attempt to repeat what Andrew of
Staritsa had done only thirty years before when he raised the pomeshchiks of Novgorod against the Moscow government. But now the boyars
would have had no one to raise against their foes; the pomeshchiks were
siding with Alexandrovsk, and the Moscow townsmen were now siding
with the pomeshchiks, not with the boyars. The gosts, the merchants, and
"all Orthodox Christendom of the city of Moscow," in answer to the gracious letter of the tsar, which was read at an assembly of the higher Muscovite merchantry, "in order that they might retain no doubt, that there
was no wrath upon them and displeasure," unanimously replied that they
"stand not for the sovereign's evildoers and traitors and themselves destroy
them." And in the embassy despatched to Alexandrovsk, along with
bishops, abbots, and boyars, we find gosts, merchants, and even simple
"common people," who, it would seem, had no place at all in a matter of
state. The Moscow townsmen gave up their allies of yesterday. For negotiations with them, in all probability, the future *oprichniks* had needed a
whole month, and their decision definitely tipped the scales to the side of
the coup. What evoked this decision is easily determined from the sequel;
commercial capital itself was associated with the oprichnina, and this
promised advantages that no amount of protection from the Princes
Shuisky could counter-balance. Soon after the coup we find merchants and
gosts acting as official agents of the Muscovite government both at Con-
stantinopole, and in Antwerp, and in England—in all the "seaboard
states," toward which they yearned so much; and they were all equipped
not only with all sorts of safe-conducts, but also with *"bologodet"* (sub-
sidy) from the tsar's treasury. "Into the oprichnina fell all the chief
(trade) routes, with a great part of the towns located along them," says
Prof. Platonov; and here he gives a very convincing list of these towns.
"Not for nothing did the English who had business with the northern provinces beg to be taken into the oprichnina; not for nothing did the Stro-

ganovs seek to be included; commercial-industrial capital, of course, needed the support of the administration that controlled the country and, as is evident, did not fear the horrors attendant upon our conception of the oprichnina." Why should capital fear what it itself had helped to create?

Just as the "reforms" had been the work of a coalition of the bourgeoisie and the boyars, the coup of 1564 was carried out by a coalition of the townsmen and the petty vassals. This explains, in all probability, one peculiarity in the tsar's letter as read at Moscow which hitherto has not attracted great attention but possesses great interest. In form the coup was an act of self-defence on the part of the tsar against his great vassals, who "had begun to betray." But these "treasonous matters" are mentioned very obscurely and only at the end of the letter. On the other hand, the document develops three points in detail. First, the conduct of the boyars during the minority of Ivan IV—"who committed treasons and caused losses to his realm before he the sovereign reached maturity." Second, that the boyars and voevodas "seized upon the sovereign's lands" and, holding great pomestyes and votchinas, by unlawful means gathered great wealth. This motif, taken straight from Peresvetov, envisaged a quite definite fact, which had already led to a partial confiscation of votchina lands three years before the coup. On January 15, 1562, Ivan IV "decreed with the boyars (not with 'all the boyars'!): whatever old votchinas are in the possession of the princes of Yaroslavl, Starodub, Rostov, Tver, Suzdal, Obolensk, Beloozero, Vorotynsk, Mosalsk, Trubetsk, Odoev, and *other serving princes,* those princes shall not sell nor exchange their votchinas." The right of these men to dispose of their lands had been reduced to a minimum; they could bequeath estates only to their sons. If there were no sons, the votchina reverted to the sovereign, who did what was necessary —"ordered his soul," *i.e.,* dealt out lands to the Church for prayers for the soul of the deceased, allotted a portion "for life" to his widow, dowries for his daughters, etc. What is more, the sovereign confiscated, without compensation, all votchinas of this category that had been sold fifty or twenty but not less than ten years before the publication of the edict. The basis for such an extraordinary measure was that under decrees even of the times of Ivan III and of Vasily III, father of Ivan the Terrible, princes' votchinas might be sold only with the licence of the grand prince: a new landholder meant a new vassal and, in accordance with widespread feudal custom, not peculiar to Russia, the suzerain must be asked for his consent. Votchina lands were simply treated as the sovereign's, and arbitrary disposal of them as embezzlement of treasury property. Finally, the third point made in the letter—it, too, occurs in Peresvetov—is the aversion of the boyars to an active foreign policy; they "did not wish to take care of all Orthodox Christendom" and did not wish to defend Christendom against the Crimea, and Lithuania, and the Germans. These were all themes popular among wide masses, and those who read or heard the proclamation did not, of course, stop to question why in his thirties the tsar had a mind to punish the boyars for sins and faults committed in the days of his youth. Had it been a palace coup organized from above, these demagogic methods would, of course, be very strange; but the point is that in December, 1564—January, 1565, as in 1547, and as in the 'thirties under the Shusikys, the masses of the people were on the stage and must be addressed in a language they could understand.

Yet the content of this proclamation, as of any other, by no means defined the current policy of those who published it. When business negotiations began between Ivan the Terrible and the Moscow deputation that had come to Alexandrovsk, the tsar put forward demands relevant to the immediate causes of the coup, demands that had nothing to do with recollections of the days of his youth. In these demands two aspects must be distinguished. In the first place, Ivan insisted on fulfilment of the promise, given freely by the merchantry of Moscow and subscribed to by the terror-stricken boyars and officials left in Moscow, namely, to surrender his foes to him unconditionally. In fulfilment of this demand in February of the same year (the negotiations had taken place, we shall remember, at the beginning of January) a number of boyars of old princely families were executed, others given the tonsure, still others banished for life to Kazan with their wives and children, while the property of all of them was confiscated. Banishments and executions at once gave into Ivan's hands a supply of land probably sufficient to remunerate the immediate participants in the coup d'état. To secure them a money salary the tsar and grand prince decreed that *for his expenses* a hundred thousand rubles (about 5,000,000 rubles gold, according to the reckoning of Professor Klyuchevsky) be taken from the treasury of the land. From this aspect the coup was only the affair of a small circle, but Ivan was serving the interests of a class. Not all the pomeshchiks could be satisfied out of the proceeds of a few banishments and a small appropriation from the treasury chest. The form devised to satisfy the "warriors" was as old-fashioned as the content of the change effected was new. In the state the sovereign could not give orders without his boyars, the suzerain without his curia; but on his "domain," in his court economy, he was as absolute as was any votchinnik at home. Conversion of half the state, and the wealthiest part of it at that, into the sovereign domain made it possible to hold sway over a vast territory without consulting the feudal aristocracy. Without violating the decrees of 1550, he might here do all that he liked, not only without the assent of "all the boyars" but without that of even a single boyar; the right of the boyar college did not, of course, extend to the sovereign's court management. And for the tsar's court, now increased to colossal proportions, a very old name was at first chosen; the tsar demanded that "from his realm be set apart an *oprichnina*." This was the name given to the estates in former times portioned out to widowed princesses "for life." Later there came into use the more accurate and newer term, *dvor* (court). In its arrangements this "dvor" was an exact copy of an old sovereign's votchina, so exact that one modern scholar has even doubted whether the oprichnina had any institutions of its own, or whether new men were not simply seated in the old institutions along with the old "clerks," for management of "oprichnina" (select) matters. While effecting a genuine revolution, the creators of the oprichnina apparently strove to conceal all juridical traces of it, and we cannot but see in this fact a conscious purpose, issuing from the same impulses as were reflected in the tsar's proclamation that we analysed above. The people needed a scapegoat, and they were assured that the coup was directed against individual persons, however numerous, the old order remaining inviolate.

The sovereign's dvor began to expand enormously, but it never came to embrace the whole country, and the *zemshchina,* which administered all that remained outside the limits of the oprichnina, was more than merely decorative. The best study of the territorial composition of the oprichnina has been made by Professor Platonov; we shall therefore describe it in his words. "The territory of the oprichnina," says this scholar, "taking form gradually, in the 1570's comprised the towns and townships lying in the central and northern parts of the state. . . . Resting to the north on the 'great sea-ocean,' the lands of the oprichnina cut into the zemshchina like a wedge, dividing it in two. On the east were left to the zemshchina the Perm and Vyatka towns, the Low country and Ryazan; on the west the border towns 'of the German frontier' (Pskov and Novgorod), 'of the Lithuanian frontier' (Veliky Luki, Smolensk, and others), and the Seversk towns. To the south these two zones of the 'zemshchina' were connected by the frontier towns and the 'wilderness.' The Moscow North, the Littoral, and two of the Novgorod pyatinas the oprichnina ruled integrally; in the central provinces its lands were interspersed with those of the zemshchina in a patchwork that is as hard to understand as to describe," but that can nevertheless be characterised in a general way. "In the oprichnina administration," says Professor Platonov in another passage, "were gathered the *old appanage lands.*" The goal toward which the law of 1562 had striven, by inches and within legal bounds, was attained three years later, all at once and by a revolutionary road; the most valuable part of the territory of the Muscovite state, together with the greatest commercial-industrial centres, became immediately an appanage of the sovereign where, unrestrained by the old boyars, the men of the "Peresvetov party" now began to hold sway. The old authority retained the worst and poorest regions; it is curious that just as Kazan had become a place of exile, so the newly-conquered lands in the west were now willingly ceded to the "men of the zemshchina." The Novgorodin "knights" from the Obonezh and Bezhets pyatinas, when these were taken into the oprichnina, received pomestyes around Polotsk, on the recently annexed and very insecure Lithuanian lands.

The tsar's edict, even in the brief résumé preserved in the official Moscow chronicle (like a great part of the official documents of his stormy time, the original edict on the oprichnina has not come down to us), states quite distinctly in whose favour and for what proximate goal all this shuffling of lands was effected. "And to give to the sovereign in the oprichnina princes and nobles and knights, of court and town, 1,000 head, *and to them to give pomestyes in those towns which he took into the opri-*

chnina," says the chronicle. Modern historians have seen in this something in the nature of the establishment of a corps of gendarmes charged with the detection of domestic sedition, the protection of the tsar, and the defence of the realm. But tempting as is this analogy, one must not yield to it. Police work, and that alone, has always been the task of gendarmes; not they—there were too few of them for that—but the standing army has constituted the material support of the government. The oprichniks represented something quite different. The detachment of a thousand knights really constituted a corps of ten or twelve thousand men, inasmuch as each appeared for service with several armed bondsmen. Not a single large landholder, even among the former appanage princes, could have such a retinue; even two or three together of the very greatest probably would not have raised so many men. Besides this mounted detachment there were in the oprichnina infantry as well—"and he ordered the *streltsy* to be to him especially," says the chronicler. To cope with a "domestic foe" such a force would have been more than sufficient; the grand prince of Moscow was now, in his single person, the very greatest of the Muscovite feudatories. The oprichnina army was a logical corollary to the oprichnina dvor of the sovereign, and, it must be added, the very possibility of forming this dvor had been conditioned by the existence of such an army; for the novelty of this part of the edict was not the appearance close to the tsar of a "thousand heads" but the quartering of them on lands unceremoniously taken from other holders—"and the votchinniks and pomeshchiks who are not to be in the oprichnina (the sovereign) bade to be removed from these towns." A detachment of a thousand had long existed, even from 1550, and in the coup of January 3, 1565, it had played exactly the same role as did the Paris garrison in the coup of December 2, 1851. This tsar's guard, founded, as we shall recall, by the boyar government as a concession to the upper crust of the pomeshchik masses, had become a powerful weapon in the struggle of the pomeshchik class against the boyars themselves. Only by its closeness to the tsar is to be explained the fact that "base-born" now standing around him dared so audaciously to raise their hands against their feudal lords of yesterday, and in the tsar's train this "picked" thousand, moving "after the tsar with men and with horses, with all service attire," was, of course, the most imposing part. In all probability, all of them, with the exception of a few individuals, were taken into the oprichnina corps, so that actually the latter represented nothing new. And as before, so also after 1565, along with its military and police significance it continued to have political significance; there entered it the "better," *i.e.,* the most influential, elements of the local bodies of nobles. As Klyuchevsky has explained in detail, they did not while in the tsar's guard lose contact with the local communities; in other words, they were the political leaders of the pomeshchik class, and distribution of oprichnina lands to them signified nothing else than that along with the old, boyar-votchina state, now more than cut in half, there arose a new, noble-pomestye state.

Clear proof that the coup meant merely the establishment of a new class régime, of which the tsar's personal authority was only a tool, and

not the personal emancipation of Ivan from the boyar tutelage that had
trammelled him, is the singular assembly that was held in Moscow in the
summer of the following year (1566). On June 28, 1566, the Tsar and
Grand Prince Ivan IV of All Rus "spoke" with Prince Vladimir of Staritsa,
with his archbishops, bishops, and the whole "Holy Synod," with all the
boyars and officials, with the princes, with the knights and military servi-
tors, "and with the gosts, and with the merchants, and with all trading
men." The subject of this conversation was a truce proposed by the Polish-
Lithuanian government on the basis of *uti possidetis*. Thus, it was proposed that Ivan the Terrible renounce his original goal, the seizure of all
Livonia. In essence, the question was put: is it worth while to keep on
fighting? And it is significant that Ivan and his new government did not
presume to decide this question upon their own responsibility but referred
it to the judgment of all those in whose name they ruled. It would, of
course, be very naïve to imagine that this "zemsky sobor of 1566," the
first sobor whose existence is historically indisputable, even remotely resembled modern popular representative bodies; the very worst of them, if
only in theory, speaks in the name of the "people," a concept alien to
feudal Europe. Mediaeval assemblies, both in Russia and in the West, represented, not the people but "estates," *états, Stände*. From this point of
view the important point about the sobor of 1566 was the rôle of two
"estates" whose political importance had hitherto scarcely been openly
recognised—the petty vassals or "nobility," and the bourgeoisie. Quantita-
tively the pomeshchiks even constituted a majority of this assembly. The
Livonian War had been decided on by the boyars, unwillingly and under
pressure from below, and now they were asking the "warriors" and the
"trading folk" whether this war should be continued. Between 1557 and
1566 lay a wide gulf. The details of the debates at the sobor, assuming
there were debates, have not come down to us. The one-day sobor was, of
course, not summoned to learn the opinions of those assembled; the pomeshchiks and the merchants were summoned because their opinions were
already known, and it was hoped that the authority of their voices would
reinforce the authority of the declarations of Muscovite diplomacy. The
sobor was, in essence, a ceremonial façade; the real negotiations took
place, of course, before the sobor met and, apparently, by no means inspired the government with the confidence breathed by the solemn
speeches at the sobor itself. The sobor decided to continue the war, come
what might; but in fact *negotiations* were continued and a few years
later terminated in a truce on the conditions proposed by the Poles. The
suzerain Ivan needed the formal promise of his new, extensive vassalage to
"die for the sovereign on horseback" in case of war, and of the trading
men to give their last red cent if need be. This promise Ivan received, and
on their speeches the military-serving and the trading men kissed the
cross. Whether or not to make the fullest use of this promise was the business of the government, which was, of course, guided by the views of its
supporters, but these views were not ascertained at the sobor.

An Evaluation of the Reign of Ivan Grozny

This evaluation of the results of Ivan's reign is typical not only of
M. Waliszewski's dashing style, but also of his keen insight and original
approach. The source is: Waliszewski, *Ivan,* pp. 394–399.

The massacres ordered by Ivan have been notoriously exaggerated by his
enemies and his detractors, the first egging on the second. Kourbski mentions the *entire destruction* of families—such as the Kolytchev, the Zabo-
lotski, the Odiévski, the Vorotynski—all of which appear in the inventories of the following century. The gaps created in the ranks of the
aristocracy by emigration were certainly much larger, and even so they
were not entirely emptied. Ivan's conduct in this particular was not dictated by any fixed principle, and he himself endeavoured to ensure the future of three great houses—the Mstislavski, the Glinski, and the Romanov—whose fidelity seemed guaranteed by lack of connections in the
country, by a material state of dependence, or by family relationships.
The two first-named families had just arrived from Lithuania, and the
last was related to the Sovereign's own house.

The principal factors in the weakening of the aristocratic element were
economic causes and political measures. In the course of the sixteenth
century, as a result of the condition of debt to which everybody had been
reduced, landed property began to crumble away of itself in the boïars'
hands. In the registers kept by a moneylender of that period, named
Protopopov, is a list of noble names, and the archives of the Monastery
of St. Cyril afford proof of the continuance of this state of things. In 1557
Prince D. D. Oukhtomski, whose credit with such persons as Protopopov
had probably become exhausted, sold the monks a village, with twenty-
six hamlets round it, for 350 roubles; three years later he received 150
roubles, and gave up possession of four more outlying places. At about the
same time the community acquired a large property, also belonging to
this family, and in 1575 it received another lot of meadows, 'for Masses';
so that, in one way or another, the whole of the Oukhtomski properties
passed into the same hands (see Rojkov, 'Agriculture . . . in the Sixteenth Century,' 1899, p. 396).

Now, this financial distress amongst the great families was the direct
consequence of the new political system, and the obligations it had cast
upon them. Universal service implied residence at Court, or near it, even
if it did not imply active military service or the performance of some official function or other. When the nobles had lived on their family properties
they had found it hard enough to draw a scanty income from them. Once
they left them, they were very soon ruined. Thereupon came the Opritchnina—that is to say, wholesale dispossession under the conditions I have
already described—and this dealt the position, economic and political, of
the persons concerned its death-blow. Ivan's system of guarantees increased the effect of emigration twofold—nay, a hundredfold, seeing that

for every fugitive there were from ten to a hundred persons who had to pay for him. Except for the Stroganovs, you will not find a single instance of a large fortune in the aristocratic class which escape this other form of massacre. If in the present day some few authentic descendants of Rurik and Guédymine, such as the Troubetzkoïs, the Galitzines, the Kourakines, the Soltykovs, the Boutourlines, still possess some worldly wealth, their opulence only dates from the eighteenth century, and from the favours of some Empress.

And thus a class which already differed from the Western aristocracies, in that the feudal principle was entirely absent from it, was completely and democratically levelled. The hierarchy of the service did indeed create new titles and fresh prerogatives, guaranteed by the *miéstnitchestvo,* but these were not corporative elements in the Western signification of the term. They rather tended to break up the family and reduce it to atoms, on which the hold of the absolute power continued, and grew perpetually stronger.

This revolution, which had seemed destined to benefit the popular element, brought it nothing but the bitterest fruit. The new system was a house of two stories, both built on the same plan. The officials were upstairs, the serfs below, and slavery everywhere. But in this matter all Ivan the Terrible did was to complete or carry on that which had been the Moscow programme for two centuries past, and the *Opritchnina* itself, was no more than an extension of the policy applied by the Tsar's predecessors to all their conquered towns and territories. It was a sort of colonization backwards. As to colonization in the normal direction, it continued to depend on private enterprise; but Ivan opened a wider field for it.

Westwards his expansive policy failed. It would not be just to cast all the responsibility for this on him. If Peter the Great, when he took the same road 150 years later, had found his way barred by a man like Batory, instead of by a madman like Charles XII., the result of the Battle of Poltava might have been very different. Eastward, Kazan, Astrakan, and Siberia make up a noble score in Ivan's favour.

From the economic point of view, the conquest of Kazan did not result in the immediate advantages that might have been expected from it. The trade of that place, which the Tartars had exaggerated in their desire to induce the Sultan to retake possession of the town, was a disappointment to the English merchants. Ivan did not fail to seek compensation elsewhere. When he offered the Swedish traders a free passage through his dominions, even for going to India, he stipulated for a similar privilege for his own subjects, in their enterprises, existing or to be undertaken, with Lübeck and even with Spain. In 1567 the chroniclers mention the departure of Russian merchants for Antwerp and London, and in 1568 English authorities mention the presence on the banks of the Thames of two such Muscovites, Tviérdikov and Pogoriélov, who were taken to be Ambassadors. They performed both offices, no doubt, and devoted their endeavours partly to diplomacy and partly to mercantile affairs.

The development of industry in Ivan's time was rather superficial;

the field was widened by the annexation of the eastern provinces. The acquisition of the Lower Volga favoured the development of fisheries. There were ninety-nine establishments of this kind at Péréiaslavl in 1562. After the occupation of the banks of the Kama by the Stroganovs, and the discovery of salt-mines near Astrakan, the salt-works there attained great importance.

Ivan's financial policy does not call for praise. It may be summed up as a series of expedients, all savouring more or less of robbery. Fletcher mentions several of these. Governors of provinces were treated with the utmost tolerance till they had gorged themselves with plunder, when they were forced to give up the spoil. The same system was applied to monasteries, which were allowed to heap up wealth in the same way. There were temporary seizures or monopolies of certain forms of produce or merchandise, thus made to bring in very large profits. Fines were imposed on officials for imaginary offences. The English diplomat tells an almost incredible story about a capful of *live flies* demanded on his way from the Moscow municipality.

The taxes themselves were managed in the most senseless manner that could have been devised. Generally speaking, every fresh need resulted in the imposition of a fresh tax, and there never was the smallest care as to fitting the burdens to the means of those who had to bear them, nor the slightest prudence as to killing the goose that laid the golden eggs. By the time the end of the reign was reached, the bird's laying-powers were very nearly exhausted.

The interests best served by the conquest of Kazan and Astrakan were those of the Church, whose borders were thus enlarged. Gourii, first Archbishop of Kazan, made a good many converts among the Tartars; but this triumph of orthodox proselytism was counterbalanced, till the close of Ivan's reign, by the prolonged resistance of the paganism still existing in the interior of his dominions, and especially in certain districts in the province of Novgorod. As to the Tsar's attempts at religious reform, which he soon abandoned or only carried on in a most perfunctory fashion, they produced no appreciable result at all, and the intellectual and moral condition of the clergy was in no way altered by them.

Yet, from a more general point of view, there was a visible increase in the intellectual life of the country. Though the schools planned in 1551 never were anything but plans, though printing did not get beyond the stage of rudimentary attempt, the author of the letters to Kourbski did none the less witness a certain upward trend of ideas, which took their flight out of the narrow walls of the cloister and the confined circle of religious discussion into the world of secular thought. This beginning of the secularizing process was one of the great conquests of Ivan's reign.

On the other hand, Ivan, even in his international dealings, could not or would not break with certain barbarous traditions which harmonized but ill with progress such as this. Just as in past times, envoys sent to his Court were often treated as if they had been prisoners of war, and the fate of his genuine prisoners of war continued to be lamentable. The happiest thing they could expect was to be sold or given to the monasteries as serfs. Occasionally they were simply thrown into the water. In 1581, Ivan gave orders that when the Swedish 'tongues'—in other words, the persons belligerents or non-belligerents, taken with a view to obtaining information—had served their purpose, they were all to be killed. Polish and Swedish captives were used as current coin in the exchanges arranged by Tartar merchants on the Constantinople markets.

But as he stood, with all his faults and vices, his errors and his crimes, his weaknesses and his failures, Ivan was popular, and his was a genuine popularity, which has stood the twofold test of time and of misfortune. This, too, is a result. In the cycle of the historic songs of Russia, the Tsar holds the place of honour, and is shown in by no means repulsive colours; he is open to every feeling of humanity—severe, but just, and even generous. True, indeed, his sacerdotal majesty lifts him up so high and surrounds him with such an aureole of glory that no critic would dare to lay his hand upon him. But we feel that, in spite of that, all the popular sympathies are with him. When he indulges in savage orgies over the corpses of the vanquished Tartars, or hands one of his boïars over to the executioner on the merest hint of suspicion, the masses are on his side; they applaud the carnage, and rejoice in their master's joy. Even when they cannot applaud, they shut their eyes respectfully, religiously, and cast a mantle of decent fiction over that which makes their consciences revolt. The populace will not admit that the Tsar killed his own son. The Tsar of the *bylines* bestows a noble reward on Nikita Romanovitch, who at the peril of his own life, saves that of the victim; for the moment the order was given the Sovereign had repented. This Tsar has some weaknesses, indeed; he is apt to be choleric, and his first instinct is not always his best. Under the walls of Kazan, whither the intentional anachronism of the poets has already brought Ermak and even Stenka Razin, Ivan taxes his artificers, who have been too slow about blowing up a mine, with treason, and threatens them with the gallows. The chiefs, cowards in this case, as always, according to the popular historians, shelter themselves behind their subordinates. But one young soldier speaks boldly in defence of his fellows, the mine blows up, and the Tsar acknowledges his own mistake and the merit of the humble hero. Passing into the conquered town, Ivan spares the Tsarine Helen, who comes out to meet him bearing bread and salt, and is content with having her baptized by force and thrust into a convent. But he has the eyes of the Tsar Simeon, who shows less goodwill and greater dignity, torn out of his head; and here again, the populace applauds the victor.

This is the theory of morals peculiar to the period to which Ivan's name is attached. The ideal it evolves is one of material greatness and brute force—a twofold postulate to which the Russian race has proved iself ready to sacrifice everything else. . . . In this other dream, Tsar and people both had their part, and they were to make it a living reality on the day when Peter took Ivan's place, and completed the incarnation which gave birth to modern Russia. But when Ivan died, this work was in the embryonic stage. His labour had been one of destruction, more especially, and he had no time to build up again. Still less had he ensured the continuity of his effort. The legacy left his country by the luckless adversary of Batory, the murderer of the Tsarevitch, his own heir, was a war with Poland and a state of anarchy. The germ was there, too, of a fresh inroad by the rivals of the Slavonic West, destined, under the shelter of the false Dmitri, to reach Moscow itself, and of a triumphant return of the aristocratic oligarchy, which, favoured by the general crumbling of the unfinished edifice, was to recover its old advantages. This was to be the history of the seventeenth century. But Peter the Great was not to guard his inheritance any better against future risks; and yet, after a fresh eclipse, Catherine was to come, even as he had come. The strength was there still, increased materially and tempered morally—the imperishable pledge of a mighty future.

The Domostroy

The *Domostroy* or household code was once considered to be the work of the priest Sylvester, adviser to Ivan Grozny. Professor Wiener, from whose work the following excerpts are quoted, believed that the code was a composite work—an interpretation corroborated by later research. Professor Wiener characterized the morality of the *Domostroy* as "one of extreme formalism," and added: "To preserve appearances before God and men is, according to this code, the chief aim in life." His translation is from a sixteenth-century document. The source is: Wiener, *Anthology,* vol. 1, pp. 126–130. Abridged.

How to Teach Children

Punish your son in his youth, and he will give you a quiet old age, and restfulness to your soul. Weaken not beating the boy, for he will not die from your striking him with the rod, but will be in better health: for while you strike his body, you save his soul from death. If you love your son, punish him frequently, that you may rejoice later. Chide your son in his childhood, and you will be glad in his manhood, and you will boast among evil persons, and your enemies will be envious. Bring up your child with much prohibition, and you will have peace and blessing from him. Do not smile at him, or play with him, for though that will diminish your grief while he is a child, it will increase when he is older, and you will cause much bitterness to your soul. Give him no power in his youth, but crush his ribs while he is growing and does not in his wilfulness obey you, lest there be an aggravation and suffering to your soul, a loss to your house, destruction to your property, scorn from your neighbors and ridicule from your enemies, and cost and worriment from the authorities.

· · ·

The Wife to Take Counsel with Her Husband

In all affairs of every-day life, the wife is to take counsel with her husband, and to ask him, if she needs anything. Let her be sure that her husband wants her to keep company with the guests she invites, or the people she calls upon. Let her put on the best garment, if she receives a guest, or is herself invited somewhere to dinner. By all means let her abstain from drinking liquor, for a drunk man is bad enough, but a drunk woman has no place in the world. A woman ought to talk with her lady-friends of handwork and housekeeping. She must pay attention to any good word that is said in her own house, or in that of her friend; how good women live, how they keep house, manage their household, instruct their children and servants, obey their husbands, and ask their advice in everything, and submit to them. And if there be aught she does not know, let her politely inquire about it. . . . It is good to meet such good women, not for the sake of eating and drinking with them, but for the sake of good converse and information, for it is profitable to listen to them. Let not a woman rail at anyone, nor gossip about others. If she should be asked something about a person, let her answer: "I know nothing about it, and have heard nothing of it; I do not inquire about things that do not concern me; nor do I sit in judgment over the wifes of princes, boyars, or my neighbors."

How to Instruct Servants

Enjoin your servants not to talk about other people. If they have been among strangers, and have noticed anything bad there, let them not repeat it at home; nor should they bruit about what is going on at home. A servant must remember what he has been sent for, and he must not know, nor answer any other questions that are put to him. The moment he has carried out his commission, he should return home and report to his master in regard to the matter he had been sent for; let him not gossip of things he has not been ordered to report, lest he cause quarrel and coldness between the masters.

If you sent your servant, or son, to tell, or do something, or buy a thing, ask him twice: "What have I ordered you to do? What are you to do, or say, or buy?" If he repeats to you as you have ordered him, all is well. . . . If you send anywhere some eatables or liquids, send full measures so that they cannot lie about them. Send your wares after having measured or weighed them, and count the money, before you send it out. Best of all, despatch under seal. Carefully instruct the servant whether he is to leave the things at the house, if the master is absent, or if he is to bring them back home. . . .

When a servant is sent to genteel people, let him knock at the door softly. If anyone should ask him, as he passes through the courtyard: "What business brings you here?" let him not give any satisfaction, but say: "I have not been sent to you; I shall tell to him to whom I have been sent." Let him clean his dirty feet before the antechamber, or house, or cell, wipe his nose, clear his throat, and correctly say his prayer; and if he does not receive an "amen" in response, he should repeat the prayer in a louder voice, twice or three times. If he still receives no answer, he must softly knock at the door. When he is admitted, he should bow before the holy images, give his master's respects, and tell his message. While doing so, let him not put his finger in his nose, nor cough, nor clean his nose, nor clear his throat, nor spit. If he absolutely must do so, let him step aside. He must stand straight and not look to either side when reporting the message; nor should he relate any matter not relevant to the message. Having done his duty, he should forthwith return home, to report to his master.

Russia at the Time of Boris Godunov

One of the most famous descriptions of Russia by a foreign observer was written by Giles Fletcher who went to Moscow as the ambassador of Queen Elizabeth of England. Western and Russian historians both count Fletcher's *The Russe Commonwealth* as a first-class source. Fletcher arrived at Moscow in 1588, four years after the death of Ivan Grozny. The weak Fedor was on the throne, but the real power was in the hands of the nobles, expecially Nikita Romanov and Boris Godunov. The excerpt from *The Russe Commonwealth* which follows was taken from Hakluyt, *Principal Navigations, etc.,* vol. 2, pp. 284–310, *passim.*

The description of the countrey of Russia, with the bredth, length, and names of the Shires.

The whole Countrey is of great length and breadth. From the North to the South (if you measure from Cola to Astracan which bendeth somewhat Eastward) it reacheth in length about 4260. verst, or miles. Notwithstanding the Emperour of Russia hath more territorie Northward, farre beyond Cola unto the River of Tromschua, that runneth a hundred verst, welnigh beyond Pechinga, neere to Wardhouse, but not intire nor clearely limited, by reason of the kings of Sweden and Denmarke, that have divers Townes there, as well as the Russe, plotted together the one with the other: every one of them clayming the whole of those North parts as his owne right. The breadth (if you go from that part of his territorie that lyeth farthest Westward on the Narve side, to the parts of Siberia Eastward, where the Emperour hath his garrisons) is 4400. verst or thereabouts. A verst (by their reckoning) is a 1000. pases, yet lesse by one quarter then an English mile. If the whole dominion of the Russe Emperour were all habitable, and peopled in all places, as it is in some, he would either hardly holde it all within one regiment, or be over mightie for all his neighbour Princes. . . .

The whole Countrey differeth very much from it selfe, by reason of the yeare: so that a man would marveile to see the great alteration and difference betwixt the Winter, and the Summer Russia. The whole Countrey in the Winter lieth under snow, which falleth continually, and is sometime of a yard or two thicke, but greater towards the North. The Rivers and other waters are all frosen up a yard or more thicke, how swift or broade so ever they bee. And this continueth commonly five moneths, viz. from the beginning of November till towardes the ende of March, what time the snow beginneth to melt. So that it would breede a frost in a man to looke abroad at that time, and see the Winter face of that Countrey. The sharpenesse of the aire you may judge of by this: for that water dropped downe or cast up into the aire congealeth into yce before it come to the ground. In the extremitie of Winter, if you holde a pewter dish or pot in your hand, or any other mettall (except in some chamber where their warme stoaves bee) your fingers will friese fast unto it, and drawe off the skinne at the parting. When you passe out of a warme roome into a colde, you shall sensibly feele your breath to waxe starke, and even stifeling with the colde, as you drawe it in and out. Divers not onely that travell abroad, but in the very markets, and streetes of their Townes, are mortally pinched and killed withall: so that you shall see many drop downe in the streetes; many travellers brought into the Townes sitting dead and stiffe in their Sleds. Divers lose their noses, the tips of their eares, and the bals of their cheekes, their toes, feete, &c. Many times (when the Winter is very hard and extreeme) the beares and woolfes issue by troupes out of the woods driven by hunger, and enter the villages, tearing and ravening all they can finde: so that the inhabitants are faine to flie for safegard of their lives. And yet in the Sommer time you shal see such a new hiew and face of a Countrey, the woods (for the most part which are all of firre and birch) so fresh and so sweete, the pastures and medowes so greene and well growen, (and that upon the sudden) such varietie of flowers, such noyse of birdes (specially of Nightingales, that seeme to be more lowde and of a more variable note then in other Countreys) that a man shall not lightly travell in a more pleasant Countrey.

And this fresh and speedy growth of the Spring there seemeth to pro- ceede from the benefite of the snow: which all the Winter time being spread over the whole Countrey as a white robe, and keeping it warme from the rigour of the frost, in the Spring time (when the Sunne waxeth warme, and dissolveth it into water) doeth so thoroughly drench and soake the ground, that is somewhat of a sleight and sandie mould, and then shin- eth so hotely upon it againe, that it draweth the hearbes and plants foorth in great plentie and varietie, in a very short time. As the Winter exceedeth in colde, so the Sommer inclineth to over much heat, specially in the moneths of June, July and August, being much warmer than the Sommer aire in England. . . .

For kindes of fruites, they have Apples, peares, plummes, cherries, red and blacke, (but the blacke wilde) a deene like a muske millian, but more sweete and pleasant, cucumbers and goords (which they call Ar- bouse) rasps, strawberies, and hurtilberies, with many other beries in great quantitie in every wood and hedge. Their kindes of graine are wheat, rie, barley, oates, pease, buckway, psnytha, that in taste is somewhat like to rice. Of all these graines the Countrey yeeldeth very sufficient with an overplus quantitie, so that wheate is solde sometime for two alteens or ten pence starling the Chetfird, which maketh almost three English bushels.

Their rie is sowed before the Winter, all their other graine in the Spring time, and for the most part in May. The Permians and some other that dwell farre North, and in desert places, are served from the parts that lye more Southward, and are forced to make bread sometimes of a kinde of roote (called Vaghnoy) and of the middle rine of the firre tree. If there be any dearth (as they accompted this last yeere Anno 1588. wheat and rie being at 13. alteens, or 5. shillings five pence starling the Chetfird) the fault is rather in the practise of their Nobilitie that use to engrosse it, then in the Countrey it selfe.

The native commodities of the Countrey (wherewith they serve both their owne turnes, and send much abroad to the great enriching of the Emperor, and his people) are many & substantiall. First, furres of all sorts. Wherein the providence of God is to be noted, that provideth a naturall remedie for them, to helpe the naturall inconvenience of their Countrey by the cold of the Climat. Their chief furres are these, Black fox, Sables, Lusernes, dun fox, Martrones, Gurnestalles or Armins, Lasets or Miniver, Bever, Wulverins, the skin of a great water Rat that smelleth naturally like muske, Calaber or gray squirrel, red squirrel, red & white fox. Besides the great quantitie spent within ye Countrey (the people clad al in furres the whole winter) there are transported out of the Countrey some yeeres by the merchants of Turkie, Persia, Bougharia, Georgia, Armenia, and some other of Christendom, to the value of foure or five hundred thousand rubbles, as I have heard of the merchants. The best Sable furre groweth in the countrey of Pechora, Momgosorskoy and Obdorskoy, the worser sort in Siberia, Perm, & other places. The blacke foxe and red come out of Siberia, white and dunne from Pechora, whence also come the white wolfe, and white Beare skin. The best Wulverin also thence and from Perm. The best Martrons are from Siberia, Cadam, Morum, Perm, and Cazan. Lyserns, Minever, and Armins, the best are out of Gallets, and Ouglits, many from Novogrod and Perm. The Beaver of the best sort breedeth in Murmonskey by Cola. Other common furres and most of these kindes grow in many, and some in all parts of the Countrey.

The second commoditie is of Waxe, whereof hath bene shipped into forreigne countreys (as I have heard it reported by those that best know it) the summe of 50000. pood yeerely, every pood conteyneth 40. pound, but now about 10000. a yeere.

The third is their Honie, whereof besides an exceeding great quantitie spent in their ordinary drinkes (which is Mead of all sorts) and their other uses, some good quantitie is caried out of the countrey. The chiefe encrease of hony is in Mordua and Cadam neere to the Cheremissen Tartar: much out of Severskoy, Rezan, Morum, Cazan, Dorogobose, and Vasma.

Fourthly, of Tallow they afoord a great waight for transportation: not onely for that their countrey hath very much good ground apt for pasturage of cattell, but also by reason of their many Lents and other fastes: and partly because their greater men use much waxe for their lights, the poorer and meaner sort birch dried in their stoaves, and cut into long shivers, which they call Luchineos. Of tallow there hath bene shipped out of the Realme a few yeeres since about 100000. pood yerely, now not past 30000. or thereabouts. The best yeeld of tallow is in the parts and territories of Smolensko, Yaruslave, Ouglits, Novogrod, and Vologda, Otfer, and Gorodetskey.

An other principall commoditie is their Losh and Cow hide. Their Losh or Buffe hide is very faire and large. Their bull and cowe hide (for oxen they make none, neither yet weather) is of a small sise. There hath bene transported by merchants strangers some yeres 100000. hides. Now it is decreased to 30000. or thereabouts. Besides great store of goates skinnes, whereof great numbers are shipped out of the countrey. The largest kinde of Losh or Buffe breedeth about Rostove, Wichida, Novogrod, Morum, and Perm. The lesser sort within the kingdome of Cazan.

An other very great and principall commoditie is their Trane oyle, drawen out of the Seal fish. Where it will not be impertinent to shewe the manner of their hunting the Seal, which they make this oyle of: which is in this sort. Towards the ende of Sommer (before the frost beginne) they goe downe with their boates into the Bay of S. Nicholas, to a cape called Cusconesse or Foxnose, where they leave their boates till the next spring tide. When the Sunne waxeth warme toward the spring, and yet the yce not melted within the Bay, they returne thither againe. Then drawing their boates over the sea yce, they use them for houses to rest and lodge in. There are commonly about 17. or 18. fleete of them, of great large boates, which divide themselves into divers companies, five or sixe boats in a consort.

They that first fine the haunt, fire a beacon, which they carry with them for the nonce. Which being espied by the other companies, by such among them as are appointed of purpose, they come altogether and compasse the Seales round about in a ring, that lie sunning themselves together upon the yce, commonly foure or five thousand in a shoale, and so they invade them every man with his club in his hand. If they hit them on the nose, they are soone killed. If on the sides or backe they beare out the blow, and many times so catch and holde downe the clubbe with their teeth by maine force, that the partie is forced to call for helpe to his fellowes.

The maner of the Seals is when they see themselves beset, to gather all close together in a throng or plumpe, to sway downe the yce, and to breake it (if they can) which so bendeth the yce that many times it taketh the sea water upon it, and maketh the hunters to wade a foote or more deepe. After the slaughter when they have killed what they can, they fall to sharing every boate his part in equall portions; and so they flay them, taking from the body the skin, and the lard or fat with all that cleaveth to the skin. This they take with them, leaving the bodies behind, and so go to shore. Where they digge pits in the ground of a fadome and an halfe deepe, or thereabout, and so taking the fat or lard off from the skinne, they throw it into the pit, and cast in among it hoat burning stones to melt it withall. The uppermost and purest is sold, and used to oile wool for cloth, the grosser (that is of a red colour) they sell to make sope.

Likewise of Ickary or Cavery, a great quantitie is made upon the river of Volgha out of the fish called Bellougina, the Sturgeon, the Severiga and the Sterledey. Whereof the most part is shipped by French and Netherlandish merchants for Italy and Spaine, some by English merchants.

The next is of Flax and Hempe, whereof there hath bene shipped (as I have heard merchants say) at the port of Narve a great part of 100. ships small and great yerely. Now, not past five. The reason of this abating and decrease of this & other commodities, that were wont to be transported in a greater quantitie, is the shutting up of the port of ye Narve towards the Finland sea, which now is in the handes and possession of the Swedes. Likewise the stopping of the passage overland by the way of Smolensko, & Plotsko, by reason of their warres with the Polonian, which causeth the people to be lesse provident in mainteining and gathering these and like commodities, for that they lacke sales. For the growth of flaxe the province of Vobsko, and the countrey about is the chiefe and onely place. For Hempe Smolensko, Dorogobose and Vasma.

The countrey besides maketh great store of salt. Their best salt is made at Stararovse in very great quantitie, where they have great store of salt wels, about 250. verst from the sea. At Astracan salt is made naturally by the sea water, that casteth it up into great hils, and so it is digged downe, and caried away by the merchants and other that wil fetch it from thence. They pay to the Emperor for acknowledgement or custome 3.d. Russe upon every hundred weight. Besides these two, they make salt in many other places of the Realme, as in Perm, Wichida, Totma, Kenitsma, Solovetsky, Ocona, Bombasey, and Nonocks, all out of salt pits, save at Solovetsky, which lieth neere to the sea.

Likewise of Tarre they make a great quantitie out of their firre trees in the countrey of Duyna and Smolensko, whereof much is sent abroad. Besides these (which are all good and substantiall commodities) they have divers other of smaller accompt, that are naturall and proper to that countrey: as the fish tooth (which they call Ribazuba) which is used both among themselves, and the Persians and Bougharians that fetch it from thence for beads, knives, and sword hafts of Noblemen and gentlemen, and for divers other uses. Some use the powder of it against poison, as the Unicornes horne. The fish that weareth it is called a Morse, and is caught about Pechora. These fish teeth some of them are almost 2. foote of length, and weigh 11. or 12. pound apiece.

In the province of Corelia, and about the river Duyna towards the North sea, there groweth a soft rocke which they call Slude. This they cut into pieces, and so teare it into thin flakes, which naturally it is apt for, and so use it for glasse-lanthorns and such like. It giveth both inwards and outwards a clearer light then glasse, and for this respect is better then either glasse or horne: for that it neither breaketh like glasse, nor yet will burne like the lanthorne. Saltpeter they make in many places, as at Ouglits, Yaruslave & Ustiug, and some smal store of brimstone upon the river Volgha, but want skil to refine it. Their iron is somewhat brittle, but a great weight of it is made in Corelia, Cargapolia, & Using Thelesna. Other mine they have none growing within ye realme.

Their beasts of strange kinds are the Losh, the Ollen, the wild horse, the beare, the wolvering, or wood dog, the Lyserne, the Beaver, the Sable, the Martron, the blacke and dunne fox, the white Beare towards the sea coast of Pechora, the Gurnstale, the Laset or Minever. They have a kinde of Squirrell that hath growing on the pinion of the shoulder bone a long tuft of haire, much like unto feathers with a far broader taile then have any other squirrels, which they move and shake as they leape from tree to tree, much like unto a wing. They skise a large space, & seeme for to flie withal, and therefore they cal them Letach Vechshe, that is, the flying squirrels. Their hares and squirrels in Sommer are of the same colour with ours, in Winter the hare changeth her coate into milke white, the squirrel into gray, whereof commeth the Calaber.

They have fallow deere, the roe bucke, & goats very great store. Their horses are but smal, but very swift & hard, they travell them unshod both winter and Sommer, without all regard of pace. Their sheepe are but smal & beare course & harsh wool. Of foule they have divers of the principal kinds: First, great store of hawks, the eagle, the gerfaulcon, the slight-faulcon, the goshawk, the tassel, the sparhawk, &c. But the principal hawke y^t breedeth in the country, is counted ye gerfaulcon. Of other foules their principal kinds are the swan tame & wilde, (whereof they have great store) the storke, the crane, the tedder of the colour of a feasant, but far bigger & liveth in the firre woods. Of feasant and partridge they have very great plentie. An owle there is of a very great bignesse, more ugly to behold then ye owles of this country, with a broad face, & eares much like unto a man.

For fresh water fish, besides the common sorts (as carp, pikes, pearch, tench, roach, &c.) they have divers kinds very good and delicate: as the Bellouga or Bellougina of 4. or 5. elnes long, the Ositrina or Sturgion, the Severiga and Sterledy somewhat in fashion and taste like to the Sturgion, but not so thicke nor long. These 4. kinds of fish breed in the Volgha, and are catched in great plenty, and served thence into the whole Realme for a great food. Of the Roes of these foure kinds they make very great store of Icary or Caveary as was said before.

They have besides these that breed in the Volgha a fish called the Riba bela, or white salmon, which they accompt more delicate then they do the red salmon, whereof also they have exceeding great plentie in the Rivers Northward, as in Duyna, the river of Cola, &c. In the Ozera or lake neere a towne called Perislave, not far from the Mosco, they have a smal fish which they cal the fresh herring, of the fashion, and somewhat of the taste of a sea-herring. Their chiefe townes for fish are, Yaruslave, Bealozera, Novogrod, Astracan, and Cazan: which all yeeld a large custome to the

Emperour every yeere for their trades of fishing, which they practise in Sommer, but sende it frozen in the Winter time into all parts of the Realme.

The chiefe cities of Russia are Mosco, Novogrod, Rostove, Volodomer, Plesko, Smolensko, Jaruslave, Perislave, Nisnovogrod, Vologda, Ustiug, Colmogro, Cazan, Astracan, Cargapolia, Columna. The city of Mosco is supposed to be of great antiquitie, though the first founder be unknownen to the Russe. It seemeth to have taken the name from the River that runneth on the one side of the towne. Berosus the Chaldean in his 5. booke telleth that Nimrod (whom other prophane stories cal Saturne) sent Assyrius, Meduc, Moscus, & Magog into Asia to plant colonies there, and that Moscus planted both in Asia and Europe. Which may make some probabilitie, that the citie, or rather the river whereon it is built, took the denomination from this Moscus: the rather because of the climate or situation, which is in the very farthest part & list of Europe, bordering upon Asia. The Citie was much enlarged by one Ivan or John, sonne to Daniel, that first changed his title of duke into King: though that honor continued not to his posterity: the rather because he was invested into it by the Popes Legate, who at that time was Innocentius the 4. about the yeere 1246. which was very much misliked by the Russe people, being then a part of the Easterne or Greeke Church. Since that time the name of this city hath growen more famous, & better knowen to the world: insomuch that not only the province, but the whole Countrey of Russia is termed by some by the name of Moscovia the Metropolite city. The forme of this City is in maner round with 3. strong wals, circuling the one within the other, & streets lying betwene, whereof the inmost wall, and the buildings closed within it (lying safest as the heart within the body, fenced and watred with the river Moscua, that runneth close by it) is all accompted the Emperors castle. The number of houses (as I have heard) through the whole Citie (being reckoned by the Emperor a little before it was fired by the Crim) was 41500. in all. Since the Tartar besieged and fired the towne (which was in the yere 1571.) there lieth waste of it a great breadth of ground, which before was wel set and planted with buildings, specially that part on the South side of Moscua, built not long before by Basilius the Emperor for his garison of souldiers, to whom he gave priviledge to drinke Mead, and beere at the dry or prohibited times, when other Russes may drinke nothing but water, and for that cause called this new city by the name of Naloi, that is skinck or poure in. So that now the city of Mosco is not much bigger then the city of London. The next in greatnes, & in a maner as large, is the citie Novograd: where was committed (as the Russe saith) the memorable warre so much spoke of in stories of the Scythians servants, that tooke armes against their masters: which they report in this sort: viz. That the Boiarens or gentlemen of Novograd & the territory about (which only are souldiers after the discipline of those countreis) had war with the Tartars. Which being wel performed & ended by them, they returned homewards. Where they understood by the way that their Cholopey or bondslaves whom they left at home, had in their absence possessed their townes, lands, houses, wives and all. At which newes being somewhat amased, and yet disdeining the villany of their servants, they made the more speed home: and so not far from Novograd met them in warlike maner marching against them. Whereupon advising what was best to be done, they agreed all to set upon them with no other shew of weapon but with their horse whips (which as their maner is every man rideth withal) to put them in remembrance of their servile condition, thereby to terrifie them, & abate their courage. And so marching on & lashing al together with their whips in their hands they gave the onset. Which seemed so terrible in the eares of their villaines, and stroke such a sense into them of the smart of the whip which they had felt before, that they fled altogether like sheepe before the drivers. In memory of this victory the Novogradians ever since have stamped their coine (which they cal a dingoe Novogrodskoy currant through al Russia) with a figure of a horsman shaking a whip aloft in his hand. These 2. cities exceed ye rest in greatnes. For strength their chiefe townes are Vobsko, Smolensko, Cazan, & Astracan, as lying upon the borders. But for situation Jaruslave far exceedeth the rest. For besides the commodities that the soile yeeldeth of pasture and corne, it lieth upon the famous river of Volgha, & looketh over it from a high banke very faire & stately to behold: whereof the towne taketh the name. For Jaruslave in that tongue signifieth as much as a faire or famous banke. In this towne (as may be ghessed by the name) dwelt the Russe king Vladimer sirnamed Jaruslave, that maried the daughter of Harald king of England, by mediation of Sveno the Dane, as is noted in the Danish story about the yere 1067.

The other townes have nothing y^t is greatly memorable, save many ruines within their wals. The streets of their cities and townes in stead of paving are planked with fir trees, plained & layd even close the one to the other. Their houses are of wood without any lime or stone, built very close and warme with firre trees plained and piled one upon another. They are fastened together with dents or notches at every corner, & so clasped fast together. Betwixt the trees or timber they thrust in mosse (whereof they gather plenty in their woods) to keep out the aire. Every house hath a paire of staires that lead up into the chambers out of the yard of streat after the Scottish maner. This building seemeth far better for their countrey, then that of stone or bricke; as being colder & more dampish then their wooden houses, specially of firre, that is a dry & warme wood. Whereof the providence of God hath given them such store, as that you may build a faire house for 20. or 30. rubbles or litle more, where wood is most scant. The greatest inconvenience of their wodden building is the aptnesse for firing, which happeneth very oft & in very fearful sort, by reason of the drinesse and fatnes of the fir, that being once fired, burneth like a torch, & is hardly quenched til all be burnt up.

Boris Godunov

Fedor, second son and successor of Ivan Grozny, was incompetent to rule. Ambitious boyars plotted to displace or succeed him and the power was seized temporarily by the boyar, Nikita Romanov, uncle of Fedor. Upon Nikita's death, authority passed to another boyar, Fedor's brother-in-law, Boris Godunov, who had been one of Ivan's chief agents. Godunov, tsar in fact, succeeded to the title after Fedor's death in 1598. His reign is the prelude to the Time of Troubles.

The following brief characterization of Godunov is translated from the writings of the French novelist and historian, Prosper Mérimée. The work from ⸻ based mainly upon Russian sources. The so⸻ *de de l'histoire de Russie— Les faux Demet*⸻ 54. Pp. 26–29.

His ambition was imn⸻ s habit was to temporize and the Russian nego⸻ irkey, and Poland which took place under his ad⸻ this. Always he advanced slowly but firmly towai⸻ iever to risk a false step. Moreover, it is entirely⸻ s not at first clear to him. If it is true that he hac⸻ lled, it is not necessarily also true that he aspire⸻ it moment; but the heir-presumptive, trained by⸻ a prince as feeble as Fedor, would one day be ;⸻ id ruin his power. Absolute master of the tsar, ⸻ behind this phantom sovereign, Boris had too much sense to hasten the moment when the last tsar of the Varangian dynasty should go to his grave.

That event had long been foreseen and it was, in fact, astonishing that Fedor, ill from infancy, lived so long. Boris had long been preparing himself for the extinction of the dynasty. All public officials were his creatures; the streltsi and the clergy were, so to speak, in his hands, and he was accustomed to think of himself as the sole head of the state. The people, who all hated him, believed in his skill and his luck; and it was an established opinion that empire could not descend to a more resourceful leader. Finally, Fedor himself regarded Boris as his inevitable successor and seemed to designate him as such to the nation. Not long before his death Fedor presented to Boris a chest filled with relics, saying: "Place your hands upon these holy relics, Regent of the Orthodox People. Rule with wisdom. You will achieve all your aims, but you will find that on this earth all is vanity and deception."

Like Richard III and other ambitious men, Boris made a show of refusing the crown when it could not in fact escape from him. Before Fedor's death, the regent forced the Boyars' Council and the important officials to take the oath of allegiance to Irene [the tsarina and Boris' sister]. But whether because of disgust with the world, or because of a secret order of her dying husband, or because of the instigation of her brother, Irene announced her intention of entering a convent. As for Boris, he haughtily declared that he wanted to abandon the affairs of state and live in retirement —knowing full well that he would not have to do so. Several times the nobility, the provincial deputies, and the clergy with the patriarch at their head, threw themselves at his feet and tearfully begged him to rule over Russia. They competed for the honor of persuading him, or rather each saw clearly the necessity for proving his devotion to Boris and as a Russian annalist said, "those who were not able to weep moistened their eyes with saliva."

The people, frightened by rumors of a Tatar invasion, joined the nobility in urging the favorite to accept his destiny. Mothers threw their suckling babies before him. A countless multitude surrounded the monastery to which Boris had retired and answered each of his refusals with wails of despair. "Have pity on me," said Boris weeping—for he could command his tears—"have pity, do not make me the victim of the throne." But this pretended resistance came to an end. Boris granted what he had always intended to grant on the ground that he was called to the throne by the will of the nation. Amidst the general enthusiasm, only the Shuiskis [rival boyars, one of whom, Basil, later became tsar] were lukewarm or even somewhat opposed; Boris never forgot that.

"The Time of Troubles"

> This section comprises accounts of the Time of Troubles by two Russian historians, Platonov and Klyuchevskii. The Platonov material was translated for this anthology by Mr. Cyril Geacintov. The source is the previously cited Prague edition of Platonov's *Uchebnik Russkoi Istorii*, Part I, pp. 164–167, 184–186. I was assisted in the translation of the Klyuchevskii material by Miss Gayle Durham. The source is: Klyuchevskii, *Kurs Russkoi Istorii* in *Sochineniya* (*Works*), vol. 3, pp. 49–54, 59–61, 86–89.

The Pretender

The peaceful life of Moscow, which had been interrupted by the famine of 1601–1603, was totally destroyed by the troubled times during the period of the Pretender. In 1603, rumors were rampant in southwestern Russia and in Poland that Dmitri Ivanovich, the "Uglitsky tsarevich" who was believed to have died in 1591, was actually alive. An individual calling himself Dmitri presented himself to the Russian prince, Adam Vishnevetski; later, he went over to the Polish lord, George Mnishek, and took up residence in Mnishek's castle at Sambor. This man was very vague and brief in the description of his background; he mentioned that he had been saved from Godunov's attempt on his life, and said that he now wanted to "ascend" to the throne of his father. He was presented to King Sigismund III of Poland, and was converted from Orthodox to Roman Catholicism. Then he was allowed to recruit troops in Sambor for his campaign against Moscow. He also established contacts with the Cossacks of the Don and of the "wild plains," and incited them against Boris [Godunov].

As news of the appearance of a pretender spread, the powers in Moscow guessed that an unfrocked monk named Gregory Otrep'ev, the son of a boyar, had taken the name of Dmitri. Orphaned at an early age, Otrep'ev had become a monk, and had wandered from monastery to monastery until he finally reached Moscow. Once there, he was accepted into the Chudov Monastery in the Kremlin, and became familiar with life in Moscow. Otrep'ev and three other monks went from Moscow to Lithuania and Poland, where Otrep'ev left the Church and began to call himself the Tsarevich Dmitri. When information about him was sent to Poland, however, it was not believed and The Pretender was allowed to proceed unhindered. Even today some people still doubt that The Pretender was Otrep'ev. Some scholars are inclined to believe that he actually was the Tsarevich Dmitri who had been shielded by the Nagimis from the assassins sent by Moscow. Others believe that he was an imposter, not Otrep'ev, but some unknown person who had accompanied Otrep'ev from Moscow to Poland. Still others simply believe that The Pretender was not even a Muscovite, but a native of western Russia who was put forward by the Poles. It is most probable, however, that The Pretender really was Otrep'ev, though he actually appears to have believed that he was a descendant of the tsars. The men who controlled him convinced him that he had once been saved from assassination, had been given a false name, and had been disguised in a monk's habit until he could grow up and be safe from Godunov. The Pretender was totally unafraid of being exposed as an imposter: behavior that further confirms the statement that he really believed himself to be the Tsarevich.

Having assembled an army, The Pretender marched on Moscow in the fall of 1604, starting his campaign in Sambor and proceeding past Kiev to Chernigov. The first few Muscovite cities in his path surrendered to him, but resistance began near Novgorod-Severskim and, finally—in the Battle of Dobrinichakh—he was defeated, routed, and forced to flee to Putivl on the outermost border of the Muscovite Empire. His cause, however, was not lost. East of Putivl, in the new towns which had been built on the plains as protection against the Tatars, Cossacks and garrison troops had been aroused by agents of The Pretender, and had revolted in the name of Tsar Dmitri. Forming an army, they marched north and occupied a small town called Kromakh. Tsar Boris' army commanders were informed of this; they left the beaten Pretender in Putivl and marched to lay siege to Kromakh. The well fortified little town did not surrender, and the siege lasted until the spring of 1605. Boris' troops, exhausted by the hard winter march, were demoralized. At this point (April, 1605) Tsar Boris unexpectedly died.

Boris' son, Fedor Borisovich, ascended the throne in Moscow, but he was still very young. Boris, by his strong personality, had been able to maintain the allegiance of Moscow and the empire. When an inexperienced young man succeeded him on the throne, however, and when his mother, the Tsarina Maria Gregorievna (the much disliked daughter of the *oprichnik* Maliuta Skuratov) usurped the powers of government, the

boyars vented their opposition to the Godunovs. The Shuiskis, the Go-
litsins, and other boyars decided to betray the Godunovs and to overthrow
them in the name of Tsar Dmitri. Once this had been accomplished, they
planned to oppose Dmitri because they did not believe him and intended
to choose a tsar according to their own wishes. This, indeed, was what the
boyars proceeded to do. They went over to The Pretender's side (near
Kromakh) pledged the whole army to him, and sent to Putivl for him.
Simultaneously, the boyar prince, Vassili Ivanovich Shuiski, who had conducted an investigation of the Tsarevich's death at Uglich, remained in
Moscow and began to say that the Tsarevich had not been killed at Uglich,
but had been saved and was now marching on Moscow. The Muscovites
rebelled against the Godunovs, overthrew Tsar Fedor Borisovich, and
killed him together with his mother, and committed his sister, Ksenia, to
a convent. They then awaited the arrival of the "true" Tsar Dmitri. He
arrived in Moscow in June, 1605.

These were the successes of The Pretender. Apparently, he had been
put up to it by certain Muscovite boyars who hated Godunov and refused
to submit to his rule. After The Pretender had been sent to Poland, he
found support there from the Polish king and clergy. The king hoped that
he would create internecine dissension in Moscow and thus sap its strength
by extending help to The Pretender. The Catholic clergy, having converted The Pretender to Roman Catholicism, expected, through him, to
achieve the subjugation of the whole Moscow Empire to the Pope. For
this purpose, Jesuits were always in The Pretender's company, and they
accompanied him all the way to Moscow. The Pretender also found some
sympathizers among the Polish lords and gentry. Some members of the
gentry joined his army, hoping for loots and honors during the conquest of
Moscow. Some Polish lords also held similar hopes. Lord Mnishek, for
example, promised to give his daughter, Marina, in marriage to The Pretender. But most of the Pretender's successes were due to Russians from
the southern borders of the Muscovite Empire: the Cossacks and the government officials residing in the newly built towns. They were all former
residents of the central provinces of the Empire where they had suffered
from the *oprichniki* and from oppressive serfdom. They hated the Muscovite rulers, and therefore revolted against Boris, hoping that the "true"
Tsar Dmitri would improve their lot and would subjugate the "evil boyars"
who were oppressing the simple people. With help from so many quarters,
The Pretender succeeded in creating troubled times in the Muscovite Empire. The boyars decided to take advantage of this situation in order, first,
to free themselves from the hated Godunovs and, subsequently, to get rid
of The Pretender as well. They succeeded in overthrowing the Godunov
family, but when Prince Vassili Ivanovich Shuiski began to contradict his
earlier statements concerning The Pretender and came out against him in
an effort to persuade the people to refuse him entry into Moscow, Shuiski
was met with disbelief and was arrested. The people organized a festive
welcome for the False Dmitri and accepted him as the true tsarevich.

The Reign and Death of the Pretender

Once in Moscow, The Pretender replaced the Patriarch Iov with the Archbishop Ignatiev of Ryazan. After his coronation, the new tsar sent for Dmitri's mother, the nun Martha who had been living in exile, and greeted her as if she were his own mother. Martha, for her part, treated him in public as if he were her own son. Those whom Boris had banished into exile were allowed to return on the occasion of the coronation; the Nagis and the Romanovs were among the first to return. While in Moscow, The Pretender remained independent of the Pope and of the Polish king even though he [the False Dmitri] had been converted to Roman Catholicism during his stay in Poland and had made many promises to both the king and the Pope. Catholicism wasn't even mentioned. The Pretender openly showed himself to be an Orthodox, and made it clear that he did not intend to convert Russia to Roman Catholicism. He also refused to cede the territory he had promised to the Polish king. He remembered only that he had promised to fight the Turks and Tatars with his Polish allies; and he therefore proceeded to prepare for a campaign in the Crimea. This did not satisfy his former friends and patrons. Both the Jesuits and the Polish diplomats who had accompanied Dmitri were now extremely dissatisfied with his actions. The Pretender, however, was attentive only to the Mnishek family into which he was to marry. The Polish government favored this marriage, hoping that Marina, who was a Catholic, would exercise the correct influence on her husband. Marina and her father went to Moscow.

The Pretender had thus evoked displeasure in Poland, and was not very well liked in Moscow either. Some foreigners who were at Dmitri's court in Moscow told of his keen intellect and of his liking for hard work—characteristics allegedly not to be found among boyars. His Russian contemporaries, however, do not mention these qualities; instead, they said that The Pretender acted quite strangely. Not only did he not behave like an emperor, he didn't even behave like a well brought up man. He was not religious, did not observe the rules of fasting, drank frequently and engaged in carousing on many occasions. Furthermore, he was too close to the Poles who had come to Moscow with him. He did not live in the manner expected of a tsar: did not rest after meals, broke his own horses, walked through the streets and went to market without an entourage; in short, did not maintain the dignity which the Muscovites expected of him. He removed experienced boyars from responsible posts and ruled with the assistance of a few favorites. Peter Fedorovich Basmanov was his best and most capable adviser; the others were minor officials or members of the Polish-Lithuanian gentry. All these things offended the Muscovites and made them resentful of The Pretender.

The people, moreover, became totally disenchanted with him over his wedding. Many guests had arrived from Poland along with the Mnishek family. Because of a lack of hostels, they were assigned to private homes. The foreign and heterodox guests behaved like lords and masters, and insulted and irritated the Muscovites. On top of this, only the foreign guests and the court officials were allowed at the wedding. Furthermore, the citizenry of Moscow was even barred from the Kremlin on the Wedding day. The offended populace was further irritated because the new empress had not adopted the Orthodox religion and because the wedding was consecrated on the eve of a holy day (May 8th), which was against all custom.

The boyars took advantage of the popular dissatisfaction with The Pretender and the Poles. Prince Vassili Ivanovich Shuiski had already called The Pretender a liar prior to his arrival in Moscow, and had tried to set the people against him, but at that time Shuiski had been tried and exiled. He was soon pardoned, however, and he, his brothers and other boyars began to plot against their tsar. They planned to sound the alarm and to incite the populace against the hated Poles. Once the anti-Polish pogrom had started in the city, the plotters could enter the Kremlin and overthrow Tsar Dmitri. The plan was successful. During the early hours of 17 May, 1606, the plotters sounded an alarm in Kitaigorod [literally, Chinatown; the section of Moscow next to the Kremlin] with the cry, "Poles are murdering boyars!" The plotters sent the mob to the houses occupied by Poles, while the plotters themselves went to the palace. Once inside, they first killed Basmanov; then they came upon The Pretender in the courts of Kremlin and killed him on the spot; then they arrested the Tsarina Marina and her entourage. After this, the boyars tried to stop the rioting and looting in the city, but were unable to restore order in Moscow before the mobs had killed over 2,000 foreigners.

The Significance and the Consequences of the Time of Troubles

Once one is familiar with the events of the Time of Troubles, it becomes easy to understand the overall development. The Time of Troubles started at the end of the Muscovite dynasty; it was caused by the dissatisfaction of various classes of Muscovites who were dissatisfied with existing living conditions in the empire. The boyars and minor princes were embittered with the persecution they had undergone under Ivan the Terrible and the Godunovs. As soon as they saw a possibility of terminating the tsarist line in Moscow, they began the fight for power and influence in order to reinstate their former rights and position at the court and in the empire. They also tried to regain the throne. Following the death of [Ivan] the Terrible and up to the coronation of Shuiski, an internal court rivalry existed between the various factions desiring to control the throne. The boyars had set up a pretender against Boris and had thereby given rise to a popular movement. This impostor gained most of his support from a class of people which can be called the Cossacks. The Cossacks were run-away peasants and serfs and were comprised of embittered people without possessions who had left their homes because of persecution by the landowners. By following the impostor, the Cossacks rebelled against the hated Muscovite government in order to take revenge for the wrongs which they had suffered at the hands of the government. They were also hoping to be rewarded by the False Dmitri with rights and privileges upon successful completion of their campaign. When however The Pretender died at the hands of the boyars, the Cossacks stopped bothering about Dmitri and simply continued the rebellion against the boyar rule of Shuiski mainly because of their hate towards the boyar oppressors and because they wanted to change the feudal laws which the peasants and serfs found unsufferable. Therefore, under Shuiski, the court rivalries for the throne and power were replaced by a general contest between the Cossacks and lower classes against the boyars and landowners. This internecine war led to a collapse of law and order and seriously disrupted the government. The Poles and the Swedes took advantage of Moscow's "dislocation" and openly intervened in the internal affairs of the Moscow government. Their action was crowned with success: ultimately the Poles gained control of Moscow and Smolensk and the Swedes gained control of Novgorod. After this had happened, a patriotic movement against foreign rulers began in Russia.

The first attempt to dislodge the Poles from Moscow was unsuccessful, because the first militia formed was composed of too many varied groups which were unfriendly to each other and were drawn from widely varying classes of people. The Cossacks quarreled with the nobles and chased them away; however, they were not strong enough by themselves to conquer Moscow. The nobles and townspeople united then and formed a single militia which took action against both the Poles and the Cossack-"thieves." They were successful in liberating Moscow and hastened to elect a tsar; slowly order returned to the country.

The Time of Troubles which had started with the end of the Moscow dynasty had thus undergone three distinct periods:

1) The struggle of the boyars for power and the throne,

2) The fight of the lower classes (the Cossacks) against the higher classes (the landowners) and

3) The fight of the Russian people against foreign enemies and internal "thieves."

The Time of Troubles, lasting almost a quarter of a century, had naturally a profound influence upon the political and social life of the Muscovite Empire. First of all, the boyars who had started this Time of Troubles, were not only unsuccessful in achieving their aim, but were, instead, completely destroyed by the Time of Troubles. Some of the major boyar families disappeared completely from sight, some died out entirely (Count Shuiski, Mstislavski, Vopotinski), others lost their influence and wealth (the Godunovs, Saltikovs) and some lost much of their power for prolonged periods of time (the Counts Golizin and Kurakin). The boyars who had been shaken during the rule of "The Terrible" were completely destroyed by the Time of Troubles. Following the Time of Troubles, ancestral boyars were replaced by simple noblemen. But the Cossacks also failed to achieve their aims. They were defeated every time they rebelled against government rule. Finally, the largest band of Cossacks under the command of Ottoman Zarutski, fled from the empire. The rest of the

Cossacks submitted to land serfdom. Zarutski perished and the Cossacks remaining on the "plain" and on the Don river stopped their attacks on Moscow and tried to live in friendly relations with Moscow.

They organized themselves into a semblance of states along the lower Don and called themselves "armies" which were under the command of elected officials (the collective term for these officials was "starshina" or, loosely translated, "the group of elders"). These groups managed their affairs in so-called "circles" (meetings). The Cossacks hunted and fished and their fighting urge was now directed against the Turks and the Tartars, temporarily abandoning their fight with the Moscow Empire.

A third change which occurred following the dissolution of Moscow's aristocracy and defeat of the Cossacks, was the emergence to power of the middle class—the noblemen and townspeople. The taking up of arms by the middle classes resulted in the liberation of Moscow and their "zemski sobor" [Land Assembly] elected a new emperor—M. F. Romanov. The Emperor's council (the boyar's duma) was composed of members of the middle classes and they also were drawn upon to staff the government jobs which were needed to conduct the affairs of the government following the Time of Troubles. This then was the result of the Time of Troubles for the Muscovite society.

The effects of the Time of Troubles were also very great for the government itself. Previous emperors regarded the empire as their "patrimony" (*i.e.,* an inherited property). The newly elected Emperor, as well as his relatives and close associates, could not have the same outlook in regard to the empire. The people and the empire itself not only did not seem to them to be their property, but had all the aspects of a formidable element which required the assistance of a "zemstvo" council for proper administration, at least until such time at which the upheaval generated, by the Time of Troubles had come to rest. This, then, is the reason why the new Emperor refused to rule without the assistance of a "zemstvo" council and why he constantly kept it at his side. The terrible devastation of the country during the time of troubles caused a lot of worries and work for the Emperor and the council. Wars had to be fought to regain control of the cities and provinces which had been occupied by the Poles and the Swedes. The council's and Emperor's every action was dictated by the consequences of the Time of Troubles. The historical chain of events which occurred in the XVII century in the Muscovite empire was directly related to the events of the Time of Troubles. This, then, was the significance and consequence of the Time of Troubles. The old order of the Moscow Empire had come to an end and a new era had begun.

Klyuchevskii's Analysis

To explain the reasons for the time of troubles means pointing out the circumstances which provoked it and the conditions which supported it for such a long time. The circumstances . . . are already well known to us: the forceful and secret suppression of the dynasty and its subsequent, artificial re-establishment by means of impostors [pretenders]. But both these circumstances and the deep, inner causes of the Time of Troubles derived their strength only because they grew in fertile soil and were carefully through inadvertently cultivated by the efforts of Tsar Ivan [IV] and Boris Godunov, the real ruler during the reign of Fedor. The fertile soil was the depressed mood of a bewildered society, a mood created by the open outrages of the *oprichnina* and the hidden intrigues of Godunov.

The Time of Troubles was precipitated by an accidental happening—the ending of the dynasty. The extinction of a family, or of a family name, whether it happens naturally or by force, is an every-day phenomenon, and in private life is scarcely noteworthy. It is, however, another matter when an entire dynasty comes to an end. In our country, such an event at the end of the sixteenth century led to a social and political struggle—political, first,—over the form of government; then, social—a conflict of social classes. The clash of political ideas was accompanied by a battle of economic conditions. The forces which supported the changing tsars and the pretenders who struggled for power were the various strata of Moscow society.

Each class sought its own tsar, or put forward its own candidate for the throne. Tsars and candidates were only standard-bearers behind whom the various political aspirations vied with each other, and behind the aspirations were the several classes of Russian society. The troubles began with the aristocratic schemes of the great boyars in opposition to the unlimited power of the new tsars. They were continued by the political ambitions of the noble guards of the capital who, in the name of political freedom for officers [*i.e.*, guardsmen], armed themselves against the oligarchical ambitions of the high-ranking aristocracy. Behind the metropolitan nobility rose the private, provincial nobility which wished to be master of the country. It carried along with it the non-governmental, provincial classes which, in the name of individual privilege—that is, in the name of anarchy—protested against any ordered government at all. Each of these stages of the Troubles was accompanied by the intervention of Cossack and Polish gangs from the Don, the Dnieper and the Vistula—the scum of the Muscovite and Polish states—who rejoiced at the opportunity for plundering in the disordered country.

The boyars were the first to try to unite the classes of the almost disintegrating society in the name of a new social order, but this new order did not coincide with the ideas of the other classes of society. Then came an attempt to avert disaster through a person, by artificially resurrecting the recently ended dynasty which had been able to restrain hostility and to unite the divergent interests of the various classes of the society. The struggle of the irreconcilable interests led to the putting forward of a pretender [to the throne]. When this effort repeatedly failed, it became evident that there remained no political bonds, no political interests under which it would have been possible to avert the disintegration of society. Yet the society did not disintegrate; only orderly government was impaired. When the political ties which bound the social order gave way, there remained still stronger national and religious bonds which, alone,

saved the society. The Cossack and Polish bands slowly but surely educated the population which they were ruining and thus finally brought
about a unification of the hostile classes, not for the sake of any form of
government, but for the sake of the national, religious, and civil security
which was being threatened by the Cossacks and the Poles. In this fashion,
although the Troubles were nourished by the discord among the landed
classes, they were ended by the struggle of all landed society against alien
interventionists in the internal, domestic struggle.

We see that two conditions, the pretendership and social disorder,
clearly operated to maintain the Troubles. These suggest where one must
look for the causes of the Time of Troubles. I have already had occasion
to note one error in Muscovite political thinking: the state, as a union of
people, could belong to no one except the people, but both the sovereign
and the people of Muscovy looked upon the Moscow state as the patrimony of the princely dynasty from whose property it had developed. In
this patrimonial-dynastic view of the state, I see one of the basic causes of
the Troubles. This error in understanding was connected with a general
immaturity or lack of political understanding. . . . The Moscow state, I
repeat, was generally regarded as an appanage, the property of the Muscovite rulers, the property of the Kalita clan which had acquired, expanded, and strengthened it during the course of three centuries. It was,
in fact, already a union of the Great Russian people; but, although men
had developed the concept of the Russian land as an entity, they had not
conceived of the state as a union of the people.

The will and the interest of the owner of the lands continued to be the
real bonds of union. One must add, however, that such a patrimonial
concept of government was not simply a dynastic pretense of the Muscovite rulers; it was the type of political thinking that was inherited from the
appanage period. At that time in our country, they did not understand the
state except in the sense of an hereditary estate, the property of the ruler
of a given dynasty. If the ordinary Muscovite of that time had been told
that the ruler's power was matched by his responsibility to serve the
general welfare and the state, ruled by the people, this would have seemed
a mishmash of confusion and an anarchy of thought. It seemed to the
people that the Muscovite state, in which they lived, belonged to the
Muscovite sovereign, not to the people of Muscovy or Russia. The inseparable concepts were not government, or state, and people; but a government, or state, and a sovereign of a given dynasty. People could more
readily imagine a sovereign without a people than a state without a
sovereign. This attitude was distinctively expressed in the political life of
the people of Muscovy.

When subjects who are bound to their rulers through the idea of the
welfare of the state recognize that the government fails to safeguard this
welfare, they protest. When servants or tenants who are bound to a master
through mutual, temporary, and conditional advantages find that they are
not receiving these advantages, they leave the master's house. But subjects who protest against authority do not abandon a state which they do

not consider to be alien to them; a servant or a tenant, however, who becomes dissatisfied with a master does not remain in the master's house because he does not think of the house as his. The people of the Moscow state acted more like dissatisfied servants or tenants than like disobedient citizens of a government. They frequently grumbled at the actions of the power which ruled them, but so long as the old dynasty existed, popular discontent did not reach the point of insurrection against authority.

The people of Muscovy worked out a special form of political protest: those who felt that they could not continue to live under the existing order did not rebel against it, but left it—"wandering apart," running away from the state. The Muscovite people, as if they felt themselves aliens in their own state or as accidental, temporary residents in a strange home, considered it possible to run away from the uncongenial owner of the home when matters became too difficult. They could not, however, reconcile themselves to rebelling against him, nor to establishing a new order in his home. Thus the bond of common relationships to the Moscow state was not the idea of general welfare, but the person of a member of a dynasty; and an ordered state was deemed possible only under a ruler of that same dynasty. Therefore, when the dynasty ended and, subsequently, the state seemed no man's property, the people lost their heads. Ceasing to understand who they were or where they were, they fell into conditions of anarchy and chaos . . . and felt compelled to revolt.

It became necessary for a *Zemski Sobor* (Land Assembly) to elect a tsar. But election by a *sobor,* because of its very novelty, was not considered to provide a sufficient foundation for a new state power. The election provoked doubts and anxieties. The announcement by the *Zemski Sobor* of the election of Boris Godunov anticipated the objection of the people who said, "We are separate from them because they are themselves creating a tsar.". . . Throughout the Time of Troubles, people could not reconcile themselves to the idea of an elected tsar. They thought that an elected tsar could not really be a tsar, that only an hereditary tsar born in the Kalita clan could be a true and legal tsar, and that elected tsars tried to attach themselves to this clan by any means possible—judicial fabrication, strained genealogy, rhetorical exaggeration. The people and the clergy solemnly greeted Boris Godunov at his election as an hereditary tsar, "wishing him good fortune in his *votchina"* [hereditary estate], and Basil Shuiski, though he formally limited his own power, signed his official acts as *Samoderzhets* [Autocrat] which had been the title of the birthright tsars.

The appearance on the throne of an elected tsar, given such an inflexibility of thinking among the ruling circles, must have seemed to the masses of the people not the consequence of a sad political necessity, but a violation of a law of nature. An elected tsar must have appeared to the masses as incongruous as an elected father or an elected mother. That is why simple minds could not accept as "natural" tsars Boris Godunov, or Basil Shuiski, or—even worse—Wladislaw, the king of Poland. These men were seen as usurpers whereas a newcomer of unknown lineage who claimed some connection with the "natural" tsar was able to satisfy the masses' dynastic consciousness and thereby win their confidence. The Time of Troubles ended only when they succeeded in finding a tsar who was linked by descent, albeit not direct, with the extinct dynasty. The lack of confidence in a popular election as an adequate legal source of supreme power was an important condition fostering the Time of Troubles. This lack of confidence [in an election] rose from the deeply ingrained conviction that the sole source of supreme authority was patrimonial inheritance within a dynasty. The inability to reconcile oneself to the idea of an elected tsar must, therefore, be recognized as a derivative cause of the Troubles. . . .

Moscow, at the end of 1611, presented a spectacle of complete and universal disruption. The Poles had taken Smolensk; a Polish detachment had burned Moscow and had fortified itself behind the remaining walls of the Kremlin and Kitaya-gorod [Chinatown]; the Swedes had taken Novgorod and had set one of their own royal candidates on the throne; the murdered, second False Dmitri had been replaced by a person named Sidorka; and the first attempt of the nobility [to rid the country of invaders] had fallen apart near Moscow after the death of Lyapunov. The country, meanwhile, remained without a government. The Boyars' Duma, which had assumed power at the death of Shuiski, abolished itself when the Poles occupied the Kremlin, though several boyars continued to meet under the chairmanship of Prince Mstislav. The government, having lost its nucleus, began to break down into basic components; almost every city acted independently, or only by correspondence with other cities. The government became a sort of formless confederation. But when the political forces were exhausted at the end of 1611, the religious and national forces which ultimately rescued the stricken country began to awaken.

Proclamations by the Archimandrite Dyonisius and the Abbot Avraham of the Troitsky Monastery placed the inhabitants of Nizhni Novgorod under the leadership of their village elder, the butcher, Kuz'ma Minin. There began to gather, summoned by the people of Nizhni Novgorod, "serving people" who had lost their posts, their pay, and, often, their lands; urban nobility; and boyars' children. Kuz'ma Minin found a leader for this group in Prince Dmitri Mikhailovich Pozharsky. In this manner there was formed the second expeditionary force against the Poles. Its military quality was not as high as the first expeditionary force, but it was well equipped, thanks to the abundant financial help generously supplied, often at considerable personal sacrifice, by the people of Nizhni Novgorod and the other cities which joined with them. The force spent four months in organizing itself; in six months it went to Moscow, adding to itself along the way many "serving people" who hoped for rewards in land. The Cossack band of Prince Trubetskoi, remnant of the first expeditionary force, stood before Moscow. This band seemed worse than the Poles to the second group who responded to Trobetskoi's offer of cooperation by saying: "We will certainly not join ourselves with the Cossacks." But it soon became clear that nothing could be accomplished without the Cossacks, and nothing important was done during the three months in which the group stayed outside of Moscow.

There were in the ranks of Prince Pozharsky over forty persons of high service rank, but only two men did great deeds and they were not "serving people." They were the monk A. Palitsin and the butcher, Minin. The former, at the request of Prince Pozharsky, persuaded the Cossacks to support the nobility at the decisive moment; the latter successfully begged three or four companies from Prince Pozharsky and, with their aid, mounted a successful attack on a small Polish detachment, commanded by the Hetman Khotkevich, which was attempting to get supplies into the Kremlin for their beleaguered comrades. Minin's brave attack, after the Cossacks had prepared the way, encouraged the nobility who then forced the Hetman to retreat. The Cossacks alone captured Kitaya-gorod in October, 1612, but the expeditionary force did not storm the Kremlin. The handful of Poles who held it, having been driven by hunger to cannibalism, gave themselves up. King Sigismund, headed for Moscow to restore it to Polish control, was driven back from Volokolamsk and forced to return home—not by the military leaders of Moscow, but by the Cossack chieftains. The noble militia once again showed small competence in the field which was supposed to be its profession and its obligation to the state. . . .

Foreigners traveling to Moscow soon after the ascension of [Tsar] Mikhail [Romanov] have left for us a horrible picture of towns and villages deserted or burned; of deserted huts, filled with corpses which remained unburied in 1615. The stench forced winter travelers to spend the night on the ice [*i.e.,* in the open]. Persons surviving the Troubles made a run for it wherever they could; civil order fell apart; all human relationships became confused. Continuing efforts were necessary to gather together the people who had run away, to resettle them in their former locations, and to get them to begin again the daily routines from which the Time of Troubles had wrenched them.

Many district lists of "serving people" . . . and land inventories which show the economic position of the "serving landowners" and the peasants have come down to us from Mikhail's day. These clearly indicate the economic reconstruction of the Muscovite state and people during the first reign of the new [Romanov] dynasty. It is possible, even before this, to see a change in the composition of the rural serf population which was the main source of state income. According to the sixteenth century records, the serf population fell into two classes in terms of property: the peasant and the landless peasant. The two were much the same except that the landless peasants either ploughed plots smaller than peasants, or were literally without land, owning only a farmhouse. The peasants had been numerically predominant over the landless peasants in the sixteenth century, but—according to the records of Mikhail's reign—after the Troubles, this relationship was changed, or even reversed, with the number of landless peasants being either equal to or greater than the number of peasants. For example, on the lands of the district "serving people" in the districts of Belev, Mtsensk, and Elets in 1622 we find 1,187 peasants and 2,563 landless peasants. This means that the Time of Troubles forced very many peasants either to reduce or to abandon their cultivated lands. The increase in the number of landless peasants meant, also, an increase in the number of abandoned fields . . . the *pomestie* of one district in Ryazin had twenty-two times more waste land than cultivated land in 1616. The monk Palitsin . . . writes that despite a three-year failure of the harvest during the reign of Godunov many persons were able to stockpile great quantities of grain, that threshing floors overflowed with straw and hay, and that during the fourteen years of the Time of Troubles when "ploughing and sowing and harvesting were foregone," and "the sword was always at everyone's throat," these persons fed themselves and others from these stores. This is evidence both of the growth of agriculture up to the Troubles and of the decline of agriculture during the Troubles.

The reordering of the rural economy and the concomitant changes in the economic status of the rural population told heavily against private landowners and especially against the provincial nobility. . . . The military capability of the "serving class" depended upon the productivity of their estates, and upon the numbers and status of the peasants who peopled the estates. In some districts, the nobles owned hereditary estates, but the great majority lived on the income from their service estates. Hereditary estates made up a quarter of the nobles' landownership in the Belev district; a little more than a fifth in Tula; one-seventeenth in Mtsensk; one one-hundred fifty seventh in Elets; and in Tver, even among the wealthiest nobles, a quarter. The estates of the district nobility were generally very poor and very sparsely populated; the average estate in the Tula district comprised 364.5 acres of arable land; in Elets, 334.8 acres; in Belev, 405 acres; and in Mtsensk, 183.6 acres. The number of tax-paying farmers, both peasants and landless peasants, averaged two per 324 acres, or one for every 162 acres of service estate land in these four districts. But do not think that all this arable land was actually tilled by the peasants and landless peasants. Only a small portion was so cultivated, and part of that was not fully worked.

In the Tver district, for example, we find a wealthy noble landowner whose service estate and hereditary holdings totaled 2,430 acres. But only 256.5 acres were cultivated; 54 acres of this were tilled by the landowner's manor serfs; 28 peasants and landless peasants, comprising 19 households, used the remaining 202.5 acres so that each household had, in round figures, 11 acres. Large-scale peasant tillage was a rare phenomenon. Moreover, many nobles in Elets and other districts were completely landless, owning only a farm with no tenant farmers, or not even that. There were, for instance, 878 registered nobles and boyar's children in the Elets district, 133 of whom were landless and 296 owned only a tenantless farm or a "wasteland." Several nobles surrendered their estates and joined the Cossacks, or became bondsmen in a boyar household, or entered a monastery as lay brothers, or—to quote the records—"fell to wallowing in taverns."

The more the service estate declined, the greater became the need to increase the pay of the *pomeshchiki* in order that they might perform required services. But increasing such payments also meant increasing the taxes which fell only upon the peasants. Because taxes were assessed on the basis of the acreage under cultivation, the peasants, being unable to carry this increased tax burden, reduced their tillage in order to pay less tax. The treasury was thereby reduced to a parlous state.

Finally, the internal difficulties of the government were exacerbated by a profound change in the attitude of the people. The new dynasty had to deal with a society far different from that which the former tsars had ruled. The disturbances of the Time of Troubles adversely affected the political attitudes of society. From the ascension of the new dynasty throughout the remainder of the seventeenth century, all social classes complained loudly of their misfortunes, their poverty, their ruination, and the abuse of power. They complained about grievances which they had long endured in patient silence. The dissatisfaction grew until, by the end of the century, it had become the dominant note in the mood of the masses. The people emerged from the storms of the Troubles more impressionable and more irritable than before; they had lost that long-suffering tolerance which had surprised foreign observers, and were no longer an instrument, silent and resigned, in the hands of the government. This change was manifested by a phenomenon not hitherto observable in the life of the Moscow state: the seventeenth century was the time in our history of popular uprisings. This phenomenon was peculiarly unexpected because it appeared during the reigns of tsars whose personal qualities and policies did not justify such action.

Sixteenth and Seventeenth Century Muscovite Diplomacy

The following selection is composed of a series of excerpts from a collaborative work written by eight members of the Soviet Academy of Sciences. Their announced purpose was to produce a history of diplomacy as distinct from what they considered to be the conventional Western histories of international relations. Their general frame of reference was, of course, determined by the official policies at the time of publication. Their charge that the earliest foreign residents in Moscow were primarily spies and informers is especially interesting in view of Soviet attitudes and actions toward diplomats, newsmen, and other visitors. The source is: Potemkin (Ed.), *Istoriia Diplomatii* (History of Diplomacy), vol. 1, pp. 196–198, 247–249, *passim*.

In the second half of the sixteenth century, the Muscovite state, which had achieved national unity during the preceding century, appeared on the international scene. At the beginning, it bore the modest title of "the Grand Duchy of Muscovy," and was a feudal monarchy. The new state, having brought vast expanses of eastern Europe under its sway, soon held an important position in the international arena. From the end of the fifteenth century, the Principality of Moscow represented a considerable force, and European diplomats found themselves faced with a new problem: to find it a place within the European state system which would be compatible with its importance.

[European diplomats, concerned with protocol, sought to define the new state as a monarchy, and proposed that the Holy Roman emperor confer the title of king on Ivan III. Ivan responded that he was sovereign by the grace of God and needed no appointment to that dignity.] . . . Ivan IV was solemnly crowned in 1547, an act which brilliantly defined the rank his state should occupy among other civilized powers.

. . . In 1453, Constantinople was taken by the Turks, and the problem of the Turkish threat was exposed in all its gravity to the European powers. Henceforward, it was the dream of Western diplomats to draw the ruler of Moscow into an alliance against the Turks. . . .

[Though accepting marriage with Zoe Paleologue and claiming thereby to be the heir of Byzantium, Ivan declined—as did his immediate successors—to enter an alliance against the Turks. This was partly because Moscow wished to have good relations with Turkey in the hope of developing trade on the Black Sea. Mostly, however, it was because Moscow regarded its most pressing diplomatic problem to be] . . . in the first place, the recovery of the Russian lands which had been seized by the united state of Poland and Lithuania. . . . Moscow declared that the "hereditary" patrimony of the Grand Prince of Moscow included all the Russian lands which had once belonged to Kiev. . . . "If your sovereign," said the Moscow boyars in 1503 to the Lithuanian ambassadors, "wishes peace and fraternity with our sovereign, he must cede to him all the patrimonies of all Russia." On its side, the Lithuanian-Polish government protested against the adoption by the Grand Prince of Moscow of the title, sovereign of all Russia.

[The other main diplomatic goals of Ivan III and Vasili III were the final dissolution of their legal dependency upon the Golden Horde, and the expansion of their territories toward the Baltic Sea. Ivan IV was equally interested in expansion to the East (Kazan and Astrakhan) and to the West (the Livonian War).]

•   •   •

The problems which had to be solved by diplomatic means became more and more complex in the sixteenth and seventeenth centuries. Certain among them (for example, the extradition of political criminals . . . the purchase of military supplies, the raising of mercenary troops, the conclusion of loans, the purchase of grain from Russia, etc.) were posed for the first time. Muscovite diplomacy in the seventeenth century also began to take an active interest in the internal affairs of foreign powers . . . thus the government of Alexis Mikhailovich broke its commercial relations with England in reprisal for the execution of Charles I . . . and refused to recognize the Commonwealth; the Tsar Alexis kept himself informed about the health of the widow of Charles I and gave pecuniary

aid to his son . . . the future Charles II. Muscovite diplomats showed a
similar hostility to the aid which the French and Danish kings gave to the
"muzhiks" of Holland against the king of England. . . .

. . .

The seventeenth century also saw the beginning of a struggle against
the foreign press with the purpose of putting an end to propaganda against
tsarist Russia. Moscow had protested to Sweden about the dispatches
published at Riga during Razin's revolt. . . . Moscow also lodged a complaint against a pamphlet, published at Reval in 1655, which depicted
Ivan Vasilievich as a tyrant and compared Alexis Mikhailovich himself
to "Erostrate" because of "his absolute tyranny in Livonia." The Treaty
of 1650 with the Republic of Poland contained a special clause concerning
the suppression of books which made hostile criticisms of the Muscovite
state; one of the pretexts alleged by the Muscovite diplomats to break the
peace with Poland was the publication "by order of the king and the
nobles of the Diet" of books "in which ignominious faults, criticisms, and
reproaches were laid to our great sovereigns, the tsars of Moscow, and to
our boyars and persons of other ranks."

The development and extension of diplomatic and commercial relations with Western nations caused the appearance in Moscow of foreign
residents and agents representing the interests of the different countries.
After 1585, one finds mention of a resident Englishman whose functions
were like those of a consul. . . . At the end of the second decade of the
seventeenth century, "Danish clerks" appeared. The Dutch Estates General received the right to establish a resident agent in 1631, but did not
exercise this right until 1678. Swedish agents were living in Moscow at
the end of 1631; those of Poland were admitted in 1673, but were there
only sporadically. Attempts by France and Brandenburg to establish their
resident agents in Moscow in 1629 were unsuccessful. These foreign representatives were officially present "in order to make personal reports
more readily than those which had to be sent by post." In reality, in addition to efforts on behalf of the commercial interests of their countrymen,
they carried out the functions of spies and informers. . . . The despatches of the Swedes who were resident in Moscow in the seventeenth
century contained valuable information on the military forces of Russia,
on trade, on popular movements, and, finally, on rival parties at the
court. . . . Moscow only began in the course of the seventeenth century
to establish permanent missions abroad, at first only in the two countries
to which she was the most closely bound, that is to say, Sweden and
Poland. . . .

The absence of permanent missions abroad made itself painfully apparent in the mediocrity of the information which Muscovite diplomacy
possessed about foreign affairs. Chemodanov, set in 1656 to the Doge
Francis, learned on arrival that "this Francis was dead . . . and that
three princes had already succeeded him." To fill this lack, foreign newspapers were imported and translated. . . . Evidently such information

was not an adequate substitute for diplomatic reports, and certain gross errors resulted. Thus, in 1687, Prince I. T. Dolgoruki left for France with the delicate mission of suggesting to Louis XIV a Franco-Russian alliance against Turkey just when France was on the verge of concluding an alliance with Turkey.

Church and State in Early Russian History

As even the Bolshevik historians have finally been forced to recognize, the Orthodox Church was a powerful and important factor in the creation and the development of the Russian state and society. The following selection is an excellent summary of the relations of church and state in the sixteenth century, together with a brief sketch of their historical connections. The source is: Mikhail M. Karpovich, "Church and State in Russian History," *The Russian Review*. Vol. 3, no. 3, pp. 10–20 (Spring, 1944). Pp. 10–14.

In the early sixteenth century an acute struggle was going on within the ranks of the Orthodox Church in Muscovy. The immediate issue was the question of church land possession. Like the Western church during the Middle Ages, the Russian Church had accumulated, in the course of the previous centuries of its existence, enormous wealth in land which for the most part belonged to the monasteries. It was against this state of affairs that a small but determined group of church reformers raised the voice of protest. Known as the "Trans-Volga Elders," the protestants were grouped around the hermitage of Sorsk, a center of ascetic monasticism, highly respected for the purity of life and the devotional zeal of its members. They had for a leader a remarkable man—Nilus of Sorsk, himself an ascetic and a mystic, a man of deep convictions and of a great strength of character. The Trans-Volga Elders, who also were referred to as the "noncovetous" monks, loudly called upon the church to give up its worldly possessions in order to achieve the Christian ideal of poverty and humility. In their eyes, a truly monastic life and management of big land estates were fundamentally incompatible.

On the other side stood the so-called "Josephites," by far the larger of the two groups, and one that enjoyed the support of the church hierarchy. To them the material wealth of the church was one of the indispensable conditions for the proper performance of its functions. The head of this faction, Joseph of Volokolamsk (hence the name of the Josephites), was the abbot of one of the richest and most influential monasteries in Muscovy. Throughout the sixteenth century this monastery played the part of a "nursery of bishops," and many of the most prominent hierarchs of the period had received their training there. Profoundly different from Nilus of Sorsk in character and outlook, Joseph too was a remarkable man, in his own way. An outstanding church administrator, he defended the retention by the monasteries of their land possessions on purely utilitarian grounds. One of his typical arguments was that the poor monasteries could not attract the better class of people, and these were needed for the building up of an educated and influential hierarchy.

Behind this controversy over the problem of church lands lay a more fundamental difference between two distinct religious types. The Josephites stood for a strict adherence to tradition, emphasized the importance of the ritual and were inclined towards a literal interpretation of religious texts. The followers of Nilus represented the spiritual trend in Russian Christianity, assigning first place to personal piety and assuming a much more liberal attitude towards the dogma and tradition.

Of particular importance was the difference between the two groups with regard to the problem of Church and State relationship. The Josephites wanted the Russian Church to be in an intimate and indissoluble alliance with the State. Preaching a doctrine of absolute loyalty to the secular power, they expected in return a full measure of state support and protection for the Church. In particular, they did not hesitate to invoke the assistance of the secular arm in the suppression of heresies. The Trans-Volga Elders differed sharply from the Josephites on this point. With a degree of tolerance surprising for their time, they rejected compulsion in matters of faith. Those who strayed away from the path of true Christianity should be brought back by persuasion, not by force. The realm of the Church, unlike that of the State, was one of spirit, and in the solution of its problems only spiritual methods could be used. Therefore, it would be better for the State not to interfere with the Church, just as the clergy should refrain from interfering in politics.

The Russian government of the period was bound to be vitally interested in this controversy within the Church. It was particularly concerned with the problem of church lands. Precisely at that time the Moscow rulers were engaged in reorganizing the system of national defense in their dominions. The new system was based on the principle of military service in return for land grants, and the government needed a sufficiently large land fund at its disposal. This is why it viewed the growth of church landownership with some alarm, and why at times it even contemplated secularization of church estates. With regard to this issue the government found itself in agreement with the followers of Nilus of Sorsk who, as is known, demanded the voluntary relinquishment by the church of its worldly possessions. And yet it could not enter into an alliance with the Trans-Volga Elders because of the other tenets held by that group. The spirit of individual freedom in which they approached the religious problems, their liberal attitude towards those deviating from Orthodoxy, and, above all, their endeavor to protect the Church from state interference and control, were hardly compatible with the centralizing and absolutist tendencies of the rising Russian autocracy. On the contrary, the government was in full sympathy with the traditionalism of the Josephites, their strict adherence to Orthodoxy, and, in particular, their advocacy of a close alliance between Church and State.

And so, a sort of unwritten concordat was concluded between the Moscow government and the leading faction of the Russian Church. For the time being, the government gave up its plan of secularizing the church estates, limiting itself to enacting legislation that tended to prevent their further growth, and in return it received the unqualified allegiance of the church hierarchy. With governmental support, the opposition movement within the Church was effectively silenced, and the Josephites achieved a complete victory over their antagonists. Under their leadership, the Orthodox Church finally became, by the middle of the sixteenth century, the official national Church of Russia, thus winning a position that it was destined to hold until the Revolution of 1917.

* * * * *

At that time the Russian Church already had over five centuries of existence behind it. In the course of this long period it played a great and creative part in the history of Russian culture and the State. Not only did it control the spiritual life of the people, being the only educational agency in the country, but it also became the chief guardian and exponent of the slowly growing idea of national unity. When, in the later part of the Middle Ages, the princes of Moscow undertook the political unification of Russia, it was the Church that rendered them the most determined and particularly effective support. It contributed to the rise of the Tsardom of Moscow by lending it its own moral prestige and, in the persons of some of its outstanding representatives, it took a direct part in the work of national consolidation. Moreover, it supplied the young Russian monarchy with a ready-made theory of divinely ordained royal absolutism which it borrowed from its spiritual parent, the Church of the Byzantine Empire.

One could expect that in virtue of this contribution the Church would emerge an equal partner in the alliance between Church and State in Russia. And yet, in reality, almost from the outset the Church became a subordinate member of the alliance, with the State firmly retaining full measure of control. In a large degree, the very nature of political theories preached by the clergy was responsible for such a result. True, in Byzantium there existed a doctrine which emphasized the equality of the spiritual and the secular power and envisaged a harmonious balance between the two, and that doctrine, too, found its way into Russia. But on the whole the main tradition of the Byzantine Empire was that of the imperial domination over the Church, and it was this tradition that was particularly familiar to the Russian hierarchs. At any rate, neither in Byzantium nor in Russia did the Church as a whole ever exhibit either a strong tendency to assert the supremacy of the spiritual power over the secular, or such a tenacity in defending itself against the encroachments of the State as were characteristic of the Roman Catholic Church in the West.

Of even greater importance were, perhaps, the specific conditions of Russia's historical development. In comparison with the relatively slow progress of royal absolutism in Western Europe, the Russian autocracy succeeded in establishing itself in a surprisingly short period of time. It arose in the process of a rapid territorial expansion of the Tsardom of Moscow, under the constant pressure of foreign menace, and it consolidated its position within the country before any of its potential domestic rivals could become strong enough to successfully challenge its supremacy. Unlike Western European absolutism, the rising Russian monarchy did not have to face either a fully developed and firmly established feudal system, or (after the early fall of the city-republic of Novgorod) any strong and prosperous urban communes. The Russian Church merely shared the fate of other social forces in the country. In spite of its riches and its privileges, it too had not developed into an independent feudal body, and in the end, it succumbed under the sway of the Tsar's autocratic power in the same way as did the other social groups and organizations.

In the early centuries of its existence the Russian Church remained in canonical dependence on the mother Church in Byzantium, and its head had to be appointed or at least confirmed in office by the Patriarch of Constantinople. Gradually, however, this dependence grew weaker and weaker, and since the destruction of the Byzantine Empire by the Turks in 1453, the Russian Church, to all practical purposes, became an independent national Church. This independence was given formal sanction with the elevation, in 1589, of the Russian Metropolitan to the dignity of the Patriarch of Moscow, recognized as an equal by the other Eastern Patriarchs. In the process of this gradual emancipation from canonical dependence on Constantinople, the practice was established of electing first the Metropolitan and then the Patriarch of Moscow at a Russian Church council. Theoretically, the Church was free in the choice of its head, but there is enough evidence to show that from the outset the elections were controlled by the State. It became customary to submit the names of the candidates for the Tsar's preliminary approval.

No wonder, therefore, that as a rule the Patriarch was not and could not feel himself to be the Tsar's equal. During the whole seventeenth century, there were only two cases when it was otherwise, but both these cases can be viewed as exceptions proving the rule.

The first of these cases was that of Patriarch Philaret (1619–33) who was the virtual co-regent with Tsar Michael (the first of the Romanovs) and was officially recognized as such. But, in addition to his outstanding ability and personal prestige, Philaret owed his exalted position to the fact that he was the Tsar's father. Two decades later a similar position was attained by Patriarch Nikon who, for a while, also acted as the Tsar's co-regent and was given the use of the sovereign title. This time the exaltation of the Patriarch was due to the remarkable ascendency that Nikon had succeeded in gaining over the mind of Tsar Alexis. Nikon, however, began to lose ground the moment he ceased to enjoy the personal favor of the Tsar. Significantly, the cause of his ruin was precisely his uncompromising insistence on the prerogatives of his office, in which, in the opinion of the Tsar, he overstepped the boundaries of the permissible. Practically alone of all the Russian hierarchs, Nikon attempted to advance in Russia the medieval Western doctrine of the supremacy of the spiritual over the secular power, but in this he was not supported by the Church. Finally he was deposed by a church council and died in disgrace. His fall might be viewed as a prelude to the final subordination of the Russian Church to the State, which took place in the reign of Peter the Great.

Where to Find More Information

ALLEN, *Ukraine*, ch. 3.

BLACK, *Rewriting*, chs. 7 & 8.

BURY, J. B. "Russia, 1462–1482," *Cambridge Modern History*. N.Y.: Macmillan, 1934 edition. Vol. 5, ch. 16.

CHARQUES, *Short History*, chs. 4–6.

CLARKSON, *History*, chs. 5–8.

DEWEY, H. "Trial by Combat in Muscovite Russia," *Oxford Slavonic Papers*. Vol. IX (1960). Pp. 21–31.

ECK, *Moyen âge*, pp. 65–493.

ECKHARDT, H. VON *Ivan the Terrible*. N.Y.: Knopf, 1949.

FLORINSKY, *Russia*, vol. 1, chs. 3, 4, 6–9.

HARCAVE, *Readings*, vol. 1, sections 12–15.

LOBANOV-ROSTOVSKY, A. *Russia and Asia*. Ann Arbor: Wahr, 1951. Intro. & chs. 1 & 2.

LYASHCHENKO, *National Economy*, pp. 172–197, 205–227.

MARTIN, *Picture History*, pp. 31–63.

MAZOUR, *Russia*, chs. 3–6.

MILIUKOV, *Outlines*, vol. 1, ch. 3; vol. 3, pp. 1–14.

NIKOLAIEFF, A. M. "Boris Godunov and the Ouglich Tragedy," *The Russian Review*, vol. 9, no. 4 (October, 1950), pp. 275–285.

PARES, *History*, chs. 4–8.

RAMBAUD, *Russia*, vol. 1, chs. 8–18.

TOLSTOY, A. *Prince Serebryani*. N.Y.: Dodd, Mead, 1892.

VERNADSKY, *Mongols and Russia*.

————. *Russia in the Dawn of the Modern Age*. (Vol. IV in his *History of Russia*.) New Haven: Yale Univ. Press, 1959.

WALSH, *Russia*, chs. 4 & 5.

WIPPER, R. Iu. *Ivan Grozny*. Moscow, 1947.

WREN, *Course*, chs. 7 & 8.

Part IV

The Seventeenth and Eighteenth Centuries

The Raskol and the Raskolniki

There occurred in the seventeenth century the beginnings of a major and lasting schism in the Russian Church. The schism, known in Russian as *raskol,* was precipitated by the efforts of the Patriarch Nikon (né Nicetas) to revise the ritual and liturgy of the church. The underlying causes and issues were, however, considerably more complicated. The inspiration for the Nikonian revisions appears to have come from clerical scholars at Kiev. This not only aroused the chauvinism of some Great Russians, but also awakened theological fears because of the successes of Roman Catholicism in the western borderlands during the sixteenth and seventeenth centuries. Tsar Alexis, who was planning an expansion of his power over the Ukraine, saw potential political advantage in conciliating the Kievan clergy, and for this reason among others supported the Nikonian reforms. Other basic causes included opposition to the growing centralization of the Russian Church, to the increasing absolutism of the Romanov regime, to the subordination of the church to the autocracy, and to a widespread psychological insecurity arising from many socio-political changes.

Nikon's insistence that the church ought to be superior to the state was not acceptable to the tsar who much preferred the Byzantine tradition of a subservient church. This, coupled with Nikon's antipathy toward the theory of the Third Rome and his personal arrogance, led Alexis to support the Nikonian reforms but to reject the reformer at a Church Council in 1666–1667. Those who refused to accept the Nikonian reforms as endorsed by the Council became known as the *raskolniki* (schismatics) or "Old Ritualists," or "Old Believers." They were anathematized and excommunicated by the church and persecuted by the state. Before the end of the seventeenth century, the *raskolniki* split into two wings: the *popovtsi,* who accepted priests; and the *bezopopovtsi,* who rejected priests. The following selection summarizes the legal position of the *raskolniki* during the seventeenth and eighteenth centuries.

139

Reprinted by permission of the publishers from Frederick Cornwallis Conybeare, *The Russian Dissenters*. Cambridge, Mass.: Harvard University Press, 1921. Pp. 226–232.

Before Peter I

No ukases were hurled directly against the Old believers until Tsar Alexis Mikhailovich issued one, which the patriarch Joseph countersigned, as well as his Metropolitans and archbishops, bishops and the entire holy synod; this condemned to the stake any and all who should insult Jesus Christ, the Virgin or the Cross. Under this law provision was duly made for hunting down and burning alive such as confronted the inquisitor with firmness and courage, while those who promptly made their peace with the church were only to be subjected to what was understood in that age as spiritual admonition, no doubt of the kind that Claverhouse administered about the same time to Scotch covenanters.

The above ukase, however, was too indefinite and too gentle for the Empress Regent Sophia, who as soon as she had disarmed her rebellious praetorian guard, the Streltsy, issued a new one proscribing the very existence of the Raskol, and making it illegal; the teachers of the Raskol were condemned to be burned alive as heretics, as were all whom they had rebaptized. The repentant, who saw the error of their ways, were to be sent to convents and enlightened by application of the knout, as also were any who sheltered them, unless they did so in ignorance, in which case they were to be heavily fined.

Peter I

The above law continued in force under Peter I, called the Great, but was not put in force by him very thoroughly, because he was preoccupied with other concerns. He was intent on opening his window towards Europe, the new capital of Petersburg, as he called it, rechristened by the late Tsar Petrograd, a change of name which, though it pleases the Pan-slavists, is not likely to be permanent. Peter I was too busy at first building a fleet of ships and developing the system of bureaucratic concentration begun a hundred years before, to turn his attention to the persecution of heretics. What is more, he may even have sympathized a little with them, for he had himself to bear the odium of abolishing the patriarchate and installing himself in its place, of tearing the veils off the faces of high-born ladies, of cutting off the curls of the Jews and the beards of Russians. Such an emperor was not, at any rate at first, disposed to make martyrs of people who were to his mind, as they would have been to Frederick the Great's or Voltaire's, cranks and ignoramuses. As long as they did not hinder his pet designs, he had little fault to find with them, and was ready to consider them as good citizens, just as he regarded the many Lutherans who put their wits at his disposal. The settlers on the Vyg even earned his good will by assisting him in his enterprises; so did those of Starodub, and he rewarded both for a time by allowing them liberty to worship as they liked.

Later on, however, Peter discovered their fanaticism. Most probably their orthodox enemies discovered it for him. Anyhow in 1714 unfriendly laws were made against them of a kind to facilitate their exploitation by the Government. As Sophia's edict stood on the statute book with its menace of rack and stake, any official could blackmail them, and they were naturally ready to bear any burdens of taxation or corvée provided only they were allowed to retain their convictions.

Peter the Great therefore began by obliging them to inscribe themselves as Raskolniks on a state-kept register and to pay double taxes. Now they regarded themselves as the Orthodox Church, and indeed had as much right to the name as Nikon and his time-serving prelates. It is not surprising therefore that many refused to register themselves in the ledgers of Anti-christ, as Ivanovski explains, "partly to avoid the extra imposts but still more *from fanaticism.*" The result was that Peter I invented ingenious penalties alike for those heretics who concealed their identity and for those who revealed it. The avowed dissenter was not to be actively molested, but to be made ridiculous in the eyes of all, *monstrari digito praetereuntium.* To that end they were, like our convicts, to wear clothes of a special cut marked with the agreeable lettering H. R. A., i.e. Heretic, Raskolnik, Apostate. They were to be denied any, even the humblest, of public offices. Their evidence could not be accepted in a court of justice except as against members of their own sect. The only function of a public kind left to them was that of collecting the double tax of their fellows in misfortune. This last improvement in their position was sanctioned July 7, 1725. Already, however, in May 1722 a fresh edict had been issued against their teachers and against any who sheltered the latter; and on July 13 of the same year another forbade runaway priests, as well as Bezpopovtsy elders, to hold any sort of religious services anywhere. The children of dissenters were to be baptized by orthodox priests, while the settlers on the Vyg, who still enjoyed certain immunities because of the services they had loyally rendered to Peter I, were in 1724 forbidden to quit their residences without passports.

The reason for all these restrictions, alien to Peter's original conceptions of his duties as a ruler, is to be sought in the hostility of the holy synod, which waxed ever more intense as the propaganda of the Raskol spread. They had hoped to extirpate it by the Draconian law of Sophia. They now demanded of the Government fresh powers to hunt down and capture the malignants.

All the above regulations applied primarily to the avowed dissenters. The task of discovering the unavowed ones was now entrusted to the clergy; the maxim 'set a thief to catch a thief,' seeming no doubt to Peter thoroughly applicable. But here the Government met with difficulty. Very many of the clergy were secretly in sympathy with the Raskol, as is shewn by the constant leakage from their ranks into those of the adversary. Many more, as underpaid men with families to support, were open to bribes. It was held necessary therefore by the Synod to frame edicts against its own clergy in case they sheltered or connived at Dissent. Those who did so were liable to forfeit their orders, to undergo corporal punishment, forced labour, etc. Civil and military officials were in turn appointed to hunt out the orthodox clergy who were lax in their duty—*Quis custodiet ipsos custodes?*—and to assist them in discharging the same, in case they were loyal to their bishops. Even the landowners were found to be infected with the Raskol poison, and were made liable to capture, and to 'admonition,' as it was tenderly called, by the spiritual authorities; and if that failed of effect to punishment and exile. The punishment—according to the old trick of the Roman inquisition—was nominally levelled, not against religious opinion, but at those who opposed the civil Government, in this case the Ukases of the Tsar. Secret police were sent to Starodub, Novgorod, Nizhigorod, Livonia and elsewhere, to keep watch not only on the quasi-orthodox clergy, but upon the landed proprietors as well. Such was the legislation of Peter the Great, and it furnished a model which succeeding Governments as a rule followed only too faithfully.

We have seen that for a time the settlers on the Vyg enjoyed exemption from the double tax along with a few other privileges; but not for long, since one of the first acts of the next ruler, Catharine I, was to impose it on them in June 1726. The new Government even entertained the plan of extirpating that community and removing its members to their original homes by force. It was eventually decided however in 1732 to pass a law or ukase condemning all members of the Raskol to be interned in monasteries, there to undergo clerical 'correction.' They were by the same ukase to be taken regularly to divine service and in case of resistance to be handed over to the civil authorities and secular arm. In 1734 they were forbidden to erect chapels or oratories for themselves, and finally in 1734 under Anna Ivanovna took place the first great hunt. The Cossacks in the course of a campaign in Poland descended upon the settlement of Vetka which had till now been out of range of the Russian Government, and 40,000 of them were driven back across the frontier into the grip of the Moscovite.

Peter III to Alexander I

We now approach the second half of the XVIIIth Century, an era of greater freedom lasting from the accession of Peter III in 1750 to the end of the reign of Alexander I in 1825, seventy-five years in all. The former monarch tried to assimilate the status of the dissenters to that of cults recognized in the empire as legitimate though not orthodox. He did not live to carry out his plan, and it devolved on Catharine II to execute so sensible and humane a project. She began by issuing an edict inviting members of the Raskol who had fled across the borders in the previous reigns to return to Russia, where such orderly and industrious people could ill be spared; she promised them in return an indemnity for any wrongs they might have committed, and instead of being shorn, as together with the Jews, they had been by Peter the Great, the right was conceded to them of wearing their beards, to the disgust of the many German barbers whom Peter's legislation had furnished with remunerative jobs. Catharine also

engaged to spare them the indignity of wearing a distinctive dress not unlike that assigned by Latin Inquisitors to the victims of an auto-da-fé. Over
and above these indulgences, the returned Raskolniks were allowed to become proprietors of land, 'royal peasants,' or, if they preferred it, trades-
men and merchants. They were however condemned to continue to pay
to the Government double taxes for a period of six years. There still remained a considerable number of settlers at Vetka in Poland, and, as she
was conducting one of the perpetual campaigns against the Poles, Catharine
seized the occasion to transport thence to their old homes another 20,000
of them. This second enforced migration gave the *coup de grace* to this
once flourishing colony of Old believers. The date of the granting of these
exemptions was 1764. At the same time Raskolniks who remained confined in monasteries were liberated. Five years later they were admitted
to the witness box in legal cases; in 1782 the double tax was abolished.

Hitherto this had been levied on avowed Raskolniks, and pressure had
been used to force them to inscribe their names in the official registers, in
consequence of which and from abhorrence of the name Raskol—for they
considered themselves to be the Orthodox Church—they had concealed
their quality. There was no longer the same reason to do so and some
began even to see an advantage in being put on the register, for once they
were inscribed upon it they were exempt from the exactions which the
authorized clergy were authorized to levy upon their flocks. Not a few even
of the orthodox inscribed themselves upon the register in order to escape
these. The Government thus found itself in a dilemma; certain of the provincial governors moreover, e.g., those of Perm and Tobolsk, represented
that the retention of the double category of Raskol and Orthodox confused the census and taxation lists and made the collecting of accurate
statistics more difficult than need be. The end of it was that the Tsarina
expunged the very name Raskol from all juridical and official documents.
The Senate approved of this step, and by an ukase of 1783 the name was
discarded in ecclesiastical lists and records as also in verbal communications. The next year, 1784, the holy Synod was induced to assent to this
reform, and in 1785 the dissenters had all their disabilities removed by a
fresh ukase which admitted them to public positions in all towns and cities.
The most enlightened of all female sovereigns in Russia and perhaps the
whole world, had won, and all the oppressive regulations of Peter I were
abrogated. At the same time permission was given to the members of the
Raskol to settle in Siberia.

After Catharine's death succeeded the brief reign of Paul (Nov. 1796
to March 1801), and then Alexander came to the throne, a man of liberal
and humane instincts. His policy towards the Raskol however was a perpetual seesaw, according as his native disposition or the sleepless hatred
of the orthodox prelates prevailed. Even under Catharine the law against
orthodox popes who joined the Raskol was maintained in all its severity,
and ukases of November 1765 and January 1776 condemned them to
ecclesiastical degradation and deprivation of their orders, and it was not
safe for them to appear in public in their true colours. At the beginning of

Alexander's reign, although the laws were not changed, the Government shewed itself more indulgent; and in many places, e.g. gorodets in the Nizhegorod Government and at Starodub, they were in 1803 openly discharging their spiritual offices. Nine years later however the Synod interfered to prevent the Popovtsy of the village of Uvanov in the Vladimirski Government from employing them, and their veto was upheld by Alexander in February 1812. Later on, in March 1822, the Sovereign crowned his inconsistencies by sanctioning the use of runaway popes in case they had been guilty of no crime and were not quitting the church in order to evade the consequences of their actions. The prelates expostulated against such mildness, but this time in vain.

The right of having their own chapels and oratories was conceded or denied under Alexander to the Raskol with similar waverings. Before Catharine II had finally lightened their yoke, the old laws forbidding them to have places of worship of their own had been reaffirmed in ukases of July 1769 and April 1778. Subsequently, it is true, the Government winked at their existence and the law was not carried out. In one case (1817) the cupola of a church would be pulled down, but the rest of it left intact. In other cases the raising of a church was allowed, but the right to hold services in it denied. It was a real triumph, however, for the Raskol in Moscow when in 1809 the legality of their Transfiguration Cemetery was upheld, and when the Minister of the Interior authorized the rebuilding of churches in the Vyatka Government and in the district of Sarapul. The Holy Synod of course fumed at the least show of tolerance, and appealed to the ukase of 1803 which, while disclaiming any desire to violate men's consciences, forbade any open exhibitions of apostasy; and in 1816 they managed to get the chapels in Fatezh in the Government of Kursk destroyed, especially any that presumed to have a bell. In 1817 the Tsar issued instructions to local authorities to forbid the erection of chapels. In 1822 a fresh edict allowed old structures to remain, but forbade the raising of new ones.

Under Alexander's régime the open celebration of their rites was also winked at, and the Raskol were freely allowed to baptize and to bury their dead until 1818, in some cases even to ring a bell to summon the faithful to worship. But stronger measures were enforced in 1820, especially against Raskol propaganda. Any public manifestation of their religion, even the conducting of a burial by a priest attired in canonicals, was forbidden in 1824. They might bury their dead, but without hymns or candles.

The Growth of Serfdom

The author of the following selection was Professor of Public Law in the University of Moscow in the late nineteenth century. He was deprived of that post by the government, despite his distinction as a scholar, on the ground that he was politically unreliable. He later was active in the Constitutional Democratic Party.

Economic serfdom was already established in Russia by the Time of Troubles, but legal serfdom did not come into existence until the Code of 1649. In the following selection, Professor Kovalevsky sketches the origins and growth of the institution. The source is: M. Kovalevsky, *Modern Customs and Ancient Laws of Russia (Being the Ilchester Lectures for 1889–90)*. London, 1891. Pp. 209–219. Slightly abridged.

An account of the origin, growth, and abolition of serfdom in Russia might easily be made to fill volumes, so vast and so various are the materials on which the study of it is based. But for the purpose now in view, that of bringing before your notice the general conclusion to which Russian historians and legists have come as to the social development of their country, perhaps a single lecture will suffice. In it I cannot pretend to do more than present to you those aspects of the subject on which the minds of Russian scholars have been specially fixed of late years.

Among the first to be considered is the origin of that system of personal servitude and bondage to the land in which the Russian peasant lived for centuries. An opinion long prevailed that this system was due solely to the action of the State, which, at the end of the sixteenth century, abolished the freedom of migration previously enjoyed by the Russian peasant and bound him for ever to the soil. This opinion, which would have made Russian serfdom an institution quite apart from that of the serfdom of the Western States of Europe, has been happily abandoned, and consequently its development becomes the more interesting, in so far as it discloses the action of those economic and social forces which produced the personal and real servitude of the so-called villein all over Europe.

The first point to which I desire to call your attention is the social freedom enjoyed by the Russian peasant in the earlier portion of mediaeval history. The peasant, then known by the name of *smerd*—from the verb *smerdet,* to have a bad smell—was as free to dispose of his person and property. He had the right to appear as a witness in Courts of Justice, both in civil and in criminal actions; he enjoyed the right of inheriting—a right, however, which was somewhat limited by the prevalence of family communism—and no one could prevent him from engaging his services to any landlord for as many years as he liked, and on terms settled by contract. Lack of means to buy a plough and the cattle which he needed for tilling the ground very often led the free peasant to get them from his landlord on condition that every year he ploughed and harrowed the fields of his creditor. It is in this way that an economic dependence was first established between two persons equally free, equally in possession of the soil, but disposing the one of a larger, the other of a smaller capital. The name under which the voluntary serf is known to the Pravda, the first legal code of Russia, is that of *roleine zakoup;* this term signifies a person who has borrowed money on condition of performing the work of ploughing (ralo means the plough) so long as debt remains unpaid.

The frequent want of the simplest agricultural implements, was also probably the chief cause, which induced more than one Russian peasant to prefer the condition of a sort of [share-cropper], whose rent, paid in kind, amounts to a fixed proportion of the yearly produce, to that of a free shareholder in the open fields and village common. The prevalence in ancient Russia of the same rude and elementary mode of farming is established by numerous charters and contracts, some of which are as late as the end of the seventeenth century, whilst others go back to the beginning of the sixteenth. It would appear that previous to that date such contracts were not put into writing, apparently on account of the small diffusion of knowledge. We are therefore reduced to the necessity of presuming the existence of these contracts solely because the intrinsic causes which brought them into existence in the sixteenth century had been in operation for hundreds of years before. The peasant, on entering into such a contract, took upon himself the obligation of paying back in the course of time the money which had been lent to him—the *serebro,* silver, according to the expression used in contemporary documents. From the name of the capital intrusted to them (the serebro) arose the surname of *serebrenik,* which may be translated silver-men, under which peasants settled on a manor were generally known; their other being *polovnik,* or men paying half of their yearly produce to the lord, although as a rule their payments did not amount to more than a quarter. So long as his debt remained unpaid the share-cropper was obliged to remunerate the landlord by villein service performed on the demesne lands of the manor. According to the German writer Herberstein, who visited Russia in the seventeenth century, the agricultural labour which the serebrenik performed for the lord very often amounted each week to a six-days' service, at any rate in summer. Contracts still preserved also speak of other obligations of the serebrenik. Such, for instance, were the obligations of cutting wood and of forwarding it on their own carts to the manor-house, and of paying certain dues on the occasion of the marriage of the peasant's daughter. Custom also required the peasant to make certain presents to his lord at Christmas and Easter, or at some other yearly festival, such for instance as that of the Assumption of the Blessed Virgin.

The peasant who chose to settle on the land of a manorial lord got the grant of a homestead in addition to that of land, and this was the origin of a sort of house-rent called the *projivnoe,* which as a rule amounted yearly to the fourth part of the value of the homestead.

As to the land ceded by the landlord to the settler who wished to live on his manor, its use became the origin of another special payment, the *obrok,* which represented a definite amount of agricultural produce. The obrok was often replaced by the obligation of doing certain fixed agricultural labour on the demesne land of the manor.

As soon as the peasant had repaid the money borrowed from the manorial lord, and had discharged all the payments required from him for the use of his land and homestead, he was authorized by custom to remove wherever he liked, of course giving up to the squire his house and his share in the open fields of the manor. At first this right of removal could be exercised at any period of the year, but this being found prejudicial to the agricultural interests of the country certain fixed periods were soon established, at which alone such a removal was allowed. Usually the end of harvest was fixed as the time when new arrangements could be entered into with regard to future agricultural labour without causing any loss to the interests of the landlord. Not only in autumn, however, but also in spring, soon after Easter, manorial lords where in the habit of permitting the establishment of new settlers on their estates, and the withdrawal of those peasants who expressed a desire to leave.

The first *Sudebnik,* the legal code published by Ivan III, in 1497, speaks of the festival of Saint George, which according to the Russian calendar falls on the 26th of November, as a period at which all removals ought to take place. Those peasants who had not been fortunate enough to free themselves from all obligations to the manor by this period were obliged to remain another year on its lands; he who was unable to repay the lord the sum borrowed was reduced to the same condition as that of the insolvent farmers of the Roman ager publicus, who, according to Fustel de Coulanges, saw their arrears of debt changed into a perpetual rent called the canon, and their liberty of migration superseded by a state of continual bondage to the land they cultivated. No Russian historian has shown the analogy existing between the origin of the Roman colonatus and that of Russian serfdom so clearly as Mr. Kluchevsky, the eminent professor of Russian history in the University of Moscow. It is to him that we are indebted for the discovery of the fact that centuries before the legal and general abolition of the right of free migration a considerable number of peasants had thus ceased to enjoy that liberty. Such was the case of those so-called "silver-men from the oldest times," (viz., *starinnii sere-brenniki*) who during the sixteenth century were already deprived of the right of free removal from no other cause but the want of money, so that the only condition on which they could withdraw from the manor on which they were was that of finding some other landlord willing to pay the money they owed, and thereby acquiring the right to remove them to his own manor.

So long as the Russian power was geographically limited to the posses- sion of the central provinces in the immediate neighbourhood of Moscow, and so long as the shores of the Volga and Dnieper suffered from almost periodical invasions of the Tartars, the Russian peasant who might wish to leave a manor could not easily have procured the land he required; but when the conquests of Ivan III, and Ivan the Terrible had reduced to naught the power of the Tartars, and had extended the Russian possessions both to the East and to South, the peasants were seized with a spirit of migration, and legislation was required to put a stop to the economic in- security created by their continual withdrawal from the manors of Inner Russia to the Southern and Eastern steppes. It is, therefore, easy to under- stand why laws to prevent the possibility of a return of peasant migration were first passed, at least on a general scale, at this period. It is no doubt true that, even at the end of the fifteenth century, to certain monasteries were granted, among other privileges, that of being free from the liability of having their peasants removed to the estates of other landlords. A charter of the year 1478 recognises such a privilege as belonging to the monks of the monastery of Troitzko-Sergievsk, which is, according to popular belief, one of the most sacred places in Russia. The financial interests of the State also contributed greatly to the change. The fact that the taxpayer was tied to the soil rendered the collection of taxes both speedier and more exact. These two causes sufficiently explain why, by the end of the sixteenth century, the removal of peasants from manor to manor had become very rare.

The system of land endowments in favour of the higher clergy and monasteries, and also of persons belonging to the knightly class, had increased to such an extent that, according to modern calculation, two-thirds of the cultivated area was already the property either of ecclesiastics or of secular grandees. It is therefore easy to understand why, during the sixteenth century, the migratory state of the Russian agricultural population came to be considered as a real danger to the State by the higher classes of Russian society. The most powerful of the nobles and gentry did their best to retain the peasants on their lands. Some went even farther, and by alleviating the burdens of villein-service, and securing a more efficent protection for them from administrative oppression, induced the peasants who inhabited the lands of smaller squires to leave their old homes and settle on their manors. It was in order to protect the small landowners from this sort of oppression that Boris Gudonov, the all-powerful ruler of Russia in the reign of Theodor Ivanovitch, promulgated a law, according to which every one was authorised to insist on the return of a peasant who left his abode, and that during the five years next following his departure. This law was promulgated in 1597. As no mention is made in it of the right previously enjoyed by the peasants of removing from one manor to another on St. George's Day, this law of 1597 has been considered by historians as the direct cause of the introduction of the so-called "bondage to the soil" (*krepostnoie pravo*). Such was certainly not its object. The right of migration on the Day of St. George was openly acknowledged by the laws of 1601 and 1602. The bondage of the peasant to the soil became an established fact only in the year 1649, when the new code of law, the so-called Ulozhenie, refused to any one the right to receive on his lands the peasant who should run away from a manor, and abolished that limit of time beyond which the landlord lost the right to reclaim the peasant who had removed from his ancient dwelling.

The number of serfs rapidly increased during the second half of the seventeenth and the eighteenth centuries, owing to the prodigality with which the Czars and Emperors endowed the members of the official class with lands, in disregard often of the previous occupation by free village communities, the members of which were forced to become the serfs of the persons who received the grant. It is in this way that Catherine II., for instance, during the thirty-four years of her reign, increased the number of serfs by 800,000 new ones, and that Paul I., in a period of four years added 600,000 to the number, which was already enormous.

Before the reign of Catherine, serfdom was almost unknown in Little Russia, where it had been abolished by Bogdan Chmelnitzky, soon after the separation of Little Russia from Poland, and in the Ukraine (the modern Government of Kharkov), where it had never before existed. In 1788 she revoked the right hitherto enjoyed by the peasants of these two provinces to remove from one manor to another. The same right of free removal was abolished a few years later in the "Land of the Don Kossacks" and among the peasants of the Southern Governments, called New Russia (Novorossia).

Class War: Bolotnikov's Rebellion

During the Time of Troubles, Ivan Bolotnikov led a rising of the unprivileged and underprivileged against the tsar and the richer boyars. This was a real class war of the "have-nots" against the "haves" and Soviet historians have not failed to emphasize the incident. The following account with its Marxist-Leninist explanation of Bolotnikov's failure is from a Soviet textbook. The source is: A. V. Shestakov (Ed.), *A Short History of the USSR.* Moscow, 1938. Pp. 55–56.

IVAN BOLOTNIKOV, THE PEASANTS' LEADER. The peasant revolt continued under the reign of Shuisky. At this time an energetic leader named Ivan Bolotnikov rose among the peasants. Bolotnikov had formerly been a serf to one of the boyars and had fled from him. He had been to Turkey and Italy, and had seen a great deal. He was a gifted military leader, and the peasants, minor serving men and Cossacks rallied to him in large numbers. He collected an army in the south, and in 1606 marched on Moscow to overthrow the boyar tsar, Vasili Shuisky, and to put a "good" tsar in his place.

In the towns and villages along the line of march the rebels captured the tsar's officials, exterminated the boyars and pomeshchiks, laid waste to their estates and destroyed the houses of the rich merchants. Detachments of small landowners, who were discontented with the tyranny of the boyars and with the boyar tsar, Shuisky, also joined Bolotnikov's army.

Bolotnikov laid siege to Moscow. The small landowners who had joined Bolotnikov soon realized that his victory would weaken the power of the landlords. During a battle outside of Moscow these landlord detachments betrayed Bolotnikov and deserted to the side of the boyars and Tsar Shuisky. Bolotnikov's army was defeated.

Bolotnikov retreated, first to Kaluga and then to Tula, in order to prepare for another attack on Moscow. Shuisky with a large army besieged Bolotnikov in Tula. The rebel army defended itself heroically, but suffered defeat. This is not surprising. The peasants at that time had no such ally and leader as the working class. Besides, the peasants themselves lacked political consciousness. They did not fight againt tsarism and landlordism, but against the bad tsar and the bad landlords. They wanted a "good" tsar and "good" landlords.

In the winter of 1607 Ivan Bolotnikov was taken prisoner by the Boyars. They put out his eyes and then took him to the river and drowned him in a hole in the ice. The conditions of the defeated peasantry became still worse. Shuisky issued new decrees increasing the state of bondage of the serfs. These decrees gave the landlords the right to search for and bring back fugitive peasants for a period of fifteen years from the time of their escape. The peasant revolts continued.

Revolts in the Towns

The following selection is also from Shestakov, *Short History*, pp. 59–61.

After the death of Tsar Michael Romanov, his son Alexei become tsar of Muscovy. By his order a heavy salt tax was introduced in 1646. This tax roused the anger of the people. Fearing a rebellion, Tsar Alexei repealed the tax. But the tax was not the only trouble. Even after it was repealed the people of Moscow rose against their oppressors. In 1648 the people of Moscow caused a "riot," as popular rebellions were called at that time. The people well remembered the wrongs inflicted upon them by the tsar's servants and officials. They demanded that the chief of these officials be surrendered to them for punishment.

The tsar promised to fulfill the demands of the rebels, but he sent his horsemen against them, who beat them with whips and trampled upon them with their horses. Then the crowds of people wrecked the houses of the most hated of the boyars and tsarist officials and killed a number of them. The rebellion was crushed by the tsar's troops. In that year, 1648, rebellions in other towns were also crushed. After this, the tsar assembled the representatives of the boyars, landlords and merchants in what was known as the Zemsky Sobor. In 1649 they passed a law granting the landlords the right to search for and bring back fugitive peasants no matter how long since they had escaped. The peasants were made complete serfs. A census was taken of all villages and peasant households. It became very difficult for a fugitive peasant to hide anywhere. At that time, also, handicraftsmen and small traders were forbidden to move from one town to another without permission.

In the towns the handicraftsmen lived in special districts called *slobodas,* according to their occupation. For example, there was a Tanners' Sloboda, Potters' Sloboda, Gunsmiths' Sloboda, etc. There were many such slobodas in Moscow, which was the largest city in the country. The narrow crooked streets of these slobodas in Moscow were lined with small houses with two or three tiny windows.

The handicraftsmen earned little. Their lives were very hard; they were robbed by the voyevodas and merchants.

The revolts of the handicraftsmen and town poor continued. These revolts assumed particularly large dimensions in Pskov and Novgorod in

1650. They were joined by the peasants. Tsar Alexei had to send a large army to suppress the revolts.

The town poor rose in rebellion also in subsequent years. For example, a great revolt broke out in Moscow in 1662. In suppressing this revolt the tsar's soldiers killed and drowned in the River Moscow several thousand rebels.

Russia, Poland, and Ukraine

The word "Ukraine" is derived from the phrase "ot kraina" which means "at the border" and the lands so designated were literally at the borders of both Russia and Poland. A bitter struggle for the control of these borderlands has gone on for centuries. One of the great heroes of Ukrainian national history is the Cossack Bogdan Khmelnitski who led a revolt against the Poles in the mid–seventeenth century. Russia was soon involved and Khmelnitski's movement, ironically, led directly to the annexation of Ukraine by Russia.

The two stories of this which follow offer a contrast in both style and interpretation. The shorter is from Shestakov, *Short History*, pp. 62–64 and is an example of Soviet historiography. The source of the longer and more balanced account is: Alfred Rambaud (L. D. Lang, Tr.), *Russia*. Two volumes. New York: F. P. Collier & Sons, 1902. Vol. 1, pp. 274–282.

Beginning with the 13th century the Ukraine gradually passed under the yoke of the Polish and Lithuanian pans. The latter transformed all the peasants into serfs. Even slight offences by their serfs they punished with death. In some of the Polish manors permanent gallows were erected. The Poles forcibly compelled the Ukrainian people to adopt their religion.

In Poland, and in Byelorussia, too, the peasants groaned under the tyranny of the pans. The serfs fled from the pans to the Dnieper, where they built small fortifications below the Rapids and called the place *Zaporozhskaya Sech,* or the Zaporozhye Cossacks. In other places, in the Ukrainian towns and villages, lived the town Cossacks. The town Cossacks as well as the Zaporozhye Cossacks were organized in regiments. Their chiefs were elected by the Cossacks. These chiefs were called hetmans.

The peasants and Cossacks frequently rose in rebellion against the Polish rulers. Even the rich Cossacks were discontented with the Poles because they robbed the land, and because of their oppression.

In 1648 a great rebellion of Cossacks and peasants broke out against the Poles. This rebellion was led by a rich town Cossack named Bogdan Khmelnitsky.

Bogdan Khmelnitsky sent his people disguised as beggars and monks to the villages of the Ukraine to rouse the peasants for the struggle against the pans. Soon the peasants rose in rebellion in all parts of the Ukraine and Byelorussia. The rebels began to wreck the mansions of the pans. The latter were compelled to split up their forces in order to fight

Khmelnitsky and the rebel peasants. Khmelnitsky succeeded in defeating the Polish troops and in capturing their chief leaders.

The news of Khmelnitsky's victories rapidly spread throughout the Ukraine, Byelorussia and Poland. The peasants rallied to Khmelnitsky's standard in large masses. One of the most outstanding of the peasant leaders was Maxim Krivonos. Khmelnitsky, however, did not want to give the peasants freedom. He himself was a landlord and owned serfs. He started negotiations with the Poles and concluded a treaty with them which granted many concessions to the Cossacks. The Poles promised to pay the Cossacks regular salaries, to supply them with arms, and not to deprive them of their liberties.

The Polish pans deceived Khmelnitsky, however, and failed to carry out their promises. Then Khmelnitsky went to war against the Poles again.

There seemed to be no prospect of the war coming to an end. The Poles were devastating the country. In order to extricate himself from his difficult position, Khmelnitsky, in 1654, concluded a treaty with Tsar Alexei of Moscow, who professed the same religion as he. In accordance with the treaty Ukraine became subject to Russia. The Cossack elders received the rights which formerly they had tried to obtain from Poland. The peasants of the Ukraine were released from the oppression of the pans. No one was now forcing an alien religion upon them. But the fact that the Ukraine was joined to Russia did not free the toilers of the Ukraine from the oppression of their elders and hetmans.

To assist Khmelnitsky, the tsar made war upon Poland. The war ended with the annexation by Russia of all the lands on the left bank of the Dnieper and of the city of Kiev.

* * * * *

We have seen that Little Russia [Ukraine], after many partial risings, only awaited a chief to break out into a general insurrection. This chief was found in Bogdan Khmelnitski,—a brave, clever, energetic, and even educated Cossack. He was owner of Soubbotovo, near Tchigirine, and had been illtreated and imprisoned by one of his neighbors, the Pole Tchaplinski, who also seized on Khmelnitski's son, a boy of ten years, and had him whipped in the public streets by his men. Khmelnitski could obtain no redress, either for himself or for his countrymen, against the Jews and the taxes. King Vladislas is said to have told him that the senators would not obey him, and, drawing a sword on paper, he handed it to Bogdan, observing, "This is the sign royal: if you have arms at your sides, resist those who insult and rob you; revenge your wrongs with your swords, and when the time comes you will help me against the pagans and the rebels of my kingdom." In the Polish anarchy of that date it is quite possible that the king may have held this language, and himself placed the sword in the hands of those whom he could not protect. Vladislas acknowledged Bogdan ataman of the Zaporogues, and in return Bogdan promised him the following year a body of 12,000 men.

Konetspolski, the gonfalonier of the Crown, and Potocki, tried to get rid of Bogdan, but he fled to the Zaporogues, and then passed over to the Khan of the Crimea, and returned to the heroes of the Dnieper with a Mussulman army. To Tatars and Zaporogues were soon added all the malcontents of Little Russia. Cossacks and people were alike determined to finish with it. Bogdan defeated the Polish generals Potocki and Kalinovski; first at the "Yellow Waters," where the registered Cossacks abandoned the Polish banners after having stabbed their hetman Barabbas, and then at Korsoun, where the Poles lost 8000 men and 41 guns. The two generals fell into the hands of Bogdan, who delivered them to the Khan of the Crimea. This double victory was the signal of a general insurrection. The orthodox clergy everywhere preached a crusade against the Jesuits and Uniates, and everywhere the peasants rose against the Polish or Polonized *pans*. The castles were demolished, the governors put to death. The Jews were in a sad strait. According to a popular song they only asked one thing —to be allowed "to escape in their shirts beyond the Vistula, abandoning their wealth to the Cossacks, and promising to teach their children to live honestly, and to covet no more the land of the Ukraine" (1648).

At this critical moment for Poland, King Vladislas died, and the Diet met at Warsaw for the new election, with all its accustomed turbulence. At this news the revolt in Little Russia increased. Wherever the nobles could defend themselves they gave back cruelty for cruelty. Jeremiah Vichne-vetski, a powerful Polonized Russian lord, took a town belonging to him by assault, and exercised the most horrible reprisals. "Make them suffer," he cried to the executioners, "they must be made to feel death;" and his Cossack prisoners were impaled. The Cossacks, who in the absence of a king expected justice from no one, broke out more violently than ever. Khmelnitsky pursued his course of success; he defeated the Poles near Pilava, and penetrated into Gallicia as far as Lemberg, a rich, half-Jewish city, which had to pay a war indemnity. He was besieging Podmostié when he learned that John Casimir was elected in the place of his brother Vladislas. The new king at once sent envoys to negotiate his submission. The commissioners promised him satisfaction for his own grievances and those of the Cossacks on condition that the insurgents were abandoned to them. "Let the peasants return to their ploughs, and the Cossacks alone bear arms," said the Poles. Bogdan could neither abandon the Cossacks, who would not hear of the register, nor the country people, whose revolt had given him the victory, to be again placed, as was proposed, under the yoke of the *pans*. "The time for negotiations is past," he said to the commissioners; "I must free the whole Russian nation from the yoke of the Poles. At first I took up arms for my own injuries—now I fight for the true faith. The people will stand by me as far as Lublin, as far as Cracow; I will not betray them." The war continued, and Bogdan summoned the Khan of the Crimea to his aid, and marched to meet the Polish army, commanded by the king in person. John Casimir found himself at Zborovo surrounded by the innumerable cavalry of the enemy. It would have been all over with him had he not purchased the defection of the Khan of the Crimea by a large sum, and the promise of an annual tribute. The Khan

then retired, recommending his ally to the clemency of the king. Khmelnitski was driven to treat; the register was re-established, but the number of
Cossacks enrolled was raised to 40,000; Bogdan was recognized hetman of
Little Russia, and the town of Tchigirine assigned to him as a residence. It
was agreed that there should be neither Crown troops nor Jews in the
localities inhabited by the Cossacks, and no Jesuits where orthodox schools
existed. The Metropolitan of Kief was to have a seat in the senate of
Warsaw.

What Bogdan had foreseen when he refused to treat really happened;
the treaty could not be executed. The number of fighting men who had
taken part in the election exceeded 40,000—were those in excess to be
relegated to the work of the fields, to the seignorial *corvée?* The people
had helped the Cossacks, were they then to be surrendered to their *pans?*
Bogdan soon found himself involved in inextricable difficulties: on one
side he violated the treaty by enrolling more than 40,000 men in his
register; on the other hand, if he executed it, he would have to begin by
inflicting death on the rebels. He wore out his popularity in performing this
ungrateful task. He preferred to take up arms, accusing the Poles of having
broken certain clauses of the treaty. This war was less successful than the
first; the Khan of the Crimea, who a second time came to the aid of the
Cossacks, a second time betrayed them, and the Cossacks were beaten at
Berestechtko. The conditions of the Peace of the White Church (*Belaïa
Tcherkof*) were more severe than those of the first peace. The number of
registered Cossacks was reduced to 20,000; and 20,000 more, thus finding
themselves excluded from the army, were thrown back upon the people.
The greater part chose rather to emigrate to Russian soil, to wander to the
Don, or to live by brigandage on the Volga.

A peace such as this was only a truce, and the Cossacks were certain to
break it as soon as they could find an ally. Bogdan wrote to entreat the
Tzar to take Little Russia under his protection. The Government of Alexis
had sought for some time a pretext for rupture with Poland. The Polish
Government, in writing to the Tzar, had not used the full royal title. Moscow never missed an opportunity for remonstrance; Warsaw assured them
that it was pure inadvertence. "Then," said the Russians, "an example
must be made of the guilty." No example was made, and the diminution of
title was used at every interchange of notes. The Court of Russia kept up
this *casus belli,* waiting for a moment to profit by it; this was found in the
appeal of Khmelnitsky. The Estates were convoked, and to them were reported the repeated insults to his Tzarian Majesty, and the persecution of
the true faith in Little Russia. It was added, that the Little Russians, if repulsed by the Tzar, would have to place themselves under the protection
of the Sultan. On this occasion the Estates declared for war. Alexis sent the
boyard Boutourline to receive the oath of the hetman, the army, and the
people of Little Russia.

It was time that the Tzar decided. Bogdan, betrayed a third time by the
Khan, had been defeated at Ivanetz on the Dniester, but on the receipt of
the news from Moscow he called the General Assembly at Peréiaslavl to

announce to them the fact. "Noble colonels; *esauls,* and centurions, and you army of Zaporogues, and you orthodox Christians," cried the hetman, "you see it is no longer possible to live without a prince. Now we have four to choose from: the Sultan of Turkey, the Khan of the Crimea, the King of Poland, and the Tzar of orthodox Great Russia, whom for six years we have not ceased to entreat to become our Tzar and lord. The Sultan is a Mussulman; we know what our brethren the orthodox Greeks suffered at his hands. The Khan is also a Mussulman, and our alliances with him have brought us nothing but trouble. It is needless to remind you of what the Polish *pans* have made us endure. But the Christian and orthodox Tzar is of the same religion as ourselves. We shall not find a better support than his. Whoever thinks otherwise may go where he likes—the way is open." The air rang with applause, the oath demanded by Boutourline was taken, and an embassy set out for Moscow, to ask the maintenance of Ukrainian liberties. The Tzar freely granted all their conditions: the army was to be raised permanently to the number of 60,000; the Cossacks were to elect their hetman; the rights of the *schliachta* and the towns were to be maintained; the administration of the towns and the imposition of taxes were to be entrusted to the natives; the hetman was to have the right of receiving foreign ambassadors, but was to signify the fact to the Tzar; and he was forbidden, without special leave, to receive the envoys of Turkey and Poland.

In May 1654 the Tzar Alexis solemnly announced in the *Ouspienski Sobor* that he had resolved to march in person against his enemy the King of Poland. He commanded that in this campaign no occasion should be given for the generals to dispute precedence. The Polish voïevodes affirm that on this occasion "Moscow made war in quite a new way, and conquered the people by the clemency and gentleness of the Tzar." This humanity, so well timed in a war of deliverance, contributed greatly to the success of the Muscovites. Polotsk, Mohilef, and all the towns of White Russia opened their gates one after the other, and Smolensk only resisted five weeks (1654). The following year the Prince Tcherkasski defeated the hetman Radziwell and began the conquest of Lithuania proper; Wilna, the capital, Grodno, and Kobno, fell successively. During this time Khmelnitski and the Muscovites invaded Southern Poland and took Lublin. All the East resounded with the Russian victories: it was said at Moscow that the Greeks prayed for the Tzar and refused obedience to any but an orthodox emperor, and that the Hospodars of Wallachia and Moldavia implored Alexis to take them under his protection.

Poland seemed reduced to the last extremity; and there was still a third enemy to fall on her. Charles X., King of Sweden, arrived and captured Posen, Warsaw, and Cracow, the three Polish capitals. This conflict of ambition was, however, the salvation of the *pospolite;* the Swede threatened the Russian conquests, and claimed Lithuania. He entered into relations with Khmelnitski, who forgot the oath he had taken; it was Charles XII, and Mazeppa enacted half a century before. The Tzar Alexis feared he had only shaken Poland to strengthen Sweden, and would not risk the reunion of these two formidable monarchies under the same sceptre. He hastened to negotiate with the Poles, who promised to elect him after the death of their present king; then he turned his arms against Sweden. The latter was the heir on the Baltic of the Livonian Order. Alexis trod in the steps of Ivan the Terrible; like him, his successes were rapid, but they as rapidly evaporated in smoke. He took Dünaburg and Kokenhusen, two old castles of the Knights; but the Russians besieged Riga in vain, and succeeded no better at Oréchek or Kexholm. The occupation of Dorpat terminated the first campaign (1656); after that, hostilities languished, and Alexis concluded a truce of twenty years, which secured him Dorpat and a part of his conquests. The affairs of Poland and Little Russia became, however, so terribly complicated, that the truce became the Peace of Cardis, by which Alexis abandoned all Livonia (1661).

The hetman Khmelnitski had more than once given his new sovereign cause for discontent. In spite of his oath, he had negotiated with Sweden and Poland. In fact, now that he had got rid of his former master, he did not want to become the vassal of a new sovereign, but to create a third Slav State between Poland and Russia, and to remain its independent sovereign. This hope was shared by the Cossacks. They had revolted against Poland because the king was weak and could not make himself respected by the aristocracy; they feared the Tzar of Muscovy would be only too strong. All government, all authority, was a burden to the free Cossack.

Bogdan, however, kept up the appearances of submission. His death was the signal of disorder. Vygovski, chancellor of the Cossack army, took the mace of the hetman, but Martin Pouchkar, the *polkovnik* of Pultowa, and the Zaporogues, refused to recognize him. Vygovski, Pouchkar, and the Zaporogue ataman denounced each other at Moscow. Vygovski caused Pouchkar to be assassinated, and made advances to Poland, to secure himself an ally against the Tzar; he also applied to the Khan of the Crimea, and defeated Prince Troubetskoï at Konotop; but after the retreat of the Khan, the majority of the Cossacks declared for Moscow, and obliged the rebel to fly to Poland. George Khmelnitski, son of the liberator, was elected hetman.

The troubles of Little Russia revived the courage of the Poles. They succeeded in expelling the Swedes, and refused to execute the treaty of Moscow. The war recommenced, and the Russinas were unfortunate. The very extremity of their misfortunes seemed to have bound the Poles together. After some slight successes, one Russian army was defeated at Polonka by the voïevode Tcharnetski, the conqueror of the Swedes; another, commanded by the boyard Cheremetief and the hetman George Khmelnitski, allowed itself to be surrounded near Tchoudnovo by the Tatars and Poles, and being deserted by the Cossacks, was forced to lay down its arms. In the north they lost Wilna and the whole of Lithuania.

Khmelnitski, had become a monk. Teteria, his successor, had done homage to the king; but the country on the left bank of the Dnieper refused to recognize him as hetman, and elected Brioukhovetski, who was devoted to Russia. John Casimir crossed the river, and was on the point of reconquering the whole Ukraine; but having been repulsed at the siege of Gloukhof, he lost all his best troops through hunger and cold in the steppes of the desert. The two empires were exhausted by a war which had already lasted ten years. The whole of Poland had been overrun by Swedes, Russians, and Cossacks. Russia had no longer money with which to pay her army, and she had recourse to a forced currency, by which a bronze coinage was given the fictitious value of silver. Everywhere were heard bitter complaints of the famine. At Moscow a riot broke out against the Miloslavskis, the kinsmen of the Tzarina, and the multitude marched to the palace of Kolomenskoé to drag them out by force. The soldiers had to fire on the rebels, and 7000 of them were killed or taken.

Notwithstanding all this, neither the Poles nor the Russians would lay down arms without being assured the possession of all that they had conquered with so many sacrifices. Poland was now attacked by two new misfortunes—the revolt of Prince Lubomirski, who had some grievance against the queen, and the death of Teteria, whose successor, Dorochenko, went over to the Sultan, and by so doing involved the Government in a war with both Turks and Tatars. It was necessary to treat with Russia, and a thirteen years' truce was concluded at Androussovo. Alexis renounced Lithuania, but kept Smolensk and Kief on the right bank of the Dnieper, and all the Little Russian left bank (1667).

The treaty with Poland did not give peace to Little Russia. Neither the Dnieper Cossacks nor the Don Cossacks could exist under the obedience and regularity essential to a modern State. The more Russia became civilized and centralized, the more she became separated from the men of the Steppe; the further the frontier of this civilized Russia advanced to the South, the nearer approached the inevitable conflict. The reign of Alexis, troubled at first by the revolts of the Muscovite cities, was now vexed by the revolts of the Cossacks.

The hetman Brioukhovetski was a devoted adherent of Russia, but he was surrounded by many malcontents. As usual, the people had not got all they had hoped by the revolution; he saw, however, in the absolute authority of the Tzar, a bulwark against the Little Russian oligarchy of the *starchina* and the *polkovniks,* and against the turbulence of the Cossacks. "God," he said to the latter, "has delivered us from you; you can no longer pillage and devastate our houses." The Cossacks and the *starchina,* or in other words, the military and aristocratic party, were still more displeased to see the Muscovite voïevodes establish themselves in the towns. The Republic of the Zaporogues already feared that it had given itself a master. Methodius, Metropolitan of Kief, encouraged the resistance of a party of the clergy who wished to remain subject to the Patriarch of Constantinople, and not to be transferred to the Patriarch of Moscow. It was Methodius who organized the rebellion; he made advances to the hetman, who opened a negotiation with Dorochenko, the ataman of the right bank, who promised to resign his office and to recognise as chief of Little Russia the man who would deliver her. The weak Brioukhovetski allowed himself to be persuaded, and at the Assembly of Gadatch, in 1668, it was decided to revolt against the Tzar, and to take the oath to the Sultan, as the men of the right bank had already done. Two voïevodes and 120 Muscovites were put to death. A short time after, Brioukhovetski was slain by order of Dorochenko, who became hetman of both banks. But of the two parties which divided Little Russia, the party of independence of the Polish and Turkish Party, and the party of Moscow, the latter was predominant on the left bank. It did not hesitate to make terms with the Tzar, and, at the price of a few concessions, a second time submitted to him entirely. Mnogogrechnyi, the new hetman, took up his abode at Batourine.

The right bank had no reason to pride itself on the policy to which it was committed by Dorochenko. It became the theatre of a terrible war between Turkey and Poland, and was cruelly ravaged by Mahomet IV. Abandoned for a moment by the weak King Michael Vichnevetski, it was conquered by his energetic successor, John Sobieski. The left, or Muscovite bank, had less to suffer, although the Sultan claimed it equally as his own possession, but the inhabitants had only to fight with their old enemies the Tatars.

Razin's Rebellion

The third major revolt of the seventeenth century was that of Stepan (Stenko) Razin. The first excerpt is from Rambaud, *Russia,* vol. 1, pp. 281–282. The second is from Shestakov, *Short History,* pp. 64–66.

The Cossacks of the Don at this period were, on the whole, tolerably quiet; but one of their number, Stenko Razine, overturned all Eastern Russia. The immigration of Cossacks of the Dnieper, expelled from their native land by war, had created a great famine in these poor plains of the Don. Stenko assembled some of these starved adventurers, and formed a scheme for the capture of Azof; but on being hindered by the *starchina* of the Dontsi, he turned towards the East, towards the Volga and the Jaïk (Oural). His reputation was wide-spread; he was said to be a magician, against whom neither sabre, balls, nor bullets could prevail, and the brigands of all the country crowded to his banner. He swept the Caspian, and ravaged the shores of Persia. The Russian Government, powerless to crush him, offered him a pardon if he would surrender his guns and boats stolen from the Crown. He accepted the offer; but his exploits, his wealth acquired by pillage, and his princely liberality created him an immense party among the lower classes, and among the Cossacks and even the *streltsi* of the towns. The lands of the Volga were always ready for a social revolution, hence the success of Razine, and later of Pougatchef. There brigands were popular and respected; honest merchants, come to the Don for trading purposes, and learning that Stenko had begun the career of a pirate, did not hesitate to join him.

In 1670, Stenko having spent all the money he had gained by pillage, went up the Don with an army of vagabonds, and thence crossed to the Volga. All the country rose on the approach of a chief already so famous. The inhabitants of Tzaritsyne opened their gates to him. A flotilla was sent against him, but the sailors and the *streltsi* surrendered, and betrayed to him their commanders. Astrakhan revolted, and delivered up its two voïevodes, one of whom was thrown from the top of a bell-tower. Ascending the Volga, he took Saratof and Samara, and raised the country of Nijni-Novgorod, Tambof, and Pensa. Everywhere in the Russia of the Volga the serfs revolted against their masters—the Tatars, Tchouvaches, Mordvians, and Tcheremisses against the domination of Russia. It was a fearful revolution. In 1671 Stenko Razine was defeated, near Simbirsk, by George Baratinski. His prestige was lost; he was pursued into the steppes, arrested on the Don, and sent to Moscow, where he was executed (1671).

His death did not immediately check the rebellion. The brigands still continued to hold the country. At Astrakhan, Vassili Ouss governed despotically, and threw the archbishop from a belfry. Finally, however, all these imitators of Razine were killed or captured, the Volga freed, and the Don became as peaceful as the Dnieper.

* * * * *

The peasants who fled to the south, to the banks of the River Don and its tributaries, formed large Cossack settlements which were called *stanitsas.*

There was no equality among the Cossacks of the Don in the middle of the 17th century. Some of the Cossacks had seized the best lands, accumulated property, began to trade, and became rich. Others remained poor. The poor Cossacks either had to go into bondage to the rich Cossacks, or to obtain their livelihood by robbery. The tsar's voyevodas hunted down the fugitives and returned them to the landlords. The poor Cossacks hated the Moscow landlords bitterly. They were roused to rebellion by the Cossack Stepan Razin.

A foreign traveller, who was in Muscovy at that time, described Razin as follows: "He is of majestic appearance and noble bearing; proud of feature, tall in stature, his face slightly pock-marked. He possessed the ability to inspire fear and love."

Stepan Razin rallied large masses of poor people to his standard. He was elected ataman, or chief. Many Cossacks and other people who were enraged against the tsar's voyevodas and the landlords joined him.

In the spring of 1670, Razin, at the head of an army of 7,000 men, attacked Tsaritsin on the Volga (now called Stalingrad) and captured that town. Here the tsar's soldiers, the *Streltsi,* came over to his side. Then he marched on Astrakhan and captured that town after a siege of two days. The rich merchants, boyars and the tsar's officials were put to death by the Cossacks. Razin threw the voyevoda of Astrakhan from the belfry of the church. In Astrakhan Razin's followers elected administrators from among the Cossacks.

With the munitions captured in Astrakhan, Razin moved up the Volga.

He captured cities and wreaked vengeance on the tsar's voyevodas and officials. He sent messengers among the peasants to call upon them to join his ranks.

In response to Razin's call, the peasants rose in rebellion, killed their landlords, burned down the manors, and joined Razin's army in whole detachments. The peoples of the Volga, the Chuvash, Tatars, Mordovians and Maris, marched with the Russian peasants. The fact that they spoke different languages did not hinder them. Their hatred for the tsar and the landlords united them into one common family.

The tsar and the landlords gathered their army and regiments of mercenary foreign soldiers and marched against Razin. Razin found it hard to contend against these well-armed forces. He gave them battle near Simbirsk. Razin was wounded. His army was defeated. With a small detachment he managed to retire to the Don. But the rich Cossacks of the Don captured him and surrendered him to the tsar. The tsar pronounced the following sentence on him: "Put him to a cruel death."

Razin was executed in Moscow in 1671.

Tsar Alexei dealt cruelly with the rebel peasants. Thousands of the rebels were hacked to pieces, whipped to death and hanged on gallows. The peasant revolt was crushed.

During the Razin rebellion, as was the case during Bolotnikov's rebellion, the peasants did not have an organized working class for their reliable ally. Nor did they understand the aim of the rebellion; they could wreck the landlords' mansions and kill the landlords, but they did not know what to do further, what new order to introduce.

This was the cause of their weakness.

Pre-Petrine Contacts with the West

Peter the Great has been so publicized as "the westernizer of Russia" that earlier Russian relations with Western Europe are often forgotten or ignored. Peter's efforts at westernization were spectacular, but as the following excerpts show, Western contacts and influences did not originate with him. The source of the first excerpt is: Rambaud, *Russia*, vol. 1, pp. 255–289, *passim*. The second is taken from: Eugene Schuyler, *Peter the Great, Emperor of Russia. A Study of Historical Biography*. Two volumes. New York: Charles Scribner's Sons, 1890. Vol. 1, pp. 199–207. Slightly abridged. (On Schuyler, see below.)

In May 1614, Ouchakof and Zaborovski had been sent to ask help from Holland in men and money. The Dutch gave them a thousand gulden, but said that they had themselves only lately ended a great war, that they could give the Tzar no substantial aid, but would do their utmost to induce the King of Sweden to make peace. Alexis Ziousine had been despatched to London in June 1613; he was ordered to narrate all the excesses committed by the Poles in Moscow, and to say to King James, "After the destruction of Moscow, the Lithuanians seized your merchants—Mark the

Englishman, and all the others—took away all their wares, subjected them to a rigorous imprisonment, and ended by massacring them." If by chance he discovered that the English were aware that it was not the Poles, but the Cossacks and the lower classes who had put Mark to death and seized on the merchandise, he was to have other excuses ready. The Tzar entreated help in money to pay the men-at-arms, and not in soldiers, as he could give them no pay. They would think themselves happy if the King of England would send the Tzar money, provisions, powder, lead, sulphur, and other munitions, to the value of about 100,000 roubles; but would content themselves with 70,000 roubles' worth, or in case of absolute necessity with 50,000. James received the envoy and his suite courteously, informed them that he was aware of the wrongs the Poles and the Swedes had inflicted on them, and ordered them three times following to cover themselves. The Russians declined to do this. "When we see thy fraternal love and lively friendship for our sovereign, when we hear thy royal words which glorify our prince, and contemplate thine eyes thus close at hand, how can we, *kholopys* as we are, put our hats on our heads at such a moment?"

In August 1614, the year following this embassy, there appeared at Moscow John Merrick, who had for long traded with the holy city, but who came this time as ambassador from James I., qualified with full powers, as prince, knight, and gentleman of the bedchamber. In an interview with Prince Ivan Kourakine he began by demanding, on the part of the English merchants, a direct communication with India by the Obi, and with Persia by the Volga and Astrakhan. Kourakine alleged that this route was unsafe, that Astrakhan had only lately been delivered from Zaroutski, and that numerous brigands still infested the Volga. When security should be established, they would open the question with King James. They then passed to the subject of mediation. John Merrick declared that the King of England had assembled his Parliament to consider the best means of helping the Tzar, but that the Parliament had as yet decided nothing, and that he had no instructions on this head. "But," said Kourakine, "can you not assure us that your sovereign will send us help in the spring?" "How can I guarantee it? The journey is long, and there is no way save that by Sweden. . . . I believe, however, he will give you aid." Merrick, having contented himself with causing the Russians to hope, returned to commercial matters: liberty of trade by the Obi and the Volga, concessions of iron and jet mines on the Soukhona, concessions of territory about Vologda for new establishments, &c. The Russian boyards continued to expatiate on the difficulty of the situation, and John Merrick went to Novgorod to negotiate with the Swedes, where he was joined by the envoys of Holland. Gustavus Adolphus, King of Sweden, had obtained some successes over the voïevodes, but he had not contented the Novgorodians, nor been able to take Pskof. The kings of Denmark and Poland were his enemies, and he may have felt a presentiment of the splendid career that awaited him in Germany. He consented to open a congress, and in 1617 concluded with Russia the Peace of Stolbovo, by which he received an indemnity of 20,000 roubles, and kept Ivangorod, Iam Koporié, and Oréchek (Schlüsselburg), but ceded Novgorod, Roussa, Ladoga, and some smaller places.

Russia had begun at last to be a European nation. Everywhere her political or commercial alliance was sought. Gustavus Adolphus, who was making preparations to play his part as the champion of Protestantism in Germany, wished to assure himself of the friendship of Russia against Poland. He represented to Michael, with much truth, that the Catholic League of the Pope, the King of Poland, and the house of Hapsburg were as dangerous to Russia as to Sweden; that if Protestantism succumbed it would be the turn of Orthodoxy, and that the Swedish army was the outpost of Russian security. "When your neighbor's house is on fire," writes the King, "you must bring water and try to extinguish it, to guarantee your own safety. May your Tzarian majesty help your neighbors to protect yourself." The terrible events of late years had only too well justified these remarks. The intrigues of the Jesuits with the false Dmitri, and the burning of Moscow by the Poles, were always present to the memory of the Russians. A treaty of peace and commerce was concluded with Sweden, and a Swedish ambassador appeared at the Court.

England had rendered more than one service to Russia. In her pressing need James I. had lent her 20,000 roubles, and British mediation had led to the Peace of Stolbovo. John Merrick considered he had the right to demand that Russia should open to English commerce the route to Persia by the Volga, and to Hindostan by Siberia. The Tzar consulted the merchants of Moscow. They unanimously replied that such a concession would be their ruin, for they could never hope to rival the wealthier and more enterprising English. They were, however, ready to sacrifice their interests to those of the empire, if the dues paid by the foreigners were essential to the treasury. John Merrick declined to pay any dues, and the negotiation was broken off. They paid him, however, the 20,000 roubles, as he assured them the King had need of them for the help of his son-in-law, the Elector Palatine.

In 1615 the Tzar sent an envoy into France, to announce to Louis XIII. his accession to the throne, and to ask his aid against Poland and Sweden. In 1629 there appeared at Moscow the ambassador Duguay Cormenin, who was commissioned to solicit for French commerce what had been refused to English trade—free passage into Persia. He also spoke of a political alliance. "His Tzarian majesty," he said, "is the head of Eastern countries and the orthodox faith; Louis, King of France, is the head of Southern countries; and the Tzar, by contracting a friendship and alliance with him, will get the better of his enemies. As the Emperor is closely allied to the King of Poland, the Tzar must be allied to the King of France. These two princes are everywhere glorious; they have no equals either in strength or power; their subjects obey them blindly, while the English and Brabançons are only obedient when they choose. The latter buy their wares in Spain, and sell them to the Russians at a high price, but the French will furnish them with everything at a reasonable rate." This negotiation for the first

Franco-Russian treaty spoken of in history had no result. As to the route to Persia, it was refused by the boyards, who said that the French might buy the Persian merchandise from the Russians.

Western influence made considerable progress during this reign. The merchants entreated that access into the interior might be forbidden to those strangers whose rivalry was their ruin; but the latter were, on the contrary, so necessary to the State and to the general progress that they had to be invited into the country by all possible means. Under Michael, more foreigners than ever came into Russia. Vinius the Dutchman established foundries at Toula for guns, bullets, and other iron weapons. Marselein the German opened similar ones on the Vaga, the Kostroma, and the Cheksna. Privileges were granted to other foreign merchants or artisans, and the only condition imposed on them was not to conceal the secrets of their industries from the inhabitants of the countries. This is another point of resemblance between this reign of reform and that of Henri IV., who also summoned to his kingdom Flemish, English, and Venetian artisans. One European import did not however, find favor in Russia—the usage of tobacco was forbidden, and snuff-takers had their noses cut off.

Learned men were also sought from Europe. Adam Olearius of Holstein, a celebrated astronomer, geographer, and geometer, was invited to Moscow. Already the Academy of Sciences of Peter the Great was foreshadowed. A cosmographical treatise was translated from Latin into Russian. The Patriarch Philarete had established at Moscow an academy where Greek and Latin, the languages of the Renaissance, were taught. The Archimandrite Dionysius of Troïtsa, who had distinguished himself in the struggle with the Poles, undertook to correct the text of the Slavonian books—a hazardous enterprise, which cost Dionysius himself a short period of persecution. Native historians continued to re-edit their chronicles, and Abraham Palitsyne, cellarer of Troïtsa, narrated the famous siege of the convent.

During this reign, when Russia was trying to assimilate herself to Europe, diplomacy naturally took rapid strides. Muscovy had entered into more or less close relations with all the Courts of the West.

In 1645, Alexis sent Gerasimus Doktourof to notify his accession to the King of England, Charles I. The Russian envoy arrived in England in the midst of the Revolution. Being received at Gravesend with great honors and the firing of guns by the company of merchants that traded with Russia, he at once inquired "where was the king?" They replied, they did not know exactly where he was, because for three or four years there had been a great civil war, and instead of the king they had now the Parliament, composed of deputies from all the orders, who governed London as well as the kingdoms of England and Scotland. "Our war with the king," said the merchants, "began for the sake of religion, when he married the daughter of the King of France. She, being a Papist, persuaded the king into various superstitious practices; it was by her counsel that the king instituted archbishops and called in the Jesuits. Many people, in order to follow the example of the king, made themselves Papists too. Besides this, the king wished to govern the kingdom according to his own will, as do the sovereigns of other States. But here, from time immemorial, the country has been free: the early kings could settle nothing: it was the Parliament, the men who were elected, that governed. The king began to rule after his own will, but the Parliament would not allow that, and many archbishops and Jesuits were executed. The king, seeing that the Parliament intended to act according to its own wish, as it had done from all time, and not at all according to the royal will, left London with the queen, without being expelled by anyone, saying that they were going away into other towns. Once out of London, he sent the queen to France and began to fight us, but the Parliament was the stronger. The Parliament is composed of two *palaty* (chambers): in one of them sit the boyards, in the other the men elected by the commons—the *sloujilié lioudi* and the merchants. Five hundred men sit in the parliament, and one orator speaks for all."

These lessons in the English Constitution could not penetrate the brain of the Russian envoy. He only recognized the king, and persisted, according to the text of his instructions, in trying to deliver his letters of credit to the king himself. "Hast thou a letter from thy sovereign, and a mission to the Parliament?" they asked him. He replied, "I have neither a letter nor a mission to the Parliament. Let the Parliament send me immediately before the king, and give me an escort, carriages, and provisions. Let the Parliament present me to him—it is to him that I will speak." His demand was naturally refused, and he wished instantly to leave for Holland, but this was not allowed.

The following year Charles I. was brought a prisoner into London. Doktourof insisted on being presented to him. His request was ill-timed. "You cannot be brought before him," they said to him; "he no longer governs anything." Doktourof then refused a dinner given to him by the Russian Company, and only yielded when the dinner was served at his own house. The Parliament, however, did not wish to interrupt the friendly relations with Russia.

Doktourof was summoned before the House of Lords on the 13th of June. At his entrance all the "boyards" took off their hats, and Lord Manchester, the "chief boyard," rose. Then Doktourof, to the general consternation, made the following speech:—"I am sent by my sovereign to your king, Charles King of England. I have been sent as a courier (*gonets*) to negotiate important affairs of State, which offer great advantages to both sovereigns and to all Christendom, and may help to maintain peace and concord. It is the 13th of June, and, since I arrived in London on the 26th of November last, I have never ceased to show you the letter of the Tzar and to beg you to allow me to go before the king. You have kept me in London without permitting me either to have an interview with the king or to return to the Tzar; and yet in all neighboring countries the route is free to all ambassadors, envoys, and couriers of the Tzar."

Manchester replied that they would explain to the Tzar by letter their reasons for acting thus. They gave him a chair, and the English "boyards" likewise seated themselves; and he began to look about the House, of which he gives a minute description in his report. He was then conducted to the House of Commons, and the dignitaries came to meet him preceded by the royal sceptre. He renewed his declarations, and then retired ceremoniously. In June 1646 he left England much discontented. Alexis could understand no more of the English Revolution than his envoy. He maintained, like Catherine II., the cause of kings against the liberty of the subjects. In May 1647 he received at Moscow Nawtingall, envoy of Charles I., who denounced the captivity of the king, and said Charles would see with pleasure the English Company deprived of its privileges, and everyone allowed to trade freely with Russia. Alexis listened to his request, and granted him, as aid to the king 30,000 *tchetverts* of corn, out of the 300,000 that were asked of him. But the English merchants settled in Russia accused Nawtingall of imposture, saying that the king's letter was apocryphal, and that the dog he had brought as a present to Alexis had never been bought by Charles I. Nawtingall was expelled in disgrace, and avenged himself by accusing his compatriots of a project of attacking Arkhangel, and of pillaging the Russian merchants. His honors as ambassador were then given back to him, but he quitted Russia.

When Alexis heard of the execution of Charles I., he published the oukase of June 1649, which, as a punishment to the regicides, forbade the English merchants to live in the cities of the interior, and confined them to Arkhangel. The Tzar furnished help in money and corn to Charles, Prince of Wales, who in 1660 became Charles II., and resumed relations with him when he ascended the throne of the Stuarts.

* * * * *

Although foreigners came to Russia from the earliest period, yet it was not until the time of Ivan III. that they arrived in great numbers. That prince received foreign artists and artisans so well that numbers of Italian architects, engineers, goldworkers, physicians, and mechanics hastened to Moscow. His marriage with the Greek Princess Sophia Palaeologos gave rise to new and more frequent relations with Italy, and he several times sent to Rome, Venice, and Milan for physicians and men of technical knowledge. It was in this way that the Cathedral of the Assumption came to be built by Aristotle Fioraventi of Bologna, that of St. Michael the Archangel by Aleviso of Milan, and the banqueting hall of the palace, and the walls and the gates of the Kremlin by other Italian architects. German miners, too, came, or were sent by Matthew Corvinus, King of Hungary, and some of them discovered silver and copper mines in Siberia.

Ivan IV., the Terrible, appreciated foreigners, and invited large numbers of them into Russia. But, besides this, it was during his reign in 1558, that an English expedition penetrated into the White Sea, and the trade with England began, which soon took great proportions, and brought to Russia many English merchants. After the conquest of Livonia and portions of the southern shore of the Baltic very many prisoners of war were sent to Moscow, and elsewhere in the interior of Russia, and were never allowed to return to their own country.

Under Ivan's son Theodore, and Boris Godunof, the intercourse with western Europe constantly increased. Favours were given, not only to the English merchants, but also to Dutchmen and Danes, to immigrants from Hamburg and the Hanse Towns. Godunof invited soldiers and officers as well as physicians and artisans. His children were educated with great deviations from Russian routine. He even thought of marrying his daughter to a Danish prince, and, when at his country estate, was fond of the society of foreigners. The so-called False Demetrius had very great inclinations toward foreigners. This was very natural, for he had been educated in Poland, and had seen the advantages of western culture. Polish manners prevailed at his court; he was surrounded by a guard of foreign soldiers; he protected all religions, especially the Catholic; he urged Russians to travel abroad, and so willingly received foreigners that a Pole, in writing about the immigration of so many foreigners into Russia, said: "For centuries long it was hard for the birds even to get into the realm of Muscovy, but now come not only many merchants, but a crowd of grocers and tavernkeepers." Under the Tsar Theodore, son of Ivan the Terrible, there were, according to Fletcher, about 4,300 foreigners in the Russian service, most of them Poles and Little Russians, but still about 150 Dutchmen and Scotchmen. In the reign of Boris Godunof, the foreign detachment in the army was composed of twenty-five hundred men of all nationalities. . . .

In the beginning of the sixteenth century, the Grand Duke Basil established the residence of his foreign body-guard, consisting of Poles, Germans and Lithuanians, on the right bank of the river Moskva, outside the town, in a place called Naleiki, in order, as Herberstein said, that the Russians might not be contaminated by the bad example of their drunkenness. Later on, this district became inhabited by Streltsi and the common people, and the Livonian prisoners of war were established by Ivan the Terrible on the Yauza, near the Pokrof gate. When Demetrius was so desperately defended by his foreign body-guard, that a Livonian, Wilhelm Furstenberg, fell at his side, the Russians said: "See what true dogs these Germans are: let us kill them all"; and during the Troublous Times, the foreigners in Moscow were subject to constant attacks from the Russians. Persecutions were organised against them, as at other times and places against the Jews. There was not a popular commotion in which threats, at least, were not made against them, and during one of the attacks the whole foreign quarter was burnt to the ground. After this, the foreigners lived within the walls, and for a while enjoyed the same privileges as Russian subjects, adopting their dress and their habits. Livonian prisoners of war had, even before the Troublous Times, made their way within the town, and had built a church or two. For some reason they incurred the wrath of the Tsar, were driven from their houses, and their property was plundered. . . .

When affairs became more settled under the Tsar Alexis, by a decree of 1652 there was a systematic settling of all foreigners in a suburb outside the town; the number of the streets and lanes was set down in the registers, the pieces of land, varying from 350 to 1,800 yards square, were set apart for the officers, the physicians, the apothecaries, the artisans and the widows of foreigners who had been in the Russian service. This suburb, which was nicknamed by the Russians Kukui, now forms the north-eastern portion of the city of Moscow, intersected by the Basmannaya and Pokrofskaya streets, and still contains the chief Protestant and Catholic churches. It is fairly depicted to us in one of the drawings made by the artist who accompanied Meyerberg's embassy in 1661. As the houses were of wood, and surrounded by gardens, this suburb had all the appearances of a large and flourishing village.

Reutenfels, who was in Russia from 1671 to 1673, estimated the number of foreigners in the country as about 18,000. Most of them lived in Moscow, but a large number inhabited Vologda, Archangel and other towns where there was foreign trade, as well as the mining districts.

The residence of the foreigners in a separate suburb naturally enabled them to keep up the traditions and customs of Western Europe much more easily than if they had mingled with the Russians. They wore foreign clothing, read foreign books, and spoke, at least in their households, their own language, although they all had some acquaintance with the Russian tongue, which sometimes served as a medium of communication with each other. The habitual use of a few Russian words, the adoption of a few Russian customs, conformity to the Russian dress and ways of thinking on some points, was the most they had advanced toward Russianisation. Rarely did they change their faith to advance their worldly prospects, although the children of marriages with Russians were brought up in the Russian church. In general, they held close to their own religion and their own modes of education. They kept up a constant intercourse with their native countries, by new arrivals, and by correspondence with their friends. They imported not only foreign conveniences for their own use, but also received from abroad the journals of the period, books of science and history, novels and poems. Their interest in the politics of their own lands was always maintained, and many and warm were the discussions which were caused by the wars between France and the Low Countries, and the English Revolution. In this way, the German suburb was a nucleus of a superior civilisation.

The influence of the foreign residents in Russia was especially seen in the material development of the country. The Russians were then, as they are now, quick to learn and ready to imitate. A Pole, Maszkiewicz, in the time of the False Demetrius, remarked that the metal and leather work of the Russians after Oriental designs could scarcely be distinguished from the genuine articles. Foreigners understood this quality of Russian workmen, and frequently endeavoured to keep their trades as a monopoly for themselves. We know that Hans Falck, a foreign manufacturer of bells and metal castings, sent away his Russian workmen when engaged in the delicate processes, in order that they might not learn the secrets of the art. The Government found it necessary, in many cases, to make contracts with foreign artisans that they should teach their trades to a certain number of Russian workmen. It was the Englishman John Merrick, first merchant and subsequently ambassador, who was one of the earliest to teach the Russians that it was better for them to manufacture for themselves than to export the raw materials. He explained to the boyars how people had been poor in England as long as they had exported raw wool, and had only begun to get rich when the laws protected the woollen manufacturers by insisting on the use of wool at home, and especially on the use of woollen shrouds, and how greatly the riches of England had increased since the country began to sell cloth instead of wool. It was in part through his influence that a manufactory of hemp and tow was established near Holmogory. In a similar way, paper-mills, glass-factories, powder-mills, saltpeter-works, and iron-works were established by foreigners. A Dane, Peter Marselis, had important and well-known iron-works near Tula, which were so productive that he was able to pay his inspector three thousand rubles a year, and had to pay to his brother-in-law, for his share, twenty thousand rubles. We can see the relative value of this, when we remember that, at that time, two to two and a half quarters of rye could be bought for a ruble, and that, twenty years later, the salary of General Gordon, one of the highest in the Russian service, was only one thousand rubles a year; while the pastor of the Lutheran church in Moscow in 1699 received annually only sixty rubles. Concessions for copper mines were also given to Marselis and other foreigners, and the Stroganofs, who possessed such great and rich mining districts on the frontier of Siberia, constantly sent abroad for physicians, apothecaries, and artisans of all kinds.

It has already been said that the foreigners in Russia were not too well pleased with the ease with which the Russians learned their trades; neither did this please foreign Governments. The famous Duke of Alva said that it was "inexcusable to provide Russia with cannon and other arms, and to initiate the Russians into the way war was carried on in Western Europe, because, in this way, a dangerous neighbour was being educated." Sigismund, King of Poland, did his best to hinder the intercourse which sprang up between Moscow and England, and wrote to Queen Elizabeth that "such commercial relations were dangerous, because Russia would thus receive war material; and it would be still worse if Russia, in this way, could get immigrants who should spread through the country the technical knowledge so necessary there. It was in the interest of Christianity and religion to protest against Russia, the enemy of all free nations, receiving cannon and arms, artists and artisans, and being initiated into the views and purposes of European politics."

It was natural that, with constant and increasing intercourse with foreigners, the Russians should adopt some of the customs which the strangers had brought with them. For a long time the foreigners were greatly laughed at for eating salads, or grass, as the peasants called it, but this habit gradually spread. In the early part of the seventeenth century, the Dutch introduced the culture of asparagus, and garden roses were first brought by the Dane, Peter Marselis. The use of snuff and of smoking tobacco was speedily acquired, much to the horror of all right-thinking and orthodox people, who saw in this a plain work of the devil; for was it not said in the Bible: "Not that which goeth into the mouth defileth a man; but that which cometh out of the mouth, this defileth a man." Many Russian nobles even adopted foreign clothes, and trimmed their hair and beard. Nikita Romanof, the owner of the boat which Peter found at Ismailovo, wore German clothes while hunting, for which he was sharply reprimanded by the Patriarch; and the conduct of Prince Andrew Koltsof-Masalsky, in cutting his hair short, in 1675, caused so much displeasure that the Tsar Alexis issued an ukase, forbidding, under heavy penalties, the trimming of one's hair or beard, or the wearing of foreign clothes. This decree soon fell into desuetude, and at the time of which we are speaking, foreign clothes and foreign habits were not at all uncommon among the Russians of the higher ranks. Even Peter himself occasionally wore foreign dress, and was severely blamed by the Patriarch for daring to appear in such costume at the deathbed of his mother. . . .

One of the most important steps in civilisation introduced by foreigners was the letter-post. Postal communications had previously existed in the interior of the country, but, even for Government purposes, they were very slow, and nearly all letters were sent by private hand, or by a chance messenger. It was in 1664 that a decree of the Tsar Alexis gave a Swede named John privileges for the organisation of an international letter-post, and in 1667 the first postal convention was made with Poland. John of Sweden was succeeded by Peter Marselis, the Dane, and he by Andrew Vinius, who first received the title of Postmaster of His Majesty the Tsar, and was ordered to conclude postal conventions with the neighbouring States. The institution of the post-office did not please all Russians as much as it did the foreigners, and, if we may judge from the continued existence of a censorship, is still looked upon with a certain degree of suspicion. The Russian political economist, Ivan Pososhkof, writing in 1701, complains:

"The Germans have cut a hole through from our land into their own, and from outside people can now, through this hole, observe all our political and commercial relations. This hole is the post. Heaven knows whether it brings advantage to the Tsar, but the harm which it causes to the realm is incalculable. Everything that goes on in our land is known to the whole world. The foreigners all become rich by it, the Russians become poor as beggars. The foreigners always know which of our goods are cheap and which are dear, which are plentiful and which are scarce. Thereupon they bargain, and know immediately how much they are obliged to pay for our goods. In this way trade is unequal. Without the post, both sides would be ignorant of the prices and the stock of goods on hand, and no party would be injured. Besides, it is a very bad thing that people know in other countries everything that happens in ours. This hole, then, should be shut up—that is, the post should be put an end to; and, it seems to me, it would be very sensible not to allow letters to be sent, even through messengers, except with a special permission each time from the proper authorities."

Early Slavophilism

Not all Russian subjects approved of the growing contacts with the West. Sometimes a desire to learn from the West seems to have been coupled with a resentment of westerners. This dichotomy was shown in the writings of Yuri Khrizhanich, a Croatian who migrated to Russia and whom many regard as the founder of Slavophilism. Much of Khrizhanich's life in Russia was, incidentally, spent in Siberian exile. He died in 1677 or thereabouts, but his works were not published until 1860. The source is: Wiener, *Anthology*, vol. 1, pp. 134–136. Abridged.

. . . The time has come for our nation to be instructed in various branches, for God has in His mercy and kindness uplifted through Russia a Slavic kingdom to glory, power and majesty, such as for splendour has never existed before among us. . . . We, too, must learn, for under the honoured rule of the Righteous Tsar and Great King Alexis Mikhaylovich we have an opportunity to wipe off the mould of our ancient barbarism, to acquire various sciences, to adopt a better organization of society, and to reach a higher well-being.

• • •

We are not possessed of an innate vivacity, nor praiseworthy national characteristics, nor sincerity of heart. For people who have such pride do not allow foreigners to command them, except by force, whereas our nation of its own free will invites foreigners to come to its country. Not one people under the sun has since the beginning of the world been so abused and disgraced by foreigners as we Slavs have been by the Germans. Our whole Slavic nation has been subject to this kind of treatment; everywhere we have upon our shoulders Germans, Jews, Scotchmen, Gypsies, Armenians, Greeks and merchants of other nationalities, who suck our blood. In Russia you will see nowhere any wealth, except in the Tsar's treasury; everywhere there is dire, bare poverty.

Pososhkov on Trade and the Peasants

The Pososhkov whom Schuyler identified as a "Russian political economist" was scarcely that. Ivan T. Pososhkov was a self-educated man, the son of a peasant, and his learning barely went beyond reading, writing, and arithmetic. This, together with native ability and shrewdness, gave him a great advantage over his fellows and enabled him to amass a large fortune from trade. One measure of Pososhkov is that his son was one of the first Russians to be sent abroad for instruction. Another measure is his *Book on Poverty and Wealth,* which gives an interesting, firsthand view of some of the norms and values of the time of Peter I. These excerpts are reprinted from Wiener, *Anthology,* vol. 1, pp. 205–210, *passim.*

. . . At the present time boyars, noblemen and their people, soldiers and peasants carry on commerce, without paying any tax, and many merchants carry on trade in their names, and pay no tax. Not half the revenue is collected, nor ever can be collected, if commerce is not to be made free from the nobles and officials, since many mighty people have taken to trade, and some who are not themselves powerful but are not subject to the magistrate.

I know, for example, one case in a Novogorod county where there are a hundred or two of merchant-peasants, and who do not pay a farthing's worth of taxes. And if a collector, seeing them, tries to collect the revenue, the gentry take the peasant's part and send the collector away more dead than alive, and the government officers look on, and dare not interfere. And there are some wealthy men, who have some five or six hundred peasants carrying on such illicit trade, and pay not a farthing to the Great Tsar. If all be arranged as I have proposed, commerce will awaken as if from a dream.

It is a very bad custom the merchant people have, to do each other wrong by cheating each other. Both foreigners and Russians are in the habit of showing good-looking wares that are badly made within or filled with bad stuff; or bad wares are mixed with wares of good quality and are sold as if of good quality, taking for them an unfair price, and greatly deceiving inexperienced people. They give wrong weights and measures, deceive in price, and do not think all that to be a sin, although they cause so much injustice to the inexperienced. Yet those who deceive are in the end ruined through their own inequity, and become impoverished. . . . In order to establish justice in the Merchant Rows, let there be appointed hundred-men and fifty-men and ten-men, and over the shop where there is an hundred-man let there be nailed a round board, painted white, so that it can be easily seen, and on that board let there be written "hundred-man." Do the same with the shop of the fifty-man and the ten-man, so that those who purchase any goods may know where to show their wares, if they should want to find out whether they have received the right weight, or measure, or whether the wares are good or bad, and whether they have paid the correct price for them.

If the merchant have received more than the worth of the wares, let him be fined a dime or two for every unfair kopeck, and let him be beaten with rods or a whip, that he may not do so again in the future; and if he repeat his offense, let the fine and the punishment be increased.

But if one give wrong measure and weight, or sell different goods from what the buyer demanded, and give him inferior goods, let his punishment be much more severe, and the fine be ten times the price of the goods.

• • •

Much might be added to the protection of the peasantry if their houses were rebuilt so that they could live more freely and peacefully; for much damage is done to them through overcrowding: if one man's house takes fire, the whole village is threatened, and frequently not a single house is left. This leads to endless poverty. If they had not been so much crowded in their settlements, they would not be so easily ruined. It is against this ruin that they ought to be protected. Let them build their houses farther from each other, nor join yard to yard, but with intervals, a few houses in a lot; the streets ought to be wide, where there is sufficient space, not less than two hundred feet in width; where the space is crowded, not less than one hundred feet in width. In this way if there should be a fire, all the neighbours would run to put it out: there being intervals between the houses, it would be easy to reach them from all sides, and as there would be little danger for the neighbouring houses, the peasants would not rush, as before, to save their own possessions, but would aid their unfortunate neighbour. As the settlements are now arranged, it is utterly impossible for the neighbours to bring aid; they rush for their own, which they cannot all save, but generally lose everything they have. Thus they are ruined and become impoverished.

Not a small degree of annoyance is caused the peasants from not having literate people among them. There are many villages of twenty to thirty houses that have not a single man that can read; if any come to them with an ukase, or without an ukase, pretending to have one, they believe him, and suffer damages; for they are all blind,—they see nothing and understand nothing. They are not able to dispute with the people that pretend having ukases, and they frequently pay unwarranted taxes to them. To guard the peasants from such losses, it seems to me, they ought to be compelled to send their children of ten years and less to some subdeacon to be instructed how to read and write. I think it would not be a bad thing if the smallest village were not without a literate man, so there ought to be a strict law compelling the peasants to have their children instructed for three or four years. And there ought to be a severe punishment for those who do not have their children taught anything for four years, or who do not have them instructed at all as they grow up.

Having learned to read and write, they will not only conduct more intelligently the affairs of their masters, but they will also be useful in the Government, being eligible as hundred-men and fifty-men, and no one would abuse them and mulct them for nothing.

Peter the Great

Many persons, ranging from pedants through scholars to popularizers, have written about Peter the Great and his reign. This was one of the most active fields in Russian historiography during the generation before the revolution, and has been sporadically emphasized by Soviet historians, especially in the years immediately after World War II. Some of their findings, as well as some of the findings of their predecessors, are gradually being incorporated into general accounts, producing some revisions in the estimate and understanding of Peter and his work. Though it obviously lacks these modifications of more recent scholarship and therefore needs revision in some parts, the best biography of Peter is still that written in the late nineteenth century by Eugene Schuyler, an American diplomatic and consular official. Schuyler's work, based on extensive research, was so accurate and so carefully done that it has been supplemented but not supplanted by later studies. The following excerpts from it deal with Peter's youth, with his journey to Western Europe, and with his reforms. The source is: Schuyler, *Peter the Great*, vol. 1, pp. 103–109, 274–286; vol. 2, pp. 348–352, 369–379. Abridged.

This was the beginning of the celebrated Preobrazhensky Regiment, even now the first regiment of the Imperial guard, and of which the Emperor is always the chief. The name Preobrazhensky was given to it first because it was formed and quartered at the palace and village of Preobrazhensky, or the Transfiguration, which, in turn, took their name from the village church. . . .

Peter entered upon his military exercises with such zest that they ceased to be mere child's play. He himself performed every exercise, giving himself no rest night or day. He stood his watch in turn, took his share of the duties of the camp, slept in the same tent with his comrades, and partook of their fare. There was no distinction made between the Tsar and the least of his subjects. When his volunteers became proficient in their discipline, he used to lead them on long marches in the neighbourhood of his country home, and went at times even as far as the Trinity Monastery at Kaliazin. As his followers were armed, these marches were in the nature of campaigns, and the troops, such as they were, were under strict military discipline, and were regularly encamped at night with the usual military precautions. In 1685, when Peter was thirteen years old, he resolved on something further, and, in order to practise the assault and defence of fortifications, began to construct a small fortress on the banks of the Yauza, at Preobrazhensky, the remains of which are still visible on the edge of the Sokolniki wood. This fort, probably at the suggestion of one of the German officers, was called Pressburg. It was built with a considerable amount of care, timber was drawn for the purpose from Moscow, and its construction took the greater part of the year. Peter named it with great ceremony, leading a procession from Moscow which included most of the court officials and nobles. All this, as has been said, brought Peter into very close relations with the foreign suburb, and the foreigners in Moscow were fond of social amusements, always accompanied, according to their habits, with beer, wine, and tobacco. Peter, who was precocious, both physically and mentally, took his full share in these entertainments and on the return feasts he gave it may be imagined that there was no stint of drink. With such society Peter gained not only knowledge of men and of the world, but his inquiring mind led him to be curious about many subjects which rarely before had troubled the head of a Russian Prince. Without regard to rank or position, he was always glad to make the acquaintance of those from whom he could learn anything, and was especially attracted by all that was mechanically curious.

Frequently, for amusement, he used to hammer and forge at the blacksmith's shop. He had already become expert with the lathe, and we have documentary evidence to prove that he had practically learnt the mechanical operation of printing as well as the binding of books. We can believe that the Electress Charlotte Sophia did not exaggerate when, in 1697, in describing her interview with Peter, she said that he "already knew excellently well fourteen trades."

All this was a school for Peter; but do not let us be led astray by the word school. Peter's military education was such as he chose to give himself, and entirely for his own amusement. There was nothing in it similar to the regular course of military training practised in a cadet school. Peter was only too glad to escape from the nursery and house to the amusements of the street and the fields. Although we know that in the Russia of that day the intellectual development of a youth did not at all keep pace with his physical growth, and that when a lad was grown to the stature of a man, he immediately assumed the duties and responsibilities of a man, though in mind he might be still a child; yet there was generally the semblance of discipline. The way in which Peter seems to have slipped through the hands of his instructors, tutors and guardians shows not only his strong self-will, but the disorganisation of his party, and the carelessness of his family. Such a training may have been useful, and, indeed, it was useful to Peter; at all events it was better than nothing; but in no sense of the term can it be considered education. This Peter himself, in later life, admitted, and the Empress Elizabeth tells how, when she was bending over her books and exercises, her father regretted that he had not been obliged or enabled to do the same.

One more word with regard to Peter's military amusements. There were, as we have said, mere amusements, and had not the regularity or the plan which subsequent chroniclers and anecdote-writers ascribe to them. In playing at soldiers, Peter followed his natural inclination, and had in his head no plan whatever for reorganising or putting on a better footing the military forces of his country. The reorganisation of the Russian army, indeed, grew out of the campaigns and exercises at Preobrazhensky; but it was not until real war began that Peter saw of what service these exercises had been to him and to others, and found that the boy-soldiers could easily be made the nucleus of an army.

. . .

The Tsar's feeling was so strong with regard to what might be learnt about ship-building in foreign countries that, after he had sent off many of his subjects to study the trade, he resolved to go himself. Without ascribing to this journey all the importance which Macaulay gave to it when he said, "His journey is an epoch in the history, not only of his own country, but of ours, and of the world," we must admit that it was a remarkable event, and one fraught with much consequence. Since the exiled Izyaslav visited the court of the Emperor Henry IV., at Mainz, in 1075, no Russian ruler had ever been out of his dominions. Peter's journey marks the division between the old Russia, an exclusive, little known country, and the new Russia, an important factor in European politics. It was also one of the turning points in the development of his character, and was the continuation of the education begun in the German suburb. In one way, it may be said that Peter's appearance in the German suburb was really more startling, and of more importance, than his journey westward, for that journey was the natural consequence and culmination of his intercourse with foreigners at Moscow.

This sudden and mysterious journey of the Tsar abroad exercised the minds of Peter's contemporaries no less than it has those of moderns. Many were the reasons which were ascribed then, and have given since, for this step. There was even a dispute among the students of the University of Thorn as to the motives which had induced the Tsar to travel. Pleyer, the secret Austrian agent, wrote to the Emperor Leopold that the whole embassy was "merely a cloak for the freedom sought by the Tsar, to get out of his own country and divert himself a little." Another document in the archives at Vienna finds the cause of the journey in a vow made by Peter, when in danger on the White Sea, to make a pilgrimage to the tombs of the Apostles St. Peter and St. Paul, at Rome. According to Voltaire, "He resolved to absent himself for some years from his dominions, in order to learn how better to govern them." Napoleon said: "He left his country to deliver himself for a while from the crown, so as to learn ordinary life, and to remount by degrees to greatness." But every authentic source gives us but one reason, and the same. Peter went abroad, not to fulfil a vow, not to amuse himself, not to become more civilised, not to learn the art of government, but simply to become a good shipwright. His mind was filled with the idea of creating a navy on the Black Sea for use against the Turks, and his tastes were still, as they had always been, purely mechanical. For this purpose, as he himself says, and as his prolonged residence in Holland shows, he desired to have an opportunity of studying the art of shipbuilding in those places where it was carried to the highest perfection, that is, in Holland, England, and Venice.

In order to give the Tsar greater freedom of action, and to save him from too much formality and ceremony, which he exceedingly disliked, an attempt was made to conceal the purpose of his journey by means of a great embassy, which should visit the chief countries of Western Europe, to explain the policy of Russia toward Turkey, and to make whatever treaties it was found possible, either for commercial purposes or for the war against the Turks. The embassy consisted of three extraordinary ambassadors, at the head of whom was General Lefort. Besides the other rewards he had received for the campaigns against Azof, he had been given the honorary title of Governor-General of Novgorod. The other ambassadors were the Governor-General of Siberia, Theodore Golovin, who had already distinguished himself by the treaty of Nertchinsk with the

Chinese; and the Governor of Bolkhof, Prokop Voznitsyn, a skilful and experienced diplomatist. In the suite of the ambassadors were twenty nobles and thirty-five others, called volunteers, who, like those previously sent, were going abroad for the study of shipbuilding. Among these was the Tsar himself. These volunteers were chiefly young men who had been comrades of Peter in his play regiments, in his boat-building, and in his campaigns against Azof. Among them may be particularly remarked Alexander Menshikof and Alexis Golitsyn, two Golovins, Simeon Naryshkin, and the Prince Alexander Bagration of Imeritia. Including priests, interpreters, pages, singers, and servants of various kinds, the suite of the embassy numbered as many as two hundred and fifty persons. The Tsar himself travelled under the strictest incognito. It was forbidden to give him the title of Majesty—he was always to be addressed simply as *Min Her* Peter Mikhailof—and it was forbidden, under pain of death, to mention his presence with the embassy.

During the absence of the Tsar, the government was entrusted to a regency of three persons—Leo Naryshkin, Prince Boris Golitsyn, and Prince Peter Prozorofsky, who were given supreme power. Prince Ramodanofsky was charged with maintaining order in Moscow, and he had verbal instructions to follow up, in the severest way, the slightest movement of discontent or rebellion. The boyar Shein, assisted by General Gordon, had charge of the defence of the southern frontier on the side of Azof, while Prince Jacob Dolgoruky succeeded the boyar Sheremetief in charge of the defences against the Tartars on the frontier of Little Russia, and was ordered to get galleys ready for the siege of Otchakof in the spring of 1698. Sheremetief, who had already served two years in that country, obtained leave of absence and permission to travel abroad.

Preparations were nearly finished for the departure of the embassy, when an unexpected delay occurred. Gordon expressed it thus in his diary: "A merry night has been spoiled by an accident of discovering treason against his Majesty." The Colonel of the Streltsi, Ivan Zickler, of foreign birth or extraction, and two Russian nobles of high rank, Alexis Sokovnin and Theodore Pushkin, were accused of plotting against the life of the Tsar. They were accused on the testimony of Larion Yelisarof, who was one of the denunciators of the alleged plot against Peter's life in 1689, when he took refuge at Troitsa. In all probability there was no plot whatever, but simply loose and unguarded talk between discontented men. Zickler had always been well treated by the Princess Sophia and Shaklovity, but when he saw the preponderance on the side of Peter he went to Troitsa and made denunciations. He did not, however, receive the reward and favour which he expected, but on the contrary, was looked upon askance, and had recently been sent to Azof. He was naturally irritated against the Tsar, and in unguarded moments probably expressed his feelings too strongly. Sokovnin was a virulent dissenter, and the brother of two ladies well known for their opposition to the Patriarch Nikon, and their encouragement of dissent in the reign of Alexis—Theodora Morozof and the Princess Avdotia Urusof. He was therefore opposed to many of

Peter's innovations; and his father-in-law, Matthew Pushkin, who had been appointed Governor of Azof, had excited the anger of the Tsar because he had refused to send his children abroad. Theodore Pushkin was one of the sons, and had uttered vague threats of revenge in case the Tsar should have his father whipped to death for his refusal, for rumours to that effect were being industriously circulated. Torture produced confessions of various kinds, and among them repetitions by Zickler of the old accusations against the Princess Sophia. The prisoners were speedily condemned, and were beheaded on the Red Place, after having their arms and legs chopped off. Their heads were exposed on stakes. The confessions of Zickler, and the renewed accusations against his sister Sophia, excited Peter's mind against the whole of the Miloslavsky family, and in his rage he even went to the length of taking up the body of Ivan Miloslavsky— who had been dead fourteen years—of dragging the coffin by swine to the place of execution, and of placing it in such a position that the blood of the criminals spurted into the face of the corpse.

Even at this time there was much popular discontent and hostile criticism of Peter. Not all of those who saw that reforms were absolutely necessary approved his measures and his conduct. A rumour was spread that the Tsar Ivan had publicly proclaimed to all the people: "My brother does not live according to the Church. He goes to the German suburb, and is acquainted with Germans." There was talk, too, of the way in which Peter had abandoned his wife and family, and family affairs probably caused the quarrel between Leo Naryshkin and the Lopukhins, the relatives of Peter's wife. What exactly happened is not known, but Peter Lopukhin, the uncle of the Tsaritsa and the Minister of the Palace, was accused of bribery and extortion, and for this, or some other cause, was exiled, together with his brothers, one of them the father of the Tsaritsa. A report was circulated among the common people, and was widely believed, that Peter had assisted with his own hands in applying the torture to his wife's uncle. One man, the monk Abraham, dared to make himself the exponent of the popular feeling, and presented to Peter a petition in which he made mention of the abandonment of his wife, of the relations which he had formed in the German suburb, and of the bad feeling which had been excited by the Tsar lowering himself to work at boats, and to appear on foot in the triumphal procession, instead of taking his proper place. As was natural, the petition gave rise to a trial; Abraham was sent to a distant monastery, and three other men who were implicated were punished with the knout, and sent to Azof.

When these trials were completed, the embassy set out, on March 20, 1697. It was intended to go first to Vienna, then to Venice and Rome, then to Holland and England, and to return by the way of Königsberg. The trouble in Poland, consequent on the interregnum, made travelling through that country dangerous, and the only way in which Vienna could be reached was by a roundabout journey through Riga, Königsberg, and Dresden. The plan was therefore changed.

The first experience of the Tsar in a foreign country was an unfortunate one. The Governor of Pskov, who had been ordered to make the arrangements for Peter's journey through Livonia, had neglected to say in his letter to Eric Dahlberg, the Governor of Riga, how many persons accompanied the embassy. Dahlberg replied, asking that, while he would do his best, he hoped they would overlook some inconveniences, as a great famine was unfortunately reigning in the country. Major Glazenap was sent to the frontier to escort the embassy, but Peter was so impatient, and travelled so fast, that they arrived at the frontier before the proper arrangements had been made to receive them. They therefore found no conveyances, and were obliged to go on to Riga in the carriages brought from Pskov, and trust to their own provisions. A short distance from Riga, light carriages and an escort were waiting for them, and they were ceremoniously received in the town with a military parade, while a guard of fifty men was placed near their lodgings. The next day the ambassadors sent two of their nobles to thank the governor for his kindness, and a return visit was paid by one of his adjutants. Immediately afterward, Peter wrote to Vinius that they "were received with great honour, and with a salute of twenty-four guns, when they entered and left the fortress." Unfortunately, the embassy was detained at Riga for a whole week by the breaking up of the ice on the Düna, which made crossing impossible. Peter preserved his incognito, and went out to see the town. His military curiosity naturally led him to inspect the fortifications and measure the width and depth of the ditches, when he was somewhat rudely ordered away by the sentinel. Discontented at this, a complaint was made, and the governor apologised, assuring Lefort that no discourtesy was intended. Lefort was satisfied, and said that the sentinel had merely done his duty. It must be remembered that Riga was a frontier town, that Livonia was an outlying province of Sweden, and that the embassy was not accredited to the Swedish court. Dahlberg was coldly, formally polite; he did all that propriety demanded, but nothing more. He knew perfectly well that the Tsar was with the embassy, but he respected his incognito. As the ambassadors did not pay him a visit in person, he did not pay a personal visit to the ambassadors. Nothing was done in the way of amusement or diversion for the Tsar, besides the first reception. The ambassadors were left to pay for their lodgings and their provisions, and to get on as best they might. They paid high prices for everything, but times were hard, and the people naturally tried to make the most they could out of the distinguished strangers. As there was nothing to be seen, either in a military or naval way, as there were no feasts or amusements of any kind prepared for him, Peter became bored, especially as he was anxious to continue his journey. He left the rest, ventured across the river in a small boat, and remained waiting two days on the other side. In a letter to Vinius, of April 18, he says: "Here we lived in a slavish way, and were tired with the mere sight of things." Nevertheless, the embassy took its leave with all form and ceremony, and crossed the river on a vessel carrying the royal flag of Sweden, and with a salute. When it was necessary to find a pretext for a war with Sweden, the reception at Riga was made one of the reasons, and even in 1709, when the siege of Riga was undertaken, Peter, after throwing the first three bomb-shells into the town, wrote to Menshikóf: "Thus the Lord God has enabled us to see the beginning of our revenge on this accursed place." We should add here that Peter's feelings about his reception at Riga probably increased with time. In other countries where he went, there was a sovereign with a court, and although, in a certain way, the Tsar was incognito, yet he was privately and familiarly received and entertained. It was unfortunate for him that his first venture was in an outlying province, the tenure of which was not too secure, and in a commercial rather than in an aristocratic city.

Mitau is now a dull provincial town, and the Hebrew signs on the street corners show the great Jewish population. Its greatest object of interest to travellers is the old Ducal Castle, almost entirely rebuilt in the last century, with its reminiscences of the residence and sudden depature of the exiled Louis XVIII., and with the mummified body of the Duke John Ernest Biren (the lover of the Empress Anne, and the ancestor of the Sagan family), which lies in its coffin attired in velvet and ruffles, but by some malice lacking the tip of the nose. In 1697 Mitau was the capital of the little Duchy of Curland, which maintained a semi-independence by becoming a fief of the Polish crown. The reigning Duke, Frederic Casimir, was an old friend of Lefort. It was with him that Lefort had served in Holland. Although he was poor, he did everything that he could to make the time pass pleasantly for Peter and for the embassy. Here the Tsar consented to give up in part his incognito, made visits to the Duke, and received them in return. A week was quickly passed in amusement and pleasure, but even with this Peter found time to exercise himself in a carpenter's shop.

From Mitau Peter proceeded to Libau, where he was detained by bad weather for a week, until he finally took passage on a small ship going to Pillau, the port of Königsberg. During his stay at Libau, he passed for the skipper of a Russian privateer, though he was able to give no satisfactory explanation to an acquaintance, who frequently met and drank with him in a small beer-shop, as to why it was a privateer, and not a merchant vessel that he commanded. Besides the beer-house, Peter often visited an apothecary's shop, and wrote to Vinius that he had seen there "a wonder which was ordinarily considered untrue, a real salamander preserved in spirits in a bottle," which he had taken out and held in his hand. The embassy proceeded by land. The Tsar went by sea, to avoid passing through Polish territory.

Blomberg, whom we have already cited about the election of Patriarch, met the embassy in Curland, and says of their entertainment: "Open tables were kept everywhere, with trumpets and music, attended with feasting and excessive drinking all along, as if his Tsarish Majesty had been another Bacchus. I have not seen such hard drinkers; it is not possible to express it, and they boast of it as a mighty qualification." Of Lefort's drinking he remarks: "It never overcomes him, but he always continues master of his reason." Leibnitz, writing from private information received from Königsberg, says much the same thing: "Lefort drinks like a hero; no one can rival him. It is feared that he will be the death of some of the Elector's courtiers. Beginning in the evening, he does not leave his pipe and glass till three hours after sunrise, and yet he is a man of great parts."

Frederick III., Elector of Brandenburg, then on the eve of transforming himself into the first King of Prussia, was greatly interested to know whether the Tsar was really with the embassy, and beside sending a secret agent into Curland to find out, he gave directions about the treatment of the embassy, in case it were simply intending to pass through his dominions, or in case it were directed also to him. Peter was therefore met at Pillau by an officer who proffered the hospitality of the Elector, but an answer was returned that there was no person of distinction on board, except the Prince of Imeritia, and that no visits could be received. A similar occurrence took place at the mouth of the Pregel, and it was not until Peter arrived at Königsberg itself that he was willing to allow himself to be known to the elector. After taking small lodgings in a street on the Kneiphof, he went out in a close carriage, late at night, and paid a visit to the Elector, entering the palace by a private staircase. The interview lasted for an hour and a half, and the sovereigns were mutually pleased. Although, in order to keep his incognito, Peter refused to receive a return visit, yet he saw the Elector several times again, and was entertained by him at his country house, witnessed a bear-fight, and appeared at a hunting party. His curiosity and vivacity, his readiness to be pleased, and his appreciation of the manners and habits of the country, made a favourable impression. He astonished by his natural capacity and his dexterity, even in playing the trumpet and the drum.

The embassy arrived eleven days after Peter, and was splendidly received. Great advantages were expected to Brandenburg from an intimacy with Russia, and the Elector, therefore, spared no money. Peter's visit is said to have cost him 150,000 thalers. Under the skilful guidance of Lefort and Von Besser, all ceremonial observances were strictly complied with, and, for the first time in the history of Russian missions abroad, there was no unseemly wrangling over points of precedence and etiquette. The members of the embassy appeared officially in Russian costume, although they wore foreign dress in private. The Elector told the Tsar afterwards that he had hard work to keep from laughing, when, according to custom, he had to ask the ambassadors how the Tsar was, and whether they had left him in good health. Peter had just before been standing at the window to see the entry of the embassy, and was well satisfied. At a supper given in honour of the ambassadors, great pleasure was caused by the fireworks, one piece representing the Russian arms, and another the victory at Azof.

The two rulers were so well disposed towards each other, that a treaty of friendship was speedily concluded. The Elector was greatly desirous that there should be inserted an article of alliance for mutual defence and protection; but the Russians were too cautious for this, and although the treaty contained clauses giving additional privileges to merchants, especially as regarded the Persian trade, and for the surrender of criminals and deserters, yet the Elector had to be satisfied with a verbal agreement and oath "not to let a favourable occasion escape of being useful to each other by giving each other their mutual help, as far as possible, against all their enemies, but particularly against the Swedes."

On June 20, after nearly a month's stay, Peter went to Pillau, with the intention of taking ship directly to Holland, for he found it more convenient to defer his visit to Vienna till his return. Before leaving, he sent a ruby of large size as a present to his host. At Pillau he was detained three weeks longer, by the necessity of watching affairs in Poland, where the interregnum consequent on the death of Sobieski had produced more than the usual trouble. The threatened intervention by the French, to support the Prince de Conti on the Polish throne, would have been greatly against the interest of Russia. The Tsar occupied his leisure with active and thorough studies in artillery, under the guidance of the chief engineer of the Prussian fortresses, Colonel Steitner von Sternfeld, who gave him a certificate of remarkable progress and knowledge.

An unfortunate incident, arising from Peter's hasty temper, marked the conclusion of his stay. He had remained a day longer to celebrate his name's-day, and had expected the Elector to visit him. He had even made some fireworks for the occasion. Frederick had been obliged to go to Memel, to meet the Duke of Curland, and therefore sent Count von Kreyzen and the Landvogt von Schacken to present his compliments and his regrets. Peter was childishly vexed, and in his disappointment at not being able to show his fireworks, vented his rage on the envoys. We took it amiss that they had left the room after dinner to "refresh themselves" after their journey, and had them brought back. Looking "sourly" at Count von Kreyzen, he remarked in Dutch to Lefort, that "The Elector was very good, but his counsellors were the devil." Then, thinking he saw a smile steal over the face of Kreyzen, who was about to retire, he rushed at him, cried, "Go! go!" and twice pushed him backwards. His anger did not cool until he had written to his "dearest friend," the Elector, a letter half of complaint and half of apology.

Instead of going by sea from Pillau to Holland, Peter went no farther than Colberg, as he was fearful of falling in with the French squadron, which was said to be escorting the Prince de Conti to Poland. From that place he travelled by land as speedily as possible, stopping only to look at the famous ironworks near Ilsenburg, and to ascend the Brocken for the view.

The journey of the Tsar produced as much commotion and excitement in the minds of curious people of that time as did those of the Sultan and Shah in our own day. Among those most anxious to form a personal acquaintance with the Tsar were the philosopher Leibnitz, who had long been interested in the widowed Electress of Hanover, granddaughter of James I. of England, and her daughter Sophia Charlotte, wife of the Elector of Brandenburg. Sophia Charlotte was on a visit to her mother, and had therefore missed the visit of Peter to Königsberg, though she had had

full accounts of it from a constant correspondent. Leibnitz was unable at
this time to see the Tsar, but the two Electresses, attended by several
young princes and members of their court, made a hasty journey from
Hanover to Koppenbrügge, through which they found Peter was to pass.
They invited him to sup with them, but it took a discussion of an hour to
persuade him to accept, and he did so only on the assurance that he would
be received in the simplest way. He finally succeeded in avoiding the
curious eyes of the attendants, and in getting into the supper-room by the
back staircase. After supper there was a dance, and the party did not
separate until four in the morning. Perhaps the princesses can tell their
own story best. Sophia Charlotte says in a letter:

"My mother and I began to pay him our compliments, but he made
Mr. Lefort reply for him, for he seemed shy, hid his face in his hands, and
said: *'Ich kann nicht sprechen.'* But we tamed him a little, and then he sat
down at the table between my mother and myself, and each of us talked
to him in turn, and it was a strife who should have it. Sometimes he replied with the same promptitude, at others he made two interpreters talk,
and assuredly he said nothing that was not to the point on all subjects that
were suggested, for the vivacity of my mother put to him many questions,
to which he replied with the same readiness, and I was astonished that he
was not tired with the conversation, for I have been told that it is not
much the habit in his country. As to his grimaces, I imagined them
worse than I found them, and some are not in his power to correct. One
can see also that he has had no one to teach him how to eat properly, but
he has a natural, unconstrained air which pleases me."

Her mother wrote, a few days afterwards:

"The Tsar is very tall, his features are fine, and his figure very noble.
He has great vivacity of mind, and a ready and just repartee. But, with
all the advantages with which nature has endowed him, it could be wished
that his manners were a little less rustic. We immediately sat down to table. Herr Koppenstein, who did the duty of marshal, presented the napkin
to his Majesty, who was greatly embarrassed, for at Brandenburg, instead
of a table-napkin, they had given him an ewer and basin after the meal.
He was very gay, very talkative, and we established a great friendship for
each other, and he exchanged snuff-boxes with my daughter. We stayed,
in truth, a very long time at table, but we would gladly have remained
there longer still without feeling a moment of *ennui,* for the Tsar was in
very good humour, and never ceased talking to us. My daughter had her
Italians sing. Their song pleased him, though he confessed to us that he did
not care much for music.

"I asked him if he liked hunting. He replied that his father had been
very fond of it, but that he himself, from his earliest youth, had had a real
passion for navigation and for fireworks. He told us that he worked himself in building ships, showed us his hands, and made us touch the callous
places that had been caused by work. He brought his musicians, and they
played Russian dances, which we liked better than Polish ones.

"Lefort and his nephew dressed in French style, and had much wit. We did not speak to the other ambassadors. We regretted that he could not stay longer, so that we could see him again, for his society gave us much pleasure. He is a very extraordinary man. It is impossible to describe him, or even to give an idea of him, unless you have seen him. He has a very good heart, and remarkably noble sentiments. I must tell you, also, that he did not get drunk in our presence, but we had hardly left when the people of his suite made ample amends."

In another letter she says:—

"I could embellish the tale of the journey of the illustrious Tsar, if I should tell you that he is sensible to the charms of beauty, but, to come to the bare fact, I found in him no disposition to gallantry. If we had not taken so many steps to see him, I believe that he would never have thought of us. In his country it is the custom for all women to paint, and rouge forms an essential part of their marriage presents. That is why the Countess Platen singularly pleased the Muscovites; but in dancing, they took the whalebones of our corsets for our bones, and the Tsar showed his astonishment by saying that the German ladies had devilish hard bones.

"They have four dwarfs. Two of them are very well-proportioned, and perfectly well-bred; sometimes he kissed, and sometimes he pinched the ear of his favorite dwarf. He took the head of our little Princess (Sophia Dorothea, ten years old), and kissed her twice. The ribbons of her hair suffered in consequence. He also kissed her brother (afterwards George II. of England, then sixteen years old). He is a prince at once very good and very *méchant*. He has quite the manners of his country. If he had received a better education, he would be an accomplished man, for he has many good qualities; and an infinite amount of natural wit."

. . .

Every time that the Tsar returned from a prolonged absence he found the administration of Russia in such a state that it was necessary to begin at once a series of trials and executions. The contrast, in this respect, between Russia and Sweden is striking. The King was absent from Sweden for fourteen years, communication with him was often difficult and interrupted, the country suffered greatly from the war, yet the regular machinery of government went on as before. In Russia, on the contrary, if the Tsar were away for a year or less, the administration became thoroughly disorganized. So far Peter had succeeded in pulling down better than in building up. He had set about this latter task several times, and now that the war was practically finished, it was necessary for him to be in earnest over it. In order to understand the state of affairs when the Tsar returned from Paris, we must go back for a few years and trace the course of the civil administration. As the negotiations for peace will still go on slowly for three years, we can the more readily turn from foreign to internal affairs.

The Senate, as we remember, was created by the Tsar on the eve of the campaign of the Pruth, in order to take his place in the internal administration of the country, and to govern during his absence. In its hands were concentrated all the powers of government of every kind. As was natural, things did not at once work smoothly. Ramodanófsky, the Governor of Moscow, had a bitter quarrel with the Senate for usurping his powers and interfering with his jurisdiction—a quarrel ending only with his death in 1713. His successor, Soltykóf, having been appointed through the influence of the senators, succeeded better; but he in turn got into a quarrel with his vice-governor and had to be changed, and under his successor Dolgorúky the disputes with the Senate began again. The Governor of Kazán complained that, while the Senate interfered in everything, it had not sufficient knowledge on which to base its decisions. His provinces were too heavily taxed because they were thought to be rich, and they had now become so poor that it was with difficulty anything could be got from them. The Tsar himself complained bitterly of the waste of time. He wrote frequent letters to "Messieurs the Senate," scolding them as one would a child or a careless servant. He reminds them of their oath of office, he tells them that they have made themselves a laughing-stock, once expresses the suspicion that they have been bribed, and threatens to hold them to strict accountability on his return. He tells them that "loss of time is like death, as hard to return as a life that is ended." He orders them while in session not to converse about matters not pertaining to the service, especially not to have idle talk or jests, "for the Senate represents the person of his Majesty." Nothing was to be done except with the consent of the whole Senate, and nothing transacted at home or privately. Everything must be written out and recorded, and no outsiders must be introduced into the Senate. The slowness of business in other departments of the Government naturally affected that of the Senate. Decrees frequently remained unattended to. In order to prevent this, Basil Zótof was in 1715 appointed a General Inspector of Decrees. It was his duty to watch over their execution and see that there were no delays. Three years later we find him complaining that the Senate pays no attention to his remonstrances, destroys his reports, transacts business without him, and does not hold regular sessions nor keep registers of all the business; that the returns are neither properly nor regularly sent from the provinces, that fines and forfeitures are not collected, that in three years nearly a million and a half of rubles remain unpaid, that fines had been imposed to the amount of 31,657 rubles, of which 3,368 only had been received, the rest having been either postponed, remitted, or not collected. Probably the Senate would not have done even as well as this, had not Prince Jacob Dolgorúky been appointed first Senator in 1712, and had he not immediately, so to speak, taken possession of that body. We remember the curious reports of his mission to France in 1687. He had been taken prisoner at the battle of Narva, and had after eleven years succeeded in escaping from Sweden. Shrewd, crafty, of violent prejudices, obstinate, and strong-willed, he could not but impose himself on his weaker colleagues, if only by force of lungs. Menshikóf was the only man who dared face him. Frank to an excess, he dared tell the truth to the Tsar, on many occasions when the truth was disagreeable. Many amusing anecdotes are told of his obstinacy.

An important change was made in the constitution and sphere of the Senate in 1718 by the institution of colleges, or, as we call them, boards of commissioners. The division of business among the old *Prikazes* or departments had come about a good deal by chance. Through the general changes, especially through the interference of the Senate, these departments had fallen into confusion, and business had been transferred at will from one to the other. This created additional delay. It was necessary to find something to take their place. Naturally, in the present turn of affairs, the first question was, How are these things done abroad? and in Stockholm and Vienna the business of the State was managed by colleges. This idea was proposed to the Tsar as long ago as 1698 by Dr. Francis Lee, but no particular attention had been paid to his proposals. In 1715 Heinrich Fick, formerly in the service of the Duke of Holstein, who had been recommended by Bassewitz to General Weyde, was secretly sent to Sweden to obtain accurate information of the constitution and working of the colleges in that country. He sent a series of reports, which were for a long time accredited to Leibnitz, who certainly had the same general idea, and had indeed, although a year later, proposed it to the Tsar. In one of these reports the functions of the colleges are compared to the works of a watch, "where one wheel brings another into movement," a comparison which naturally pleased the Tsar. The great difficulty of introducing such a system of wheels into Russia was to find the proper men to work them, and it was thought at first that recourse must be had to foreigners. For this purpose General Weyde, in the same year, was instructed to hire learned foreigners, skilled in jurisprudence and administration. Veselófsky in Vienna had similar orders. He was to search especially for persons speaking Slavonic languages, one from each college at Vienna, and at the same time was to ask the Jesuit School at Prague to translate certain books, which would be of use to the new administration. There seems, however, to have been very few who were willing to go to Russia in such capacity; and therefore, in August, 1717, an effort was made to find Swedish prisoners of war who had learnt Russian well enough, and had other necessary qualities, to take service. Finally, in 1719, with the same end in view, thirty or forty Russians were sent to Königsberg to study German and jurisprudence.

At the end of 1717 the plan had made such progress that nine colleges were instituted, although it was only in 1720 that they got into thorough working order. These colleges or commissions were those of Foreign Affairs, Revenue, Expenditure, Control, Justice (including Internal Affairs), War, Admiralty, Commerce, and Mines and Manufactures; under the presidency respectively of Count Golófkin, Prince Dimítri Golítsyn (the Governor of Kief), Count Musin-Puskin, Prince Jacob Dolgorúky, Count Matvéief (who had finished his diplomatic career), Prince Menshikóf, Admiral Count Apráxin, Tolstói, and General Bruce. All the presidents—who were equivalent to Ministers—were Russian, with the exception of General Bruce in the College of Mines and Manufactures, there being no Russian fit for the place. The vice-presidents were all foreigners, except Baron Shafirof in the College of Foreign Affairs. The whole institution was so un-Russian that several colleges even bore foreign names, as *Kammer, Staats-Control, Justitz Collegium, Berg Collegium.* The presidents appointed councillors, assessors, writers, translators, &c., of whom a small fixed number could be foreigners. All business was to be transacted in full meeting of the members, as in the Senate, and the presidents were also to have seats in the Senate itself. These new wheels at first revolved very badly, and stopped one another more than they put one another in motion. In the College of Foreign Affairs, the vice-president did not wish to sit and discuss with persons whom he called the creatures of Count Golofkin. In others there were disputes, as was very natural between the Russians and the foreigners. That these institutions worked badly can be seen readily enough from the protocols of their sessions, and it did not escape the notice of all foreigners. Vockerodt, a competent contemporary, says: "It was soon shown that there had been too much haste, and that in the transaction of business there was more confusion to be expected than good order and promptitude. The chanceries in the provinces, from which business must come to the colleges in St. Petersburg, still remained on the old footing, and although instructions were sent to them how they must forward their reports and accounts, the old Russian clerks could not understand them, and thus caused much disorder. The Russian councillors in the colleges, even if they understood the concerns of their country, still could not immediately get a clear idea of the new method, and the Germans were seldom able to show them, partly because they did not understand the Russian language, and partly also because the Swedish forms were as little known to them. Therefore the Tsar in 1722 was obliged to make a second change in his new colleges, to dismiss most of the foreigners, and to put the colleges themselves, though still keeping the German names, on a footing which came considerably nearer the old one, and indeed did not differ from it in anything except the number of members, which hindered rather than advanced the prompt transaction of business, since no member was allowed to work at home or read over the case except in full session, and then give his vote, and that in those chanceries where there were accounts of revenue and expenditure proper books were kept in the commercial style."

. . .

"The Tsar, pitying the peoples of his realm, zealous to root out unjust, disastrous, general burdens and crafty thefts from the State treasury, having ascertained that great falsifications and thefts are increasing the public burdens and injuring the interests of the State, and that by this many people of every station, but most of all the peasants, are becoming impoverished and ruined," &c., &c. So began one of the Tsar's decrees in 1713; but the Tsar really knew very little of the sufferings of the people. Indeed, how could he? What were the Russian serfs at that time, that anyone should interest themselves in them except as mere draft animals, machines for labour, and objects of taxation? The revenue of Russia which for 1709 had been calculated at 3,026,128 rubles had risen in 1725 to 10,186,707 rubles, the ruble having depreciated fifteen per cent. in value. At the end of Peter's reign the regular army numbered 210,000 men, and the fleet contained forty-eight ships of the line and eight hundred smaller vessels, manned by 28,000 men. This result could not have been reached without immense and oppressive taxation, and, as we have already seen, nearly everything possible was taxed. Besides that, the recruiting and the way it was carried on, the building of St. Petersburg, the construction of the fortresses, the digging of canals, and the opening of harbours had cost the lives of hundreds of thousands of men. To escape harsh treatment and death many more had run away. Strahlenberg tells us that to escape the oppression of the tax officials, who collected the taxes in the times of the year worst for agriculture, and seized the draft horses of the peasants, at least a hundred thousand men had fled to Poland, Lithuania, Turkey, and the Tartars. Others say two hundred thousand. The figures may be doubted, but the general fact remains true. Whole villages ran away to the frontiers or hid in the woods. As the maintenance of a large army rendered both men and money necessary, the pursuit of the fugitive serfs, and of unwilling and runaway conscripts, was carried on diligently throughout the whole of Peter's reign. All other means of raising revenue proving insufficient, even the monopolies of trade producing unsatisfactory results, recourse was had to a poll-tax—imposed on males only—which fell chiefly on the peasants, as the nobles, the clergy, and their families, the inhabitants of the Baltic provinces, the Bashkirs and the Lapps were exempted from it. This amounted to 120 kopeks per head on the inhabitants of towns, 114 kopeks on the crown and church peasants, the odnodvórtsi, or peasant proprietors, and the inhabitants of the Ukraine, and 74 kopeks on the other taxpayers. The census ordered in 1719 to regulate the imposition of the poll-tax served to strengthen greatly the bonds of serfage. There had been hitherto a legal distinction between household slaves and serfs or peasants attached to the soil, but the department of serfage, charged with the registration of slaves and the maintenance of this distinction, had been abolished in 1704, and consequently all the peasants were inscribed indiscriminately on the census lists as serfs, became thenceforth the absolute property of the landed proprietors, and could be bought and sold. As the proprietors were made responsible for the poll-tax and the furnishing of recruits, it is easy to understand what power they were given over these wretched labourers. The laws establishing manufactures introduced a new kind of serfdom, where the peasant was separated from the land, and rendered a simple slave attached to a manufactory. To be sure, a decree was issued in 1721 forbidding the sale of serfs as such without land—the theory of Russian law being that, when land was sold, the serfs naturally went with it—but even in this very decree there was added "should such sale be absolutely necessary, they should be sold by families and not individually." Pososhkóf, himself a peasant and a contemporary of Peter, shows throughout his economical treatise how great was the oppression of the peasantry, and how little it was known to the Tsar. Foreigners, however, perceived it. Vockerodt wondered at the patience of the oppressed people, and questioned "whether some patriot will not arise before one expects, and find means to bring the complaints and sighs of the subjects to the steps of the throne." Weber, in a ciphered despatch to the Elector of Hanover, says: "Everything in this realm will have a fearful end, because the sighs of so many million souls against the Tsar rise to heaven, and the glowing sparks of rage concealed in every man lack nothing but a fair wind and a conductor." The real history of the Russian people at this time is, however, only to be found in the archives of the Secret Tribunal of Preobrazhénsky, and in the memoirs of traditions of the dissenters in the north and east.

The poll-tax had the merit of being simple and easily collected; but it replaced a tax on arable land, much better in principle, which had existed from the earliest times, was in thorough conformity with Russian ideas, and had been gradually developed and was capable of still further development and improvement. The inequality and injustice of the poll-tax—or tax on *souls,* as it was technically called—struck contemporaries. Pososhkóf opposed it, and recommended a land-tax. He thought this could not be permanent, and that the money spent on the census was therefore wasted. Two years after Peter's death Catherine appointed a commission to find means for diminishing the poll-tax, or substituting for it a land or house-tax. Her death put an end to the project.

In spite of the great increase of revenue and the constant economy practised by the Tsar, yet—owing to wars as well as bad harvests—the treasury was sometimes so low that it was necessary to recur to extraordinary measures, such as are now practised only in Turkey. In the winter of 1723 the Government officials were paid in furs and other Government wares instead of money. It was not so easy then for the Government to contract loans. A subsequent decree says that "when money is absolutely necessary, and when no other way of raising it is found, the sum must be deducted proportionally from the salaries of the officials, spiritual as well as temporal, except foreign artisans and soldiers and sailors." A few months later, besides raising the excise on spirits and the price of stamped paper, one-fourth was deducted from the pay of all officials, and the rations of officers were either reduced by half or withheld altogether.

In endeavoring to find ways of improving the revenues and of increasing the general well-being of the country, Peter was certainly in earnest and energetic. In some respects he was an adherent of the mercantile or protective theory, as far as he understood it; but it requires a strong imagination to find any real or consequent system in his commercial policy. He did things as they occurred to him. If when travelling abroad he saw something which he thought useful for Russia, he at once adopted it, without further thought as to whether its introduction was easy or not. Hence many trials which were soon abandoned, many measures which contradicted each other. Peter himself admitted that there was no branch of administration which he found so difficult to understand as economy and commerce. When the Dutch resident was pressing for a new commercial treaty, and had met with nothing but delay, Osterman at last said: "Between ourselves, I will tell you the whole truth. We have not a single man who understands commercial affairs at all. But I can assure you that the Tsar is now occupying himself with this matter." As concerns the accumulation of precious metals, the policy of Peter would certainly satisfy the most rigid adherent of the mercantile system. In 1714 he forbade the exportation of silver. The next year this order was repeated. Four years later, merchants who crossed the frontier were searched to see whether they took with them ducats, specie, thalers, or silver, and the coin was confiscated. Not even silver or copper small money was allowed to go out of the country. In 1721, a proposition had been made by the Mining College, and approved by the Tsar, that worked or unworked silver should never be exported. This decree was repeated two years later, with the addition of the punishment of death for its violation. None of these did any good, for the exportation of precious metals constantly increased. In those days the system of the easy transfer of money by paper had not reached its present development. The import of gold and silver was not only allowed, but Peter tried to increase it by freeing it from duty. At the same time it was not allowed to introduce any small Russian coin, on the ground that it would probably be counterfeit. Russians were not permitted to sell their wares to foreigners for Russian money, but must receive always foreign money. Peter even said that he would heartily thank the man who could show him how to keep money in the country, and many decrees say nearly the same thing.

The measures for the improvement of the economical condition of Russia had reference chiefly to mining, manufactures, and the regulation of commerce. Very little attention was paid to agriculture, which was apparently thought to be such a natural and simple condition of man that it needed none. One decree, however, orders the grain to be reaped with scythes and not with sickles, and the peasants were commanded, under heavy penalties for disobedience, to use hoes of new construction. Tobacco culture was introduced into the south, efforts were made to increase the production of flax and hemp, and it was forbidden to burn the grass in the steppes. To improve the wool shepherds introduced from Silesia, and sheep farmers, especially in Little Russia, were ordered to tend their flocks on the Silesian plan. An attempt was also made to improve the breed of horses in the south. To forests, as we have seen, the Tsar paid much more attention, but chiefly because he needed the trees for shipbuilding. The wilful destruction of forests, or even sometimes the necessary use of trees for timber, was forbidden by a series of severe decrees, in which the penalty of death was frequently threatened. On the Neva and the shore of the Finnish Gulf, as a warning, gallows were built every five miles, on which offenders against the forest laws were at once strung up. In St. Petersburg itself a birch grove stood on the site of the present bazaar. When, in spite of all laws, many inhabitants cut wood there, Peter resolved to hang every tenth man among the guilty and to knout the rest, but this severity was fortunately alleviated at the request of Catherine. Immense quantities of timber were used by the Government itself. So much went to the construction of the harbour works at Reval and Baltic Port, the latter of which was left unfinished, that Vockerodt said they had ruined the forests of Livonia and Esthonia and in 1720 Peter wrote to Repnin to forbid the export of wood from Pernan because the forest was disappearing.

In a decree of 1723 Peter thus explains the causes of the slow development of manufactures. "Either our decrees are not accurately observed, or there are few people who wish to go into the business. Manufacturers too are ruined by goods brought from abroad. For instance, a peasant discovered a dye called 'Florence lake.' I had artists try it. They said that it was only inferior to the Venetian, and quite equal to the German; some said even better. A good deal of it was made, and no other manufacturers also complain. Therefore it is necessary to look after this sharply and to communicate with the College of Commerce and, if it does not look after it, then to protest to the Senate and state the matter to us, for other nations greatly envy our manufactories and try by all means to ruin them by bribery, as many examples show. That there are a few people wishing to go into business is true, for our people are like children, who never want to begin the alphabet unless they are compelled to by their teacher. It seems very hard to them at first, but when they have learnt it they are thankful. So in manufacturing affairs we must not be satisfied with the proposition only, but we must act and even compel, and help by teaching, by machines, and other aids, and even by compulsion, to become good economists. For instance, where there is fine felt we should compel people to make hats, by not allowing the sale of felt unless a certain number of hats are made." Always force, always compulsion. Peter seems to have found no better way for dealing with even such a delicate matter as commerce, where people are governed entirely by their own interests, and where a slight fear of loss, especially if caused by Government interference, counteracts an almost certain hope of profit. Force was of little avail to promote Russian industry. High import duties, bounties, privileges and monopolies did more, but Russian manufactures never took a high rank in Peter's day nor indeed for long after.

On the whole the constant Government interference, the prohibitions of exports and imports, so suddenly and frequently established, changed, and withdrawn, the minute regulations, the paternal supervision, did more harm than good to Russian trade, and lessened instead of increased the wealth of the country. Many interests were sacrificed in these commercial experiments. Thus in 1701 two foreigners were commissioned to make hats in the German style out of beaver skins and wool, and the exportation of the raw material or its sale to foreigners was forbidden, though only two years before two Dutchmen had been given a twelve years' privilege for the purchase and exportation of wool. In 1705 woolen factories were doing so well that Peter wrote to Menshikóf: "They are making cloth, and this business is making good progress, and God gives excellent results, so that I have made a caftan for myself for the holidays." In 1715 he hoped that in five years' time there would be cloth enough made to stop the importation, and in 1718 he ordered that the uniforms for all the soldiers in garrison should be made out of Moscow cloth. Another decree of the same year ordered "the servants of the Boyars to wear livery or clothes of cloth of Russian manufacture and not foreign, the same to be the rule for the lower class of townspeople, who must in future content themselves with soldier's cloth. If there is not enough cloth for the Boyars' servants, then let them use serge, double if necessary. Either diminish the gold galloon or forbid it altogether, for it is beginning to be a habit to wear much of it, whence there is a loss not only to private people but also to the State, for the English are richer than we, and do not wear much of it." About the same time the use of gold and silver stuffs was forbidden during the war. Old stuffs could be worn out but no new could be made. The importation of gold lace and stuffs worked with gold and silver was forbidden, but their manufacture was allowed at St. Petersburg to not more than 2,200 pounds of silver in one year, and later still the importation was again permitted. The importation of serge was forbidden, as well as of stockings, the latter to encourage a Frenchman who had started a factory at Moscow. The hemp and flax industries went through a number of vicissitudes. With his idea of exporting only manufactured products and not raw material, Peter forbade the exportation of hemp and flax seed, the great staples of Russia, except in the shape of oil. The oil, however, was so bad that none would buy it, and the prohibition of export was removed. At the same time he was trying to extend by compulsion the culture of flax and hemp. The course of trade too was arbitrarily changed. At times all the flax and hemp must be sent to St. Petersburg; at others part could be sent to Archangel; at others still it must all be sold to the Government. To encourage honesty an admixture of stones in a bale of hemp was punished with death. The needs of the Fleet were so great that the manufacture of sail cloth took good proportions. The Government factories were nearly ruined by bad management, and it became necessary to give them into private hands. In 1712 the Tsar forbade the weaving of the narrow linen commonly used in Russia, and, with entire forgetfulness of the fact that the home market is the most important, for the sake of a possible export to England and her colonies, ordered all linen to be made at least a yard wide. The narrow linen made after that date was to be confiscated, and the informer was promised ten kopeks for each ell of linen he discovered. In 1718 this prohibition was withdrawn, and linen of all widths was allowed to be made; but again there was a change, and the export of narrow linen was forbidden (as if indeed it would have been exported without a demand for it). In spite of this paternal care, the linen industry languished. When long after, in 1762 and 1764, the restrictions on trade were removed, the export of flax and hemp increased, and they now constitute nearly one-fifth of the whole export. In order to encourage the manufacture of silk, Baron Shafírof and Tolstói were given a privilege for the manufacture of silk goods. The importation from abroad was entirely forbidden, and no European silk could even be worn, and they had the

right of importing Asiatic raw silk free of duty; yet the business went on
so badly that a limited importation (100,000 rubles) without duty of foreign silk goods was allowed to them for two years, in order to set the factory going again. The prospect, however, was so poor that they sold their
privilege to private merchants for 20,000 rubles. One of the chief exports
of Russia at that time was leather. In 1716 at least five million pounds
were brought to Archangel for shipment, and its quality had long been
famous. But the Tsar was dissatisfied with it on the ground that it was not
sufficiently durable and waterproof, and with the best of intentions did
what he could to break up the trade. In 1715 he forbade the manufacture
of Russian leather, and ordered it henceforth to be made on the German
plan, to teach which a sort of tanning-school was opened at Moscow,
master-workmen being sent from Reval, who instructed the Russians, from
the factories of the interior. If after two years of trial anyone made leather
on the old system he was to be sent to Siberia and his property confiscated.
The mining industry fared better owing to the great richness of the ores
discovered in the Ural. Mining privileges were given to Nikíta Demídof,
the blacksmith of Tula, in 1702, who set to work vigorously and became so
rich that, on the birth of the Tsarévitch Peter, he presented him with a
hundred thousand rubles as "tooth-cutting money." In 1720 he was ennobled. The Stróganofs increased their already great fortune in the same
region, and Alexander Stróganof was created a Baron in 1712. Even the
Government mines prospered under the excellent management of General Hennin and Basil Tatíistchef.

The general state of the country was not such as to encourage either
manufacturers or merchants. The officials had been so long acustomed to
look down upon the trading classes as low sorts of beings, that they made
no scruples of harassing them and seizing their property. The large factories which were started by great nobles with the assistance of the State
were safe, but the smaller ones frequently suffered from exactions and irregularities, and dared not complain. The safest way was to obtain the
protection of some powerful person, but this after a time was strictly forbidden. Thus we find that many wealthy merchants had got themselves
registered as servants of the Princess Natalia, or even of the Tsaritza
Catherine; and when they were obliged to go back to their shops, they
complained that the taxes were such that they were unable to live and
carry on their trade as before. We may judge how necessary such protection sometimes was, from the case of the merchant Bogomólof, who was a
well-known and rich man in Moscow; had much silver, gold, and jewels;
had given much to the construction of a monastery where he hoped to be
buried; had lent money to various high placed personages; and among
others, had been on friendly terms with Prince Boris Golítsyn, who frequently visited him. One day Sergius, son of Boris, came to visit Bogomólof; and, finding him alone with a young nephew, ordered all the servants
out of the house, sent him off to a monastery in the country, forced him to
become a monk, and in fact robbed him of all his property.

It is almost useless to recount the vain attempt to introduce the German system of guilds among the Russian workmen, in which all laws and lessons of historical development were disregarded. Yet the old Russian *artel* —a sort of mutually-guaranteeing, mutually-protecting company of artisans—lay ready to hand, waiting only for development. Nor need more particular mention be made of the hundreds of Russian artisans sent abroad by the Government to learn trades. Many found it pleasanter to stay where they were. Of those who returned, the majority, finding themselves isolated among their countrymen, soon fell back into the old ways.

Peter's Administrative Reforms

The diagram is a schematic presentation of the results, at least on paper, of Peter the Great's efforts to modernize his government. It is based upon a chart published in N. P. Eroshkin, *Ocherki istorii gosudarstvennyikh uchrezdenii dorevolutsionnoi Rossi (An Outline History of State Institutions in Prerevolutionary Russia)*. Moscow, 1960.

THE SENATE AND THE STATE APPARATUS, 1711-1725

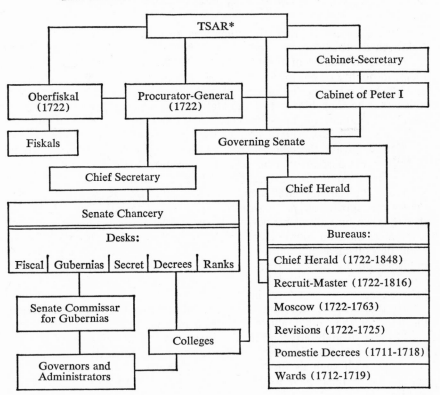

*Title changed to Emperor in 1722

Prince Menshikov

Among Peter's boon companions, none was more favored than Menshikov whom the tsar raised to great power. During the reign of Catherine I, he was the power behind the throne and aspired to be more, affiancing his daughter to Peter II. But when Peter II came to power, he stripped Menshikov of his powers, honors, and titles and exiled him to Siberia. The following description of Menshikov is from a contemporary source: General Manstein, *Memoirs of Russia, Historical Political and Military from the Year MDCCXXVII to MDCCXLIV.* (*Introduction by David Hume.*) London, 1770. Pp. 10–13.

The general opinion on the origin of Menzikoff is, that his father was a peasant, who had placed him, at Moskow, with a pastry-cook, and that he carried about little pies, singing along the streets; that the Emperor Peter I. having stopped to speak to him, he had pleased him with the wit and liveliness of his repartees. Upon this he put him servant to Monsieur Le Fort; thence he took him about his own person, and by degrees made his fortune.

Others again say, that his father was an officer in the service of the Czar, Alexis Michaëlowitz, and that as it is not extraordinary to see gentlemen serve in stables of the Czar, Menzikoff had also been employed in them, in quality of one of the head-grooms: that Peter having often spoke to him; had taken notice of the wit and shrewdness of his answers, insomuch that he took him out of the stables, and placed him as a more immediate attendant on himself; when, observing great talents in him, he had, in a few years, raised him to the first posts in the empire.

I have always thought the first of these opinions the nearest to the truth; for it is certain, that he was of an obscure birth, and that he began with being a common servant; after which the Emperor placed him as a private soldier in the first company of regular troops, which he raised under the appelation *preprovojdenie* [Preobrazhenskii]. Peter I. having thence taken him about his person, gave him his entire confidence, in such a manner, that, on many occasions, Menzikoff governed Russia with the same despotism as his master. His credit had, however, been greatly diminished during the last years of the reign of Peter I. and it is believed, that if that Emperor had lived some months longer, there would have been changes at court, and in the ministry.

By the following character, any one may decide which preponderated, the good or the bad qualities of Prince Menzikoff.

He was strongly attached to his master, and to the maxims of Peter I. for civilizing the Russian nation; affable and polite towards strangers; that is to say, with such as did not pretend to have more wit than himself; neither did he misbehave to those of the Russians who showed submission to him. He treated all who were his inferiors with gentleness, never forgetting a service done him. Brave withal, he gave, on occasions of the greatest dangers, incontestable proofs of the necessary personal courage. Wherever he had once taken a friendship, he continued a zealous friend.

On the other hand, he was possessed with a boundless ambition; he could not endure a superior or an equal, and less yet one that he could suspect of pretending to surpass him in understanding. His avarice was insatiable. He was an implacable enemy. He did not want for natural wit; but having had no education, his manners were rather coarse. His avarice had led him into several disagreeable explanations with Peter I. who had sometimes condemned him to pay arbitrary fines: notwithstanding which, there was found, on his imprisonment, the value of three millions of rubles, in jewels, in plate, and ready money.

He had a son and two daughters: she who had been betrothed to the Emperor died, before her father, in exile; the other was married, under the reign of the Empress Anne, with the General Gustawus Biron, brother to the Duke of Courland, and died in the beginning of the year 1737. The son is major in the guards. So long as his father was in favor and prosperity, all the world allowed him a great deal of wit, though he was but a child; since the disgrace and death of his father, there are few persons in the whole empire of Russia that have less than he.

Menzikoff, who, from the lowest condition, had been raised to the highest stations of life, would have finished his career with honor, if he had not been so infatuated with ambition, as to seek to place his posterity on the throne of Russia. It is the same rock against which all the favorites that followed him have struck, and sunk like him, as will hereafter be shown.

The Empress Anne

Following the death of Peter II, the State Council, which was dominated by the Dolgoruki and Golitsin families, met to choose a sovereign and sought to use this opportunity to limit the autocratic power to the advantage of the nobility. Their choice fell upon Anne of Courland, niece of Peter I, to whom they offered the throne provided she would accept certain limitations. Anne first accepted the offer with its strings attached and then, sure of the crown, thanks to the support of other nobles, renounced the conditions. The following account of this abortive palace revolution is from Manstein, *Memoirs,* pp. 26–35, *passim.*

The council of state, the senate, and such of the principal generals of the army as were then at Moscow, assembled immediately after the decease of Peter II. and sat in close committee in a chamber of the palace of Kremlin. The high-Chancellor Goloskin announced to the assembly the death of the Emperor, and as soon as he had done speaking, the Prince Demetrius Michaelowitz Gallitzin got up, and said, that *"since, by the demise of Peter II. the whole male line of Peter I. was extinct, and that Russia had suffered extremely by despotic power, to the prevalence of which the great number of foreigners brought in by Peter I. had greatly contributed, it*

would be highly expedient to limit the supreme authority by salutary laws,
and not to confer the imperial crown on the new Empress that should be
chosen, but under certain conditions;" concluding with putting the question
to the whole assembly, whether *"they did not approve this proposal?"*
They all assented to it, without any of the least opposition. Upon which
the Prince Basilius Loukitsch Dolgoroucki proposed the duchess dowager
of Courland; alleging, that as the crown was now falling to female, it was
but just to prefer the daughter of the Czar Iwan, the elder brother of
Peter I. to those of this Emperor; that though the duchess of Mecklenburgh
was the eldest, it was to be considered that she was married to a foreign
Prince, whereas the Duchess of Courland was actually a widow, and, not
being above thirty-six years of age, might marry, and give heirs to Russia.

The true reason, however, for preferring the duchess of Courland was,
that she being at Mittau, the remoteness of that place would afford time
for firmer establishment of the republican system.

All the votes then united in her favor, and it was agreed, that the
Council of State, which was at that time constituted of seven members, of
whom the majority were the Dolgorouckis or their relations, should have
the whole power, and the assembly framed the following articles:

1st. That the Empress Anne was to reign only in virtue of the resolves,
upon deliberation of the privy-council.

2d. That she should not declare war nor make peace on her own authority.

3d. That she would not lay any new tax, or bestow any post or place of
consequence.

4th. That she would punish no gentleman with death unless he was
duly convicted of his crime.

5th. That she should not confiscate anyone's property.

6th. That she should not alienate or dispose of any lands belonging to
the crown.

7th. That she should not marry, nor choose an heir, without asking,
upon all these points, the consent of the privy-council.

The assembly then chose three members to notify to the Empress her
accession to the throne, and to propose to her the conditions under which
she should reign.

In the instructions given to the deputies, it was enjoined to them, to
require of the Empress that she should sign the above articles, and that she
should not bring her favorite with her to Moscow, Biron, gentleman of the
chamber.

•   •   •

The council of state imagined they had sufficient precaution against the
restoration of despotic government, having exacted from the whole army
an oath, that it would not serve the Empress but conjointly with the senate.
Moreover, before the assembly broke up, they had forbidden, under pain
of death, the acquainting the new Empress of any thing that had been
debated and resolved. She was not to receive advice of her election, and of

the conditions under which she was to mount the throne, but at first hand from the deputies.

. . .

The Empress consented, without making any difficulty, to the signing of whatever the deputies presented to her on the part of the privy-council. She did not even oppose the leaving her favorite behind her at Mittau, and got immediately in readiness to set out for Moscow.

Her Majesty came on the 20th of February to a village called All Saints, situated two leagues from Moscow, where she stopped for five days. As soon as she was arrived there the high-chancellor, at the head of the members of the privy-council, repaired thither, and presented her with the ribbon of St. Andrew, and star, in a gold bason. As soon as the Empress saw it, she said, "it is true, I had forgot to put the order on;" and taking it with her own hands out of the bason, she made one of her attendants put it on her, without suffering any members of the privy-council to help her on with it; and when the high-chancellor was beginning to harangue her, she stopped him, and prevented his going on.

On the same day she appointed the Prince Soltikoff, a very near relation to the mother of the Empress, lieutenant-colonel of the guards. This was the first act of authority she took since her accession to the throne. The rest of her conduct, after her arrival at Moscow, gave many members of the council and of the senate reason to think that she was satisfied with the restrictions laid upon despotic power. She signed anew all that the council of state required, and affected to submit cheerfully to all the conditions.

Her secret conduct was very different from this her public one. Her favorite, whom, at the requisition of the council, she had left behind, was arrived at Moscow; and she took all the pains imaginable to form a strong party. She tried to engage the guards, by her liberality to those who daily did duty about her person. In short, she left no arts or managements unemployed towards effectuating her purpose of creating misunderstandings among the members of the council of state. Everything succeeded to her wish. It had been remarked to them, that the family of the Dolgorouckis, and its connections, would be the only persons that would be benefited by the smallness of the Empress's influence; that they had tied up her hands only to establish the more firmly the power which they had acquired under Peter II; that there were already of that family many of the members of the privy-council, and of the senate; that, little by little, the number would go on augmenting; and that they ought to reflect on the conduct of that family, after the death of the late Emperor, at which time they had aspired to transmit the imperial crown to their family, in which not having been able to succeed, they had not given up the hope of bringing it about in time, by their circumscription of the supreme power.

Neither was it omitted the instilling a mistrust into the lesser nobility, which is very numerous in Russia, by giving them to understand, that none of them stood any chance of obtaining any preferment of the least consequence, while the council of state should have all the power in their hands; as each member would make a point of procuring the most considerable employments for his respective relations and creatures; and that, properly speaking, they would be slaves of the council: whereas, if the Empress was to be declared sovereign, the least private gentleman might pretend to the first posts of the empire, with the same currency as the first Princes: that there were examples of this under Peter I when the greatest regard was paid to true merit; and that if that Prince had done acts of severity, he had been obliged to it; besides, that the lesser nobility had nowise suffered by him; on the contrary, they had recovered their consequence under his reign.

Such hints thrown out, with proper discretion, did not fail of producing the expected effect. The guards, who, even to the private soldiers, are constituted of hardly any but the nobles of the country, formed meetings. Several hundreds of country-gentlemen assembled at the houses of the Princes Trubetszkoi, Boraitinski, and Kzerkasky, as being those in whom they had the greatest confidence, and who were in the interest of the Empress. These did not fail of animating them more and more, till, on the 8th of March, they judged them ripe for the point at which they wanted them. It was then that these Princes, at the head of six hundred gentlemen, went to wait on the Empress; and having obtained an audience, entreated of her to order the council of state and the senate to assemble for the examination of certain points touching the regency. The Empress having consented, she ordered, at the same time, Count Soltikoff, lieutenant-general and lieutenant-colonel of the guards, to have all the avenues well guarded, and not to permit any one to go out of the palace. The guards were also commanded to have their pieces loaded with ball; and special care was taken to acquaint all those who came to court, of the precautions which had been ordered.

While these arrangements were taking, the council of state and the senate were assembled. The Empress gave orders that both these bodies should appear before her. These Princes then having repaired to the presence-chamber, or hall, with the canopy; the count Mattweof, advancing towards her Majesty, spoke, and said, That he was deputed by the whole nobility of the empire to represent to her, that she had been, by the deputies of the council of state, surprised into the concessions she had made; that Russia having for so many ages been governed by sovereign monarchs, and not by council, all the nobility entreated her to take into her own hands the reins of government; that all the nation was of the same opinion, and wished that the family of her Majesty might reign over them to the end of time.

The Empress, at this speech, affected great surprize: "How?" (said she) "was it not then with the will of the whole nation that I signed the act presented to me at Mittau?" Upon which the whole assembly answered, "No." At this she turned towards Prince Dolgoroucki, and said to him, "How came you then, Prince Basilius Loukitch, to impose on me so?" She then ordered the high-chancellor to go and bring her the writings which she had signed. This being done, she made him read them with an audible voice; and at each article she stopped him, and asked if such an article was for the good of the nation. The assembly having to all and each of these constantly answered "NO;" she took the deeds out of the hands of the high-chancellor, and tore them, saying, "These writings then are not necessary." She declared at the same time, "That as the empire of Russia had never been governed but by one sole monarch, she claimed the same prerogative as her ancestors had had, from whom she derived her crown by right of inheritance, and not from the election of the council of state, as they had pretended; and that whoever should oppose her sovereignty should be punished as guilty of high treason." This declaration was received with applause, and nothing was heard all over the town but acclamations and shouts of joy.

Russian Intervention in Poland

Active Russian intervention in Polish domestic affairs began long before Catherine the Great effected the partitioning of that unhappy nation. The Empress Anne, for example, supported her candidate for the Polish crown (the Elector of Saxony) by armed invasion of Poland. Here is a contemporary account of the start of that adventure. The source is: Manstein, *Memoirs,* pp. 66–69.

The disturbances of Poland began with the year 1733. The King, Augustus II. who had repaired to Warsaw to hold a diet extraordinary, died there the 11th of February. The archbishop of Gnezen, primate of the kingdom, took the regency, and convened the diet of convocation, in which it was unanimously stipulated to give the exclusion to all foreign Princes, and to elect none but a *piaste,* or native nobleman.

The courts of Vienna and of Petersburgh at first much approved of this resolution of the diet, and gave orders to their embassadors to express their satisfaction at it to the republic, but to add, at the same time, that they could never suffer King Stanislaus to be chosen, who had been, by the result of a diet, declared incapable of the crown. These two courts were, at that time, very far from a disposition in favor of the Elector of Saxony: on the contrary, there had for some years, prevailed so great a coolness in them towards him, as was not unlikely to have brought on a war, if the death of the King had not prevented it. As to the court of Vienna, the cause of dispute was, that he had not only refused to sign the Pragmatic Sanction, but had even entered into a close connection with France against the interests of the house of Austria. As to Russia, its motives of discontent were, the King's not having acted according to the views of the court of Petersburgh in the affairs of Courland; besides which, the primate, and a part of the nobility, who had suspected the King of designs upon the liberty of Poland, had applied to Russia, imploring its assistance in case of his undertaking any thing against the republic.

Affairs soon changed aspect. The new Elector of Saxony found means to appease the court of Vienna, by signing the Pragmatic Sanction; and as to Russia, he promised to conform to the will of the Empress with regard to the affairs of Courland so that both courts united to procure him the crown of Poland. Their embassadors had orders to declare, especially to the primate, that they would recognize no other King of Poland than the Elector of Saxony, and that her Russian Majesty would support the election of that Prince with all her forces, in case of the republic's not taking such a resolution with a good grace.

The court of Petersburgh had caused two bodies of troops to be assembled, the one in Ukraine, on the frontiers of Lithuania, the other in Livonia, upon those of Courland. In the mean while, France had spared neither pains nor money to get King Stanislaus elected. The primate, and the greatest part of the nobility, seeing that the Russians signified their commands to them in the tone of masters, and that the point insisted on was nothing less than such a compulsion to receive the law from foreign powers as totally destroyed the *liberum veto,* which was the great essential of the Polish liberty, united in favor of Stanislaus. They wrote accordingly to France to hasten his departure, that he might come to Poland in time enough to be present at the proclamation.

The diet of election began on the twenty-fifth of August, and continued, though often not without violent contestations, till the twelfth of September, when Stanislaus Leckzinski was, for the second time, elected King of Poland, unanimously by all the gentlemen who were at the *kola,* or field of election. This Prince had arrived on the ninth, and had kept *incognito* in the house of the French ambassador. The primate, and all the nobility of his party, now imagined that they had triumphed over all opposition, and were in hopes, that though the courts of Vienna and Petersburgh might not be pleased with their procedure, they could never, however, carry the point of overturning the act of almost the whole nation.

The Courts of Vienna and Petersburgh had been duly informed of the schemes of France, and cabals of the primate. The Empress of Russia had caused to be played off all the springs of policy imaginable, to embarrass and retard the election of Stanislaus, in the hope that, by gaining time, the Elector's party would increase, and that he might be chosen King without the necessity of coming to an open rupture. Her ambassadors at Warsaw had orders to spare neither fair promises nor money to weaken the French party. She wrote to the states of Lithuania, and made a mention to them of the concern she took in the maintenance of the liberty of the republic. Her aim was to persuade the senators of the grand dutchy to detach themselves from Poland. She did not, however, entirely succeed. There were but a few who came into a separation, and retired on the other side of the Wistula, to a village called Praag. The bishops of Cracovia, of Posnania, the Princes Wiesnowiski, and some others, were of the number, which altogether appeared but a small one in comparison of the rest of the nobility. And yet it was these that gave the first impulse to the whole machine, and placed Augustus III. on the throne of Poland. Some of the separatists had aspired to the crown for themselves, but finding that they could not succeed, they united to procure it for the Elector of Saxony, rather than suffer it quietly in the possession of King Stanislaus.

They wrote to Petersburgh, and requested the protection of Russia against the primate and the French party. The Empress, who only wanted a pretext for sending troops into Poland, could not have wished a fairer one than the being called in by the Poles themselves. Upon this, she sent orders to Count Lacy to enter Lithuania, at the head of twenty thousand men. On receipt of them, he advanced in hasty marches towards Warsaw, in the hope that he should arrive in time enough to hinder the proclamation of King Stanislaus. But the primate had taken his measures too well. In the meanwhile, the malcontent nobility went out to meet Count Lacy, and on the thirtieth of September came along with him to the banks of the Wistula. They proposed passing the river, and to repair directly to the field of election, but the Poles of the contrary party had broken down all the bridges, as soon as Stanislaus had retreated to make himself master of the town of Dantzick.

Not to lose time then, they proceeded to the election of the Elector of Saxony, near the village of Comiez, upon the same field, where Henry of Valois (the Third of France) had been chosen. It was on the fifth of October that this great affair was determined, on the eve of the day fixed to be the last of the diet of election. About fifteen senators and six hundred gentlemen were present at it.

A Palace Revolution

> Just before her death, the Empress Anne named the infant Ivan as her successor under the regency of Biren, Duke of Courland. The latter plotted to secure the throne for his family by the marriage of his son to the Princess Elizabeth. One of Biren's associates, Marshal Münnich, was disappointed in his hopes of preferment and entered into a plot against the regent. The outcome was the disposal of Biren in favor of Ivan's mother, Anne. This coup d'état, typical of the "Reign of the Women," is described by Manstein who took part in it. The source is: Manstein, *Memoirs*, pp. 268–273.

When the marshal was returned from court, he told his aid-de-camp general, the lieutenant-colonel de Manstein, that he should have occasion for his service the next day, very early in the morning. Accordingly, at two, after midnight, he sent for him. They both got into a coach together by themselves, and repaired to the winter-palace, where the Emperor and his father and mother were lodged after the death of the Empress. The marshal and his aid-de-camp entered the apartment of the Princess, by the door of the wardrobe. There he made madamoiselle Mengden, lady of honor, and favorite of the Princess, get up. When Munich had explained himself to her, she went in and waked their Highnesses; but it was the Princess alone that came out to him. They had but a moment's talk. The marshal ordered Manstein to call all the officers who were on guard at the

palace, for the Princess to speak to them. These being come, her Highness
represented in a few words to them the injuries which the regent made the
Emperor, herself, and her husband suffer; adding, that as it was impossible, and even shameful, for her to endure such insults any longer, she was
resolved to have him apprehended, and had given marshal Munich the
commission of it; so that she hoped that the officers would be so good as to
follow all his orders, and assist him to the best of their power. The officers
made not the least difficulty of obeying the Princess in whatever she required of them; upon which, giving them her hand to kiss, and embracing
them all, they went down the stairs with the marshal, and got the guard
under arms.

Count Munich told the soldiers what was in agitation; and all, with one
accord, answered him, That they were ready to follow him wherever he
would lead them. They were ordered to load their muskets, and an officer
with forty men were left on guard with the colors. The other eighty
marched with the marshal to the summer-palace, where the regent still
resided.

About two hundred paces from this house, this troop halted, and the
marshal sent Manstein to the officers of the regent's guard to acquaint
them of the Princess Anne's intention: they made no more difficulty than
the others had done, and even offered their assistance to seize the duke, if
it was necessary.

Upon this, the marshal told the same lieutenant-colonel Manstein, to
put himself, with an officer, at the head of twenty men, to enter the palace,
to seize the duke; and in case of his making any the least resistance, to
massacre him without mercy.

Manstein entered the palace; and not to make too much noise, he
made the detachment follow him at a distance. All the centinels suffered
him to pass in without any opposition; for, as he was personally known to
all the soldiers, they imagined he might be sent to the duke upon some
affair of consequence, so that he crossed the guards, and got as far as the
apartments, without any difficulty. But as he did not know the particular
room in which the duke lay, he was all on a sudden extremely embarrassed
where to go, so as to avoid all noise and suspicion, neither would he ask
any one the question, though he met with some servants who were waiting
in the ante-chamber. After some moments meditation, he resolved to keep
advancing through the apartments, in the hope he should at length find
out the apartment he was seeking. And so it happened in fact; for, after
he had gone through two chambers, he was come to a door that was locked;
luckily for him, this was a folding door, and the servants had neglected to
fasten it, by sliding the bolts at the top and bottom, so that he easily forced
it open. In the chamber, he found a great bed, in which the duke and
duchess were lying, buried in a profound sleep. Not even the noise he had
made in forcing open the door had waked them. Manstein having got close
to the bed, drew the curtains, and desired to speak with the regent. Upon
this, both started up in a surprise, and began to cry out aloud, judging
rightly enough that he was not come to bring them any good news. Man-

stein happening to stand on the side on which the duchess lay, the regent threw himself out of bed, on the ground, certainly with an intention to hide himself under the bed; but this officer springing quickly round to the other side, threw himself upon him, and held him fast embraced till the guards came in. The duke having at length got upon his legs again, and wanting to disengage himself from their hold, distributed blows with his double fist to the right and left; to which the soldiers made no return but with strokes from the but-end of their muskets; and throwing him down again on the floor, they crammed a handkerchief into his mouth, and bound his hands with an officer's sash; then they led him, naked as he was, to the guard-room, where they covered him with a soldier's cloak, and put him into a coach of the marshal's, that was waiting for him. An officer was placed in it by the side of him, and he was carried to the winter-palace.

While the soldiers were struggling with the duke, the duchess was got out of bed in her shift, and, running after him as far as into the street, when a soldier took her in his arms, and asked Manstein, what he should do with her. He bid him carry her back to her chamber; but the soldier not caring, it seems, to take the trouble of it, threw her down on the ground, in the midst of the snow, and there left her. The captain of the guard, finding her in this piteous condition, made her clothes be brought to her, and reconducted her to the apartments she had always occupied.

As soon as the duke was thus on the way to the winter-palace, the same colonel, Manstein, was sent to seize his younger brother, Gustavus Biron, who was then at Petersburgh. He was lieutenant-colonel of the Ishmaëlow regiment of guards. But this expedition required somewhat more of precautionary measures than the first; for Gustavus Biron was beloved in his regiment, and had a guard of it in his house, consisting of a serjeant and twelve men. And, accordingly, the centinels made at first some resistance, but they were soon laid hold of, and threatened with death if they made the least noise. After which, Manstein went into the bedchamber of Biron, and made him get up, telling him, that he had an affair of great consequence to impart to him. Having then drawn him to the window, he acquainted him with his orders of arrest. Biron wanted to open the window, and began to cry out; but he was instantly let to know that the duke was seized, and under confinement, and that himself would be killed on the least resistance. The soldiers, who had waited in the adjoining room, came in directly, and satisfied him that there was nothing for him but to obey. They gave him a furred cloke, put him into a sledge, and he too was carried to the winter-palace.

At the same time colonel Koneingsfelt, one of the adjutants of the marshal, who had joined him when he was returning with the duke, was sent back to apprehend count Bestucheff.

As for the duke, he was put into the room of the officers of the guard. His brother and count Bestucheff had each a separate room, where they remained till four o'clock in the afternoon, till the duke, with all his family (except his eldest son, who was then sick, and who staid till his recovery at Petersburgh) were carried to the fort of Schluiselburgh. The other two prisoners were sent to places at a small distance from the capital, where they were kept till after their examination.

As soon as the duke was seized, order was sent to all the regiments that happened to be then at Petersburgh, to be put under arms, and to assemble round the palace. The Princess Anne then declared herself Grand-Duchess of Russia, and regent of the empire during the minority of the Emperor. She at the same time put on the collar of the order of St. Andrew, and every one took a new oath of fidelity, in which the Grand-Duchess was mentioned by name, which had not been done in that imposed by the regent. There were none that did not make great demonstrations of joy, at seeing themselves delivered from the tyranny of Biron; and from that moment everything was quiet. Even the piquets were taken away, which the duke of Courland had posted in the Streets to prevent commotions during his regency; and yet there were some, who, at the very moment of that event, prognosticated that it would not be the last revolution; and that those who had been the most active in bringing this about, would be the first that would be overset by another. Time has shown that they were not in the wrong.

Elizabeth Seizes the Throne

> Following the seizure of Biren by General Münnich, Princess Anne became regent. Münnich resigned in March, 1741, leaving confusion worse confounded, and Sweden took advantage of Russia's weakness to declare war upon her. The only hope of the patriotic Russian nobility seemed to be Peter's younger daughter, Elizabeth. Urged and aided by the Guards, Elizabeth made a successful coup d'état on December 6, 1741. The account which follows was written by "a learned man, an accomplished linguist, but a mediocre historian." It gives, however, a vivid picture of the palace revolution which made Elizabeth an empress. The source is: R. Nisbet Bain, *The Daughter of Peter the Great. A History of Russian Diplomacy and of the Russian Court under the Empress Elizabeth Petrovna, 1741–1762*. New York: E. P. Dutton and Co., 1900. Pp. 50–61.

On December 6th, 1741, La Chetardie, the French Ambassador at St. Petersburg, wrote as follows to Amelot, the French Minister of Foreign Affairs, as to the prospects of a *coup d'etat* in favour of the Tsarevna Elizabeth: "An outbreak, the success of which can never be morally certain, especially now that the Swedes are not in a position to lend a hand, would, prudently considered, be very difficult to bring about, unless it could be substantially backed up." That very same evening, Elizabeth, without any help from without, overthrew the existing government in a couple of hours, a circumstance carefully to be borne in mind, as many historians, rashly relying on certain ex-post-facto statements by La Chetardie, have credited that diplomatist with a leading part in the revolution which placed the daughter of Peter the Great on the Russian throne. As a matter of fact La Chetardie, beyond lending the Tsarevna 2,000 ducats instead of the 15,000 she demanded of him, took no part whatever in the actual *coup d'etat,* which was as great a surprise to him as it was to everyone else. The merit and glory of that singular affair belong to Elizabeth alone.

It must also be observed that, from the first, Elizabeth had taken a much saner view of the situation than any of her foreign advisers, and all along, despite much fear and faltering, she seems to have never been without the comforting persuasion that her courage would rise to the level of her necessities. Thus, when the Swedish Minister, Nolcken, suggested that she should rally all her partisans and arrange everything before hand, even to the choosing of a leader for the enterprise, she objected, very pertinently, that the inveterate distrust with which every Russian regarded every other Russian, rendered any such combination impossible. To even attempt it would be sufficient to ruin everything. It were far better, she said, to win over her partisans one by one, and make each of them believe that he was contributing equally to the glory of the enterprise. To prevent any jealousy, moreover, she meant to head the Guards herself when the moment for action arrived. "I know very well," she concluded, "that you suspect me of weakness, but I will not be false to my blood, I will show myself worthy to be the daughter of Peter the Great." Yet nearly twelve months had elapsed since these brave words were spoken, and still nothing had been done. Elizabeth's vacillation was intelligible enough, it is true. The least evil which she knew would befall her in case of failure, was life-long seclusion in a monastery, and this to a Princess "who," to use Mr. Finch's elegant expression, "had not an ounce of nun's flesh about her," was the most terrible prospect in the world. She was ready to endure much before risking such a contingency, but a point was reached at last beyond which even her endurance refused to go.

On Dec. 4th, the Tsarevna and most of the Foreign Ministers attended a crowded reception at the Winter Palace. The Regent, who appeared to be unusually perturbed that evening, withdrew early into an inner chamber, and shortly afterwards Elizabeth was summoned to her presence. No sooner did the Grand Duchess perceive her cousin than she exclaimed: "Matushka! what is this I hear of you? They tell me that you are in correspondence with the enemies of our country, and that your doctor is intriguing with the French Minister."—Elizabeth protested, with well-feigned astonishment, that this was the first she had heard of it, adding that she knew her duty better than to break the oath she had sworn to the young Emperor. But the Regent was not so easily mollified. "Madam," said she, adopting a harder tone, "I am about to request the King of France to recall M. de la Chetardie, and I must therefore request you never again to receive him at your house."—"Never again!" exclaimed Elizabeth, piqued in her turn. "I might refuse to see him once or twice perhaps, but to promise never to see him again is impossible."—"But I insist upon it!" cried Anne.—"My cousin," retorted Elizabeth, "you are Regent, and have but to command to be obeyed. Surely it would be much simpler if you were to order Count Ostermann to tell La Chetardie ex-

pressly not to visit me any more."—By this time both Princesses were
growing warm, and had raised their voices, and while the Regent had recourse to threats, Elizabeth took refuge in tears. At the sight of her cousin's
distress, the Regent was herself visibly affected, and the agitated ladies
finally composed their quarrel in each other's arms, Elizabeth swearing
eternal fidelity, and the Regent professing implicit faith in her loyalty.
Nevertheless this scene seems to have at last opened the eyes of the
Tsarevna to the imminence of her danger. She knew very well that the
indolent and foolishly good-natured Regent would never have taken such
a high hand with her unless prompted to do so, and she rightly suspected
the hand of Ostermann in the affair. She was confirmed in her suspicions
next day by another still more significant event. On the morning of Dec.
5th, the Government issued orders to all the regiments of the Guards in
the capital to hold themselves in readiness to march to the seat of war
within four-and-twenty hours, as the Swedish general, Levenhaupt, was
reported to be advancing rapidly towards Viborg. This however, was a
mere pretext. Ostermann was well aware that Levenhaupt was still in his
cantonments at the other end of Finland; the manoeuvre was simply intended to render Elizabeth defenceless, and there can be little doubt that
the astute old Minister intended to arrest the Tsarevna as soon as the
Guards were gone.

That same night, at about 10 o'clock, a hurried and anxious conference
was held at the Tsarevna's house, after Lestocq, her surgeon, had reconnoitered the town and made certain that all the lights in the Winter Palace
and in Ostermann's house had been extinguished. The only persons present besides Lestocq, were the Princess's Kammerherr, Michael Ilariono-
vich Vorontsov; her old music-master, Herr Schwarz; her favourite, and
future husband, Alexius Razumovsky, and Alexander and Peter Shuvalov,
two of the gentlemen of her household. No monarch ever had more devoted servants than these men were to prove to Elizabeth; but they were,
all of them, subaltern spirits who looked to their mistress to take the initiative, and now, at the supreme moment, it seemed as if she were about to
yield to a sudden fit of panic, for she began to expatiate on the dangers
they were likely to run. "Truly, Madam," replied Vorontsov, "the affair
demands no little daring, but where shall we look for it if we cannot find it
in the blood of Peter the Great?" At these words the Tsarevna recovered
her sangfroid, and turning to Lestocq, ordered him to send at once for the
twenty most resolute grenadiers of the Guard, whom he had already bought
with the ducats of the French Ambassador, and, upon their arrival between eleven and twelve, they were admitted into the presence of the
Tsarevna, and she asked them point-blank if she could absolutely rely
upon their fidelity. "Yes, Matushka! we are ready to die for you," they
exclaimed, whereupon she bade them withdraw for a moment, and,
flinging herself down before an ikon of the Saviour, made a solemn vow to
God that if her enterprise succeeded, she would never sign a death-warrant
as long as she lived. Then rising from her knees and taking a cross in her
hand, she went out to the soldiers and said: "If God be merciful to us and

to Russia, I will never forget your devotion. Go now to the barracks, assemble your comrades with all speed and secrecy, and await my arrival, I will be with you immediately." When they had gone she returned to her oratory, and remained on her knees in silent prayer for nearly an hour, till Lestocq, growing anxious, reminded her of the danger of further delay, and handed her the insignia of the order of St. Catherine (a decoration cherished by her as having been instituted in honour of her beloved mother), which she put on forthwith, and a silver cross, which she concealed about her person. He also persuaded her to wear a mail cuirass beneath her clothes, escorted her to a sledge which was already waiting at the door, and took his seat himself by her side, while Vorontsov and one of the Shuvalovs mounted up behind, and Razumovsky remained in the house to keep order. It was close upon two o'clock in the morning when they set off on their adventurous drive through the silent snow-covered streets of the city to the Preobrazhensky Barracks, where nearly two hundred of the Guards were already awaiting them. Immediately on dismounting, Elizabeth snatched a spontoon from one of the soldiers, and led the way into the messroom, ordering first of all, however, that all the drums in the barracks should be slit up, so that nobody could give the alarm. The men crowded after her, and when they were all assembled, she exclaimed: "My children, you know whose daughter I am! It is my resolve this night to deliver you and all Russia from our German tormentors. Will you follow me?"—"Matushka!" they cried enthusiastically, "we will follow thee to the death, and as for the *nyemtsui,* we will cut them to pieces!"—"Nay, my children," replied Elizabeth, "if you hurt a hair of their heads, I will not go one step with you. There must be no bloodshed. What we are going to do we do simply for the benefit of our country."— Having thus restrained their savage zeal within due limits, she knelt down, all present following her example, and producing her silver cross, held it aloft and exclaimed: "I swear before Heaven to die for you, will you swear to die for me?"—"We swear!" thundered the Grenadiers.—"Then let us go!" cried the Tsarevna, rising, "and remember, my children, whatever befall, no bloodshed!"—By this time her escort of grenadiers had swelled to nearly 400, all of them with bayonets screwed on and grenades in their pockets. Her first care was to despatch well-mounted messengers to the barracks of the Semenovsky and Ismailovsky Guards, bidding the soldiers assemble before her house as speedily as possible, and there await further orders; then, at the head of the Preobrazhensky Regiment, she proceeded on her way to the Winter Palace where the Regent was reposing in absolute security. As she passed through the grand avenue of the Nevsky Prospect on her way thither, she had the persons of the Vice-Chancellor, Count Golovkin and Baron Mengden, who resided there, secured in their beds, and, on arriving at the end of the avenue leading to the Admiralty, she sent three separate detachments of grenadiers to arrest Count Ostermann, his three brothers-in-law the Streshnevs, all of whom were generals, and Field Marshal Münnich who lived at the other end of the city. At this point, moreover, in order to stimulate the zeal of her men, she descended from

her sledge, and walked on foot in their midst, but the grenadiers soon
perceiving that their "Matushka" had much difficulty in keeping pace with
them, lifted the by no means ethereal form of their little mother on to their
shoulders and so carried her the remainder of the distance, to the gates of
the Winter Palace.

The guards in the barracks of the Winter Palace were surprised in
their slumbers, and Elizabeth did not allow them a moment's time for
reflection. "Wake up, my children!" she cried, "and listen to me. You
know who I am, and that the crown belongs to me of right. Will you follow
me?"—Most of the men responded with shouts of devotion, but four sub-
altern-officers and one private hesitated, and she ordered then to be arrested on the spot. Her command was not only instantly obeyed, but was
even in danger of being exceeded, for the loyal grenadiers in their fiery
zeal would have bayoneted their lukewarm comrades there and then, had
not the Princess struck up their weapons with her pike. The backsliders
having been safely secured, Elizabeth proceeded, like a prudent general,
to marshal and distribute her forces for the final assault. Dispatching
numerous small detachments of her grenadiers to guard all the staircases
and other exits, she ascended the grand staircase at the head of the remainder of the party, after once more solemnly adjuring them to use no
violence. The guards in front of the Grand Duchess's apartments made no
resistance, and Elizabeth entering the bedroom, found Anne Leopoldovna
asleep in bed with Julia Mengden by her side. "Awake, my sister!"
cried Elizabeth, gently shaking the slumbering ex-Regent, who started up
exclaiming: "What, is it you, Sudaruinya?" Then perceiving the helmets
of the grenadiers behind the Princess, she guessed the truth and quietly
submitted, merely begging that no harm should be done to her children,
and that she should not be separated from her friend Julia. Elizabeth
assured her cousin that neither she nor her children had anything to fear,
and she bade the grenadiers convey the Grand Duchess to her own litter.
The persons of the infant Tsar and his lately born sister, Catherine, were
then secured, and they were both brought in to Elizabeth. Taking them in
her arms, she kissed them both, exclaiming: "Poor children, it is not you,
but your parents, who are to blame." They were then placed, with their
nurses, in a second sledge and driven to Elizabeth's own palace, she following closely behind them in her own sledge with Anna Leopoldovna
and Julia Mengden. The seizure and abduction of the ex-Regent and her
children had been effected in less than half an hour, indeed so smoothly,
swiftly and noiselessly had the whole revolution proceeded, that, as late as
eight o'clock the next morning, very few people in the city, except the
confederates, were aware that Elizabeth Petrovna had, during the previous
night, been raised to the throne of her father, on the shoulders of the
Preobrazhensky Grenadiers.

On regaining her mansion, Elizabeth despatched Lestocq, Vorontsov
and Schwarz to all parts of the city, to summon the notables, civil and
ecclesiastical, to her presence. The Commander-in-Chief, Field Marshal
Lacy, was one of the first to be advised of the change. "To which party do

you belong?" enquired the emissaries of the Tsaritsa. "To the party in power," responded the prudent old Irishman, without the slightest hesitation, and he immediately hastened to Elizabeth's mansion in order to place his services at the disposal of the new Empress. He found her surrounded by the chief dignitaries of the realm, holding her first council, the immediate results of which were a new oath of Allegiance and a skilfully worded manifesto, the joint production of the lately recalled ex-Minister, Alexius Bestuzhev, and Count Brevern, Ostermann's private secretary, who had already deserted his life-long benefactor, to the effect that her Majesty, moved by the prayers of her faithful subjects, had accepted the throne in order to put an end to the prevalent confusion caused by the late government. At eight o'clock the oath and manifesto were ready, the Council rose, and the Empress, after declaring herself Colonel of the three regiments of the Guards, and investing herself with the insignia of St. Andrew, appeared in the midst of the distinguished mob which was already thronging her ante-chambers, and received the congratulations of the nobility, gentry and high officials with a gracious *bonhomie* which won every heart. Then, despite the Arctic severity of the weather, she ordered the windows to be thrown open, stepped out on the balcony, and showed herself to the people who crowded the square below. She was received with a loud burst of enthusiasm, the like of which had not been heard in St. Petersburg since the death of Peter the Great.

After sufficiently gratifying the curiosity of the populace, Elizabeth retired to rest for a short time, and then proceeded in state to the Winter Palace, which had, in the meantime, been prepared for her reception. The din of salvoes from the citadel, and the still louder roar of the joyous multitude that thronged the line of route, marked her triumphal progress. Indeed so dense was the throng that the Court dignitaries had to leave their carriages and fight their way into the Palace, on foot. After hearing a Te Deum at the Imperial chapel, in the midst of her grenadiers, whose captain, at their urgent petition, she had consented to become, the Empress held a reception. The new oath was then administered to the Guards and to all the civil, military and ecclesiastical functionaries, and couriers were despatched to all parts of the realm announcing her Majesty's happy accession.

The confederates and adherents of the new sovereign were rewarded with a promptness and a liberality only to be expected of the most bountiful of Princesses; the favourites, Peter and Alexander Shuvalov, were made Generals and Colonels in the Guards; Alexius Razumvosky became a Lieutenant-Colonel and a Kammerherr, and Lestocq was made the Empress's first body-physician, a Privy Councillor and Director of the College of Medicine, with a salary of 7,000 rubles. He also received her Majesty's portrait set in brilliants worth 20,000 rubles. Twelve thousand rubles were distributed among the soldiers of the Preobrazhensky Regiment, which received at the same time the title of the Imperial Body Guard, with a new uniform; and nine thousand rubles were distributed among the soldiers of the Semenovsky and the Izmailovsky Regiments respectively. All the officers of these regiments were raised in rank, the very corporals becoming captains, while each private was made a lieutenant, ennobled and gratified with a small estate. All persons proscribed for political offences during the last two reigns were recalled to Court and restored to favour. Conspicuous among them was the aged Field Marshal Vasily Vladimirovich Dolgoruki, one of the victims of Anne's cruelty, who was released from his dungeon at Narva, where he had languished for ten years, to preside over the War Office. Moreover, he and his family had their estate restored to them, and their wives and daughters were appointed to considerable posts near the Empress's person, along with the female relations of their old rivals, the Golitsuins. Biren also was released, but, by the advice of La Chetardie, he was forbidden the Court and ordered to live quietly on an estate which was bestowed upon him, with an honourable maintenance.

Yet this bloodless revolution, this pleasing picture of a liberated nation rejoicing around the idolized monarch of its choice, was not without its sinister touch of tragedy, and chief among its victims was the man to whom, next after Peter the Great, belongs the honour of having laid the foundations of modern Russia. Ostermann could indeed expect little mercy from a Princess whom all his life long he had consistently neglected and despised. Perhaps Elizabeth's good nature might ultimately have got the better of her resentment, but La Chetardie was constantly at her elbow to keep alive her wrath against the most formidable enemy of the French system in Russia, and so the illustrious statesman was sacrificed. At first he so far abased himself as to address a couple of appealing letters to the Empress, which were treated as "very mean and paltry performances"; but during the subsequent farcical proceedings, dignified with the name of a trial, before a tribunal presided over by the personal enemies of the accused, he comported himself with a quiet resignation not without dignity.

The Empress Elizabeth

The followed detailed description of Elizabeth and some of her associates was written by R. Nisbet Bain. The source is: Bain, *Daughter of Peter the Great*, pp. 134–145. Abridged.

Elizabeth Petrovna, although no longer the ravishing, exquisite madcap, "always on the hop," whom grave diplomatists judicially pronounced to be the most exquisite creature in existence, was still one of the most handsome, one of the most fascinating women in Europe. Lord Hyndford described her in her 38th year as "worthy of the admiration of all the world." Catherine II tells us that at forty her somewhat puissant, but marvellously well-proportioned, figure appeared to admiration in male attire, while all the movements of the stately Tsaritsa were so graceful that one could gladly have gazed upon her for ever. Nothing else in the room seemed worth looking at when she was gone. Her once brilliant complexion, indeed, now needed the assistance of cosmetics; but her large blue eyes, "so like a merry bird's," were as brilliant as ever, while her luxuriant hair, of the richest auburn hue, was the crowning charm of a singularly majestic and imposing liveliness. But her salient, her most irresistible attraction was a natural kindliness expressing itself in a ready courtesy, an impulsive sympathy, which came straight from the heart. La Chetardie frequently alludes to her as debonaire, and that delightful word exactly describes her. She was gentle, affable, and familiar with all who approached her, yet always with a due regard to her dignity, and her playful gaiety was without the slightest tinge of malice. It was good to be with her, folks said. She seemed to radiate joyousness. Catherine II also possessed a charm of manner which was well-nigh irresistible, but with her benevolence was always more or less a matter of profound calculation. It was not so with Elizabeth. To make people happy was a necessity of her nature; she loved to see smiling faces around her, and considered that distress of every kind had an imperative claim upon her. Her horror of bloodshed made the very idea of war hateful to her, and she wept bitterly at the news of every victory won by her arms. She took care that her soldiers were so well-clad that casualties from stress of weather were almost unknown, and on receiving intelligence of the earthquake at Lisbon, she offered to rebuild part of the city at her own cost, though she had no diplomatic relations with Portugal. We have seen how at the beginning of her reign, she resolved to abolish capital punishment. The Ukaz to that effect was, by the advice of her Ministers, never promulgated, lest malefactors should multiply; but she took care to commute every capital sentence as it came before her. Again, when Peter Shuvalov submitted to her his codification of the Russian laws, which bristled with cruel and vexatious fiscal penalties, the Empress indignantly declared that it was "written not with ink, but with blood," and refused to sign it. One of her most engaging qualities was her fondness for young people, children especially, and all little folk were passionately devoted to her. She also very frequently gave children's parties, eighty to ninety little couples sitting down to supper with their governors and governesses at separate tables. The Princess Dashkova tells us that she took "the affectionate interest of a good godmother" in the private affairs of the youth and maidens of her Court, and, matchmaker as she was, repeatedly helped struggling young lovers out of their pecuniary difficulties. On one occasion, the Princess, then a mere child, was so affected by the tone of maternal tenderness with which the Empress congratulated her on her engagement, that she burst into tears, whereupon Elizabeth, tapping her gently on the shoulder and at the same time kissing her cheek, said with a smile: "Come, come, my child; compose yourself, or all your friends will fancy I have been scolding you." For, like most warmhearted people, the Tsaritsa had a naturally quick and impetuous temper, and, when fairly roused, would scold and bully for an hour at a time, without stopping to pick her words, till she grew purple in the face. Yet when the paroxysm was over, she was as radiant as ever; never bore the slightest resentment, even under the most trying circumstances; and the words "Vinovata, Matushka!" uttered with becoming contrition, always disarmed her. And if hasty and choleric, she was also just, equitable, and a great peacemaker. It is one of her chief glories that, so far as she was able, she put a stop to that mischievous contention of rival ambitions at Court, which had disgraced the reigns of Peter II, Anne and Ivan VI, and enabled Foreign Powers to freely interfere in the domestic affairs of Russia. Her Ministers had not only to serve her, but to live in harmony with one another. We have already seen how she protected the Bestuzhevs against Lestocq and Trubetskoi, and how she would not sacrifice Vorontsov to Bestuzhev; we shall see presently how, for a long time, she held the balance equally between the Chancellor's party and the Shuvalovs.

Nevertheless this bright picture has its darker side. One of the chief faults imputed to the Empress Elizabeth is her indolence. Lord Hyndford, on one occasion, complains of "this lady's mortal backwardness in all sorts of business or anything that requires one moment's thought or application," and although there is much of exaggeration, there is also something of truth, in this accusation. No doubt, as Solovev justly observes, her backwardness was not always due to indolence, but to a conscientious endeavour to consider doubtful questions from every possible point of view, and it is quite certain that, under the pressure of emergency, she took infinite pains to disentangle truth from falsehood, and would decide nothing till she had quite satisfied her own mind as to the subject in debate. It must also be remembered that, even judged by the low standard of her own age, she was very ignorant, and therefore obliged to lean a good deal upon the opinions of others. But, after making every possible allowance, we cannot altogether acquit her of neglect of affairs. Frequently she left the most important documents unread and unsigned for months together, and Bestuzhev used bitterly to complain that she would not attend to business without a great deal of coaxing. There was the less excuse for her, moreover, because she had always plenty of time upon her hands. Literature naturally had no attraction for a Princess who regarded all reading (except the perusal of devotional books printed in very large type) as injurious to health. And then she lived in such a haphazard way. She had no fixed times for lying down or getting up, and her meals were uncertain and irregular. A large portion of each day was spent in gossiping in her private apartments with her favourite women, Maura Egorovna Shuvalova, Anna Karlovna Vorontsova, Nastasia Mikhailovna Izmailovna, and a certain Elizabeth Ivanovna, a mysterious and not altogether reputable old lady whom the Tsaritsa frequently employed on dark and dubious errands, and whom the witty Stroganov therefore dubbed "Le ministere des affairs étranges," in contradistinction to the Grand Chancellor, who was "Le ministere des affaires étrangeres." Her devotions, however, for she rigorously observed the innumerable feast and fast days of the Orthodox Church, occupied no small part of her leisure. In the summer she hawked and hunted, and, in winter, took horse exercise in the vast covered riding-school built in the reign of Anne for the favourite Biren. She was an excellent shot, a fearless and graceful rider, and could, in her best days, outwalk the strongest of her guardsmen. Nor was she altogether without æsthetic tastes, being passionately fond of music and the drama, and taking a great interest in architecture. No other Russian Sovereign ever erected so many churches, and the celebrated Winter Palace, Rastrelli's master-piece, was built under her supervision, though she did not live long enough to inhabit it.

But building was by no means her most costly pastime. For every hun-dred rubles she expended on the permanent embellishment of her capital, she wasted a thousand on the transitory pleasures of her Court. Lavish to the verge of extravagance, and loving pomp and show with all the ardour of a sensuous, semi-barbarous Oriental, it was the great delight of Eliza-beth Petrovna to pose as the majestic central figure of brilliant assemblies and gorgeous pageants, and her court was indisputably the most splendid in Europe. Her cousin Anne, before her, had indeed astonished foreigners by the gorgeousness of her appointments, but Anne's crude and bizarre magnificence lacked the veneer of grace, elegance and refinement which characterized the court of Elizabeth. For, though in many respects a Rus-sian gentlewoman of the old school, and intensely patriotic, Elizabeth Petrovna was far more intelligent and receptive than Anne Ivanovna, and, especially where her pleasures were concerned, borrowed freely from the luxuries of the Western civilization. Hence the accusation of reckless extravagance so often and so justly brought against her by Prince Shcher-batov and other laudatores temporis acti. Sir Cyril Wych, as early as 1742, when Elizabeth was still comparatively economical, described the Court of St. Petersburg as the most expensive in Europe, and protested that his allowance could not meet even current expenses. This extravagance mani-fested itself principally in the habiliments, equipages, retinue and banquets of the gentry and nobility, the Empress herself setting the example in this respect. She is said to have changed her clothes half-a-dozen times a day, and although she lost 4,000 dresses at the great Moscow conflagration of 1747, fifteen thousand more were found in her wardrobes after her death, most of which had only been worn once. And the Empress took care that her courtiers should live up to this high standard of display. At the wedding of the Grand Duke Peter, all public officials were given a year's salary in advance that they might be able to make a brave show on the occasion, and a special ukaz laid down sumptuary regulations for the pageant. Every member of the first and second class in the table of grades was to have two heydukes and not less than eight lacqueys attached to each of his car-riages, and as many more as he could afford. But the jeunesse dorée of Peterhof and Tsarkoe Selo needed little prompting. Their natural vanity and luxuriousness met the Tsaritsa's wishes half way. It soon became the ambition of every young Russian noble to outshine his neighbour, and at last even the most expensive galloon was generally looked down upon as common and vulgar. Sergius Naruishkin, accounted the greatest dandy of the age in Russia, won great favour by going to the wedding of the Grand Duke, in a carriage inlaid all over, even to the wheels, with crystal mir-rors, and wearing a caftan ablaze with jewels, the back of which was made to imitate a tree, the trunk being represented by a broad golden hand in the middle of his body, while the branches were indicated by lines of silver running up the sleeves to the wrists, and the roots by similar lines running down to the knees of the breeches. The immensely wealthy Ivan Chernuishev, who had travelled widely and did more than any other man to import foreign luxury into Russia, used to order twelve suits at a time, and the very liveries of his pages were of cloth of gold. Yet even he could not compete with Count Alexander Razumovsky and his brother Cyril. The elder Razumovsky was the first to wear diamond buttons, buckles and epaulets; while Count Cyril, on being appointed Grand Hetman of the Cossacks, departed for Glukhov, the seat of his Government, where he lived in regal state, with an immense retinue which included a bodyguard, a troupe of actors, and half-a-dozen French cooks, including the famous chef, Barridian, who received a salary of 500 rubles (£125), and was considered even superior to Duval the chef of Frederick the Great. On one occasion Cyril bought up 100,000 bottles of wine, including 6,800 bottles of the best champagne, then a fashionable novelty, which he freely distributed among his friends. Far less generous was Chancellor Bestuzhev, whose immense cellar was, after his death, given by Catherine II to Prince Orlov, who sold it for an incredible sum. Prince Shcherbatov instances it as a sign of the degeneracy of the times, that pineapples and English horses were first introduced into Russia, at enormous expense, by Peter Shuvalov, who lived so recklessly that he left behind him a million rubles' worth of debts, although his standing income for years was 400,000 rubles (£100,000). Peter Shuvalov was particularly proud of the magnificence of his dessert; his brother Alexander, on the other hand, boasted that he was the chief propagandist of champagne in Russia. Then there was Field Marshal Stephen Apraksin who had hundreds of suits of clothes, a jewelled snuff-box for every day in the year, and required more than five hundred horses to drag his private baggage when he took the field against the King of Prussia; and Count Peter Borisovich Sheremetev, the richest man in the Empire, whose dresses were heavy with gold and silver, and who always went about surrounded by a whole army of domestics almost as brilliantly attired as himself. It is recorded of him that he kept such an ample table that once, when the Empress and her by no means tiny court looked in upon him unawares, he was able to entertain them all sumptuously with what was actually provided for the use of his household on that particular day. The lesser nobles naturally imitated the magnates, and the result was a rapid declension from the simplicity of the old Russian mode of life, and a growing fondness for costly and unnecessary exotic luxuries which ministered to vanity and dissipation with often the most serious consequences. This was bad enough, but still worse remained behind, for the Court of Elizabeth was not only the most extravagant, it was also the most licentious in Europe, and for this also the Empress must be held primarily responsible.

The Emancipation of the Nobles

> On the death of Elizabeth in December, 1761 (O.S.), the crown went
> to her nephew, Peter, who as Tsar Peter III proved himself wholly in-
> competent to rule. Early in his reign, Peter freed the nobility from the
> obligation of state service which had been laid upon them by Peter
> the Great. This action was, of course, very popular with the nobility,
> and Catherine, whose power depended upon the favor of this group,
> reaffirmed and extended the grant by her Charter of the Gentry in
> 1785. The following selection is an excerpt from the ukase of
> Peter III. The source is: William Tooke, *The Life of Catherine II,
> Empress of all the Russias.* (First American edition.) Two volumes.
> Philadelphia, 1802. Vol. I, pp. 513-515.

WE PETER III, &c. The troubles and inconveniences experienced by the
wise sovereign, our late dear grandsire, Peter the Great, of immortal
memory, in his endeavours for the good of his country, and for procuring
his subjects a competent knowledge, as well in military discipline, as in
civil and political affairs, are known to all Europe, and the greater part of
the globe.

In the attainment of this end, he found it necessary to begin by convincing the Russian nobility, which is the first body of the state, of the
immense advantages possessed by the nations well versed in the sciences
and the arts, over those people who continue benighted in ignorance and
sloth. The state of things at that time imperiously demanded, that he
should oblige his nobility to enter the military service, and engage in civil
functions; that he should send them to travel into foreign countries, that
they might get a tincture of the useful arts and sciences, and therefore he
established, in his own country, schools and academies, that the seeds of
these his salutary regulations, might be cherished in their growth, and
more speedily matured. The nobility had the less reason to complain of
the constraint thus laid upon them, as, independently of the utility, both
public and private, that naturally resulted from it, it was their duty to
concur with the wishes of an emperor to whom they were under so many
obligations.

The execution of these projects seemed at first to be attended with the
utmost difficulty. They were intolerable to the nobility, who saw themselves obliged to abandon a soft and indolent life, to quit their dwellings, to
serve in war and in peace, and to enrol their children for future services.
Several members of their body withdrew from the service, and were therefore deprived of their estates, which were confiscated, and that for the best
of reasons. They rendered themselves criminal towards their country,
which they basely deserted.

These excellent ordinances, though at the beginning inseparable from
certain methods of constraint, have served as a model to all the successors
of Peter the Great, and especially to our dear aunt, the empress Elizabeth

Petrovna, of glorious memory; who determined to follow the example of her father, encouraged, by a special protection, the advancement of the arts and sciences. Of this we are now reaping the fruits; and every impartial man will agree, that they are considerable. Manners have been improved; minds indifferent to the happiness of the country have been roused from their fatal lethargy, and have habituated themselves to reflect on the public welfare; zeal in the service is augmented; generals, already valiant, are become experienced; intelligent ministers; enlightened magistrates; in a word, patriotism, love and attachment to our person, activity in all offices and posts, and every generous sentiment, are now the happy lot of the Russian nation. For all these reasons, we have judged it to be no longer necessary to compel into the service, as hitherto has been the practice, the nobility of our empire.

In consideration whereof, in virtue of the full power to us granted by God, and of our imperial especial grace, we grant to the Russian nobility, from this moment and forever, in the name of all our successors, permission to take service in our empire, as well as in all those of the European powers in alliance with us; and to this end we have given the following ordinance as a fundamental law, &c.

[Then follow nine articles concerning the terms on which liberty of resignation, of travelling abroad, of entering the service, &c. may be asked for and granted: concluding thus:]

Granting as we do, graciously and to perpetuity, to our nobility this franchise, making it a fundamental and unalterable law, we promise them equally on our imperial word, and in the most solemn manner, to observe the present ordinance sacredly and irrevocably, in all its tenor, and to maintain the prerogatives therein expressed. . . . Our successors on the throne ought not to alter it in any manner. The execution of our said ordinance being the principal support of the imperial throne, we hope that from gratitude for this benefit, the Russian nobility will serve us faithfully and zealously; and that, instead of withdrawing from our service, will enter it with eagerness, and that they will carefully educate their children. . . . We therefore command all our faithful subjects, and true sons of the country, to despise and avoid those who have wasted their time in idleness, and who have not educated their children in the useful sciences, as people who have never had the public good at heart, who shall have no access to our court, nor be admitted to the publick assemblies and the national festivities.

Given at St. Petersburg, Feb. 18, 1762.

Catherine's Coup d'État: Report of the British Ambassador

Catherine the Great had no legal right to the Russian throne. She came to power through a successful coup d'état against her husband, Peter III. The coup was originally planned to take place at Elizabeth's death, but that event found the conspirators unready. The arrest of one of them and the fear of complete discovery precipitated the coup in 1762. It was a palace revolution, made by some of the nobles among whom the most prominent were the Orlov brothers. The following account of the event was sent to London by the British agent in St. Petersburg. The source is: A. D. Collyer (Ed.), *The Despatches and Correspondence of John, Second Earl of Buckinghamshire, Ambassador to the Court of Catherine II, 1762–1765.* Two volumes. Published for the Royal Historical Society. London: Longmans, Green and Co., 1900/01. Vol. 1, pp. 60–63.

MR. KEITH TO MR. GRENVILLE. St. Petersburg: July 12, 1762. I have the honour to transmit to you the manifesto published by authority, with the translation, in which you will see that great stress is laid upon the shameful peace concluded with their enemy, notwithstanding which, as Baron Goltz, who attended the Emperor to the last, was returning to town, he was met on the road by M. Alsuffiew, who, by order of the Empress, assured him that he had nothing to fear, and that he might either return to Oranienbaum for a day or two, or proceed to Petersburg, a proper escort being appointed to attend him at either place; but he, choosing the town, is now at his house here in perfect freedom, and, what is most remarkable, M. Alsuffiew assured him that the Empress was perfectly well disposed towards cultivating his Prussian Majesty's friendship. The Hetman was, I hear, with General Villebois and M. Panin, the great Duke's Governor, the principal persons in bringing about this revolution, and under them the brothers Orlow were the most trusted and the most active; but the most singular circumstance of the whole is that the place of rendezvous was the house of the Princess Dashkow, a young lady not above twenty years old, daughter to Count Roman Larevonetz Woronzow, sister to the late favourite Elizabeth, and niece to the Chancellor. It is certain that she bore a principal share in contriving and carrying on the conspiracy, from the beginning to the conclusion of it.

Of all men the Hetman seemed to possess the greatest share of the unfortunate Emperor's affection, and two days before his fall he dined at Marshal Rosamowsky's country house, and was, upon that occasion, received and served with the greatest marks of duty, zeal, and attachment on the part of both brothers; and when he returned to Oranienbaum the Hetman went straight to Peterhof to concert matters with the Empress. It is a dispute what part the Chamberlain, Shouvalow, had in this affair.

On Friday evening, before the Empress left the town, she despatched an officer to bring back Count Bestucheff to Petersburg, and it is thought he will have a considerable share in the administration. In the meantime M. Panin is the person that takes most upon him, though both the Chancellor, Count Woronzie, and the Vice-Chancellor, Prince Galitzing, continue in their places; the former came to town on Friday evening, and, going directly to Court, was tolerably well received and promised the Empress's protection. However, at his own desire he had two officers of the Guards put about him for the first two days, but now they are taken off, and he goes on in the functions of his office. His lady was not at Court till

Sunday (having continued with the Emperor till the end, and having even been at Cronstadt with him), and when she kissed the Empress's hand she took off her riband of St. Catherine, and, offering it to her Imperial Majesty, said she had never asked for it, and now laid it at her feet; but the Empress most obligingly took it, and with her own hand put it again over the Countess Woronzow's shoulder.

With regard to the motives of this Revolution, it is plain that the taking away the Church lands was the principal, joined to the neglect of the clergy. The next was the severe discipline which the Emperor endeavoured to introduce amongst the troops, especially the Guards, who had been accustomed to great idleness and licence, and the discontent amongst them was heightened by the Resolution his Imperial Majesty had taken of carrying a great part of that corps into Germany with him in his expedition against Denmark, which was a measure disagreeable to the whole nation, who stomached not greatly their being drawn into new expenses and new dangers for recovering the Duchy of Schleswig, which they considered a trifling object in itself, and entirely indifferent to Russia; and this after the Emperor had just sacrificed the conquests made by the Russian arms (and which might have been of great importance to this Empire) to his friendship for the King of Prussia, which however, their desires of peace would have made them not only put up with, but approve. Several other little circumstances, greatly exaggerated and artfully represented and improved, contributed to the fall of this unhappy Prince, who had many excellent qualities, and who never did a violent or cruel action in the course of his short reign; but who, from an abhorrence to business, owing to a bad education and the unhappy choice of favourites who encouraged him in it, let everything run into confusion, and by a mistaken notion he had conceived of having secured the affections of the nation by the great favours he had so nobly bestowed on them after his first mounting the throne, fell into an indolence and security that proved fatal to him.

To conclude, not only I, but several persons of sense and discernment thought they could perceive latterly in this Prince a considerable change from what he was for some months after his accession, and that the perpetual hurry in which he lived, and the flattery he met with from the vile people about him, had in some measure affected his understanding.

I must own that I had no apprehension that this revolution would happen so soon, but I was always of opinion that if he left his dominions he ran a great risk of never returning to them, and for that reason I made use of every means I could think of to divert him from that expedition. Sometimes by insinuations to himself, and sometimes by representing the danger to others who had the honour to approach his person—whether they did their duty on this point, particularly Prince George, I cannot say; but if they did, the event has shown that it was all to no purpose.

Catherine's Coup: Her Own Account

This account of the palace revolution which brought Catherine to the Russian throne is in her own words. It is an excerpt from her letter of August, 1762 to Stanislaw Pontiatowski, her lover whom she later made King of Poland. The source is: R. Nisbet Bain, *Peter III, Emperor of Russia. The Story of a Crisis and a Crime*. New York: E. P. Dutton and Co., 1902. Pp. 191–197.

. . . It is six months ago since my accession to the throne was first put in hand. Peter III. had lost the little wit he had. He ran his head against everything. He wanted to break up the Guards, and with that intent led them out to war; he meant to substitute for them the Holstein troops which were to have remained in town. He wanted to change his religion, marry Elizabeth Vorontsov and shut me up.

The day of the celebration of the peace with [Prussia], after having publicly insulted me at table, he ordered my arrest the same evening. My uncle, Prince George, got this order retracted, and from thenceforth I lent an ear to the propositions which had been made to me [ever] since the death of the Empress [Elizabeth].

The [original] design was to seize him in his apartments and shut him up as was done with the Princess Anne and her children. He went off [however] to Oranienbaum. We were sure of a great number of the captains of the Guards. The fate of the secret was in the hands of the three brothers Orlov. . . . They are extremely determined people and much beloved by the common soldiers, having served in the Guards. I am under great obligation to these people, all Petersburg is my witness.

The minds of the Guards were made up and at last 30 to 40 officers and 10,000 of the common soldiers were in the secret. There was not a traitor to be found among them during the three weeks [before the revolution], there were four separate parties among them, whose chiefs met together as an executive; the real secret was in the hands of the three brothers. Panin wanted the revolution to be in favour of my son, but they would not consent anyhow.

I was at Peterhof, Peter III. was making merry and dwelling at Oranienbaum. It had been agreed that in case of treason, his return should not be proclaimed. Their zeal for me did what treason might have done. On the [27th July, O. S.] a report spread among the troops that I was arrested. The soldiers began to stir, one of our officers calmed them. Then a soldier went to a captain called Passek, chief of one of the [four] parties, and told him that it was certainly all up with me, he assured him he had news [to that effect]. This soldier, alarmed about me, then went to another officer, who was not in the secret, and told him the same thing. Alarmed to hear that an officer had sent away this soldier without arresting him, he posted off to his major. The major caused Passek to be arrested—and the whole regiment was instantly agog. The report [of this affair] was sent the same

night to Oranienbaum. All our conspirators were alarmed. They immediately resolved to send the second brother Orlov to me to bring me into town,
and the other two [Orlovs] secured the town, telling everybody I was coming.

The Hetman [Razumovsky], Volkonsky and Panin were in the secret.
I was sleeping calmly at Peterhof at 6 o'clock in the morning of the 28th
[July O. S.] The day had been a very disturbing one for me as I knew all
that was going on. [Suddenly] Alexius Orlov enters my room and says
quite gently: "It is time to get up; all is ready for your proclamation." I
demanded some details. "Passek is arrested," said he. I hesitated no longer.
I dressed myself quickly without making my toilet and got into the carriage
which he had brought with him. Another officer, dressed up as a valet, was
at the carriage door, a third met us some versts from Peterhof.

Five versts from the town I met the elder Orlov with the younger
Prince Bariatinsky. Orlov gave up his carriage to me, for my horses were
done up, and we got out at the barracks of the Ismailovsky Regiment. [At
the gates] were only twelve men, and a drummer, who began sounding an
alarm, when the soldiers came running out, kissing me, embracing my
hands and feet and clothes, and calling me their deliverer. Then they began swearing allegiance to me. When this had been done, they begged me
to get into the carriage, and the priest, cross in hand, walked on in front.
We went [first] to the [barracks of the] Semenovsky Regiment, but the
regiment came marching out to meet us, crying, Vivat! Then we went to
the church of Kazan, where I got out. Then the Preobrazhensky Regiment
arrived, crying, Vivat! "We beg your pardon," they said to me, "for being
the last. Our officers stopped us, but here are four of them whom we have
arrested to shew you our zeal. We want what our brothers want." Then the
horse-guards arrived frantic with joy, I never saw anything like it, weeping
and crying at the deliverance of their country. . . . I went to the new
Winter Palace where the Synod and the Senate were assembled. A manifesto and a form of oath were hastily drawn up. Then I went down and
received the troops on foot. There were more than 14,000 men, guards and
country regiments. As soon as they saw me they uttered cries of joy which
were taken up by an innumerable crowd. I went on to the old Winter
Palace to take [my] measures and finish [the business], there we took
counsel together, and it was resolved to go to Peterhof, where Peter III.
was to have dined with me, at their head. All the great roads had been
occupied and rumours came in every moment.

I sent Admiral Talisin to Cronstadt [to secure that fortress]. Then the
Chancellor Vorontsov arrived to reproach me for my departure [from
Peterhof]; they took him off to church to swear him in. Prince Trubetskoi
and Count Shuvalov also arrived from Peterhof in order to collar the regiments and kill me. They were taken off to swear the oaths without the least
resistance.

After having sent off our couriers and taken every precaution, towards
10 o'clock in the evening I put on a uniform of the Guards. Having been
proclaimed Colonel, with inexpressible acclamations, I took horse and we

left only a very few of each regiment behind to protect my son, whom we left in town. I set out at the head of the troops, and we marched all night towards Peterhof. On reaching a little monastery on the way, the Vice-Chancellor arrived with a very flattering letter from Peter III. I had forgotten to say that on leaving town, three soldiers of the Guards, sent from Peterhof to distribute a manifesto among the people, came to me and said: "Here! take what Peter III. has entrusted us with, we give it to you. We are very glad of the opportunity of joining our brethren."

After the first letter came a second, the bearer whereof, General Michal Ismailov, threw himself at my feet and said: "Do you take me 'or an honest man?" On my replying, "Yes!" "Well," says he, "it is pleasant to have to do with sensible folk. The Emperor offers to resign. I will bring to you [a form of abdication] after a very few alterations. I will save my country from a civil war without any difficulty."

I charged him with this commission, and off he went to accomplish it. Peter III. abdicated, at Oranienbaum, in full liberty, surrounded by 5000 Holsteiners, and came with Elizabeth Vorontsov, Gudovich and Ismailov to Peterhof, where, to protect his person, I gave him five officers and some soldiers. . . . Thereupon I sent the deposed Emperor to a remote and very agreeable place called Ropsha, 25 versts from Peterhof, under the command of Alexius Orlov, with four officers and a detachment of picked good-natured men, whilst decent and convenient rooms were being prepared for him at Schlusselburg. But God disposed otherwise. Fear had given him a diarrhœa which lasted three days and passed away on the fourth; in this [fourth] day he drank excessively, for he had all he wanted except liberty. Nevertheless, the only things he asked me for were his mistress, his dog, his Negro and his violin; but for fear of scandal [sic] and increasing the agitation of the persons who guarded him, I only sent him the last three things.

The hemorrhoidal colic which seized him affected his brain: two days he was delirious, and the delirium was followed by very great exhaustion, and despite all the assistance of the doctors, he expired whilst demanding a Lutheran priest. I feared that the officers might have poisoned him, so I had him opened, but it is an absolute fact that not the slightest trace of poison was found inside him. The stomach was quite sound, but inflammation of the bowels and a stroke of apoplexy had carried him off. His heart was extraordinarily small and quite decayed. . . .

It would take a whole book to describe the conduct of each of the leaders. The Orlovs brilliantly distinguished themselves by their faculty of ruling the minds of men, by their prudent audacity, by [their attention to] great and petty details, and by their presence of mind. They have a great deal of common-sense and generous courage. They are enthusiastic patriots, very honest folk, passionately attached to my person and united as never brothers were united before. There are five of them in all, but only three were here. . . . The Princess Dashkof, younger sister of Elizabeth Vorontsov, though she would like to attribute to herself all the honour [of the affair], being acquainted with some of the chiefs, was looked upon askance because of her parentage, and being but 19 had no authority at all, and although she pretends that she was the chief intermediary all along, yet the real fact is that everyone had been in [direct] communication with me six months beforehand, before she even knew their names. But she has a meddlesome humour together with a great deal of ostentation, and our principal men hate her exceedingly. It was only a few feather-brains who let her into the secret and told her all they knew, which was very trumpery. Nevertheless, they say that Ivan Ivanovich Shuvalov, the lowest and most cowardly of men has written to Voltaire that a woman 19 years old, has changed the government of this Empire. I beg of you to undeceive this great writer. Five months before she knew anything it was necessary to conceal from the Princess Dashkov [the nature of] the modes of communication between myself and others, and during the last four weeks she was told as little as possible.

The strength of mind of Prince Bariatinsky, who concealed the secret from his dearly beloved brother, the late Emperor's adjutant . . . deserves praise.

In the Horse-Guards, an officer named Chitrov, aged 22, and an under officer, 17 years old, named Potemkin, directed everything with discernment, courage and energy.

That is pretty much the history of this affair and I assure you that everything was done under my direct personal orders. At the last moment I hurried up because the departure [of the Emperor] for the country prevented the execution [of the plot], and everything had been ripe for a fortnight.

The late Emperor, when he heard of the tumult in town, was prevented by the young women of his suite from following the advice of old Field Marshal Münnich, who advised him to throw himself into Cronstadt, or set off for the army with a few followers. When he *did* go in his galley to Cronstadt the fortress was already ours in consequence of the good conduct of Admiral Talizin, who caused General Devier to be disarmed, this Devier being already on the spot on the Emperor's behalf when Talizin arrived. An officer of the port, on his own initiative, threatened to fire point-blank at the galley of this unfortunate Prince.

At last, then God has brought everything to pass according to His predisposition. The whole thing is rather a miracle than a fact foreseen and arranged beforehand, for so many felicitous combinations could not have coincided unless God's hand had been over it all.

. . . Be assured, too, that hatred of foreigners was the leading principle of the whole affair, and that Peter III. himself passed for a foreigner.

Adieu, there are some very strange situations in this world.

Catherine's Accession Manifesto

Catherine announced her usurpation of power by the following manifesto which she had printed and distributed in St. Petersburg. The source is: Tooke, *Life of Catherine II,* vol. 1, pp. 518–519.

By the grace of God, Catharine II, empress and autocratrix of all the Russias, &c.

All true sons of Russia have clearly seen the great danger to which the whole Russian empire has actually been exposed. First, the foundations of our orthodox Greek religion have been shaken, and its traditions exposed to total destruction; so that there was absolutely reason to fear, that the faith which has been established in Russia from the earliest times, would be entirely changed, and foreign religion introduced. In the second place, the glory which Russia has acquired at the expense of so much blood, and which was carried to the highest pitch by her victorious arms, has been trampled under foot by the peace lately concluded with its most dangerous enemy. And lastly, the domestic regulations, which are the basis of the country's welfare, have been entirely overturned.

For these causes, overcome by the imminent perils with which our faithful subjects were threatened, and seeing how sincere and express their desires on this matter were; we, putting our trust in the Almighty and his divine justice, have ascended the sovereign imperial throne of all the Russias, and have received a solemn oath of fidelity from all our loving subjects.

St. Petersburg, June 28, 1762.

Herzen's Estimate of Catherine

> Alexander Herzen was one of the most famous of the nineteenth century non-Marxist socialists of Russia. By virtue of his beliefs, he was early forced into exile, and spent most of his adult life away from his native land. From his exile he edited the famous underground newspaper, *The Bell* (*Kolokol*). He also wrote profusely and was instrumental in founding the Free Russian Press in London. The following excerpt is from his introduction to the memoirs of the Empress Catherine II. The source is: *Memoirs of the EMPRESS CATHERINE II Written by Herself. With a Preface by A. Herzen.* New York: D. Appleton and Company, 1859. Pp. 13–16.

And now, after all that has been said, let the reader picture to himself what must have been the nature of the medium into which destiny had cast this young girl, gifted, as she was, not only with great talent, but also with a character pliant, though full of pride and passion.

Her position at St. Petersburg was horrible. On one side was her mother, a peevish, scolding, greedy, niggardly, pedantic German, boxing her ears, and taking away her new dresses to appropriate them to her own use; on the other, the Empress Elizabeth, a coarse and grumbling virago, never quite sober, jealous, envious, causing every step of the young Princess to be watched, every word reported, taking offence at everything, and all this after having given her for a husband the most ridiculous Benedict of the age.

A prisoner in the palace, she could do nothing without permission. If she wept for the death of her father, the Empress sent her word that she had grieved enough. "That her father was not a king, that she should mourn him longer than a week." If she evinced a friendship for any of her maids of honour, she might be sure the lady would be dismissed. If she became attached to a faithful servant, still more certain was it that that servant would be turned away.

Her relations with the Grand Duke were monstrous, degrading. He made her the confidante of his amorous intrigues. Drunk from the age of ten, he came one night in liquor to entertain his wife with a description of the graces and charms of the daughter of Biren; and as Catherine pretended to be asleep, he gave her a punch with his fist to waken her. This booby kept a kennel of dogs, which infested the air, at the side of his wife's bedchamber, and hung rats in his own, to punish them according to the rules of martial law.

Nor is this all. After having wounded and outraged nearly every feeling of this young creature's nature, they began to deprave her systematically. The Empress regards as a breech of order her having no children. Madame Tchoglokoff speaks to her on the subject, insinuating that, *for the good of the state,* she ought to sacrifice her scruples, and concludes by proposing to her a choice between Soltikoff and Narichkine. The young lady affects simplicity and takes both—nay, Poniatowsky into the bargain, and thus was commenced a career of licentiousness in which she never halted during the space of forty years.

What renders the present publication of serious consequence to the imperial house of Russia is, that it proves not only that this house does not belong to the family of Romanoff, but that it does not even belong to that of Holstein Gottorp. The avowal of Catherine on this point is very explicit —*the father of the Emperor Paul is Sergius Soltikoff.*

The Imperial Dictatorship of Russia endeavours in vain to represent itself as traditional and secular.

One word before I close.

In perusing these Memoirs, the reader is astonished to find one thing constantly lost sight of, even to the extent of not appearing anywhere—it is *Russia and the People.* And here is the characteristic trait of the epoch.

The Winter Palace, with its military and administrative machinery, was a world of its own. Like a ship floating on the surface of the ocean, it had no real connection with the inhabitants of the deep, beyond that of eating them. It was the *State for the State.* Organized on the German model, it imposed itself on the nation as a conqueror. In that monstrous barrack, in that enormous chancery, there reigned the cold rigidity of a camp. One set gave or transmitted orders, the rest obeyed in silence. There was but one single spot within that dreary pile in which human passions reappeared, agitated and stormy, and that spot was the domestic hearth; not that of the nation—but of the state. Behind that triple line of sentinels, in those heavily ornamented saloons, there fermented a feverish life, with its intrigues and its conflicts, its dramas and its tragedies. It was there that the destinies of Russia were woven, in the gloom of the alcove, in the midst of orgies, *beyond* the reach of informers and of the police.

What interest, then, could the young German Princess take in that *magnum ignotum,* that people *unexpressed,* poor, semi-barbarous, which concealed itself in its villages, behind the snow, behind bad roads, and only appeared in the streets of St. Petersburg like a foreign outcast, with its persecuted beard, and prohibited dress—tolerated only through contempt.

It was only long afterwards that Catherine heard the Russian people seriously spoken of, when the Cossack Pougatcheff, at the head of an army of insurgent peasants, menaced Moscow.

When Pougatcheff was vanquished, the Winter Palace again forgot the people. And there is no telling when it would have been again remembered had it not itself put its masters in mind of its existence, by rising in mass in 1812, rejecting, on the one hand, the release from serfdom offered to it at the point of foreign bayonets, and, on the other, marching to death to save a country which gave it nothing but slavery, degradation, misery—and the oblivion of the Winter Palace.

This was the second memento of the Russian people. Let us hope that at the third it will be remembered a little longer. A. HERZEN. London, *November 15th,* 1858.

The British Ambassador Describes Catherine

The Earl of Buckinghamshire, British ambassador to Catherine's court, sent his government two descriptions of the empress. The first was written soon after his arrival in St. Petersburg in 1762; the second, shortly before his departure from there in 1765. The source is: Collyer, *Despatches,* vol. 1, pp. 100–104; vol. 2, pp. 273–276.

Her Imperial Majesty is neither short nor tall; she has a majestic air, and possesses that happy mixture of dignity and ease which at once enforces respect and sets men at their ease. Formed with a mind and a body capable of acquiring every accomplishment, and enforced retirement gave her more leisure to cultivate them than is usually allotted to princes, and qualified her, as she charmed the eye in gay society, to delight the understanding in more serious moments. This period of constraint, which lasted several years, and the agitation of mind and continual fatigues which she has undergone since her accession, have deprived her charms of their freshness. Besides, she has never been beautiful. Her features were far from being so delicately and exactly formed as to compose what might pretend to regular beauty, but a fine complexion, an animated and intelligent eye, a mouth agreeably turned, and a profusion of glossy chestnut hair produce that sort of countenance which, a very few years ago, a man must have been either prejudiced or insensible to have beheld with indifference. She has been, and still is, what often pleases and always attaches more than beauty. She is extremely well made, the neck and hands remarkably beautiful, and the limbs so elegantly turned as equally to become the dress of either sex. Her eyes are blue, their vivacity tempered by a languor in which there is much sensibility and no insipidity. She has the air of paying no attention to what she wears, yet she is always too well drest for a woman who is entirely indifferent to her appearance. A man's dress is what suits her best; she wears it always when she rides on horseback. It is scarce credible what she does in that way, managing horses, even fiery horses, with all the skill and courage of a groom. She excels, too, in the serious as well as livelier dances. She expresses herself with elegance in French, and I am assured that she speaks Russian with as much precision as German, which is her native language, and that she has a critical knowledge of both languages. She speaks and reasons with fluency and precision, and some letters which must have been of her own composing have been admired and applauded by the scholars of the nation in whose language they were wrote.

Reading made her amusement in the retirement in which she lived in the days of the late Empress. The history and the interests of the European Powers are familiar to her. When she spoke to me of English history, I perceived that what had struck her the most was the reign of Elizabeth. Time will show where such an emulation may lead her. Finding herself superior in information and argument to most of those about her, she thinks she is equally so to everybody, and, understanding clearly what she has learnt, she sometimes thinks herself mistress of what she has not. When she was on board the Admiral's ship at Cronstadt, her imperial standard flying, and flattered with the inexperienced grandeur of commanding more than twenty large ships, she disputed with me which end of a man-of-war went first—a circumstance which indeed she was not obliged to know—but the actual situation made the doubt ridiculous.

Much stress is laid upon her resolution, particularly in the instance of dethroning her husband. Desperate situations make cowards valiant. She was compelled either to ruin him or to submit herself to that confinement which she knew had long been in deliberation. Those who know her well say she is rather enterprising than brave, and that her appearance of courage arises sometimes from a conviction of the pusillanimity of her enemies, at others from her not seeing her danger. She certainly is bolder than the generality of her sex, but I have seen her twice very much afraid without reason: once when she was getting out of boat into a ship; the other time, upon hearing a little noise in the ante-chamber at Court. But when the occasion requires it she dares all, and in many critical and dangerous situations her courage has never failed her. Yet she has all the delicacy of her sex. To see her is to know that she could love, and that her love would make the happiness of a lover worthy of her.

Two capital errors, which are equally evident and inexcusable, are the meanness with which she submits to the ill-bred inattention of Orlow, and the little affection she shows to the Grand Duke.

The amusements of her retirement, into which she enters with a youthful spirit, are trifling beyond expression, and much the same which children in other countries leave off at twelve years old.

Those who are most in her society assure me that her application to business is incredible. The welfare and prosperity of her subjects, the glory of her empire, are always present to her; and to all appearance her care will raise the reputation and power of Russia to a point which, at present, they have never reached, if she does not indulge too much in far-fetched and unpractical theories, which interested or ignorant people are too ready to suggest to her. Her foible is too systematic, and that may be the rock on which she may, perhaps, split. She embraces too many objects at once; she likes to begin, regulate, and correct projects all in a moment. Indefatigable in everything that she undertakes, she obliges her ministers to work incessantly. They argue, make plans, and sketch out a thousand schemes, and decide upon nothing. Among those who hold the first rank in her confidence, some will be found who have experience, but few if any who possess superior talents. There is, however, one of her Majesty's secretaries who has knowledge, wit, and even application, when women and the pleasures of the table—which always demand his first cares—give him any leisure for business.

Unwilling to touch so tender a string, I have deferred till the last speaking of the Revolution and the most melancholy catastrophe which succeeded.

The Empress has frequently talked to me of her husband, and, without exaggerating his indiscretions, pointed out those which principally occasioned his ruin. Once, in her absence, I saw his picture in her cabinet; it was without a frame and stood upon the floor, as if brought in for her to look at. The Vice-Chancellor told me it was a strong likeness. I examined it with attention, and could not help running over in my mind the hard fate of the heir of Russia, Sweden, and Holstein, who, with many defects in his understanding, had none in his heart.

The Vice-Chancellor seemed surprised at my silent attention, and asked me what employed my thoughts. Was it so difficult to guess?

When this is considered as a portrait drawn by one who knew her and who wished with candour to steer the middle course between calumny and adulation, who will not mourn the steps she took to raise herself to Empire, and the fatal measures which the worst of her followers judged necessary to secure her in that throne she fills so well?

Many, and some of the deepest hue, are the blemishes which shade a character otherwise so amiable. Her enemies, and particularly the French and Austrians, have taken every method to place them in the strongest light, and, not contented with those which were known to be true, and others but too probably, they have sought to blacken her still more with fictions which have almost been generally received, even by those from whom her political disposition might claim a fairer hearing. She is accused of dethroning her husband; of usurping that empire of which, even from her own declaration, she could only pretend to be Regent; of causing her husband to be put to death; of changing the whole system of her Empire in order to make one of her former lovers king of Poland; and, lastly, of contriving the murder of the late Prince Ivan. That her present favourite is the fourth person she has distinguished is as certain as that she was persuaded to receive the first by the Empress Elizabeth, who thought her nephew incapable of begetting children; and possibly anyone who is acquainted with the abandoned scenes which passed at that Court will wonder that a young, lively woman, who had long seen debauchery sanctified by usage and the highest example, should want any persuasion at all. When I allow that the seizing the Crown herself does not admit of justification, nor even of palliation, that adopting the most favourable and improbable supposition that her husband was put to death, not only without her order, but contrary to her intention, her not clearing up the fact and punishing the guilty at any risk is unpardonable. Shall I incur a suspicion of partiality when I assert that the folly and imprudence of the ill-fated Emperor, his avowed intention of confining her, his further plan of setting aside the Great Duke, his ill-conceived expedition against the Danes, his mean, subservient adulation of the King of Prussia, which in the end must have been destructive to his country, and lastly, the insults she was hourly exposed to from his abandoned mistress—too powerful an incentive of that feminine resentment which so often decides the fate of empires—may, in a great measure, apologise for her conduct so far as removing him from the throne?

. . .

To assert that some time ago I should have thought it an easy task to draw a full and just character of the Empress, and that now, having frequent opportunities of seeing her in the hours of dissipation when the veil of restraint and ceremony was thrown off, the undertaking puzzles and embarrasses me, has something the air of a paradox, which, however, is easily solved by mentioning that then I knew only the great outlines and was unacquainted with the little weaknesses and inconsistencies which almost efface some and shade many of those eminent qualities which adorn her. It is impossible to consider the general tenour of her conduct, since she placed herself upon the throne, without tracing evident marks of a laudable ambition to distinguish herself; to make her subjects happy at home and respectable abroad; to encourage arts, sciences and commerce; to form by a liberal education the young nobility of both sexes; to extend in a great degree the same advantages to inferior ranks; to improve the public revenue without oppressing individuals; to check the tyranny with which the clergy distressed their vassals; and to introduce that ease of society, that urbanity and general good breeding which prevail in other European nations; in a word, to transmit her name with glory to posterity, and by the use she makes of empire to palliate the means by which she has acquired it.

In the course of two years, though hourly alarmed by the attempts of her enemies, she has exerted her good offices for the general pacification of Europe; she has given a King to Poland, established a sovereign in Courland, and greatly contributed to the overturning of the so long prevailing French system in Sweden. These are facts of which it is as necessary to labour the proof as it would be vain to contest the reality, and surely it is greatly to be lamented that vanity, self-sufficiency, avarice, and a taste for trifling pleasures should cloud so bright a future?

The expenses of the Court are in some instances retrenched to a degree of meanness, and many persons of the first rank seize officiously the first pretence to retire from Petersburg, as, receiving no longer the same presents from the Sovereign, they cannot afford to pay the daily-increasing price of every article of consumption.

Political intrigue and fruitful imaginations have variously accounted for her most imprudent journey to Riga; in fact, it was determined by the desire of a little mind to make a naval parade, to enjoy the pageantry and adulations with which the provinces received her, and to see a sovereign of her own creating at her feet. Deaf to the friendly advice which combated her inclination, she was obstinate to prove her steadiness.

Her face and figure are greatly altered for the worse since her accession. It is easy to discover the remains of a fine woman, but she is now no longer an object of desire. The many who wish to arraign the conduct and vilify the character of this Princess tax her with the same disposition to debauchery as sullied the reign of her predecessor. This makes it necessary to say something on the subject, and succinctly state such information as upon the strictest inquiry I have obtained, which when candidly considered may palliate though not justify her conduct. She had been married some years to the Grand Duke without being with child, and, as this was supposed to arise from the inability of her husband, distant hints were thrown out by the Empress, which were not taken. At last she sent her confidante, Madame Shouvalow, to inform the Grand Duchess that if she did not soon contrive to produce an heir to the Empire she must expect to be divorced. After some hesitation she yielded. One Soltikow (now abroad) was the man pitched upon, and he is said to be the father of the present Grand Duke. The first scruples being got over, the rest followed but too naturally. Soltikow having left the country, the solitude in which she generally lived made every possible amusement necessary, and General Chernichow and, soon after, Poniatowski enjoyed her favour. Orlow was one of the young people who entered early into the conspiracy to place her upon the throne. She saw him frequently; the beauty of his person, and his particular affection for her, of which she has since declared she had long been sensible, induced her to yield. Her being with child at the time of the Revolution was a circumstance which, as her husband never approached her, made it necessary to hasten that event. She was brought to bed of a son at Moscow some months after. The child is under the care of Schurin at Petersburg, where her Imperial Majesty has sometimes visited him.

Catherine's Manifesto on Pugachev

Catherine, in 1773, faced a full-scale revolt of malcontents under the leadership of Emelian Pugachev, a Cossack of the Don. A capable and inspiring leader, Pugachev welded many discontented groups into a large army. Mastering the Ural and Volga areas, the rebels moved westward toward Moscow, gathering strong peasant support on the way. Catherine's generals, aided not a little by a famine in the Volga region, gradually destroyed the rebel forces. Pugachev was captured and executed in 1775. Catherine issued the following manifesto at the beginning of the revolt. The source is: Tooke, *Life of Catherine II*, vol. 2, pp. 425–427.

By the grace of God, we Catharine II, empress and autocratrix of all the Russias, &c. make known to all our faithful subjects, that we have learnt, with the utmost indignation and extreme affliction, that a certain Kozak, a deserter and fugitive from the Don, named Ikhelman Pugatshef, after having traversed Poland, has been collecting, for some time past, in the districts that border on the river Irghis, in the government of Orenburg, a troop of vagabonds like himself; that he continues to commit in those parts all kinds of excesses, by inhumanly depriving the inhabitants of their possessions, and even of their lives; and that in order to draw over to his party, hitherto composed of robbers, such persons as he meets, and specially the unhappy patriots, on whose credulity he imposes, he has had the insolence to arrogate to himself the name of the late emperor Peter III. It would be superfluous here to prove the absurdity of such an imposture, which cannot even put on a shadow of probability in the eyes of sensible persons: for, thanks to the divine goodness, those ages are past, in which the Russian empire was plunged in ignorance and barbarism; when a Griska, an Outreper, with their adherents, and several other traitors to their country, made use of impostures as gross and detestable, to arm brother against brother, and citizen against citizen.

Since those eras, which it is grievous to recollect, all true patriots have enjoyed the fruits of public tranquillity, and shudder with horror at the very remembrance of former troubles. In a word, there is not a man deserving of the Russian name, who does not hold in abomination the odious and insolent lie by which Pugatshef fancies himself able to seduce and to deceive persons of a simple and credulous disposition, by promising to free them from the bonds of submission, and obedience to their sovereign, as if the Creator of the universe had established human societies in such a manner as that they can subsist without an intermediate authority between the sovereign and the people.

Nevertheless, as the insolence of this vile refuse of the human race is attended with consequences pernicious to the provinces adjacent to that district; as the report of the flagrant enormities which he has committed, may affright those persons who are accustomed to imagine the misfortunes of others as ready to fall upon them, and as we watch with indefatigable care over the tranquillity of our faithful subjects, we inform them by the present manifesto, that we have taken, without delay, such measures as are the best adapted to stifle the sedition: and in order to annihilate totally the ambitious designs of Pugatshef, and to exterminate a band of robbers, who have been audacious enough to attack the small military detachments dispersed about those countries, and to massacre the officers who were taken prisoners, we have dispatched thither, with a competent number of troops, general Alexander Bibikof, general in chief of our armies, and major of our regiment of life guards.

Accordingly we have no doubt of the happy success of these measures, and we cherish the hope that the public tranquillity will soon be restored, and that the profligates who are spreading devastation over a part of the government of Orenburg, will shortly be dispersed. We are moreover persuaded, that our faithful subjects will justly abhor the imposture of the rebel Pugatshef, as destitute of all probability, and will repel the artifices of the ill-disposed, who seek and find their advantage in the seduction of the weak and credulous, and who cannot assuage their avidity but by ravaging their country, and by shedding of innocent blood.

We trust, with equal confidence, that every true son of the country will unremittedly fulfil his duty, of the contributing to the maintenance of good order and of public tranquillity, by preserving himself from the snares of seduction, and by duly discharging his obedience to his lawful sovereign. All our faithful subjects, therefore, may dispel their alarms and live in perfect security, since we employ our utmost care, and make it our peculiar glory, to preserve their property, and to extend the general felicity.

Given at St. Petersburg, Dec. 23, 1773, O.S.

Catherine's Enlightenment

> Catherine's pride in her "enlightenment" is well known. The two letters which follow are illustrative of this aspect of her character. The first was written to Voltaire in answer to a request for her aid to some victims of persecution; the second was written to Vladimir Orlov, Director of the Academy of Science at St. Petersburg. The source is: Tooke, *Life of Catherine II*, vol. 1, pp. 425, 556–557.

SIR, The brightness of the northern star is a mere aurora borealis. It is nothing more than giving to a neighbour something of our own superfluity. But to be the advocate of human kind, the defender of oppressed innocence; by this you will be indeed immortalized. The two causes of Calas and Sirven have procured you the veneration due to such miracles. You have combated the united enemies of mankind, superstition, fanaticism, ignorance, chicane, bad judges, and the power lodged in them, all together. To surmount such obstacles, required both talents and virtue. You have shown the world that you possess both. You have carried your point. You desire, sir, some relief for the Sirven family. Can I possibly refuse it? Or, should you praise me for the action, would there be the least foundation for it? I own to you, that I should be much better pleased if my bill of exchange could pass unknown. Nevertheless, if you think my name, unharmonious as it is, may be of any service to those victims of the spirit of persecution, I leave it to your discretion; and you may announce me, provided it be no way prejudicial to the parties.

• • •

MONS. COUNT ORLOV, Having been informed that in the summer of the year 1769, the planet Venus will pass over the sun, I write you this letter, that you may acquaint the Academy of Sciences on my part, 1. That it is my pleasure that the academy should procure the observations to be made with the utmost care; and that I desire, in consequence, to know, 2. which are the most advantageously situated places of the empire that the academy has destined for this observation; to the end that, in case it should be necessary to erect any buildings, workmen, etc. may be sent, and proper measures be taken. 3. That if there be not a sufficient number of astronomers in the academy for completing the observations in the places pitched upon by the academy, I propose, and take upon me to find out, among my marine subjects, such as, during the interval between the present time and the transit of Venus, may be perfected in the habit of observing, under the eyes of the professors, so as to be employed to advantage in this expedition, and to the satisfaction of the academy. You will, Mr. Count, transmit me the answer of the academy, with its full opinion about every thing above, that I may give orders for the whole without loss of time. Moscow, 3d March, 1767. Catharine.

Lomonosov

Mikhail Vasilevich Lomonosov died three years after Catherine became empress, so chronologically he belongs in the reign of Elizabeth. The literary "school" which he founded was, however, a major feature of the artistic and intellectual life of Catherine's time. Her generation esteemed Lomonosov as a poet. Later generations honor him more for his development of a Russian literary language and for his pioneering work in the sciences. He is considered the first of the great Russian scientists. The prose selection below is an excerpt from a letter to his patron, Shuvalov, written in 1753. The poetry reflects his scientific interests as well as his philosophy and his literary skill. Both selections are from: Wiener, *Anthology*, vol. 1, pp. 245, 253–254.

Letter

First, as to electricity: There have lately been made here two important experiments, one by Mr. Richmann by means of the apparatus, the other by me in the clouds. By the first it was proved that Musschenbroek's experiment with a strong discharge can be transferred from place to place, separating it from the apparatus for a considerable distance, even as much as half a mile. The second experiment was made on my lightning apparatus, when, without any perceptible thunder or lightning, on the 25th of April, the thread was repelled from the iron rod and followed my hand; and on the 28th of the same month, during the passage of a rain cloud without any perceptible thunder or lightning, there were loud discharges from the lightning apparatus, with bright sparks and a crackling that could be heard from a great distance. This has never been noticed before, and it agrees completely with my former theory of heat and my present one of electric power, and this will serve me well at the next public lecture.

. . .

Evening Meditations on Seeing the Aurora Borealis

The day retires, the mists of night are spread
Slowly o'er nature, darkening as they rise;
The gloomy clouds are gathering round our heads,
And twilight's latest glimmering gently dies:
The stars awake in heaven's abyss of blue;
Say, who can count them?—Who can sound it?—Who?

Even as a sand in the majestic sea,
A diamond-atom on a hill of snow,
A spark amidst a Hecla's majesty,
An unseen mote where maddened whirlwinds blow,
And I midst scenes like these—the mighty thought
O'erwhelms me—I am nought, or less than nought.

And science tells me that each twinkling star
That smiles above us is a peopled sphere,
Or central sun, diffusing light afar;
A link of nature's chain:—and there, even there,
The Godhead shines displayed—in love and light,
Creating wisdom—all-directing might.

Where are thy secret laws, O Nature, where?
In wintry realms thy dazzling torches blaze,
And from thy icebergs streams of glory there
Are poured, while other suns their splendent race
In glory run: from frozen seas what ray
Of brightness?—From yon realms of night what day?

Philosopher, whose penetrating eye
Reads nature's deepest secrets, open now
This all-inexplicable mystery:
Why do earth's darkest, coldest regions glow
With lights like these?—Oh, tell us, knowing one,
For thou dost count the stars, and weigh the sun!

Whence are these varied lamps all lighted round?—
Whence all the horizon's glowing fire?—The heaven
Is splendent as with lightning—but no sound
Of thunder—all as calm as gentlest even;
And winter's midnight is as bright, as gay,
As the fair noontide of a summer's day.

What stores of fire are these, what magazine,
Whence God from grossest darkness light supplies?
What wondrous fabric which the mountains screen,

Whose bursting flames above those mountains rise;
Where rattling winds disturb the mighty ocean,
And the proud waves roll with eternal motion.

Vain is the inquiry—all is darkness, doubt:
This earth is one vast mystery to man.
First find the secrets of this planet out,
Then other planets, other systems scan!
Nature is veiled from thee, presuming clod!
And what canst thou conceive of Nature's God?

Tatishchev on Russian History

Vasili N. Tatischev was also a link of sorts between Catherine's reign
and those of her predecessors. Entrusted by Peter the Great with several research projects, Tatishchev collected and studied many historical documents. Later, he also studied some foreign sources of Russian
history, and on the basis of these studies wrote a *History of Russia*.
This aroused so little interest in Russia that Tatishchev vainly sought
to have the work published in England. It was finally published during
the reign of Catherine the Great. The source is: Wiener, *Anthology*,
vol. 1, pp. 222–223.

As regards the usefulness of Russian history it must be remarked, that, as
is the case with all other histories, the knowledge of one's own history and
geography is more important for any nation or region than that of foreign
histories; at the same time it must be kept in mind that without the knowledge of foreign histories, one's own is not clear and sufficient: 1. That the
writer of contemporary history cannot know all the external influences for
good and bad; 2. That the writers frequently are compelled, out of fear, to
suppress, or change, or modify some very important circumstances of contemporary history; 3. That from passion, love, or hatred, they describe
quite differently from what were the actual occurrences, and that the facts
are frequently related more correctly and in detail by outsiders. Thus, in
my present work, the first part, dealing with the Russian antiquity, has
mainly been drawn from foreign sources for lack of native writers, and in
the other parts many errors and lacunae have been corrected and filled
out from foreign sources. European historians accuse us of having no old
history, and of knowing nothing of our antiquity, simply because they do
not know what historians we possess, and though some have made a few
extracts, or have translated from them a passage here and there, others,
thinking that we have no better ones than those quoted, despise them.
. . . I wish to say emphatically that all the famous European historians
will not be able to know or tell anything correctly of our many antiquities,
no matter what their efforts in Russian history may be, if they do not read
our sources. . . . This history is not only of use to us Russians, but also
to the whole learned world, in order that by it the fables and lies invented

by our enemies, the Poles and others, for the sake of disparaging our ancestors may be laid bare and contradicted.

Such is the usefulness of history. But everybody ought to know, and this is easily perceived, that history describes not only customs, deeds and occurrences, but also the consequences resulting from them, namely, that the wise, just, kind, brave, constant and faithful are rewarded with honour, glory and well-being, while the vicious, foolish, evildoers, avaricious, cowardly, perverse and faithless will gain eternal dishonour, shame and insult: from which all may learn how desirable it is to obtain the first and avoid the second.

The Historian Shcherbatov

Catherine's patronage of scholarship was demonstrated, among other ways, by her concern for historical and archival materials. One of her projects was the ordering of the archives of Peter the Great, a task which she gave to Prince M. M. Shcherbatov. Though educated in the Western manner, Shcherbatov was essentially a Slavophile who attributed much which he did not like about the Russia of his day to the reforms of Peter I. This thesis he expounded in a book entitled, *On the Corruption of Manners in Russia,* from which the following excerpt is taken. The book was so critical of the court that Shcherbatov did not publish it, and the work did not appear in print until 1858 when Herzen published it in London. The source is Wiener, *Anthology,* vol. 1, p. 290.

Although Russia, through the labours and care of this Emperor [Peter I], has become known to Europe and has now weight in affairs, and her armies are properly organized, and her fleets have covered the White and Baltic seas, so that she has been able to conquer her old enemies and former victors, the Poles and the Swedes, and has gained fine districts and good harbours; although the sciences, arts and industries began to flourish in Russia, and commerce to enrich her, and the Russians were transformed from bearded men into clean-shaven ones, and exchanged their long cloaks for short coats, and became more sociable and accustomed to refinement; yet at the same time the true attachment to the faith began to disappear, the mysteries fell into disrepute, firmness was weakened and gave way to impudent, insinuating flattery; luxury and voluptuousness laid the foundation for their domination, and with it selfishness began to penetrate the high judicial places, to the destruction of the laws and the detriment of the citizens. Such is the condition of morals in which Russia was left after the death of the great Emperor, in spite of all his attempts, in his own person and through example, to ward off the encroachment of vice.

Novikov and Radishchev, "Radicals" or "Liberals"?

Catherine was much attracted to the Western liberalism of her day, and encouraged its development in Russia during the early years of her reign. She sponsored a satirical journal, modeled upon *The Spectator,* and she sent promising young men to study in Western Europe.

Among those who responded to this encouragement were N. I. Novikov and A. N. Radishchev. Novikov, the leading Freemason of Moscow, devoted himself to the publishing and dissemination of books and
to the encouragement of young writers. For a short time he was the
publisher of a satirical journal entitled, *The Drone*. Radishchev, one
of the first to be trained in Europe, distinguished himself as an honest
and able civil servant. In 1790, he wrote and circulated a manuscript
called *Journey from St. Petersburg to Moscow*, in which he not only
advocated serf emancipation, but also spoke very critically of autocracy. Catherine punished him by exile to Siberia. She also imprisoned
Novikov, partly at least because of her growing suspicions of the
Masonic Order. The first of the two following selections is an excerpt
from an essay by Novikov which he published in *The Drone* under
the title, "Recipe for His Excellency, Mr. Lacksense." The second
selection is an excerpt from Radishchev's *Journey*. Both are reprinted
from Wiener, *Anthology*, vol. 1, pp. 332, 367–369.

This nobleman suffers from a quotidian fever of boasting of his family. He
traces his family tree to the beginning of the universe, and hates all those
who cannot prove their aristocratic blood at least five hundred years back,
and loathes to speak with those whose nobility is only a hundred years old
or less. He shakes with fever the moment somebody mentions burghers or
peasants in his presence. In opposition to the modern current appellation,
he does not even honour them with the name "low-born," but in the fifty
years of his fruitless life he has not yet been able to find a proper term for
them. He does not travel to church nor in the streets, for fear of a dead
faint which would unavoidably fall upon him the moment he met an igno-
ble man. Our patient complains hourly against fate for having destined
him to share the same air, sun and moon with the common people. He
wishes there were no other beings on the whole globe but aristocrats, and
that the common people should all be annihilated. He had repeatedly
handed in projects to that effect, and they had been highly praised for the
good and novel ideas contained therein, though many rejected them, because the inventor demanded three million roubles in advance in order
to execute his plans.

   Our aristocrat hates and loaths all the sciences and arts, and regards
them as a disgrace for any noble gentleman. In his opinion a blueblood
can know everything without having learned it; but philosophy, mathematics, physics and all other sciences are trifles that are below a nobleman's
attention. Books of heraldry and letters patent that have just escaped the
dust-pile and mould are the only books which he continually reads by
spelling out. . . .

                                •   •   •

   A few steps from the road I noticed a peasant who was ploughing his
field. It was warm; I looked at my watch: it was twenty minutes to one. I
left the city on Saturday, so it was Sunday then. The peasant that was
ploughing evidently belonged to a landowner that did not receive any tax

from him. The peasant was ploughing with great care; evidently the field did not belong to the master. He was turning the plough with remarkable ease.

"God aid you!" I said as I approached the ploughman, who did not stop but finished the furrow he had begun.

"God aid you!" I repeated.

"Thank you, sir!" said the ploughman as he cleaned the ploughshare and transferred the plough to a new furrow.

"You are, of course, a dissenter, since you work on Sunday."

"No, sir, I make the correct sign of the cross," he said, and showed me his three fingers put together; "but God is merciful and does not want a person to starve, as long as he has a family and sufficient strength."

"Have you not any time to work during the week, that you work on a Sunday, and at that in a great heat?"

"In the week, sir, there are six days, and we have to work for the manor six times a week, and in the evening we haul the hay from the meadows, if the weather is good; and on holidays the women and girls go to the woods to gather mushrooms and berries. God grant a rain this evening," he added as he made the sign of the cross. "Sir, if you have any peasants, they are praying for the same."

"I have no peasants, my friend; and so nobody curses me. Have you a large family?"

"Three sons and three daughters. My eldest is ten years old."

"How do you manage to get enough grain, if you have only the Sundays to yourself?"

"Not only the Sundays—the nights are ours too. We need not starve, if we are not lazy. You see, one horse is resting; and when this one gets tired, I'll take the other, and that's the way I make my work count."

"Do you work the same way for your master?"

"No, sir! It would be sinful to work the same way; he has in his fields one hundred hands for one mouth, and I have but two hands for seven mouths, if you count it up. If you were to work yourself to death at your master's work, he would not thank you for it. The master will not pay the capitation tax; he will let you have no mutton, no hempen cloth, no chicken, no butter. Our people are fortunate in those places where the master receives a rent from the peasant, particularly without a superintendent! It is true, some good masters ask more than three roubles for each soul, yet that is better than tenant labour. They are now in the habit of letting farms out of renters who, being poor, flay us alive. They do not give us our own time, and do not let us go out in the winter to work for ourselves, because they pay our capitation tax. It is a devilish idea to let one's peasants do work for somebody else! There is at least a chance of complaining against a superintendent, but to whom is one to complain against a tenant?"

"My friend! You are mistaken: the laws do not permit to torture people."

"Torture, yes! But, sir, you would not want to be in my hide!" In the meantime the ploughman hitched another horse to his plough and, bidding me good-bye, began a new furrow.

The conversation with this agriculturist awakened a multitude of thoughts in me. Above all, I thought of the inequality of the peasant's condition. I compared the crown peasants with those of the proprietors. Both live in villages, but while the first pays a stated tax, the others have to be ready to pay whatever the master wishes. The first are judged by their peers; the others are dead to the laws, except in criminal matters. A member of society only then is taken cognisance of by the Government that protects him when he violates the social bond, when he becomes a criminal! That thought made all my blood boil. Beware, cruel proprietor! On the brow of every one of your peasants I see your condemnation.

Catherine's *Instructions*

Catherine II was heir to a particular tradition and practice which dated from the reign of Peter I. The particular tradition was that the sovereign favored a general legal reform, especially a codification of the laws; the practice was to keep committees at work drafting and re-drafting a code. Catherine followed the pattern by appointing (in 1767) a Commission to Draft a New Code of Laws. She added her personal touch by supplying this commission with a set of *Instructions* prepared by herself. The commission failed to produce a legal reform despite this special guidance, but the *Instructions* added to Catherine's reputation as an "enlightened monarch."

Most of the *Instructions*, as Catherine freely admitted, were borrowed from the writings of Montesquieu, Beccaria, Bielfield, and others, and a surprising number of pedants have found nothing better to do than to trace the origins of the 655 items which make up the *Instructions*. The samples below were chosen to show the range of Catherine's concern and the nature of this famous document.

The source is: W. R. Reddaway (Ed.), *Documents of Catherine the Great*. New York: Macmillan, 1931. Pp. 215–309, 322–329, *passim*.

1. The Christian Law teaches us to do mutual Good to one another, as much as possibly we can.

2. Laying this down as a fundamental Rule prescribed by that Religion, which has taken, or ought to take Root in the Hearts of the whole People; we cannot but suppose, that every honest Man in the community is, or will be, desirous of seeing his native Country at the very Summit of Happiness, Glory, Safety, and Tranquillity.

3. And that every Individual Citizen in particular must wish to see himself protected by Laws, which should not distress him in his Circumstances, but, on the Contrary, should defend him from all Attempts of others, that are repugnant to his fundamental Rule.

4. In order therefore to proceed to a speedy Execution of what *We*

expect from such a general Wish, *We,* fixing the Foundation upon the above first-mentioned Rule, ought to begin with an Inquiry into the natural Situation of this Empire.

8. The Possessions of the Russian Empire extend upon the terrestrial Globe to 32 Degrees of Latitude, and to 165 of Longitude.

9. The Sovereign is absolute; for there is no other Authority but that which centers in his single Person, that can act with a Vigour proportionate to the Extent of such a vast Dominion.

10. The Extent of the Dominion requires an absolute Power to be vested in that Person who rules over it. It is expedient so to be, that the quick Dispatch of Affairs, sent from distant Parts, might make ample Amends for the Delay occasioned by the great Distance of the Places.

11. Every other Form of Government whatsoever would not only have been prejudicial to Russia, but would even have proved its entire Ruin.

12. Another Reason is: That it is better to be subject to the Laws under one Master, than to be subservient to many.

15. The Intention and End of Monarchy, is the Glory of the Citizens, of the State, and of the Sovereign.

16. But, from this Glory, a Sense of Liberty arises in a People governed by a Monarch; which may produce in these States as much Energy in transacting the most important Affairs, and may contribute as much to the Happiness of the Subjects, as even Liberty itself.

18. The intermediate Powers, subordinate to, and depending upon the supreme Power, form the essential Part of monarchical Government.

19. *I* have said, that the intermediate Powers, subordinate and depending, proceed from the supreme Power; as in the very Nature of the Thing the Sovereign is the Source of all imperial and civil Power.

23. This Care, and strict Execution of the Laws, can be nowhere so properly fixed as in certain Courts of Judicature, which announce to the People the newly-made Laws, and revive those, which are forgotten, or obsolete.

24. And it is the Duty of these Courts of Judicature to examine carefully those Laws which they receive from the Sovereign, and to remonstrate, if they find any Thing in them repugnant to the fundamental Constitution of the State, &c. which has been already remarked above in the third Chapter, and twenty-first Article.

25. But if they find nothing in them of that Nature, they enter them in the Code of Laws already established in the State, and publish them to the whole Body of the People.

26. In Russia the Senate is the political Body, to which the Care and due Execution of the laws is confided.

29. These Instructions will prevent the People from transgressing the Injunctions of the Sovereign with impunity; but, at the same Time, will protect them from the Insults, and ungovernable Passions of others.

30. For, on the one Hand, they justify the Penalties prepared for those who transgress the Laws; and, on the other, they confirm the Justice of that Refusal to enter Laws repugnant to the good Order of the State, amongst

those which are already approved of, or to act by those Laws in the Administration of Justice, and the general Business of the whole Body of the People.

32. It is the greatest Happiness for a Man to be so circumstanced, that, if his Passions should prompt him to be mischievous, he should still think it more for his Interest not to give Way to them.

33. The Laws ought to be so framed, as to secure the Safety of every Citizen as much as possible.

34. The Equality of the Citizens consists in this; that they should all be subject to the same Laws.

39. The political Liberty of a Citizen is the Peace of Mind arising from the Consciousness, that every individual enjoys his peculiar Safety; and in order that the People might attain this Liberty, the Laws ought to be so framed, that no one Citizen should stand in Fear of another; but that all of them should stand in Fear of the same Laws.

67. Civil Liberty flourishes, when the Laws deduce every Punishment from the peculiar Nature of every Crime. The Application of Punishment ought not to proceed from the arbitrary Will, or mere Caprice of the Legislator, but from the Nature of the Crime; and it is not the Man, who ought to do Violence to a Man, but the proper Action of the Man himself.

119. The Laws, which condemn a Man upon the Deposition of one Evidence only, are destructive to Liberty. There was a Law made in the Time of the Heirs of Constantine I, by which the single Evidence of one Man in a high Station is taken for sufficient Proof of the Guilt of the Party accused; and for this Reason, the Evidence of others, in relation to the very same Affair, are not allowed to be heard. By the Will of this Legislator, the Decision was dispatched in a very quick and very strange Manner. They decided the Affair according to the Figure the Evidence made, and they judged of his Figure according to the Dignity of his Rank.

210. Proofs from Fact demonstrate to us, that the frequent Use of capital Punishment never mended the Morals of a People. Therefore, if *I* prove the *Death* of a Citizen to be neither *useful* nor *necessary to Society in general, I* shall confute *those* who *rise up against* Humanity. *I* repeat here, *to Society in general;* because the Death of a Citizen can *only* by useful and necessary in *one* Case; which is, when, though he be *deprived* of Liberty, yet he has *such Power* by his *Connections,* as may *enable* him to raise Disturbances dangerous to the publick Peace. This Case can happen only, when a People either loses, or recovers their Liberty; or in a Time of Anarchy, when the *Disorders* themselves hold the *Place* of Laws. But in a Reign of Peace and Tranquillity, under a Government established with the united Wishes of a whole People; in a State well fortified agains/ external Enemies, and protected within by strong Supports; that is, by its own internal Strength and virtuous Sentiments rooted in the Minds of the Citizens; and where the whole Power is lodged in the Hands of a Monarch; in such a State, there can be *no* Necessity for *taking away the Life of* a Citizen. The twenty Years Reign of the Empress *ELIZABETH PETROVNA* gives the Fathers of the People a more illustrious Example for Imitation than a Reign of the most shining Conquests.

214. He who disturbs the publick Peace, who refuses to submit to the Laws, who breaks through those Ties, by which People are united in Society, and reciprocally defend each other, ought to be excluded from the Community; that is, to become *politically dead.*

222. The most certain Curb upon Crimes, is not the *Severity* of the Punishment, but the absolute Conviction in the People, that Delinquents will be *inevitably* punished.

265. Russia is not only *greatly* deficient in the *number* of her Inhabitants; but at the same Time, extends her Dominion over *Immense* Tracts of Land; which are neither peopled nor improved. And therefore, in a Country so circumstanced, *too much* Encouragement can never be given to the *Propagation* of the human Species.

266. The Peasants generally have twelve, fifteen, and even twenty Children by one Marriage; but it rarely happens, that one *Fourth* of these ever attains to the *Age* of Maturity. There must therefore be some Fault, either in their Nourriture, in their Way of Living, or Method of Education, which occasions this *prodigious* Loss, and disappoints the *Hopes* of the Empire. How flourishing would the State of this Empire be, if we could but ward off, or *prevent* this fatal Evil by proper Regulations!

272. The more happily a People live under a Government, the more easily the Number of the Inhabitants increases.

274. Wherever the Inhabitants can enjoy the Conveniences of Life, there Population will certainly increase.

275. *But a Country, which is so overwhelmed with Taxes, that the People, with all their Care and Industry, can with the utmost Difficulty find Means for procuring a bare Subsistance, will, in length of Time, be deserted by its Inhabitants.*

295. Agriculture can never flourish there, where no Persons have any Property of their own.

296. This is founded upon a very simple Rule: *Every Man will take more Care of his own Property, than of that which belongs to another; and will not exert his utmost Endeavours upon that, which he has Reason to fear another may deprive him of.*

314. Machines, which serve to shorten Labour in the mechanick Arts, are not always useful. If a Piece of Work, wrought with the Hands, can be afforded at a Price, equally advantageous to the Merchant and the Manufacturer; in this Case, Machines which shorten Labour, that is, which diminish the Number of Workmen, will be greatly prejudicial to a populous Country.

350. It is impossible to give a general Education to a very numerous People, and to bring up all the Children in Houses regulated for that Purpose; and, for that Reason, it will be proper to establish some *general Rules,* which may serve *by Way of Advice* to all Parents.

358. The Husbandmen, who cultivate the Lands to produce Food for People in every Rank of Life, live in Country Towns and Villages. *This is their Lot.*

359. The Burghers, who employ their Times in mechanick Trades, Commerce, Arts, and Sciences, *inhabit the Cities*

360. *Nobility* is an Appellation of *Honour,* which distinguishes all those who are adorned with it from every other Person of *inferior Rank.*

494. In such a State as *Ours,* which extends its Sovereignty over so many different Nations, to forbid, or not to allow them to profess *different Modes* of Religion, would greatly indanger the Peace and Security of its Citizens.

525. *To render this difficult Affair more easy; these Instructions are to be read over once, at the Beginning of every Month, in the Commission for composing the new Code of Laws, and in all the subordinate Committees, which depend upon it; particularly the respective Chapters and Articles intrusted to their Care, till the Conclusion of the Commission.*

526. *But as no perfect Work was ever yet composed by Man; therefore, if the Commissioners should discover, as they proceed, that any Rule for some particular Regulations has been omitted, they have Leave, in such a Case, to report it to Us, and to ask for a Supplement.*

Catherine and the French Revolution

The fears and apprehensions which led Catherine to deal so harshly with Novikov and Radishchev were aroused partly by Pugachev's revolt and more particularly by the French Revolution. The effects which the revolution had on her were brilliantly summarized—mostly through skillful use of quotations from Catherine's letters—in Kasimerz Waliszewski, *The Romance of an Empress: Catherine II of Russia.* New York: D. Appleton and Co., 1894. Pp. 246–261. Samples from this are printed below.

In 1769 the cause of liberty had no more enthusiastic defender in Europe than the Empress of Russia.

• • •

In 1781 Catherine comes forward on behalf of Necker. His famous *Compte rendu,* which is practically an act of accusation against the administration of royal finances, that is to say against royalty itself, enchants and delights her. She does not doubt that heaven has destined the able Genevese for the salvation of France.

Certainly she has not much love, just then, either for France or for the turn that things are taking there; but in her hostile feelings the court holds as large, if not larger, a place than the people, and the old *regime* foundering under the rising flood of social claims has no part in her favor. . . .

Hearing . . . [of the] "Assembly of Notables," she sees in it only an imitation of her own legislative commissions. She invites Lafayette to visit her at Kief. To open her eyes on what is being prepared by the Lafayettes, it needs the thunderclap of the taking of the Bastille. Then she begins to understand what is in the air, and the *Gazette de St-Petersbourg.* which had been silent on the Assembly . . . and the Tennis Court Oath, breaks out in indignant protestations: "Our hand shakes with horror," etc. The rest of the article may be imagined. . . .

"One never knows if you are living in the midst of the murders, carnage, and uproar of the den of thieves who have seized upon the government of France, and who will soon turn it into Gaul as it was in the time of Caesar. But put them down! When will this Caesar come? Oh, come he will, you need not doubt." [January 13, 1791—letter to Grimm]

. . .

When news of the death of Louis XVI reaches her, Catherine . . . is cut to the heart; she betakes herself to bed, in a sort of fever, and she cries,
"The very name of France should be exterminated! Equality is a monster. It would fain be king!" [February 1, 1793—letter to Grimm]
This time the holocaust is complete. Voltaire is sacrificed with the rest. And in the words and writings of the Empress there are almost savage calls to vengeance, the most extravagant projects of repression. . . .

From this moment Catherine's ideas underwent a rapid change, and it is curious to follow, in her correspondence and her confidential conversation, the progress of this evolution. In June 1790 Grimm, who has not yet had time to perceive the change which is coming over the Empress's mind, asks for her portrait on behalf of Bailly, offering in exchange that of the revolutionary hero of the day. Catherine replies—
"Listen; I cannot accede to your request, and it is as little suitable for the mayor who has dismonarchised France to have the portrait of the most aristocratic Empress in Europe, as it would be for her to send it to the dismonarchising mayor; it would be to place both the dismonarchising mayor and the *aristocrasissime* Empress in contradiction with themselves and their functions, past, present, and future."
And two days after—
"I repeat that you are not to give to the dismonarchising mayor the portrait of the greatest aristocrat in Europe; I would have nothing to do with Jean Marcel, who will be strung up *a la lanterne* some day soon."
Here is a complete throwing overboard of republicanism. It is not so with regard to philosophy, to which the Empress still clings. She endeavors to find out how far it is responsible for the present events—

June 25, 1790.
To GRIMM.
"The National Assembly should burn all the best French authors, and all that has carried their language over Europe, for all that declares against the abominable mess that they have made. . . . As for the people and its opinion, that is of no great consequence!"

Where to Find More Information

ALLEN, *Ukraine*, ch. 4.

ANTHONY, K. *Catherine the Great*. Garden City: Garden City Publishing, 1925.

BAIN, R. N. "Peter the Great and His Pupils," *Cambridge Modern History*. Vol. 5, ch. 17.

————. "Russia under Anne and Elizabeth," *CMH*, vol. 6, ch. 10.

BLACK, *Rewriting*, ch. 9.

CHARQUES, *Short History*, chs. 7–9.

CLARKSON, *History*, chs. 9–14.

CURTISS, *Church and State*, pp. 15–32.

FLORINSKY, *Russia*, vol. 1, chs. 10–23.

GOGOL, N. *Taras Bulba*. Everyman's Library.

GRAY, I. *Peter the Great*. Philadelphia: Lippincott, 1960.

GRUNWALD, C. DE *Peter the Great*. N.Y.: Macmillan, 1956.

HARCAVE, *Readings*, vol. 1, sections 16–23.

HRUSHEVSKY, *Ukraine*, chs. 14 & 16.

HUNTINGTON, W. C. "Michael Lomonosov and Benjamin Franklin," *The Russian Review*. Vol. 18, no. 4 (October, 1959), pp. 294–306.

KLYUCHEVSKY, V. *Peter the Great*. Vintage Russian Library.

LASERSON, M. M. *The American Impact on Russia, 1784–1917*. N.Y.: Macmillan, 1950. Chs. 1–4.

LOBANOV-ROSTOVSKY, *Russia and Asia*, chs. 3 & 4.

————. *Russia and Europe*. Durham: Duke Univ. Press, 1947. Chs. 1 & 2.

LORD, R. H. *Second Partition of Poland*. Cambridge: Harvard Univ. Press, 1915. Intro.

LYASHCHENKO, *National Economy*, pp. 248–304.

MAROGER, D. (Ed.) *The Memoirs of Catherine the Great*. N.Y.: Macmillan, 1955.

MARTIN, *Picture History*, pp. 64–107.

MAVOR, J. *Economic History of Russia*. 2 vols. N.Y.: Dutton, 1925. Vol. 1, chs. 2 & 3.

MAZOUR, *Russia*, chs. 7–13.

MILIUKOV, *Outlines*, vol. 1, chs. 3–6; vol. 3, chs. 1 & 2.

O'BRIEN, C. B. *Russia Under Two Tsars, 1682–1689*. Berkeley: Univ. of Calif. Press, 1952.

PARES, *History*, chs. 9–15.

PUTNAM, P. *Seven Britons in Imperial Russia*. Princeton: Princeton Univ. Press, 1952.

RAMBAUD, *Russia*, vol. 1, chs. 19–21; vol. 2, chs. 1–11.

SOLOVEYTCHIK, G. *Potemkin*. N.Y.: Norton, 1947.

TOLSTOY, A. *Peter I*.

WALSH, *Russia*, chs. 6–9.

WREN, *Course*, chs. 9–15.

Part V

The Reigns of Paul, Alexander I, and Nicholas I

~~~~~~

Life and Manners in the Late Eighteenth Century

> The distinguished English observer and student of Russia, William Tooke, made a detailed, firsthand study of the land and peoples, the government, and Russian society in general in the latter part of the eighteenth century. His Russian hosts honored Tooke and recognized the value of his studies by electing him to membership in The Free Economical Society of St. Petersburg and the Imperial Academy of Sciences. The published report of his studies fills three sizable volumes and is a valuable source of information about many aspects of life in Russia under Catherine and Paul. The selections below describe the appearance of the people and many of the norms and values of the era. The source is: W. Tooke, *View of the Russian Empire During the Reign of Catherine the Second, and to the Close of the Present Century*. Three volumes. London, 1799. Vol. 1, pp. 332–334, 341–352, 355–368, 371–376, 379–381; vol. 2, pp. 128–133, 252–256.

The People

The Russians are a moderate-sized, vigorous, and durable race of men. The growth and longevity of this people are very different in different districts; but in general rather large than small, and they are commonly well-built. It is very rare to see a person naturally deformed; which doubtless is chiefly owing to their loose garments and the great variety of bodily exercises. All the sports and pastimes of the youth have a tendency to expand the body and give flexibility to the muscles.

Easy as it is occasionally by comparison to discriminate the Russian by his outward make from other Europeans, it will, however, be found very difficult to point out the principal lineaments of the national physiognomy, as speaking features are in general extremely rare. The following may be deemed common and characteristical: A small mouth, thin lips, white teeth, little eyes, a low forehead; the nose has a great variety of forms; it is most frequently seen to be small and turned upwards. The beard is almost always very bushy; the colour of the hair varies through all the shades from dark brown to red, but it is seldom quite black. The expression of the countenance is gravity and good-nature or sagacity.—Hearing and sight are usually very acute; but the other senses more or less obtuse by manner of living and climate. The gait and gestures of the body have a peculiar and often impassioned vivacity, partaking, even with the mere rustics, of a certain complaisance and an engaging manner.

The same features, on the whole, are conspicuous in the female sex, but in general improved, and here and there actually dignified. A delicate skin and a ruddy complexion are in the vulgar idea the first requisites of beauty; in fact fine rosy cheeks are perceived more commonly among the Russian women than in other countries, but no where is paint so essential an article of the toilet as here, even among the lowest classes of the people. As the growth of the Russian ladies is not confined by any bandages, stays, or other compresses, the proportions of the parts usually far exceed the line which the general taste of Europe has prescribed for the contour of a fine shape.—The early maturity of girls, at which they generally arrive in the twelfth or thirteenth year, is only to be accounted for, in so cold a climate, by the frequent use of hot baths, which, while it accelerates this expansion, also brings on an early decay of beauty and solidity of bodily frame. Married women seldom retain the fresh complexion and the peculiar charms of youth beyond the first lying-in. By their baths, their paint, and the great submission in which they live with their husbands, the moderate share of beauty with which nature has endowed these daughters of the northern earth is generally faded at an age when the husband is just entering his prime.

The bodily frame of the Russians is excellent. Their happy organization, their cheerful and blithe temper, that hardness which they oppose to every inconveniency, the natural simplicity of their manner of living, and their rude, but dry and wholesome climate, procure to the great mass of the people a degree of physical complacency of which few other nations can boast.—The Russians are endowed with a vitality, of which an instance has scarcely ever yet been found in any other country, as we have seen in the foregoing section. If the Englishman or the Spaniard excels the Russian in bodily strength, the latter is superior to them by far in the endurance, or in the patient suffering of severer hardships. Hunger and thirst, want of accommodation and repose the Russian can bear longer than any other nation.—In all the lower classes, the soldiery excepted, a healthy old age is very common; lively old men of a hundred years are in all parts of Russia no unusual appearance, but probably the number of them would be far greater if the propensity to dram-drinking were not the occasion of so great a mortality in the middle periods of life.

The general disposition of the people is gay, careless even to levity, much addicted to sensuality, quick in comprehending whatever is proposed, and not less prompt in its execution; ingenious in finding out means of abridging their work; in all their occupations ready, alert, and dexterous. Violent in their passions, they easily mistake the golden mean, and

not infrequently rush into the contrary extreme. They are attentive, resolute, bold, and enterprising. To trade and barter they have an irresistible
impulse. They are hospitable and liberal, frequently to their own impover-
ishment. Anxious solicitudes about the future here cause but a few grey
pates. In their intercourse with others, they are friendly, jovial, complai-
sant, very ready to oblige, not envious, slanderous, or censorious, and
much given to secrecy. From their natural and simple way of life, their
wants are few, and those easily satisfied, leaving them leisure for recrea-
tions and repose; and the constant cheerfulness of their temper frees them
from troublesome projects, procures them satisfaction in all situations,
keeps them healthy and strong, and brings them to an undisquieted, contented, brisk, sometimes a very advanced old age.

. . .

Thus far we are enabled to ground the calculation of the number of
the people on actual enumerations; but for the state of the unnumbered
classes, and for the increase of the population, as well by the great acquisitions since the year 1783, as by the very considerable surplus of the births,
and the numerous accessions of foreign colonists, we have only probable
and partly-authenticated data to proceed upon, as the result of the fifth
revision, in 1796, if it be published, is not yet come to hand. In the meantime, the following calculations, made with the greatest nicety of examination, may well be admitted to supply that defect.
By the revision of 1783, there were in the said 41 governments,
  computing the female sex as equal to the male, of registered
  persons 25,677,000
The amount of the Kozaks of the Don and the Euxine, according
  to the most authentic private accounts, at least   220,000
For the unnumbered tribes and classes at the time of the fourth
  revision, we cannot, without the highest improbability, allow
  less than 1.500,000
Consequently, the Russian Empire, in the year 1783, might have
  inhabitants amounting all together to 27,397,000
According to the results deduced from experiments and observations on the fruitfulness and mortality in Russia, this mass must
  of itself have increased annually more than half a million. If,
  in order to keep as far as possible from all exaggeration, we de-
  duct the half of this surplus of births, to allow for the diminution
  it may have suffered by an extraordinary mortality, as by war;
  there remains for every year an increase of 25,000 new citizens,
  which, exclusively of all ascending proportion, in 12 years makes
  a sum total of   3,000,000
The new acquisitions since the year 1783, or the present nine vice-
  royalties of Taurida, Minsk, Bratzlau, Vosnesensk, Podolia,
  Volhynia, Courland, Vilna, and Slonim, contain, according to a
  legitimated statement already mentioned   5,755,000
Consequently, we may admit, by the most moderate estimate, the
  population of the Russian Empire at present to be 36,152,000
  or in a round sum thirty-six millions of persons.

Of this prodigious mass the greater part by far belongs to European Russia. The five governments of Perm, Ufa, Kolhyvan, Tobolsk, and Irkutsk, comprehended under the general name of Siberia, contain all together, according to the revision-lists, only 2,215,000, or, with the unnumbered classes and tribes, perhaps above three millions and a half of inhabitants. The population of the European part is therefore about fourteen times greater; and the Russian Empire, which in regard to its superficial contents mostly belongs to Asia, must in regard to its population be reckoned as belonging to Europe.

On the scale of the population of the European states, Russia holds the second place, having in this respect only the Ottoman Empire above it, which is usually admitted to have 49 millions of inhabitants, whereof 8 millions are stated to be in Europe, 36 in Asia, and 5 in Africa. Excluding the parts of both these countries which lie out of Europe from this comparison, it will follow that Russia has the largest population of all the states of Europe.—The countries which come nearest to the Russian Empire in this regard, are the Germanic States, which may be admitted at 26 millions; France, to which we may still notwithstanding the havoc brought on by various means since the Revolution, allow 25 millions; and the states of Austria, which may be taken at about an equal number. Of the neighbouring states whose relative interests are of importance to Russia, Prussia and Sweden are the most remarkable. The former, with its lately acquired possessions in Poland and the circle of Franconia, has about the fourth; the latter the eleventh part of the population of the Russian Empire.

. . .

Living Conditions

The employments of the female sex, both in town and country, vary but little from those in the neighbouring countries. They see to the cleanliness of the house, spin, weave linen and coarse cloth on frames, in quality but little inferior to what is brought from Germany; they bleach, full, and colour, knot the ends of the threads for a span long, for table-cloths, neckcloths, &c. make felt, bake bread every day &c. In general they are kept closer to work, and fare harder than is customary among their European neighbours.

The country market-towns and hamlets are commonly open; are mostly built in irregular streets, with little kitchen-gardens and large yards to the houses. They are situated on the banks of the rivers, as the digging of wells is not in practice: as in most parts pebbles are not to be had in any considerable quantity, the roads and streets are frequently made of timbers, or bauks laid close together having the upper-part made flat with the hatchet. They contain many, not large, but good-looking churches, mostly of brick and plaister. The monasteries in and near the towns, from their strong walls, massy gates, and numerous church-towers, have the appearance of castles. The fortresses dispersed about the country, have seldom earth-ramparts, mostly batteries of bauks laid one on the other, in the same manner as they build their houses; and about these a low palisade. The canons stand on the gates, and upon the angles of the ramparts or batteries on wooden carriages. Their design is to keep the tributary tribes in awe, and the neighbouring nomades from the borders. Ostrogs, or houses surrounded with a palisade of upright pointed bauks, are either in towns, where they serve as prisons for criminals, or stand solitary in various parts of the country, for the same purpose as the fortresses.

Villages of very various dimensions, and parishes are situated on the margin of rivers, brooks, lakes, and sometimes on mere morasses and springs. The parishes, or church-villages, are sometimes very extensive; and contain, it may be 500 or even 1000 and more farms, from 3 to 7 churches, many of brick, markets, and trafficking places. Large villages are frequently called slobodes; but many slobodes are less than church-villages: the houses are ranged in straight streets, and the streets mostly laid with timbers.

The proper Russian architecture is alike in towns and villages. A messuage consists of a dwelling-house, a few little store-rooms, stables, and a stew, or hot-bath, by which the yard is inclosed. All these structures are built of bauks, unhewn, placed on one another, and notched into each other at the four corners; sometimes, though but rarely, on a brick foundation; these houses are covered with boards, and when the owner can afford it, with oak shingles. The meanest dwelling-houses consist solely of one little room, which therefore has the door to the street. In it is an oven, taking up almost one fourth part of the whole space; adjoining to it, of equal height with the oven, is a broad shelf of board. The top of the oven and this shelf are the sleeping places of the family. The light is admitted into these houses through two or three holes in the walls furnished with shutters, or through a little window of muscovy-glass, or only of bladder, oiled linen or paper. The smoke finds its way out as well as it can through these apertures in the wall. These rooms, as may well be supposed, are as black as a chimney; and, as all the household functions are performed in them, such as baking, cooking, washing, &c. it is hardly possible to keep them clean. They are called, with the utmost propriety of speech, black-rooms. Under the floor of the room is a cellar.

A complete town or country-house, for the sake of having a cellar, stands raised a fathom above the ground, and has a black-room and a white-room, and between the two, a small passage. The black-room has frequently a chimney to the oven, and a window of glass or marienglas; but the white-room has the oven of tiles, or bricks covered with plaster. The entrance, by a covered flight of wooden steps to the aforementioned passage, is from the back-yard, not from the street.

The magazines or store-rooms are small detached huts, for provisions, corn, in short all the necessary stores. The stables are mere hovels or sheds, open to the yard, or at most fronted with wattles, paid with mortar; in the latter case they are called pokleti. The bathroom resembles a detached black-room. It stands alone; has an oven like the other, smoke-holes, a water-tub, brushes, and benches raised one above another in the form of a scaffold. The corn-kilns are without the towns and villages. Places thus built must be very liable to raging fires; and, when once they break out, they rarely leave anything unconsumed.

The household-furniture, both in town and country, even among people of opulence, is very simple. In the room, which, with very few exceptions, is, at the same time, the kitchen, are a table, benches, the shelf, which serves for the dormitory, and in the corner one or more holy figures. The rich have a great many of them, some with rims of beaten silver. Before these, lamps or wax-candles are kept constantly burning, or at least on all the festivals, which amounts to nearly the same thing; so that many of these summer-rooms have the appearance of little chapels. Culinary utensils, and those for the use of the table, are as few as can well be conceived. As vehicles they make use of quite small open one-horse carts, or somewhat larger, and half covered over like a child's cradle, also with one horse, without shafts, so that a collateral horse can at any time be put to; both kinds of such a simple mechanism, that almost any boor can make a new one or at least repair the defects of the old one even upon the road. They are extremely light and commodious. ―――― Splinters, like laths, of fir or very dry birchwood are much more commonly used for giving light in the room, after dark, than tallow-candles.

As the country towns, in general, progressively endeavour to imitate the Residence, one perceives from time to time loftier houses of wood or brick spring up, built in a superior style, with fashionable furniture within, gardens laid out in a regular method, &c.

The inferior houses are much pestered with domestic vermin; besides the common house-rat and mouse, they swarm with water-rats, bats, large beetles very frequent, crickets, bugs, fleas in abundance; various kinds of very troublesome flies, gnats, moths, bullmoths, wood-lice; in southern low places frogs, toads, and tadpoles; in Siberia little beetles; about the Tsheremtshan, lapland beetles.

The preparation of their victuals is so simple, that foreigners do not easily bring themselves to relish it, but adhere to the customary way of dressing their food in their own countries. Fresh meats with watery sauce, or baked pastries of common crust, with minced-meat, or whole fish, fish with water and salt, without other sauce, cabbage and roots chopped together, cabbage-soup, which is never omitted, meagre fish and flesh soups, cool-drinks, quas, with eggs, minced-meat, and leeks, pancakes, soup of ground hemp and linseed, millet-soup and grits, turned milk with meal and sour milk, &c. almost all seasoned with onions, leeks, garlic, and sometimes pimento, are their ordinary dishes. Where Tartars dwell, they use likewise a few wild roots, especially dog-tooth, lily-roots, and others. For the evening repast are served up nuts, orchard-fruits, and the several wild fruits produced by the country round; blackberries, strawberries, sloes, &c. At an entertainment of their friends and acquaintance they provide a surprising variety of these kinds of dishes. The lower sort feed very poorly at all times, but particularly in the fasts. In large towns, the table in good houses is becoming more luxurious and fashionable from day to day.

The most common domestic drink is quas, a liquor prepared from pollard, meal, and bread, or from meal and malt, by an acid fermentation. It is cooling and well-tasted. Corn-spirits, and rectified corn-spirits, supply the place of wine. In good houses, fruit-wines, raspberry-wine, cherry-wine, bilberrywine, &c. from the juices of those fruits, mead and brandy made by fermentation, which are pleasant enough to the palate. Brown beer and metheglin are more in use than braga or white cloudy beer brewed from malted millet or wheat, with hops, and busa or white unhopped wheat-beer. Tea is in very general use. The true russian tea is a concoction of honey, water, and spanish pepper, and drank warm. It tastes well and cheers the stomach. Many even of the common people drink chinese tea, sweetened with honey or sugar. Persons of distinction keep their tables supplied with meats and drinks entirely in the foreign taste, hire french cooks, &c. as in other countries. Tobacco is but little used.

In the article of dress they adhere as faithfully, in the country towns and villages, to the manners of their fathers, as they do in food and lodging. The noblesse, all the officers in the civil department; and, besides the light troops, the soldiery all over the empire, the merchants of the chief towns and those who trade with them, the mine-owners, and almost all the people of quality throughout the empire, dress after the german fashion; and the ladies, even in the remotest and most retired parts of the country, appear more modishly attired than would easily be imagined. The burghers and mercantile class, however, generally speaking, stick close to the national dress, no less than the peasantry. Of this I shall speak a little more particularly.

The men let their beards grow, which are commonly long and bushy: the hair is cut and combed: their shirt is short, without any sort of collar, and made of white, blue, or red linen. Their trousers are loose, and tied below the knees. The shirt usually hangs over the trousers, and is girt round the waist with a string. Stockings are not so commonly worn by the lower class of people, as leg-wrappers, which they tie about their feet and legs with pack-thread, so as to make them look very thick. Shoes are worn by the better sort, and mat-slippers by the common people; but half-boots are in very general use. Over the shirt they wear a short breast-cloth, or a vest furnished with buttons. The coat is made so big as to allow of one side lapping over the other before, with little buttons, close sleeves, and a collar. The skirt is made with gathers at the hips, and reaches below the calves of the legs, and the garment is girt round with a sash that passes twice round the body. At the sash commonly hangs a long-bladed knife, in a sheath. The covering for the head is either a flat fur-cap, with a narrow brim; or, in other places, a cap which forms a bag of a span in depth, in which they keep their handkerchief on their head. In summer they go with flapped high-crowned dutch hats, ornamented with a narrow ribband of some gaudy colour. The materials of the dress vary according to the rank and circumstances of the wearer; the rich wear fine broad cloth, sometimes decorating the edges with gold cording, and little silver buttons for fastenings; common people clothe themselves in homespun cloth; in the summer in linen, made likewise at home. A well-dressed Russian makes a very good figure. In winter the common people wear sheep-skins, with the woolly side turned inwards; the better sort put on furs of a higher price.

The habits of the clergy, as well in their everyday wear, as when officiating at the altar, are in the oriental style; the latter of different colours, often in brocade, mostly very rich. The monks are always clad in black, and are also distinguishable by their high pasteboard caps, wound about with crape.

The women wear stockings or leg-wrappers, and shoes like the men, sometimes likewise picked-pointed slippers. The lower class frequently go barefoot, or simply in slippers on their naked feet: their shifts are white; but in Dauria the female peasants put on silk-coloured shifts of gauze or cotton; they fasten about the neck with a collar, and are decorated with fancied ornaments of needle-work: the vest is close about the neck without sleeves, and fits tight to the body down to the hips; from the hips it spreads without gathers and reaches down to the shoes; on the facing it is garnished with a thick row of little buttons from the top to the very bottom; it is however girt with a sash, to which the bunch of keys is suspended. The quality of the saraphan is various according to circumstances: of glazed linen, kaitaka, silks, frequently edged with fur, or lined with it throughout. The dress of the lower sort of females in winter is more complete, consisting of coarse cloth, or sheep skin, with sleeves. Another dress is the usual woman's gown, and a contushe without sleeves. The dushagrek is also worn on the saraphan, without a gown. In the winter they wear furs made after the manner used in Poland, with pointed sleeves. As this is usually a present made by the bridegroom, and the best piece of dress, the common people, in order to make a show of it, go, the whole summer through, to church, to make visits, &c. in the pelice. They also wear necklaces of corals, pearls, or golden chains, ear-rings of precious stones, and decorate their fingers and wrists with rings and bracelets.

The head-dress is somewhat different in different districts. The girls in general wear their hair uncovered more than the women; the former plait it in three plaits, with ribbands and beads tied to the point of them. In Tver, Novgorod, &c. they wear a band across the forehead, bedizoned with pearls and beads of various colours, which gives the appearance of a tiara or open coronet. At Voronets and the parts adjacent, both women and girls wear coifs made to fit the head, with cheek-pieces and tresses. About the Oka, at Murom, and the country round, the caps are in the form of an upright crescent. In the governments of Mosco, Yaroslaf, Kaluga, and the circumjacent parts, the coif has a stiff flap before, like a jockey-cap, which is decorated with tresses, pearls, and various-coloured stones. On this they hang in the tartarian fashion, a veil; but which they usually keep thrown back. The veil is generally of silk, set off with gold or silver lace. In their ordinary dress, they tie on the veil over the hair, without any cap. In western Russia caps are in use that are a kind of fillet, with tresses, pearls, and stones. Numbers wear caps having a stiff rim one or two inches broad, like a small skreen or a flapped hat. Persons of consequence, in towns, wind pieces of silk about their heads in such manner to let the hair hang down in ringlets from under it; and these head-dresses have very much the resemblance of a high turban. A complete woman's attire is very dear, but remarkably handsome.

Paint is as necessary an article in the dress of a Russian lady, as linen. The freshest and ruddiest young woman of the place puts on both white and red; and, as this practice is prejudicial to natural beauty, therefore such antiquated dames as would not appear hideous are forced to continue it. Fine white paint is made of pulverized marcasite; more commonly white-lead. The rouge in the shops seems to be compounded of florentine-lake and talc, with powder of marcasite; red tiffany is also very much worn. The village-toasts gather the roots of onosma echioides Linn. or of lithospermum arvense, which, after being dried, they moisten with their tongue, and then rub their cheeks with it; or they extract the colour with boiling water and alum from the rind of these roots. Some rub their cheeks with river-spunge, till the skin is sufficiently thinned or inflamed for being transparent to the blood. From the toilet, however, we will now retire with awe, and presume no farther to pry into its mysteries.

They have usually two meals in the day; in the forenoon about nine o'clock and in the afternoon at three. The family at these times eat all together; and, when it is numerous, first the males and afterwards those of the other sex. They allow themselves but a short time at table, and are easy and cheerful. Even among the inferior people the table-linen, platters and vessels are kept in great cleanliness. If strangers sit down with them there are very copious potations. Intoxication is not disgraceful, and even among people of good condition, if a lady be overtaken in liquor, it is no subject of reproach. They are never quarrelsome or scurrilous in their cups, but friendly, jovial, courteous, speak in praise of the absent, and boast of their friendship, and those that are not able to stand, find ready assistance from those that can. On journies, merchants and others take their food with remarkably few formalities. In towns and great village-stations, women sit in the street, near public-houses, with tables having roast and boiled meat, fish, piroggees, cabbage-soup, cucumbers, bread, and quas, consequently a superb and every where a cheap repast, which is taken standing, and always accompanied with a glass or two of brandy.

To hot and cold bathing they are so habituated from their earliest infancy that the practice is indispensable. They usually go into the hot-bath once a week, besides other frequent occasions, such as, after a slight indisposition, hard work, on returning from a journey, and the like. They use the bath very hot, heating the room with large stones made glowing red, and raising a vapour by repeatedly throwing water upon them; the room all the while being so tight that no particles of heat or vapour can transpire. The bather lies extended naked upon a mat thrown on one of the shelves of the scaffold already described, which the higher he ascends the greater the heat he feels. When he has thus lain perspiring for some time, the waiter of the bath, generally a female, comes and washes his body all over with hot water, scourges and rubs him with bunches of leafy birch, wipes him with cloths, and then leaves him to lie and sweat as long as he chooses. Numbers of them run from the hot bath into the cold water flowing by, and in winter roll themselves in the snow, without deriving any bad consequences from it.

The intercourse between the sexes is more free than elsewhere, particularly in the country, on account of the contracted space of their habitations and sleeping room, their baths, the simplicity of their conversation, and their artless songs. The behaviour of husbands toward their wives is, in general, comparatively with european manners, rough and austere. The wives must work hard, and are often obliged to be the tame spectators of their husband's intemperance and irregularities without daring to complain; but to this they are so early accustomed that they are seldom heard to vent a murmur even while smarting under very tyrannical treatment. In larger towns, however, and even among people of condition, the lady is in a quite contrary predicament; and they are either very much slandered or many a kind husband sometimes gets a rap of the slipper. It is a maxim with parents of the common class, never to become dependent on their children; and therefore keep the management of the house in their own hands, till they die. Indeed the laws of the land are more favourable to widows and mothers than they are in other countries.

With substantial people the marriage-contract is made with mercantile punctuality; the common sort enter into the nuptial state, for its peculiar purposes, as young as they can; and, as housekeeping is not expensive, and as education is neither attended with cost nor trouble, they live as much at their ease as before. The betrothing is performed with ecclesiastical rites, generally eight days previous to the marriage, and is indissoluble. During this interval, the bride is only visited by the bridegroom, and the girls of her acquaintance, who amuse her with singing. On the last evening the young women bring the bride into the hot-bath, where they plait and tie up her hair, all the while singing ballads descriptive of her future happiness.

The marriage is solemnized in the church, before the altar, whither they proceed, with the figure of some saint carried before them. During the ceremony a crown is put on each of their heads. The priest, with due forms, changes their rings, reads to them an admonition of their reciprocal duties, gives them to drink of a cup in token of the present union of their fortunes, and dismisses them with his blessing.

At their return from church the father of the bride presents the young couple with a loaf of bread and some salt, accompanied with a wish that they may never know the want of either, for which they thank him on their knees. They then sit down to supper, and when the shift that the bride is to put on has been inspected, the new-married pair are put to bed. This shift is produced the next day to the guests, who, upon seeing the tokens of virginity upon it, felicitate the mother of the bride on that fortunate event. All things considered, it need not be mentioned that these tokens never fail to appear. This day passes with far more jollity than the former, as the young woman, being now freed from all restraint, can bear a part in the sports and entertainments of the company.

Dancing is a diversion every where followed. Even the common people, who here are not apt to become stiff with work, dance to admiration. They generally dance to the voice. The universal dance of the country consists in frequent genuflexions of the man, and a gentle step in proper cadence of the woman. It is pantomimic and very engaging. The woman lays her arms on her breast crosswise, beckons to the man with her fingers, shrugs her shoulders, and glides by him hanging down her head, with some sideglances, without giving of hands. In another dance, the man and woman shew a repugnance to each other; they reciprocally pass by with averted and disdainful looks; make faces of derision at one another as their backs are towards them; turn about and shew by their looks and gestures an ambiguous aversion. The dove-dance exhibits an imitation of the coaxing airs of turtle-doves or lovers. Generally one stands still to the other; presently the man dances about with vehement motion, while the woman proceeds in gentle and delicate movements. Polish dances are also much in use, not only in the Ukraine, but in most other parts of the country, likewise during the winter evening-companies are very common. They consist in absurd and ridiculous masquerades by young people. They sometimes, though but rarely, put on disguises, humorously represent grotesque and romantic stories, imitate particular persons and animals, and usually indulge themselves in coarse and licentious buffooneries. After these comedies, or masquerades, which are sometimes omitted, the party amuse themselves with singing, dancing, playing for stakes, and always with eating and drinking.

They are very much attached to gymnastic diversions. In severe winter-nights the ladies make sledge-parties, in which there is always much vehement singing. The swing and round-abouts are diversions of the easter holidays. The former is carried to great perfection; five or six people stand or sit, one behind another on a plank, which is swung to a great height. Instead of a plank, some of these swings have wooden lions, swans, bears, coaches, chairs, sofas, &c. The girls divert themselves in summer in jumping on a board, resting in the middle on a block of wood as a fulcrum; one standing on each end of this board, they alternately bound one another up to a surprising height. The diversion of the ice-hills has been described in a former section of this work. Wrestling and boxing are another diversion, though very awkwardly performed. Ringing the bells, on church and court holidays, is a species of exercise of which they are remarkably fond; but they produce nothing like harmony from them. The sole excellency consists in striking the clappers the oftenest.

Agriculture

Agriculture, therefore, is not so generally the business of the peasantry in Russia as in other countries. However, on the whole it is carried on to so great an extent, as not only to furnish the nations of the empire that eat bread with that article, and the prodigious quantities of corn, at a very moderate price, consumed by the brandy-distilleries; but also can export a great superfluity to foreign countries. Even from the 55th to the 60th deg. of north lat. in Siberia, are large tracts of arable land, mostly fertile, good crops of hay, and spacious forests. More to the north, cultivation is less to be depended on, and the whole system of rural economy is very liable to failures, and attended with great difficulties. Throughout Russia every village has its proper territory, and every estate its allotted inclosures and commons. In the less cultivated plains of Siberia, every man takes as much ground from the open steppes as he can manage. When such a portion of ground is exhausted, the countryman lets it lie fallow for a year or two, goes and turns up another piece, and so proceeds. Frequently these little strips of ground lie scattered at 20, 50, and even 80 versts distance from the village. The size of these fields is measured eastwards, each of which being 60 fathom long and 40 wide; but in some parts, and all over the Ukraine, they are 80 fathom in length and 40 in breadth.

In Russia and Siberia they cultivate winter rye and summer rye, winter-wheat only in Russia as far as the Kama, summer-wheat both in Russia and Siberia; barley, spelt-barley, or bear-barley, plentifully in Russia; oats, in Russia and Siberia; few pease, still fewer vetches and beans; a great deal of buck-wheat; in Siberia tartarian buck-wheat, millet, and the grain called panicum germanicum, only in Russia.

The manure depends much on the quality of the soil, climate, and greater or inferior population. In well peopled regions the fields are dunged, because the husbandman can afford them but little respite; in fertile districts, however, of less numerous habitations, the good arable land endures no dung, requiring only after every 5 or 10 years use, 3, 4, or 5 years rest. Such powerful soil is found in different parts of the governments of Simbirsk and Penza, and about Ufa and Orenburg, as also in the southern steppes of Siberia, in the steppes of the Iset, the Ishim, the Baraba, about Irkutsk and in southern Dauria. The corn, after dunging, shoots up into high straw, and bears no solid ears. The most ungrateful soils are in Finnland, Archangel, and the north of Russia, also the north and north-eastern parts of Siberia, in Kamtshatka, &c. They rarely yield an increase above threefold, and often entirely fail by the intenseness of the frost. The common land brings an increase of from 5 to 8 fold, and the fresh broke pieces in the above-mentioned steppes for some years successively will give an increase of 10 up to 15 fold.

The country people generally make use of the little Russian or Livonian one-horse plough. For winter corn they plough twice, for summer corn only once, and always quite flat. On some lands the corn is first strewn, then ploughed in, and harrowed smooth with an additional horse by the side of the other; by which method one man, with two poor feeble horses, can rid a good bit of ground. In woody districts the boors make new land in the swedish manner, by burning the forests, which if they let alone for three or four years will all be covered over again with young trees and saplings.

The corn is cut with sickles, in which employment the women and children assist. They bind it in little sheaves, set it up on the fields in shocks, and carry it home in winter on sledges. They then dry it in small wooden kilns, with a smouldering fire, which they keep burning in a hole near the kiln, and the smoke whereof rushes into it. The corn thus dried, is spread upon the ice of a river, or a floor wetted with water, where it is threshed with light flails, then stored in little barns; and, what remains over from domestic uses, is conveyed to town, which is sometimes a hundred, nay two hundred, or even four hundred versts distant; where it is sold, not by measure, but by weight; rye and wheat as well as meal, in mat-sacks of 8 pood, and, especially in Siberia, at an inconceivably low price. In Krasnoyarsk, for example, where it is particularly cheap, a pood of rye meal will sell for 2 to 3 kopeeks; or about a penny. Wheat flour 5 kopeeks, and so of the rest. In Irkutsk they are about three times dearer.—In many parts of the country every boor has his own water-mill built by himself, with a horizontal water-wheel. In cold regions the straw is given to the cattle; but in the southern parts, where the cattle remain out all the winter, it is left to rot.

The villagers, with whom winter provender is a requisite, have hay-fields, bordering on the banks of lakes and rivers, in brakes and fens of the forests. In order to get rid of the old withered grass, the dry weeds, twigs, and light stuff, for warming the ground, and for manuring it with wood-ash, they set it on fire, as they are apt to do with the meadow-lands of the steppe in spring; though, on account of the great mischief occasioned by this practice to the forests, whole versts of them being frequently burnt at once, it is strictly prohibited. When the steppes and meadow-lands are thus on fire, the appearance they make, especially at night, is truly tremendous; the fire works its way in all directions, frequently in lines that extend farther than the eye can reach, and fill the horizon in such manner with smoke, that one may look steadfastly at the sun the whole day through. The grass is mowed with very small scythes, and not before the month of July, that it may have time to reach its full growth and scatter its feed.

Besides corn, they grow flax, in large quantities, chiefly on the shores of the Volga; but most of all in the government of Varoslaf, where one sees flax-fields, as elsewhere corn-fields; the next in the produce of flax are the governments of Mosco and Kazan. It is thought that the common flax would not prosper in Siberia; nevertheless some poles, settled about the Irtish and In Dauria upon the Selenga, cultivate valakhian flax with good success. The perennial flax, frequent in the south of Siberia, is entirely unheeded, though it might be propagated to great advantage.

Hemp is indigenous in all the south and middle of Russia and Siberia, and in all these parts is propagated in great abundance, both on account of its material, for linens, sail-cloth, &c. and of the oil expressed from its feed, of which an amazing quantity is consumed for food during the fasts, and, as well as the hemp itself, exported annually to a great amount.

Woad likewise grows wild in southern Russia and Siberia; it is gathered in the Ukraine and employed in staining and dying. It is also cultivated, but only in the government of Penza, and about the Don.

Tobacco is planted almost only in the Ukraine; but there in great abundance.

Hops are propagated by the villagers only in small quantities, in the

governments of Kazan, Nishney-Novgorod, &c. and in Siberia in the province of Irkutsk. They are plentifully supplied with the wild sort, which
thrives almost every where, among the bushes that grow about the banks of
rivers, in brakes and low forests.

But little account is made of orchards except in the chief towns: however they are seen about the towns and villages, on the Volga from the
region round Mosco down the river to Astrakhan, along the Oka, and the
other rivers on the right of the Volga and the inferior parts of the river
Ural, and all over the Ukraine, where orchard fruits are cultivated with
great diligence and success. After all the attempts that have been made, no
fruit-trees will thrive in Siberia. Something of a country wine is made about
the Don, in Little Russia, on the Terek, and on the Volga, near Saratof,
and especially about Astrakhan. Every villager has a little kitchen-garden
adjoining to his cottage, particularly for the growth of cabbages, turnips,
bete, carrots, cucumbers, radishes, onions, and leeks, a few potatoes,
some dill, gourds, and melons, indispensable to him on account of the
numerous fast-days. Water-melons are cultivated in surprising numbers in
the south-eastern parts of Russia, from the Don to the Ural, especially on
the Volga, in open fields got from the steppes, and are eaten raw, or salted
like cucumbers.

The forests, which are scattered sparingly about the southernmost parts
of Russia, in the northern extremities above the 60th degree, are not seen.
They are very common in the middle regions of Russia and in Siberia, and
consist alternately of the fir, the pine, the white fir, the white and black
poplar, the aspin, the ash, the alder, the birch, the beech, the oak, the
linden, the mountain-ash, the elm, the willow, the palm-willow, and several
others: also in the caucasean mountains a great variety of fruit-trees
walnuts, and a kind of red wood; in Siberia and in lofty mountains the
larch, the siberian cedar, and balsam-poplar, every where employing a
great number of hands. Almost every villager is a carpenter, who builds his
own house of balku or trunks of trees, makes wharfs on the navigable
rivers, and whatever else belongs to the carpenter's trade. In the upper
parts of the Oka and its superior rivers, and on the rivers to the left of the
Volga, from the Unsha as far as the Kama, their chief employment is to
strip the linden of its bark; the inner rind whereof, they work up into
baskets for sledges and carts, or make a light covering to their houses of it,
to the sheds where the salt is kept in heaps; little huts for sleeping in upon
the floats and vessels that go down the rivers, &c. All sorts of household
cups, baskets, and the like, are made of it, in common use throughout the
whole empire; and the making of what we call russia-mats, trays, troughs,
ladles, skimmers, spoons, &c. of the linden wood, is a great part of their
business. A no less number gain their livelihood merely by preparing the
birch-tar, not to mention the occupation of so many in stripping all kind
of trees of their bark for the several uses of the tanneries, particularly the
youft-manufactories, and the burning of wood for charcoal, which is sent
to the mines, and the different storehouses belonging to government.

In the breeding of cattle, the countryman is directed by climate and pasturage. In regions where the cattle must be stalled and foddered during the winter, the boor has at most but a scanty herd; where they can stay out in the open steppe all the winter, or the greater part of it; as in the south of Siberia, a man is often master of 300 horses, not fewer sheep, somewhere about half the number of horned cattle, always a few swine, and a great deal of poultry; sometimes geese and ducks.

The russian horses are of a middling size, with large heads, long flabby ears, not very handsome, but spirited, strong, and hardy. The horned cattle are little and brisk. The cows give but little milk, and that is poor and thin. In little Russia the oxen are used for draught. Every where about Archangel there is a fine breed of large cows, brought originally from Holland, and are not found to degenerate in the least. The true russian sheep are distinguishable from the common sort by their short tail, not above the length of three inches. Their wool is coarse, but better than that of the broad-tailed kirghistzian sheep, and would probably improve in some of the dry steppes. There are nowhere any particular sheep-folds; that is, there are no people who make it their sole business to breed and fatten them. It is never the practice to milk the ewes. Hogs, dogs, and cats, are of the ordinary kinds.

The poultry are housed all the winter in the cottage, under the hearth and the sleeping-benches, for the sake of having Easter-eggs. The goose is not in all places the common domestic species; many keep wild geese. They catch the young before they can fly, fatten them, and kill them in autumn. On the approach of spring, they catch others, and thus save themselves the winter's feed. In Siberia at times one sees the white-headed little goose tamed. Besides, and instead of the domestic duck, some cottagers keep the wood-duck, the red duck, the muscovy duck, and several other species. Doves and pigeons nestle about the villages, without owners. Turkey-fowl are very common among the poultry in the southern parts of Russia, and wherever there is a good market for them in the large towns.

Securing the Dynasty

The Empress Catherine, intent upon assuring the continuance of her dynasty, arranged for the eighteen-year-old tsarevich to marry a princess of Hesse-Darmstadt. It was neither a fruitful nor a happy marriage, and when the Grand Duchess Natalie died in childbirth, Catherine promptly set about finding a new wife for Paul. The choice fell on the Princess Sophie of Würtemburg. Prince Henry of Prussia was the intermediary and, later, escorted Paul to the couple's first meeting. Matters moved fast. Sophie was confirmed in the Russian Church, and rebaptized as the Grand Duchess Maria Federovna. She preserved a personal record of these happenings in private notes which she entitled, "Interesting Dates." The source is: N. K. Shilder, *Imperator Pavel Pervyi. Istoriko-biograficheskii ocherk* (*The Emperor Paul I. Historical-biographical sketch*). St. Petersburg, 1901. P. 540.

On 26 March, new style, (1776) which was 15 March, old style, the hereditary prince [Henry] came to Monbeillard.

16/27 March, I am promised.

17/28 March, he left.

3/14 May, the first courier of the King came.

16/27 June, I left my dear Etupe forever.

10/21 July, I saw the Grand Duke for the first time.

12/23 July, my marriage was announced.

I left Reinsberg 1/12 August.

I arrived at Carscosello [Tsarskoe Tselo] 31 August/11 September.

My profession of faith was made 14/25 September.

My promises 15/26 September,

and my wedding 26 September/7 October, 1776.

Paul's Children and Catherine II

The marriage of Paul and Maria Federovna fulfilled Catherine's dynastic intentions. The first two children born of the marriage were sons—Alexander and Constantine—and soon after their births Catherine took them away from their parents in order that she might have full control of them. At the end of 1786, the empress made known her intention of having the two little grandsons accompany her on her famous journey to the "New Russia," *i.e.*, to the newly annexed Ukraine. This led to an interchange of letters between the parents and the grandmother—letters which were rather pathetic on the one side, firm and somewhat callous on the other. The source is: Shilder, *Imperator*, pp. 555–559.

1. The Grand Duke Paul and the Grand Duchess Maria Federovna to the Empress Catherine II.

It is with the most lively distress that we address these lines to Your Imperial Majesty, having just learned that she plans to be accompanied by our sons on the grand tour which she is about to undertake. In the first moments of distress and sorrow, we are too upset by this news and too disturbed to express ourselves orally, so we have taken pen to write you, Madame, our feelings on the subject. The idea of being separated from Your Imperial Majesty for six months is itself painful to us, duty has obliged us, Madame, to respect your silence about this trip and to refrain from expressing our distress; but news of the order you have given to prepare our sons for this journey has put the finishing stroke to our sorrow, for the idea, Madame, of being separated from you and from them, is too much for us. Our experience, which we have spoken of, and our recollection of what we suffered during a similar absence, does not permit us to accept the idea we find in this new case. Read these lines with indulgence and with kindness. Note particularly, Madame, the spirit in which we address you; we appeal to your mother's heart, that it be our judge, and we do not fear refusal.

We venture to expose to you, Madame, the picture of our pain, our fears, our uneasiness about this journey by our children; that you will understand our distress easily, Madame, recall how we felt on the eve of our departure for foreign countries. The incident was such that the recollection of the leave which we then took of Your Imperial Majesty and our children, who were then in their early infancy, produces in us the most vivid emotions, and we do not feel strong enough to bear a repetition. Our fears, Madame, center on the health of our children whose tender age makes doubtful their ability to withstand the fatigues of a long trip, undertaken at the height of winter, and the change of climate; moreover, our boys have not yet had all those sicknesses which ordinarily affect children; we are also worried that the trip, and the distractions which will naturally accompany it, will interfere with the progress of their education. There, Madame, is a sincere and accurate exposure of our innermost feelings; and Your Imperial Majesty is too just, too good, she has a heart too tender not to consider the prayers of a father and a mother who, next to the attachment and respect they have for you, know no emotions stronger than the tenderness they have for their children.

2. The Empress Catherine's Reply.

My very dear children. A mother who sees her children sorrowful can only advise them to moderate their grief, not to nourish somber and distressing thoughts, not to give way to sadness induced by an active imagination, but to seek the help of reason which can soften such grief and calm fears. Your children are yours, they are mine, they are the state's. From their earliest babyhood, it has been my duty and my pleasure to take the tenderest care of them. You have more than once told me by word of mouth and by writing that you regard the care which I have given them as a genuine good fortune for your children which has given them the greatest happiness. I love them tenderly. Here is how I reasoned: separated from you, it will be a consolation to me to have them near me. Of [your] five [children], three will stay with you; would you have me alone, in my old age, deprived for six months of the pleasure of having some of my family with me? In regard to their health, I am firmly persuaded that the tour will strengthen them in body and soul; between January and April the climate of Kiev differs from here only in having several weeks more of spring. The progress of their education will not suffer at all because their tutors will accompany them. For the rest, I am deeply aware of the tender sentiments you bear me, and I embrace you both with all my heart.

3. Paul and Maria Federovna to the Empress Catherine II.

We have read the letter which Your Imperial Majesty sent us with gratitude and the deepest appreciation. If the thought of separation causes us feelings of pain, it is within her [Majesty's] power to soothe them and to replace them by others, pleasant and comforting; we are yours, Madame, even more than our children, and this is a cherished happiness for us. Take us with you, Madame, and we will be near you and our sons. As to our daughters, they no longer need physical care, and the presence of their father and mother is no longer necessary to them; we shall be able to carry on with equanimity if we are not separated either from you or from our sons. This is the outpouring of our hearts which are entirely yours, these are the sentiments of those who are, my very dear mother, your children.

4. The Grand Duchess Maria Federovna to Prince Potemkin.

You have so often assured me, Prince, of your attachment [to me] and of your desire to fulfil my wishes that I confidently address this letter to you. The matter concerns me so much that I believe I can not do better than to speak to you myself. I am concerned about my children; in a word, the greatest service you could render us would be to save us the pain of finding ourselves separated from them for six months while they make the trip with Her Majesty. My husband and I addressed ourselves jointly to her as soon as we knew that our sons were to make this trip; we represented to her the danger and the difficulty which this would cause them, and the inexpressible grief which the separation would cause us. It was painfully clear from the response that Her Imperial Majesty condescended to return to us that she intended, nevertheless, to persist in her decision. Seeing this, we asked her, in a second letter, for the boon of making the trip ourselves in order that we should be separated neither from her nor from our sons.

Her Majesty contented herself with a word of response, telling us in general the difficulties which this plan would cause. As far as we are concerned, these would be inconsequential because we would need no retinue, and are ready to stay at Kiev, or in any other city which the Empress selects, while Her Majesty travels in the Crimea, where my sons are not bound to be so that during this time they would be alone, far away from both their grandmother and their parents. There matters have rested. We continue to hope that Her Majesty will heed our prayers, and that the indispositions which have beset our sons, one after the other, will finally change her decisions in this respect. But different circumstances, about which it is useless to trouble you, show us that Her Majesty persists [in her plans], and my maternal heart no longer dares hope. Only you, Prince, can come to our help by supporting our case and our prayers before the Empress. I have told you all this in detail so that you can understand what has happened and can judge what you can do in this matter. We have charged Saltykov, at different times, to say to Her Majesty that, knowing her goodwill, we can only count on that and persist in the righteous hope that she will deign to heed our prayers either to leave our sons here, or to allow us to accompany her. I beg you, Prince, to urge these same requests before Her Majesty, and I can only tell you that success—even the steps you take to achieve this—will give you an eternal right to our gratitude. Maternal feelings lead me to address these lines to you, pledging the obligations we will be under to you for success in something so dear to our hearts and which touches us so closely. It is with pleasure that I repeat to you on this occasion the assurances of my esteem and affection.

Two European Monarchs Describe Paul

Paul and Maria Federovna, traveling incognito under the titles, which obviously fooled no one, of the Count and Countess of the North, spent fourteen months in Western Europe during 1781/1782. The impressions which the imperial couple made on Joseph II of Austria and Leopold of Tuscany are in marked contrast to the descriptions presented in most Russian sources.

The first selection below consists of excerpts from a long letter written by Joseph II to Leopold, his brother, advising the latter on how to treat the visiting Russians. The second selection is made up of excerpts from a letter from Leopold to Joseph, reporting on the visit to Tuscany. Both selections are translations from Shilder, *Imperator*, pp. 546–553, *passim.*

I

The Grand Duke and the Grand Duchess possess uncommon abilities and a knowledge sufficiently broad so that they have a strong desire to see and to learn . . . nothing will please them more than being allowed to see everything as it really is [literally, without paint and without preparation], without hiding defects which, in any event, could not escape their keenness. . . .

Your conversations [with them] ought to touch on everything which seems good to you; the subject of the education of your children, which I know is very close to your heart, will certainly be interesting to them in all its details because they are very sensible and careful parents.

Because their life is very regular, and because the Grand Duke's health is not as strong as one might wish, late nights and undue fatigue should be carefully avoided. It seems desirable to arrange matters so that they do not have to go out before nine or ten in the morning, and even more important that they should be able to retire by ten or eleven at night. . . .

Everything which is really beautiful—whether by reason of its antiquity, or its special nature, or its form, or its richness of construction—interests them intensely; one must never crowd too much [sightseeing] into one day, but allow them time to make a detailed examination of the objects, choosing those which are the most unusual and interesting.

Public establishments, whether charitable or educational, have been of interest to them; and because they try to profit from everything they see, one must not refuse them details but, on the contrary, furnish them with all details, carefully written out . . . they will appreciate these contributions to the usefulness and pleasure of their tour.

It is necessary to note that His Imperial Highness, the Grand Duke, knows no Italian; and that Madame the Grand Duchess understands Italian but cannot speak it. It is worth trying very hard to assure that those who accompany them or who explain what they are going to see should know French.

The Grand Duke does not dance; Madame the Grand Duchess dances, but does not care for it. . . .

Good music appears to please Their Imperial Highnesses, and so does a good play—especially if it does not last too long or too late; but for the reason mentioned above, a play in Italian, in which there is no singing, can scarcely amuse the Grand Duke.

Military and naval objects will certainly be their favorites, [but they are also interested in] trade, industry, and manufacturing. . . .

II

The Count of the North, . . . in addition to a great deal of spirit, talent and thoughtfulness, also possesses the ability fully to understand things and ideas, and to understand thoroughly all aspects and circumstances. . . . It is necessary to behave openly, sincerely, and straightforwardly with him so that he does not become distrustful and suspicious. [Joseph also noted that Paul and Maria became suspicious if they thought items were being concealed from them.] I believe that he is very industrious, and particularly that he has a great deal of toughness in his thinking. . . . [he is] very firm, resolute, and decided, when he has taken a position; certainly [he is] not a man to let himself be managed by anyone. It appears, in general, that he does not care much for strangers, and that he will become even more severe and inclined to discipline, to subordination without limit, to regularity and precision.

In his conversations, he has never mentioned his situation nor the Empress [Catherine]; what he has not concealed from me is that he does not approve all the great projects and innovations which have been made in Russia, and which, in fact, are more nominal than real. On the subject of the Empress' project to expand at the expense of the Turks and to re-establish the empire of Constantinople, he has not concealed from me how much he disapproves of this project and of all projects to enlarge an empire which is already vast, which needs to ponder its domestic problems, to put aside all useless ideas of conquest which serve only to acquire glory without any real advantages [but] on the contrary, make them always weaker. On this subject, I am persuaded that he spoke sincerely.

[Leopold noted the continuing attachment of the Russian couple to Prussia, and their continuing suspicion of Austria.] He did not try to dissimulate his opinion that the portion of Poland taken by Russia was the poorest of the three while that which we [Hapsburgs] had acquired was the richest, most beautiful, and most fertile. . . . He many times spoke to many persons [of his suspicion that his correspondence was being intercepted and read] although I tried to disabuse him of this suspicion. He was particularly disturbed because he had received no letters from Panin since leaving Vienna although he had written by every post, and that he had rarely heard from Prince Repnin, to whom he is equally attached. [Continuing in this vein, Leopold reported how well informed the Russians were on persons and happenings in Vienna, and how Paul had charged Austria with suborning Russian officials.] I protested that I knew nothing about this and he replied: "Well, I know them, and I will name them. Prince Potemkin . . . Bezborodko . . . Bakunin . . . Counts Simon and Alexander Vorontsov and M. Markov. . . . I name them because I am sure that they know that I know, and that as soon as I can I will crush them ruthlessly and chase them out."

[Leopold then told his brother that Paul and Maria not only kept personal records of everything which seemed important to them, but also had kept themselves informed on happenings in Leopold's family.] For example, concerning business relative to the future marriage of my son, they looked in their notebooks and read to me: H. M. the Emperor told us in so many words such and such a thing in the presence of so and so on this day at that hour. I assure you, and you can well believe, that I was greatly astonished and redoubled my precautions. . . .

The count is a man who likes firm positions and holds them tenaciously once he has taken them.

The Murder of Paul

Alexander I, like his grandmother, Catherine II, was elevated to the throne as the result of a palace revolution which involved the murder of his predecessor. The predecessor in Alexander's case was his father, Paul, and throughout his life, Alexander was haunted by a sense of guilt over his complicity in the murder. The following version of the murder is Alexander's own, as he told it to his friend and confidant, Prince Czartoryski. The source is: Adam Gielgud (Ed.), *Memoirs of Prince Adam Czartoryski and his Correspondence with Alexander I.* Second edition. Two volumes. London, 1888. Vol. 1, pp. 227 ff. Abridged.

Then he spoke to me of his father's death with inexpressible grief and remorse. We often returned to this subject, and Alexander gave me full details of it which I shall repeat below, together with information communicated to me by other actors in the tragedy.

Alexander told me that the first man who spoke to him about the plans of the conspirators was Count Panin, and he never forgave him. Panin was one of the chief leaders of the conspiracy which brought about Paul's death, though he did not actually take part in it. During my previous stay in the Russian capital I had never met him. When I returned to St. Petersburg, I first made his acquaintance. Apart from other reasons, the Count's exterior, would I think, almost have alone been sufficient to make friendship impossible. I have often been struck by his icey expression; his impassive countenance, on a body as straight as a spike, did not induce one to address him. I saw him but little, however, and my judgment of his character might have been erroneous and even unjust.

The two Counts Panin and Pahlen were at that time the strongest heads of the Empire. They saw further and more clearly than the other members

of Paul's Council, to which both of them belonged; and they agreed to
initiate Alexander into their plans. It would not have been prudent to attempt anything without being assured of the consent of the heir to the
throne. Devoted fanatics or enthusiasts might no doubt have acted otherwise. By not implicating the son in the dethronement of his father, by exposing themselves to a certain death, they would have better served both
Russia and the prince who was to be called upon to govern her; but such a
course would have been almost impracticable, and it would have demanded an audacity and antique virtue which in these days very few men
possess. Pahlen obtained a secret audience for Panin with the Grand-
Duke. Panin represented to Alexander the evils from which Russia was
suffering and would continue to suffer if Paul continued to reign. He said
that Alexander's most sacred duty was to his country, and that he must not
sacrifice millions of people to the extravagant caprices and follies of a
single man, even if that man was his father; that the life, or at least the
liberty, of his mother, of himself, and of the whole of the Imperial family
was threatened by Paul's inconceivable aversion for his wife, from whom
he was entirely separated; that this aversion increased from day to day, and
might prompt him to the most outrageous acts; and that it was therefore
necessary to save Russia, whose fate was in Alexander's hands, by depos-
ing Paul, which would be the only means of preventing him from inflicting
greater calamities on his country and his family, and securing to him a
quieter and more happy life. This speech produced a great impression on
Alexander, but it did not convince him. It required more than six months
to enable his tempters to obtain his consent to their plans.

It was a thousand pities that a prince so anxious and so well qualified
to be a benefactor of his country did not hold entirely aloof from a conspiracy which resulted almost inevitably in his father's assassination. Russia certainly suffered much under the almost maniacal Government of
Paul, and there are no means in that country of restraining or confining a
mad sovereign; but Alexander felt and exaggerated in his own mind all his
life the sombre reflection of the crime committed on his father, which had
fallen on himself, and which he thought he could never wipe out. This in-
effaceable stain, although it was brought about solely by his inexperience
and his total and innocent ignorance of Russian affairs and the Russian
people, settled like a vulture on his conscience, paralysed his best faculties
at the commencement of his reign, and plunged him into a mysticism sometimes degenerating into superstition at its close.

It must be admitted that the Emperor Paul was Precipitating his country into incalculable disorders and into a complete deterioration of the
Government machine. The principal officials and other officers of rank
were more or less convinced that the Emperor had fits of mental alienation.
His rule became a reign of terror. He was hated even for his good qualities,
for at bottom he desired justice, and this impulse sometimes led him to do a
just thing in his outburst of rage; but his feeling of justice was blind and
struck at all without discrimination; always passionate, often capricious
and cruel, his decrees were constantly suspended over the heads of officers,

and made them detest the man who filled their lives with uncertainty and terror. The conspiracy had the sympathy of all, for it promised to put an end to a regime which had become intolerable. The deposition, if not the murder, of Paul had become inevitable in the natural course of events. Although everybody sympathized with the conspiracy, nothing was done until Alexander had given his consent to his father's deposition.

Those who approached Alexander after the murder often feared that his mind would be affected. I think I was of some use in preventing him from succumbing to the weight of the terrible thought that pursued him. Temporarily he found some consolation in the absorption of all his faculties, but I am certain that toward the end of his life it was the same terrible thought that so depressed him, filling him with a disgust of life and a piety which was perhaps exaggerated, but which is the sole possible and real support in the most poignant grief. When we returned to this sad topic in our conversation, Alexander often repeated to me the details of the plans he had formed to establish his father in the palace of St. Michael, and afterwards to enable him as much as possible to reside in the imperial palaces in the country. . . . He judged of his father by himself. There was always in his noble character, a feminine element, with its strength and weaknesses. He often used to make plans which could not be realized, and on this idealistic foundation he raised complete structures which he made as perfect as possible. Nothing was more impracticable—especially in Russia—than the romantic means which Alexander was devised of rendering his father happy, while depriving him of his crown and of the possibility of tormenting and ruining the country. Alexander was not only young and inexperienced; he had almost the blind and confiding inexperience of childhood, and this characteristic remained with him for some years until it was destroyed by the realities of life.

A Friendly Description of Alexander I

The author of the following flattering descriptions of Alexander I was his intimate and devoted friend, the Countess de Choiseul-Gouffier. The countess, who was born at Vilna in Russian Poland, was the daughter of a wealthy landowner. She first met the tsar in 1812 and their friendship lasted until his death. The source is: Mme. la Comtesse de Choiseul-Gouffier (M. B. Patterson, Tr.), *Historical Memoirs of the Emperor Alexander I and The Court of Russia.* Second edition. Chicago: A. C. McClurg and Co., 1901. Pp. 82–83, 25.

Notwithstanding the regularity and delicacy of his features, the brightness and freshness of his complexion, his beauty was less striking at first sight, than that air of benevolence and kindness which captivated all hearts and instantly inspired confidence. His tall, noble, and majestic form, which often stooped a little with grace, like the pose of an antique statue, already threatened to become stout, but he was perfectly formed. His eyes were blue, bright and expressive; he was a little short-sighted. His nose was straight and well shaped, his mouth small and agreeable. The rounded contour of his face, as well as his profile, resembled that of his august mother. His forehead was somewhat bald, but this gave to his whole countenance an open and serene expression, and his hair, of a golden blond, carefully arranged as in the heads on antique cameos or medallions, seemed made to receive the triple crown of laurel, myrtle, and olive. He had an infinity of shades of tone and manner. When he addressed men of distinguished rank, it was with dignity and affability at the same time; to persons of his retinue, with an air of kindness almost familiar; to women of a certain age, with deference; and to young people, with an infinite grace, a refined and attractive manner, and a countenance full of expression.

This prince in his early youth had had his hearing seriously impaired by the report of a discharge of artillery, in consequence of which his left ear was somewhat deaf, and he usually turned the right toward the speaker to hear better.

· · ·

Alexander loved to learn. He had a remarkable memory and quick, penetrating, and refined perceptions. In his early years he showed a taste for military science, occupying himself zealously with what he was pleased to call his service, following exactly and observing punctiliously the strictest discipline and subordination. He possessed in a high degree the love of order and work. That which one could not help most admiring in him was the perfect evenness of his temper, a quality very rare and very valuable in a sovereign, which had for its source the goodness of his heart. Nothing could change the sweet benevolence which showed itself in his face as well as in his actions.

Alexander spoke several languages, especially French, with elegance and fluency. His manners were charming. A certain timidity was noticeable in his early youth. No one ever possessed to a greater degree the happy gift of gaining all hearts; and no one, I am sure, could have seen Alexander and heard him speak without saying to himself, "How happy I should be to call this man my friend!"

Alexander's Character

Prince Adam Czartoryski, author of the following sketch of Alexander, was a brilliant Polish statesman who was drafted into the service of Paul in 1796. He served Paul well and was on intimate terms with him. Later he was intimately associated with Alexander whom he served in various official and unofficial capacities. Their close friendship continued throughout the tsar's lifetime although Czartoryski did not hold office throughout the period. His comments upon Alexander are of especial interest due to the closeness of the two men. The source is: Gielgud, *Memoirs, etc.,* vol. 1, pp. 118–120.

His opinions were those of one brought up in the ideas of 1789, who wishes to see republics everywhere, and looks upon that form of government as the only one in conformity with the wishes and the rights of humanity.

Although I was myself at that time very enthusiastic—although born and brought up in a Republic where the principles of the French Revolution had been accepted with ardour—yet I had constantly to moderate the extreme opinions expressed by Alexander. He held, among other things, that hereditary monarchy was an unjust and absurd institution, and that the supreme authority should be granted not through the accident of birth but by the votes of the nation, which would best know who is most capable of governing it. I represented to him the arguments against this view, the difficulty and the risks of an election, what Poland had suffered from such an institution, and how little Russia was adapted to or prepared for it. I added that now at any rate Russia would not gain anything by the change, as she would lose the man who by his benevolent and pure intentions was most worthy of acceding to the throne. We had incessant discussions on this point. Sometimes during our long walks we talked of other matters. We turned from politics to nature, of whose beauties the young Grand-Duke was an enthusiastic admirer. One had to be a great lover of nature to discover its beauties in the country we walked in; but everything is relative in this world, and the Grand-Duke flew into ecstasies about a flower, the greenness of a tree, or the view over an undulating plain. There is nothing uglier or less picturesque than the neighbourhood of St. Petersburg. Alexander loved gardens and fields, and was fond of agriculture and the rustic beauty of village girls; the occupations and labours of the country, a simple, quiet, and retired life in some pretty farm, in a wide and smiling landscape —such was the dream he would have liked to realise, and to which he was always returning with a sigh.

I knew well that this was not the thing best suited to him; that for so high a destiny more elevation, force, ardour, and self-confidence were necessary than Alexander seemed to possess; that it was not right for a man in his position to wish to rid himself of the enormous burthen which was reserved for him, and to yearn for the pleasures of a quiet life. It was not enough to perceive and feel the difficulties of his position; he should have been filled with a passionate desire to surmount them. These reflections occasionally presented themselves to my mind, and even when I felt their truth, they did not diminish my feelings of admiration and devotion for Alexander. His sincerity, his frankness, his self-abandonment to the beautiful illusions that fascinated him, had a charm which it was impossible to resist. Moreover, he was still so young that his character might yet gain the qualities in which it was defective; circumstances and necessities might develop faculties which had not the time or the means of showing themselves; and although he was afterwards much changed, he retained to the last a portion of the tastes and opinions of his youth.

Many people—my countrymen especially—in later years reproached me for having placed too much confidence in Alexander's assurances. I have often maintained against his detractors that his opinions were sincere. The impression produced by the first years of our relations could not be effaced. Assuredly, when Alexander, at the age of eighteen, spoke to me with an effusiveness which relieved his mind, about opinions and sentiments which he concealed from everybody else, it was because he really felt them, and wished to confide them to someone. What other motive could he have had? Whom could he have wished to deceive? He certainly followed the inclination of his heart and expressed his real thoughts.

Besides our political discussions, and the ever-welcome topic of the beauties of nature, and the dream of a quiet country life after the destinies of free Russia should have been secured, Alexander had also a third object to which he ardently devoted himself, and which was not at all in accordance with the others, namely, the army, which was his hobby, as it was that of his father, the Grand-Duke Paul.

The Education of Alexander

The source is: Gielgud, *Memoirs, etc.*, vol. 1, pp. 127–132.

It is certainly astonishing that Catherine, who took pleasure in the thought that Alexander would continue her reign and her glory, did not think of preparing him for this task by familiarising him in his early youth with the various branches of government. Nothing of the sort was attempted. Perhaps he would not have acquired very correct information on many things, but he would have been saved from the want of occupation. Yet it would seem that either the Empress and her council had no such idea, or that the former did not at least insist upon its being carried out. Alexander's education remained incomplete at the time of his marriage, in consequence of the departure of M. de la Harpe. He was then eighteen years old; he had no regular occupation, he was not even advised to work, and in the absence of any more practical task he was not given any plan of reading which might have helped him in the difficult career for which he was destined. I often spoke to him on this subject, both then and later. I proposed that he should read various books on history, legislation, and politics. He saw that they would do him good, and really wished to read them; but a Court life makes any continued occupation impossible. While he was Grand-Duke, Alexander did not read to the end a single serious book. I do not think he could have done so when he became Emperor, and the whole burthen of a despotic government was cast upon him. The life of a Court is fatiguing and yet idle. It furnishes a thousand excuses for indolence, and one is constantly busy in doing nothing. When Alexander came to his rooms it was to take rest and not to work. He read by fits and starts, without ardour or zeal. The passion of acquiring knowledge was not sufficiently strong in him; he was married too young, and he did not perceive that he still knew very little. Yet he felt the importance of useful study, and wished to enter upon it; but his will was not sufficiently strong to overcome the daily obstacles presented by the duties and unpleasantnesses of life. The few years of his early youth thus passed away, and he lost precious opportunities which he had in abundance so long as Catherine was alive, and of which he might have recovered a part even under the Emperor Paul.

While he was Grand-Duke, and even during the first years of his reign, Alexander remained what his education had made him, and was very different from what he became later on when he followed his natural propensities. It must be concluded that nature had endowed him with rare qualities, as notwithstanding the education he had received he became the most amiable sovereign of his age and the cause of Napoleon's fall. After having reigned for some years, and acquired the experience entailed by the necessity of at once taking the management of important affairs of State and by constant intercourse with men in office, people were surprised to find him not only an accomplished man of the world, but an able politician, with a penetrating and subtle mind, writing without assistance excellent letters on complicated and difficult subjects, and always amiable, even in the most serious conversations. What would he have become had his education been less neglected and more adapted to the duties which were to occupy his life? M. de la Harpe was the only man that can be mentioned with praise among those to whom the education of the two Grand-Dukes was entrusted. I do not know exactly who were the persons directed by Catherine to select their tutors; probably they were some encyclopædists of the clique of Grimm or the Baron d'Holbach.

M. de la Harpe does not seem to have directed Alexander into any serious course of study, though he had acquired so much influence over the Grand-Duke's mind and heart that I believe he could have made him do anything. Alexander derived from his teaching only some superficial knowledge; his information was neither positive nor complete. M. de la Harpe inspired him with the love of humanity, of justice, and even of equality and liberty for all; he prevented the prejudices and flatteries which surrounded him from stifling his noble instincts. It was a great merit in M. de la Harpe to have inspired and developed these generous sentiments in a Russian Grand-Duke, but Alexander's mind was not penetrated by them; it was filled with vague phrases, and M. de la Harpe did not sufficiently make him reflect on the immense difficulty of realising these ideas—on the thorny task of finding means to obtain possible results. He was, however, merely charged with Alexander's literary education; the choice which was made of those who were to look after his moral training was extraordinary. Count Nicholas Soltykoff, who was a subaltern during the Seven Years' War and had not since seen any active service (which did not prevent him from attaining the highest rank in the army), was the superintendent of the education of the two Grand-Dukes. Short, with a large head, affected, nervous, and of health so delicate that it required constant attention (he could not wear braces, and constantly hitched up his breeches like a sailor) he had the reputation of being the most astute courtier in Russia. When Catherine discovered that her favourite Momonoff had formed intimate relations with one of her maids of honour, she ordered the culprits to come before her, had them married, and then expelled them from her Court; after which Soltykoff at once introduced to her Plato Zuboff, who speedily became Momonoff's successor. The elevation of Zuboff so angered Prince Potemkin that he declared he would go to

St. Petersburg to extract this tooth (*zub* means tooth in Russian); but he died before he could carry out his intention, and Soltykoff remained in high favour with the Empress. He was not only the channel by which her messages and admonitions were conveyed to the young princes; he also acted as intermediary whenever Catherine had anything to communicate to the Grand-Duke Paul. Soltykoff used to omit or soften any words which seemed too disagreeable or severe in the orders or the reproaches of his Imperial mistress, and he did the same with regard to the replies he had to convey to her. This gave satisfaction to both sides; he alone knew the truth, and took good care not to tell it. There was perhaps some merit in doing this successfully, but Count Soltykoff was certainly not the man to direct the education of the young heir to the throne, or to make a salutary impression on his character.

Besides Count Soltykoff, each of the two princes had a special director of studies with assistants. The selection of the two directors was even more extraordinary than that of the chief superintendent. The one attached to Alexander was Count Protasoff, whose only merit was to be the brother of the *demoiselle â portrait,* an old favourite of the Empress as to whose functions, though she was a good woman at heart, there were all sorts of extraordinary anecdotes. Constantine's special director was Count Sacken, a weakminded man who was the object of incessant ridicule on the part of his pupil. Count Protasoff may justly be said to have been a complete imbecile; Alexander did not laugh at him, but he had never the smallest esteem for him. The assistant directors were selected solely by favour, with the exception of Mouravieff, whom Alexander when he ascended the throne made his secretary for petitions, and afterwards appointed curator of the schools of the Moscow district. He was a worthy man and was said to be well informed, but he was so timid as to be almost incapable of transacting business. I should also not omit Baron Budberg, who some years later succeeded me as Minister of Foreign Affairs.

Such surroundings could only produce a bad effect on the young princes, and the qualities displayed by Alexander are the more astonishing and praiseworthy, as he developed them notwithstanding the education he had received and the examples which were before his eyes.

A Feminine View of Alexander's Russia

During the Napoleonic Wars two young ladies of a distinguished Anglo-Irish family, Catherine and Martha Wilmot, paid an extended visit to Russia as guests of the famous Princess Dashkov. Their hostess was a most remarkable woman, an intimate of Catherine II, a gifted writer, the founder and the first president of the Russian Academy. Exiled by Paul to one of her distant estates, she was allowed to return to the vicinity of Moscow by Alexander I. With such a hostess, the Wilmot sisters had a most unusual opportunity to observe Russian life at firsthand. The source is: The Marchioness of Londonderry and M. M. Hyde (Eds.), *The Russian Journals of Martha and Catherine Wil-*

mot, 1803–1808. London: Macmillan and Co., Ltd., 1934. Pp. 146–147, 199–201.

. . . There is a Small Meadow opposite to my Windows in which 150 Mowers are mowing this moment, Men & Women. All the Men are clothed in white linnen Jacket & trowsers (no that's a fib, white trousers & a Shirt border'd at bottom with the scarlet work of the Peasants & likewise on the Shoulders, girdled round the waist with a guady girdle). The effect is excessively picturesque, and those who imagine the Russ peasantry sunk in sloth & misery imagine a strange falsehood. Wou'd to God our Paddys (dear Spalpines & Broaganeers that they are, for on my *oath* I doat down upon them) were half as well clothed or fed the year round as are the Russians. There is *for & against* in every state, but take the two Nations to Rob''s touchstones, "Have they eneough to eat, to drink?" "Have they Houses, firing & a bed to lie on?" and trust me the *Bears* would triumph, oh beyond comparison. If they are *Slaves* 'tis likewise the Master's interest to treat them kindly. His population constitutes his riches, & he who neglects or oppresses his subjects becomes their victim & sinks himself. Those indeed who class with Servants are different there. A Master's caprice comes in contact with every act of his Domestics, and as they *cannot be dischar'd* corporal punishment must be sometimes inflicted. Oh Zandy, there's what we Islanders cannot even bear to think of. Yet to sum up all in one word, the greatest punishment that can be inflicted is to be "given for a Soldier." 'Tis probably therefore that the former situations could not be *very* miserable, *& on ne peut desirer ce qu'on ne cannoit pas.* . . .

I believe I never mention'd Troitska. It is a fine place, the Princess has made it herself, and situated in the midst of 16 Villages belonging to her. Three thousand Peasants, "my subjects" (as she calls them) live most happily under her absolute power; and of all the blessed hearted beings that ever existed on that subject she is the most blessed (excepting your Mother). There are two hundred servants, taking in all denominations inside and outside, in this establishment, more than a hundred horses, two hundred stock of cows, and everything else in proportion. The Church establishment too belongs to her, and is built at the back of the House. A lovely wood belonging to the estate 9 miles long and 4 broad is within a few yards of the place inhabited by Wolves, and in it the Princess and I lost our way yesterday evening for an hour and half. A beautiful river winds all through the grounds and serpentines amidst the entire estate. However Troitska is a dead flat almost, and to the cultivation alone its beauty is attributable. An immense quantity of ground is laid out under shrubberies and all sorts of pleasure grounds completely in the English stile. The House is enormous with wings on either side which are only connected by balconies raised on iron railings up to the 2nd Story. Matty and I inhabit one of these wings and Anna Petrovna the other. 20 bearded Men are now busily employ'd in making a temporary wooden passage from the hall door to the door of our Castle, as in winter (strange to say) they had provided for no internal communication so much was sacrificed to the appearance of the outside.

There are a hundred whimsical and most ridiculous peculiarities of custom, such as letting you provide your own bed cloaths, in a Palace even! We have our own sheets, blankets and Quilts which we give to the washer-woman with our wearing apparel, and they would look upon one as extraordinary to expect the House was to provide for these things, as you would if I laid myself up at Glanmire and sent for your gown to wear as a matter of right. (Black eneough you'd look at me and soon eneough you'd shew me the door in case of such an outrage!) In fact this system of each person having a seperate little establishment is observ'd in more ways than that, for saucepans, candles, candlesticks, tea and coffee equipage and a hundred &c. &c. are regularly found in the care of the *Femmes de Chambre;* and I might lock my Castle door, or Anna Petrovna or Matty, and we have provisions to keep the Citadel a week in flourishing health. The system of hoards is without bounds, and presents appropriate to this comical system are perfectly the fashion. The Princess sent up a pair of silver candlesticks on our arrival here and a store of wax candles! I expected a spit or gridiron next, but tho' not exactly so we all got presents! When I left London I laid in as many beads, necklaces, and trinkets as if I was going to trade with Otahiete, and they are almost exhausted already amongst the band of Damsels who attend the Chambers fair. To be sure Eleanor comes in for costly offerings in return, but it is a torment and horrid waste of money, for bawbles accumulate without mercy; and besides one scarcely has the liberty of choice as on certain days they must be given and receiv'd or else outrage the customs of the Country and give universal offence. Matty has already provided 14 volumes beautifully bound in green and gold for Anna Petrovna's Easter gift; she has seen them and look'd them over, but till the day comes she is not to receive or acknowledge them.

In the midst of this immense Establishment and in the center of riches and honours I wish you were to see the Princess go out to take a walk, or rather to look over her subjects! An old brown great coat and a silk handkerchief about her neck worn to rags is her dress, & well may it be worn to rags for she has worn it 18 years and will continue to do so as long as she lives because it belong'd to Mrs. Hamilton. Her originality, her appearance, her manner of speaking, her doing every description of thing, (for she helps the masons to build walls, she assists with her own hands in making the roads, she feeds the cows, she composes music, she sings & plays, she writes for the press, she shells the corn, she talks out loud in Church and corrects the Priest if he is not devout, she talks out loud in her little Theatre and puts in the Performers when they are out in their parts, she is a Doctor, an Apothecary, a Surgeon, a Farrier, a Carpenter, a Magistrate, a Lawyer; in short she hourly practices every species of incongruity, corresponds with her brother, who holds the first post in the Empire, on his trade, with Authors, with Philosophers, with Jews, with Poets, with her Son, with all her Relations, and yet appears as if she had her time a burthen on her hands) altogether gives me eternally the idea of her being a Fairy! And I protest it is not jokingly I say so, for the impression never quits me for a moment. The marvellous contradiction too of her speaking like an Infant in her broken English and with her unaccountable expressions! She is unconscious whether she speaks French, English or Russian, and mingles these in every sentence. She speaks German and Italien equally well, but her pronounciation is not clear which takes from the pleasure I shou'd otherwise receive from her conversation. I have just finish'd reading Voltaire's, Diderot's, Garrick's & the Abbe Raynall's letters to her. She has promised me the Empress Catherine's, and I have also read a good part of her life written by herself. Indeed it is necessary to qualify oneself with the knowledge of public things and characters in Russia since the time of Catherine, since the Princess alludes to them perpetually and her mind wanders so naturally back to the Court & Study & Toilet & Boudoir of Catherine that I am beginning to fancy I recollect her habits of life & conversation & that I was a party concern'd in the revolution. By the by, the principal reception room at Troitska is ornamented with an immense picture of Catherine on Horseback in uniform taken the very day of her husband's destruction, & the P^{ss} says a perfect resemblance. Besides this there are Portraits of her in every room.

The Unofficial Committee (I)

One of the most discussed institutions of the first years of the reign of Alexander I was a group of young men—all reputedly liberal and close to the emperor—who formed what was known as the Unofficial, or the Secret Committee. Count Paul Alexandrovich Stroganov appears to have been the originator of the committee, and to have persuaded the tsar to bring it into being. The following selections have been translated from Stroganov's own records of the genesis and work of the committee. Stroganov's papers were edited and published by an imperial amateur of history, the Grand Duke Nicholas Mikhailovich. The collection is titled: *Count Paul Alexandrovich Stroganov. (1774–1817) Istoricheskoe Izledovanie Epokhi Imperatora Aleksandra I (Historical Revelations of the Epoch of Alexander I)*. Three volumes. St. Petersburg, 1903. The material below is from volume II, pp. 5–8 *passim*, 10–11, 15–22 *passim*, 28–32 *passim*, 61–64, 70, 76, 80, 102–103, 115–118 *passim*, 120, 166–168 *passim*, and 174. The first four items deal with the genesis of the committee; the remainder, with some of its work.

Stroganov Reports a Conversation with Alexander (April, 1801)

The Emperor began by giving me some details on his manner of working. In the final analysis, this comes down to the Emperor's deciding immediately every subject on which he works. Everything which requires the meeting of several parties is taken to the Council in order that the matter may be discussed in the presence of all who are attached to the different branches of administration and may consequently be modified as required by their respective interests. . . .

I spoke to him next concerning my idea that he should begin [reforms] by considering the administration [of the government] before making a real constitution, and that the one should result from the other. He approved. He told me that one of the most important bases of the work ought to be the establishment of the famous rights of the citizen. I observed to him that I thought this should be only relatively the work of the committee; he seemed to be of my mind. I told him that it seemed to me that all these rights were summed up in the maxim that every citizen ought to be guaranteed his property and the unlimited right to do anything which did not injure another. He seemed to agree absolutely on this point. . . .

Stroganov's General Plan for Work on the Reform with the Emperor

The first principle to establish is that this reform must be entirely His Majesty's, and it is necessary to take all measures so that no one questions the work. This principle ought to be developed in such fashion as to leave no room for doubt on any case which might arise.

Next, it is necessary to make a plan of the goal at which one wishes to arrive, so that, in the course of affairs one has a platform on which to stand in order not to contradict the principles one wishes to see firmly established. Then it is necessary to move on to the work of the reform and to attack it regularly; to begin by setting up the committee, establishing the bases and the plan of the work, etc.

The reform, to be done well, must be carried out first in the administration which ought to be ordered in all its parts relative to a guarantee of property and liberty of action, so long as it does not injure another; as to this last, the limits beyond which injury to another occurs should be defined by law because everything which the law does not forbid is permitted (and a law should never be retroactive). Once established on a solid basis, it is a question only of finding a barrier which will not allow arbitrary power to destroy this order. This barrier ought to be found in already existing institutions; to create a new order of things in this regard seems to me to be very dangerous, and giving prestige to some ancient privileges will, it appears to me, erect a sufficient safeguard.

A carefully followed plan is required; the Emperor must explain in each case how he wishes the work to proceed; those who cooperate with him must be secretly appointed; their work must be so accomplished that it is the Emperor and no one else who organizes his country; it is necessary that the Emperor so conduct himself in public that the whole world will be persuaded that everything remains on its ancient foundation and that he does not wish any innovation.

The first thing now is to get the Emperor to explain his projects and the manner of the reform; if he believes that it must start with a constitution, this idea must be opposed; then he must be made to realize that he must not permit anyone to sidetrack the idea of reform.

The Emperor presently busies himself with much too much detail. He is so occupied with details that this is all he can do; scarcely enough time remains to consider reforms which are, however, so important that they require almost all his time. His work seems to me to be poorly organized; he occupies himself with his ministers, one after another and never all together; for his sake and theirs, he needs to set up a council and attend its discussions.

Essay on the System to Follow in Reforming the Administration of the Empire

The welfare of the people, in order to be solidly established, must be based on the principles of domestic prosperity which, in turn, depend on the justice of the bases of administration and not on empty glory which bears a great influence abroad.

Your Majesty, convinced of this truth, wishes to occupy himself with the reform of our government; this is a difficult task but worth doing, and the law-giver who, after long, hard work, reaches some parts of his general goal is sure to merit the blessings of his people, the admiration of the wise, and the title of benefactor of his country.

Your Majesty will not be able to accomplish this honorable task by his own efforts alone; he will doubtlessly deem it necessary to have collaborators. How shall these persons cooperate in order to achieve the desired results? [After a somewhat pretentious discourse of several pages, Stroganov concludes:] . . . three things must form the basic principles of the committee: 1) the general basis, after which everything else ought to be combined, *secrecy;* 2) regular work with Your Majesty, organized in such fashion as not to arouse curiosity; 3) Finally, the necessity that all members be kept informed about administration.

The Emperor's Principles Concerning Reform

His Majesty appears to approve the principle that he should be the sole author of the reform. . . .

He wishes that one of the bases of the committee's work be the fixing of the rights of man; he seemed to me to feel that this ought not to be only for the committee.

He seemed to me to accept the definition of a constitution which would prevent arbitrary power from changing a law and would fix the way in which such a change could be made.

He wishes one of the tasks to be to find a way under which nothing but merit is needed for advancement.

It appeared to me that he willingly adopted as the basis of the rights of the citizen the definition of liberty and ownership without injury to others.

Results of the Work on May 9th

His Majesty declared that he approved the principles I had enunciated. In developing this, he expanded most on the formation of the committee and on the way of working which would suit him. He seemed to approve beginning the reform in administration. . . . In regard to the formation of the committee, His Majesty named to it Count Kochubey, Prince Czartoryski, M. Novosiltsev, and myself. He agreed that the committee should meet regularly with him. We can get to work as soon as M. Novosiltsev arrives, without waiting for Czartoryski. . . .

His Majesty wishes someone to acquire an exact knowledge of all the constitutions which have been promulgated, that these be examined, and that ours be composed upon the principles of all. . . . Before implementing the constitution, [His Majesty feels] that it is necessary to codify the laws in such fashion that they shall be simple, orderly, not contradictory, and comprehensible to all . . . after that, the constitution can be implemented. There was a commission for this work in the time of Catherine II and in the time of Paul I, but its work was interrupted or reduced, and His Majesty wishes to restore its vigor.

Another project which he is considering is to restore the power of the Senate, and he wishes to charge the First Department with self-examination as to how it lost its rights and how these can be restored. . . .

Results of a Committee Meeting with the Emperor, 24 June 1801

. . . His Majesty having agreed that we should first have a look at the actual condition of all parts of the Empire in order to judge more knowingly the illness, if I may so phrase it, and the method of treatment to be followed, M. Novosiltsev was charged with this work, and since the task required considerable time, His Majesty consented to look first at parts of the whole.

. . . The first great division of the task, as unanimously recommended by all, was to report on the actual state of affairs, then to proceed to reform the different parts of the administration . . . and finally to crown these different institutions by an open guaranty—a constitution embodying the true spirit of the nation. These three principles formed the three major divisions of the whole task.

[They proposed to examine, first, the defense posture of the empire; next, its relations with foreign powers; then, to consider domestic affairs —trade, communications, agriculture, industry, administration, justice, finances, and legislation.] That was the division of the first part of the general task. We began today with a report on the navy. . . . His Majesty accepted the report and said that the poor state of the navy was due to the head of its administration. His Majesty said that this person had never had any merit other than that of having been attached to the dead emperor, which was the only reason he received the appointment. . . .

His Majesty, speaking of the Senate and of the reform which his order on the subject should bring about, expressed a fear that this action on his part might not lead to the result he desired, and said he thought . . . [this committee] ought to provide him with a precise regulation. It was pointed out to him that it would be very easy to include in the report, which was to be made to him, those principles of which His Majesty spoke: seeking to discover the true spirit of the establishment of the

Senate and being guided thereafter by this in seeking the proper means of fulfilling that goal either through existing regulations or, if these do not serve, by proposing to His Majesty those which will achieve the end he proposed. His Majesty approved this idea. . . .

His Majesty then spoke of the need of naming as senators only persons capable of filling the post worthily and he added that his difficulties in such choices were considerable, and that he had considered having every gubernia name two candidates and choosing the senators from this general list. M. Novosiltsev, in approving the idea of His Majesty, made him see, however, the disadvantage involved in this method which would produce only really honest men who might lack the understanding required for so important a post. His Majesty appeared impressed by this thought, and the conference ended with the observation that it was necessary to determine the nature of the illness before proceeding to remedies.

His Majesty left, and a second meeting was set for the following Monday.

> Stroganov's records cover eighteen additional meetings of the Unofficial Committee in 1801 and twenty more meetings in 1802. Despite the original intentions of Stroganov, and perhaps of the tsar, to make the committee what in modern parlance would be called a "high-level study group," or a "long-range planning body," the group soon found itself discussing personalities and daily problems. Among the subjects discussed in the committee's sessions were: army morale, foreign relations, the tsar's visits to Moscow ("the second capital"), internal passports, the behavior of some officials, the use of military officers as civilian administrators, the acquisition of land by the peasants, the privileges and rights of the nobility, the reform of the senate, and the transformation of the old "colleges" into ministries. The last two were, in fact, the only two major reforms which grew out of the work of the committee. The next several excerpts illustrate the committee's dealings with several subjects.

Foreign Relations (10 July, 1801)

One could conclude from this conversation of His Majesty concerning foreign relations that his principles are to use great frankness in negotiations, not to ally himself with anyone by treaties; in regard to France, to seek to put a check on her ambition but without offending her in any way; to behave well toward England since she is our natural friend.

Peasant Land Acquisitions (23 July, 1801)

The discussion turned to those articles which concerned giving peasants the power to acquire villages. His Majesty, though approving the spirit of the articles, appeared to doubt that this act would have the desired effect because the landowners were always the same: they would always find ways of extorting this property [from the peasants] either by threat or other means. Thereupon it was observed to His Majesty that he was certainly correct, but that this was only a first step, which had no drawbacks because they already made such acquisitions through intermediaries who often cheated them, and that the proposed method would do away with this abuse of the peasants. His Majesty agreed fully. . . .

"Nothing to Present" (29 July, 1801)

Today, Monday, we went into His Majesty's office after dinner. According to the work plan which we had proposed, we should have continued to consider the state of the Empire, but M. Novosiltsev had nothing ready for today and did not wish to present only bits and pieces, and Count Kochubey had nothing to present so the day was spent in dealing with current affairs. . . .

Peasants and Serfs (4 November, 1801)

For some time, several persons, notably LaHarpe and Mordvinov, but especially the latter, had spoken to the Emperor of the necessity of doing something for the peasants who, having no civil rights, were reduced to the most deplorable condition. This had to be done very gradually, and the first step proposed by Mordvinov was to permit those peasants who were not serfs to buy land. The Emperor agreed with him, but he wished that these same peasants instead of just being able to buy land could also purchase serfs. The serfs, being owned by persons not of gentle rank, would be subject to more moderate discipline and would not be their slaves, as were the serfs belonging to gentlemen. This would be a step very much to the benefit of the serfs. The Emperor would also outdo Mordvinov by letting the middle class buy serfs. It seemed to us that being allowed to buy land and serfs at the same time was too great an innovation.

A Council of Ministers (18 November, 1801)

The discussion then turned to the subject of the Council [of Ministers]. Several persons, notably Count Simon Vorontsov, frequently wrote from London that the Council should deal with all matters, that this was the custom in every country. He cited the example of England where every matter of any importance was always resolved by the entire cabinet and not by one minister after consultation with the king. He added that this was the best way to avoid having a minister surprise the emperor, or give him incorrect ideas, or persuade him to take the wrong measures. [Vorontsov had in mind Count Panin who, he charged, had abused the Emperor's confidence and had presented matters from a false point of view.] . . .

The situation with us is different . . . so that it would be imprudent to bring all matters indiscriminately before the Council. . . . It is necessary that no one should be able to say that the Emperor is subordinate to the Council or under its guardianship. That would have many disadvantages because there is a general spirit of confidence in the Emperor and of distrust of the Council. [It was suggested that some matters be handled by the Council, some by the emperor, and that] In affairs which required secrecy, the Emperor should name a committee of two or three trustworthy persons with whom he could consult.

His Majesty seemed to approve these general propositions, but he wanted a much more precise proposal on the distribution of business—matters which ought to go to the Council, and matters which he ought to hear. Such a distinction, he said, would remain secret and . . . only for his own guidance. In order to facilitate [the making of such distinctions] he promised to give us a list of his occupations together with the names of the recording secretaries. It would then be possible to depict the separation of affairs.

(21 November, 1801). We were supposed to have a special session to-day so that His Majesty could present to us his ideas on what should be submitted to the Council. His Majesty had sent us a list, as promised, but it was so incomplete that the work which was to be based on it was incomplete also. On the Whole, it said no more than that the Council should meet more than once a week.

Serf Problem (20 January, 1802)

M. Novosiltsev said that two Livonian landowners had given him some suggestions in regard to a way of adjusting the rights of landlords over their peasants, but that the military governor of Riga would almost certainly not allow these matters to be discussed [in the local assembly (Landtag)] unless the Emperor advised him to place no obstacle in the way of such discussion. Our discussion was on whether the Emperor should allow such discussion to take place.

M. Novosiltsev thought that there would be no ill effects from such action since the proposition had already been made in the reign of Paul without bad results. Moreover, the assurance given by the two landowners that most of the owners would consent provided, he thought, an additional reason for allowing the discussion to take place. Sooner or later, he said, it would be necessary to take this first step, otherwise one could not begin general emancipation. Now the owners themselves had started it, and in such fashion that an entire province would give an example to the rest of the Empire. . . . . . . he thought that the Emperor should not intervene formally, but should not forbid them to concern themselves with the matter.

Prince Czartoryski was inclined to agree. Count Kochubey regarded this as a very delicate question which required serious consideration. He feared that such a discussion in one of the provinces would be dangerous in view of the already too great reputation of the Emperor for favoring peasant emancipation. He proposed to consult the Council. . . . [Stroganov opposed giving the Landtag permission to discuss the subject, not because he wanted to stop emancipation, but because he felt that so important a matter should be discussed in the Unofficial Committee and not in a provincial assembly.] . . . As the matter seemed delicate, and since each continued to urge his own opinion, His Majesty decided to consult others, Count Vorontsov among them, and directed Novosiltsev to undertake this. Thus ended the discussion on this point.

The University of Moscow (*3 February, 1802*)

Among other things discussed was the improvement of the University of Moscow. Many things in that University had been inadequate; among other problems, the funds given it had remained at the level established when it was founded; considering how the prices of everything had risen, these funds were no longer adequate. Professors' salaries had also remained as they were originally which meant that they were at very much too low a scale. All these matters have now been taken care of: the funds increased; the professors' salaries raised. It is proposed to purchase a house to be set aside as a residence for professors and other employees.

The Unofficial Committee (II)

Another and briefer account of the Unofficial Committee was left by Prince Adam Czartoryski, a member of the committee. (The reader will have noted some references to Czartoryski in the Stroganov papers.) Czartoryski was also actively concerned with the reform of the senate and the modernization of the administration by the replacement of the colleges with ministries modeled after those existing in the West. Here are portions of Czartoryski's account of the Unofficial Committee and of these two reforms. The source is: Gielgud, *Memoirs, etc.*, vol. 1, pp. 257–258, 260–263, 267, 279–280, 291–310, 322–325. Adapted.

General

In order to remedy the discrepancy between Alexander's opinions and his acts, he established a Secret Council composed of persons whom he regarded as his friends and believed to be animated by sentiments and opinions in conformity with his own. The first nucleus of this Council was formed by the young Count Paul Strogonoff, M. de Novosiltzoff, and myself. We had long been in near relations with each other, and these now became more serious. The necessity of rallying round the Emperor and not leaving him alone in his desire of reform drew us more closely together. We were regarded for some years as models of intimate and unshakeable friendship. To be superior to every personal interest, and not to accept either presents or distinctions, was the principle of our alliance. Such a principle could not take root in Russia, but it was in accordance with the ideas of Alexander's youth and inspired him with special esteem for his friends. I was the sole author of the principle, which indeed was specially suited to my peculiar position. It was not always liked by my companions, and the Emperor himself afterwards grew tired of servants who wished to distinguish themselves by refusing to accept rewards which were so eagerly sought by everyone else.

The understanding between us had, as I have shown, begun at the coronation of the Emperor Paul at Moscow, and we had for a long time been on intimate terms, as we met daily at Count Strogonoff's. The fourth member admitted by the Emperor to the Secret Council was Count Kotchoubey.

We were privileged to dine with the Emperor without a previous invitation and we used to meet two or three times a week. After coffee and a little conversation, the Emperor used to retire, and while the other guests left the palace, the four members of the Secret Council entered through a corridor into a little dressing-room, which was in direct communication with the private rooms of their Majesties, and there met the Emperor. Various plans of reforms were debated; each member brought his ideas, and sometimes his work, and information which he had obtained as to what was passing in the existing administration and the abuses which he had observed. The Emperor freely expressed his thoughts and sentiments, and although the discussions at these meetings for a long time had no practical result, no useful reform was tried or carried out during Alexander's reign which did not originate in them. Meanwhile the Official Council, namely, the Senate and the Ministers, governed the country in the old way. Directly the Emperor left his dressing-room he came under the influence of the old Ministers, and could do nothing of what had been decided upon in the Secret Council; it was like a masonic lodge from which one entered the practical world.

This mysterious Council, which was not long concealed from the suspicions, or ultimately from the knowledge, of the Court, and was designated "the young men's party," grew impatient at not obtaining any result whatever from its deliberations; it pressed the Emperor to carry out the views he had expressed to us and the proposals he considered desirable and necessary. Once or twice an attempt was made to induce him to adopt energetic resolutions, to give orders and make himself obeyed, to dismiss certain superannuated officials who were a constant obstacle to every reform and to put young men in their place. But the Emperor's character inclined him to attain his end by compromises and concessions, and moreover he did not yet feel sufficiently master of the position to risk measures which he thought too violent. In our Council, Strogonoff was the most ardent, Novosiltzoff the most prudent, Kotchoubey the most time-serving, and I the most disinterested, always striving to curb undue impatience. Those who urged the Emperor to take immediate and severe measures did not know him. Such a proposal always made him draw back, and was of a nature to diminish his confidence. But as he complained of his Ministers and did not like any of them, an attempt was made in the Council, before inducing him to change them, to discuss abstract considerations of reform which had previously occupied us. Strogonoff accepted the post of Procurator of the First Department of the Senate; and Novosiltzoff was appointed one of the Emperor's secretaries, a place which gave him many advantages, as every letter addressed to the Emperor passed through his hands, and he had a right to publish the Emperor's ukases. His special department, however, was at first to deal with promotors of public undertakings, who are sometimes men of talent, but more often adventurers of very doubtful honesty who flock to Russia from abroad at the beginning of each new reign. This was a duty for which he was qualified by his varied knowledge in matters of finance and industry, and it was at the same time a school which did much to form his character. I must not here forget the fifth member of the Secret Council, M. de la Harpe, Alexander's tutor, who had come on a visit to his former pupil. He did not take part in the after dinner meetings, but he used to have private conversations with the Emperor, and frequently handed to him memoranda reviewing all the branches of the administration. These memoranda were first read at the secret sittings, and afterwards passed on from one member of the Council to the other to be considered at leisure, as they were interminably long. M. de la Harpe was at that time about forty-four years of age; he had been a member of the Swiss Directory, and always wore the uniform of that appointment, with a large sword fastened to an embroidered belt outside his coat. We were all of opinion that he did not merit his high reputation and the esteem in which Alexander held him. He belonged to the generation of men nourished with the illusions of the last part of the eighteenth century, who thought their doctrine a sort of philosopher's stone, or universal remedy which removed all difficulties to the regeneration of society. M. de la Harpe had his own particular panacea for Russia, and he explained it in such diffuse papers that Alexander himself had not the courage to read them. One of his favourite phrases was *organisation réglementairs;* an important idea no doubt, but he used to repeat it so often and with such emphasis that it was at last attached to him as a sort of nickname.

• • •

During the summer of 1801 the Secret Council continued to meet. The only measure it decided upon before the coronation was the dismissal of Count Panin, whose participation in the conspiracy which brought about the death of Paul filled Alexander with dislike and suspicion. After much discussion it was resolved that Panin should be succeeded as Minister of Foreign Affairs by Count Kotchoubey, but should be allowed to remain at St. Petersburg. The Emperor, wishing to avoid disagreeable scenes, treated Panin as a Minister up to the last moment, and this again was interpreted as a sign of duplicity. The Emperor's will was notified as to Panin by letter, then Kotchoubey entered upon his duties to the great satisfaction of Alexander and of our council.

• • •

The Emperor was at that time beginning to pay special attention to foreign affairs. Kotchoubey, the Foreign Minister, had adopted a system which he believed to be in entire conformity with the Emperor's opinions and views, and at the same time with his own. This was to hold Russia aloof from European affairs, and to keep on good terms with all foreign Powers, so as to devote all her time and attention to internal reforms. Such was indeed the Emperor's wish and that of his intimate advisers, but none of them had adopted it with more conviction, or maintained it with more persistence, than Kotchoubey. Russia, he used to say, is great and powerful enough both as regards population and extent of territory, and geographical position; she has nothing to fear from any one so long as she leaves other Powers in peace; and she has too often mixed herself up with matters which did not directly affect her. Nothing had happened in Europe but she claimed to have a part in it; she had made costly and useless wars. The Emperor Alexander was now in such a fortunate position that he could remain at peace with all the world and devote himself to internal reforms. It was at home, not abroad, that Russia could make immense conquests, by establishing order, economy, and justice in all parts of her vast empire, and by making agriculture, commerce, and industry flourish. European affairs and European wars were of no advantage whatever to the numerous inhabitants of the Russian Empire; they only lost their lives through them or had to furnish new recruits and taxes. What was necessary to their prosperity was a long peace and the incessant care of a wise and pacific administration—a task eminently suited to the Emperor, with his ideas of reform and liberal government.

This system was somewhat similar to that advocated by the English radicals. The idea is plausible and not without a basis of truth, but it has the disadvantage of reducing to insignificance and humiliation the State which follows it too literally, as by so doing it incurs the risk of becoming the vassal and tool of more enterprising and active States. Moreover, a consistent adherence to such a system would require much tact and firmness to avoid damaging compromises, which, in the then existing state of European relations, would have become almost inevitable.

Alexander's Dream of Reforms

At length the Emperor's vague and floating ideas were consolidated into a practical shape. All the eccentric views which were mere fireworks were abandoned, and Alexander had to restrict his wishes to the realities and possibilities of the moment. He consoled himself by indulging in his hours of leisure, which were daily becoming more rare, in hopes of progress which enabled him not to give up entirely the dreams of his youth. These dreams seemed to me like a tree transplanted into a dry and arid soil and deprived of its exuberant vegetation, whose despoiled trunk puts forth a few weak branches and then perishes. The Emperor's first step was to issue an ukase or manifesto to restore the authority and dignity of the Senate; this was a prudent course, calculated to predispose the public for the changes which were to follow. In speaking of the Senate he spoke a language which the Russians understood and which flattered the nobility; it was already the Supreme Court of Justice and Administration, for although every order of the Emperor, whether written or spoken, had the force of law, they had (especially those relating to general administration and the civil and criminal law) all to be addressed to the Senate, which was entrusted with the task of publishing them and seeing to their due execution. The various departments of the Senate were charged not only with trying on final appeal the civil and criminal cases of the empire, but also with punishing contraventions of the administrative regulations. It had the right of issuing ukases of its own founded on those of the Emperor, and, when necessary, explaining and developing them; and it presented him with reports for his approval. The governors and financial authorities of the provinces were under its direct supervision, and it was their duty to send to the Senate regular and formal reports upon which the sovereign gave such orders as he pleased. It was accordingly called "The Senate administering the Empire." Its vague functions, partly judicial and partly executive, were not in accordance with modern ideas, being so cumbrous in form that they retarded and might even embarrass the course of government; but there was no way of touching this ancient organisation without exposing internal affairs to even greater confusion, as the institution of the Senate had become part of the routine and the habits of the government machine. The Senate was consequently allowed to retain its administrative functions, though it was intended to let them fall by degrees into desuetude. All its powers were confirmed in pompous terms of which the author was Vorontzoff, and to them was added the right of making representations on the Emperor's ukases. It was at the same time laid down that all the Ministers should make detailed reports of their functions which the Emperor would send to the Senate for its opinion.

This, it was hoped, would be a first step in the direction of national and representative government. The idea was to deprive the Senate of its executive powers, to leave it those of a Supreme Court of Justice, and gradually to convert it into a sort of upper chamber to which would afterwards be attached deputies of the nobility who, either as part of the chamber or as a separate body, would, for the Emperor's information, state their views on the management of affairs by the Ministers and on the laws which were in existence or in preparation. This plan was never carried out, and what really happened was very different.

Those who think that the Senate of St. Petersburg can ever be of any importance for the destinies of Russia are entirely mistaken, and only show that they do not know Russia. The Russian Senate in its present form is less able than any political body in the world to make itself respected or to act on its own initiative. It can neither give an impulse nor even receive one, it is a marionette which one can move about as one pleases, but which has no motive power of its own.

Those who are tired of official life and wish to retire and live quietly in idleness are the sort of people who seek the appointment of Senator. The Senate thus becomes a receptacle for the indolent and the superannuated; all its work is done by the procurators and the secretaries, who decide questions at their pleasure and then take the decisions to the Senators, who as a rule sign them without reading them. These decrees are drawn up in a more diffuse and tedious style even than the official documents of other countries; the minutes in each case fill an immense volume, and it would require some courage to read them. One or two Senators who do read the decrees that are submitted to them for signature are spoken of with admiration as heroes. It is evident that such a political body is incapable of undertaking or following up any reform.

After laying the first stone of the edifice of a regulated legislative power, and devising a limit to the autocratic power, the Emperor turned his attention to the organisation of his government, so as to make its action more enlightened, more just, and more methodical. The government machine was irregular and intermittent in its action, and the administration was a chaos in which nothing was regulated or clearly defined. The only administrative authorities that were recognised were the Senate and the Committees of War, of the Navy, and of Foreign Affairs. These were not deliberative or consultative bodies; one of the members of each committee, usually the president, brought the reports of the committee to the sovereign and then informed it of his decisions. The Procurator-General united in his person the offices of Minister of the Interior, of Police, of Finance, and of Justice; but sometimes the sovereign created separate departments, and the Empress Catherine placed the conquered provinces under the direction of one of her favourites, such as Potemkin or Zuboff, who were independent of the Senate and reported direct to the sovereign. Moreover, when the reports of the Senate and the various committees were handed to the sovereign by the Ministers or other high functionaries of State, they were often put away in a drawer, and after some time had elapsed a decision totally opposed to the one suggested was issued. Thus there was practically no bar to the caprice of the sovereign. Paul, who thought he was a great general, and was especially jealous of any control over the army apart from his own, appointed one of his aides-de-camp in whom he had confidence to examine and submit to him all the proposals of the War Committee, and all promotions and appointments. The direction of Foreign Affairs was nominally entrusted to a committee of three members, each of whom worked with the sovereign separately, and had the management of some particular question which was kept a secret from his colleagues. This post was much sought after, and Catherine's favourites obtained some magnificent presents from foreign powers by employing for a negotiation, with which they had been charged by the Empress, one of the members of the Foreign Affairs Committee on whose complaisance they could rely. This was the case with Prince Zuboff and Count Markoff, who were handsomely rewarded for advocating the two last partitions of Poland.

In the time of the Emperor Paul foreign affairs were often directed by his favourite aides-de-camp. The Vice-Chancellor or the eldest of the members of the committee only had the direction of the administrative and financial branch, and of the current correspondence. This system suited an able sovereign like the Empress Catherine, who, notwithstanding its disadvantages and a complete absence of unity, still ultimately carried out a consistent policy. Paul, with his incessant caprices and changes of mind, yet had a most decided, almost furious, will which all the wheels of the government machine had at once to obey. But with a sovereign of vacillating character it is evident that the system of administration above described must lead to serious evils. The Emperor was continually exposed to making mistakes, to seeing only one side of a question; he was liable to be confused by a mass of opinions from persons many of whom had an interest in not letting him know the whole truth; and he could never advance towards a definite object. Russia therefore had reason to be grateful to the Emperor Alexander and those whose advice he then followed for having sought to introduce more order and method in the Imperial administration.

The object of the reform was to establish a system somewhat similar to those adopted in most other European States by separating the departments, defining their limits, assembling in each department matters of the same kind, centralising their management, and thereby augmenting the responsibility of the principal functionaries of State. It was hoped among other things that this would be an efficacious means of checking the numberless abuses and frauds which are the curse of Russia. The Emperor accordingly created for the first time Ministries of the Interior and of Police, of Finance, of Justice, of Public Instruction, of Commerce, of Foreign Affairs, of War, and of the Navy. As to the War Department, Alexander continued the system adopted by his father, insisting that everything relating to the army, down to the smallest appointment, should emanate direct from the sovereign, and that the army should know it. The post of aide-de-camp charged with the management of the *personnel* of the army became gradually converted, in imitation of Napoleon, into that of Major-General, so as to show that Russia always considers herself in a state of war, and wishes to be in position to make war at any moment. In the manifesto establishing the changes above referred to, it was stated that all the Emperor's ukases were in future to be countersigned by one of the Ministers—an attempt to introduce the principle of responsibility—and the Ministers were directed to meet in a council, in which they were to discuss the most important questions of State. This was a new administrative machine superior to the Senate, which retained all its functions and was invested with new ones; but those which related to administration properly so called, became in its case almost purely formal. By the creation of the new Ministers the administrative authority of the Government was concentrated, while hitherto it had not had any legal or definite status except in the person of the sovereign. The Council of State also was not changed, although some of its most eminent members became Ministers. The Emperor continued occasionally to refer to this Council various disagreeable or complicated questions, in order to give it something to do, and not let it die too soon; but it speedily perished through its insignificance, and Alexander afterwards created another Imperial Council on quite a different and much more extensive plan.

These changes, which elsewhere would seem the very A B C of politics, seemed at that time to the Russians novel and immense. The manifesto made much noise in the whole Empire and especially in the salons of St. Petersburg and Moscow; each man had his own opinion of it, and the majority judged it not by its intrinsic merits or the benefits it might confer on the State, but by the effect it would be likely to have on their own advancement. Those who obtained places approved it, while those who remained in the cold criticised the juvenile infatuation that wished to change the old and venerable institutions under which Russia had become great. The personages high in office who had not been consulted, and did not expect so considerable a change, were taken by surprise, finding themselves eclipsed by those who during the reign of Paul and the beginning of that of Alexander had held aloof. They strove to vent their disappointment by smiling with pity at the young men who were trying to reform the Empire, and at the foolishness of some older men who consented to be the instruments of a servile and awkward imitation of foreign institutions. The easy good-nature of the Emperor encouraged these criticisms, so far as they were possible in Russia, and they found a certain amount of support in the Empress Dowager, who was annoyed, without admitting it, at not having been more consulted by her son and at not being able to influence his decisions. She perceived in all these novelties a germ of liberalism whose development she feared, and her salon became a centre of opposition where people came to express their discontent.

The head of the new administration was Count Alexander Vorontzoff, who was made Foreign Minister, and also Chancellor—a title which had not been given to any one for years. Kotchoubey had entirely to reorganise an administration which had been long neglected, and which in the more distant provinces was without any direction or supervision, and given up to all the abuses arising from the ignorance and cupidity of subordinate officials. It was a noble and arduous task, and if he did not succeed as well as he had wished, it was not for want of zeal or good will. He began by organising his office, dividing it into several sections, each of which had to deal with a distinct branch of the vast department. He invited the assistance of all the able and experienced officials he could find, and endeavoured to raise in general estimation the post of Governor of a province by appointing in that capacity men whose character and position afforded guarantees of integrity, and who, though inexperienced in official work, were likely soon to obtain the necessary knowledge. It seemed as if order was going to break through the chaos, and the immediate effects of the change were soon felt by the people. One of the reforms he introduced was in the supply of salt, which in Russia is a matter of great importance. This was not nominally a Government monopoly, but the Government alone was able to supply salt to all parts of the Empire by obtaining it from the salt marshes or distilling it from sea-water. Kotchoubey took steps to reduce the cost of production and of conveyance to the lowest possible point, so as to enable the people to buy salt more cheaply, and the Government to be repaid its expenses.

The new Finance Minister was Count Vasilieff, a capable and honest official who had in financial matters been the right hand of Prince Viaziemskoy, the only Procurator-General who had been mentioned with praise at the time of the Empress Catherine. In the various changes which had taken place since the Prince's death in 1794, M. Vasilieff, as treasurer of the Empire, had been indispensable; he was a steady worker, appreciated new ideas, and adopted them when he thought they were opportune. All the branches of the public revenue, the brandy traffic, the Imperial Bank, etc., were comprised in this department, to which was added the mines department, which had been reorganised on a large scale.

The functions of Minister of Justice were united to those of Procurator-General of the Senate. General Beklescheff did not wish to stop in this department, as it had been deprived of the greater part of its functions by the creation of the Ministers of the Interior and of Finance; and he was succeeded by the Senator Dzierzanin. He was the personal choice of the Emperor, without communication with the Secret Council. A worthy man, and the writer of some much admired lyrics which were full of swing and passion, he was imperfectly educated and knew no language but Russian. The Emperor had been attracted to him by his ardent sentiments and poetic dreams, not being able to resist fine phrases; the vaguer they were the better they pleased him, as he could then easily assimilate them to his hopes, which also were not very clear. He liked expressions of energetic liberalism, and was especially attracted by admiration of himself when it was couched in the language of devotion to the cause of humanity.

The Emperor had direct and special relations with certain persons whom he himself introduced at our meetings; he liked to patronise them and defend them against objections raised sometimes by people who knew them more intimately. It gave him pleasure to have these relations without the knowledge of his friends, who already at that time had begun to displease him because they were so united among themselves. Yet it was absolutely necessary to introduce members of "the young men's party" into the administration, for all Alexander's hopes rested upon them for the zealous continuation and accomplishment of the reforms he had at heart. Kotchoubey was provided for, but what was to be done with the others? It would be too much to make them Ministers, and it was accordingly decided that assistants to the Ministers should be appointed; in this way the Emperor's friends would be able to direct their chiefs in accordance with the Emperor's views, and to keep him fully acquainted with what was going on.

Count Paul Strogonoff was at his request appointed assistant to the Minister of the Interior, and Novosiltzoff obtained the post of assistant to the Minister of Justice, retaining his former appointment of Secretary of the Emperor. This gave Novosiltzoff the most important place in the administration, as it was through him that the Emperor was to begin the work of reforming jurisprudence and the existing laws. He was well qualified for the task, as he had studied jurisprudence and political economy in England, and had more good use of the opportunities thereby afforded him of becoming conversant with those subjects. No one in Russia was at that time his superior in that administrative knowledge which was then only to be obtained by reading French and English works. His practical mind rejected all vain theories; he possessed skill and tact in dealing not only with individuals, but with the Russian public, which he knew thoroughly. He had bad qualities also; but these had not yet developed themselves. One of his greatest merits was that he seconded Alexander's wishes as to the improvement of the condition of the peasants, and he drew up the first ukase on this subject. He also reconstituted the commission for the revision of the law. This commission had been formed by the Empress Catherine, who thereby gained the flattering appreciation of Voltaire and the Diderots; but the only result was the publication of the philanthropic and philosophical instructions addressed by Catherine to the commission. It was dissolved soon after, and its proceedings were never made public. The new commission was organised by Novosiltzoff with the assistance of a German jurist, Baron Rosenkampf, on a vast and well-conceived plan. It was directed to codify all the existing Russian laws, which were very numerous and often contradicted each other, classifying them according to subjects, omitting such as were obsolete, and adding new ones when necessary, but taking care to retain in the new codes all that had entered for many years into the life of the Russian people, even if not quite reconcilable with the ideas of modern jurisprudence. The system adopted was somewhat similar to that of Justinian; but the task of the Russian codifiers was far more difficult than that of the Roman ones. The latter merely had to select and classify out of a somewhat confused mass of laws, most of which were admirable examples of wisdom and legislative science, while in Russia the laws were not only confused, but in many respects defective and insufficient. For such a work not only jurists, but real legislators were wanted. A similar code was to be prepared for the outlying provinces of the Empire, such as Livonia, Esthonia, Courland, and the Polish provinces of Little Russia, each of which had its own particular language, laws, and customs.

This great undertaking was begun methodically and pursued for some time with activity; Novosiltzoff was allowed by the Minister of Justice to make it his exclusive occupation. The classifications were prepared by Baron Rosenkampf, and so long as they were adhered to the work progressed; but it did not produce the results which were expected of it. This is usually the case in Russia; if there is no immediate result, the persons entrusted with the execution of the work are changed, and it has to be begun over again.

I was the only member of the Secret Council who remained without employment. Alexander offered me, with Count Vorontzoff's concurrence, the post of assistant to the Minister of Foreign Affairs, and all my friends, the Emperor especially, pressed me to accept the offer. I hesitated for a long time, feeling how much surprise and dissatisfaction such an appointment would cause in Russia. The Emperor observed that during my mission to the King of Sardinia I had made myself favourably known by my despatches, and that my nomination to the Foreign Office ought not therefore to be a matter of astonishment, besides which Count Vorontzoff, who alone had a right to be consulted on the subject, had consented to my becoming his assistant. I replied that he (the Emperor) knew more than anyone my feelings with regard to my country; that they could never change, and that I had some reason to fear that they might be incompatible with the duties of the appointment he wished to give me; the safest and most proper course, therefore, would be for me not to accept it. To this

Alexander rejoined that he did not at present anticipate any such contradiction as that which I feared; that I should always be at liberty to give up my post if such a contradiction were to arise; and that, on the contrary, he thought that events would occur which would be favourable to my views. He added some very flattering expressions with regard to my qualifications for the post. It is every man's duty, he said, to pay his debt to humanity; when one has talents one must not refuse to employ them in the most useful way. I still declined, but Alexander was bent on my taking the appointment; this was one of his irresistible fancies which nothing could induce him to abandon until they were satisfied. His persistence and kindness to me were such that at length I yielded, on the express condition that I should be allowed to resign the appointment directly its functions should become incompatible with my feelings as a Pole. My chief object in this was, by spending some years in the Emperor's service, to prove to him my sincere attachment and my gratitude for his friendship and confidence. I accepted with some sadness, as by so doing I was entering on a new career full of pitfalls which would retain me at St. Petersburg.

Reforms in Practice: the Senate

The progress of internal reform in Russia was abruptly stopped by an unexpected incident. Count Severin Potocki, who, as I said above, was a great admirer of the Emperor, often addressed memoranda to him on various subjects. The Senate had received from the Emperor, among other important prerogatives, the right of making representations to him, but it had hitherto not made any use of this right. Count Severin naturally thought the Emperor was sincere in his liberal opinions; the Emperor himself thought so; and the Count therefore imagined it would be a good thing, and would please his Imperial master, if the Senate were prompted to exercise its prerogatives. For this an opportunity soon presented itself. Although almost every noble in Russia entered the army, he was not obliged to do so, and could leave it when he thought proper. This double privilege was granted by Peter III in an ukase for which many blessed his memory. Alexander, however, restricted the privilege to nobles who held the rank of officers, those below that rank were obliged to serve for twelve years. This was looked upon as an attack on the guaranteed rights of the nobility, and produced a deep and painful sensation. The Minister of War, an old military bureaucrat of low origin, was said to be the author of the new ukase, and Count Severin Potocki proposed to the Senate that it should address representations to the Emperor on this violation of the nobles' charter. His proposal was read to the general assembly of all the departments, and the senators, seeing that one of the confidential advisers of the Court was taking the initiative in the matter, and that his opinion was warmly supported by Count Strogonoff, thought they could safely vote in its favour. They gladly did this, under the impression that by so doing they could without danger assume an air of independence in a matter to which it was believed the Emperor did not attach any serious importance. Count Severin's proposal was adopted, notwithstanding the opposition of the Procurator-General (Minister of Justice), which was supposed to be feigned in order to give more appearance of reality to the little scene which it was believed had been got up for the occasion. Count Strogonoff, who was deputed with two other senators to take the representations of the Senate to the Emperor, readily set out on his mission; but the deputation was received by Alexander very coldly, and Strogonoff, disconcerted and not knowing what to say, withdrew. The Emperor sharply reprimanded the Senate, ordered it not to meddle with things which did not concern it, and directed it by a new decree to carry out the very ukase against which it had appealed. To my great astonishment that it was Novosiltzoff who was the agent of the Emperor's move of the Senate in the direction of liberalism sufficed to discourage people whose generous aspirations were not, it must be admitted, very strong. The Senate did not again attempt any independent action, and its rights became a dead letter. At my first interview with the Emperor after this incident, I could not help smiling at his extreme alarm in presence of the new attitude of the Senate. My jocular remarks on this point were ill received by Alexander, and I believed they left in his mind a certain anxiety as to my liberal tendencies which afterwards came back to him. This was an indication of Alexander's true character, which then appeared to me in a novel and unfortunately too real light. Grand ideas of the general good, generous sentiments, and the desire to sacrifice to them part of the Imperial authority, and resign an immense and arbitrary power in order the better to secure the future happiness of the people, had really occupied the Emperor's mind and did so still, but they were rather a young man's fancies than a grown man's decided will. The Emperor liked forms of liberty as he liked the theatre; it gave him pleasure and flattered his vanity to see the appearances of free government in his Empire; but all he wanted in this respect was forms and appearances; he did not expect them to become realities. In a word, he would willingly have agreed that every man should be free, on the condition that he should voluntarily do only what the Emperor wished.

Reforms in Practice: Education

The creation of a Ministry of Public Instruction was a remarkable innovation in Russia which was fruitful of great and salutary results, and posterity will owe gratitude both to Alexander and to the young men, then so much criticised, who supported him in his plans and gave them practical shape by dividing into special branches the confused organisation which was then in existence. Nothing could be more wretched or insufficient than public instruction in Russia up to the reign of Alexander. There was an Academy of Science at St. Petersburg which owed its only celebrity to the presence of some learned men whom the Government had brought to the Russian capital from abroad. Euler came when he was already an old man, and died there soon after. The transactions of this Academy were for the most part written in the French and German languages; it had no relations whatever with the country, and exercised no influence on its progress. At Moscow there was a university which was equally isolated, and was attended by not more than a hundred students maintained at the expense of the Government. The only other educational establishments in Russia proper were the so-called "National Schools." The teaching in these schools was bad and extremely meagre; the teachers were poor wretches whom idleness and *ennui* had rendered drunkards, and no respectable person sent his children to them. The establishment of the Ministry of Public Instruction completely changed all this. The existing universities of Moscow, Wilna, and Dorpat were better endowed, and three new ones were created—those of St. Petersburg, Kharkoff, and Kazan,—each forming an educational centre for a prescribed district, in which it directed all the educational arrangements. The University of Wilna was exclusively Polish, and during the next few years the whole of Russian Poland was covered with schools in which Polish feeling freely developed itself. This University, to which I appointed the most distinguished literary and scientific men of the country, and some eminent professors from abroad, directed the movement with admirable zeal and intelligence, and its consequences, which the Russians afterwards deeply regretted, seemed at that time to flow naturally from the Emperor's generous intentions with regard to the Poles. The University of Kazan was to look after the instruction of the Tartars and of Siberia generally. Each university had its curator, and the curators formed a council of public instruction, the President of which was the Minister. The persons appointed to these posts by the Emperor were such as to give a hope that the work of public instruction would be pushed forward with zeal and success. General Klinger, commandant of one of the cadet corps, was appointed curator of Dorpat. He was a distinguished German author, with liberal opinions which might almost be called utopian, although he had been in the service of the greatest despots; his intentions, however, were good, and he was full of zeal for the advancement of science and instruction. His eccentric and dreamy views were expressed with a German bluntness which gave him an appearance of frankness and energy, and all this had gained him Alexander's favour. Count Severin Potocki was appointed Curator of the University of Kharkoff, which was the centre of a district the inhabitants of which were strongly desirous of obtaining the means of instruction. Count Severin, as a Pole, had been treated with great consideration by Alexander when he was Grand-Duke; he had been admitted, like my brother and myself, into his familiar circle, and was one of his most enthusiastic admirers. The Emperor appointed him not only curator of Kharkoff, but also senator of the third department of the Senate, which issued decisions on appeals against measures taken by the administrations of the Polish provinces. Count Severin obtained some celebrity in Russia as a senator and in his capacity of curator he showed zeal and perseverance.

The universities which were most progressive were Wilna, Dorpat, and Kharkoff. The nobility of Livonia, Esthonia, and Courland did not look with favour upon the University of Dorpat, which had declared itself the protector of the peasants and the bourgeoisie. One of the professors of this university was named Parot; he was a worthy man who expressed boundless attachment to the Emperor Alexander, and was very anxious about his health. Once Madame Parot sent a waistcoat, woven by herself, which she said would preserve the Emperor's life. Parot begged him to wear it, and by such manifestations of affection he gained Alexander's favour, and had private conferences with him during his frequent journeys to St. Petersburg. The Curator of Moscow was M. de Mouravieff, one of the gentlemen formerly attached to Alexander's service when he was Grand-Duke, and also his former secretary. He was a worthy man, but excessively timid and quite devoid of energy. The Emperor appointed him assistant to the Minister of Instruction in order that it should not be said that young men only performed the duties of assistant, and that these posts were created only for the members of the Secret Council. Novosiltzoff was appointed Curator of St. Petersburg. As there was already in that capital a faculty of medicine dependent on the Ministry of the Interior, and a faculty of law could not be established before the commission for the revision of the laws had terminated its labours, Novosiltzoff for the present confined himself to establishing a faculty of philosophy, with the special object of training professors of the exact sciences, of administration, and of literature. This faculty began brilliantly by turning out some distinguished pupils, but they did not afterwards realize the hopes that had been formed of them, and the institution perished without leaving any durable results. A university with privileges and endowments would have better maintained itself, as was shown by the universities of Moscow and Kharkoff, which, though they declined, were still active in the midst of the indifference and oblivion by which they were long surrounded.

The Napoleonic Invasion

Alexander I bought time by the Treaties of Tilsit of 1807. That time ran out when on the 23d of June, 1812, Napoleon led his army of 600,000 troops across the River Nieman into Russia. Two days later, Alexander issued to his army the propaganda appeal which is printed below. The source is: General Sir Robert Wilson (H. Randolph, Ed.), *Narrative of Events during The Invasion of Russia by Napoleon Bonaparte, and the Retreat of the French Army, 1812.* London, 1860. Pp. 23–24. Sir Robert was the official British military observer attached to the Russian armies at the time of the invasion.

Proclamation to the Army

Wilna, the 25th of June, 1812. We had long observed on the part of the Emperor of the French the most hostile proceedings towards Russia, but we had always hoped to avert them by conciliatory and pacific measures. At length, experiencing a continued renewal of direct and evident aggression, notwithstanding our earnest desire to maintain tranquillity, we were compelled to complete and assemble our armies. But even then we flattered ourselves that a reconciliation might be effected while we remained on the frontiers of our empire and, without violating one principle of peace, were prepared only to act in our own defence: all these conciliatory and pacific measures could not preserve the tranquillity which we desired. The Emperor of the French, by suddenly attacking our army at Kowno, has been the first to declare war. As nothing, therefore, could inspire him with those friendly sentiments which possessed our bosoms, we have no choice but to oppose our forces to those of the enemy, invoking the aid of the Almighty, the witness and the defender of the truth. It is unnecessary for me to recall to the minds of the generals, the officers, or the soldiers, their duty and their bravery. The blood of the valiant Slavonians flows in their veins. Warriors! you defend your religion, your country, and your liberty! I am with you. God is against the aggressor.

> Within a month after the start of the Napoleonic invasion, Alexander found it necessary to issue a general appeal to his subjects and a special call to the city of Moscow. These examples of early nineteenth-century war propaganda are from: Wilson, *Narrative,* pp. 46–50.

First Proclamation

To the Nation. The enemy has passed the frontiers, and carried his arms into the interior of Russia. Since perfidy cannot destroy an empire which has existed with a dignity always increasing for so many generations, he has determined to attack it by violence, and to assault the empire of the Czars with the forces of the continent of Europe.

With treason in the heart and loyalty on the lips, he flatters the ears of the credulous and enchains their arms; and if the captive perceives fetters under the flowers, the spirit of domination discovers itself; and he calls forth war to assure the work of treason! But Russia has penetrated his views. The path of loyalty is open to her: she has invoked the protection of God; she opposes to the plots of her enemy an army strong in courage, and eager to drive from her territory this race of locusts who consume the earth, and whom the earth will reject, finding them too heavy a burden to sustain.

We call our sufficient armies to annihilate the enemy. Our soldiers who are under arms are like lions who dart on their prey; but we do not disguise from our faithful subjects that the intrepid courage of our warriors actually under arms needs to be supported by an interior line of troops. The means ought to be proportioned to the object; and the object placed before you is to overthrow the tyrant who wishes to overthrow all the earth.

We have called on our ancient city of Moscow, the first capital of our empire, to make final efforts, and she is accustomed to make them, by sending her sons to the succour of the empire. After her, we call on all our subjects of Europe and Asia to unite themselves for the cause of humanity! We call on all our civil and religious communities to co-operate with us by a general rising against the universal tyrant.

Wherever in this empire he turns his steps he will be assured of finding our native subjects laughing at his frauds, scorning his flattery and his falsehoods, trampling on his gold with the indignation of offended virtue, and paralyzing, by the feeling of true honour, his legions of slaves. In every noble Russian he will find a Pojarskoi, in every ecclesiastic a Palistyn, in every peasant a Minin.

Nobles! you have been in all ages the defenders of our country! Holy Synod! and you members of your Church! you have in all circumstances by your intercession called down upon our empire the Divine protection! Russian people! intrepid posterity of Slavonians! it is not the first time that you have plucked out the teeth from the head of the lion, who sprung on you as upon a prey, and met his own destruction! Unite yourselves! carry the cross in your hearts and the sword in your hands, and human force never can prevail against you.

I have delegated the organization of the new levies to the nobles of every province; and I have charged with the care of assembling the brave patriots who will present themselves of their own accord for the defence of the country the gentlemen amongst whom the officers will be chosen. The number of those who will be assembled ought to be sent to Moscow, where they will be made acquainted with the commander-in-chief.

Given at our camp of Polotzk, the 18th of July, 1812.

(Signed) ALEXANDER.

Second Proclamation

To our ancient City and Capital of Moscow. The enemy, with a perfidy without parallel, and with forces, equal to his immeasurable ambition, has passed the frontiers of Russia. His design is to ruin our country. The Russian armies burn with desire to throw themselves upon his battalions and to punish by their destruction this perfidious invasion; but our paternal regard for our faithful subjects will not permit us to allow so desperate a sacrifice. We cannot suffer that our brave soldiers should immolate themselves thus upon the altar of this Moloch! We are ready to contend with him in the open field, man against man in equal combat, he for his ambition, we for our country.

Fully informed of the bad intentions of our enemy and of the great means he has prepared for the execution of his projects, we do not hesitate to declare to our people the danger of the empire; and to call on them to destroy, by their patriotic efforts, the advantages that the aggressor hopes to draw from our present inferiority in number.

Necessity commands the gathering of new forces in the interior, to support those which are in the presence of the enemy, determined to perish or to form a barrier between him and the liberty of our country. To assemble these new armies, we address ourselves to the ancient capital of our ancestors—to the city of Moscow! She was always the sovereign seat of all the Russias, and the first in every moment of public danger to send forth from her bosom her courageous children to defend the honour of the empire. As the blood flows invariably towards the heart of heroes to recall valour to their energetic souls, the children of our country also from the surrounding provinces spring towards her, seeking in her breast the lessons of courage, with which they ought to defend their children on the material bosom and save the tombs of their fathers from a sacrilegious violation!

The existence of your name in the list of nations is threatened—the enemy announces the destruction of Russia!

The safety of our holy Church and the throne of the Czars, the independence of the ancient Muscovite empire, all loudly proclaim that the object of the appeal will be received by our faithful subjects as a sacred law.

We will not delay to appear in the midst of our faithful people of Moscow, and from this centre we will visit the other portions of our empire to advise upon and direct the armaments.

May the hearts of our nobles and of the other orders of the state, propagate the spirit of this holy war that is blessed by God, and fight under the banners of this holy Church! may the filial zeal extend from Moscow to the extremities of our dominions! The nation then, assembled round its monarch, may defy the thousand legions of the perfidious aggressor; then the evils which he has prepared for you will recoil on his own head; and Europe, delivered from slavery, will hail the name of Russia.

Camp of Polotzk, the 18th of July, 1812.

(Signed) ALEXANDER.

> Despite Alexander's exhortations, things did not go well with the Russian armies which proved themselves unable to beat back the Napoleonic drive. The Russian army was all but broken at Borodino and shortly thereafter Napoleon entered Moscow. Here is Alexander's proclamation after that event. The source is: Wilson, *Narrative,* pp. 191–194.

Proclamation

The enemy entered Moscow the 15th of September.

It might be expected that consternation should be general at this news, but let us disdain a pusillanimous despondency. Let us swear rather to redouble our perseverance and our courage; let us hope that, whilst combating in a cause so just as ours, we may direct upon the heads of our enemy the calamities he is heaping up for our destruction. Moscow, it is true, is in their hands, but our army is not disgraced or dispersed. The General-in-chief has yielded to a necessity, but only to reunite with advancing forces, and then to snatch from the enemy his ephemeral triumph.

We know and feel how grieved all the hearts of the faithful Russians will be at the desolation of our provinces and the ancient capital of the empire, but the enemy occupies only its ramparts. Deserted by its inhabitants—stripped of its treasures—it resembles no more a peopled city, but a vast tomb, in which the merciless invader may erect his throne.

This haughty destroyer of kingdoms on entering Moscow flattered himself that he was the arbiter of our destinies, and might dictate peace at his will; but his presumption is already foiled: he has found in Moscow not only no aid for his domination, but not even the means of subsistence.

Our forces augment every day. They occupy all the roads, and destroy all the detachments of the enemy in search of food:

He will soon be convinced of the fatal error which led him to consider the possession of Moscow as the subjection of the empire; and famine will compel him to attempt an escape through a country of which our intrepid warriors with closed roads will bar the passage.

Look at the condition of this enemy: he entered Russia at the head of more than three hundred thousand men, but how is that force composed?

Is there any national unity in this multitude?

No! the different nations who march under his standards do not serve him from attachment or patriotism, but servile fear.

Already the disorganising effect of his principle of fusion is apparent.

Half the army is destroyed by Russian valour, by desertion, by want of discipline, by sickness and hunger!

The pride of the conqueror is doubtless increased by the apparent success of his enterprise, but the "end crowns the work."

Through the whole course of his invasion he has not found a spot where a Russian from terror has fallen at his feet.

Russia is attached to the paternal throne of her Sovereign, who extends over her the guardian arm of his affection.

She is not accustomed to the yoke of oppression. She will not endure a foreign domination. She will not surrender the treasurers of her laws, her religion, and independence. She is ready to shed the last drop of her blood in their defence. This sentiment is ardent and universal.

It has manifested itself by the prompt and voluntary organisation of the people under the banner of patriotism! Under such an ægis, where can there be any ground for a disgraceful fear? Can there be a man in the empire so base as to despair, when vengeance is the rallying word of the state?—when the enemy, deprived of all resources, sees his numbers daily diminishing, and a powerful nation environing him, with an army in his front and rear intercepting his supplies and retreat?

Can a true Russian feel alarm? Has Spain not broken her chains, and menaced the integrity of the French empire? Does not the greatest portion of Europe, degraded and plundered by the ruler of France, serve him with a reluctant heart, and turn an impatient regard on us for the signal of general deliverance?

Does not France herself sigh for the termination of a sanguinary war, in which she has been involved by a boundless ambition?

Does not an oppressed world look to us for example and encouragement, and can we shrink from such an honourable mission as is confided to us? No; let us rather kiss the hand that has selected us to act as the leaders of nations in the struggle for independence and virtue.

Too long has humanity been afflicted by the calamities of war, and the cruelties of this horrible ambition; but we will brave it, for our freedom and the interests of mankind.

We will enjoy the noble sentiment of a good action; immortal honour shall be the recompense of a nation enduring all the ills of a savage war, and contending with courage and constancy to obtain a durable peace, not only for herself, but for those unhappy countries which the tyrant is now forcing to fight in his quarrel.

It is glorious—it is worthy a great people to render good for ill.

Almighty God! is the cause for which we are battling not just? Cast an eye of compassion on our holy church. Preserve to this people its courage and constancy. Suffer it to triumph over its adversary and Thine. May it be in Thy hand the instrument of his destruction—and in delivering itself, redeem the freedom and independence of nations and kings.

(Signed) ALEXANDER.

> General Sir Robert Wilson did not fall into the error, which entrapped many Western military experts in 1940–1941, of underestimating the Russian army. Here is a portion of one of his confidential reports to Earl Cathcart, written late in August, 1812, when everything seemed to be going against the Russians. The source is: Wilson, *Narrative*, pp. 385–386. Abridged.

The Russian Army

I have had occasion to ascertain that great improvements have been made in the Russian commissariat department, and that the medical department is also in rapid progress to a respectable system; but I have seen with regret that the interior economy of this army is still very distant from necessary method and order.

The columns of march, notwithstanding General Barclay's commands and, I may add, example—considering his station, are still encumbered with immense numbers of private carriages: and I verily believe several thousand Cossacks are employed in the service of officers.

The duties of our divisionary assistant Quartermasters-general are not known, or never performed.

No ground is ever previously reconnoitered by the junior staff, no roads examined, no reports made of the local conveniences or inconveniences of the proposed post, camp, or quarters.

The pioneers' duty is equally neglected. No bridges are ever repaired to anticipate the necessity; no additional passages are made over the numerous little marshy rivulets that intersect the road, so that the line of march unnecessarily extends for miles, is frequently interrupted for hours, confusion daily prevails, and ruin would ensue if the enemy were enterprising.

I have seen moments when one thousand five hundred daring men would have accomplished that which Buonaparte, with one hundred and fifty thousand, will not achieve when the Russian army is arrayed in order of battle.

I have mentioned to your Lordship that the Russian ammunition-waggons were not calculated to descend hilly ground without great delay and much risk.

General Kutaisow, who commands the artillery, has now, however, accepted my suggestion, and I am to order, at the St. Petersburg arsenal, staples to fix on the shafts, and straps to connect the breechings with that support.

Without this arrangement, the top of the collar affords the only resistance, for there is no breast-strap to connect the lower part of the collar with the belly-bands; consequently, as the horse leans back, the collar flies forward and upward to the end of the shafts.

It is true that iron shoes, to lock or fix the wheels, ought to have been with each waggon, but these have been long broken away; and if they remained, the driver must always have dismounted to set and to unloosen them.

I have also General Kutaisow's request to procure dragropes, after the English fashion, for the guns. At the present the Russians use cords that wound the hands and afford no purchase.

I have been thus particular in making your Lordship acquainted with the result of my observations and my impressions, that your Lordship may be enabled to form an opinion of the character and temper of the force which is engaged in this awful contest. Its excellences are manifold, and its means are equal to final success. Its defects and imperfections are of a nature to be corrected as soon as qualified persons are charged with the superintendence of its interior arrangements.

> It is fitting that this series should end on a note of triumph. By January, 1813, Napoleon had been routed and his troops driven from Russian soil. Two days before he led his victorious army across the western frontier to pursue the French across Europe, Alexander issued the following order to his soldiers. The source is: Wilson, *Narrative,* pp. 368–369.

Victory Proclamation

Merecz, 13th Jan., 1813. Soldiers, The year has ended—a year for ever memorable and glorious—one in which you have trampled in the dust the pride of the insolent aggressor.

The year has passed, but your heroic deeds survive.

Time will not efface their trace. They are present to your contemporaries—they will live with their posterity.

You have purchased at the price of your blood the deliverance of your country from the hostile powers leagued against its independence.

You have acquired rights to the gratitude of Russia, and to the admiration of mankind. You have proved by your fidelity, your valour, and your perseverance, that when hearts are filled with the love of God, and devotion to their Sovereign, the efforts of the most formidable enemies resemble the furious waves of the ocean, which break in impotent lashings against indestructible rocks, and leave behind only confused sounds.

Soldiers! desirous of distinguishing all those who have participated in these immortal exploits, I have ordered medals of silver to be struck, which have been blessed by our holy Church. They bear the date of the memorable year 1812: suspended to a blue ribbon, they will decorate the warrior breasts which have served as bucklers of the country.

Each individual of the Russian army is worthy to bear this honourable recompense of valour and constancy.

You have all shared the same fatigues and dangers; you have had but one heart, one mind; you will all be proud to wear the same distinction; it will proclaim every where that you are the faithful children of Russia,—children on whom God the Father will pour his benedictions.

Your enemies will tremble on seeing these decorations: They will know that under these medals hearts are beating, animated with unconquerable valour, and imperishable, because it is not based upon ambition or impiety, but on the immutable foundation of patriotism and religion.

(Signed) ALEXANDER.

Alexander's Mysticism

During the latter part of his reign, Alexander I was much attracted to and influenced by religious mysticism. The following brief quotation from the Manifesto which he issued on the conclusion of the Peace of Paris in 1814 is illustrative of this aspect of the man. The source is: Paul LaCroix, *Histoire de la vie et du regne de Nicolas Ier Empereur de Russe*. Three volumes. Paris, 1864–1866. Vol. 1, pp. 82–83.

Thus the All Powerful has put an end to our unhappiness, has illuminated our country in the eyes of future generations, and has granted the wishes of our heart. In addressing to heaven fervent and respectful prayers of thanks to the Author of all good, we order that solemn thanksgiving shall be returned throughout the length and breadth of our empire. We are convinced that Russia, on her knees before the throne of the Eternal One, will pour out tears of joy.

The Problem of Succession

Tsarevich and heir-presumptive to Alexander I was his brother Constantine Pavlovich. But Constantine, who long served as governor of Warsaw, divorced his wife and married a woman not of royal blood. The divorce and re-marriage were with the consent of Alexander, but imperial law prohibited children of this second union from inheriting the throne. At least partly because of this, Constantine determined to renounce the throne for himself. Alexander agreed to the renunciation and in a secret manifesto named his brother Nicholas Pavlovich as his successor. Because this arrangement was not published, considerable confusion arose when Alexander I died in 1825. It was precisely this situation which made possible the Decembrist Rising.

The following selections set forth the pertinent letters and other documents in the case. They are arranged in chronological order. The source is: LaCroix, *Histoire*, vol. 1, pp. 238–239, 239–240, 244–247, 326–327, 328–329, 346, 363, 395–399, 401–402.

CONSTANTINE TO ALEXANDER. Encouraged by all the proofs of the infinitely sympathetic disposition of your Imperial Majesty toward me I dare once more lay at your feet, Sire, a most humble prayer.

Not finding in myself the genius, the talents, nor the force necessary to be elevated to the Sovereign dignity to which I would have the right by my birth, I beg your Imperial Majesty to transfer this right to whom it would come after me, and thus to assure forever, the security of the empire. As to me, I will add by this renunciation a new guarantee and a new force to the engagement which I have voluntarily and solemnly contracted on the occasion of my divorce from my first wife.

All the circumstances of my own situation, bearing more and more upon this measure, prove to the Empire and to the entire world the sincerity of my sentiments.

Deign, Sire, to accept with good will my prayer; help me secure the consent of our Imperial Mother to this plan and sanction it with your Imperial assent.

In the sphere of private life, I shall pledge myself always to serve as an example to your faithful subjects, and to all those who are animated by a love for our dear country.

I am with a profound respect for your Majesty.

> Your most faithful subject and brother
> Constantine Tsarevich
>
> St. Petersburg,
> 14/26 January, 1822.

ALEXANDER'S REPLY. Very dear brother: I have read your letter with all the attention that it merited. Having always fully appreciated the high sentiments of your heart, I found nothing in your letter to make me change my judgment. It has given me a new proof of your sincere attachment to the Empire, and of your solicitude for its continued tranquility.

In accordance with your desire I presented your letter to our beloved Mother; she has read it with the same recognition of the noble motives which guided you. Having taken into consideration the reason which you set forth, we both agree that you should be given full liberty to follow your immutable resolution, and we pray the All Powerful to bless the consequence of a purpose so pure.

I am ever your affectionate brother,

> Alexander
> St. Petersburg,
> 2/14 February, 1822.

MANIFESTO OF ALEXANDER I ON THE SUCCESSION. By the grace of God, we, Alexander I, Emperor and Autocrat of all The Russias, etc., etc., etc., make it known to our faithful subjects:

From the moment of our coming to the throne of all the Russias, we have constantly realized that it was our duty toward all powerful God not only to guarantee and increase during our life, the happiness of our country and our people, but also to prepare for and to assure their security and their good fortune after us by a clear and precise designation of our successor according to the laws of our Imperial House and the interests of the Empire. We could not name him immediately as our predecessors had done, but waited in the hope that it would perhaps please Providence to give to us an heir to the throne in a direct line. But as the years have gone on, it has more and more seemed to us our duty to place our throne in such a position that it will not remain vacant even momentarily.

While we bear this solitude in our heart, our well beloved brother, the Tsarevich and Grand Duke Constantine, obeying only the impulse of his own free will, has addressed to us the demand that we transfer his right to the sovereign dignity, a position to which he would one day be elevated by his birth, to the head of some person who might possess this right after him. He showed at the same time his intentions to give a new force to the additional act relative to the succession of the throne which was promulgated by us in 1820, an act voluntarily and solemnly recognized by him insofar as that act was of concern to him.

We are profoundly touched by the sacrifice which our well beloved brother has believed that he ought to make in his own interests for the consolidation of the fundamental laws of our Imperial House, and the ineffable tranquility of the Empire of all the Russias. Having invoked the aid of God, having seriously reflected upon a subject as dear to our heart as it is important for the Empire, and finding that the statutes which exist on the order of the succession to the throne do not deprive those who have the right, of the power to renounce it, since in this special circumstance it does not present any difficulty in the order of hereditary succession to the throne, we have with the consent of our distinguished Mother, in turn the supreme head of the Imperial family to which we belong, and by the absolute power which we hold from God Himself, have ordered and shall order:

First, the voluntary act by which our brother, the Tsarevich and Grand Duke Constantine, renounces his rights to the throne of all the Russias shall be irrevocable. The said act of renunciation shall be, in order to insure its being known, preserved in the Cathedral of the Assumption in Moscow and in the three high Courts of our empire, in the Holy Synod, in the Council of the Empire, and in the Directing Senate. Secondly, following the strict provision of the statute on the succession to the throne, be it known that our successor shall be our second brother, the Grand Duke Nicholas.

In consequence, we have the well founded hope that on the day when it shall please the King of Kings to recall us, following the common law of all mortals, from our temporal reign to eternity, the properly constituted authorities of the Empire to whom we have made known our irrevocable wish in this matter will hasten to swear submission and fidelity to the em-

peror whom we have just designated as heir to the invisible crown of the
Empire of all the Russias, of the Kingdom of Poland, and of the Grand
Duchy of Finland. As to us, we ask all our faithful subjects, that, with the
same sentiment of affection with which we have considered our first responsibility on earth to be the care given to their constant prosperity, they
address fervent prayers to our Lord Jesus Christ that He might deign, in
His infinite sympathy, to receive our soul in His eternal kingdom.

Given at Tsarskoe-selo, the sixteenth of August [O.S.] year of Grace
1823 and of our reign the 23rd.

Alexander.

CONSTANTINE TO THE EMPRESS MOTHER. Very gracious Sovereign and
Beloved Mother; It is with the deepest affliction of the heart that I have received at 7 o'clock in the evening . . . the news of the decease of our beloved Sovereign and my benefactor the Emperor Alexander. . . .

The position in which this unhappiness places me imposes upon me the
duty of spreading before your Imperial Majesty with complete frankness
my true sentiments on this essential point.

Your Imperial Majesty is not unaware that following only my own impulse I asked the Emperor Alexander of glorious memory, for the authority
to renounce my right to the succession to the throne, and that I received in
consequence an Imperial autograph rescript, dated the second/fourteenth
of February, 1822, and of which I send here a copy, by which the Emperor
gave his absolute assent to this demand, adding that your Imperial Majesty
would be also advised, and that he himself would confirm it in conversation.

The absolute orders of the Emperor were that the supreme rescript mentioned above would stay in my hands under a secret seal until the death of
his Majesty.

. . . I consider it an obligation to cede my right to the throne, in accordance with the dispositions of the Act of the Empire on the order of
succession in the Imperial family, to his Imperial Highness, the Grand
Duke Nicholas and to his heirs.

It is with the same frankness that I feel it my duty to declare that, not
having changed my mind, I should esteem myself very happy if, after more
than thirty years of service consecrated to the Emperors, my brother and
my father of glorious memory, it should be permitted to me to continue
these services to his Majesty, the Emperor Nicholas, with the same deep
veneration, with the same burning zeal which has animated me on all
occasions, and which shall move me until the end of my days.

After having expressed my sentiments which are as true as they are
irrevocable, I place myself at the feet of your Imperial Majesty, and very
humbly beg the honor of a gracious acceptance of the present letter, and
ask that you will notify him [Nicholas] of that part of it which pertains to
him in order that it may be placed into execution with all the force and all
the will of his Imperial Majesty, my deceased Sovereign and benefactor, as

well as with the assent of your Imperial Majesty. I am taking the liberty of submitting herewith a copy of the letter which I have addressed simultaneously with this to his Majesty, the Emperor Nicholas.

I am with the deepest veneration, very gracious Sovereign and very much beloved Mother,

> Your humble and most submissive son
> Constantine,
> Warsaw, 25 November/7 December, 1825.

CONSTANTINE TO NICHOLAS. Very dear brother: It is with an inexpressible affliction that I received at 7 o'clock in the evening the unhappy news of the death of our beloved Sovereign, of my benefactor, the Emperor Alexander.

. . . it is my duty to inform you that I have simultaneously addressed to Her Imperial Majesty, our well-beloved mother, a letter announcing to her my irrevocable resolution to cede to you my rights of succession to the Imperial Throne of All the Russias. [This action is taken] by authority of an autograph rescript which I received from the Emperor on 2 [14] February, 1822 in answer to a letter which I had written him renouncing my succession to the Imperial Throne. This letter had been shown to our mother and had been accepted by her—a fact she herself deigned to confer to me.

After this declaration, I regard it as a sacred duty to beg very humbly of your Imperial Majesty, that you would deign to accept from me first, my oath of royalty and fidelity, and permit me to expose to you that I have not raised my wishes to any new dignity or any new title—that I desire only to save that of tsarevich with which I have been honored for my services to our father.

My unique good fortune will always be that your Imperial Majesty deigns to accept the assurances of my most profound veneration and of my devotion without limit, sentiments of which I offer as a pledge more than 30 years in the faithful and zealous service, to their Majesties the Emperors, my brother and my father, of glorious memory. It is with the same sentiments that I shall not cease to the end of my days, to serve your Imperial Majesty and his descendants in my function and my proper place.

I am with the most profound veneration, Sire, of your Imperial Majesty, the most faithful subject,

> Constantine
> Warsaw, 25 November/7 December 1825

NICHOLAS TO CONSTANTINE. My Dear Constantine: I bow before my sovereign, after having pronounced together with those persons who found themselves before me, the oath which is due him. . . . In the name of heaven do not abandon us, and do not desert us!

Your brother and your faithful subject in life and in death,

> Nicholas
> 27 November/9 December 1825

CONSTANTINE TO NICHOLAS. Your Aid de camp, my dear Nicholas, has just given me your letter. I have read it with the most vivid chagrin. My decision sanctified by him who was my benefactor and my Sovereign, is irrevocable. I am not able to accept your proposal to hasten my departure for St. Petersburg, and I warn you that I shall leave Warsaw only to retire to some greater distance, if everything is not arranged following the will of our deceased Emperor.

> Your faithful brother and sincere friend,
> Constantine
> Warsaw, 6/18 December

EDICT OF NICHOLAS. By the grace of God, we, Nicholas, Emperor and Autocrat of all the Russias, etc. make known to all our faithful subjects:

In the affliction of our heart, in the middle of the general sadness which surrounds us, we, our Imperial house and our dear country, humiliate ourselves before the impenetrable decrees of the Most High, it is from Him alone that we seek our strength and our consolations. He has just called to Him the Emperor Alexander I, of glorious memory, and we have all lost a father and a sovereign, who for twenty-five years has worked for the well-being of Russia and us. . . .

In consequence of all these acts [the change in succession], and after the fundamental law of the Empire on the order of succession, with a heart full of respect for the impenetrable decrees of Providence who leads us, We ascended the throne of our ancestors, the throne of the empire of all the Russians, and those of the kingdom of Poland and the Grand Duchy of Finland which are inseparable, and we order:

1. That the oath of fidelity be taken to us and to our heir, His Imperial Highness Alexander, our well beloved son;

2. That the epoch of our accession to the throne shall be dated from the 19th November 1825 [O.S.] . . .

Given in our imperial residence of St. Petersburg, the 12th/24th of December in the years of grace, 1825 and of our reign the first.

> Nicholas

Karamzin's History

Editor, novelist, poet, and, lastly, historian—that was the literary career of N. M. Karamzin. Appointed historiographer in 1803, Karamzin brought out the first volume of his eight-volume *History of the Russian Empire* in 1815. The brief excerpt which follows emphasizes, not unfairly, Karamzin's strong nationalism. An adviser to both Alexander I and Nicholas I, Karamzin believed firmly in the autocracy. He also believed with equal firmness that an autocrat had obligations to act, not out of personal whim, but for the good of the state. The source is: Wiener, *Anthology,* vol. 2, pp. 39–40.

. . . The Greeks and the Romans may captivate our imagination: they belong to the family of the human race and are no strangers to us in their virtues and in their weaknesses, in their glory and in their calamities; but the name of a Russian has a special attraction for us: my heart beats more strongly for Pozharski than for Themistocles or Scipio. Universal history by its great recollections embellishes the world in our eyes, but Russian history embellishes our country in which we live and feel. How attractive are to us the banks of the Volkhov, Dnieper, Don, when we know what has taken place upon them in remote antiquity! . . . The shadows of bygone centuries everywhere draw pictures before us.

Outside of their special value for us, sons of Russia, its annals have universal interest. Let us cast a glance at this unique Empire: thought staggers! Rome in all her majesty . . . could never equal it. Is it not wonderful how a land that is disrupted by eternal barriers of Nature, by immeasurable deserts and impenetrable forests, by cold and hot climates, how Astrakhan and Lapland, Siberia and Bessarabia, could have formed one empire with Moscow? And is that mixture of its inhabitants less wonderful, that composite and heterogeneous mass of varying degrees of civilisation? Like America, Russia has its savages; like other countries of Europe, it displays the fruits of a protracted civil existence. One need not be a Russian, one need only think, in order to read with curiosity the traditions of a nation that by daring and courage has obtained the dominion over the ninth part of the world, has discovered countries, heretofore unknown, has entered them in the universal system of geography and history, and has enlightened them through God-sent faith, without violence, without atrocities practiced by the other devotees of Christianity in Europe and America, but merely by dint of good example.

"Who Lives Happily in Russia?"

The astringent satire of the poet N. A. Nekrasov forms an interesting contrast to the cloying sentimentalities of Karamzin. Nekrasov belongs to another generation, both literally and figuratively speaking. Though he began to write during the reign of Nicholas I, and was for a time editor of *The Contemporary*, his most productive years were in the reign of Alexander II. The lines below are reprinted from his poem, "Who Lives Happily in Russia?" The source is: Wiener, *Anthology*, vol. 2, pp. 353–359, *passim*.

What year it was,—you figure out!
What land it was,—you guess yourself!
Upon a level country road
Were gathered seven muzhiks:
They all had masters whom they served
In the Government of Strained-too-hard,
The county called Enduring-much
The district Fallowlandedness,

In villages hard by:
In Patchedupville and Raggedtown,
In Emptyville and Freezingtown,
In Burnedupville, and Hungerville,
And in Cropfailingthorpe;

They met and quarrelled straight away:
"Who lives in Russia happily
And to his heart's content?"
Roman declared—"The landowner,"
Demyan declared—"The bureaucrat,"
Luka declared—"The Priest."
"The merchant with his goodly paunch,"
The Gubin brothers both declared,
Ivan and Mirotdor.
But old Pakhom looked gloomily
Upon the ground, and said at last:
"The gentleman of noble birth,
"The minister of the Emperor,"
While Prov declared: "The Tsar."

. . .

Beside the road, right in the wood,
The peasants sat them down. . . .
The vodka came in proper time;
There also somehow came some food,—
A feast for the muzhiks!
Three glasses each man had to drink;
They ate,—and quarrelled once again:
Who lives in Russia happily
And to his heart's content?

. . .

Nicholas and Repression

Liberal historians have often referred to the reign of Nicholas I as "the period of outward repression and inner liberation." The repression was exemplified by the notorious Third Section of His Majesty's Own Chancery and by the censorship. This description of the repression under Nicholas was written by the great Czech scholar and statesman, Thomas G. Masaryk. The source is: T. G. Masaryk, *The Spirit of Russia.* Two volumes. New York: Macmillan and Co., 1919. Vol. 1, pp. 106–109, 111–113.

In this sketch it would be difficult to give an adequate idea of the abominable stupidity and provocative brutality that characterised reaction under Nicholas. For the utterance of liberal ideas conflicting with the official

program, leading men were simply declared insane. This happened to Čaadaev (Chadayev) and to a number of officers inclined towards revolutionary notions. In one case Nicholas had the death announced of a certain
Engelhardt whose sentence had in reality been commuted to imprisonment
for life; his wife was compelled to wear mourning; and the very number of
his grave in the churchyard was entered in the records. When the poet
Ševčenko (Tsevchenko) and his associates were sentenced in 1847 as
members of the slavophil Cyrillo-Methodian Union, the tsar aggravated
the punishment in the case of Ševčenko, to whom the use of writing materials was denied. In his diary the poet complains that while the pagan
Augustus permitted Ovid to write, this indulgence was forbidden to himself
by the Christian ruler. Not merely was the tsar chief officer of police, but
in his own exalted person he revised the sentences of the courts. In the year
1837 two Jews were condemned to death in Odessa because, from fear of
the plague, they had attempted to escape across the frontier. Nicholas
commuted the death penalty as follows: "The convicts are to run the
gauntlet—a thousand men—twelve times. God be thanked, with us the
death penalty has abolished, and I will not reintroduce it." This is but one
among numerous instances of the theocratic sovereign's power of self-
deception and of his cruelty—for who had proposed that the decabrists
(Men of December or Dekabristi) should be quartered and who had commuted their punishment to hanging? In the year 1838 a student gave the
director of the surgical academy a box on the ear. He was sentenced to run
the gauntlet—five hundred men—three times. Nicholas revised the sentence thus: "To be carried out in the presence of all the students of the
academy. Subsequently the offender, instead of being sent to Siberia, is to
spend ten years, wearing fetters, in the disciplinary battalion at Kronstadt."
It is hardly necessary to add that though there was no capital punishment,
the men thus sentenced died under the blows of the soldiers.

The severities of Nicholas were hardly credible. The wives of the decabrists who followed their husbands to Siberia were not permitted to return
to Russia after the death of these; those among the decabrists who lived
on into the reign of Alexander II received amnesty from that ruler. Only to
one like Nicholas was it possible to have sane men declared insane, or to
inflict upon Dostoevskii the tortures of a death sentence.

Here is an additional contribution to the psychology, perhaps it would
be better to say the psychopathology, of Tsar Nicholas. A young man
wrote a satire upon contemporary student life. The work was circulated in
manuscript, and a copy fell into the hands of the emperor, who was especially incensed at the strictures upon the church and political institutions.
He sent for the author and compelled him to read the composition aloud to
himself and the minister for education. After a severe reprimand, wherein
the writing was stigmatised as a product of decabrist sentiment, Nicholas
kissed his victim upon the forehead and dismissed him with the sentence
that he was to serve at the front, the minister's advocacy averting a worse
issue. The tsar granted the offender the privilege of writing to his sover-

eign in order to recount progress on the right path. He availed himself of
this privilege to beg for pardon, or at least for a mitigation of punishment,
but his petitions were disregarded, and his biographers tell us how the unhappy man was tantalized, how in his despair he took to drink, and how
finally he died of consumption, at the age of two and thirty years. We learn
from Poležaev's verses what the age of Nicholas seemed to reflective minds.

Reforms, properly speaking, were unknown in the reign of Nicholas.
Much was done to safeguard order, and especial attention was devoted to
the army. Under the guidance of Speranskii, legislation was codified in
1833, a new criminal code was issued (1845), and the ministry of the state
domains was founded (1837). In 1839, in order to promote the efficiency
of centralisation, the village replaced the volost as the administrative unit.

I must not omit to mention that under Nicholas the use of the rod in
punishment was abolished, the lash taking its place (1845). Humani-
tarian considerations, however, were not solely determinative, for those
chastised with the rod were no longer fit for military service.

Some of the changes introduced in this reign were beneficial. For example, educational reform was forced upon the Jews, and thereby some of
the Jews had opened to them the path to general culture.

Naturally, the reaction under Nicholas was based upon the state church,
just as happened in Austria and Prussia, and quite in accordance with the
teachings of de Maistre, de Bonald, Görres, Gentz, and the various other
theorists of the antirevolutionary restoration and reaction.

All independent thought was to be inexorably suppressed; higher education was to be reduced to the minimum of essential knowledge; philosophy and literature, attempts at general culture and at the attainment of
a philosophic outlook upon the universe, were to be stifled in the germ.
Count Uvarov, minister for education from 1833 to 1849, addressing the
governing committees of the schools, announced his advent to office in the
following terms: "It is our joint task to secure that the culture of the nation
shall be carried on in the unified spirit of Orthodoxy, autocracy and
patriotism." Yet more thoroughly did Uvarov, in the course of the same
year, formulate this trinitarian doctrine as "the main principle of the social
system of education," writing as follows: "Amid the rapid decay of religious
and civil institutions in Europe, amid the widespread diffusion of revolutionary ideas, it becomes our duty to establish the foundations of the fatherland so firmly that they cannot be shaken. We must find a basis from
which right conduct can spring; we must discover energies which will develop the distinctive characteristics of Russia, and will ultimately enable
our country to assemble the sacred heritage of nationality into a compact
whole, to which we must anchor our salvation. How fortunate is it that
Russia has preserved ardent faith in those saving principles in default of
which right conduct is impossible, without which an energetic and worthy
life is unknown. A Russian devoted to his fatherland is as little willing to
permit the subtraction of a single dogma from our Orthodox faith as he
would be to allow the theft of a pearl from the crown of Monomachus.

Autocracy is the main condition of Russia's political existence. In conformity with these two national bases is the third basis, equally important and equally strong—patriotism.". . .

Hardly had Nicholas become tsar when he abolished the chair of philosophy at Moscow university. Driving past the university on one occasion, looking very serious, he pointed to the building and said, "There is the wolf's den." The less developed universities were dealt with in accordance with this estimate. A fuller activity had begun at the universities during the liberal epoch of Alexander I, with the issue of the studies' ordinance of 1804, although even then the police outlook towards these institutions was not abandoned. In 1835 Uvarov reorganised the universities in conformity with his general program, making the study of theology and ecclesiastical history obligatory in all faculties. In 1850, owing to the alarm inspired by the revolution of 1848, certain disciplines, and notably the study of European constitutional law, were banished from the university as deleterious; whilst philosophy was reduced to courses upon logic and psychology which had in future to be delivered by theologians, the pretext given for the change being "the blameworthy development of this science by German professors." The historian Granovskii was not permitted to lecture on the Reformation. The number of students was restricted to three hundred. The object of universities was announced to be, "the education of loyal sons for the Orthodox church, of loyal subjects for the tsar, and of good and useful citizens for the fatherland." Not until the days of Alexander II were these and other reactionary measures abrogated. Nevertheless, even during the reign of Nicholas one new university was founded, at Kiev in 1833, for these "wolves' dens" were indispensable to the civil administration and the army.

Reform of the higher schools (1847) was effected in conformity with the restrictions imposed on the universities. The study of classical tongues was discontinued lest youth should be corrupted by the reading of Greek authors who had written in republics. In this connection we may refer to a European example of the same way of thinking. Napoleon III held the like view of Greek authors, and Nicholas might have appealed to the French emperor for support. But reaction in Russia works and thinks from day to day only. In 1854 classical studies were partially reintroduced, the idea being that Greek and Latin fathers of the church would inspire refractory youths with due veneration for the official program.

The history of recent Russian literature is filled with stories of the oppression which great writers had to suffer under Alexander and still more under Nicholas. The work of Griboedov, Puškin, Lermontov, and Gogol was hindered in every possible way. Banishment was a frequent penalty. Books were mutilated by the censorship. Newspapers were suppressed, among them an opposition journal edited by Ryléev and Marlinskii, and entitled "Poljarnaja Zvězda" (Polar Star, a name chosen later by Herzen for his organ). In the "Moskovskii Telegraf," Polevoi adopted an opposition standpoint from 1825 onwards, and was able to continue his journalistic advocacy of liberal ideas down to 1834, but this "Revue des décabristes" was in the end suppressed by Uvarov. I record, not in jest but in earnest, that this minister for education and president of the Academy of Sciences expressed a strong desire that Russian literature should cease to exist. Almost all notable authors suffered during the reign of Nicholas. I have previously referred to Čaadaev and Ševčenko. Bělinskii was unable to print his first drama. Puškin was informed of the tsar's exalted disapproval.

Puškin's aristocratic inclinations led him astray not infrequently, and he experienced a shortsighted pleasure when Polevoi's newspaper was suppressed, for he regarded the Moscow journalist as "unduly jacobin." Polevoi was one of the non-aristocratic *raznocinčy* (unclassed, plebian). In 1845 the tsar seriously thought of having obstacles imposed to the entry of the *raznocinčy* into the higher schools.

The events of 1848 caused intense anxiety to Nicholas, and a regular witches' sabbath of reaction was inaugurated. The members of the Petraševcy group (the two Dostoevskiis, Pleščeev, Durov, etc.) were all prosecuted; measures were taken against Saltykov; Ostrovskii, Turgenev, Kirěevskii, Homjakov, and Herzen, successively fell into disfavour— Turgenev's offence being an obituary notice of Gogol! It was forbidden to mention the very name of Bělinskii, and those who wished to refer to him had to employ circumlocutions!

Censorship was developed to an almost incredible extent. There were twenty-two distinct censorships. Criticism of the government and of official proceedings was absolutely prohibited. Even those who at a later date were considered pillars of reaction, even such men as Bulgarin, were now suspect as revolutionaries; Pogodin suffered the same fate; to the ultra-reactionaries, Uvarov actually seemed insufficiently reactionary, and he had to resign his position as minister for education. Upon a ministerial report which included the word "progress," Nicholas wrote the comment, "Progress? What progress? This word must be deleted from official terminology.". . .

Kireevski's Slavophilism

Ivan Kireevski (1806–1856) is generally considered to have been the first proponent of Russian Slavophilism. Returning to Russia after an education in Western Europe which left an enduring imprint on him, Kireevski became enamoured with the myths of Russia's unique past and particular mission. He and his followers developed an expanded, nineteenth-century version of the "Theory of the Third Rome." T. G. Masaryk, in his famous book, *The Spirit of Russia,* gave the following summary of Kireevski's views. Extreme as these may seem, it should be noted that Kireevski was both less hostile to the West and less doctrinaire than were most later Slavophils. The source is: Masaryk, *Spirit,* vol. 2, pp. 242–243.

In its intimate nature Russia differs from Europe. The contrast between the two civilisations is determined by religious and ecclesiastical differences.

It is the contrast between faith, and knowledge inimical to faith; between tradition and criticism; between eastern Orthodoxy, on the one hand, and Roman Catholicism and predominantly German Protestantism, on the other. Orthodoxy is for Russia the buckler of revealed religion; the Orthodox creed is the mystical expression of absolute and divinely revealed religious truth. European Catholicism, and above all Protestantism, made an unfortunate attempt to show that divine revelation was in conformity with reason, the net result of this rationalism being to destroy the faith of the western church and to divide the human spirit against itself. Culture, too, as based upon the faith and upon the church, differs in Russia and in Europe. The dominant philosophy of Russia is that of the Greek fathers of the church, but in Europe scholasticism and the essentially Protestant philosophy which sprung from scholasticism have been the mainsprings of culture. For this reason Russian art has its peculiar characteristics, for to it beauty and truth are one, whereas in Europe the conception of abstract beauty leads to visionary untruths.

The Russian state has grown organically out of the commune, the mir; the European state originated through armed occupations and the subjugation of foreign peoples. Moreover, modern parliamentarism with its majority rule is merely the continuation of the materialist principle of government.

Russian law, too, has developed organically out of the convictions of the people, whereas European law, imposed by the Roman conquerors, finds its climax in outward legalism and in the formalism of the letter.

Above all, therefore, the relationship of state to church differs in Russia and in Europe. The Russian state is entirely distinct from the church, the former having none but secular tasks to fulfil. The European state is merged into the church; the church usurps power over temporal affairs and neglects spiritual affairs. "Holy Russia" does not signify what the politically Holy Roman Empire had signified; Holy Russia is a treasure house for relics.

In Russia property is communal (the mir), for the individual has a value as such; in Europe the individual is valueless, for the meaning of European private property is that the human being is adscript to the soil— it is the soil which has value, not the individual.

In Russia, consequently, the family has an entirely different constitution from that which obtains in Europe. The Russian family is patriarchal; by the ties of blood its members are associated to form a moral unity from which have originated by organic growth the commune and ultimately the state with its patriarchal ruler. The European family is individualistic and therefore egoistic; it leads to the emancipation of women and children.

Russian life is simple, but Europe seeks luxury and comfort. Political economy is the science of the life of material enjoyments.

The Russian finds genuine civilisation, Old Russian, Slavic, prepetrine civilisation, upon the land; its sustainer is the peasant, the muzik, the community at large. The European has his modern civilisation, whose focus is in the town, and whose sustainer is the bourgeois. Bourgeois industrialism dominates social life; bourgeois philanthropy is essentially the outcome of egoistic calculation.

The fruits of these differing outlooks and activities are likewise fundamentally diverse. The Russian is spiritually unified; though he never fails to be aware of his imperfections, his conscience gives him repose and satisfaction. The European has a conviction that he is perfect, and yet has no feeling of happiness or satisfaction, for his spiritual nature is utterly disunited, and he is plunged into scepticism and unbelief; but without faith it is impossible to live.

The "Literary Circles"

> The "outer repression" of Nicholas' reign compelled the tiny group of liberal and radical intelligentsia to resort to the stratagem of "circles." These were small, rather informal groups which met ostensibly to discuss literary matters, such meetings being precariously permissible under "the Nicholas system." The discussions did deal with literature, but soon moved from literary to philosophical subjects and thence to politics. The groups took themselves very seriously, and so did the secret police who kept them under surveillance, often disrupted their meetings, and usually broke up the "circles" by sending the participants into exile.
>
> Alexander Herzen, who was himself exiled for his part in one of the circles, left a description of the institution. The Sungarov to whom Herzen refers was a government official, N. P. Sungarov, who founded a secret circle whose members thought of themselves as followers of the Decembrists. The circle was broken up by the police in the early 1830's. Sungarov was sentenced to hard labor; the other members were either exiled or kept under police surveillance. Nicholas Vladimirovich Stankevich organized and led a circle at Moscow University. Herzen once described Stankevich as "Hegel's first disciple in the Moscow circle . . . one of the idle people who accomplished nothing . . . sickly in constitution and gentle in character, a poet and a dreamer." He died in Italy in 1840.
>
> The excerpt is from: Alexander Herzen, *Selected Philosophical Works*. Moscow, 1956. Pp. 536–541.

We have spoken many times of the stagnation that followed the crisis of 1825. The moral level of society sank, development was interrupted, everything progressive and energetic was effaced. Those who remained— frightened, weak, distracted—were petty and shallow; the worthless generation of Alexander occupied the foremost place. As time went on they changed into cringing officials, lost the savage poetry of revelry and aristocratic ways together with every shadow of independent dignity; they served assiduously, they made the grade, but they never became high dignitaries in the full sense of the word. Their day was over.

Under this great world of society, the great world of the people main-

tained an indifferent silence; nothing was changed for them—their plight
was bad, indeed, but not worse than before—the new blows were not intended for their scourged backs. *Their time had not yet come.* It was
between this roof and this foundation that our children were the first to
raise their heads—perhaps because they did not suspect how dangerous it
was; anyway, by means of these children, Russia, stunned and stupefied,
began to come to life again.

What impressed them was the complete contradiction of the *words* they
were taught with the *realities* of life around them. Their teachers, their
books, their university spoke one language which was intelligible to heart
and mind. Their father and mother, their relations, and all their surroundings spoke other things with which neither mind nor heart was in agreement, but with which the powers that be and pecuniary interests were in
accord. Nowhere did this contradiction between education and real life
reach such proportions as mong the nobility of Russia. The uncouth German student with his round cap covering a seventh part of his head, with
his world-shaking sallies, is far nearer to the German *Spiessbürger* than is
supposed, while the French *collégien,* thin with vanity and emulation is
already *en herbe l'homme raisonnable, qui exploite sa position.*

The number of educated people amongst us has always been extremely
small; but those who were educated have always received an education,
not perhaps very thorough, but fairly general and humane: it humanized
them all. But a *human* being was just what the bureaucratic hierarchy or
the successful maintenance of the landowning regime did not require. The
young man had either to dehumanize himself—and the greater number
did so—or to stop short and ask himself: "But is it absolutely essential to
go into the service? Is it really a good thing to be a landowner?" After that
for some, the weaker and more impatient, there followed the idle existence
of a cornet on the retired list, the sloth of the country, the dressing-gown,
eccentricities, cards, wine, etc.; for others a time of ordeal and inner
travail. They could not live in complete moral disharmony, nor could they
be satisfied with a negative attitude of withdrawal; awakened thought demanded an outlet. The various solutions of these questions, all equally
harrassing for the young generation, determined their distribution into
various circles.

Thus, for instance, our little circle was formed in the university and
found Sungurov's circle already in existence. His, like ours, was concerned
rather with politics than with learning. Stankevich's circle, which came
into existence at the same time, was equally near and equally remote from
both. It followed another path, and its interests were purely theoretical.

Between 1830 and 1840 our convictions were too youthful, too ardent
and passionate, not to be exclusive. We could feel a cold respect for
Stankevich's circle, but we could not come into closer contact with it. They
traced philosophical systems, were absorbed in self-analysis, and found
peace in a luxurious pantheism from which Christianity was not excluded.
The stuff of our dreams was woven out of ways of organizing a new league
in Russia on the pattern of the Decembrists and we looked upon knowl-

edge as merely a means. The government did its best to strengthen us in
our revolutionary tendencies.

In 1834 the whole of Sungurov's circle was sent into exile and—
vanished.

In 1835 we were exiled. Five years later we came back, hardened by
our experience. The dreams of youth had become the irrevocable determination of maturity. That was the heyday of Stankevich's circle. Stankevich
himself I did not find in Moscow—he was in Germany; but it was just at
that moment that Belinsky's articles were beginning to attract universal
attention.

On our return we measured our strength with them. The battle was an
unequal one for both sides; origins, weapons, and language—all were
different. After fruitless skirmishes we saw that it was our turn now to
undertake serious study and we too set to work upon Hegel and the German philosophy. When we had made a sufficient study of it, it became
evident that there was no ground for dispute between us and Stankevich's
circle.

The latter was inevitably bound to break up. It had done its bit—and
had done it most brilliantly; its influence on the whole of literature and
academic teaching was immense—one need but recall the names of
Belinsky and Granovsky; Koltsov was formed in it; Botkin, Katkov, and
others belonged to it. But it could not remain an exclusive circle without
lapsing into German doctrinairism—men who were alive and Russian had
no leanings that way.

In addition to Stankevich's circle, there was another one, formed during our exile, and, like us, it was at swords' points with Stankevich's circle;
its members were afterwards called Slavophils. The Slavophils approached
the vital questions which occupied us from the opposite side, and were far
more absorbed in practical work and real conflict than Stankevich's circle.

It was natural that Stankevich's society should split up between them
and us. The Aksakovs and Samarin joined the Slavophils, that is, Khomyakov and the Kireyevskys. Belinsky and Bakunin went over to us. Stankevich's closest friend, one most kindred to his spirit, Granovsky, was one
of us from the day he came back from Germany.

If Stankevich had lived, his circle would nonetheless have broken up.
He would himself have gone over to Khomyakov or to us.

By 1842 the sifting in accordance with natural affinity had long been
over, and our camp stood in battle array face to face with the Slavophils.
Of that conflict we will speak elsewhere.

In conclusion I will add a few words concerning those elements of
which Stankevich's circle was composed; that will throw some light on the
strange underground currents which were silently undermining the strong
crust of the Russo-German regime.

Stankevich was the son of a wealthy Voronezh landowner, and was at
first brought up in all the ease and freedom of a landowner's life in the
country; then he was sent to the Ostrogozhsk school (and that was something quite original). For fine natures a wealthy and even aristocratic edu-

cation is very good. Comfort gives unbound freedom and scope for growth and development of every sort, it saves the young mind from premature anxiety and apprehension of the future, and provides complete freedom to pursue the subjects to which it is drawn.

Stankevich's development was broad and harmonious; his artistic, musical, and at the same time reflective and contemplative nature showed itself from the very beginning of his university career. It was to his artistic temperament that Stankevich owed his special faculty, not only of deep and warm understanding, but also of reconciling, or as the Germans say "transcending" contradictions. The craving for harmony, proportion, and enjoyment makes Germans indulgent as to the means; to avoid seeing the well they cover it over with canvas. The canvas will not withstand any pressure, but the yawning gulf does not trouble the eye. In this way the Germans reached pantheistic quietism and there they rested tranquilly. But such a gifted Russian as Stankevich could not have remained "tranquil" for long.

This is evident from the first question which involuntarily troubled Stankevich immediately after he left the university.

His university studies were finished, he was left to himself, he was no longer led by others; *he did not know what he was to do.* There was nothing to go on with, there was no one and nothing around that could appeal to a live mind. A youth, taking stock of his surroundings and having had time to look about him after school, found himself in the Russia of those days as a lonely traveller might awakening in the steppe; you may go where you will—there are tracks to follow, there are bones of those who had perished, there are wild beasts and the emptiness on all sides with its dull menace of danger—it is easy to perish and impossible to struggle. The only thing one can do honestly and enjoy doing it is study.

And so Stankevich persevered in the pursuit of learning. He imagined that it was his vocation to be an historian, and he took to Herodotus; as was to be expected nothing came of that.

He would have liked to be in Petersburg in which there was so much of *new* activity and to which he was attracted by the theatre and its nearness to Europe; he would have liked also to be an honorary superintendent of the school at Ostrogozhsk. He resolved to be of use in that "modest office"—but that proved to be even less of a success than his study of Herodotus. He was in reality drawn to Moscow, to Germany, to his own university circle, to his own interests. He could not exist without kindred spirits around him (another proof that there were at hand no interests congenial to him). The craving for sympathy was so strong in Stankevich that he sometimes invented intellectual sympathy and talents and saw and admired in people qualities which they completely lacked.

But—and in this lay his personal power—he did not often need to have recourse to such fictions—at every step he did meet people worthy of admiration, he *knew how* to meet them, and every one to whom he opened his heart remained his passionate friend for life; to everyone Stankevich's influence meant either an immense benefit or an alleviation of his burden.

Herzen's Self-Exile

> After a period of imprisonment, followed by exile to Perm and Vyatka, Herzen returned to Moscow and resumed his place among the radical intelligentsia. Inheriting a large fortune on the death of his father, Herzen became a voluntary exile, living in Italy, France, and England. The letter below, written from Paris in 1849, is his explanation to his friends of why he left Russia to live in Western Europe. The source is: Herzen, *Selected Philosophical Works,* pp. 340–347.

Our separation will continue for a long time, perhaps for ever. At the present moment I do not wish to return, and I do not know whether I will have a chance to do so later. You have been expecting me and I am in duty bound to explain the situation. If I owe anyone at all an explanation for my absence, or for my conduct, it is, of course, to you, my friends.

An insurmountable repugnance and a strong inner voice, a prophetic voice, forbids me from crossing the borders of Russia, particularly now when the monarchy, exasperated and frightened by all that is going on in Europe, redoubles its fury in suppressing every intellectual movement, and brutally curtains off sixty million people from mankind liberating itself, barring out with its black, iron hand, covered with Polish blood, the last ray of light faintly illuminating a small number of them. No, my friends, I cannot cross the boundary of this kingdom of darkness, arbitrariness, silent torpor, secret murders, gagged torture. I shall wait until the power, weary with fruitless efforts and enfeebled by the resistance it has provoked, recognizes *something* in the Russian individual worthy of respect.

Please, don't misunderstand me: it is not pleasure or diversion, nor even personal safety that I have found here. Indeed, I do not know who could, today in Europe, find either pleasure or diversion; diversion during earthquakes, pleasure during a desperate struggle. You could sense the sorrow in every line of my letters; life here is very difficult. Venomous hatred is intermingled with love; gall with tears; a feverish agitation saps the whole organism. The time of illusions and hopes is over. There is nothing here in which I believe save a handful of people, a few ideas and the fact that the movement cannot be stopped. I see the inevitable downfall of the old Europe and regret nothing that exists, neither the heights attained by her education, nor her institutions. There is nothing in this world that I love more than that which it chastises, nothing that I respect more than that which it executes and yet I stay here only to suffer doubly —from my own grief and from its grief and to perish, perhaps, at its downfall and ruin towards which it is rushing headlong.

Why then do I stay here?

I stay because that struggle is going on *here.* Here, in spite of the blood and tears, social problems are being worked out; and painful and burning as the suffering here is, it is articulate. The struggle is open and above-

board. No one hides. Woe betide the vanquished but at least they will
have given battle. They are not gagged before they have had their say. The
tyranny is great but the protest is thundering; the warriors are often sent
to the galleys, chained hand and foot—but with head upraised and their
right to free speech not denied them. Where the world has not been lost,
the cause has not yet been lost. It is this open struggle, this free speech
that keeps me here. For its sake I am willing to sacrifice everything. I give
up you, my friends, part of my fortune and, perhaps, my very life to march
in the ranks of the vigorous minority "persecuted, but invincible."

It is for this free word that I have broken, or rather, for time, loosened my blood ties with the people in whom I found such rich response
to all that is light and dark in my heart, whose tongue and songs are my
tongue and songs, and I stay in a country where only the bitter cry of the
proletariat and the desperate bravery of its friends arouse my deep sympathy.

This decision has cost me dear. You know me—and will believe me. I
have stifled my heartache. My heart has been torn by the struggle, and I
have made my decision not as a hotheaded youth but as a man who has
long reflected over the step taken, weighing all that he loses. It took me
many months of hesitation and deliberation to arrive at a decision and I
have finally decided to sacrifice everything

To human dignity,
To free speech.

I cannot let myself be influenced by consideration of the consequences.
They lie beyond my power. They depend rather on the power of autocratic caprice which goes to the lengths of its arbitrary compass which has
traced not only our words, but our steps as well. It lay, however, within
my power not to obey, and I did not.

To go against one's convictions when it can be avoided is immoral.
Passive submission now becomes almost impossible. I have witnessed two
revolutions. I have too long been a free man to suffer myself again to be
enchained. I have lived through popular movements and have grown accustomed to free speech. Am I again to become a serf? Never, not even
for the sake of suffering together with you! If it were necessary to prevail
over myself for the sake of a common cause, I might have found the
strength. But where is this common cause of ours at the moment? There,
at home, you have no ground on which a free man can stand. So how can
you call me back? To a struggle—I gladly agree! But to martyrdom, to
futile silence, to submission—under no circumstances! Ask anything you
like of me, but don't ask me to be double-faced; don't compel me to act
the loyal subject. Respect in me the liberty of the individual.

Personal freedom is a magnificent thing; *by it and by it alone* can a
nation achieve its true freedom. Man must respect and honour his freedom in himself no less than in his neighbour or in the people at large. If
you are convinced of this then you will agree that it is my right and my
duty to remain here; that it constitutes the only way in which an individual

in our country can voice his protest; that it is the sacrifice he must make for the sake of human dignity. But if you will qualify my staying here as desertion, and forgive me only because you love me, that will mean that you have not yet completely liberated yourselves.

I am well aware what objection may be raised from the point of view of sentimental patriotism and civic affectation; but I cannot accept these superannuated views. I have outgrown them. I have extricated myself from them and it is precisely against them that I am fighting. This rehash of Roman and Christian reminiscences interfere most of all with the establishment of true conceptions of freedom—conceptions that are sound, clear and mature. Fortunately customs and long evolution in Europe compensate for some of the absurd theories and absurd laws. People here live on soil fertilized by two civilizations; the path, trodden by their ancestors in the course of two and a half thousand years, was not futile, and much that is human has sprung up in spite of externalities and the official system.

In the worst days of European history we find some respect for the individual and a certain recognition of his independence, certain rights conceded to talent, to genius. Vile as the German Government of those days was, Spinoza was not exiled. Lessing was not flogged nor forced into the army. In this respect shown not only to sheer physical force, but to moral force as well, in this involuntary recognition of the individual lies one of the greatest humanistic principles of life in Europe.

Europe never regarded its citizens residing abroad as criminals or anyone emigrating to America as a traitor.

Not so in our country. The individual at home ever oppressed and neglected has never made as much as an attempt to get a hearing. Free expression of opinion at home was always regarded as an insolence; independence as sedition. The individual was absorbed in the state; was dissolved in the commune. The revolution effected by Peter I replaced the antiquated landlord rule of Russia by the European bureaucratic system. Everything that could be transferred from the Swedish and German codes was; everything that could be transplanted from Holland, a land of free municipalities, to an autocratic government of rural communes was borrowed. But the unwritten, moral restraints on the government, the instinctive recognition of the rights of individuals, the right of thought, of truth, could not be transplanted and were not. Slavery in Russia increased with education; the state grew, improved, but the individual in no way profited by the process. Indeed, the stronger the state grew, the weaker did he become. The European forms of administration and of the judiciary, military and civil organization have developed into a monstrous, hopeless despotism. If Russia were not so vast and that borrowed system of government had not been built so haphazardly and amorphously, one could then say without exaggeration that not a soul with any sense of personal dignity could have remained in Russia.

Corrupted by the complete absence of resistance, power went on occasions to outrageous lengths, unparalleled in the history of any other country. You know the extent of it from stories about Emperor Paul, a poet of his craft. Discard the capricious, the fantastic in Paul and you will see that he is by no means original and the principles inspiring him are exactly those to be found not only in all the tsars but in every governor, police inspector or landlord. All fourteen ranks of the famous bureaucratic hierarchy are becoming ever more drunk with the certainty of their own immunity. Every act of power, every relation of a superior to a subordinate is a flagrant exhibition of gross insolence, of the humiliating certainty that the individual will stand for anything: the recruitment repeated for three times, the law on foreign passports, flogging in the school for engineers. Thus Little Russia accepted serfdom in the eighteenth century; thus all Russia, finally, believed that people could be sold and resold without a question, without even being asked by anybody on what legal grounds all this was done, not even by those who were being sold. The government at home is more self-assured and unrestrained than it is in Turkey or in Persia. There is nothing to restrict it, no traditions of the past: for it has disowned its own past, and has no concern for that of Europe. It has no respect for its people, knows nothing of the general culture of mankind, and battles against the present. Hitherto, at least, the government was ashamed of its neighbours and looked up to them; now it sets itself up as an example to all oppressors and aspires to be their mentor.

We saw the worst possible period of the imperial regime. We grew up under terror, under the black wings of the secret police, and were mutilated by hopeless oppression. We have barely survived. But is that not too little? Has the time not come to loosen our hands and tongue for activity which would serve as an example? Has the time not come to awaken the slumbering consciousness of the peoples? And surely it is impossible to awaken it by whispering, or remote allusions, when shouting and blunt words are barely audible? Open, frank acts are required: December 14 made so violent an impression on young Russia precisely because it took place in St. Isaac's Square. But now not only the square, but the written word, or the lecturer's chair have all grown impossible in Russia. An individual working in secrecy or his protest from afar is all that is now left open to us.

I stay here not only because I find it repugnant to allow myself to be pinioned on crossing the borders, but also in order to work. I cannot live with folded arms anywhere; here I have no other work but that of *our cause*.

He who has, for more than twenty years, nurtured in his breast a single thought, suffered for it and lived for it; he who has wandered from prison to prison, from one place of exile to another, who owes to this thought the finest moments of his life, the most inspiring meetings, will not abandon it. Nor will he make it dependent on external factors and the degree of longitude and latitude. Quite the other way round. Here I am more useful. Here I am your uncensored speech, your free press, your chance representative.

All this seems new and unusual only to us; actually it has had many precedents. In all countries, faithful and active people used to emigrate at the beginning of a revolution, when thought was still feeble and the material power unbridled: their free words came from afar and this fact in itself lent their words weight and authority, for behind the words you could see the self-sacrificing deeds. The force of their words grew with the distance, as does the impetus of a stone, dropped from a high tower. Emigration is the first symptom of the approaching revolution.

Besides, Russians abroad have one more task to fulfil. It is indeed time to acquaint Europe with Russia. Europe does not know us; she knows our government, our façade and nothing more; conditions are extremely propitious for accomplishing this. It would not become Europe to drape herself majestically in the robes of disdainful ignorance. *Das vornehme Ignorieren* of Russia would not become Europe now that she has felt the despotism of the petit bourgeoisie and the Algerian Cossacks, now that she has been kept in a state of siege from the Danube to the Atlantic Ocean, and her prisons and galleys have been filled with people persecuted for their convictions. Let Europe become more closely acquainted with a nation whose youthful strength she felt in battles even though she eventually emerged the victor; let us tell Europe of this mighty and still enigmatic people which has so unobtrusively formed a country of sixty million and has grown so strong and tremendously large without departing from the principle of communal organization, and was the first to preserve it through the various stages of state development; about a people which, in some astonishing way, was able to come out intact from under the yoke of the Mongolian hordes and of German bureaucrats, from under the disciplinary stick of the corporal of the barracks and from under the degrading whip of the Tatars, a people which retained its fine character, clear mind and vigorous nature in spite of the oppression of serfdom, and which responded to the tsar's edict to promote education within a century with the genius of Pushkin. Let the Europeans become acquainted with their neighbour; they only fear him. It would be well for them to know what they fear.

Hitherto we have been unpardonably modest and conscious of our enslaved condition. We were apt to forget all that was good, full of hope and promise in the life of our people. We waited for a German in order to introduce ourselves to Europe. Is that not a disgrace?

Will I have the time to accomplish something? I don't know—I hope so!

Farewell, my friends, for long—give me your hands and your help. I need both the one and the other. And then, who knows? So much has happened in recent times! Perhaps that day when we shall gather as of old in Moscow and clink our glasses unafraid "To Russia and blessed liberty," *is not so far off* as it seems.

My heart refuses to believe that that day will not come; it is wrung at the thought of eternal separation, at the thought that I shall not see those streets which I paced so often full of my youthful dreams, those houses which are so interwoven with my memories, our Russian villages, our

peasants whom I missed so much at the southernmost part of Italy. . . .
No, it cannot be. But what if it is so? Then I bequeath my toast to my
children. Dying in an alien land, I shall preserve my faith in the future of
the Russian people, and bless it from my place of voluntary exile!

Vissarion Grigoreyevich Belinsky

V. G. Belinsky (1811–1848) was perhaps the outstanding literary critic
of nineteenth-century Russia. Certainly, he was a giant among the in-
telligentsia of Nicholas' reign, and his influence and inspiration long
outlived him. Here are two descriptions of Belinsky by fellow intel-
lectuals, Herzen and Nicholas Gavrilovich Chernishevsky. Herzen
and Belinsky were contemporaries; Chernishevsky was almost half a
generation younger. Herzen's description, which appears first below,
was originally published in 1855 in *Polyarnya Zvezda* (*North Star, or
Pole Star*), a journal which he published in London. Its emphasis is
upon the man. Chernishevsky's description, which emphasizes Belinsky's ideas and work, was first published in 1856 in *Sovremennik*
(*The Contemporary*), a literary journal which owed most of its fame
to Chernishevsky's contributions to it as writer and editor. The sources
are, respectively: Alexander Herzen, *Selected Philosophical Works*,
pp. 527–530; and N. G. Chernyshevsky, *Selected Philosophical Essays*.
Moscow, 1953. Pp. 493–499, *passim*.

Belinsky's essays were awaited with feverish impatience by the younger
generation of Petersburg and Moscow beginning with the 25th of every
month. Half a dozen times the students would drop in at the Coffee house
to ask whether the *Otechestvenniye Zapiski* [Fatherland Notes] had
been received; the heavy volume was snatched from hand to hand. "Is
there an article by Belinsky?" And if there was, it was devoured with
feverish interest, with laughter, with disputes . . . and three or four cults
or *reputations* were no more.

Skobelev, the governor of the Fortress of Peter and Paul, might well say
in jest to Belinsky when he met him in Nevsky Prospect: "When are you
coming to us? I have a nice warm little cell all ready reserved for you."

I have spoken in another book of Belinsky's development and of his
literary activity; here I will only say a few words about the man himself.

Belinsky was very shy and quite lost his head in an unfamiliar or very
large company; he knew this and did the most absurd things to try and
conceal it. K. once persuaded him to go to visit a lady; as they approached
her house Belinsky became more and more depressed, kept asking whether
they could not go some other day, and pleaded having a headache. K.,
who knew him, would accept no excuse. As soon as they got out of the
sledge on their arrival, Belinsky tried to run off, but K. caught him by the
overcoat and led him to be introduced to the lady.

He sometimes put in an appearance at Prince Odoyevsky's literary
and diplomatic evenings. At these there were crowds of people who had
nothing in common except a certain apprehension of and aversion for each

other: officials from the Embassies and Sakharov, the archaeologist, painters and A. Meyendorf, the economist, several councillors of the cultured sort, Ioakinf Bichurin from Pekin, people who were half-gendarmes and half-literary men, others who were wholly gendarmes and not at all literary men. A. K. was so conspicuous for his silence there that generals took him for an authority. The hostess was secretly distressed by her husband's vulgar tastes, and yielded to them as much as Louis Philippe at the beginning of his reign indulged the tastes of his electors by inviting to the balls at the Tuileries whole *rez-dechaussée* of bracemakers, grocers, shopkeepers, shoemakers, and other worthy citizens.

Belinsky was utterly lost at these parties, between some Saxon ambassador who did not understand a word of Russian and some officer of the Third Department who understood even words that were not uttered. Belinsky usually felt out of sorts for two or three days afterwards and cursed the man who had persuaded him to go.

One Saturday, on New Year's Eve, Odoyevsky took it into his head to mix punch *enpetit comité* after the principal guests had left. Belinsky would certainly have gone away, but he was prevented by a barricade of furniture; he had somehow got stuck in a corner, and there was a little table before him with wine and glasses on it; Zhukovsky in white gold-braided trousers sat in front of him, off to one side. Belinsky suffered patiently for a long time, but, seeing no chance of escape, he began pushing the table quietly; it yielded at first, then lurched over and fell with a bang on the floor, while the bottle of Bordeaux very deliberately emptied its contents over Zhukovsky. He jumped up with the red wine trickling down his trousers; there was a great to-do, a servant rushed up with a napkin to rub the wine over the other parts of the trousers, and another to pick up the broken wineglasses. . . . While this bustle was going on Belinsky disappeared and ran home more dead than alive.

Dear Belinsky! How long he remained upset by such incidents, with what horror he used to recall them, walking up and down the room and shaking his head.

But that shy man, that frail body contained a mighty spirit, the spirit of a gladiator! Yes, he was a powerful fighter! He could not preach or lecture, what he needed was argument. If he was not contradicted, if he was not stirred to irritation, he did not speak well; but when he was touched to the quick, when his cherished convictions were challenged, when the muscles of his cheeks began to quiver and his voice trembled, then he was worth seeing; he pounced upon his opponent like a panther, he tore him to pieces, made him look ridiculous and pitiful, and incidentally developed his own thought, with extraordinary force, with extraordinary poetry. The discussion would often end in blood coming from the sick man's throat; pale, gasping, his eyes fixed on the man with whom he was speaking, he would lift his handkerchief to his mouth with shaking hand, and stop, deeply mortified, crushed by his physical weakness. How I loved and pitied him at those moments!

Worried financially by unscrupulous literary agents, morally fettered by the censorship, surrounded in Petersburg by people little sympathetic to him, and consumed by a disease to which the Baltic climate was fatal, he became more and more irritable. He shunned outsiders, was savagely shy, and sometimes spent weeks together in gloomy inactivity. Then the publishers sent note after note demanding copy, and the enslaved writer, grinding his teeth, took up his pen and wrote those biting articles throbbing with indignation, those indictments which so impressed their readers.

Often, utterly exhausted, he would come to us to rest, and lie on the floor playing with our two-year-old child for hours together. While we were only the three of us things went swimmingly, but if there came a ring at the door, his face began working all over and he would look about him uneasily, searching for his hat; though he often remained out of Slavic weakness. Then a word, an observation that went against his grain would lead to the most curious scenes and disputes. . . .

Once on Passion Week he went to dine with a writer and Lenten dishes were served. "Is it long," he asked, "since you have grown so devout?" "We eat Lenten fare," answered the writer, "simply for the sake of the servants." *"For the sake of the servants?"* said Belinsky, and he turned pale. "For the sake of the servants?" he repeated and rose. "Where are your servants? I'll tell them that they are deceived, any open vice is better and more *humane* than this contempt for the weak and uneducated, this hypocrisy in support of ignorance. And do you imagine that you are free people? You are to be bracketed with all the tsars and priests and slave-owners. Good-bye, I don't eat Lenten fare for the edification of others, I have no *servants!"*

. . .

Belinsky was a vigorous and resolute man; he spoke with great energy and extreme animation, but it would be an absurd mistake to call him, as some have done, a man of immoderate demands and hopes. His demands and hopes both sprang from the needs and circumstances of our activities; therefore, for all their vigour, they were extremely moderate. What interests us here is Russian literature, therefore, it is of literature that we shall speak. Belinsky admired the *Inspector General* and *Dead Souls*. Let us think well and ask: could a man of immoderate desires admire these works? Can it really be that Gogol's sarcasm knows no limits? On the contrary, it is sufficient to recall even Dickens, not to speak of the French writers of the last century, to be forced to admit that Gogol's sarcasm is very modest and restrained. Belinsky wanted our literature to develop, but what were the limits of his demands and hopes? Did he demand that our literature should before our very eyes become as deep and as rich as, say, contemporary French or English literature (although both are far from perfect)? Not at all. He said plainly that at the present time this was impossible and it was no use thinking about it. It was already a good thing, in his opinion, that our literature was beginning to look something like literature. He thought that the progress it was making was very rapid and praiseworthy. This rapidity of our development was a constant source of joy to him, and yet, truth to tell, progress was rather slow: as in 1846, so in 1856, we are still far from the "maturity" towards which we are striving. Yes, Belinsky was a very patient and moderate man. Numerous examples of this can be quoted. They are to be found on every page of his essays. It would also be wrong to imagine that his criticism was too severe; on the contrary, he was very lenient. True, he could not fail to detect flaws, and he expressed his opinions about them without mincing his words; but if a work he was reviewing possessed the least bit of merit, he was ready for the sake of it to excuse all the flaws for which some excuse could be found. It is doubtful whether any of our Russian critics was as tolerant towards other people's opinions as he was. If the convictions concerned were not absolutely absurd and harmful he always spoke of them with respect, no matter how much they differed from his own. Numerous examples of this can be quoted. We shall point to one, which we will have to discuss, viz., his controversy with the Slavophiles, in which he always displayed far more goodwill than his opponents did. He was even gratified by the increase in the number of adherents to this school. (Incidentally, Belinsky was mistaken in thinking so: it has now been revealed that Slavophilism is incapable of attracting followers.) Similarly, he was quite ready to recognize all the merits of literary works that were not written in the spirit which in his opinion most conformed to the requirements of our literature, if only these works possessed positive merits. By way of example we recall his review of Mr. Goncharov's *An Ordinary Story*. We give as an appendix to this essay an excerpt from Belinsky's last review of Russian literature. It will remind the reader that Belinsky did not recognize "pure art" and deemed it the duty of art to serve the interests of life. And yet, in this review he speaks with equal goodwill of Mr. Goncharov's novel, in which he perceives a striving for nothing but so-called pure art, and of another novel, which appeared at about the same time, written in the spirit which Belinsky liked most; if anything, he was even more indulgent towards *An Ordinary Story*. We can also recall the extreme sympathy with which Belinsky always spoke about Pushkin, although he totally disagreed with his conceptions. It is superfluous, however, to quote more examples, for a multitude of them will occur to everybody who has retained a clear recollection of Belinsky's essays.

The opinion that Belinsky was not very moderate in his conceptions, or that he denounced every mode of thought that differed from his own, is totally unjust. Anybody can easily convince himself of this by perusing a few of his essays. There have been quite a considerable number of fanatics in our literature, but far from resembling them in any way, Belinsky always waged a most resolute struggle against them, irrespective of the colour of their fanaticism, or of the party they belonged to. He denounced the fanatics of the so-called "tendency" as sternly as he denounced the fanatics of the opposite school. As an example, it is sufficient to recall how emphatically he expressed his disapproval of the publication in book form of the works of two young poets of that day who sang about how "mankind, weeping tears of blood, will awaken," and about the necessity of "punishing the priests of falsehood."

How could the opinion have arisen that Belinsky was not a man of very moderate opinions about our literature and the problems connected with it, when a perusal of his essays will absolutely convince everybody that his conception of things was exactly the same as that of nearly all right-minded people in our times? Here, much must be attributed to the unfounded accusations levelled against him by his personal enemies whose pride had been hurt by his criticism. They called him an extremist on the same grounds, and with the same lack of justification, as they asserted that he attacked our old writers, when, as a matter of fact, he sought to restore their fame. But the causes that gave rise to the opinion which we regard as unjust cannot be limited to these personal and petty motives.

Belinsky's demands were very moderate, but they were firm and consistent, and were expressed with animation and vigour. Needless to say, the sternest judgment can be covered up with flowery phrases. Belinsky, a man of straightforward and resolute character, disdained such devices. He wrote what he thought, concerned only for truth, and employing precisely the words that most exactly expressed his thoughts. What was bad he bluntly called bad, disdaining to conceal his judgment with diplomatic reservations and ambiguous hints. That is why people to whom every word of truth seems harsh, no matter how moderate it may be, regarded Belinsky's opinions as harsh. This cannot be helped; many people always regard straightforwardness as harshness. But those who understand what they read know very well that Belinsky's desires and hopes were very modest. In general, he demanded nothing beyond what would seem to be absolutely necessary for every man with a developed mind. This explains the strong sympathy accorded him among our public, which, in general, is very moderate in its desires.

It was not Belinsky's habit to yield in debate with his opponents, and there was not a single case of a debate not ending in the utter defeat of his opponent on all points. Not a single literary debate ended without Belinsky's opponent losing the respect of the best part of the public. But it is only necessary to recall what opinions he combated to have to admit that these debates could not have ended otherwise. Belinsky combated only opinions that were positively harmful and utterly mistaken. It is impossible to point to a single case of his taking up the cudgels against opinions that were harmless, or not absurd. Consequently, it was not he but his opponents who were to blame if the debates (usually not started by Belinsky) ended in their utter defeat. Why did they defend opinions that could not and should not have been defended? Why did they protest against obvious truths? Why did they so often strive to carry literary problems into the sphere of law court accusations? All the cases in which Belinsky conducted vigorous debate come under the following definition: Belinsky said that $2 \times 2 = 4$; for this he was accused of being ignorant, of lacking taste, of being disloyal. It was hinted that the paradox he proclaimed—

namely, that $2 \times 2 = 4$—that, for example, Pushkin's works are of higher artistic merit than Derzhavin's, and that *A Hero of Our Time* is superior to *Brynsky Forest* * or *Simeon Kirdyapa* †—that this terrible paradox would have the direst consequences for the Russian language, for our national literature, and that—who can tell!—the whole world was threatened with mortal danger by such unfounded and malicious invention. In repelling such attacks, it could not, of course, be admitted that the attackers had even a particle of truth on their side. Had they chosen something that was doubtful for the object of their indignation, had they observed any one-sidedness or oversight on the part of Belinsky, the debate might have been conducted differently. Whether he agreed or disagreed with his opponents' remarks, he would readily have admitted that what they said was not altogether devoid of common sense, that their opinions were worthy of respect. Whenever he found that he was mistaken, he was the first unhesitatingly to expose the mistake. But what could he do when, for example, one of his opponents expressed indignation at the complete absence of convictions in Belinsky's essays, when that same opponent asserted that Belinsky did not understand the meaning of the words he wrote—later he reiterated that Belinsky was borrowing his conceptions from him (when, in fact, the opposite was the case, as will be obvious to every one who compares the old *Moskvityanin* with the *Otechestvenniye Zapiski*)—when others objected to Belinsky's alleged disrespect towards Derzhavin and Karamzin (whose merits he was the first to appraise), and so forth? Here, with all his readiness to be compliant, he could not fail to see that his opponents' remarks contained not a spark of truth, and he could not possibly refrain from saying that they were utterly mistaken. Such also was the situation when Belinsky started a controversy. Could he refrain from saying that the opinions he challenged were totally devoid of foundation when those opinions were something like the following: Gogol is a writer destitute of talent. The best character in *Dead Souls* is Chichikov's coachman Selifan. Hegelian philosophy was borrowed from Vladimir Monomachus' *Precept*. Writers like Mr. Turgenev and Mr. Grigorovich deserve to be pitied for not taking Russian life for the content of their works. Lermontov was an imitator of Mr. Benediktov and was weak in versification. Dickens' novels are monstrous examples of mediocrity. Pushkin was a bad writer. The greatest poets of our age are Victor Hugo and Mr. Khomyakov. Mr. Solovyov knows nothing of Russian history. The Germans must be exterminated. Chapter VII of *Eugene Onegin* is a slavish imitation of one of the chapters of *Ivan Vyzhigin*.‡ Gogol's best work is his *Evenings on a Farm* (in the opinion of some) or his *Correspondence with Friends* (in the opinion of others), the rest are much feebler. England perished in 1827, or thereabouts, so that not a trace of her existence has remained, just as no trace has remained of Plato's Atlantis. England is the

* One of the historical novels by Zagoskin.—*Ed.*
† A historical novel about fourteenth century Russia by Polevoi.—*Ed.*
‡ A novel by F. Bulgarin.—*Ed.*

only virile state in Western Europe (the opinion of the same writer who discovered that she had perished). The wicked West is decaying and we must as quickly as possible regenerate it with the wisdom of Skovoroda. Byzantium must be our ideal. Education is harmful, and so on and so forth. Can even a particle of truth be found in such opinions? Can any concessions be made to them? Does objecting to them mean displaying intolerance? When a person who imagined he was a scientist and who exercised great influence on a magazine which made a speciality of attacking Belinsky and the *Otechestvenniye Zapiski* took it into his head to assert that Galileo and Newton had turned astronomy on to a false road, was it possible to argue against him in the following strain: "There is much truth in what you say. We must admit that there were errors in our former conceptions of astronomical laws. But while agreeing with you on the main thing, we must say that some of the details of your remarks are not quite clear to us"? To have spoken like that would have meant betraying the obvious truth and making oneself a general laughingstock. Was it possible to speak in such a strain in respect to opinions, samples of which we quoted above, and which, in their way, are no better than the repudiation of Newton's theory? No, here it was impossible to combine denial with compliance, because it was impossible to discover anything resembling the truth in what the opponents had said. With respect to such opinions, no middle course can be taken: either say nothing about them, or say right out, without equivocation, that they totally lack foundation. The attacks on Galileo and Newton could, of course, have been ignored—there was no danger that anybody would be misled by them. The other opinions, however, were not so innocuous—it was necessary to expose their unsoundness. Does the fact that Belinsky could not agree that Gogol was a mediocre writer and that drunken Selifan must be regarded as being representative of the Russian people show that he was intolerant?

The people who took up the cudgels against Belinsky attacked truths that were only too obvious and important. Belinsky attacked only opinions that were positively absurd and pernicious. Being a man of firm convictions and of straightforward character, he expressed his opinions vigorously.

But whoever confuses these qualities with extreme opinions is totally mistaken. On the contrary, Belinsky expressed his opinions with exceptional force precisely because, in essence, they were very moderate.

Belinsky on Nationalism and the Petrine Reforms

Having seen Belinsky through the eyes of Herzen and Chernishevsky, the reader may wish to look for himself, and the next three selections will enable him to do so. The first two, which appear under this subtitle, are excerpts from Belinsky's lengthy review of two multivolume works on Peter the Great. The Soviet editors state that they have restored the review which had been "unmercifully garbled by tsarist censorship deletions" at the time of its original publication in 1841.

The reader will note that although Slavophilism is not explicitly mentioned, Belinsky's remarks constitute an implicit argument against the Slavophil position. The source is: V. G. Belinsky, *Selected Philosophical Works*. Moscow, 1956. Pp. 118–120, 145–147.

Two words are current in the Russian language which have a synonymous meaning: one is the native Russian *narodnost,* the other is a Latin word which we have derived from the French—*nationality*. But we are firmly convinced that there can be no two words in any language so identical in meaning, so perfectly synonymous, that one could be wholly substituted for the other. Still less likely is it that a foreign word should survive in a language which possesses a word of its own expressing the same idea: if not a big difference, there is always at least a shade of difference in their signification. So with the words *narodnost* and *nationality:* they may be synonymous in meaning, but they are certainly not identical, and the difference between them is far greater than nuance. *"Narodnost"* bears the same relation to "nationality" as the species or lower conception to the genus or higher, more general conception. When we speak of *the people* we have in mind the lower strata in the polity, while *nation* betokens the conglomerate body of all social estates and conditions. There may be yet no nation in the *people,* but the nation has a people. The songs of Kirsha Danilov possess *narodnost;* the poetry of Pushkin is national: the former are within reach of the highest (most educated) classes of society as well, but the latter is within reach only of the highest (most educated) classes of society and is beyond the intelligence of the people in the close and strict sense of the word. The educated grandee of our days understands the speech and affairs and way of life of his bearded ancestor of pre-Petrine days; but if his ancestor arose from his grave he would not understand anything in the life of his shaven descendant. Every educated man today, no matter how remote he stands in form and even essence from the life of the people, well understands the muzhik without lowering himself to his level, but the muzhik can understand him only by rising to his level or by the other descending to his apprehension. Yet no foreigner, unless he was born and bred in Russia, will understand the Russian muzhik even though he knew the language well enough to make himself a name in Russian literature. Consequently there is something *in common* between our past and our present, between the grandee in his time-honoured cloak and with flowing beard and the grandee in frock coat and with shaven chin, between the muzhik, townsman and bearded merchant and the *barin* (having a European education). But this common trait is not *narodnost,* but *nationality*. The latter easily understands the former (for, being the higher form, it incorporates it), but in order to make itself understood to *narodnost* nationality must bend down to it. The utter supremacy of *narodnost* necessarily presupposes within the polity a condition of natural immediacy, a condition of patriarchy, when the difference between the social estates consists not so much in form as in shades of form, but certainly not in essence. Such was the condition of Russia prior to Peter the Great. Read Koshikhin, and you will see that the wedding of the last village muzhik was the same as the first boyar; the difference was merely a matter of abundance of viands, costliness of clothing, in short, the importance and sum of expenditure. The same knout hung over both the muzhik and the boyar, for whom it was a misfortune, but not dishonour. The serf easily understood his master, the boyar, without the slightest strain on his intelligence; the boyar understood his serf without need of coming down to his intellection. The same corn brandy cheered the hearts of both: the only difference was that one drank an inferior grade and the other a pure grade of liquor. One and the same mead tickled the palate of the one and the other: the only difference was that one drank it from a wooden tankard or iron scoop, the other from a gold or silver goblet. And suddenly by the will of Peter everything underwent a swift and sweeping change: as little as did the common Russian man understand the new words in vogue: *victoire, rang, armée, general en chêf, admiral, Hofmarschal* and so on— so little did he understand the language and ways of his sovereign, and lord, or for that matter of any army officer with his *honneur,* his *menuet,* his *breeches* and other new-fangled ideas. The higher still understood the lower, but the lower was no longer capable of understanding the higher. The people was divorced from the gentility and soldiery. There was no longer a people in the politic sense, there was a nation. The foreign word became indispensable and unconsciously came into common use, receiving the right of citizenship in the vocabulary of the Russian language.

. . .

Some people impute to Peter the Great's reforms the mischievous effect of having placed the nation in a singular position by divorcing it from its native sphere and throwing it off its ground of innate horse sense without having inoculated real Europeanism. Despite the fallacy of this view, it possesses a foundation and is at least worthy of being refuted. Indeed, while the reformation released, as it were, the spiritual powers of such talented men as Sheremetev, Menshikov and others, it made sort of posers and scrapers out of the majority. Naturally, the old boyars, endowed with inborn intelligence and strong character, who refused to take an example from a man like Romodanovsky and to relinquish their staidly-cut costume and discard stern and ancient custom, looked with profound contempt on those new-fledged and home-bred Europeans who, through lack of practice, got their legs entangled in their sword, dropped their cocked hat from under their arm, trod on the ladies' toes when coming up to kiss their hand, needlessly, parrot-fashion, employed foreign words, substituted for courtesy rude and impudent gallantry and, as sometimes happened, put their clothes on the wrong way. Even today, though in another shape, vestiges of this sham, distorted Europeanism still survive: these forms sans ideas, that courtesy sans respect to self and others, that urbanity sans aesthetics, that foppery and *lionhood* sans elegance: notorious Ivan Alexandrovich Khlestakov, made famous by Gogol, is a type of that kind of *Europeans* of our days. Our Gallomaniacs, Anglomaniacs, lions, wild asses, *petit-maîtres,* agriculturists, comfortists could easily step into Gogol's comedy, some to chat with Anna Andreyevna about life in the capital and the rubbing of shoulders with ambassadors and ministers, some to debate on France and Turkey's political relations with Russia with the Postmaster Shpekin and the Judge Lyapkin-Tyapkin. It was a consequence of Peter's reformation that the great intellect of Lomonosov is so jejune and rhetorical in poetry, and that our literature up to Pushkin, with the exception of Krylov, is servilely imitative, colourless and of no interest to foreigners. Yes, that is all true, but it would be as absurd to blame Peter for it as it would be to blame the physician who, in order to cure a sick man of the fever, first weakens and utterly debilitates him by bloodletting and plagues him when convalescent by a strict diet. The point is not whether Peter made us half-Europeans and half-Russians, consequently neither Europeans nor Russians: the point is are we always to remain in this characterless condition? If *not,* if we are destined to become European Russians and Russian Europeans, we should not reproach Peter, but rather wonder how he could have accomplished such a gigantic, such an unprecedented task! And so the crux of the matter consists in the words "shall we"—and we can answer firmly and explicitly that we not only *shall be,* but are already *becoming* European Russians and Russian Europeans, that we have been becoming so since the reign of Catherine II, and are making progress therein day by day. We are today the pupils and no longer the zealots of Europeanism, we no longer wish to be either Frenchmen, or Englishmen, or Germans, we want to be Russians in the European spirit. This consciousness is permeating all spheres of our activity and made itself strikingly manifest in our literature with the advent of Pushkin, that great, independent and sheerly national talent. The fact that the final great act—the utter permeation of our *narodnost* by Europeanism—has still not been accomplished and will not be accomplished for a long time, merely goes to prove that Peter has carried out in thirty years a task that is giving work to whole centuries. That is why he is a giant among giants, a genius among geniuses, a king among kings. Napoleon himself had a rival in antiquity—Julius Caesar: our Peter has neither rivals nor models since the beginning of the world; he is akin and equal to no one but himself. And this great task was accomplished by the unqualified adoption of forms and words: the form is not always the idea, but often leads to it; the word is not always the need, but often leads to it. Our literature began with the form without the idea, originated not out of the national spirit, but out of sheer imitation, yet we should not despise our imitative literature without it we would not have had Pushkin. From literature we can make a premise to everything else. Peter the Great's soldiers did not understand why they were being trained in military drill and crammed with the articles; they just senselessly obeyed their paternal commanders—and well!—the result of this senseless obedience and aping of the foreign military was the taking of Azov, the victories at Lesnaya and Poltava, the conquest of Sweden's Baltic provinces. Our first representatives of polite society shocked European society by their Tatarism, but there soon appeared people who could be considered its adornment and who amazed the Parisians by their refinement and good breeding.

The building of St. Petersburg is also placed by many to the discredit of its great founder. It is said: on the margin of a vast realm, on swamps, in a terrible climate, with the sacrifice of many workmen's lives, many were forced against their wishes to build their homes there and so on and so forth. All this is not quite groundless, but the question is, was it necessary, and was it avoidable? Peter had to abandon Moscow—the beards hissed at him there; he had to secure a safe haven for Europeanism, make the visitor welcome in the bosom of the family, so that he may quietly and unobtrusively influence Russia and act as the lightning conductor for ignorance and bigotry. For such a haven he required an entirely new and traditionless soil, where his Russians would find themselves in an utterly new environment in which they could not help but recast their customs and habits of their own accord. He had to introduce them to foreigners, join them together by ties of service, commerce and fellowship, place them on a footing of permanent contact. For that purpose he needed the conquered ground, which would become the home both for foreigners who could not be enticed to Moscow in great numbers and for Russians who were only reluctant at the beginning to settle there. . . .

Belinsky's Letter to Gogol

> One of the major manifestations of the "inner liberation" of Nicholas' reign had been the early work of Nicholas Gogol (1809–1852), first of the great Russian prose writers. In his *Revisor* and in his *Dead Souls,* Gogol brilliantly and effectively attacked the evils of serfdom and the abuses of the bureaucracy; but his later work, *Correspondence with Friends,* was a vigorous blast against the peasants. It was this "new Gogol" whom Belinsky so scathingly denounced in this letter. Equally scathing was his denunciation of serfdom and the Russian system. Such outspoken attacks could not have been made in Russia. The letter was written in Europe where Belinsky had gone, as his letter notes, in hope of finding a cure. It was first published by Herzen in 1855 in *Polyarnaya Zvezda* (London); and despite the government's strenuous efforts to prevent it, the letter had wide, clandestine circulation in Russia. The source is: Belinsky, *Selected Philosophical Works,* pp. 536–546.

You are only partly right in regarding my article as that of an angered man: that epithet is too mild and inadequate to express the state to which I was reduced on reading your book. And you are entirely wrong in ascribing that state to your indeed none too flattering references to the admirers of your talent. No, there was a more important reason for this. One could suffer an outraged sense of self-esteem, and I would have had sense enough to let the matter pass in silence were that the whole gist of the matter; but one cannot suffer an outraged sense of truth and human dignity; one cannot keep silent when lies and immorality are preached as truth and virtue under the guise of religion and the protection of the knout.

Yes, I loved you with all the passion with which a man, bound by ties of blood to his native country, can love its hope, its honour, its glory, one of the great leaders on its path of consciousness, development and progress. And you had sound reason for at least momentarily losing your equanimity when you forfeited that love. I say that not because I believe my love to be an adequate reward for a great talent, but because I do not represent a single person in this respect but a multitude of men, most of whom neither you nor I have ever set eyes on, and who, in their turn, have never set eyes on you. I find myself at a loss to give you an adequate idea of the indignation which your book has aroused in all noble hearts, and of the wild shouts of joy which were set up on its appearance by all your enemies—both the non-literary—the Chichikovs, the Nozdrevs and the mayors . . . and by the literary, whose names are well known to you. You see yourself that even those people who are of one mind with your book have disowned it. Even if it had been written as a result of deep and sincere conviction it could not have created any other impression on the public than the one it did. And it is nobody's fault but your own if everyone (except the few who must be seen and known in order not to derive pleasure from their approval) received it as an ingenious but all too unceremonious artifice for achieving a sheerly earthly aim by celestial means. Nor is that in any way surprising; what is surprising is that you find it surprising. I believe that is so because your profound knowledge of Russia is only that of an artist, but not of a thinker, whose role you have so ineffectually tried to play in your fantastic book. Not that you are not a thinker, but that you have been accustomed for so many years to look at Russia from your *beautiful far-away;* and who does not know that there is nothing easier than seeing things from a distance the way we want to see them; for in that *beautiful far-away* you live a life that is entirely alien to it, you live in and within yourself or within a circle of the same mentality as your own which is powerless to resist your influence on it. Therefore you failed to realize that Russia sees her salvation not in mysticism, not asceticism, not pietism, but in the successes of civilization, enlightenment and humanity. What she needs is not sermons (she has heard enough of them!) or prayers (she has repeated them too often!), but the awakening in the people of a sense of their human dignity lost for so many centuries amid the dirt and refuse; she needs rights and laws conforming not with the preaching of the church but with common sense and justice, and their strictest possible observance. Instead of which she presents the dire spectacle of a country where men traffic in men, without even having the excuse so insidiously exploited by the American plantation owners who claim that the Negro is not a man; a country where people call themselves not by names but by sobriquets, such as Vanka, Vaska, Steshka, Palashka; a country where there are not only no guarantees for individuality, honour and property, but even no police order, and where there is nothing but vast corporations of official thieves and robbers of various descriptions. The most vital national problems in Russia today are the abolition of serfdom and corporal punishments and the strictest possible observance of at least those laws which already exist. This is even realized by the government itself (which is well aware of how the landowners treat their peasants and how many of the former are annually done away with by the latter), as is proven by its timid and abortive half-measures for the relief of the white Negroes and the comical substitution of the single-lash knout by a cat-o'-three tails.

Such are the problems which prey on the mind of Russia in her apathetic slumber! And at such a time a great writer, whose beautifully artistic and deeply truthful works have so powerfully contributed towards Russia's awareness of herself, enabling her as they did to take a look at herself as though in a mirror—comes out with a book in which he teaches the barbarian landowner in the name of Christ and Church to make still greater profits out of the peasants and to abuse them still more. . . . And you would expect me not to become indignant? . . . Why, if you had made an attempt on my life I could not have hated you more than I do for these disgraceful lines. . . . And after this, you expect people to believe the sincerity of your book's intent! No! Had you really been inspired by the truth of Christ and not by the teaching of the Devil you would certainly have written something entirely different in your new book. You would have told the landowner that since his peasants are his brethren in Christ, and since a brother cannot be a slave to his brother, he should either give them their freedom, or, at least, allow them to enjoy the fruits of their own labour to their greatest possible benefit, realizing as he does, in the depths of his own conscience the false relationship in which he stands towards them.

And the expression: *"Oh, you unwashed snout, you!"* From what Nozdrev and Sobakevich did you overhear this, to give to the world as a great discovery for the edification and benefit of the muzhiks, whose only reason for not washing is that they have let themselves be persuaded by their masters that they are not human beings? And your conception of the national Russian system of trial and punishment, whose ideal you have found in the foolish saying that both the guilty and innocent should be flogged alike? That, indeed, is often the case with us, though more often than not it is the man who is in the right who takes the punishment, unless he can ransom himself, and for such occasions another proverb says: *guiltlessly guilty!* And such a book is supposed to have been the result of an arduous inner process, a lofty spiritual enlightenment! Impossible! Either you are ill—and you must hasten to take a cure, or . . . I am afraid to put my thought into words! . . .

Proponent of the knout, apostle of ignorance, champion of obscurantism and Stygian darkness, panegyrist of Tatar morals—what are you about! Look beneath your feet—you are standing on the brink of an abyss! . . . That you base such teaching on the Orthodox Church I can understand: it has always served as the prop of the knout and the servant of despotism; but why have you mixed Christ up in this? What in common have you found between Him and any church, least of all the Orthodox Church? He was the first to bring to people the teaching of freedom, equality and brotherhood and set the seal of truth to that teaching by martyrdom. And this teaching was men's *salvation* only until it became organized in the Church and took the principle of Orthodoxy for its foundation. The Church, on the other hand, was a hierarchy, consequently a champion of inequality, a flatterer of authority, an enemy and persecutor of brotherhood among men—and so it has remained to this day. But the meaning of Christ's message has been revealed by the philosophical movement of the preceding century. And that is why a man like Voltaire who stamped out the fires of fanaticism and ignorance in Europe by ridicule, is, of course, more the son of Christ, flesh of his flesh and bone of his bone, than all your priests, bishops, metropolitans and patriarchs—Eastern or Western. Do you mean to say you do not know it! It is not even a novelty now to a schoolboy. . . . Hence, can it be that you, the author of *Inspector General* and *Dead Souls,* have in all sincerity, from the bottom of your heart, sung a hymn to the nefarious Russian clergy which you rank immeasurably higher than the Catholic clergy? Let us assume that you do not know that the latter had once been something, while the former had never been anything but a servant and slave of the secular powers; but do you really mean to say you do not know that our clergy is held in universal contempt by Russian society and the Russian people? Of whom do the Russian people relate obscene stories? Of the priest, the priest's wife, the priest's daughter and the priest's farm hand. Does not the priest in Russia represent for all Russians the embodiment of gluttony, avarice, servility and shamelessness? Do you mean to say that you do not know all this? Strange! According to you the Russian people is the most religious in the world. That is a lie! The basis of religiousness is pietism, reverence, fear of God. Whereas the Russian man utters the name of the Lord while scratching himself somewhere. He says of the icon: *if it isn't good for praying it's good for covering the pots.*

Take a closer look and you will see that it is by nature a profoundly atheistic people. It still retains a good deal of superstition, but not a trace of religiousness. Superstition passes with the advances of civilization, but religiousness often keeps company with them too; we have a living example of this in France, where even today there are many sincere Catholics among enlightened and educated men, and where many people who have rejected Christianity still cling stubbornly to some sort of god. The Russian people is different; mystic exaltation is not in its nature; it has too much common sense, a too lucid and positive mind, and therein, perhaps, lies the vastness of its historic destinies in the future. Religiousness with it has not even taken root among the clergy, since a few isolated and exclusive personalities distinguished for such cold ascetic reflectiveness prove nothing. But the majority of our clergy has always been distinguished for their fat bellies, scholastic pedantry and savage ignorance. It is a shame to accuse it of religious intolerance and fanaticism; rather could it be praised for an exemplary indifference in matters of faith. Religiousness with us appeared only among the schismatic sects who formed such a contrast in spirit to the mass of the people and were so insignificant before it numerically.

I shall not dilate on your panegyric to the affectionate relations existing between the Russian people and its lords and masters. I shall say point-blank: that panegyric has met sympathy nowhere and has lowered you even in the eyes of people who in other respects stand very close to you in outlook. As far as I am concerned, I leave it to your conscience to admire the divine beauty of the autocracy (it is both safe and profitable), but continue to admire it judiciously from your *beautiful far-away:* at close quarters it is not so attractive, and not so safe. . . . I would remark but this: when a European, especially a Catholic, is seized with a religious ardour he becomes a denouncer of iniquitous authority, similar to the Hebrew prophets who denounced the iniquities of the great ones of the earth. With us on the contrary: no sooner is a person (even a reputable person) afflicted with the malady which is known to psychiatrists as *religiosa mania* than he begins to burn more incense to the earthly god than the heavenly one, and so overshoots the mark in doing so that the former would fain reward him for his slavish zeal did he not perceive that he would thereby be compromising himself in society's eyes. . . . What a rogue our fellow the Russian is! . . .

Another thing I remember you saying in your book, claiming it to be a great and incontrovertible truth, that literacy is not merely useless but positively harmful to the common people. What can I say to this? May your Byzantine God forgive you that Byzantine thought, unless, in committing it to paper, you knew not what you were saying. . . . But perhaps you will say: "Assuming that I have erred and that all my ideas are false, but why should I be denied the right to err and why should people doubt the sincerity of my errors?" Because, I would say in reply, such a tendency has long ceased to be a novelty in Russia. Not so very long ago it was drained to the lees by Burachok and his fraternity. Of course, your book shows a good deal more intellect and talent (though neither of these elements is very richly represented) than their works; but then they have developed your common doctrine with greater energy and greater consistence, they have boldly reached its ultimate conclusions, have rendered full need to the Byzantine God and left nothing for Satan, whereas you, wanting to light a taper to each of them, have fallen into contradiction, upholding for example, Pushkin, literature and the theatre, all of which, in your opinion, if you were only conscientious enough to be consistent, can in no way serve the salvation of the soul but can do a lot towards its damnation. . . . Whose head could have digested the idea of Gogol's identity with Burachok? You have placed yourself too high in the regard of the Russian public for it to be able to believe you sincere in such convictions. What seems natural in fools cannot seem so in a man of genius. Some people have been inclined to regard your book as the result of mental derangement verging on sheer madness. But they soon rejected such a supposition, for clearly that book was not written in a single day, or week, or month, but very likely in one, two or three years; it shows coherence; through its careless exposition one glimpses premeditation, and the hymn to the powers that be nicely arranges the earthly affairs of the devout

author. That is why a rumour has been current in St. Petersburg to the
effect that you have written this book with the aim of securing a position as
tutor to the son of the heir apparent. Before that your letter to Uvarov
became known in St. Petersburg, wherein you say that you are grieved to
find that your works about Russia are misinterpreted, then you evince dissatisfaction with your previous works and declare that you will be pleased
with your own works only when the tsar is pleased with them. Now judge
for yourself, is it to be wondered at that your book has lowered you in the
eyes of the public both as a writer and still more as a man? . . .

You, as far as I can see, do not properly understand the Russian public.
Its character is determined by the condition of Russian society in which
fresh forces are seething and struggling for expression, but weighed down
by heavy oppression and finding no outlet, they induce merely dejection,
weariness and apathy. Only literature, despite the Tatar censorship,
shows signs of life and progressive movement. That is why the title of writer
is held in such esteem among us, that is why literary success is easy among
us even for a writer of small talent. The title of poet and writer has long
since eclipsed the tinsel of epaulettes and gaudy uniforms. And that especially explains why every so-called liberal tendency, however poor in talent, is rewarded by universal notice, and why the popularity of great talents
which sincerely or insincerely give themselves to the service of orthodoxy,
autocracy and nationality declines so quickly. A striking example is Pushkin who had merely to write two or three verses in a loyal strain and don
the *kamer-junker's* livery to suddenly forfeit the popular affection! And
you are greatly mistaken if you believe in all earnest that your book has
come to grief not because of its bad trend, but because of the harsh
truths alleged to have been expressed by you about all and everybody.
Assuming you could think that of the writing fraternity, but then how do
you account for the public? Did you tell it less bitter home truths less
harshly and wish less truth and talent in *Inspector General* and *Dead
Souls?* Indeed the old school was worked up to a furious pitch of anger
against you, but *Inspector General* and *Dead Souls* were not affected by it,
whereas your latest book has been an utter and disgraceful failure. And here
the public is right, for it looks upon Russian writers as its only leaders, defenders and saviours against Russian autocracy, orthodoxy and nationality,
and therefore, while always prepared to forgive a writer a bad book, will
never forgive him a pernicious book. This shows how much fresh and
healthy intuition, albeit still in embryo, is latent in our society, and this
likewise proves that it has a future. If you love Russia rejoice with me at the
failure of your book! . . .

I would tell you, not without a certain feeling of self-satisfaction, that
I believe I know the Russian public a little. Your book alarmed me by the
possibility of its exercising a bad influence on the government and the censorship, but not on the public. When it was rumoured in St. Petersburg that
the government intended to publish your book in many thousands of copies
and to sell it at an extremely low price my friends grew despondent; but I
told them there and then that the book, despite everything, would have no

success and that it would soon be forgotten. In fact it is now better remembered for the articles which have been written about it than for the book itself. Yes, the Russian has a deep, though still undeveloped, instinct for truth.

Your conversion may conceivably have been sincere, but your idea of bringing it to the notice of the public was a most unhappy one. The days of naive piety have long since passed, even in our society. It already understands that it makes no difference where one prays, and that the only people who seek Christ and Jerusalem are those who have never carried Him in their breasts or who have lost Him. He who is capable of suffering at the sight of other people's sufferings and who is pained at the sight of other people's oppression, bears Christ within his bosom and has no need to make a pilgrimage to Jerusalem. The humility which you preach is, first of all, not novel, and, secondly, it savours on the one hand of prodigious pride, and on the other of the most shameful degradation of one's human dignity. The idea of becoming a sort of abstract perfection, of rising above everyone else in humility, is the fruit of either pride or imbecility, and in either case leads inevitably to hypocrisy, sanctimoniousness and Chinaism. Moreover, in your book you have taken the liberty of expressing yourself with gross cynicism not only of other people (that would be merely impolite) but of yourself—and that is vile for if a man who strikes his neighbour on the cheek evokes indignation, the sight of a man striking himself on the cheek evokes contempt. No, you are not illuminated, you are simply beclouded; you have failed to grasp either the spirit or the form of Christianity of our time. Your book breathes not the true Christian teaching but the morbid fear of death, of the devil and of hell!

And what language, what phrases? "Every man hath now become trash and a rag"—do you really believe that in saying *hath* instead of *has* you are expressing yourself biblically? How eminently true it is that when a man gives himself wholly up to lies, intelligence and talent desert him. Did not this book bear your name, who would have thought that this turgid and squalid bombast was the work of the author of *Inspector General* and *Dead Souls?*

As far as it concerns myself, I repeat: you are mistaken in taking my article to be an expression of vexation at your comment on me as one of your critics. Were this the only thing to make me angry I would have reacted with annoyance to this alone and would have dealt with all the rest with unruffled impartiality. But it is true that your criticism of your admirers is doubly bad. I understand the necessity of sometimes having to rap a silly man whose praises and ecstasies make the object of his worship look ridiculous, but even this is a painful necessity, since, humanly speaking, it is somehow awkward to reward even false affection with enmity. But you had in view men who, though not brilliantly clever, are not quite fools. These people, in their admiration of your works, have probably uttered more ejaculations than talked sense about them; still, their enthusiastic attitude toward you springs from such a pure and noble source that you ought not to have betrayed them neck and crop to both your common enemies and accused them into the bargain of wanting to misinterpret your works. You, of course, did that while carried away by the main idea of your book and through indiscretion, while Vyazemsky, that prince in aristocracy and helot in literature, developed your idea and printed a denunciation against your admirers (and consequently mostly against me). He probably did this to show his gratitude to you for having exalted him, the poetaster, to the rank of great poet, if I remember rightly for his "pithless, dragging verse." That is all very bad. That you were merely biding your time in order to give the admirers of your talent their due as well (after having given it with proud humility to your enemies)—I was not aware; I could not, and, I must confess, did not want to know it. It was your book that lay before me and not your intentions: I read and reread it a hundred times, but I found nothing in it that was not there, and what was there deeply offended and incensed my soul.

Were I to give free rein to my feelings this letter would probably grow into a voluminous notebook. I never thought of writing you on this subject though I longed to do so and though you gave all and sundry printed permission to write you without ceremony with an eye to the truth alone. Were I in Russia I would not be able to do it, for the local "Shpekins" open other people's letters not merely for their own pleasure but as a matter of official duty, for the sake of informing. This summer incipient consumption has driven me abroad, (and Nekrasov has forwarded me your letter to Salzbrunn which I am leaving today with Annenkov for Paris via Frankfort-on-Main). The unexpected receipt of your letter has enabled me to unburden my soul of what has accumulated there against you on account of your book. I cannot express myself by halves, I cannot prevaricate; it is not in my nature. Let you or time itself prove to me that I am mistaken in my conclusions. I shall be the first to rejoice in it, but I shall not repent what I have told you. This is not a question of your or my personality, it concerns a matter which is of greater importance than myself or even you; it is a matter which concerns the truth, Russian society, Russia. And this is my last concluding word: if you have had the misfortune of disowning with proud humility your truly great works, you should now disown with sincere humility your last book, and atone for the dire sin of its publication by new creations which would be reminiscent of your old ones.

Chernishevsky to His Sons

The following excerpt is from a letter to his sons, Alexander and Michael, written from Siberia, to which Chernishevsky had been exiled in 1878. The letter, more in the nature of a disquisition than a bit of family correspondence, discussed at length an essay on geometrical axioms, written by the German scientist Helmholtz. The quoted material forms a preface to a scathing criticism of what Chernishevsky termed "Helmholtz's nonsense." The source is: Chernyshevsky, *Selected Philosophical Essays,* pp. 515–517.

In every trade or profession, the majority of specialists are ignorant of everything except the narrow technique of their particular occupation. For example, the majority of shoemakers are ignorant of everything except shoemaking. But an ignoramus must have something to boast about. A man of broad views and sentiments finds sufficient pride in the fact that he is a man. An ignorant shoemaker, however, is little interested in the fact that he is a man. He can make shoes within the scope of his views and sentiments, this is the only thing he can understand, like, and take pride in; and if you give him only half an hour for self-praise, you will hear him teach you, and through you the whole human race, that shoemaking is the most important occupation in the world, and that shoemakers are the greatest benefactors of the human race.

The same will be said about his trade by an ignorant tailor, an ignorant hairdresser, an ignorant bricklayer, an ignorant carpenter, and by ignorant men of every other trade.

But the artisans of these and similar trades, shoemakers, tailors, and so forth, very rarely find patient, respectful, credulous and grateful listeners to their self-praise. If we wanted to hear their wild outpourings about their being our greatest benefactors, we would have to arrange a private interview with them with no one else present. Otherwise we would not hear anything truly remarkable, for at the first word of the feeble and still hesitant opening of his didactic speech the boaster would be interrupted by a burst of laughter and would be crushed by the sarcasm of the people whom we had carelessly invited to be present at the experiment.

This is not the lot of those professional people who are specialists in occupations that are held in higher esteem than shoemaking, hairdressing or carpentry. The public listens to these highly-respected people with awe. And thanks to its professionally boastful intonation, their self-praise is a constant source of instruction and pleasure to the human race, which bows down to the ground in gratitude to its benefactors.

There are many kinds of these highly-esteemed professions. For example, architecture, painting, sculpture, and so forth; music, singing, dancing and so forth; jurisprudence, and so forth, history, and so forth.

You know that the celebrated dancer Vestris did, indeed, regard himself as the benefactor of the whole of France, and of the whole of the civilized world. He was a genial chatterbox, and it was only his vain chatter that distinguished him from the ordinary specialists. In essence, the ideas of all ignorant experts in all occupations are on a par with Vestris' naive chatter.

My dear friends, please remember that I am speaking of all those who boast about their particular occupations. I am no more unjust to musicians than to lawyers, to dancers than to preachers of morals. I say that all sing the same hymn of self-praise, except that the terminology of one is different from that of another.

If I now speak about ignorant naturalists, and about ignorant astronomer-mathematicians in particular, I shall not be more unjust to them than to other esteemed ignorant specialists. I do not think in the least that their ignorance is more reprehensible than that of painters or lawyers, vocalists and dancers, or preachers. And their self-praise is not more absurd, not worse or more harmful. I must speak about them only because it is they and not the dancers and musicians who set out to teach the human race what Newton's hypothesis is. Had mankind turned to lawyers or dancers and not to naturalists, and to the astronomer-mathematicians in particular, for an opinion on this question, I would not in these pages have troubled the naturalists, and the astronomer-mathematicians in particular, I would not even have mentioned them, but would have censured the lawyers and dancers for their ignorance.

But mankind has no inkling that it would hear from lawyers and dancers an opinion on Newton's hypothesis not less scientific and not less sound than the one they hear from Messrs. astronomer-mathematicians and company, namely: "Newton's hypothesis is a hypothesis." What could be simpler than that? And what vocalist or dancer, or even a washerwoman would find any difficulty in expressing it?

And I would censure even a washerwoman, or a peasant woman, for expressing an opinion like that as severely as I censure the astronomer-mathematicians, for the question of Newton's hypothesis is so easy that it would be disgraceful even for a peasant woman not to be able to understand it if she were asked to express an opinion after she had been given an hour or two to hear the facts and to think about them.

But those gentlemen the naturalists, and those gentlemen the astronomer-mathematicians in particular, have assured the credulous majority of educated people that there is something in the "question"—question!—of Newton's hypothesis that cannot be grasped by anybody except specialists in natural science, especially mathematics; that there is something in this "question," to answer which no mathematics is required except the multiplication tables, for which an answer can be found even by an illiterate person unacquainted with figures, who counts with the aid of the words that designate figures in ordinary language; who adds instead of multiplying, and adds with the aid of his fingers. Those gentlemen the specialists have taken the matter out of the hands of the bulk of the educated people and have proclaimed themselves the sole judges of the "question" of Newton's hypothesis—the question!—which is as much a question as whether twice two is really four. It was their pleasure to present the matter in this way. And because it was their pleasure to make the matter entirely dependent upon themselves, I am compelled to speak about them.

I am not doing so of my own free will, they compel me to do so.

My dear children, it is hard and painful for your father to speak in this way about the majority of the naturalists, and in this case, mainly about the majority of mathematicians.

But what can he do? Those gentlemen compel him to do so. There is a limit to everything, so there must surely be a limit to the ignorance of the specialists. And there is a limit to every reasonable man's compliance and indulgence.

Nicholas' Codification of Law

The "inner liberation" of Nicholas' reign refers in general to the literary and artistic advances which took place in that period. It could also be stretched to cover his efforts toward reform, among which the codification of law was perhaps the most progressive. This task was carried out by the Second Section of His Majesty's Own Chancery, headed by Mikhail Speransky. The published codification filled forty-five volumes. A condensation and digest was also published. Here are Nicholas' instructions to Speransky concerning the bases for the codification. The source is: LaCroix, *Histoire*, vol. 3, pp. 38–39.

1. To exclude from the body of law all those which are obsolete.

2. To exclude also those which are only identical repetitions of previous laws, always giving preference to the most complete text.

3. To conserve scrupulously the letter of the law and reproduce in a single text the sense of all the laws which treat of the same matter.

4. To indicate exactly the ukases from which each particular law is composed.

5. Of two laws in contradiction, to give the preference to the most recent, following the principle which establishes that all new law virtually abrogates the law which preceded it.

6. Each part of the work of the Commission ought to be submitted for revision to the ministers and the administrations in their respective specialties, committees established for that purpose being charged with this revision. A superior committee composed of senators and high functionaries under the presidency of the Minister of Justice will be set up to examine the civil and criminal laws.

7. Russia having laws of two kinds, those which act throughout the empire and those essentially local whose action is circumscribed in some provinces, there should be besides the body of general law, two bodies of provincial law, one for the government of the West, and one for that of the Baltic.

8. The codification of the laws in fixing legislation for its passage should leave a considerable latitude for the future when new needs will bring forth new laws.

Economic Development Under Alexander and Nicholas

The dramatic happenings in the reigns of Alexander I and Nicholas I have so occupied attention that the economic changes in Russia during this period have been somewhat neglected. The following selection is an exception to this generalization. The source is: N. A. Rozhkov, "Ekonomicheskoe razbitie Rossii v pervoi polovin XIX veka," *Istoriya Rossii v XIX vek (Russian History in the 19th Century)*. Nine volumes. St. Petersburg, n.d. Vol. 1, pp. 138–142. Slightly abridged.

The outstanding feature of the economic history of Russia in the first part of the nineteenth century or, more correctly, until the fall of landlordism, was undoubtedly the much greater speed and breadth than before of the development of trade and a money economy. There had been a marked development of money economy in sixteenth-century Russia, but this process took place very slowly and affected comparatively small groups at the beginning. Only with the nineteenth century began the transfer from agrarian economy to the second stage, when the majority of the people became accustomed to trading, to producing for market and to satisfy the owners' desires to purchase products of foreign labor, and also learned to carry their goods to market with a view to trade.

The outstanding characteristic economic feature of this epoch was first of all the change in trade statistics. The value of Russian exports increased from 75 million rubles at the beginning of the nineteenth century to 230 million rubles on the eve of the peasant reform; at the same time, imports of foreign goods reached 200 million rubles whereas at the opening of the century such imports had not exceeded 52 million rubles. The most important of the Russian exports were grain and, in general, the products of the land, livestock and the products of livestock, lumber, etc. The importance of the grain exports is apparent from the following figures: Between 1800 and 1845, grain exports comprised 15 to 16 per cent of the value of all Russian exports; between 1846 and 1860, 30 to 35 per cent. The average exports of grain in the decade preceding 1846 did not exceed 454 thousands of tons, but in the next ten years it was 918 thousand tons a year, so that there is noted a huge increase—amounting to 88 per cent—as compared to the preceding decade. It is wholly clear that the development and improvement of their industries by the advanced Western European countries toward the middle of the nineteenth century, were sharply felt in their demand for Russian grain, chiefly wheat.

So much wheat was exported, mostly from the South Russian ports, that the Black Sea ports—Odessa and Taganrog—attained first place in the export of farm products, surpassing the Baltic ports. The export of linseed and hops also increased. In 30 to 40 years even the Caucasus (*i.e.,* the northern part, which belonged to Russia) exported significant quantities of linseed through the port of Taganrog. The value of lumber exports in 1815 amounted to 1,320,000 silver rubles; in 1850, it reached 2,745,000 silver rubles (increasing over 100 per cent). Livestock and the products of livestock (tallow, bristles and hides) were exported in 1825 to the value of 15,885,000 rubles; by 1850, this had increased to 17 million silver rubles.

Corresponding developments are observable in the case of foreign imports. It is impossible to find a better illustration of the movement toward money economy than this: in 1820, the total import of machines into Russia was 10 thousand silver rubles; in 1850, 2,221,000. The value of imports of foreign woolen goods into the country rose from 1,500 silver rubles in 1815 to 39,000 in 1850.

Side by side with this, and, it is even possible to say, of more rapid growth than this, was the domestic trade. Previously it had been the custom not only among the peasants, but also among the land and serf owners, to satisfy their needs by products entirely of home manufacture—not buying but making such goods at home as coarse homespun cloth and homemade linen. Little by little, these primitive textiles were replaced by purchasing finer fabrics. As late as 1804, several landowners in the Moscow province had factories whose products were intended only "for domestic consumption" or for "our own use," but gradually the largest landowners increased their estate factories and mills to produce for market. There were, for example, in the same province of Moscow: the cloth factories of Prince Khovanski and Princess Golitsin; the silk and paper factories of Belavin; and the linen mills of Prince Dolgoruki and Count Protasov. The value of domestic trade had already increased to 260 million silver rubles by 1812. At the Nizhni-Novgorod Fair in 1824 there had been offered for sale, goods valued at 40,500,000 rubles. By 1838, this had increased to 129,200,000 rubles. There was also a rapid increase in mercantile capital: in the province of Moscow in 1822, the total of this capital approached 27 million rubles, but eleven years later (in 1833) it reached 39 million—an increase of 45 per cent in the short space of one decade. Improvements were made in the ways of communication. A beginning was made in railway construction and in steam navigation of the Volga, the Dnieper, and other rivers. But chiefly what strikes one as the most outstanding characteristic of this development of money economy was the division of labor among the various territorial divisions of the state—a division which inevitably led to the exchange of goods and the revival of trade.

The comparatively less fertile northern and central sections of Russia greatly needed quantities of foodstuffs which they could not raise for themselves. According to the evidence of Baron Haxthausen, who traveled through Russia in the 1840's, some provinces such as Iaroslavl did not produce half enough food for its people. Furthermore, Kaluzhskaia Province in 1822 was already buying foodstuffs from Orel and Tula Provinces. On the other hand, southern Russia traded much foodstuff to the East. Thus, the regions of what was then Orienburg Province, which now belongs in the enlarged Province of Ufa, during the 1820's and thereafter, sent much grain by boat on the Kama and the Volga. Livestock was also sold from there to the Kazak and Simbirsk lands along the Volga. Moreover, this trade involved not only the land and serf owners, but also all the people. . . .

This trade took place even among distant parts of the country. Kharkhov, Poltava, Ekaterinoslav, and Kherson Provinces provided timber for the rest of Russia. Little Russia and New Russia in 1854 consumed Great Russian goods to the value of about 80 million silver rubles. These imports went to the numerous fairs of Little Russia, of which there were 425 a year in Kharkhov, and 372 a year in Poltava. Goods were sent to Little Russia from Moscow, Vladimir, Kostroma, Iaroslavl, Riazin, Tula, Nizhni-Novgorod, Orel, Kalzhska, and even from the West—from the provinces of Smolensk, Grodnensk, and Lifland; from the South—Bessarabia, Crimea, Ekaterinoslav; and East from the Don and Voronezh Provinces. In the mid-nineteenth century, Pavlov and Worms purchased the iron which they needed for their metal industries from the Urals through the medium of the Nizhni-Novgorod fairs. In the town of Pestiaki, Vladimir Province, the women knit stockings and sold them in Siberia and elsewhere to the value of 120 thousand rubles a year. The materials for the stockings—wool to the amount of 225 tons—were purchased in the provinces of Astrakhan, Orienburg, Saratov, and in the military colonies of the Don.

In short, the division of Russia into the central and northern non-agrarian regions, and the southern agrarian and livestock areas was clearly marked. Each helped the other in economic relations and neither could live without the other. They formed a unit, a coherent economic whole, an indispensable pillar for the development of money economy.

. . .

The publisher of the journal "The Russian Farmer," in 1838, printed the statement that: as to agriculture in Russia, "it stands almost motionless," while manufacturing "attained an amazing development." Without doubt this phrase satisfactorily echoes the impressions of the contemporaries who observed the economic development of Russia in the first half of the nineteenth century. But it is also, without doubt, contrary to fact in two respects. First, to avow that the development of Russian manufacturing at that time was "amazing" is an obvious exaggeration. Second, it is a pretense that agrarian economy was "motionless." As a matter of fact, while manufacturing developed rather quickly, it did not develop amazingly or even astonishingly fast. Its growth came as a necessary prerequisite to money economy. In an important branch of manufacturing—the cotton industry—the amount of cotton manufactured increased sixteen times during the first fifty years of the nineteenth century. Smelting of iron in the same period increased from 144 thousand tons to 288 thousand tons a year. Rapid progress in the textile industry also bears witness to this fact. There were in Russia in 1850, 492 textile factories. Between 1820 and 1830 the number of factories in Russia had increased from three to four thousand, and the number of workers in these plants rose from 170 thousand to 240 thousand. During the 1840's, one such village as Ivanov in the Shuiski district provided work for 42 thousand people and produced cotton goods to the value of 23,400,000 paper rubles. The first Russian sugar beet refinery was built in 1802. By 1845 there were 206 sugar refineries with a production of 8,712 tons. Three years later, in 1848, the number of refineries had increased to 340, and the amount produced to 16,200 tons. . . .

Thus in 1812, agricultural products were valued at 23,400,000 silver rubles; livestock and its products at 17,800,000; the products of extractive industries at 7,200,000 and manufactured goods at 10,800,000. The corresponding figures for 1850 were: agriculture—44,700,000 silver rubles; livestock and its products—23,500,000 rubles; the extractive industries—7,300,000; and manufactured goods—11,300,000 rubles.

A Firsthand Report on European Russia in 1843

The Baron von Haxthausen, an astute and experienced observer, made an extensive tour through European Russia in 1843. His particular interest was in the economy of the country and the most valuable parts of his study were those which dealt with agriculture, trade, and industry. He was, however, curious and observant about all those aspects of Russian life which came to his attention. Among other qualities, Haxthausen was one of the first foreign observers to take a special interest in that important and peculiar Russian institution, the *mir*. The first two excerpts from his published report deal with that subject.

Haxthausen's study was published originally in a ponderous, three-volume German edition which was entitled, *Studien über die innern Zustände, das Volksleben, und insbesondere die ländlichen Einrichtung Russlands*. The first two volumes were published in 1847; the third, in 1852. More than a dozen years later, Robert Farie, Esq. published an abridged English translation from which the selections below are reprinted. The order of the material has been changed, as the page citations show, and some adaptations have been made. Subheadings have been added for clarity, and material which has been extensively abridged has been enclosed in brackets.

The source is: Baron von Haxthausen (Robert Farie, Tr.), *The Russian Empire, Its People, Institutions and Resources*. Two volumes. London, 1856. Vol. 2, p. 229; vol. 1, pp. 133–135, 119–121; vol. 2, pp. 229–231; vol. 1, pp. 16–18, 101–102, 106–107, 113, 114, 115, 118, 127, 136–137, 142, 145–146, 148–149, 152–153, 154, 163, 164–165, 169–172, 174–175, 183–184, 190, 215–216, 236–238.

The Mir

The Russian *Mir* has a different signification in the language of business, the law, and of the educated classes, from what it has in that of the people. In the first place it is identical with the French word *Commune,* being the aggregate of persons living together in the same place, the police jurisdiction of a city, town, or village; but the meaning is quite different in the common conception of the people. Even the literal signification of the word *Mir* indicates the sacredness of the idea, denoting both Commune and World: the Greek *Cosmos* is the only equivalent to the Russian word. I can recollect no German or Romantic proverb in which the power, right, and sacredness of the Commune are recognized; the Russian language has a great number:—

> God alone direct the Mir.
> The Mir is great.
> The Mir is the surging billow.
> The neck and shoulders of the Mir are broad.
> Throw everything upon the Mir, it will carry it all.
> The Mir sighs, and the rock is rent asunder.
> The Mir sobs, and it re-echoes in the forest.

A thread of the Mir becomes a shirt for the naked.
No one in the world can separate from the Mir.
What is decided by the Mir must come to pass.
The Mir is answerable for the country's defence.

The Mir and the Land

The Russians say that the earth belongs to the Creator, and has been granted by Him to Adam and his descendants. Successive generations inherited the possession; and as their numbers increased they occupied a greater extent of the earth's surface, which they shared under the Divine guidance in the world's history. The country now called Russia fell to the progenitor of the Russians; and his descendants, remaining united under the head of their race, and thus constituting a people, spread over the territory which has thus by the providence of God become their property. The disposal of it, as in a family, belongs to the father, the head of the race, the Czar; an individual has a right to share in it only so long as he lives in unity with the Czar and his people. The soil is the joint property of the national family, and the father or Czar has the sole disposal of it, and distributes it among the families into which the nation in the course of time has been divided. A joint occupancy of the whole could only exist when the people led a nomadic life: when they became settled, a portion was assigned to each family, which occupied its share under a separate head. The right of the family thus arose in a manner quite analogous to that of the nation. The property is a family property, belonging equally but undivided to all the members of the family,—the father having the disposal and distribution of the produce. If a member insists on a division, he receives his portion, but loses all claim upon the joint possession; he is paid off and excluded, and thenceforth constitutes a new family. The families thus remained for many generations under their respective heads, and became family communes.

The Commune is still considered in law to form a family. If a stranger comes to reside in a village, he is adopted. Every member has an equal claim upon the joint and undivided communal property; the distribution of the produce rests with the fathers, the "White-heads" or Starosta (Elders). A member cannot possess private property in the land and therefore cannot bequeath it; but his sons, by virtue of their birth into the family, have an immediate right to a share in the joint property and its usufruct.

Communal Land Distribution

The principle is, that the whole of the land (tillage, meadows, pasture, woods, streams, etc.) belongs to the population regarded as a unity, and every male inhabitant has a right to an equal share. This share is therefore constantly changing; for the birth of every boy creates a new claim, and the shares of those who die revert to the Commune. The woods, pastures, hunting-grounds, and fisheries remain undivided, and free to all the inhabitants; but the arable land and meadows are divided, according to their value, amongst the males. This equal division is of course difficult, as the soil differs in quality, and portions of it may be distant or inconveniently situated. There are however in each Commune skilfull land-surveyors, without any education but what has been acquired from the traditional habits of the place, who execute the work to the satisfaction of all. The land is first divided, according to its quality, position, or general value, into sections, each possessing on the whole equal advantages; the sections are then divided into as many portions, in long strips, as there are shares required, and these are taken by lot. This is the usual plan, but each District, and frequently each Commune, has its local customs. In the Government of Yaroslaf, for instance, many of the Communes have peculiar measuring rods, which are almost regarded as sacred; they correspond with the quality of the soil, the rod for the best land being the shortest, and that for the worst the longest: the shares therefore vary in size, but are equal in value.

The preceding remarks apply to the free Communes, to whom the land belongs as their own property: these are very numerous, all the Cossack Communes for instance being of this class. The principle however is the same whether the peasants are owners of the land, or merely tenants as on the Crown estates, or only attached to the soil, as in the case of the serfs. . . . Equal division prevails in Russia, even among the private serfs, who in Great Russia were formerly always, and still are generally, placed upon *obrok*. . . . It is, however somewhat modified in the case of those who have to perform *corvées* for the proprietor. The following is the most ancient method of cultivating an estate by the labour of the serfs, and one which is still adopted in Great Russia when they are unable to pay the *obrok* and the proprietor is consequently obliged to set up a farming establishment of his own. The latter sets apart for himself a portion of the estate, at most one-third or one-fourth; and the remainder is retained by the peasants, who are required to cultivate without payment the part reserved by the proprietor. They manure the land, plough and harrow it, reap the crop and carry it to market, at their own expense. . . .

Where the *obrok* is paid, every male receives an equal share of the land (the father takes it for his infant son), and each must undertake to pay an equal share of the tax. Where the *corvée* system prevails, of course the boys and old men cannot work, and have no claim to the land, which is given as an equivalent for labour. . . .

> Some of Haxthausen's comments in the following excerpt, which is largely interpretive, should be taken *cum grano salis*.

The Peasant and the Tsar

The patriarchal government, feelings, and organization are in full activity in the life, manners, and customs of the Great Russians. The same unlimited authority which the father exercises over all his children is possessed by the mother over her daughters: the same reverence and obedience are shown to the Communal authorities, the Starostas and the White-heads, and to the common father of all, the Czar. The Russian addresses the same word to his real father, to the Starosta, to his proprietor, to the

Emperor, and finally to God, viz. Father; in like manner he calls every Russian, whether known to him or not, Brother.

The common Russian entertains no slavish, but simply a childlike, fear and veneration for the Czar; he loves him with devoted tenderness. He becomes a soldier reluctantly, but, once a soldier, he has no feeling of vindictiveness for the coercion exercised upon him, and serves the Czar with utmost fidelity. The celebrated expression "Prikazeno" (It is ordered), has a magical power over him. Whatever the Emperor commands must be done; the Russian cannot conceive the impossibility of its execution; the orders of the Police even are not worded *Zaprestcheno* (It is forbidden), but *Ne prikazeno* (It is not ordered). The profound veneration felt for the Czar is also shown in the care of everything belonging to him; the Russian has the deepest respect for *Kaziomne,* or property of the Czar. "Kaziomne does not die, does not burn in fire, or drown in water," says a Russian proverb.

There is scarcely an instance recorded of any collectors of the Crown taxes, who often traverse the country with considerable sums of money, being attacked and robbed. In the north, in the Government of Vologda, where the morals of the people are still particularly pure and simple, and great confidence and honesty prevail, when a collector enters a village, he taps at each window and calls out, "Kaza!" Then each person brings out his Crown tax for the year and throws it into the open bag: the collector does not count the money, being well assured that he is never cheated. If his visit is in the night, he enters the first substantial house, places the money-bag under the image of the Saint, looks for a place to rest on, and sleeps with perfect assurance of finding his money safe in the morning.

The patriarchal ruler or Czar appears necessary to the very existence of the people; we never find an insurrection against the Government or Czardom, but only against certain persons, and generally upon the grounds of legitimacy, as in the instance of the false Demetrius or Pugatchef, who represented himself as the exiled Peter III, or as in the insurrection of 1825. The people have shown invariable obedience to every government, even to that of the Mongols; they frequently indeed complain of supposed wrongs, but there the matter ends.

The Czar is the father of his people; but the descent, and even the sex, of the sovereign is indifferent to them. The Empress Catherine II, a foreign princess, experienced the same veneration and attachment as princes born in Russia; she became nationalized on assuming the Czardom. This profound veneration for authority passes to the person of every one who assumes the office of Czar.

• • •

Local Government

The communal organizations of the Crown peasants have undergone some alterations in recent times. At the head of each village has always stood, and still stands, the Starosta, chosen by the peasants from among

themselves; under him, and as his assistants, are the Tenth-men, each
chosen by ten heads of families: these remain usually one year on duty, although by law they ought to be elected every month. In very small villages
there is often only a Tenth-man at the head: these have no salary, but the
Starostas receive sums varying up to 175 roubles, according to the number of inhabitants. Here and there, even in former times, several villages
constituted an Associated Commune; this is now the universal organisation.
Formerly the head of the Associated Commune, the Starshina, was the oldest Starosta of the villages; he is now elected by the collective heads of
houses of all the villages; every ten houses electing two heads of families,
and these appointing the Starshina. The latter receives a salary of 300 to
400 roubles. As many villages as contain together about 500 or 600 heads
of families are united into one, and form an Associated Commune, which
appoints the recruits for the army, who were formerly taken by general
levies, so many from every thousand inhabitants.

The union of several Associated Communes constitutes a district, at the
head of which stands the chief; he too is elected, and for three years. The
Chief of the Circle must give in writing his opinion upon the choice, and
the Governor confirms it. He may be re-elected if no complaints are made
against him.

Several Districts form a Circle, which is presided over by an officer of
state, the Chief of the Circle, who is named by the Minister. He belongs
to the 7th or 8th class of civil servants, and has an assistant, who is of the
9th class. The Chiefs of Circles are under the head of the department of
Domains in each Government.

Each village has a tribunal, composed of the Starosta and two assistants, who are likewise elected. It has the right to inflict 25 blows with a
stick, and to fine to the amount of 5 roubles; it also decides cases of *meum*
and *teum* but not of heritable property. It exercises no criminal jurisdiction, but only presents informations, instructions, issues writs of arrest, etc.

The [Chief of the District] and two assistants, who are likewise
elected, form the District Tribunal. This constitutes an appeal court from
the communal tribunal; but it can only diminish, not augment the punishments inflicted by the latter.

. . .

A Farm

From hence we went to a small village in the neighbourhood, and
examined the farm of one of the peasants. The gable-end of the house
faced the street. Next to it was a long narrow courtyard with a gate. This
house had also an entrance from the street, which is not very usual; the
door was situated on the left, with another small one on the right, for the
lower story of the house in which are the smaller animals. We ascended a
staircase, to the dwelling room, which had no other furniture than a bench
running round it. Opposite the door in the corner stood the image of the
saint, with a lamp burning under it; and on the walls were some shelves,

upon which were placed all kinds of vessels and utensils. Spinning-wheels and hand-looms testified to the widely disseminated linen manufacture in this district. An enormous stove, built up with bricks, filled one third of the room; this in winter is a sleeping-place; beside it a small staircase led down to the lower part of the house, which serves as a store, and where the smaller animals, fowls and swine, take up their abode in the night; in winter also the cows are milked here. On the other side of the staircase are some closets, with very small windows, receptacles for all sorts of things, such as boxes—one for each member of the family, containing clothes. In summer the family generally sleep here. The stove of the dwelling-room serves for cooking, and is always heated, even in summer. Immediately adjoining the house is the stable for the cattle, into which is an entrance from the house: it is covered with two roofs, so that the house and the stable had three roofs, one lower than the other. Here stand the horses and cows, separated by partitions, but not by walls; in the winter it is very cold, but to this they are accustomed.

Behind the stable stands a building in which the carts and agricultural implements are kept. Here the supply of salt and meal is also stored, and a strong padlock is put upon the door. Some paces distant, but in a line with it, is a covered cellar, containing cabbages, fruits, etc., then a small cabbage-garden, with the granary at the end, then the spot where the peasant places his grain before putting it in the granary and dries the hay; the last of this row of buildings is always the bath-house. . . .

It might be imagined that the dwelling would be very dirty, the atmosphere mephitic,—with so many animals and a low, heated room,—but it was not so; the air was purer than I could have expected, to which the constantly burning fire and open windows contributed; moreover the room was kept so clean and neat that it was a pleasure to see.

. . .

The Village of Veliko

. . . The land and its inhabitants had been the property of seven sisters, three of whom were already dead; the rest did not live here, and having no agricultural establishment, had placed the peasants upon *obrok;* not however laying the tax upon the separate families, but upon the township at large as a tribute, porportioned to its population, the extent and quality of arable land conceded, together with the meadows, woods, and manufacture (an extensive one of linen is carried on), in the township. The amount of this tribute was calculated, first, from the rent derivable from the land; secondly, from the number of individuals to whom it was granted; thirdly, from the peculiar resources of skill and industry with which the inhabitants carry on certain branches of manufacture.

. . .

The buildings are such as are usual in small towns; there is also a bazaar, some good modern houses, which testify to the well-being of the inhabitants, and a considerable manufactory of linen. The inhabitants do not themselves spin, but buy the yarn. The weaving of fine linen is paid for at the rate of 7d. per arshine (28 inches); and even a woman, if a good weaver, can with ease earn 11d. to 1s. 4d. a day. These are high wages, and quite disproportionate to the price of agricultural produce; for, in good years, the price of 5¾ bushels of rye falls generally as low as 4s. 6d.

• • •

This place possesses a well-arranged school which the priest had undertaken to conduct.

• • •

A considerable horse-fair is held here annually, although there are not 50 horses in the place. Veliko Selo is a peasant village, but has no agriculture; its inhabitants manufacture linen, but grow no flax; there is a horse-fair, but they have no horses.

• • •

In one of the peasant houses we found a tailor working at a kaftan; and we were told that in some villages in this government the entire population are tailors. At certain times, generally in the winter, they travel about for work; and on arriving at a village they work from house to house, until all the inhabitants appear in new trim: then they go to another village. They are paid by piece-work, not by day wages: for making a grey coat they receive from 5½d. to 8d., and for a blue kaftan from 1s. 10d. to 3s. 9d., in addition to their board.

> This final selection from Haxthausen's report is composed of excerpts from various sections of his report. They have been abridged and adapted.

Notes on Russian Economy

In the central parts of the empire, in the country of the "black soil," the fertility is so great that manure is not required; the land is ploughed only once, often indeed the surface is scarcely disturbed: thus but little capital is required for tillage and manure, and in abundant years, seed-corn costs only about tenpence a bushel. Meadow improvements are rare, and fruit-trees are hardly anywhere to be seen. Sheep are seldom reared among the peasantry, cattle only to a limited extent, and horses are cheap. In the Government of Yaroslaf the usual price of a good farm horse is about £2. A Russian peasant builds his house entirely without assistance, and obtains the timber gratis from the woods of his Commune; the whole cost is scarcely fifteen shillings. Thus in the greater part of Russia the capital invested in agriculture is hardly worth taking into account; permanency of occupation is therefore by no means of the same importance as in the rest of Europe.

Generally speaking, in the greater part of the empire the soil has very little value of itself. Here it is valued only as a basis for human industry. Until the last few years it was customary to make contracts, sales, donations, and bequests, with reference merely to the number of peasant families,—in such or such a village so many peasants were sold, bequeathed, etc.; the land was regarded only as an appendage to the human beings upon it.

. . .

The peasants in this part of the Government of Yaroslaf practise the simple three-course husbandry. From the end of June to the beginning of August the winter-field is supplied with manure, which frequently lies four to six weeks before it is plowed in. The land is then broken up with the heavy plow, and harrowed; the winter corn is sown, and the soil afterwards turned over with the light fork-plough. The summer-field is not ploughed again in the autumn by the peasants, but this occurs sometimes on estates where a better system of cultivation has been introduced. The summer seed-time is over by the middle of May. In the field-labour an almost military order prevails. On the same day, at the same hour, the peasants all proceed to their ploughing etc., and return home in the same manner; this regularity is not compulsory, but arises spontaneously from their social and imitative disposition: the influence of communal life is everywhere manifest.

In the township of Veliko Selo the wealthiest of the inhabitants are linen-manufacturers; agriculture is left to the poor, and is in a very rude state. In order to retain the stubble-fields for pasturage as long as possible, as well as on account of the short summer and the inferior breed of horses, the land is ploughed only once,—immediately after manuring and before sowing. Complaints are made that the meadows are either too dry, or marshy and sour; but neither drainage nor irrigation has been attempted, although the soil presents no difficulties. . . . The rearing of cattle and sheep is but little attended to, and the horned cattle are inferior. The horses of the peasants are small, but the landowners and richer class of peasants possess a larger and stronger breed. . . . A considerable quantity of hemp and flax is grown in these districts. . . . Potatoes have only been introduced about five years among the peasants, as they considered the cultivation of them sinful; these people are now however becoming accustomed to them, and on the nobles' estates they are even used as food for cattle.

The forests are not under any regular management; those belonging to proprietors who live upon their estates are, to some extent, protected; but in the villages which pay *obrok* they are given up to the unrestrained use of the peasants, who cut down the trees recklessly, and a scarcity of wood begins already to be felt.

. . .

Ribinsk is 54 miles from Yaroslaf, and is the centre of the internal trade of Russia. All the various products brought by the Volga and its tributary streams, and destined for St. Petersburg have here to be re-embarked in smaller vessels to be sent on the canals. These commodities arrive here in 1700 or 1800 large vessels, and are re-laden upon 6000 barges and boats, and thus sent on to St. Petersburg; the value of the commodities is said to amount to forty or fifty million roubles. Before the formation of the canals which unite St. Petersburg with the Volga, Ribinsk was an insignificant township, whose inhabitants paid an obrok either in fish or money. When it rose to the rank of a city the obrok was remitted, and the inhabitants now pay only the usual poll-tax to the Crown, in addition to the town rates, which amount to 50,000 or 60,000 roubles. At the present time, it contains more than 600 merchants of the three guilds. The retail trade is carried on by the small burghers and by the Raznotchinstzi, a class between the burghers and the peasants. . . . Among the labourers here is a class called Burlaki, whose occupation is to tow the vessels on the river. They are a robust and active race of men, and have formed themselves into communes and artels, with leaders, Starostas, and masters, whom they elect. For the journey from Samara to Ribinsk (a distance of 650 miles, but not less than 1000 by the river) a Burlak receives 70 roubles; for the journey from Nizhni Novgorod (perhaps 460 miles), 50 roubles. A Burlak, when fortunate, can perform the journey between Samara and Ribinsk three times in the course of the summer; he has then perhaps 70 roubles left; but if, through adverse circumstances, he only makes the trip twice, he generally consumes all he earns.

. . .

[At Yaroslaf we visited some of the manufactories.] The work-people are paid by the piece: for weaving shirt linen, they receive 6 copecks per arshine, and a woman can with ease weave from ten to 12 arshines a day. For weaving table-linen a man is paid one rouble ten copecks per arshine, and can earn two roubles a day. A man who was weaving towelling told us he could produce from 40 to 50 arshines, and was paid 34 copecks per arshine. . . . I believe that compared with the price of food, the wages of labour are nowhere so high as in Russia.

. . .

[In the Government of Yaroslaf (one of the most interesting provinces of the empire from the point of view of my study), the soil is not fertile and the climate is severe, but the situation along the Volga is favorable. Trade and commerce of all kinds pay well while agriculture yields no profits. Labour which in the countries on the Danube is spread over seven months, here, on account of the short summer has to be concluded in four months. Work which could be done in the former area with four men and four horses, here would require seven men and seven horses. The net return on labour and capital for an estate north of the Volga would be about half that for an estate of equal size and fertility in Mainz. Actually, the land at Mainz will return six to seven times the seed; that along the Volga at Yaroslaf, hardly three times the seed.]

Agricultural operations can be carried on only in the four summer months: during this period, all the labour is employed, but in the remaining eight months, as far as agriculture is concerned, it is completely at rest. The consequence has been, from the earliest times, a remarkable development

of manufacturing industry, as well in the country as in the towns. . . .
This industry was originally applied only to the raw produce of the district,
which was converted into manufactures and carried to market by the inhabitants and producers in the eight winter months, during which agriculture left them at leisure. . . . The majority of serfs in this Government
have always been *obrok* peasants. . . . This gave an extraordinary stimu-
lus to manufacturing. Agriculture yielded only a bare subsistence, but no
profit, and money had to be procured for the payment of the *obrok*. The
raw products fetched low prices, but all the manufactured articles high
ones. . . . Thus these raw products were converted into commodities; and
carpenters, wheel-wrights, makers of wooden shoes, bast-weavers, tar-boil-
ers, boat builders, spinners and weavers of linen and sailcloth, ropemakers,
saddlers, curriers, and shoe makers, brought to market their various articles
in wood, hemp, flax and leather. These artisans however did not live scattered amongst the population, working only for the supply of the immediate
wants of a neighbourhood; they worked together as in a factory, and produced articles for the markets; and in this way the remarkable spirit of association was developed, grounded upon the organization of the Russian
Communes. . . .

The various trades have mostly formed themselves into separate Communes: for instance, all the inhabitants of one village are shoemakers, those
of another are smiths, etc. . . . The members of the artisan communes
also constantly assist each other with their capital and labour; purchases
and sales are transacted in common, and they send their commodities together to the markets and towns, where they have shops for the sale of them.

. . .

I will give here some statistical tables of the year 1841, of the five Circles of the Government of Yaroslaf.

Circle	No. of villages in 21 sq. miles	Av. No. of houses in each village	Av. No. of inhabitants in each village	Av. No. of acres to each village
Poshekhon	9	13	83	1417
Mologa	8	16	124	1803
Ribinsk	21	11	63	634
Mishkin	16	15	114	840
Uglitch	15	13	99	940

Circle	Average No. of Acres to Each Male Inhabitant			
	Arable	Meadow	Good Wood	Bad Wood
Poshekhon	9.31	2.03	9.72	12.62
Mologa	6.07	1.35	9.31	11.14
Ribinsk	6.75	.90	6.75	1.42
Mishkin	8.10	.81	.25	4.86
Uglitch	6.30	.90	2.16	9.45

It is manifest from this that agriculture cannot maintain the inhabitants in these districts. In the Circle of Uglitch there are about six acres of arable land to each male inhabitant; 2½ being here reckoned the average grain producers, the calculation stands as follows:

2 acres sown with rye (after deducting the seed) 7   bushels
1 acre sown with barley (after deducting the seed) . . . . . . 3½ bushels
                                                                                                      10½ bushels

The remaining acre is sown with oats for the cattle. 7 bushels of rye give 387 pounds of bread; 3½ bushels of barley give 169 pounds of bread:— total 556 pounds.

The principal food of the Russian people consists of bread; potatoes are unknown in most districts; cabbage is the only vegetable which is much used. Animal food, milk, and butter are little eaten. In the army, each soldier receives 2½ pounds of bread a day. A healthy Russian peasant cannot subsist without three pounds; in the harvest he eats five pounds; and in White Russia even as much as seven pounds. If women, old people, and children are counted, one pound and a half must be reckoned for each individual of the population. A man and woman, according to this calculation, require on an average 1094 pounds of bread in the year. There is always a deficit therefore of 538 pounds of bread for each couple, or of 22,855,000 pounds of bread . . . for the whole population of the Circle, which can only be supplied by importations from other districts, and therefore only with the aid of auxiliary occupations and manufacturing profits, to enable the people to purchase these supplies.

In the northern districts, Olonetz, Vologda, Archangel, there is a tolerably dense population and little agriculture. The most important sources of production and employment are furnished by the forests: wood for shipbuilding, logs, planks, pitch, tar and turpentine. These employments occupy the population during the winter and the short season of spring floods, but the people have little to do in the summer. . . . They therefore proceed in large numbers to the regions further south and assist the inhabitants in field labour and the harvest for wages. [Such migratory workers earn from sixty to eighty roubles for the four summer months.]

[The number of these migratory workers cannot be ascertained with certainty, but they are many. Some go away for short periods, some for longer, and some permanently. All of them customarily retain their communal rights and continue to be inscribed in the Revision lists of their homes. In one unusual instance, of the 9500 male souls inscribed in the Commune; 7000 are go-aways.]

These traveling artisans remain together, according to their respective trades, in the large towns, and form artisan communes. When any work is to be done, the cleverest among them assume the office of contractors. If a house is to be built, a contractor is sought. He makes the bargain and concludes the contract. Then he collects his comrades, and agrees with them as to their assistance and share of the profits. If the project is expensive, he goes to his native village and bets the money necessary for the undertaking.

The people of the village, who share in the profit, collect the money and hand it to the contractor. They merely pledge their word, and all depends upon their mutual truth and fidelity; cases seldom or never occur of their defrauding one another. These are ordinary, uneducated people, who can often neither read nor write, but possess a remarkable technical genius. . . .

A large number of these young travelers are pedlars. Perhaps the greater number are carriers. A considerable number, particularly those from the neighbourhood of Rostof, are gardeners. A large number of persons go to Moscow and St. Petersburg as bakers. Others become drivers, joiners, carpenters, etc. . . .

Fairs in Russia are numerous and important. There are 37 large fairs in the Government of Yaroslaf. In 1842 goods to the value of six million silver roubles were exposed for sale in these fairs, and about two-thirds of them were sold. . . .

In the year 1839, there were 105 modern factories in Yaroslaf; in the year 1842, 158 factories with an annual production valued at 2,430,000 silver roubles. . . . There is also considerable trade. Corn, flour and iron are brought from the south and east, and sent to the north and west; on the other hand wine and colonial products come from St. Petersburg, and are sent to western Siberia. The great water and land highways cross each other here. The value of the whole trade is estimated at four million silver roubles. . . .

The people of Kubensk are unable to supply the labour necessary in summer, and procure assistants from the districts further north; one of these servants receives for the summer months his board and sixty roubles; a day-labourer with his horse is paid in seed-time 2s. 3d., in the hay-harvest 1s. 10 d., and without a horse 11d. to 2s. 3d.; the day-labour of a woman during harvest is paid 7d. to 9d.

In winter, as soon as the snow has become hard, the men employ themselves in trade, and the transport of mercantile commodities. But in the spring and harvest also, when there is sufficient water, they carry on some trade upon the lake, which is connected with navigable rivers. They likewise convey from their own farms grain, vegetable, hides, tallow, and fish (from the lake). The vegetables they dispose of mostly in Vologda, but the other articles they convey to the Volga, and even to St. Petersburg, whence they bring back other commodities as return cargo, for their own trade and that of others. The gardens alone are said, by the sale of vegetables, to yield on an average a surplus of £3 13s. to each household. The villagers therefore are generally in easy circumstances, and often very rich, a fortune of 40,000 to 50,000 roubles being not at all infrequent. . . .

In driving through the fields of some of the small villages (never of the larger ones), I observed that after every five to eight strips of arable land there was always a ridge of turf; this is from a foot to 18 inches broad, and forms the boundary of the two pieces of land. On inquiry I found that in these very small villages the yearly division of land did not exist, or had been given up, but that the ground was allotted once for all, a part to each house. Each portion is divided into as many strips as there are houses in the village, and then the whole portion is parted from the next by the green ridge. This is the only exception to the popular mode of dividing the land I have found.

.   .

The Polovnik system may be briefly explained as follows. The land is let to a free tenant farmer for a term of years on condition of his delivering yearly to the landlord half the produce. The word *Polovnik* is derived from *polovinia,* half. In certain areas of North Russia, there have been of old some families belonging to the nobles, but they possess no land with serfs living upon it: they however, as well as a number of citizens in the towns, own large districts and entire villages as their own property, without the right of cultivating them by serfs but only according to the Polovnik law— by letting them to peasant farmers for the half or a certain part of the produce. The contracts are from 6 to 20 years. Each party is free at the conclusion of the contract or a year's notice, to dissolve the relation. The contract is extremely simple in form: the parties appear before the Circle Court, and cause to be inscribed in the Polovnik books, which are kept there, this declaration:—"Mr. W . . . . has granted to the peasants N. N. N. the village of A. and the land annexed to it, according to Polovnik law, for 6, 10, or 20 years." . . .

The village of Vizena is well built, and contains several stone houses. . . . At the last Revision there were 1820 souls in the village Commune. I have remarked that the majority of the inhabitants form an association of boot and shoe-makers. There are also six glue and two wax-light manufactories, and 8 large ones in which carpets and felt boots are prepared from horse and cow hair, a branch of industry carried on in many of the houses as a subsidiary occupation. At the Fair of Nizhni Novgorod a quantity of these, valued at 50,000 roubles are sold, and in smaller fairs in the vicinity an additional quantity amounting to 10,000 or 20,000 roubles. About 500 members of the Commune are always absent with passports; they wander about in search of work as far as Saratof, Astrakhan, Uralsk, and even into the interior of Siberia. Some remain away ten or fifteen years, others establish themselves permanently in various towns, never returning to their homes; they do not however cease to belong to the Commune, but pay their taxes here, and retain their houses, gardens, and communal rights, which they let out or deliver over to some other person.

Two hundred of the inhabitants proceed every year to the Fair at Nizhni Novgorod, and remain there two months, working and selling the goods belonging to the villagers. There is a great disparity of wealth among the inhabitants. Formerly there was more wealth than at present, two peasants possessing each above 500,000 roubles; but there are even still 15 houses whose trade receipts amount to between 20,000 and 50,000 roubles.

The Prince has imposed a certain tax upon the inhabitants and leaves it to the Commune to divide this among them. They have elected one Whitehead for every 100 souls, who taxes the members of the Commune according to their means, the richer ones paying for so many souls.

The Russian American Company

> The Russian American Company was first chartered in 1799, and sporadically over two generations its activities formed a point of contact between imperial Russia and the United States. The following account of the company is based on Russian sources. It was prepared by Vladimir Gsovski *et alii,* and was published under the title, *Russian Administration of Alaska and The Status of the Alaskan Natives.* 81st Congress, 2d session. Senate Document No. 152. Washington: Government Printing Office, 1950. Pp. 4–6, 9–10, 29–30. Footnotes omitted.

Finally, the Russian American Company came into being as a result of a merger of the Shelikhov and Golikov Company with that of the Mylnikov Company (called also the Company of Irkutsk.) Two acts preceded this merger which are, however, of little importance because they were soon superceded by the Charter and four other acts promulgated on July 8, 1799, granting the Russian American Company a monopoly of trade and administration in Russian possessions in America for twenty years.

By the promulgation of the Charter a second period in the Russian administration of Alaska was opened which may be called the period of Baranov rule. Baranov was one of the pioneers and traders who opened up Alaska for Russian penetration. He administered the Russian colonies of America in the name of the Russian American Company since its establishment, from 1799 till 1818. He developed the trade of the Company considerably and under him Russians penetrated as far as Hawaii and California. He established strict order in the colonies but did not, and probably could not, change the evil practices of his subordinates.

. . .

Baranov was discharged in 1818, a criminal investigation was instituted against him, and he died on his way to Russia where he was to face a trial. Lieutenant Captain Gagemeister of the Russian Navy took the office of Administrator General and since that time, until the purchase of Alaska, this office was held only by higher officers of the Navy.

On the other hand, Baranov's rule marked the rise in profits of the Company and in the Russian expansion. He established a settlement in California, Fort Ross near San Francisco, in 1811. The expedition of a Dr. Scheffer, an adventurer in the services of the Company, succeeded in obtaining the consent of Tomari, the chief of one of the Hawaiian islands, to become a Russian subject and subject his territory to Russian sovereignty. This adventure threatened to bring Russia into conflict with England and was abandoned by the order of Alexander I. Fort Ross threatened for a long time to aggravate the relations of Russia with Spain, later Mexico and the United States. In view of the local and international situation, it did not fulfill the expectations of an advance post for expansion and a base for supply of Alaskan colonies with agricultural produce or a ground for catching otters. Its abandonment was ordered in 1839 and carried out in 1841.

. . .

From its inception the Russian American Company was intended to be an instrument of government policy with the appearance of a private company. In forcing a merger of companies trading in Alaska in the 1790's and establishing one monopolistic concern, the Russian government pursued certain political aims in addition to a desire to conserve the wildlife, the main wealth of the country, and to check the abuses of independent traders. The government wished to stimulate Russian expansion in the Pacific but here it met the competition of a similar expansion of the British Empire and later the United States. Any establishment of an outright governmental administration in Alaska and the stationing of armed forces over there might have led to an open conflict which the Russian government wished to avoid. Thus, in creating the Russian American Company, the Russian statesmen sought to apply the experience of the British East Indian Company. As it was stated in a resolution of the State Council in 1841, "the Russian American Company is a commercial establishment but it is also in a way a government authority."

The mixed character of the company was reflected in the original organization of the management of its affairs. But in time the governmental control became more and more pronounced. Under the Charter of 1799, in addition to the directors elected by the shareholders there was also a special "correspondent" or "protector" of the Company by appointment of the Emperor. He acted in the capacity of a representative of the Company before the Emperor and also as the government supervisor of the activities of the Company. Resanov, thus appointed, belonged to the high bureaucracy but was also one of the important shareholders, being related by marriage to Shelikhov's family.

In 1804 the office of correspondent was replaced by a Provisional Committee of three shareholders which, "in deciding the confidential political matters," enjoyed the powers of the general meeting of the shareholders. The elected members of the committee were the Ministers [sic] of the Navy, the Deputy Minister of the Interior, and a Privy Councillor holding an important post with the Ministry of Foreign Affairs. The provisional committee was reorganized on October 16, 1813, into a Special Council for the guidance of the political aspect of the activities of the company which, as stated by the report of the Board of Directors in 1812, would be "above the authority of directors managing the business side of the affairs of the Company."

The business men—"merchants" in the Russian terminology of the time —who were the founders of the Company gradually withdrew from the management. The first Board of Directors consisted of four merchants, two representing the Shelikhov group and two the Mylniukov [sic]. The latter two soon withdrew and among five directors elected under the third Charter of 1844 we find only one "merchant," Kusov, a survivor from the Board of the previous period. The other four comprised one vice admiral, one lieutenant general, one major general in active service, and one rear admiral retired. From 1857 on, no "merchants" are to be found among the directors.

In 1802 the commissioned officers and sailors of the Navy were allowed to take employment with the Company and, at the same time, to retain their status in active service. One half of their salary was paid by the government. The second Charter of 1821 allowed any person in military or civil service to maintain his status while joining the service of the Company.

Under the Charter of 1799 the Company was given the status of an independent government department with the duty "to report directly to His Majesty" on its activities. But on December 15, 1811, the Company was placed under the Division of Industry and Domestic Commerce (*Departament Manufaktur*) of the Ministry of the Interior, and together with this division it was transferred in 1819 to the Ministry of Finance under which it remained until the sale of Alaska.

At the time of the creation of the Company as well as later, the international situation induced Russia at one time or another to be on friendly terms with her rivals in the Pacific, Great Britain, and the United States. These political motives invariably overbalanced the commercial interests of the Russian American Company in case of a conflict.

. . .

. . . the Company was regarded as a convenient instrument of Russian expansion in the Far East. When the services of the Company were needed the government did not hesitate to grant financial aid in one form or another. The reason for the subvention was well formulated in 1849 by Muraviev, then Governor of Siberia, as follows:

"In my opinion the existence of the Russian American Company is needed by the government at least for the time being because the taking over of the administration of the North American possessions would require considerable expenses both in a lump sum and annually. It must also be borne in mind that our administration and forces in Kamchatka and the Okhotsk Sea are still in a situation that would make their expansion to the American coast premature. I dare say, on the other hand, that the abandonment of our American possessions will not conform to the aims of the government. Both these considerations lead to the conclusion that the government is forced to render aid to the Company in its present, as is known to me, difficult financial situation."

Among the most important services rendered by the Company to the government in the middle of the 19th century was that of the preparation of regaining from China the region of the Amur River abandoned some time before. Before taking any steps in this direction, the exploration of the navigability of the Amur River and its estuary was necessary. The Russian government was afraid that such open invasion of Chinese territory would induce Great Britain to ask from China further concessions in addition to those under the Nanking Treaty of 1842, which was undesirable from the Russian standpoint. Thus the vessels of the Company undertook the task of the exploration of the river Amur. Trade missions were sent to this region by the Company which also founded several Russian settlements in the region. These activities continued until 1858 when the region was ceded to Russia by China under the Aigun Treaty. Then the services of the Company were no longer needed.

135—galley—36600—Readings in Russian History, 4th Ed.—L & M

Likewise, during the Crimean War, the Board of Directors of the Russian American Company, using its status of a private company, made a "neutrality agreement" with the Hudson Bay British Company, thus protecting the Russian possessions from the attack by the British Navy against which the few Russian vessels in the Alaskan waters were helpless. It may be mentioned in this connection that the administration of the Russian colonies, being uninformed of the "neutrality" agreement of the central Board of Directors entered in its turn into a fictitious sale contract with businessmen from San Francisco. Under this contract a fictitious sale of the property of the Russian American Company to the "Russian American Company in San Francisco" was stipulated for $7,000,000, the exact amount of money paid later for Alaska by the American Government. Although it was signed by both parties no action on its basis had been taken because it became completely superfluous in view of the above-mentioned "neutrality" agreement.

Where to Find More Information

ASKENAZY, S. "Russia," *Cambridge Modern History*. Vol. 10, ch. 13.
———. "Poland and the Polish Revolution," *CMH*, vol. 10, ch. 14.
BLACK, *Rewriting*, ch. 10.
CHARQUES, *Short History*, chs. 10–13.
CHEVIGNY, H. *Lord of Alaska*. N.Y.: Viking, 1943.
CLARKSON, *History*, chs. 15 & 16.
DRAGE, G. "Russia and the Levant," *CMH*, vol. 11, ch. 9, pt. 1.
FLORINSKY, *Russia*, vol. 1, ch. 24; vol. 2, chs. 25–32.
GOGOL, N. *Dead Souls*. Signet Classic.
GRUNWALD, C. de *Tsar Nicholas I*. N.Y.: Macmillan, 1955.
HARCAVE, *Readings*, vol. 1, sections 24–28.
HECHT, D. *Russian Radicals Look to America, 1825–1894*. Cambridge: Harvard Univ. Press, 1947.
HERZEN, A. (J. Duff, Ed.) *The Memoirs of Alexander Herzen*. New Haven: Yale Univ. Press, 1923.
KARPOVICH, M. M. *Imperial Russia, 1801–1917*. N.Y.: Holt, 1932. Pp. 1–34.
KOHN, H. *The Mind of Modern Russia*. New Brunswick: Rutgers Univ. Press, 1955.
KORNILOV, A. *Modern Russian History*. 2 vols. in 1. N.Y.: Knopf, 1943. Vol. 1 chs. 3–19.
LASERSON, *American Impact*, chs. 5–8.
LOBANOV-ROSTOVSKY, *Russia and Asia*, chs. 5 & 6.
———. *Russia and Europe*, chs. 3–13.
MARTIN, *Picture History*, pp. 108–143.
MAZOUR, A. G. *The First Russian Revolution, 1825*. Berkeley: Univ. of Calif. Press, 1937.
———. *Russia*, chs. 14–16.
MILIUKOV, *Outlines*, vol. 2, ch. 2.
PARES, *History*, chs. 16–18.
STSCHEPIN, E. "Russia under Alexander I and the Invasion of 1812," *CMH*, vol. 9, ch. 16.
TARLE, E. *Napoleon's Invasion of Russia*. N.Y.: Oxford Univ. Press, 1942.
TOLSTOY, L. *The Cossacks*. World's Classics Series.
———. *War and Peace*. (Many editions.)
TOMPKINS, S. R. *Alaska*. Norman: Univ. of Okla. Press, 1945. Chs. 1–14.
TURGENEV, I. S. *The Hunting Sketches*. Signet Classic.
WALSH, *Russia*, chs. 10–13.
WREN, *Course*, chs. 16–20.
ZETLIN, M. *The Decembrists*. N.Y.: International Univ. Press, 1960.

CONTENTS OF VOLUME II
From Alexander II to the Soviet Period